Fodor's 98

Florida

The complete guide, thoroughly up-to-date

Packed with details that will make your trip

The must-see sights, off and on the beaten path

What to see, what to skip

Mix-and-match vacation itineraries

City strolls, beach excursions, countryside adventures

Smart lodging and dining options

Transportation tips, distances and directions

Key contacts, savvy travel tips

When to go, what to pack

Clear, accurate, easy-to-use maps

Books to read

Fodor's Travel Publications, Inc.
New York • Toronto • London • Sydney • Auckland
www.fodors.com/

Fodor's Florida '98

EDITOR: Andrea Lehman

Editorial Contributors: Pamela Acheson, Rob Andrews, David Brown, Marianne Camas, Catherine Fredman, Kendall Hamersly, Herb Hiller, Ann Hughes, Alan Macher, Diane Marshall, Gary McKechnie, Valerie Meyer, Peter Oliver, Heidi Sarna, Helayne Schiff, M. T. Schwartzman (Gold Guide editor), Dinah Spritzer, Rowland Stiteler, Geoffrey Tomb

Editorial Production: Laura M. Kidder

Maps: David Lindroth, *cartographer;* Robert Blake, *map editor*

Design: Fabrizio La Rocca, *creative director;* Guido Caroti, *associate art director;* Jolie Novak, *photo researcher*

Production/Manufacturing: Mike Costa

Cover Photograph: Bob Krist

Design: Between the Covers

Copyright

Special Sales

Fodor's Travel Publications are available at special discounts for bulk purchases for sales promotions or premiums. Special editions, including personalized covers, excerpts of existing guides, and corporate imprints can be created in large quantities for special needs. For more information, contact your local bookseller or write to Special Markets, Fodor's Travel Publications, 201 East 50th Street, New York, NY 10022. Inquiries from Canada should be directed to your local Canadian bookseller or sent to Random House of Canada, Ltd., Marketing Department, 1265 Aerowood Drive, Mississauga, Ontario L4W 1B9. Inquiries from the United Kingdom should be sent to Fodor's Travel Publications, 20 Vauxhall Bridge Road, London SW1V 2SA, England.

PRINTED IN THE UNITED STATES OF AMERICA

10 9 8 7 6 5 4 3 2 1

CONTENTS

Maps

ON THE ROAD WITH FODOR'S

WE'RE ALWAYS THRILLED to get letters from readers, especially one like this:

It took us an hour to decide what book to buy and we now know we picked the best one. Your book was wonderful, easy to follow, very accurate, and good on pointing out eating places, informal as well as formal. When we saw other people using your book, we would look at each other and smile.

Our editors and writers are deeply committed to making every Fodor's guide "the best one"—not only accurate but always charming, brimming with sound recommendations and solid ideas, right on the mark in describing restaurants and hotels, and full of fascinating facts that make you view what you've traveled to see in a rich new light.

About Our Writers

Our success in achieving our goals—and in helping to make your trip the best of all possible vacations—is a credit to the hard work of our extraordinary writers.

On her way to the Caribbean, former New York publishing exec **Pamela Acheson** stopped in the Sunshine State and fell in love, after discovering that there's much more to it than Walt Disney World. She likes nothing better than to drive around to neat little towns, undiscovered beaches, and other less-traveled places as she writes about her new home.

Ann Hughes, former editor of *Indiana Business* magazine and a contributing editor to other travel and trade publications, is a passionate golfer. She lives in northwest Florida, which has more courses than you can swing a club at.

Starting behind an old manual typewriter at his hometown newspaper, **Alan Macher** has written everything from human-interest stories to speeches. He makes his home in Boca Raton, where he can play tennis and bike along Route A1A year-round.

Intrepid traveler and intrepid shopper **Diane Marshall** was formerly editor and publisher of the newsletter "The Savvy Shopper: The Traveler's Guide to Shopping Around the World." From her home in the Keys, she has written for numerous travel guides, newspapers, magazines, and on-line services.

Gary McKechnie is a former stand-up comedian turned ad copywriter turned travel writer turned video producer turned travel writer. He knows Florida and he knows a good joke when he sees one.

New This Year

This year, Fodor's joins Rand McNally, the world's largest commercial mapmaker to bring you a detailed color map of Florida. Just detach it along the perforation, and drop it in your tote bag.

On the Web, check out Fodor's site (http://www.fodors.com/) for information on major destinations around the world and travel-savvy interactive features. The Web site also lists the 80-plus radio stations nationwide that carry the *Fodor's Travel Show,* a live call-in program that airs every weekend. Tune in to hear guests discuss their wonderful adventures—or call for answers to your most pressing travel questions.

How to Use This Guide

Organization

Up front is the **Gold Guide,** an easy-to-use section divided alphabetically by topic. Under each listing you'll find tips and information that will help you accomplish what you need to in Florida. You'll also find addresses and telephone numbers of organizations and companies that offer destination-related services and detailed information and publications.

The first chapter in the guide, Destination: Florida helps get you in the mood for your trip. What's Where gets you oriented, New and Noteworthy cues you in on trends and happenings, Pleasures and Pastimes describes the activities and sights that really make Florida unique, Fodor's Choice showcases our top picks, and Festivals and Seasonal Events alerts you to special events you'll want to seek out.

Chapters in *Florida '98* are arranged by region. Since it covers a big city, the Miami chapter begins with an Exploring section, which is subdivided by neighborhood; each subsection recommends a walking or driving tour and lists sights in alphabetical order. Each regional chapter is divided by geographical area; within each area, towns are covered in logical geographical order and, within town sections, all restaurants and lodgings are grouped together.

To help you decide what to visit in the time you have, all chapters begin with recommended itineraries; you can mix and match those from several chapters to create a complete vacation. The A to Z section that ends all chapters covers getting there, getting around, and helpful contacts and resources.

Icons and Symbols

★ Our special recommendations
✕ Restaurant
🏠 Lodging establishment
⚠ Campgrounds
☺ Good for kids (rubber duckie)
☞ Sends you to another section of the guide for more information
✉ Address
☎ Telephone number
FAX Fax number
☉ Opening and closing times (those we give don't apply on holidays; if you're visiting then, call ahead)
💰 Admission prices (those we give apply only to adults, except in Chapter 8; elsewhere substantially reduced fees are almost always available for children, students, and senior citizens)

Numbers in white and black circles—②
and ❷, for example—that appear on the maps, in the margins, and within the tours correspond to one another.

Dining and Lodging

The restaurants and lodgings we list are the cream of the crop in each price range. Price categories are as follows:

For restaurants:

CATEGORY	COST*
$$$$	over $50
$$$	$35–$50
$$	$20–$35
$	under $20

per person for a three-course meal, excluding drinks, service, and 6% sales tax (more in some counties)

For hotels:

CATEGORY	COST*
$$$$	over $160
$$$	$100–$160
$$	$60–$100
$	under $60

All prices are for a standard double room, excluding 6% sales tax (more in some counties) and 1%–4% tourist tax.

Hotel Facilities

We always list the facilities that are available—but we don't specify whether they cost extra: When pricing accommodations, always ask what's included. In addition, assume that all rooms have private baths unless otherwise noted.

Restaurant Reservations and Dress Codes

Reservations are always a good idea; we note only when they're essential or when they are not accepted. Book as far ahead as you can, and reconfirm when you get to town. Unless otherwise noted, the restaurants listed are open daily for lunch and dinner. We mention dress only when men are required to wear a jacket or a jacket and tie. Look for an overview of local habits in the Gold Guide and in the Pleasures and Pastimes section that follows each chapter introduction.

Credit Cards

The following abbreviations are used: **AE**, American Express; **D**, Discover; **DC**, Diners Club; **MC**, MasterCard; and **V**, Visa.

Please Write to Us

You can use this book in the confidence that all prices and opening times are based on information supplied to us at press time; Fodor's cannot accept responsibility for any errors. Time inevitably brings changes, so always confirm information when it matters—especially if you're making a detour to visit a specific place. In addition, when making reservations be sure to mention if you have a disability or are traveling with children, if you prefer a private bath or a certain type of bed, or if you have specific dietary needs or any other concerns.

Were the restaurants we recommended as described? Did our hotel picks exceed your expectations? Did you find a museum we recommended a waste of time? If you have complaints, we'll look into them and revise our entries when the facts warrant it. If you've discovered a special place that we haven't included, we'll pass the information along to our correspondents and have them check it out. So send us your feedback, positive *and* negative: E-mail us at editors@fodors.com (specifying the name of the book on the subject line) or write the Florida editor at Fodor's, 201 East 50th Street, New York, New York 10022. Have a wonderful trip!

Karen Cure
Editorial Director

Florida

Gulf of Mexico

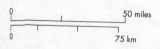

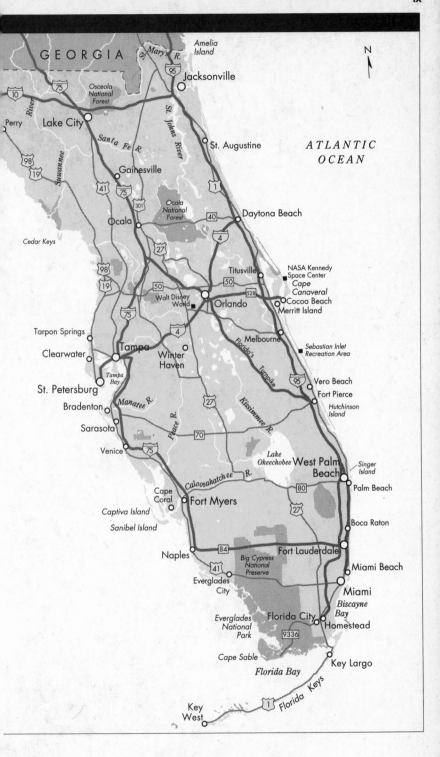

The United States

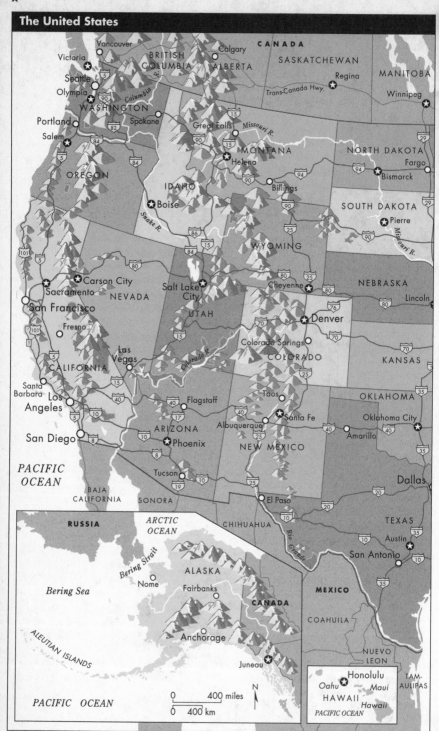

ONTARIO
QUÉBEC
NEW BRUNSWICK
CANADA
Fredericton
Québec
MAINE
Montréal
Augusta
MINNESOTA
Duluth
Ottawa
Montpelier
Concord
VT.
N.H.
Boston
MICHIGAN
Lake Huron
Toronto
Lake Ontario
Albany
Hartford
MASS.
R.I.
Providence
WISCONSIN
Green Bay
St. Paul
Buffalo
NEW YORK
CONN.
New York
Minneapolis
Milwaukee
Lansing
Lake Erie
Madison
Cleveland
Detroit
PENNSYLVANIA
Trenton
N.J.
IOWA
Lake Michigan
Chicago
Pittsburgh
Harrisburg
Philadelphia
Des Moines
OHIO
DEL.
Dover
Omaha
ILLINOIS
INDIANA
Columbus
MD.
Baltimore
Annapolis
Springfield
Indianapolis
Charleston
Washington, D.C.
Topeka
Cincinnati
Frankfort
WEST VIRGINIA
Richmond
Kansas City
Jefferson City
St. Louis
Louisville
VIRGINIA
Norfolk
MISSOURI
KENTUCKY
Raleigh
Nashville
NORTH CAROLINA
Tulsa
ARKANSAS
Memphis
Tennessee R.
Columbia
SOUTH CAROLINA
ATLANTIC OCEAN
Little Rock
Birmingham
Atlanta
GEORGIA
Savannah
MISSISSIPPI
Montgomery
Jackson
ALABAMA
Jacksonville
Baton Rouge
Mobile
Tallahassee
FLORIDA
Orlando
Houston
New Orleans
LOUISIANA
Bahama Islands
Gulf of Mexico
Miami
Nassau

Lake Superior
Lake Michigan
Mississippi R.
Ohio R.
Savannah R.
Hudson

N

0   500 miles

0   800 km

SMART TRAVEL TIPS A TO Z

Basic Information on Traveling in Florida, Savvy Tips to Make Your Trip a Breeze, and Companies and Organizations to Contact

A
AIR TRAVEL

MAJOR AIRLINE OR LOW-COST CARRIER?

Most people choose a flight based on price. Yet there are other issues to consider. Major airlines offer the greatest number of departures; smaller or regional carriers—including low-cost and no-frill airlines—usually have a more limited number of flights daily. Major airlines have frequent-flyer partners, which allow you to credit mileage earned on one airline to your account with another. Low-cost airlines offer a definite price advantage and fewer restrictions, such as advance-purchase requirements. Safety-wise, low-cost carriers as a group have a good history, but **check the safety record before booking** any low-cost carrier; call the Federal Aviation Administration's Consumer Hotline (☞ Airline Complaints, *below*).

➤ MAJOR AIRLINES: **American** (☎ 800/ 433–7300). **Continental** (☎ 800/ 525–0280). **Delta** (☎ 800/221–1212). **Midway** (☎ 800/446–4392). **Northwest** (☎ 800/225–2525). **Southwest** (☎ 800/435–9792). **TWA** (☎ 800/221–2000). **United** (☎ 800/241–6522). **US Airways** (☎ 800/428–4322).

➤ REGIONAL AIRLINES: **Carnival Air Lines** (☎ 800/824–7386) to Fort Lauderdale, Fort Myers, Miami, Orlando, Tampa, and West Palm Beach. **Midwest Express** (☎ 800/452–2022) to Fort Lauderdale, Fort Myers, Orlando, and Tampa. **ValuJet** (☎ 770/994–8258 or 800/825–8538) to Fort Lauderdale, Fort Myers, Jacksonville, Orlando, Tampa, and West Palm Beach.

➤ FROM THE U.K.: **American** (☎ 0345/ 789–789). **British Airways** (☎ 0345/ 222–111). **Continental** (☎ 0800/ 776–464) via Newark. **Delta** (☎ 0800/414–767). **Northwest** (☎ 0990/561–000) via Detroit or Minneapolis. **TWA** (☎ 0800/222–222) via St. Louis. **United** (☎ 0800/ 888–555). **Virgin Atlantic** (☎ 01293/ 747–747).

GET THE LOWEST FARE

The least-expensive airfares to Florida are priced for round-trip travel. Major airlines usually require that you **book in advance and buy the ticket within 24 hours,** and you may have to **stay over a Saturday night.** It's smart to **call a number of airlines, and when you are quoted a good price, book it on the spot**—the same fare may not be available on the same flight the next day. Airlines generally allow you to change your return date for a fee of $25–$50. If you don't use your ticket you can apply the cost toward the purchase of a new ticket, again for a small charge. However, most low-fare tickets are nonrefundable. To get the lowest airfare, **check different routings.** If your destination or home city has more than one gateway, compare prices to and from different airports. Also price off-peak flights, which may be significantly less expensive.

To save money on flights from the United Kingdom and back, **look into an APEX or Super-PEX ticket.** APEX tickets must be booked in advance and have certain restrictions. Super-PEX tickets can be purchased at the airport on the day of departure—subject to availability.

DON'T STOP UNLESS YOU MUST

When you book, **look for nonstop flights** and **remember that "direct" flights stop at least once.** Try to **avoid connecting flights,** which require a change of plane. Two airlines may jointly operate a connecting flight, so ask if your airline operates every segment—you may find that your preferred carrier flies you only part of the way.

USE AN AGENT

Travel agents, especially those who specialize in finding the lowest fares, can be especially helpful when booking a plane ticket. When you're quoted a price, **ask your agent if the price is likely to get any lower.** Good agents know the seasonal fluctuations of airfares and can usually anticipate a sale or fare war. However, waiting can be risky: The fare could go *up* as seats become scarce, and you may wait so long that your preferred flight sells out. A wait-and-see strategy works best if your plans are flexible, but if you must arrive and depart on certain dates, don't delay.

In winter, when seat availability shrinks and prices climb, a savvy travel agent may be able to secure you an otherwise-elusive excursion-fare ticket. Since airlines often set aside seats for travelers going abroad, **ask your agent to book passage to a foreign destination with a change in Florida and discard the overseas legs.**

AVOID GETTING BUMPED

Airlines routinely overbook planes, knowing that not everyone with a ticket will show up, but sometimes everyone does. When that happens, airlines ask for volunteers to give up their seats. In return these volunteers usually get a certificate for a free flight and are rebooked on the next flight out. If there are not enough volunteers the airline must choose who will be denied boarding. The first to get bumped are passengers who checked in late and those flying on discounted tickets, so **get to the gate and check in as early as possible,** especially during peak periods.

Always **bring a photo ID to the airport.** You may be asked to show it before you are allowed to check in.

ENJOY THE FLIGHT

For better service, **fly smaller or regional carriers,** which often have higher passenger-satisfaction ratings. Sometimes you'll find leather seats, more legroom, and better food.

For more legroom, **request an emergency-aisle seat;** don't however, sit in the row in front of the emergency aisle or in front of a bulkhead, where seats may not recline.

If you don't like airline food, **ask for special meals when booking.** These can be vegetarian, low-cholesterol, or kosher, for example.

COMPLAIN IF NECESSARY

If your baggage goes astray or your flight goes awry, complain right away. Most carriers require that you file a claim immediately.

➤ AIRLINE COMPLAINTS: U.S. Department of Transportation **Aviation Consumer Protection Division** (✉ C-75, Washington, DC 20590, ☎ 202/366–2220). **Federal Aviation Administration (FAA) Consumer Hotline** (☎ 800/322–7873).

AIRPORTS

Because Florida is dotted with both major and regional airports, you can usually pick one quite close to your destination and often choose from a couple of nearby options. If you're destined for the north side of Dade (metro Miami), **consider flying into Fort Lauderdale–Hollywood International;** it's much easier to use than Miami International.

➤ MAJOR AIRPORTS: **Fort Lauderdale–Hollywood International** (☎ 954/359–1200). **Miami International** (☎ 305/876–7000). **Orlando International** (☎ 561/825–2001). **Palm Beach International** (☎ 561/471–7420). **Tampa International** (☎ 813/870–8700).

B

BOOKS

If you plan to spend time at the beach, **bring along some good books about Florida** to get you in the mood. Or, if you'll be doing a lot of driving, **pick up some audiotapes** (some of these titles are available on cassette).

Suspense novels that are rich in details about Florida include Pulitzer Prize winner Edna Buchanan's *Miami, It's Murder* and *Contents Under Pressure;* Les Standiford's *Done Deal,* about violence in the Miami construction business; former prosecuting attorney Barbara Parker's *Suspicion of Innocence;* Clifford Irving's *Final Argument;* Elmore Leonard's *La Brava;* John D. MacDonald's *The Empty Copper Sea;* Joan Higgins's *A Little Death Music;* and Charles Willeford's *Miami Blues.* James W.

Hall features Florida in many of his big-sellers, such as *Mean High Tide*, the chilling *Bones of Coral*, and *Hard Aground*.

Marjorie Kinnan Rawlings's classic, *The Yearling*, poignantly portrays life in the brush country, and her *Cross Creek* re-creates the memorable people she knew there. Peter Matthiessen's *Killing Mister Watson* re-creates turn-of-the-century lower southwest Florida.

Look for *Princess of the Everglades*, a novel about the 1926 hurricane by Charles Mink, and *Snow White and Rose Red* and *Jack and the Beanstalk*, Ed McBain's novels about a gulf city attorney. *The Tourist Season* is Carl Hiaasen's immensely funny declaration of war against the state's environment-despoiling hordes; he has also written *Double Whammy*, *Skin Tight*, *Native Tongue*, and *Strip Tease*.

Other recommended titles include Roxanne Pulitzer's *Facade*, set against a backdrop of Palm Beach; Peter Dexter's *The Paperboy*; Pat Booth's *Miami*; Sam Harrison's *Bones of Blue Coral* and *Birdsong Ascending*; T. D. Allman's *Miami*; Joan Didion's *Miami*; David Rieff's *Going To Miami*; Alice Hoffman's *Turtle Moon*; *Scavenger Reef* and *Florida Straits*, by Laurence Shames; *To Have and Have Not*, by Ernest Hemingway; *The Day of the Dolphin*, by Robert Merle; and *Their Eyes Were Watching God*, by Zora Neale Hurston.

Among recommended nonfiction books are *The Commodore's Story* by Ralph Munroe and Vincent Gilpin, a luminous reminiscence about the golden years (pre-railroad) of Coconut Grove; *Key West Writers and Their Homes*, by Lynn Kaufelt; *The Everglades: River of Grass*, by Marjory S. Douglas; *The Other Florida*, by Gloria Jahoda; and *Florida's Sandy Beaches*, University Press of Florida. Mark Derr's *Some Kind of Paradise* is an excellent review of the state's environmental follies; John Rothchild's *Up for Grabs*, equally good, is about Florida's commercial lunacy. Good anthologies include *The Florida Reader: Visions of Paradise* (Maurice O'Sullivan and Jack Lane, eds.), *The Rivers of Florida* (Del and Marty North, eds.), and *Subtropical Speculations: An Anthology of Florida Science Fiction* (Richard Mathews and Rick Wilber, eds.).

BUS TRAVEL

Greyhound passes through practically every major city in Florida. For schedules and fares, **contact your local Greyhound Information Center.**

➤ BUS LINES: Greyhound (☎ 800/ 231–2222).

C

CAMERAS, CAMCORDERS, & COMPUTERS

Always **keep your film, tape, or computer disks out of the sun.** Carry an extra supply of batteries, and **be prepared to turn on your camera, camcorder, or laptop** to prove to security personnel that the device is real. Always **ask for hand inspection of film,** which becomes clouded after successive exposure to airport x-ray machines, and **keep videotapes and computer disks away from metal detectors.**

➤ PHOTO HELP: Kodak Information Center (☎ 800/242–2424). *Kodak Guide to Shooting Great Travel Pictures* (available in bookstores or from Fodor's Travel Publications, ☎ 800/533–6478; $16.50 plus $4 shipping).

CAR RENTAL

Rates in Miami begin at $31 a day and $160 a week for an economy car with air conditioning, an automatic transmission, and unlimited mileage. Rates in Orlando begin at $30 a day and $149 a week. Rates in Fort Lauderdale begin at $31 a day and $143 a week. Rates in Tampa begin at $33 a day and $126 a week. This does not include tax on car rentals, which is 6%.

➤ MAJOR AGENCIES: **Alamo** (☎ 800/ 327–9633, 0800/272–2000 in the U.K.). **Avis** (☎ 800/331–1212, 800/ 879–2847 in Canada). **Budget** (☎ 800/527–0700, 0800/181181 in the U.K.). **Dollar** (☎ 800/800–4000; 0990/565656 in the U.K., where it is known as Eurodollar). **Hertz** (☎ 800/ 654–3131, 800/263–0600 in Canada, 0345/555888 in the U.K.). **National InterRent** (☎ 800/227– 7368; 0345/222525 in the U.K., where it is known as Europcar Inter-Rent).

➤ LOCAL FIRMS: **Aapex Rent A Car** (☎ 954/782–3400) in Fort Lauderdale. **Florida Auto Rental** (☎ 954/764–1008 or 800/327–3791) in Fort Lauderdale. **InterAmerican Car Rental** (☎ 305/871–3030) in Fort Lauderdale, Miami Beach, Orlando, and Tampa. **Pinellas Rent-A-Car** (☎ 813/287–1872 or 800/526–5499) in Tampa–St. Petersburg. **Snappy Car Rental** (☎ 407/859–8808) in Orlando. **Tropical Rent-a-Car** ☎ 305/294–8136) in Key West. **Ugly Duckling Rent-A-Car** (☎ 407/240–7368 or 800/843–3825) in Orlando.

CUT COSTS

Florida is a bazaar of car rentals, with more discount companies offering more bargains—and more fine print—than any other state in the nation. For the best deal, **look for the best combination rate for car and airfare.**

To get the best deal, **book through a travel agent who is willing to shop around.** When pricing cars, **ask about the location of the rental lot.** Some off-airport locations offer lower rates, and their lots are only minutes from the terminal via complimentary shuttle. You also may want to **price local car-rental companies,** whose rates may be lower still, although their service and maintenance may not be as good as those of a name-brand agency. Remember to ask about required deposits, cancellation penalties, and drop-off charges if you're planning to pick up the car in one city and leave it in another.

Also **ask your travel agent about a company's customer-service record.** How has it responded to late plane arrivals and vehicle mishaps? Are there often lines at the rental counter, and, if you're traveling during a holiday period, does a confirmed reservation guarantee you a car?

Be sure to **look into wholesalers,** companies that do not own fleets but rent in bulk from those that do and often offer better rates than traditional car-rental operations. Prices are best during off-peak periods.

➤ RENTAL WHOLESALERS: **Auto Europe** (☎ 207/828–2525 or 800/223–5555).

NEED INSURANCE?

When driving a rented car you are generally responsible for any damage to or loss of the vehicle. Before you rent, **see what coverage you already have** under the terms of your personal auto-insurance policy and credit cards.

For about $14 a day, rental companies sell protection, known as a collision- or loss-damage waiver (CDW or LDW) that eliminates your liability for damage to the car; it's always optional and should never be automatically added to your bill.

In most states you don't need CDW if you have personal auto insurance or other liability insurance. However, **make sure you have enough coverage to pay for the car.** If you do not have auto insurance or an umbrella policy that covers damage to third parties, purchasing liability insurance and CDW or LDW is highly recommended.

BEWARE SURCHARGES

Before you pick up a car in one city and leave it in another, **ask about drop-off charges or one-way service fees,** which can be substantial. Note, too, that some rental agencies charge extra if you return the car before the time specified on your contract. To avoid a hefty refueling fee, **fill the tank just before you turn in the car,** but be aware that gas stations near the rental outlet may overcharge.

MEET THE REQUIREMENTS

In the United States you must be 21 to rent a car, and rates may be higher if you're under 25. You'll pay extra for child seats (about $3 per day), which are compulsory for children under five, and for additional drivers (about $2 per day). Residents of the U.K. will need a reservation voucher, a passport, a U.K. driver's license, and a travel policy that covers each driver, in order to pick up a car.

CHILDREN & TRAVEL

CHILDREN IN FLORIDA

Be sure to plan ahead and **involve your youngsters** as you outline your trip. When packing, include things to keep them busy en route. On sightseeing days try to schedule activities of special interest to your children. If you are renting a car don't forget to **arrange for a car seat** when you reserve.

HOTELS

Florida may have the highest concentration of hotels with organized children's programs in the United States. Activities range from simple fun and recreation to shell-hunting on Marco Island at Marriott's Marco Island Resort and learning about the Keys' environment from marine-science counselors at Cheeca Lodge. Sometimes kids' programs are complimentary; sometimes there's a charge. Not all accept children in diapers, and some offer programs when their central reservations services say they don't. Some programs are only offered during peak seasons or restrict hours in less-busy times. It always pays to **confirm details with the hotel in advance.**

➤ FORT LAUDERDALE: **Marriott's Harbor Beach Resort's Beachside Buddies** (⊠ 3030 Holiday Dr., Fort Lauderdale, FL 33316, ☎ 954/525–4000 or 800/228–9290), ages 5–12.

➤ THE KEYS: **Cheeca Lodge's Camp Cheeca** (⊠ MM 82, OS, Box 527, Islamorada, FL 33036, ☎ 800/327–2888), ages 6–12. **Sheraton Key Largo Resort's Keys Kids Club** (⊠ MM 96.9, BS, 97000 Overseas Hwy., Key Largo, FL 33037, ☎ 305/852–5553 or 800/325–3535), ages 5–12.

➤ MARCO ISLAND: **Marriott's Marco Island Resort's Beach Bandits** (⊠ 400 S. Collier Blvd., Marco Island, FL 33937, ☎ 800/228–9290), ages 5–13. **Radisson Suite Beach Resort's Radisson Rascals** (⊠ 600 S. Collier Blvd., Marco Island, FL 33937, ☎ 800/333–3333), ages 3–12.

➤ MIAMI AREA: **Sonesta Beach Resort's Just Us Kids** (⊠ 350 Ocean Dr., Key Biscayne, FL 33149, ☎ 800/766–3782), ages 5–13.

➤ NORTHEAST FLORIDA: **Amelia Island Plantation's Sunday Night at the Movies and Kids Night Out** (⊠ 3000 First Coast Hwy., Amelia Island, FL 32034, ☎ 904/261–6161 or 800/874–6878), ages 3–12.

➤ ORLANDO AREA: **Delta Orlando Resort's Wally's Club Kids Creative Center** (⊠ 5715 Major Blvd., Orlando, FL 32819, ☎ 800/877–1133), ages 6–12. **Holiday Inn Maingate East** (⊠ 5678 Space Coast Hwy., Kissimmee, FL 32741, ☎ 407/396–4488 or 800/465–4329), ages 3–12. **Holiday Inn Sunspree Resort Lake Buena Vista's Camp Holiday** (⊠ 13351 Rte. 535, Orlando, FL 32821, ☎ 800/366–6299), ages 2–12. **Hyatt Regency Grand Cypress Resort's Camp Gator** (⊠ 1 Grand Cypress Blvd., Orlando, FL 32819, ☎ 407/239–1234 or 800/228–9000), ages 5–12. **Renaissance Orlando Resort's Shamu's Playhouse** (⊠ 6677 Sea Harbor Dr., Orlando, FL 32821, ☎ 407/351–5555 or 800/468–3571), ages 2–12.

➤ PALM BEACH AND THE TREASURE COAST: **Club Med's Sandpiper** (⊠ Port St. Lucie [mailing address: 40 W. 57th St., New York, NY 10019], ☎ 800/258–2633), Baby Club ages 4–24 months, Mini Club ages 2–11. **Indian River Plantation Beach Resort's Pineapple Bunch Children's Camp** (⊠ 555 N.E. Ocean Blvd., Hutchinson Island, Stuart, FL 34996, ☎ 561/225–6990 or 800/947–2148), ages 4–12, plus a teen program.

FLYING

As a general rule, infants under two not occupying a seat fly free. If your children are two or older **ask about children's airfares.**

In general the adult baggage allowance applies to children paying half or more of the adult fare.

According to the FAA it's a good idea to use safety seats aloft for children weighing less than 40 pounds. Airlines, however, can set their own policies: U.S. carriers allow FAA-approved models but usually require that you buy a ticket, even if your child would otherwise ride free, since the seats must be strapped into regular seats. Airline rules vary regarding their use, so it's important to **check your airline's policy about using safety seats during takeoff and landing.** Safety seats cannot obstruct any of the other passengers in the row, so get an appropriate seat assignment as early as possible.

When making your reservation, **request children's meals or a free-standing bassinet** if you need them; the latter are available only to those seated at the bulkhead, where there's enough legroom. Remember, however, that bulkhead seats may not have their own overhead bins, and there's no storage space in front of you—a major inconvenience.

GROUP TRAVEL

If you're planning to take your kids on a tour, look for companies that specialize in family travel.

➤ FAMILY-FRIENDLY TOUR OPERATORS: **Rascals in Paradise** (✉ 650 5th St., Suite 505, San Francisco, CA 94107, ☎ 415/978–9800 or 800/872–7225).

CONSUMER PROTECTION

Whenever possible, **pay with a major credit card** so you can cancel payment if there's a problem, provided that you can provide documentation. This is a good practice whether you're buying travel arrangements before your trip or shopping at your destination.

If you're doing business with a particular company for the first time, **contact your local Better Business Bureau and the attorney general's offices** in your state and the company's home state, as well. Have any complaints been filed?

Finally, if you're buying a package or tour, always **consider travel insurance** that includes default coverage (☞ Insurance, *below*).

➤ LOCAL BBBs: **Council of Better Business Bureaus** (✉ 4200 Wilson Blvd., Suite 800, Arlington, VA 22203, ☎ 703/276–0100, FAX 703/525–8277).

CUSTOMS & DUTIES

ENTERING FLORIDA

Visitors age 21 and over may import the following into the United States: 200 cigarettes or 50 cigars or 2 kilograms of tobacco, 1 liter of alcohol, and gifts worth $100. Prohibited items include meat products, seeds, plants, and fruits.

ENTERING CANADA

If you've been out of Canada for at least seven days you may bring in C$500 worth of goods duty-free. If you've been away for fewer than seven days but more than 48 hours, the duty-free allowance drops to C$200; if your trip lasts 24–48 hours, the allowance is C$50. You may not pool allowances with family members. Goods claimed under the C$500 exemption may follow you by mail; those claimed under the lesser exemptions must accompany you.

Alcohol and tobacco products may be included in the seven-day and 48-hour exemptions but not in the 24-hour exemption. If you meet the age requirements of the province or territory through which you reenter Canada you may bring in, duty-free, 1.14 liters (40 imperial ounces) of wine or liquor *or* 24 12-ounce cans or bottles of beer or ale. If you are 16 or older you may bring in, duty-free, 200 cigarettes and 50 cigars; these items must accompany you.

You may send an unlimited number of gifts worth up to C$60 each duty-free to Canada. Label the package UNSOLICITED GIFT—VALUE UNDER $60. Alcohol and tobacco are excluded.

➤ INFORMATION: **Revenue Canada** (✉ 2265 St. Laurent Blvd. S, Ottawa, Ontario K1G 4K3, ☎ 613/993–0534, 800/461–9999 in Canada).

ENTERING THE U.K.

From countries outside the EU, including the United States, you may import, duty-free, 200 cigarettes or 50 cigars; 1 liter of spirits or 2 liters of fortified or sparkling wine or liqueurs; 2 liters of still table wine; 60 milliliters of perfume; 250 milliliters of toilet water; plus £145 worth of other goods, including gifts and souvenirs.

➤ INFORMATION: **HM Customs and Excise** (✉ Dorset House, Stamford St., London SE1 9NG, ☎ 0171/202–4227).

D

DINING

One cautionary word: Raw oysters have been identified as a problem for people with chronic illness of the liver, stomach, or blood, or who have immune disorders. Since 1993, all Florida restaurants serving raw oys-

SMART TRAVEL TIPS

THE GOLD GUIDE / SMART TRAVEL TIPS

ters are required to post a notice in plain view of all patrons warning of the risks associated with consuming them.

DISABILITIES & ACCESSIBILITY

TIPS & HINTS

When discussing accessibility with an operator or reservationist, **ask hard questions.** Are there any stairs, inside *or* out? Are there grab bars next to the toilet *and* in the shower/tub? How wide is the doorway to the room? To the bathroom? For the most extensive facilities meeting the latest legal specifications, **opt for newer accommodations,** which are more likely to have been designed with access in mind. Older buildings or ships may offer more limited facilities. Be sure to **discuss your needs before booking.**

➤ ACCESSIBLE ATTRACTIONS, RESTAURANTS, AND HOTELS: *Great American Vacations for Travelers with Disabilities* (available in bookstores or from Fodor's Travel Publications, ☎ 800/533–6478; $19.50).

➤ COMPLAINTS: **Disability Rights Section** (✉ U.S. Dept. of Justice, Box 66738, Washington, DC 20035-6738, ☎ 202/514–0301 or 800/514–0301, FAX 202/307–1198, TTY 202/514–0383 or 800/514–0383) for general complaints. **Aviation Consumer Protection Division** (☞ Air Travel, *above*) for airline-related problems. **Civil Rights Office** (✉ U.S. Dept. of Transportation, Departmental Office of Civil Rights, S-30, 400 7th St. SW, Room 10215, Washington, DC 20590, ☎ 202/366–4648) for problems with surface transportation.

TRAVEL AGENCIES & TOUR OPERATORS

The Americans with Disabilities Act requires that travel firms serve the needs of all travelers. That said, you should note that some agencies and operators specialize in making travel arrangements for individuals and groups with disabilities.

➤ TRAVELERS WITH MOBILITY PROBLEMS: **Access Adventures** (✉ 206 Chestnut Ridge Rd., Rochester, NY 14624, ☎ 716/889–9096), run by a former physical-rehabilitation counselor. **Hinsdale Travel Service** (✉ 201 E. Ogden Ave., Suite 100, Hinsdale, IL 60521, ☎ 630/325–1335), a

travel agency that benefits from the advice of wheelchair traveler Janice Perkins. **Wheelchair Journeys** (✉ 16979 Redmond Way, Redmond, WA 98052, ☎ 206/885–2210 or 800/313–4751), for general travel arrangements.

➤ TRAVELERS WITH DEVELOPMENTAL DISABILITIES: **Sprout** (✉ 893 Amsterdam Ave., New York, NY 10025, ☎ 212/222–9575 or 888/222–9575, FAX 212/222–9768).

DISCOUNTS & DEALS

Be a smart shopper and **compare all your options before making a choice.** A plane ticket bought with a promotional coupon may not be cheaper than the least expensive fare from a discount ticket agency. For high-price travel purchases, such as packages or tours, keep in mind that what you get is just as important as what you save. Just because something is cheap doesn't mean it's a bargain.

LOOK IN YOUR WALLET

When you use your credit card to make travel purchases you may get free travel-accident insurance, collision-damage insurance, and medical or legal assistance, depending on the card and the bank that issued it. American Express, MasterCard, and Visa provide one or more of these services, so **get a copy of your credit card's travel-benefits policy.** If you are a member of the American Automobile Association (AAA) or an oil-company-sponsored road-assistance plan, always **ask hotel or car-rental reservationists about auto-club discounts.** Some clubs offer additional discounts on tours, cruises, or admission to attractions. And don't forget that auto-club membership entitles you to free maps and trip-planning services.

DIAL FOR DOLLARS

To save money, **look into "1-800" discount reservations services,** which use their buying power to get a better price on hotels, airline tickets, even car rentals. When booking a room, always **call the hotel's local toll-free number** (if one is available) rather than the central reservations number—you'll often get a better price. Always ask about special packages or corporate rates.

➤ AIRLINE TICKETS: ☎ 800/FLY–4–LESS. ☎ 800/FLY–ASAP.

➤ HOTEL ROOMS: **Accommodations Express** (☎ 800/444–7666). **Central Reservation Service** (CRS; ☎ 800/548–3311). **Hotel Reservations Network** (HRN; ☎ 800/964–6835). **Players Express Vacations** (☎ 800/458–6161). **RMC Travel** (☎ 800/245–5738). **Steigenberger Reservation Service** (☎ 800/223–5652).

SAVE ON COMBOS

Packages and guided tours can both save you money, but don't confuse the two. When you buy a package your travel remains independent, just as though you had planned and booked the trip yourself. Fly/drive packages, which combine airfare and car rental, are often a good deal.

JOIN A CLUB?

Many companies sell discounts in the form of travel clubs and coupon books, but these cost money. You must use participating advertisers to get a deal, and only after you recoup the initial membership cost or book price do you begin to save. If you plan to use the club or coupons frequently you may save considerably. Before signing up, find out what discounts you get for free.

➤ DISCOUNT CLUBS: **Entertainment Travel Editions** (✉ Box 1068, Trumbull, CT 06611, ☎ 800/445–4137; $28–$53, depending on destination). **Great American Traveler** (✉ Box 27965, Salt Lake City, UT 84127, ☎ 800/548–2812; $49.95 per year). **Moment's Notice Discount Travel Club** (✉ 7301 New Utrecht Ave., Brooklyn, NY 11204, ☎ 718/234–6295; $25 per year, single or family). **Privilege Card International** (✉ 201 E. Commerce St., Suite 198, Youngstown, OH 44503, ☎ 330/746–5211 or 800/236–9732; $74.95 per year). **Sears's Mature Outlook** (✉ Box 9390, Des Moines, IA 50306, ☎ 800/336–6330; $14.95 per year). **Travelers Advantage** (✉ CUC Travel Service, 3033 S. Parker Rd., Suite 1000, Aurora, CO 80014, ☎ 800/548–1116 or 800/648–4037; $49 per year, single or family). **Worldwide Discount Travel Club** (✉ 1674 Meridian Ave., Miami Beach, FL 33139, ☎ 305/534–2082; $50 per year family, $40 single).

Three major interstates lead to Florida. I–95 begins in Maine, runs south through the Mid-Atlantic states, and enters Florida just north of Jacksonville. It continues south past Daytona Beach, the Space Coast, Vero Beach, Palm Beach, and Fort Lauderdale, eventually ending in Miami.

I–75 begins in Michigan at the Canadian border and runs south through Ohio, Kentucky, Tennessee, and Georgia, then moves through the center of the state before veering west into Tampa. It follows the west coast south to Naples, then crosses the state, and ends in Fort Lauderdale.

California and all the most southern states are connected to Florida by I–10, which moves east from Los Angeles through Arizona, New Mexico, Texas, Louisiana, Mississippi, and Alabama; it enters Florida at Pensacola and crosses the northern part of the state to Jacksonville.

SAFETY

Before setting off on any drive, **make sure you know where you're going** and carry a map. When you rent your car or at your hotel **ask if there are any areas that you should avoid.** Always **keep your doors locked,** and ask questions only at toll booths, gas stations, or other obviously safe locations. Also, **don't stop if your car is bumped from behind** or if you're asked for directions. One hesitates to foster rude behavior, but at least for now the roads are too risky to stop any place you're not familiar with (other than as traffic laws require). If you'll be renting a car, **ask the car-rental agency for a cellular phone.** Alamo, Avis, and Hertz are among the companies with in-car phones.

SPEED LIMITS

Speed limits are 55 mph on state highways, 30 mph within city limits and residential areas, and 55–70 mph on interstates and Florida's Turnpike. Be alert for signs announcing exceptions.

G

➤ GUIDES TO GAY- AND LESBIAN-FRIENDLY TRAVEL: *Fodor's Gay Guide to the USA* and *Fodor's Gay Guide to*

South Florida (available in bookstores or from Fodor's Travel Publications, ☎ 800/533–6478; $19.50 and $11).

➤ TOUR OPERATORS: **R.S.V.P. Travel Productions** (✉ 2800 University Ave. SE, Minneapolis, MN 55414, ☎ 612/379–4697 or 800/328–7787), for cruises and resort vacations for gays. **Toto Tours** (✉ 1326 W. Albion Ave., Suite 3W, Chicago, IL 60626, ☎ 773/274–8686 or 800/565–1241, FAX 773/274–8695), for groups.

➤ GAY- AND LESBIAN-FRIENDLY TRAVEL AGENCIES: **Advance Damron** (✉ 1 Greenway Plaza, Suite 800, Houston, TX 77046, ☎ 713/682–2002 or 800/695–0880, FAX 713/888–1010). **Club Travel** (✉ 8739 Santa Monica Blvd., West Hollywood, CA 90069, ☎ 310/358–2200 or 800/429–8747). **Islanders/Kennedy Travel** (✉ 183 W. 10th St., New York, NY 10014, ☎ 212/242–3222 or 800/988–1181). **Now Voyager** (✉ 4406 18th St., San Francisco, CA 94114, ☎ 415/626–1169 or 800/255–6951). **Skylink Women's Travel** (✉ 3577 Moorland Ave., Santa Rosa, CA 95407, ☎ 707/585–8355 or 800/225–5759), serving lesbian travelers. **Yellowbrick Road** (✉ 1500 W. Balmoral Ave., Chicago, IL 60640, ☎ 773/561–1800 or 800/642–2488).

H
HEALTH

BEACH SAFETY

If you are unaccustomed to strong subtropical sun, you run a risk of sunburn and heat prostration, even in winter. So **hit the beach before 10 or after 3.** If you must be out at midday, **limit strenuous exercise, drink plenty of liquids, and wear a hat.** Even on overcast days, ultraviolet rays shine through the haze, so **use a sunscreen with an SPF of at least 15,** and have children wear a waterproof SPF 30 or better.

While you're frolicking on the beach, **steer clear of what looks like blue bubbles on the sand.** These are either jellyfish or Portuguese man-of-wars, and their tentacles can cause an allergic reaction.

Before swimming, **make sure there's no undertow.** Rip currents, caused

when the tide rushes out through a narrow break in a sandbar, can overpower even the strongest swimmer. If you're caught in one, resist the urge to swim straight back to shore—you'll never make it. Instead, stay calm, swim parallel to the shore until you are outside the current's pull, and then work your way in.

DIVERS' ALERT

Schedule your scuba diving so you **do not fly within 24 hours of diving.**

I
INSURANCE

Travel insurance is the best way to **protect yourself against financial loss.** The most useful policies are trip-cancellation-and-interruption, default, medical, and comprehensive insurance.

Without insurance you will lose all or most of your money if you cancel your trip, regardless of the reason. It's essential that you **buy trip-cancellation-and-interruption insurance,** particularly if your airline ticket, cruise, or package tour is nonrefundable and cannot be changed. When considering how much coverage you need, look for a policy that will cover the cost of your trip plus the nondiscounted price of a one-way airline ticket, should you need to return home early. Also **consider default or bankruptcy insurance,** which protects you against a supplier's failure to deliver.

Citizens of the United Kingdom can buy an annual travel-insurance policy valid for most vacations during the year in which it's purchased. If you are pregnant or have a preexisting medical condition, make sure you're covered. According to the Association of British Insurers, a trade association representing 450 insurance companies, it's wise to buy extra medical coverage when you visit the United States.

If you have purchased an expensive vacation, comprehensive insurance is a must. It's wise to **look for comprehensive policies that include trip-delay insurance,** which will protect you in the event that weather problems cause you to miss your flight, tour, or cruise. A few insurers sell waivers for preexisting medical conditions. Companies that offer both features include Access America, Carefree Travel Insurance, Travel Guard International, and Travel Insured International (☞ *below*).

Always **buy travel insurance directly from the insurance company;** if you buy it from a travel agency or tour operator that goes out of business you probably will not be covered for the agency or operator's default, a major risk. Before you make any purchase, **review your existing health and home-owner's policies** to find out whether they cover expenses incurred while traveling.

➤ TRAVEL INSURERS: In the U.S., **Access America** (✉ 6600 W. Broad St., Richmond, VA 23230, ☎ 804/285–3300 or 800/284–8300), **Carefree Travel Insurance** (✉ Box 9366, 100 Garden City Plaza, Garden City, NY 11530, ☎ 516/294–0220 or 800/ 323–3149), **Near Travel Services** (✉ Box 1339, Calumet City, IL 60409, ☎ 708/868–6700 or 800/ 654–6700), **Travelex Insurance Services** (✉ 11717 Burt St., Suite 202, Omaha, NE 68154-1500, ☎ 402/ 445–8637 or 800/228–9792, FAX 402/491–0016), **Travel Guard International** (✉ 1145 Clark St., Stevens Point, WI 54481, ☎ 715/345–0505 or 800/826–1300), **Travel Insured International** (✉ Box 280568, East Hartford, CT 06128-0568, ☎ 860/ 528–7663 or 800/243–3174), **Wallach & Company** (✉ 107 W. Federal St., Box 480, Middleburg, VA 20118, ☎ 540/687–3166 or 800/237– 6615). In Canada, **Mutual of Omaha** (✉ Travel Division, 500 University Ave., Toronto, Ontario M5G 1V8, ☎ 416/598–4083, 800/268–8825 in Canada). In the U.K., **Association of British Insurers** (✉ 51 Gresham St., London EC2V 7HQ, ☎ 0171/600– 3333).

L

LODGING

Florida has every conceivable type of lodging—from tree houses to penthouses, mansions for hire to hostels. Recession has discouraged wildfire expansion, but even with occupancy rates inching above 70%, there are almost always rooms available, except maybe at Christmas and other holidays. Affordable lodgings can be found in even the most glittery resort towns, typically motel rooms that may cost as little as $30–$40 a night; they may not be in the best part of town, mind you, but they won't be in the worst, either (perhaps along busy highways where you'll need the roar of the air-conditioning to drown out the traffic). Since beachfront properties tend to be more expensive, **look for properties a little off the beach.** Still, many beachfront properties are surprisingly affordable, too, as in places like Olde Naples in the far southwest and Amelia Island in the far northeast.

Children are welcome generally everywhere in Florida. Pets are another matter, so **inquire ahead of time if you're bringing an animal with you.**

In the busy seasons—over Christmas, from late January through Easter, and during holiday weekends in summer—always **reserve ahead for the top properties.** St. Augustine stays busy all summer because of its historic flavor. Key West is jam-packed for Fantasy Fest at Halloween. If you're not booking through a travel agent, call the visitors bureau or the chamber of commerce in the area where you're going to check whether any special event is scheduled for when you plan to arrive. If demand isn't especially high for the time you have in mind, you can often **save by showing up at a lodging in mid- to late afternoon**—desk clerks are typically willing to negotiate with travelers in order to fill those rooms late in the day. In addition, **check with chambers of commerce for discount coupons for selected properties.**

APARTMENT & VILLA RENTALS

If you want a home base that's roomy enough for a family and comes with cooking facilities, **consider a furnished rental.** These can save you money, however some rentals are luxury properties, economical only when your party is large. Home-exchange directories list rentals (often second homes owned by prospective house swappers), and some services search for a house or apartment for you (even a castle if that's your fancy) and handle the paperwork. Some send an illustrated catalog; others send photographs only of specific properties, sometimes at a charge. Up-front registration fees may apply.

➤ RENTAL AGENTS: **Europa-Let/Tropical Inn-Let** (✉ 92 N. Main St., Ashland, OR 97520, ☎ 541/482–5806 or 800/462–4486, FAX 541/482–0660). **Hideaways International** (✉ 767 Islington St., Portsmouth, NH 03801, ☎ 603/430–4433 or 800/843–4433, FAX 603/430–4444; $99 per year), a travel club whose members arrange rentals among themselves. **Hometours International** (✉ Box 11503, Knoxville, TN 37939, ☎ 423/690–8484 or 800/367–4668). **Property Rentals International** (✉ 1008 Mansfield Crossing Rd., Richmond, VA 23236, ☎ 804/378–6054 or 800/220–3332, FAX 804/379–2073). **Vacation Home Rentals Worldwide** (✉ 235 Kensington Ave., Norwood, NJ 07648, ☎ 201/767–9393 or 800/633–3284, FAX 201/767–5510).

CAMPING & RV FACILITIES

For information on camping facilities, **contact the national and state parks and forests you plan to visit and the Florida Department of Environmental Protection** (☞ Parks & Preserves, *below*).

To find a commercial campground, **pick up a copy of the free annual "Florida Camping Directory,"** which lists 220 campgrounds, with 66,000 sites. It's available at Florida welcome centers, from the Florida Tourism Industry Marketing Corporation (☞ Visitor Information, *below*), and from the Florida Association of RV Parks & Campgrounds.

➤ CAMPING ASSOCIATION: **Florida Association of RV Parks & Campgrounds** (✉ 1340 Vickers Dr., Tallahassee, FL 32303-3041, ☎ 904/562–7151, FAX 904/562–7179).

CONDOS

➤ CONDO GUIDE: *The Condo Lux Vacationer's Guide to Condominium Rentals in the Southeast* (Vintage Books/Random House, New York; $9.95), by Jill Little.

HOME EXCHANGES

If you would like to exchange your home for someone else's, **join a home-exchange organization,** which will send you its updated listings of available exchanges for a year and will

include your own listing in at least one of them. Making the arrangements is up to you.

➤ EXCHANGE CLUBS: **HomeLink International** (✉ Box 650, Key West, FL 33041, ☎ 305/294–7766 or 800/638–3841, FAX 305/294–1148; $78 per year).

HOTELS & MOTELS

Wherever you look in Florida, it seems, you'll find lots of plain, inexpensive motels and luxurious resorts, independents alongside national chains, and an ever-growing number of modern properties as well as quite a few timeless classics. In fact, since Florida has been a favored travel destination for some time, vintage hotels are everywhere, both grand edifices like The Breakers and the Boca Raton Resort & Club, both in Boca Raton; the Biltmore in Coral Gables; and the Casa Marina in Key West and smaller, historic places, like the Miami River Inn in downtown Miami, the Governors Inn in Tallahassee, and the New World Inn in Pensacola.

➤ HOTEL AND MOTEL ASSOCIATION: **Florida Hotel & Motel Association** (✉ 200 W. College Ave., Box 1529, Tallahassee, FL 32301-1529, ☎ 904/224–2888).

INNS & B&BS

Small inns and guest houses are increasingly numerous in Florida. Many offer bed-and-breakfast in a homelike setting; in fact, many are in private homes, and their owners treat you almost like family.

➤ HISTORIC INN ASSOCIATION: **Inn Route, Inc.** (✉ Box 6187, Palm Harbor, FL 34684, ☎ FAX 813/786–9792 or 800/524–1880).

➤ REFERRAL AND RESERVATION AGENCIES: **Bed & Breakfast Co., Tropical Florida** (✉ Box 262, Miami, FL 33243, ☎ FAX 305/661–3270). **Bed & Breakfast Scenic Florida** (✉ Box 3385, Tallahassee, FL 32315-3385, ☎ 904/386–8196). **RSVP Florida & St. Augustine** (✉ Box 3603, St. Augustine, FL 32085, ☎ 904/471–0600). **Suncoast Accommodations of Florida** (✉ 8690 Gulf Blvd., St. Pete Beach, FL 33706, ☎ 813/360–1753).

VACATION OWNERSHIP RESORTS

Vacation ownership resorts sell hotel rooms, condominium apartments, and villas in weekly, monthly, or quarterly increments. The weekly arrangement is most popular; it's often referred to as "interval ownership" or "time sharing." Of more than 3,000 vacation ownership resorts around the world, some 500 are in Florida, with the heaviest concentration in the Walt Disney World/Orlando area. Non-owners can rent at many of these resorts by contacting the individual property or a real-estate broker in the area.

M

MONEY

ATMS

Before leaving home, **make sure that your credit cards have been programmed for ATM use.**

➤ ATM LOCATIONS: Cirrus (☎ 800/424–7787). Plus (☎ 800/843–7587).

P

PACKING FOR FLORIDA

The northern part of the state is much cooler in winter than the southern part. However, always **take a sweater or jacket,** just in case.

The Miami area and the Tampa–St. Petersburg area are warm year-round and often extremely humid in summer months. Be prepared for sudden summer storms, but keep in mind that plastic raincoats are uncomfortable in the high humidity.

Dress is casual throughout the state, with sundresses, jeans, or walking shorts appropriate during the day; **bring comfortable walking shoes or sneakers** for theme parks. A few restaurants request that men wear jackets and ties, but most do not. Be prepared for air-conditioning working in overdrive.

You can generally swim year-round in peninsular Florida from about New Smyrna Beach south on the Atlantic coast and from Tarpon Springs south on the Gulf Coast. Be sure to **take a sun hat and sunscreen** because the sun can be fierce, even in winter and even if it is chilly or overcast.

Bring an extra pair of eyeglasses or contact lenses in your carry-on luggage, and if you have a health problem, **pack enough medication** to last the entire trip. It's important that you **don't put prescription drugs or valuables in luggage to be checked;** it might go astray.

LUGGAGE

In general you are entitled to check two bags on flights within the United States. A third piece may be brought on board, but it must fit easily under the seat in front of you or in the overhead compartment.

Airline liability for baggage is limited to $1,250 per person on flights within the United States. On international flights it amounts to $9.07 per pound or $20 per kilogram for checked baggage (roughly $640 per 70-pound bag) and $400 per passenger for unchecked baggage. Insurance for losses exceeding these amounts can be bought from the airline at check-in for about $10 per $1,000 of coverage; note that this coverage excludes a rather extensive list of items, which is shown on your airline ticket.

Before departure, **itemize your bags' contents** and their worth, and label the bags with your name, address, and phone number. (If you use your home address, cover it so that potential thieves can't see it readily.) Inside each bag, **pack a copy of your itinerary.** At check-in, **make sure that each bag is correctly tagged** with the destination airport's three-letter code. If your bags arrive damaged or fail to arrive at all, file a written report with the airline before leaving the airport.

PARKS & PRESERVES

NATIONAL PARKS

You may be able to **save money on park entrance fees** by getting a discount pass. The Golden Eagle Pass ($25) gets you and your companions free admission to all parks for one year. (Camping and parking are extra). Both the Golden Age Passport, for U.S. citizens or permanent residents age 62 and older, and the Golden Access Passport, for travelers with disabilities, entitle holders to free entry to all national parks plus 50% off fees for the use of many park facilities and services. Both passports are free; you must show proof of age and U.S. citizenship or permanent residency (such as a U.S. passport, driver's license, or birth certificate) or proof of disability. All three passes are available at all national park entrances. Golden Eagle and Golden Access passes are also available by mail.

➤ PASSES BY MAIL: **National Park Service** (✉ U.S. Dept. of the Interior, Washington, DC 20240).

STATE PARKS

Florida's Department of Environmental Protection (DEP) is responsible for hundreds of historic buildings, landmarks, nature preserves, and parks. When requesting a free *Florida State Park Guide,* mention which parts of the state you plan to visit. For information on camping facilities at the state parks, ask for the free "Florida State Parks, Fees and Facilities" and "Florida State Parks Camping Reservation Procedures" brochures. Responding to cutbacks in its budget, the DEP established Friends of Florida State Parks, a citizen support organization open to all.

➤ STATE PARKS INFORMATION: **Florida Department of Environmental Protection** (✉ Marjory Stoneman Douglas Bldg., MS 535, 3900 Commonwealth Blvd., Tallahassee, FL 32399-3000, ☎ 904/488–2850, FAX 904/488–3947; Friends of Florida State Parks ☎ 904/488–8243).

PRIVATE PRESERVES

➤ FLORIDA SANCTUARY INFORMATION: **National Audubon Society** (✉ Sanctuary Director, Miles Wildlife Sanctuary, R.R. 1, Box 294, W. Cornwall Rd., Sharon, CT 06069, ☎ 203/364–0048). **Nature Conservancy** (✉ 222 S. Westmonte Dr., Suite 300, Altamonte Springs, FL 32714, ☎ 407/682–3554; offices at ✉ 250 Tequesta Dr., Suite 301, Tequesta, FL 33469, ☎ 561/744–6668; ✉ 201 Front St., Suite 222, Key West, FL 33040, ☎ 305/296–3880; ✉ 225 E. Stuart Ave., Lake Wales, FL 33853, ☎ 941/678–1551; ✉ 625 N. Adams St., Tallahassee, FL 32301, ☎ 904/222–0199; ✉ Comeau Bldg., 319 Clematis St., Suite 611, West Palm Beach, FL 33401, ☎ 561/833–4226).

CANADIANS

A passport is not required to enter the United States.

U.K. CITIZENS

British citizens need a valid passport to enter the United States. If you are staying for fewer than 90 days on vacation, with a return or onward ticket, you probably will not need a visa. However, you will need to fill out the Visa Waiver Form, 1-94W, supplied by the airline.

➤ INFORMATION: **London Passport Office** (☎ 0990/210–410) for fees, documentation requirements, and to request an emergency passport. **U.S. Embassy Visa Information Line** (☎ 0891/200–290, 50p per minute) for U.S. visa information. **U.S. Embassy Visa Branch** (✉ 5 Upper Grosvenor St., London W1A 2JB; send a self-addressed, stamped envelope) for U.S. visa information. Write the U.S. **Consulate General** (✉ Queen's House, Queen St., Belfast BTI 6EO) if you live in Northern Ireland.

S

To qualify for age-related discounts, **mention your senior-citizen status up front** when booking hotel reservations (not when checking out) and before you're seated in restaurants (not when paying the bill). Note that discounts may be limited to certain menus, days, or hours. When renting a car, **ask about promotional car-rental discounts,** which can be cheaper than senior-citizen rates.

➤ EDUCATIONAL TRAVEL PROGRAMS: **Elderhostel** (✉ 75 Federal St., 3rd Floor, Boston, MA 02110, ☎ 617/426–7788).

Recreational opportunities abound throughout Florida. The Governor's Council on Physical Fitness and Sports puts on the Sunshine State Games each July in a different part of the state.

➤ GENERAL INFORMATION: **Florida Department of Environmental Protection** (✉ Office of Greenways, MS 585, 3900 Commonwealth Blvd.,

Tallahassee, FL 32399-3000, ☎ 904/487-4784) for information on bicycling, canoeing, kayaking, and hiking trails. **Florida Sports Foundation** (✉ 107 W. Gaines St., Suite 466, Tallahassee, FL 32399-2000, ☎ 904/488-8347) for guides on baseball spring training, boating, fishing, golf, and scuba diving.

➤ MARINE CHARTS: **Tealls, Inc.** (✉ 111 Saguaro La., Marathon, FL 33050, ☎ 305/743-3942, FAX 305/743-3942; $7.95 set, $3.60 each individual chart).

BIKING

For bike information, **check with Florida's Department of Transportation (DOT),** which publishes free bicycle trail guides, dispenses free touring information packets, and provides names of bike coordinators around the state.

➤ BICYCLE INFORMATION: **DOT state bicycle-pedestrian coordinator** (✉ 605 E. Suwannee St., MS 82, Tallahassee, FL 32399-0450, ☎ 904/487-1200).

CANOEING & KAYAKING

You can canoe or kayak along 1,550 mi of trails encompassing creeks, rivers, and springs. Both the DEP (☞ General Information, *above*) and outfitter associations provide information on trails and their conditions, events, and contacts for trips and equipment rental.

➤ OUTFITTERS AND OUTFITTING ASSOCIATIONS: **Canoe Outpost System** (✉ 2816 N.W. Rte. 661, Arcadia, FL 33821, ☎ 941/494-1215), comprising five outfitters. **Florida Canoeing and Kayaking Association** (✉ Box 20892, West Palm Beach, FL 33416, ☎ 561/575-4530). **Florida Professional Paddlesports Association** (✉ Box 1764, Arcadia, FL 34265, no phone).

FISHING

In Atlantic and gulf waters, fishing seasons and other regulations vary by location and species. You will need to **buy a license for both freshwater and saltwater fishing.** Nonresident fees for a saltwater license are $30. Nonresidents can purchase freshwater licenses good for seven days ($15) or for one year ($30). Typically, you'll pay a $1.50 surcharge at most any marina,

bait shop, Kmart, WalMart, or other license vendor.

➤ FISHING INFORMATION: **Florida Game and Fresh Water Fish Commission** (✉ 620 S. Meridian St., Tallahassee, FL 32399-1600, ☎ 904/488-1960) for the free *Florida Fishing Handbook* with license vendors, regional fishing guides, and educational bulletins. **Florida Sea Grant Extension Program** (✉ Bldg. 803, University of Florida, Gainesville, FL 32611, ☎ 904/392-5870) for varied publications.

HORSEBACK RIDING

➤ DUDE RANCH: **Happy Wrangler Dude Ranch** (✉ 7586 S.W. 90th Ave., Bushnell, FL 33513, ☎ 352/793-3833).

➤ HORSEBACK RIDING INFORMATION: *Horse & Pony* (✉ 6229 Virginia La., Seffner, FL 33584, ☎ 813/621-2510). **Sunshine State Horse Council** (✉ Box 4158, North Fort Myers, FL 33918, ☎ 813/731-2999).

JOGGING, RUNNING, & WALKING

Local running clubs all over the state sponsor weekly public events.

➤ CLUBS & EVENTS: **USA Track & Field–Florida** (✉ Attn. Event Marketing & Management Intl., 1322 N. Mills Ave., Orlando, FL 32803, ☎ 407/895-6323, FAX 407/897-3243; send SASE for listings). **Miami Runners Club** (✉ 7920 S.W. 40th St., Miami, FL 33155, ☎ 305/227-1500, FAX 305/220-2450) for South Florida events.

PARI-MUTUEL SPORTS

➤ SCHEDULES: Department of Business & Professional Regulations **Division of Pari-Mutuel Wagering** (✉ 8405 N.W. 53rd St., Suite C-250, Miami, FL 33166, ☎ 305/470-5675, FAX 305/470-5686).

TENNIS

➤ TOURNAMENT AND EVENT SCHEDULES: **United States Tennis Association Florida Section** (✉ 1280 S.W. 36th Ave., Suite 305, Pompano Beach, FL 33069, ☎ 954/968-3434, FAX 954/968-3986; yearbook $11).

WILDERNESS & RECREATION AREAS

Florida is studded with trails, rivers, and parks that are ideal for hiking, bird-watching, canoeing, bicycling, and horseback riding.

➤ PUBLICATIONS: **"Florida Trails: A Guide to Florida's Natural Habitats"** (available from Florida Tourism Industry Marketing Corporation, ☞ Visitor Information, *below*) for bicycling, canoeing, horseback riding, and walking trails; camping; snorkeling and scuba diving; and Florida ecosystems. *Florida Wildlife Viewing Guide* (available from Falcon Press, ✉ Box 1718, Helena, MT 59624, ☎ 800/ 582–2665; $7.95 plus $3 shipping), by Susan Cerulean and Ann Morrow, for marked wildlife-watching sites. **"Recreation Guide to District Lands"** (available from St. Johns River Water Management District, ✉ Box 1429, Palatka, FL 32178-1429; free) for marine, wetland, and upland recreational areas.

STUDENTS

➤ STUDENT IDs AND SERVICES: **Council on International Educational Exchange** (CIEE; ✉ 205 E. 42nd St., 14th Floor, New York, NY 10017, ☎ 212/822–2600, FAX 212/822–2699), for mail orders only, in the United States. **Travel Cuts** (✉ 187 College St., Toronto, Ontario M5T 1P7, ☎ 416/979–2406 or 800/667–2887) in Canada.

➤ HOSTELING: **Hostelling International—American Youth Hostels** (✉ 733 15th St. NW, Suite 840, Washington, DC 20005, ☎ 202/783–6161, FAX 202/783–6171; membership $25). **Hostelling International—Canada** (✉ 400-205 Catherine St., Ottawa, Ontario K2P 1C3, ☎ 613/ 237–7884, FAX 613/237–7868; membership C$26.75). **Youth Hostel Association of England and Wales** (✉ Trevelyan House, 8 St. Stephen's Hill, St. Albans, Hertfordshire AL1 2DY, ☎ 01727/855215 or 01727/845047; membership £9.30).

➤ STUDENT TOURS: **Contiki Holidays** (✉ 300 Plaza Alicante, Suite 900, Garden Grove, CA 92640, ☎ 714/ 740–0808 or 800/266–8454).

T

LONG DISTANCE

AT&T, MCI, and Sprint long-distance services make calling home relatively convenient and let you avoid hotel surcharges. Typically you dial an 800 number in the United States.

➤ TO OBTAIN ACCESS CODES: **AT&T USADirect** (☎ 800/874–4000). **MCI Call USA** (☎ 800/444–4444). **Sprint Express** (☎ 800/793–1153).

TIPPING

Whether they carry bags, open doors, deliver food, or clean rooms, hospitality employees work to receive a portion of your travel budget. In deciding how much to give, **base your tip on what the service is and how well it's performed.**

In transit, tip an airport valet $1–$3 per bag, a taxi driver 15%–20% of the fare.

For hotel staff, recommended amounts are $1–$3 per bag for a bellhop, $1–$2 per night per guest for chambermaids, $5–$10 for special concierge service, $1–$3 for a doorman who hails a cab or parks a car, 15% of the greens fee for a caddy, 15%–20% of the bill for a massage, and 15% of a room service bill.

In a restaurant, give 15%–20% of your bill before tax to the server, 5%–10% to the maître d', 15% to a bartender, and 15% of the wine bill for a wine steward who makes a special effort in selecting and serving wine.

TOUR OPERATORS

Buying a prepackaged tour or independent vacation can make your trip to Florida less expensive and more hassle-free. Because everything is prearranged, you'll spend less time planning.

Operators that handle several hundred thousand travelers per year can use their purchasing power to give you a good price. Their high volume may also indicate financial stability. But some small companies provide more personalized service; because they tend to specialize, they may also be more knowledgeable about a given area.

A GOOD DEAL?

The more your package or tour includes, the better you can predict the ultimate cost of your vacation.

Make sure you know exactly what is covered, and **beware of hidden costs.** Are taxes, tips, and service charges included? Transfers and baggage handling? Entertainment and excursions? These can add up.

If the package or tour you are considering is priced lower than in your wildest dreams, **be skeptical.** Also, **make sure your travel agent knows the accommodations** and other services. Ask about the hotel's location, room size, beds, and whether it has a pool, room service, or programs for children, if you care about these. Has your agent been there in person or sent others you can contact?

BUYER BEWARE

Each year consumers are stranded or lose their money when tour operators—even very large ones with excellent reputations—go out of business. So **check out the operator.** Find out how long the company has been in business, ask several agents about its reputation, and **don't book unless the firm has a consumer-protection program.**

Members of the National Tour Association and United States Tour Operators Association are required to set aside funds to cover your payments and travel arrangements in case the company defaults. Nonmembers may carry insurance instead. Look for the details, and for the name of an underwriter with a solid reputation, in the operator's brochure. Note: When it comes to tour operators, **don't trust escrow accounts.** Although there are laws governing charter-flight operators, no governmental body prevents tour operators from raiding the till. For more information, *see* Consumer Protection, *above.*

➤ Tour-Operator Recommendations: **National Tour Association** (NTA; ✉ 546 E. Main St., Lexington, KY 40508, ☎ 606/ 226–4444 or 800/755-8687). **United States Tour Operators Association** (USTOA; ✉ 342 Madison Ave., New York, NY 10173, ☎ 212/599–6599).

USING AN AGENT

Travel agents are excellent resources. When shopping for an agent, however, you should **collect brochures from several sources;** some agents'

suggestions may be skewed by promotional relationships with tour and package firms that reward them for volume sales. If you have a special interest, **find an agent with expertise in that area** (☞ Travel Agencies, *below*). Don't rely solely on your agent, who may be unaware of small-niche operators. Note that some special-interest travel companies only sell directly to the public and that some large operators only accept bookings made through travel agents.

SINGLE TRAVELERS

Prices for packages and tours are usually quoted per person, based on two sharing a room. If traveling solo, you may be required to pay the full double-occupancy rate. Some operators eliminate this surcharge if you agree to be matched with a roommate of the same sex, even if one is not found by departure time.

GROUP TOURS

Among companies that sell tours to Florida, the following are nationally known, have a proven reputation, and offer plenty of options. The classifications used below represent different price categories, and you'll probably encounter these terms when talking to a travel agent or tour operator. The key difference is usually in accommodations, which run from budget to better, and better-yet to best.

➤ Deluxe: **Globus** (✉ 5301 S. Federal Circle, Littleton, CO 80123-2980, ☎ 303/797–2800 or 800/221–0090, FAX 303/347–2080). **Tauck Tours** (✉ Box 5027, 276 Post Rd. W, Westport, CT 06881-5027, ☎ 203/ 226–6911 or 800/468–2825, FAX 203/ 221–6828).

➤ First-Class: **Caravan Tours** (✉ 401 N. Michigan Ave., Chicago, IL 60611, ☎ 312/321–9800 or 800/ 227–2826, FAX 312/321–9845).

➤ Budget: **Cosmos** (☞ Globus, *above*).

PACKAGES

Like group tours, independent vacation packages are available from major tour operators and airlines. The companies listed below offer vacation packages in a broad price range.

➤ AIR/HOTEL/CAR: **American Airlines Fly AAway Vacations** (☎ 800/321–2121). **Continental Vacations** (☎ 800/634–5555). **Delta Dream Vacations** (☎ 800/872–7786, FAX 954/357–4687). **United Vacations** (☎ 800/328–6877). **US Airways Vacations** (☎ 800/455–0123).

➤ CUSTOM PACKAGES: **Amtrak's Great American Vacations** (☎ 800/321–8684).

➤ HOTEL ONLY: **SuperCities** (✉ 139 Main St., Cambridge, MA 02142, ☎ 800/333–1234).

➤ SELF-DRIVE: **Budget WorldClass Drive** (☎ 800/527–0700, 0800/181181 in the U.K.).

➤ FROM THE U.K.: **British Airways Holidays** (✉ Astral Towers, Betts Way, London Rd., Crawley, West Sussex RH10 2XA, ☎ 01293/723–111). **Jetsave Travel Ltd.** (✉ Sussex House, London Rd., East Grinstead, West Sussex RH19 1LD, ☎ 01342/312–033). **Key to America** (✉ 1–3 Station Rd., Ashford, Middx. TW15 2UW, ☎ 01784/248–777). **Kuoni Travel** (✉ Kuoni House, Dorking, Surrey RH5 4AZ, ☎ 01306/742–222). **Virgin Holidays Ltd.** (✉ The Galleria, Station Rd., Crawley, West Sussex RH10 1WW, ☎ 01293/617–181).

THEME TRIPS

➤ ADVENTURE: **Outdoor Adventures** (✉ 1625 Emerson St., Jacksonville, FL 32207, ☎ 904/393–9030, FAX 904/399–2883).

➤ FISHING: **Anglers Travel** (✉ 3100 Mill St., #206, Reno, NV 89502, ☎ FAX 702/853–9132). **Cutting Loose Expeditions** (✉ Box 447, Winter Park, FL 32790, ☎ 407/629–4700 or 800/533–4746). **Fishing International** (✉ Box 2132, Santa Rosa, CA 95405, ☎ 707/539–3366 or 800/950–4242, FAX 707/539–1320).

➤ GOLF: **Golfpac** (✉ Box 162366, Altamonte Springs, FL 32716-2366, ☎ 800/327–0878, FAX 407/260–8989). **Great Florida Golf** (✉ Box 590, Palm Beach, FL 33480, ☎ 561/820–9336 or 800/544–8687). **Stine's Golftrips** (✉ Box 2314, Winter Haven, FL 33883-2314, ☎ 813/324–1300 or 800/428–1940, FAX 941/325–0384).

➤ LEARNING: **Earthwatch** (✉ Box 9104, 680 Mount Auburn St., Watertown, MA 02272, ☎ 617/926–8200 or 800/776–0188, FAX 617/926–8532) for research expeditions. **Oceanic Society Expeditions** (✉ Fort Mason Center, Bldg. E, San Francisco, CA 94123-1394, ☎ 415/441–1106 or 800/326–7491, FAX 415/474–3395).

➤ MUSIC: **Dailey-Thorp Travel** (✉ 330 W. 58th St., #610, New York, NY 10019-1817, ☎ 212/307–1555 or 800/998–4677, FAX 212/974–1420).

➤ SAILING SCHOOLS: **Annapolis Sailing School** (✉ Box 3334, 601 6th St., Annapolis, MD 21403, ☎ 410/267–7205 or 800/638–9192). **Offshore Sailing School** (✉ 16731-110 McGregor Blvd., Fort Myers, FL 33908, ☎ 813/454–1700 or 800/221–4326, FAX 813/454–1191).

➤ SPAS: **Spa-Finders** (✉ 91 5th Ave., #301, New York, NY 10003-3039, ☎ 212/924–6800 or 800/255–7727).

➤ SPORTS: **Championship Tennis Tours** (✉ 7350 E. Stetson Dr., #106, Scottsdale, AZ 85251, ☎ 602/990–8760 or 800/468–3664, FAX 602/990–8744). **Spectacular Sport Specials** (✉ 5813 Citrus Blvd., New Orleans, LA 70123-5810, ☎ 504/734–9511 or 800/451–5772, FAX 504/734–7075).

➤ YACHT CHARTERS: **Huntley Yacht Vacations** (✉ 210 Preston Rd., Wernersville, PA 19565, ☎ 610/678–2628 or 800/322–9224, FAX 610/670–1767). **Lynn Jachney Charters** (✉ Box 302, Marblehead, MA 01945, ☎ 617/639–0787 or 800/223–2050, FAX 617/639–0216). **The Moorings** (✉ 19345 U.S. 19 N, 4th Floor, Clearwater, FL 34624-3193, ☎ 813/530–5424 or 800/535–7289, FAX 813/530–9474). **Ocean Voyages** (✉ 1709 Bridgeway, Sausalito, CA 94965, ☎ 415/332–4681 or 800/299–4444, FAX 415/332–7460). **Russell Yacht Charters** (✉ 404 Hulls Hwy., #175, Southport, CT 06490, ☎ 203/255–2783 or 800/635–8895). **SailAway Yacht Charters** (✉ 15605 S.W. 92nd Ave., Miami, FL 33157-1972, ☎ 305/253–7245 or 800/724–5292, FAX 305/251–4408).

TRAIN TRAVEL

Amtrak provides north–south service on two routes to the major cities of

Jacksonville, Orlando, Tampa, West Palm Beach, Fort Lauderdale, and Miami and east–west service through Jacksonville, Tallahassee, and Pensacola, with many stops in between on all routes.

➤ RAIL LINE: **Amtrak** (☎ 800/872–7245).

A good travel agent puts your needs first. Look for an agency that specializes in your destination, has been in business at least five years, and emphasizes customer service. If you're looking for an agency-organized package or tour, your best bet is to choose an agency that's a member of the National Tour Association or the United States Tour Operators Association (☞ Tour Operators, *above*).

➤ LOCAL AGENT REFERRALS: **American Society of Travel Agents** (ASTA; ✉ 1101 King St., Suite 200, Alexandria, VA 22314, ☎ 703/739–2782). **Alliance of Canadian Travel Associations** (✉ Suite 201, 1729 Bank St., Ottawa, Ontario K1V 7Z5, ☎ 613/521–0474, FAX 613/521–0805). **Association of British Travel Agents** (✉ 55–57 Newman St., London W1P 4AH, ☎ 0171/637–2444, FAX 0171/637–0713).

➤ CHEAP RATES FROM THE U.K.: **Flight Express Travel** (✉ 77 New Bond St., London W1Y 9DB, ☎ 0171/409–3311). **Trailfinders** (✉ 42–50 Earls Court Rd., London W8 6FT, ☎ 0171/937–5400). **Travel Cuts** (✉ 295A Regent St., London W1R 7YA, ☎ 0171/637–3161).

Travel catalogs specialize in useful items, such as compact alarm clocks and travel irons, that can **save space when packing.**

➤ MAIL-ORDER CATALOGS: **Magellan's** (☎ 800/962–4943, FAX 805/568–5406). **Orvis Travel** (☎ 800/541–3541, FAX 540/343–7053). **TravelSmith** (☎ 800/950–1600, FAX 415/455–0329).

U

The U.S. government can be an excellent source of inexpensive travel information. When planning your trip, **find out what government materials are available.**

➤ PAMPHLETS: **Consumer Information Center** (✉ Consumer Information Catalogue, Pueblo, CO 81009, ☎ 719/948–3334).

For general information about Florida's attractions, contact the office below; welcome centers are located on I–10, I–75, I–95, and U.S. 231 (near Graceville) and in the lobby of the New Capitol in Tallahassee. For regional tourist bureaus and chambers of commerce see individual chapters.

➤ STATE: **Florida Tourism Industry Marketing Corporation** (✉ Box 1100, 661 E. Jefferson St., Suite 300, Tallahassee, FL 32302, ☎ 904/487–1462, FAX 904/224–2938).

➤ IN THE U.K.: **ABC Florida** (✉ Box 35, Abingdon, Oxon. OX14 4TB, ☎ 0891/600–555, 50p per minute; send £2 for vacation pack).

W

Florida is a state for all seasons, although most visitors prefer October–April, particularly in southern Florida.

Winter remains the height of the tourist season, when southern Florida is crowded with "snowbirds" fleeing cold weather in the North. (It did snow in Miami once in the 1970s, but since then the average snowfall has been exactly 00.00 inches.) Hotels, bars, discos, restaurants, shops, and attractions are all crowded. Hollywood and Broadway celebrities appear in sophisticated supper clubs, and other performing artists hold the stage at ballets, operas, concerts, and theaters. From mid-December through January 2, Walt Disney World's Magic Kingdom is lavishly decorated, and there are daily parades and other extravaganzas, as well as overwhelming crowds. In the Jacksonville and Panhandle area, winter is off-season—an excellent bargain.

For the college crowd, spring vacation is still the time to congregate in Florida, especially in Panama City Beach and the Daytona Beach area;

SMART TRAVEL TIPS / THE GOLD GUIDE

Fort Lauderdale, where city officials have refashioned the beachfront more as a family resort, no longer indulges young revelers, so it's much less popular with college students than it once was.

Summer in Florida, as smart budget-minded visitors have discovered, is often hot and very humid, but along the coast, ocean breezes make the season quite bearable and many hotels lower their prices considerably. In the Panhandle and central Florida, summer is peak season. Theme park lines shrink only after children return to school in September. Large numbers of international visitors keep year-round visitation high at theme parks.

For senior citizens, fall is the time for discounts for many attractions and hotels in Orlando and along the Pinellas Suncoast in the Tampa Bay area.

CLIMATE

➤ FORECASTS: **Weather Channel Connection** (☎ 900/932–8437, 95¢ per minute from Touch-Tone phone).

What follows are average daily maximum and minimum temperatures for major cities in Florida.

KEY WEST (THE KEYS)

Jan.	76F	24C	May	85F	29C	Sept.	90F	32C
	65	18		74	23		77	25
Feb.	76F	24C	June	88F	31C	Oct.	83F	28C
	67	19		77	25		76	24
Mar.	79F	26C	July	90F	32C	Nov.	79F	26C
	68	20		79	26		70	21
Apr.	81F	27C	Aug.	90F	32C	Dec.	76F	24C
	72	22		79	26		67	19

MIAMI

Jan.	74F	23C	May	83F	28C	Sept.	86F	30C
	63	17		72	22		76	24
Feb.	76F	24C	June	85F	29C	Oct.	83F	28C
	63	17		76	24		72	22
Mar.	77F	25C	July	88F	31C	Nov.	79F	26C
	65	18		76	24		67	19
Apr.	79F	26C	Aug.	88F	31C	Dec.	76F	26C
	68	20		77	25		63	17

ORLANDO

Jan.	70F	21C	May	88F	31C	Sept.	88F	31C
	49	9		67	19		74	23
Feb.	72F	22C	June	90F	32C	Oct.	83F	28C
	54	12		72	22		67	19
Mar.	76F	24C	July	90F	32C	Nov.	76F	24C
	56	13		74	23		58	14
Apr.	81F	27C	Aug.	90F	32C	Dec.	70F	21C
	63	17		74	23		52	11

1 Destination: Florida

CATCH IT WHILE YOU CAN

ONLY YESTERDAY the world depicted in photos and displays at the Museum of the Florida Keys teems with bird and fish life, deer and gators, scrub flats laced by mangroves, and landscape randomly canopied by palm and hardwood hammocks. Over all hang the pewter skies of dawn, the blue skies of balmy afternoons, purple storms of summer, and red-orange sunsets. Rimming the shore for 220 mi is the reef, a magical other world beneath the sea.

But outside the museum, along the Overseas Highway, that splendor is eclipsed by motels, gas stations, RV parks, fast-food chains, convenience stores, shell shops, dive shops, and dives.

Florida these days is struggling to redress a century of environmental disaster. The state has lost more than half its wetlands and much of its upland forests, more than half its waters have been contaminated, and its coasts have been cankered with concrete. Lake bass carry dangerous levels of mercury, and the catch of bay shrimp continues to dwindle.

For more than 100 years, Florida's allure has engendered Florida's ruin. Drawn by the state's natural bounty and warm winters, early developers ravaged the state's bird populations, tore out its orchids, burned tree snail habitats, and massacred gators. The winter climate continues to draw hundreds of new year-round residents daily—swelling Florida's population to fourth place in the nation at a rate likely to surpass New York by the turn of the century.

It all began in 1513 when Juan Ponce de León stumbled on the peninsula that became Florida, in his now legendary search for a Fountain of Youth. But long before what amounted to Spanish invasion, Native Americans had discovered the area's restorative springs, rich fishing and hunting grounds along both coasts, and life-sustaining lakes and rivers. Spain named the region la Florida, land of flowers. But the Spanish never stopped to smell the fragrance: Florida disappointed them. Gold was what they were after, and Florida produced none.

Even after acquisition by the United States in 1821 and following statehood in 1845, Florida attracted few permanent settlers. Except for cotton plantations that spread south from Georgia and railroads that linked Atlantic and gulf ports to facilitate commerce in cotton and timber, settlement of the state had to wait for the end of the Civil War.

What would become the Sunshine State came into its own only in the last two decades of the 19th century. One early visionary was Ralph Middleton Munroe, a Staten Island yacht designer who shared Ralph Waldo Emerson's idea that humans had gotten the civilizing process wrong and needed to start over in wilderness. Finding his own piece of wilderness, Munroe settled at Jack's Bight, where he formed the community of Coconut Grove. He convinced early Grove settlers Charles and Isabella Peacock to open an inn, which in the winter of 1882–83 became the first lodging along Florida's lower east coast. When the inn was later closed, Munroe himself began putting up winter guests. His Camp Biscayne for years drew an intellectually prominent clientele, attracted by hospitality and the clean bay waters. Coconut Grove, when annexed into Miami in 1925, became the oldest district in that city. Although in the 1990s the Grove has become a playground for the rich and famous, it remains a sanctuary of vital Florida spirit.

Munroe's thoughtful style of development was the exception rather than the rule. State government, eager to overcome a legacy of debt, usually cast its lot with entrepreneurial monopolists eager to exploit Florida's resources. Chief among them were railroaders Henry Plant and Henry Flagler. Plant heaped sophistications on a barely civilized Gulf Coast; Flagler more grandly tamed the east.

The partner of John D. Rockefeller in Standard Oil, Flagler was one of the richest men in America, notorious for his ruthless and sometimes corrupt methods. When his sickly wife required a winter in the sun, he brought her to Florida. In 1884, widowed and remarried to his deceased wife's former nurse, he returned to St. Augustine and recruited a pair of New York architects to design the grandest hotel Florida had ever seen: the Ponce de León Hotel, opened in 1888. (Henry Plant did much the same thing for the west coast when he opened his $3 million Tampa Bay Hotel in 1891.)

Moving down the coast, Flagler bought an entire island, burned out the inhabitants, and created the opulent new American Riviera he called Palm Beach. His magnificent Royal Poinciana Hotel opened in 1894, and the Breakers—another of his great creations—remains, rebuilt, among Florida's finest accommodations.

Healthy vigorous people began coming to enjoy the climate, and sports and outdoor activities became a vital part of Florida vacations. Flagler indulged winter visitors with imaginative forms of recreation. Laborers pedaled wicker rickshaws. Sportier types raced their new motorcars on the hard-packed sand of Ormond and Daytona beaches.

Henry Plant, meanwhile, at another of his west-coast resorts, paved the first asphalt track for the newly popular sport of racing bicycles, and lavished an entire golf course—the first in Florida conceived as a resort amenity—on his immense Belleview Hotel, as popular today (now the Belleview Mido) as ever, on the bluffs of Clearwater Bay.

In 1896 Flagler brought his railroad to Miami (until then an Indian trading post). At the turn of the century, seized by his own manifest destiny, he began ruthlessly extending tracks to Key West. He proceeded unmindful of the havoc construction wreaked on the fisheries of Florida Bay and denying responsibility for the slavelike treatment of his workers. He even left crews unprepared for the 1906 hurricane that killed 200 railroad employees. But the railroad lived on, reaching Key West six years later. Flager, from then on hailed as one of history's great engineers, had little time to enjoy his accolades. He died within the year.

But his engineering achievement was just one example of Florida's quickly changing landscape. The draining of the Everglades was underway, and the sale of homesites floating in flooded swamplands to unsuspecting northerners had begun. Citrus planters extended cultivation from along the lower St. Johns River south into the lakes district, fouling the water with pesticides. Phosphate mining lowered the water table and reduced to trickles the flows of springs that for years had supported the state's spa resorts. But even as the state's natural beauty was eroding, tourism grew.

ALMOST 100 YEARS after Flagler's railroad extended tourism to the Keys, Walt Disney created another empire. Florida granted Disney extraordinary tax breaks and near-sovereign control over rule-making throughout his fiefdom. (Many of those controls are still in place.) Typically, a compliant Orlando newspaper remained silent when it learned about Disney's plans in the early 1960s. The newspaper owner helped keep secret Disney's quiet acquisition of 28,000 acres for $5.5 million. The rest has been tourism magic. But Disney's environmental record has been mixed—on the one hand being fined for disrupting the natural environment and on the other, acquiring the vast Walker Ranch for public preservation. What may seem to outsiders as a disinterest in the state's invaluable natural assets, the grow-at-all-cost mentality that attracted Walt Disney World continues throughout Florida. In 1994 former owner of Blockbuster Video, Wayne Huizenga, faced only mild challenge in his attempts to create a Disneylike sports-and-entertainment empire in a well-field site west of Miami and Fort Lauderdale, an effort subsequently abandoned by a Blockbuster Video corporate successor.

The pluses have a way to go to catch up to the long accumulation of minuses, but simply because not everything has yet been trashed, what's left of Florida's natural beauty will continue to dazzle those who never knew the state's better days.

As Florida has grown disenthralled with its potentate developers, citizens have become more aware of the environmental problems facing the state. In reaction voters are demanding more green legislation, more parks and trails, and greater support of both culture and sports. Sports franchises ratify Florida's emergence from the ranks of the minor leagues. The state now supports eight major-league teams, including football's Miami Dolphins and basketball's Orlando Magic. Bahamians, who make up one of Florida's largest contingent of overseas visitors, fly over early each June to celebrate with mainland kin the annual Bahamian heritage festival called Goombay. In February, Latins come from around the Americas for Carnaval Miami and its hip-swiveling finale, the salsa-spiced Calle Ocho Festival. November's annual Miami Book Fair is now the largest book event in America.

SPORTS LOVERS COME for the Breeders Cup at Fort Lauderdale's Gulfstream Park and for the winter polo season at the Palm Beach Polo and Country Club, as music lovers come for the London Philharmonic Orchestra's biannual summer seasons in Daytona Beach. As many as can find a room anywhere within 50 mi pack Key West for the annual Halloween Fantasy Fest.

In Fort Lauderdale, downtown's 1¼-mi Riverwalk is a magical setting for shaded promenades and alfresco entertainment, and there are new performing-arts and fine-arts venues. Along the beachfront—for years infamous for spring-break debauchery—2½ mi of shore road attest to the good life by the sea. Farther up the east coast, the rich and famous of Palm Beach County and the Treasure Coast willingly pay higher taxes to support and patronize their arts and recreational facilities, which are unequaled in the state.

In Miami—the big bad boy of Florida cities, its image tar-brushed by real-world Miami Vice—the South Beach Art Deco District has been expanded to include a revived Lincoln Road Mall. In Coconut Grove, CocoWalk and Mayfair malls, with their shops and smart bistros, have renewed that sense of life-as-art that dates from Ralph Munroe's days. To the far west is Everglades National Park.

Along the lower west coast in Naples, both the grandest hotels and baronial new residential estates lie to the back or to the side of coastal wetlands. Yet even here, mangroves are dying where marshes front the posh new communities, linked only by boardwalks to the beach. Lee County, farther north, stands out for its nature preserves, shelling beaches, and unbridged barrier islands. Since 1988 the county has collected ⅓ of its tourist-development tax solely to buy, protect, and improve beaches and parks.

Sarasota's downtown and Tampa's Ybor City stand out as the best revived urban neighborhoods of the west coast. Downtown Tampa shows off its aquarium, a mix of museums, and big recreational facilities among its office high-rises, while downtown St. Petersburg has a beautiful park-lined waterfront.

Where beaches are few or where railroaders never laid track, along the mid-Gulf Coast north of Tampa Bay, nine counties have banded together as the "Nature Coast," to flaunt their lakes and bubbling springs, hilly inland stretches, and marshes. In upper midstate, 11 counties now constitute the "Original Florida," a region that includes America's landmark Suwannee River and Cross Creek, the setting for Marjorie Kinnan Rawlings's classic novel *The Yearling*. Nearby Paynes Prairie provides habitat for sandhill cranes and bison. At the Devil's Millhopper you can descend a 221-foot walkway to the bottom of a 120-foot deep sinkhole, and at O'Leno State Park watch the Santa Fe River swirl underground. At Ichetucknee State Park you can tube the mighty "Itch." Nearby you can dive into a dozen or more pellucid springs.

The Panhandle region has many of the state's most beautiful parks—Florida Caverns, Falling Waters, Natural Bridge, Eden State Gardens, Maclay State Gardens, and Torreya State Park—and Florida's finest beaches, including top-rated Grayton in south Walton County. And nearby, beside another white beach, is Seaside, perhaps America's most acclaimed new resort. With its shell- and picket-lined lanes too narrow for automobiles, Seaside harks back to early 20th-century town planning, trying to recapture that old-fashioned sense of community, leisure pace, and human scale. Seaside is just one of the answers that Florida is attempting for its problems.

East across the top of the state, St. Augustine and Fernandina Beach are two of the state's most historic towns. Metropolitan Jacksonville, Florida's largest city in land mass, is site of the most ambitious public-private effort to maintain natural preserves, centered on the 46,000-acre Timucuan Ecological and Historic Preserve, which, at Fort Caroline, includes Europe's earliest settlement site in North America. In downtown Orlando, Lake Eola Park has become the healthy heart of the city with a $900,000 amphitheater, swan boats, night-lit fountain, and landscaping. Church Street Station has helped bring downtown back to life, and the active theater, art, and music community north of downtown shows there is more to Orlando than theme parks.

The search continues for a solution to Florida's environmental distress. In one attempt at remedy, tourism promoters increasingly aim to attract visitors to natural resources—state parks, beaches, nature preserves, rivers—with the hope that politicians will accordingly pay more attention to preserving these resources. Although new, stronger coalitions have formed among hotel owners, the fishing industry, and environmentalists that may forestall worsening disaster, these same groups fight among themselves over a management plan for the new Florida Keys National Marine Sanctuary. The forecast for Florida's future is still unclear.

The ever-increasing threat to natural habitats by development shows that it is a small world after all. Still, much natural beauty remains. Enjoy it while you can.

–Herb Hiller

NEW AND NOTEWORTHY

Disney's Animal Kingdom

The opening of Walt Disney World's fourth major theme park, set for mid-1998, is virtually guaranteed to overshadow any other new entries in the Orlando theme-park sweepstakes. Disney is betting considerable millions that its newest park will not only bring a new crop of tourists, but will also attract a large share of repeat visitors who'll want to check out the new kid on the block.

Delray Beach

Joining the flock of Florida communities to go upscale, Delray Beach has redone itself as a sophisticated beach town with an active historic preservation movement. Atlantic Avenue, the main drag, is now bordered by palm-dotted brick sidewalks, perfect for strolling between the beach and the avenue's shops, art galleries, and restaurants.

Pro Sports

Floridians love their teams, and what's not to love. The relatively young Florida Panthers of the NHL made it to the Stanley Cup finals in 1996, and the even younger NFL Jacksonville Jaguars made it to the AFC championships the next year. A new arena for the Panthers is being constructed in Sunrise, in Broward County, and a new waterfront arena for the Miami Heat is being talked about, if not actually built. In 1999, the Super Bowl is due back in Miami.

WHAT'S WHERE

The Everglades

Created in 1947, this national park in the southernmost extremity of the peninsula preserves a portion of the slow-moving "River of Grass"—a 50-mi-wide stream flowing through marshy grassland en route to Florida Bay. Biscayne National Park, nearby, is the largest national park in the continental United States with living coral reefs.

The Florida Keys

This slender necklace of landfalls off the southern tip of Florida is strung together by a 110-mi-long highway. The Keys have two faces: one a wilderness of flowering jungles and shimmering seas amid mangrove-fringed islands dangling toward the tropics, the other a traffic jam with a view of billboards, shopping centers, and trailer courts. Embrace the first; avoid the latter. Come here for beaches, deep-sea fishing, snorkeling and diving, and the balmy, semitropical weather.

Fort Lauderdale and Broward County

Once known for its wild spring breaks, this southern Florida city on the east coast is newly chic. Just as the beach has renewed itself, so has downtown—with residential construction and an emerging cultural arts district.

Miami and Miami Beach

In the 1980s, a stylized television cop show called *Miami Vice* brought notoriety to this southernmost of big Florida cities; South Beach put it on the map again in the 1990s with its revamping of the Art Deco District. Stomping ground for celebrities such as Madonna and Sylvester Stallone, the city has gone from an enclave of retired northeasterners to an international crossroads with a Latin beat. Don't miss Coconut Grove, the South Florida mainland's oldest settlement. It's chic and casual, full of bistros, cafés, and galleries.

Northeast Florida

The northeast corner of the state is an area of remarkable diversity. Only a short drive separates the 400-year-old town of St. Augustine from the spring-break and autoracing mecca of Daytona Beach. In between are slender barrier islands—some relatively pristine, all with fabulous beaches. Inland is the university town of Gainesville, Ocala horse country, and the backwoods scrub made famous by Marjorie Kinnan Rawlings.

Palm Beach and the Treasure Coast

For 100 years, high society has made headlines along South Florida's Atlantic shore from Palm Beach to Boca Raton—part of the Gold Coast. The coast north of Palm Beach County, called the Treasure Coast, is also worth exploring. Comprising Martin, St. Lucie, and Indian River counties, it's dotted with nature preserves, fishing villages, and towns with active cultural scenes.

The Panhandle

With its magnolias, live oaks, and loblolly pines, northwest Florida has more in common with the Deep South than with the Florida of the Everglades. Even the high season is different: By May, when activities are winding down south of Tampa, the Panhandle is just gearing up. The fabulous beaches, however, are a constant. A recent coastal research study named Perdido Key State Recreation Area, St. Joseph Peninsula State Park, and St. George Island State Park among the top 20 beaches in the country.

Southwest Florida

This region is subtropical to the core. It's most noted for Sanibel Island, a low-key spot that's home to world-class shelling, and Naples, a once-sleepy fishing village that's developed fast. Unlike the east coast, much of the building here has been inland of the mangrove swamps, and the area prides itself on the number of access points along its 41 mi of strand.

The Tampa Bay Area

The west coast cities of Tampa and St. Petersburg are diverse and busy. Inland is typical suburban sprawl, tempered by a bit of Africa (the Busch Gardens theme park). To the north, along what's billed as the Manatee Coast, are extensive nature preserves and parks. Tarpon Springs has been known for its Greek population for decades, Ybor City for its Cuban community. South of the bay, the cities of Sarasota and Bradenton—and the offshore keys that line the Gulf Coast—feel like the restful resort towns they are, plus Sarasota has a thriving arts community.

Walt Disney World and the Orlando Area

When Walt Disney chose 28,000 acres in central Florida as the site of his eastern Disneyland, he forever changed the face of a cattle-and-citrus town called Orlando. Today, Disney isn't the only show in town: Universal Studios, Sea World, and Church Street Station give Mickey a run for his money. It's easy to spend weeks here lost in these artificial worlds.

PLEASURES AND PASTIMES

Beaches

Florida possesses many top beaches, and no point in the state is more than 60 mi from salt water. The long, lean peninsula is bordered by a 526-mi Atlantic coast from Fernandina Beach to Key West and a 792-mi coast along the Gulf of Mexico and Florida Bay from Pensacola to Key West. If you were to stretch Florida's convoluted coast in a straight line, it would extend for about 1,800 mi. What's more, if you add in the perimeter of every island surrounded by salt water, Florida has about

8,500 mi of tidal shoreline—more than any other state except Alaska. Florida's coastline comprises about 1,016 mi of sand beaches.

Along the Atlantic Coast from the Georgia border south through the Daytona Beach area the beaches are broad and firm. In Daytona Beach you can drive on them (though the number of cars is restricted). Some beachfront communities in this area charge for the privilege; others provide free beach access for vehicles.

Major hurricanes in the last several years have caused considerable beach erosion on all of Florida's coasts, and the usual cycle of seasonal tides and winds has so far been slow to repair the damage. Major beach-rehabilitation projects have been completed or are near completion in Fort Lauderdale, the Sunny Isles area of north Dade County, Miami Beach, Key Biscayne, and several west coast barrier islands. The experimental renourishing of beaches in metro Miami's Surfside and at John U. Lloyd Beach State Recreation Area is a continuing project.

In the Florida Keys, coral reefs and prevailing currents prevent sand from building up to form beaches. The few Keys beaches are small, narrow, and generally have little or no sandy bottom. An exception is the beach at Bahia Honda State Park.

The waters of the Gulf of Mexico are somewhat murky, and Tampa Bay is polluted, though improving. But the Gulf Coast beaches are beautiful. The Panhandle is known for its sugary white sand; around Sarasota the sand is particularly soft and white. The barrier islands—especially Sanibel—off Fort Myers are known for excellent shelling.

Although the state owns all beaches below the high-tide line, even in front of hotels and private resorts, gaining access to them can be a problem along much of Florida's coastline. You must pay to enter and/or park at most state, county, and local beachfront parks. Where hotels dominate the beach frontage, public parking may be limited or nonexistent.

Biking

Florida has many cyclists on the road traveling many miles. The key to cycling's popularity is the terrain—flat in the south and gently rolling along the central ridge and in much of the Panhandle. Most cities of any size have bike-rental shops, which are good sources of information on local bike paths.

Florida's Department of Environmental Protection has developed three overnight bicycle tours of different areas of the state. The tours vary in length between 100 and 450 mi (for two to six days of cycling) and use state parks for rest stops and overnight camping. The office can also provide information on recreational cycling trails, rail-trails, and the rim trail atop the levee around Lake Okeechobee. They can also provide you with a list of the more than 30 Bicycle Coordinators in the state who have current information on local bike maps and activities.

Canoeing

The Everglades has areas suitable for flatwater wilderness canoeing that are comparable to spots in the Boundary Waters region of Minnesota. Other popular canoeing rivers include the Blackwater, Econlokahatchee, Juniper, Loxahatchee, Peace, Oklawaha, Suwannee, St. Marys, and Santa Fe. The Florida Department of Environmental Protection provides maps and brochures on 1,550 miles of canoe trails in various parts of the state. Also contact individual national forests, parks, monuments, reserves, and seashores for information on their canoe trails. Local chambers of commerce have information on trails in county parks. The best time to canoe in Florida is winter, the dry season, when you're less likely to get caught in a torrential downpour or become a snack for mosquitoes.

Dining

Florida's cuisine changes as you move across the state, based on who settled the area and who now operates the restaurants. You can expect seafood to be a staple on nearly every menu, however, with greater variety on the coasts, and catfish, frogs' legs, and gator tail popular around inland lakes and at Miccosukee restaurants along the Tamiami Trail. Florida has launched some big-league culinary stars. Restaurateurs like Fort Lauderdale's Mark Militello are nationally acclaimed, while others who got their start here, such as Douglas Rodriguez, formerly of Yuca when it was in Coral Gables, have gone on to glory in Manhattan.

South Florida's diverse assortment of Latin American restaurants offers the distinctive national fare of Argentina, Brazil, Colombia, Cuba, El Salvador, Mexico, Nicaragua, and Puerto Rico, and it's also easy to find island specialties born of the Bahamas, Haiti, and Jamaica. A new fusion of tropical, Continental, and nouvelle cuisine—some call it Floribbean—has gained widespread popularity. It draws on exotic fruits, spices, and fresh seafoods. The influence of earlier Hispanic settlements remains in Key West and Tampa's Ybor City.

All over Florida, Asian cuisine no longer means just Chinese. Indian, Japanese, Pakistani, Thai, and Vietnamese specialties are now available. Continental cuisine (French, German, Italian, Spanish, and Swiss) is also well represented all over Florida.

Every Florida restaurant claims to make the best Key lime pie. Pastry chefs and restaurant managers take the matter very seriously—they discuss the problems of getting good lime juice and maintaining top quality every day. Traditional Key lime pie is yellow, not green, with an old-fashioned graham cracker crust and meringue top. The filling should be tart and chilled but not frozen. Some restaurants serve their Key lime pie with a pastry crust; most substitute whipped cream for the more temperamental meringue. Each pie will be a little different. Try several. It is, after all, a vacation.

Fishing

Opportunities for saltwater fishing abound from the Keys all the way up the Atlantic Coast to Georgia and up the Gulf Coast to Alabama. Many seaside communities have fishing piers that charge admission to anglers (and usually a lower rate to spectators). These piers generally have a bait-and-tackle shop. It's easy to find a boat-charter service that will take you out into deep water. Some of the best are in the Panhandle, where Destin and Fort Walton Beach have huge fleets. The Keys, too, are dotted with charter services, and Key West has a big sportfishing fleet. Depending on your taste, budget, and needs, you can charter anything from an old wooden craft to a luxurious, waterborne palace with state-of-the-art amenities.

Inland, there are more than 7,000 freshwater lakes. The largest—448,000-acre Lake Okeechobee, the third-largest natural lake in the United States—is home to bass, bluegill, speckled perch, and succulent catfish (which the locals call "sharpies"). In addition to the state's many natural freshwater rivers, South Florida also has an extensive system of flood-control canals. In 1989 scientists found high mercury levels in largemouth bass and warmouth caught in parts of the Everglades and in Palm Beach, Broward, and Dade counties, and warned against eating fish from those areas. Those warnings remain in effect, and warnings have been extended to parts of northern Florida.

Golf

Except in the heart of the Everglades, you'll never be far from one of Florida's nearly 1,100 golf courses. Palm Beach County, the state's leading golf locale, has 150 courses, and the PGA, LPGA, and National Golf Foundation all have headquarters in the state. Many of the best golf courses in Florida (☞ Chapter 2) allow visitors to play without being members or hotel guests.

Especially in winter, you should reserve tee times in advance. Ask about golf reservations when you make your lodging reservations.

Horseback Riding

Trail and endurance riding are popular throughout the state. Sixteen Florida parks and recreation areas include horse trails, while five parks have overnight facilities for campers and their horses. Amelia Island offers horseback riding on the beach. Florida's only dude ranch is in Bushnell. Equestrians meet twice a year, during the fall in Altoona in the Ocala National Forest, and during the spring at a location that changes annually.

Jogging, Running, Walking

All over Florida, you'll find joggers, runners, and walkers on bike paths and city streets—primarily in the early morning and after working hours in the evening. Some Florida hotels have their own running trails; others provide guests with information on measured trails in the vicinity. The first time you run in Florida, be prepared to go a shorter distance than normal because of higher heat and humidity.

Two major Florida festivals include important running races. Each year in December the Orange Bowl 10K, one of the state's best-known running events, brings world-class runners to Miami. In April, as part of the Florida Keys annual Conch Republic Celebration, runners congregate near Marathon on one of the world's most spectacular courses for the Seven Mile Bridge Run. Other major events include the Office Depot Corporate Challenge, which attracts 15,000 runners to Miami the first week of May, and the Heart Run, which takes place February 4 each year in Fort Lauderdale.

National and State Parks

Although Florida is the fourth-most-populous state in the nation, more than 10 million acres of public and private recreation facilities are set aside in national forests, parks, monuments, reserves, and seashores; state forests and parks; county parks; and nature preserves owned and managed by private conservation groups. All told, Florida now has some 3,500 mi of trails, encompassing 1,550 mi of canoe and kayak trails, about 670 mi for bicycling and other uses, 900 mi exclusively for hiking, about 350 exclusively for equestrian use, plus some 30 mi of purely interpretive trails, chiefly in state parks. An active greenways development plan, which seeks to protect wildlife habitat as much as foster recreation, identified 150 greenways in use or under development by 1995.

On holidays and weekends, crowds flock to Florida's most popular parks—some on islands that are accessible only by boat. Come early or risk being turned away. In winter, the flocking crowds are replaced by northern migratory birds descending on the state. Many resident species breed in the warm summer months, but others (such as the wood stork) time their breeding cycle to the winter dry season. In summer, mosquitoes are voracious and daily afternoon thundershowers add to the state's humidity, but it's during the early part of this season that sea turtles come ashore to lay their eggs and you're most likely to see frigate birds and other tropical species.

NATIONAL PARKS➤ In 1993 **Fort Jefferson National Monument** in the Dry Tortugas was declared a national park. **Everglades National Park** was established in 1947, and **Biscayne National Park** in 1980. Other natural and historic sites in Florida under federal management include **Big Cypress National Preserve** in the Everglades, **Canaveral National Seashore** in central Florida, **Castillo de San Marcos National Monument** in north Florida, **De Soto National Memorial** in Bradenton, the 46,000-acre **Timucuan Ecological & Historic Preserve** on the St. Johns River in Jacksonville, **Fort Matanzas National Monument** south of St. Augustine, and **Gulf Islands National Seashore** in northwest Florida. The federal government maintains no centralized information service for its natural and historic sites in Florida.

NATIONAL FORESTS➤ The federal government operates three national forests in Florida. The **Apalachicola National Forest** encompasses 557,000 acres of pine and hardwoods across the northern coastal plain. The 336,000-acre **Ocala National Forest** includes the sandhills of the Big Scrub. Cypress swamps and numerous sinkhole lakes dot the 157,000-acre **Osceola National Forest.**

NATIONAL WILDLIFE REFUGES➤ National wildlife refuges in Florida include the **Great White Heron National Wildlife Refuge, Crocodile Lakes National Wildlife Refuge,** and **National Key Deer Refuge** in the Keys; **Pelican Island National Wildlife Refuge** (America's first) in Indian River County; **Loxahatchee National Wildlife Refuge** near Palm Beach; **J. N. "Ding" Darling National Wildlife Refuge** in southwest Florida; and **Merritt Island National Wildlife Refuge.** The federal government also operates the **Key Largo National Marine Sanctuary, Looe Key National Marine Sanctuary,** and the **Florida Keys National Marine Sanctuary,** largest in the national system.

STATE PARKS➤ The Florida Department of Environmental Protection manages hundreds of historic buildings, landmarks, and nature preserves as well as beaches, recreation areas, and parks as part of an expanding state park system.

PRIVATE NATURE PRESERVES➤ Wood storks nest at the National Audubon Society's **Corkscrew Swamp Sanctuary** near Naples. At the **National Audubon Society Wildlife Sanctuary** on Lake Okeechobee, a concessionaire operates boat tours. Audubon also controls more than 65 other Florida properties, including islands, prairies, forests, and swamps. Visitation at these sites is limited.

The Nature Conservancy admits the public to five of its preserves: the 6,267-acre **Apalachicola Bluffs & Ravines Preserve** in Liberty County; **Blowing Rocks Preserve,** with its unique anastasia limestone rock formations; the 970-acre **Cummer Sanctuary** in Levy County; the 4,500-acre **Tiger Creek Preserve,** near Lake Wales in Polk County; and the 150-acre **Spruce Creek Preserve,** which has restored historic buildings, in Volusia County.

Pari-Mutuel Sports

Florida has a big variety of venues for sports you can lawfully bet on. These include 18 greyhound race tracks, six tracks for harness and Thoroughbred racing, and five jai-alai frontons.

Scuba Diving and Snorkeling

South Florida and the Keys attract most of the divers and snorkelers, but the more than 300 statewide dive shops schedule drift-, reef-, and wreck-diving trips for scuba divers all along Florida's Atlantic and Gulf coasts. The low-tech pleasures of snorkeling can be enjoyed throughout the Keys and elsewhere where shallow reefs hug the shore.

Inland in north and central Florida, divers explore more than 100 grottoes, rivers, sinkholes, and springs. In some locations, you can swim near endangered manatees ("sea cows"), which migrate in from the sea to congregate around warm springs during the cool winter months.

Shopping

ANTIQUES➤ Antiques lovers should explore beautifully restored Havana, just north of Tallahassee; Micanopy, south of Gainesville off I–75; the Antiques Mall in St. Augustine's Lightner Museum; Beach Street in Daytona Beach; downtown and along the outskirts of Mount Dora, near Orlando; U.S. 17/92 between Orlando and Winter Park; U.S. 1 north of Dania Beach Boulevard in Dania; and S.W. 28th Lane and Unity Boulevard in Miami (near the Coconut Grove Metrorail station).

CITRUS FRUIT➤ Fresh citrus is available most of the year, except in summer. Two kinds of citrus grow in Florida: the sweeter and more expensive Indian River fruit, from a thin ribbon of groves along the east coast, and the less-costly fruit from the interior, south and west of Lake Okeechobee.

Citrus is sold in ¼, ½, ¾, and full bushels. Many shippers offer special gift packages with several varieties of fruit, jellies, and other food items. Some prices include U.S. postage; others may not. Shipping may exceed the cost of the fruit. If you have a choice of citrus packaged in boxes or bags, take the boxes. They are easier to label and harder to squash.

NATIVE AMERICAN CRAFTS➤ Native American crafts are abundant, particularly in the southern part of the state, where you'll find billowing dresses and shirts, hand-sewn in striking colors and designs. At the Miccosukee Indian Village, 25 mi west of Miami on the Tamiami Trail (U.S. 41), as well as at the Seminole and Miccosukee reservations in the Everglades, you can also find handcrafted dolls and beaded belts.

SEASHELLS➤ The best shelling in Florida is on the beaches of Sanibel Island off Fort Myers. Shell shops, selling mostly kitschy items, abound throughout Florida. The largest such establishment is the Shell Factory, near Fort Myers. The coral and other shells sold in shops in the Florida Keys have been imported for sale because of restrictions on harvesting these materials.

Tennis

Many Florida hotels have a resident tennis pro and offer special tennis packages with lessons. Many local park and recreation departments throughout Florida operate modern tennis centers like those at country clubs, and most such centers welcome nonresidents, for a fee.

FODOR'S CHOICE

Beaches

★**Canaveral National Seashore, New Smyrna Beach to Titusville.** With its 24 mi of undeveloped coastline and miles of wind-swept dunes, this 57,000-acre park is remarkable—all the more so because its beach is virtually empty. Check on the lively ranger programs, with everything from canoe trips to turtle talks.

★**Grayton Beach, near Destin.** Blue-green waters, white sand beaches, and salt marshes make it one of the most scenic spots along the Gulf Coast. There's also camping and snorkeling.

★**St. Andrews State Recreation Area, eastern tip of Panama City Beach.** This highly visited park has an artificial reef that creates a calm, shallow area perfect for young children.

★**South Lido Park, Sarasota.** These 130 acres of sugary sand draw everyone from bird-watchers to anglers to picnickers.

Historic Sites

★**Castillo de San Marcos National Monument, St. Augustine.** The 300-year-old fort comes complete with moat, turrets, and 16-foot-thick walls. For a big boom, watch one of the artillery demonstrations, held periodically on the gun deck.

★**Edison's winter home and museum, Fort Myers.** With everything just as the inventor left it, you can imagine him tinkering around to build the first phonograph.

★**Morikami Museum and Japanese Gardens, Delray Beach.** The leading U.S. center for Japanese and American cultural exchange is housed in a model of a Japanese imperial villa. On display is a permanent exhibition on the area's Yamato Colony, a turn-of-the-century settlement of immigrant Japanese farmers.

★**Vizcaya Museum and Gardens, Coconut Grove.** The estate of industrialist James Deering, overlooking Biscayne Bay, has an Italian Renaissance–style villa containing Renaissance, Baroque, Rococo, and Neoclassical art and furniture.

Hotels

★**Casa Grande, Miami Beach.** It's the first hotel on Ocean Drive and still the best for both style and trend—and with spacious baths. $$$$

★**Registry Resort, Naples.** Sure there are sumptuously decorated rooms, exceptional service, and 3 mi of glistening white beach awaiting you after a walk through a mangrove forest, but there's also a Sunday brunch that makes others pale in comparison. $$$$

★**Ritz-Carlton Amelia Island.** Ritz-Carltons may be known for stylish elegance, superb comfort, and excellent service, but this one

also comes with a pristine beach, its own golf course, and the outstanding and unusual Grill restaurant. $$$$

★**Sandestin Beach Resort, Destin.** This 2,600-acre resort is a town unto itself. Accommodations range from simple to extravagant, and all rooms have a view, either of water, golf course, or bird sanctuary. $$–$$$$

★**Hibiscus House, West Palm Beach.** An excellent value, especially along this stretch of coast, this antiques-filled B&B in the Old Northwood Historic District is enhanced by its knowledgeable owners, who work exceedingly hard at both hospitality and historic preservation. $–$$

Restaurants

★**Cafe des Artistes, Key West.** Chef Andrew Berman's brilliant tropical version of French cuisine is served in a series of intimate dining rooms filled with tropical art and an upstairs, outdoor patio. $$$

★**Mark's Place, North Miami Beach.** The deco-style dining room is as much a feast for the eyes as owner-chef Mark Militello's absolutely fresh, contemporary Florida fare is a feast for the palate. $$$

★**Armadillo Cafe, Davie.** The atmosphere is as creative and fun as the award-winning Southwestern-style South Florida seafood. $$

★**Columbia, Tampa.** Flamenco dancing and paella set the scene at this Ybor City institution. $$

★**Le Coq au Vin, Orlando.** The traditional French cuisine is as expertly prepared as any you'll find in the area, but the setting, in a small but charming house, is delightfully unstuffy. $$

Scenes and Views to Remember

★**Everglades National Park from the tower on Shark Valley Loop.** This 50-foot observation tower yields a splendid panorama of the wide River of Grass as it sweeps southward toward the Gulf of Mexico.

★**Inland waterway, Sanibel.** Scattered here are dozens and dozens of tiny mangrove islets, a lovely sight.

★**Ocean Drive in the Art Deco District, Miami Beach.** Feast your eyes on brilliantly restored vintage Art Deco hotels at every turn. Since their restoration, this palm-lined beachfront has been hopping 24 hours a day.

★ **Sunset scene at Mallory Square, Key West.** Here, sunset draws street performers, vendors, and thousands of onlookers to Mallory Dock and the eponymous square nearby.

★ **Sunshine Skyway across Tampa Bay.** One of the world's great monumental sculptures carries six lanes of traffic soaring across the mouth of Florida's largest estuary.

Theme Parks and Attractions

★ **Busch Gardens, Tampa.** Two of the world's largest roller coasters, good shows, and live animals are loosely brought together under a turn-of-the-century Africa theme at these 335 acres.

★ **Florida Aquarium, Tampa.** Follow the path of a drop of water, and along the way see exhibits on springs and wetlands, bay and barrier beach, a spectacular coral reef, and the Gulf Stream and open ocean.

★ **Spaceport USA, Cocoa Beach.** Here is the home of the real Apollo 13. A garden of old rockets, current launch facilities and Space Shuttle sites, great films, and exhibits illuminating the romance of the early space program make this one of Florida's best entertainment bargains.

★ **Universal Studios Florida, Orlando.** It's saucy, sassy, and hip, with great special effects—a grown-up theme park packed with thrill rides.

★ **Walt Disney World, Orlando.** It's everything it's cracked up to be—and there's more of it every year.

FESTIVALS AND SEASONAL EVENTS

WINTER

Dec. ➤ **Month-long Victorian Seaside Christmas** takes place oceanside on Amelia Island (☎ 904/277–0717).

Mid-Dec. ➤ **Christmas in St. Augustine** is a three-week festival with caroling, tours of turn-of-the-century churches and cottages, and musical performances (☎ 904/829–5681).

Mid-Dec. ➤ **Walt Disney World's Very Merry Christmas Parade in the Magic Kingdom** celebrates the season at the Magic Kingdom (☎ 407/931–7369).

Mid-Dec. ➤ **Winterfest Boat Parade** is on the Intracoastal Waterway, Fort Lauderdale (☎ 954/767–0686).

Late Dec. ➤ **Coconut Grove King Mango Strut** is a parody of the Orange Bowl Parade (☎ 305/858–6253).

Early Jan. ➤ **Polo Season** opens at the Palm Beach Polo and Country Club (☎ 561/793–1440).

Jan. 6 ➤ **Greek Epiphany Day** includes religious celebrations, parades, music, dancing, and feasting at the St. Nicholas Greek Orthodox Cathedral in Tarpon Springs (☎ 813/937–6109).

Mid-Jan. ➤ **Art Deco Weekend** spotlights Miami Beach's historic district with an Art Deco street fair, a 1930s-style Moon Over Miami Ball, and live entertainment (☎ 305/672–2014).

Mid-Jan. ➤ **Martin Luther King, Jr., Festivals** are celebrated throughout the state—including Orlando (☎ 407/246–2221).

Mid-Jan. ➤ **Taste of the Grove Food and Music Festival** is a popular fundraiser put on in Coconut Grove's Peacock Park by area restaurants (☎ 305/444–7270).

Late Jan. ➤ **Miami Rivers Blues Festival** takes place on the south bank of the river next to Tobacco Road (☎ 305/374–1198).

Feb. ➤ **Edison Festival of Lights,** in various locations around Fort Myers, celebrates Thomas A. Edison's long winter residence in the city (☎ 941/334–2550).

Feb. ➤ **Florida Strawberry Festival,** in Plant City, has for more than six decades celebrated the town's winter harvest with two weeks of country-music stars, rides, exhibits, and strawberry delicacies (☎ 813/752–9194).

Feb. ➤ **Gasparilla Festival** celebrates the legendary pirate's invasion of Tampa with street parades, an art festival, and music (☎ 800/448–2672).

Feb. ➤ **International Carillon Festival** takes place at the Bok Tower Gardens, Lake Wales (☎ 941/676–1408).

Feb. ➤ **Olustee Battle Festival,** in Lake City, is the second-largest Civil War reenactment in the nation after the one in Gettysburg (☎ 904/752–3610 or 904/758–1312).

Feb. ➤ **Speed Weeks** is a three-week celebration of auto racing that culminates in the famous Daytona 500, at the Daytona International Speedway in Daytona Beach (☎ 904/254–2700 or 800/854–1234).

Mid-Feb. ➤ **Coconut Grove Art Festival** is the state's largest (☎ 305/447–0401).

Mid-Feb. ➤ **Florida Citrus Festival and Polk County Fair,** in Winter Haven, showcases the citrus harvest with displays and entertainment (☎ 941/967–3175).

Mid-Feb. ➤ **Florida Manatee Festival,** in Crystal River, focuses on both the river and the endangered manatee (☎ 352/795–3149).

Mid-Feb. ➤ **Florida State Fair,** in Tampa, includes carnival rides and 4-H competitions (☎ 813/621–7821).

Mid-Feb. ➤ **Miami Film Festival,** sponsored by the Film Society of America, is 10 days of international, domestic, and local films (☎ 305/377–3456).

Last full weekend in Feb. ➤ **Labelle Swamp Cabbage Festival** is a salute to the state tree, the cabbage palm (☎ 941/675–0125).

Feb.–Mar. ➤ **Winter Equestrian Festival,** at the Palm Beach Polo and Country Club in West Palm Beach, includes more than 1,000 horses and three grand-prix equestrian events (☎ 561/798–7000).

SPRING

EARLY MAR.➤ Annual Sanibel Shell Fair, which runs for four days starting the first Thursday of the month, is the largest event of the year on Sanibel Island (☎ 941/472–2155).

EARLY MAR.➤ Azalea Festival is a beauty pageant, arts and crafts show, and parade held in downtown Palatka and Riverfront Park (☎ 904/328–1503).

EARLY MAR.➤ Bike Week, one of Daytona's biggest annual events, draws 400,000 riders from across the U.S. for 10 days of races, plus parades and even coleslaw wrestling (☎ 904/255–0981).

EARLY MAR.➤ Carnaval Miami is a carnival celebration staged by the Little Havana Tourist Authority (☎ 305/644–8888).

MID-MAR.–EARLY MAY➤ Springtime Tallahassee is a major cultural, sporting, and culinary event in the capital (☎ 904/224–5012).

MID-MAR. AND EARLY JULY➤ Arcadia All-Florida Championship Rodeo is professional rodeo at its best (☎ 941/494–2014 or 800/749–7633).

LATE MAR.➤ Blessing of the Fleet is held by the bay in St. Augustine on Palm Sunday (☎ 904/829–5681).

LATE MAR.–EARLY APR.➤ Concourse d'Elegance, held at the Ritz-Carlton Amelia Island on Easter weekend, shows off over 150 exquisitely preserved collector cars (☎ 904/277–1100).

EARLY APR.➤ Delray Affair is the biggest event in the area and features arts, crafts, and food (☎ 561/278–0424).

APR.➤ Arts in April is a series of visual- and performing-arts events produced by independent Orlando arts organizations (☎ 407/425–0277).

MID-APR.➤ Cedar Key Sidewalk Arts Festival is celebrated in one of the state's most historic towns (☎ 352/543–5600).

LATE APR.➤ River Cities Festival, a three-day event in Miami Springs and Hialeah, focuses attention on the Miami River and the need to keep it clean (☎ 305/887–1515).

LATE APR.–EARLY MAY➤ Conch Republic Celebration in Key West honors the founding fathers of the Conch Republic, "the small island nation of Key West" (☎ 305/296–0123).

LATE APR.–EARLY MAY➤ Daytona Beach Music Festival, held over four consecutive weekends, features concerts by marching bands, jazz and stage bands, an orchestra, and men's, women's, and mixed choirs (☎ 800/881–2473).

LATE APR.–EARLY MAY➤ Sun 'n' Fun Festival, in Clearwater, includes a bathtub regatta, golf tournament, and night-time parade (☎ 813/462–6531).

MAY➤ Shell Air & Sea Show draws more than 2 million to the Fort Lauderdale beachfront for performances by big names in aviation, such as the navy's Blue Angels and the air force's Thunderbirds (☎ 954/467–3555).

FIRST WEEKEND IN MAY➤ Sunfest, in West Palm Beach, includes a wide variety of cultural and sporting events (☎ 561/659–5980 or 800/833–5733).

MID-MAY➤ Arabian Nights Festival, in Opa-locka, is a mix of contemporary and fantasy-inspired entertainment (☎ 305/758–4166).

MID-MAY➤ Tropicool Fest draws thousands to more than 30 concerts as well as arts and sports events for two weeks all around Naples (☎ 941/262–6141).

MEMORIAL DAY WEEKEND➤ Florida Folk Festival takes place in White Springs at the Stephen Foster State Folk Culture Center (☎ 904/397–2192).

SUMMER

FIRST WEEKEND IN JUNE➤ Miami-Bahamas Goombay Festival, in Miami's Coconut Grove, celebrates the city's Bahamian heritage (☎ 305/443–7928 or 305/372–9966).

EARLY–MID-JUNE➤ Billy Bowlegs Festival, in Fort Walton Beach, is a week of entertaining activities in memory of a pirate who ruled the area in the late 1700s (☎ 800/322–3319).

EARLY–MID-JUNE➤ International Mangrove Fest, in Naples, is an ecotourism event that combines musical concerts, kid's activities, sand-sculpting contests, canoe tours through the mangroves, and a program of activities by the Nature Conservancy (☎ 941/594–6038).

JULY 4➤ **Firecracker Festival,** in Palm Bay, is one of the state's most colorful Independence Day celebrations (☎ 407/727–0457).

MID-JULY➤ **Hemingway Days,** in Key West, includes plays, short-story competitions, and a Hemingway look-alike contest (☎ 305/294–4440).

EARLY AUG.➤ **Annual Wausau Possum Funday & Parade** is held in Possum Palace, Wausau (☎ 904/638–1460).

LABOR DAY➤ **Worm Fiddler's Day** is the biggest day of the year in Caryville (☎ 904/548–5571).

EARLY SEPT.➤ **Anniversary of the Founding of St. Augustine** is held on the grounds of the Mission of Nombre de Dios (☎ 904/829–8379).

EARLY SEPT.➤ **Annual Outdoor Art Show,** in Gainesville, is a weekend sidewalk show displaying the works of artists from around the state (☎ 352/376–6062).

OCT.➤ **Destin Seafood Festival** gives you two days to sample smoked amberjack, fried mullet, and shark kabobs (☎ 800/322–3319).

OCT.➤ **Fort Lauderdale International Boat Show,** the world's largest show based on exhibit size, displays boats of every size, price, and description at the Bahia Mar marina and four other venues (☎ 954/764–7642).

OCT.➤ **Jacksonville Jazz Festival** is three days of jazz performances, arts and crafts, and food, plus the Great American Jazz Piano Competition (☎ 904/353–7770).

MID-OCT.➤ **Biketoberfest** is highlighted by championship racing at the Daytona International Speedway, the Main Street Rally, concerts, and swap meets that last four days (☎ 904/255–0415).

MID-OCT.➤ **Boggy Bayou Mullet Festival** is a three-day hoedown in celebration of the "Twin Cities," Valparaiso and Niceville, and the famed scavenger fish, the mullet (☎ 904/678–1615).

MID-OCT.➤ **Cedar Key Seafood Festival** is held on Main Street in Cedar Key (☎ 352/543–5600).

MID-OCT.➤ **Fall RiverFest Arts Festival** takes place downtown along the St. Johns River in Palatka (☎ 904/328–8998).

LATE OCT.➤ **Fantasy Fest,** in Key West, is a no-holds-barred Halloween costume party, parade, and town fair (☎ 305/296–1817).

EARLY NOV.➤ **Florida Seafood Festival** is Apalachicola's celebration of its famous oyster harvest, with oyster-shucking-and-consumption contests and parades (☎ 904/653–9419).

EARLY NOV.–LATE FEB.➤ The **Orange Bowl** and **Junior Orange Bowl Festival,** in the Miami area, are best known for the King Orange Jamboree Parade and the Orange Bowl Football Classic but also include more than 20 youth-oriented events (☎ 305/371–3351).

MID-NOV.➤ **Jensen Beach Pineapple Festival** is at the Martin County Fairgrounds (☎ 561/334–3444).

MID-NOV.➤ **12th Annual Miami Book Fair International,** the largest book fair in the United States, is held on the Miami-Dade Community College Wolfson Campus (☎ 305/237–3258).

2 The Florida Fifty

Golfing Throughout the State

With more courses than any other state, Florida is a golfer's paradise. The warm climate makes for year-round play on hundreds of courses, from which we've chosen the 50 best from all corners of the state.

Updated by
Ann Hughes

HOW COULD GOLFERS FEEL UNDER PAR in the sunshine state? One out of every 10 rounds of golf played in the United States is played here, and golfers visit Florida more than any other state. Florida is twice as popular as its nearest rivals, Arizona and South Carolina, and three times as popular as runners-up California and North Carolina.

But there is plenty of green to go around. Florida has more golf courses than any other state. The present count tallies 1,098, with another 63 courses either planned or under construction. According to National Golf Foundation figures, Palm Beach County, with 147, has more courses than any other county in the country.

Many of Florida's courses are private. Still, at last count roughly two-thirds were either public, "semiprivate," or private but offering limited access for nonmembers (for example, courses extending privileges to guests of nearby hotels). So if you're on your way to Florida to play golf, you'll have more than 600 places in which to get teed off.

A big part of the appeal of Florida golf is its year-round availability. Although a few courses might close for a day or two in fall to reseed greens and a few in northern Florida might delay morning tee times in winter when there's frost, it's still fair to say that you can find a fairway here 365 days a year. That's why a large number of touring professionals—including Jack Nicklaus, Gary Player, and Payne Stewart—have settled here.

What sort of play can you expect? It's no state secret that Florida is flat. With its highest elevation at 345 feet, it can't claim many naturally rolling courses. The world's leading golf-course designers, including Tom Fazio, Jack Nicklaus, and Ed Seay, have added the rolls and undulations that nature omitted. No designer, however, has been more notable in this regard than Pete Dye, pioneer of stadium-style courses, designed for large tournament audiences.

Deep rough is uncommon as a penalizing element in Florida play, short rough is especially prevalent during winter, and water and sand are common. Often lakes and canals have to be carved out to make fairways. Although Florida fairways are characteristically wide, greens tend to be heavily bunkered or protected by water. A diabolically popular invention of Florida course builders is the island green surrounded by water. Sand is also a natural part of the Florida environment, although a special fine-grain sand is sometimes imported; it isn't unusual to come across a hole in Florida with 10 or more traps, and several courses have more than 100 traps each. On the other hand, because the sandy soil drains well, the playing surface is more forgiving of iron shots than denser, clay-rich soil. What this adds up to is a premium on accuracy when it comes to approach shots.

Wind also comes into play in Florida, particularly at courses near the state's 3,000 mi of coastline. Inland, it swirls and becomes unpredictable as it moves through tall pine and palm trees.

Finally, keep in mind that for most of the year, Florida greens are seeded with Bermuda grass. If you're familiar with putting on the bent-grass greens found in other parts of the country, you may find that the speed (on the slow side) and grain of Bermuda greens takes getting used to.

Florida Golf Courses

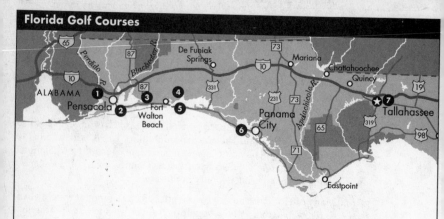

Gulf of Mexico

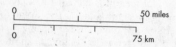

Panhandle

Bluewater Bay Resort, **4**
Killearn Country Club & Inn, **7**
Marriott's Bay Point Resort, **6**
The Moors, **3**
Perdido Bay Resort, **1**
Sandestin Beach Resort, **5**
Tiger Point Golf & Country Club, **2**

Northeast Florida

Amelia Island Plantation, **8**
Golden Ocala Golf Club, **15**
Indigo Lakes Golf Club, **14**
Ponte Vedra Inn & Club, **10**
Radisson Ponce de León Golf and Conference Resort, **12**
Ravines Golf & Country Club, **11**
Sheraton Palm Coast, **13**
Tournament Players Club at Sawgrass, **9**

Orlando Area

Falcon's Fire Golf Club, **20**
Grand Cypress Golf Resort, **19**
Grenelefe Golf & Tennis Resort, **22**

Mission Inn Golf & Tennis Resort, **17**
Palisades Country Club, **18**
Timacuan Golf & Country Club, **16**
Walt Disney World Resort, **21**

Tampa Bay Area

Bloomingdale Golfers Club, **27**
Buffalo Creek, **28**
Innisbrook Hilton Resort , **25**
Plantation Golf & Country Club, **31**
Plantation Inn & Golf Resort, **23**
The Resort at Longboat Key, **29**
Saddlebrook Resort Tampa, **26**
Sun 'n Lake Golf Club, **30**
World Woods Golf Club, **24**

Southwest Florida

Cape Coral Golf & Tennis Resort, **33**
Eastwood Golf Club, **32**
Lely Flamingo Island Club, **35**
Naples Beach Hotel & Golf Club, **36**
Pelican's Nest Golf Course, **34**

Palm Beach

Boca Raton Resort & Club, **43**
Boynton Beach Municipal Golf Course, **42**
Breakers Hotel Golf Club, **39**
Emerald Dunes Golf Club, **40**
Indian River Plantation Beach Resort, **37**
Palm Beach Polo and Country Club, **41**
PGA National Resort & Spa, **38**

Fort Lauderdale

Bonaventure Country Club, **45**
Colony West Country Club, **46**
The Oaks Golf & Racquet Club, **44**

Miami

Don Shula's Hotel & Golf Club, **49**
Doral Golf Resort and Spa, **48**
Links at Key Biscayne, **50**
Turnberry Isle Resort & Club, **47**

The Florida Fifty

In a state with nearly 1,100 courses, coming up with a mere 50 recommendations isn't easy. Even after discounting nine-hole courses, par-3 (sometimes called "executive") courses, courses that are private, and those with policies for public play that are unusually restrictive, hundreds of top-notch courses remain.

A sampling of what is available, from inexpensive municipal courses to luxurious resort courses, this index includes those repeatedly cited among Florida's best. This does not mean these are the only ones worth playing. Also, although just one course has been highlighted at each of the multicourse resorts cited (for example, Doral, Grand Cypress, PGA National), other courses at these resorts may also be among Florida's best. For that reason, the *total* number of holes at any resort is listed, not just the holes of the featured course.

Yardages listed are of the featured course and are intended as an indication of one course's length relative to others; yardages are calculated from the championship, or blue, tees. The championship length represents a course at its most difficult. Courses are typically 400 to 800 yards shorter from the regular men's tees and between 1,000 and 1,500 yards shorter from the regular women's tees. With its large retirement population, Florida also has many facilities with "seniors" tees, usually in front of the regular men's tees and often designated as gold. A few designers—notably Jack Nicklaus—include five or more sets of tee boxes to make courses playable for everyone.

The United States Golf Association (USGA) ratings are also from the championship tees and indicate a course's relative difficulty; the rating is the average a scratch (0-handicap) golfer should expect to score. Any course with a rating of two or more strokes higher than par is considered especially demanding and generally suitable only for experienced golfers. If you're less experienced, look for courses with ratings below par.

Keep in mind that a golf course tends to be a work-in-progress; holes are often lengthened or shortened, greens are rebuilt, traps added, and so forth. The statistics and descriptions here were accurate at the time of publication, but courses may have undergone changes—even major overhauls—by the time you play them.

Because Florida courses tend to be flat, most are easy to walk, but unfortunately for people who enjoy walking, this is rarely an option anymore. Carts are usually required, although a few courses allow late-afternoon players to walk and some public courses allow you to stroll between holes. The official reason is that carts speed up play, which is generally true. Operators, however, concede that cart rental means extra revenue. A note for anyone interested in walking, when and where it is permitted: In Florida, where the "golf community" is a pervasive concept, distances *between* holes can be substantial, a real-estate ploy to allow more space for course-side homes and condos.

Greens fees are per person, regular-season rates, with mandatory cart fees (per person) included, where applicable. Greens fees, especially at resort courses, can be as much as 50% more during the high season—which runs generally from February to May—and substantially lower in slow summer months.

Many resorts offer golf packages, with greens fees included at a considerable discount. There are also companies specializing in golf packages.

Most courses (even some municipal ones) have dress codes. The standard requirement is a collared shirt and long pants (often no jeans) or Bermuda-length shorts. Although many courses are less than militant in dress-code enforcement, come prepared to play by the rules.

Prices quoted in the following chart refer to greens fees:

CATEGORY	COST
$$$$	over $75
$$$	$50–$75
$$	$20–$50
$	under $20

The Panhandle

Bluewater Bay Resort. Generally ranked by golf magazines among the top courses in the state's northwest, the Tom Fazio–designed layout features thick woods, water, and marshes on four nine-hole courses that combine to make six different 18-hole routes. ⊠ *1950 Bluewater Blvd., Niceville 32578,* ☎ *904/897–3241 or 800/874–2128. Yardage: 6,803. Par: 72. USGA rating: 73.7. Total holes: 36.* ▥ *Greens fees $$. Cart optional after 1. Restaurant, driving range, accommodations.*

Killearn Country Club & Inn. Gently rolling fairways and clusters of large oak trees give this course its distinctive character. ⊠ *100 Tyron Circle, Tallahassee 32308,* ☎ *904/893–2144. Yardage: 7,025. Par: 72. USGA rating: 73.9. Total holes: 27.* ▥ *Greens fees $$. Cart optional. Special policies: must be an inn guest or member. Restaurant, accommodations.*

Marriott's Bay Point Resort. The Lagoon Legend course is a watery monster, with the beast coming into play on 16 holes. Completed in 1986, the Lagoon Legend has been rated by magazines among the top courses in the U.S. ⊠ *100 Delwood Beach Rd., Panama City Beach 32411,* ☎ *904/235–6909 or 800/874–7105. Yardage: 6,942. Par: 72. USGA rating: 75.3. Total holes: 36.* ▥ *Greens fees $$$. Cart mandatory. Special policies: tee times available 2 months in advance for resort guests; lower greens fees for resort guests. Restaurant, driving range, accommodations.*

The Moors. Home of the PGA Seniors Emerald Coast Classic, this course has pot bunkers and native grasses bordering the broad fairways, creating a unique blend of Scottish and Florida-style golf. ⊠ *3220 Avalon Blvd., Milton 32583,* ☎ *904/994–2744 or 800/727–1010. Yardage: 6,871. Par: 70. USGA rating: 72.9. Total holes: 18.* ▥ *Greens fees $$. Cart optional. Special policies: tee times available 3 days in advance. Restaurant, driving range, accommodations.*

Perdido Bay Resort. This course demands accuracy: On the par-5 11th, for example, water lines both sides of the fairway and the front of the green. ⊠ *1 Doug Ford Dr., Pensacola 32507,* ☎ *904/492–1223 or 800/874–5355. Yardage: 7,154. Par: 72. USGA rating: 73.8. Total holes: 18.* ▥ *Greens fees $$–$$$. Cart mandatory. Special policies: tee time preference for resort guests and members. Restaurant, driving range, accommodations.*

Sandestin Beach Resort. The Links course requires play around and across canals on most of its holes. After little water on the first three holes, the fourth—a par-5 of 501 yards and ranked as one of Florida's toughest—is flanked by a lagoon and marsh. ⊠ *9300 U.S. 98W, Destin 32541,* ☎ *904/267–8211 or 800/277–0800. Yardage: 6,710. Par: 72. USGA rating: 72.8. Total holes: 63.* ▥ *Greens fees $$$. Cart optional. Special policies: tee time preference and reduced greens fees for resort guests. Restaurants, driving range, accommodations.*

Tiger Point Golf & Country Club. In the design of the East Course, Jerry Pate and Ron Garl built many "spectator mounds," a relatively modern design feature that frames greens. ⊠ *1255 Country Club Rd., Gulf Breeze 32561,* ☎ *904/932–1333. Yardage: 7,033. Par: 72. USGA rating: 73.8. Total holes: 36.* ⊠ *Greens fees $$. Cart mandatory. Special policies: tee times available a week in advance. Restaurant, driving range.*

Northeast Florida

Amelia Island Plantation. The Tom Fazio–designed Long Point Course is unusual for Florida: It features water on only three holes. Cedars, oaks, marshes, and ocean views make for unusually scenic play. ⊠ *3000 First Coast Hwy., Amelia Island 32034,* ☎ *904/261–6161 or 800/874–6878. Yardage: 6,775. Par: 72. USGA rating: 72.9. Total holes: 45.* ⊠ *Greens fees $$$$. Cart mandatory. Special policies: must be a resort guest. Restaurant, driving range, accommodations.*

Golden Ocala Golf Club. Ron Garl designed this course with several "replica" holes, including one of the famed, par-3 Postage Stamp hole at Royal Troon, Scotland, and also of the 12th and 13th holes at Augusta National, home of the Masters. ⊠ *7340 U.S. 27 NW, Ocala 34482,* ☎ *352/622–0172. Yardage: 6,755. Par: 72. USGA rating: 72.2. Total holes: 18.* ⊠ *Greens fees $$. Cart mandatory. Special policies: tee times available 2 weeks in advance. Driving range.*

Indigo Lakes Golf Club. Indigo Lakes is distinguished by its oversize greens, each averaging more than 9,000 square feet. ⊠ *312 Indigo Dr., Daytona Beach 32114,* ☎ *904/254–3607. Yardage: 7,123. Par: 72. USGA rating: 73.5. Total holes: 18.* ⊠ *Greens fees $$–$$$. Cart mandatory. Special policies: tee times available a week in advance. Restaurant, driving range, accommodations.*

Ponte Vedra Inn & Club. Designed by Robert Trent Jones, Sr., the Ocean Course features an island hole—the 147-yard 9th, said to have inspired Pete Dye's design of the 17th at the nearby TPC Stadium Course—and plays tough when the wind is up. ⊠ *200 Ponte Vedra Blvd., Ponte Vedra Beach 32082,* ☎ *904/273–7710 or 800/234–7842. Yardage: 6,593. Par: 72. USGA rating: 71.5. Total holes: 36.* ⊠ *Greens fees $$$. Cart mandatory. Special policies: must be an inn guest or guest of member. Restaurant, driving range, accommodations.*

Radisson Ponce de León Golf and Conference Resort. This is an older-style Florida course, originally designed by Donald Ross. Here marshland tends to be more of a backdrop to play than a hazard, as opposed to newer courses, where marshy areas are often converted into ponds or lakes that are very much in play. ⊠ *4000 U.S. 1N, St. Augustine 32095,* ☎ *904/824–2821. Yardage: 6,823. Par: 72. USGA rating: 72.9. Total holes: 18.* ⊠ *Greens fees $$–$$$. Cart mandatory. Special policies: tee times available a week in advance. Restaurant, driving range, accommodations.*

Ravines Golf & Country Club. Trees, rolling terrain, and deep ravines are atypical in Florida, where longer, flat courses with many water hazards are the norm. ⊠ *2932 Ravines Rd., Middleburg 32068,* ☎ *904/282–7888. Yardage: 6,733. Par: 72. USGA rating: 72.4. Total holes: 18.* ⊠ *Greens fees $$. Cart mandatory. Special policies: tee times available a week in advance. Restaurant, driving range, 18-hole putting course, accommodations.*

Sheraton Palm Coast. The Matanzas Woods course, one of several open to resort guests, is an Arnold Palmer/Ed Seay design, featuring rolling fairways and large greens. ⊠ *398 Lakeview Blvd., Palm Coast 32137,* ☎ *904/446–6330 or 800/874–2101. Yardage: 6,985. Par: 72. USGA* *rating: 73.3. Total holes: 72. ✉ Greens fees $$. Cart mandatory. Restaurant, driving range, accommodations.*

Tournament Players Club at Sawgrass. With 99 holes, this is one of Florida's largest golfing compounds. The Pete Dye–designed TPC Stadium Course—famed for its island 17th hole—vexes even top pros who compete in the Tournament Players Championship. ✉ *110 TPC Blvd., Ponte Vedra Beach 32082, ☎ 904/273–3235 or 800/457–4653. Yardage: 6,857. Par: 72. USGA rating: 74. Total holes: 99. ✉ Greens fees $$$$. Cart mandatory. Special policies: must be a hotel guest, member, or guest of member. Restaurant, driving range, accommodations.*

Orlando Area

Falcon's Fire Golf Club. This layout designed by respected golf architect Rees Jones features strategically placed fairway bunkers that demand accuracy off the tee. ✉ *3200 Seralago Blvd., Kissimmee 34746, ☎ 407/397–2777. Yardage: 6,901. Par: 72. USGA rating: 72.5. Total holes: 18. ✉ Greens fees $$$–$$$$. Cart mandatory. Special policies: tee times available a week in advance. Restaurant, driving range.*

Grand Cypress Golf Resort. The New Course is a Jack Nicklaus re-creation of the famed Old Course in St. Andrews, Scotland—hidden in the fairways are "pot" bunkers deep enough to have stairs for entry and exit. ✉ *1 N. Jacaranda, Orlando 32836, ☎ 407/239–4700. Yardage: 6,773. Par: 72. USGA rating: 72.2. Total holes: 45. ✉ Greens fees $$$$; $10 reduction for walkers. Cart optional. Special policies: must be a resort guest; tee times available 2 months in advance. Restaurant, driving range, accommodations.*

Grenelefe Golf & Tennis Resort. Length is the key here: The West Course, designed by Robert Trent Jones, Sr., plays to 7,325 yards from the championship tees. An absence of water hazards (there are just two ponds) ease the challenge—a little. ✉ *3200 Rte. 546, Haines City 33844, ☎ 941/422–7511 or 800/237–9549. Yardage: 7,325. Par: 72. USGA rating: 75.4. Total holes: 54. ✉ Greens fees $$$$. Cart mandatory. Special policies: tee times available 90 days in advance for resort guests. Restaurant, driving range, accommodations.*

Mission Inn Golf & Tennis Resort. Originally built 70 years ago, this course is a mixed bag, featuring island greens typical of Florida as well as elevated tees and tree-lined fairways more characteristic of courses in the Carolinas and the Northeast. ✉ *10400 Rte. 48, Howey-in-the-Hills 34737, ☎ 352/324–3885 or 800/874–9053. Yardage: 6,860. Par: 72. USGA rating: 73.5. Total holes: 36. ✉ Greens fees $$$. Cart mandatory. Special policies: tee times available a week in advance. Restaurant, accommodations.*

Palisades Country Club. Overlooking Lake Minneola, this Joe Lee–designed course is known for its roller-coaster-like fairways and generous landing areas. ✉ *16510 Palisades Blvd., Clermont 34711, ☎ 352/394–0085. Yardage: 7,004. Par: 72. USGA rating: 73.8. Total holes: 18. ✉ Greens fees $$. Cart mandatory. Special policies: tee times available a week in advance. Restaurant, driving range.*

Timacuan Golf & Country Club. This is a two-part course designed by Ron Garl: Part I, the front nine, is open, with lots of sand; Part II, the back nine, is heavily wooded. ✉ *550 Timacuan Blvd., Lake Mary 32746, ☎ 407/321–0010. Yardage: 7,019. Par: 72. USGA rating: 73.5. Total holes: 18. ✉ Greens fees $$$. Cart mandatory. Special policies: tee times available 3 days in advance. Restaurant, driving range.*

Walt Disney World Resort. Where else would you find a sand trap shaped like the head of a well-known mouse? There are five championship courses here—all on the PGA Tour. *Golf Digest's* pick as Florida's seventh-best layout, the Osprey Ridge course, designed by Tom Fazio, incorporates elevated tees and greens and rolling fairways with a relaxing tour into forested, undeveloped acreage. ✉ *1950 W. Magnolia Palm Dr., Lake Buena Vista 32830,* ☎ *407/824–2270. Yardage: 7,101. Par: 72. USGA rating: 73.9. Total holes: 99.* 🍴 *Greens fees $$$$. Cart mandatory. Special policies: tee times available 60 days in advance for resort guests, a week in advance for the public. Restaurant, driving range, accommodations.*

Tampa Bay Area

Bloomingdale Golfers Club. Playing on this water- and tree-lined course can be like playing in an open-air aviary, because there are, reportedly, more than 60 bird species (including a bald eagle) in residence on the course. For golfers, however, birdies and eagles are hard to come by. ✉ *4113 Great Golfers Pl., Valrico 33594,* ☎ *813/653–1823. Yardage: 7,165. Par: 72. USGA rating: 74.4. Total holes: 18.* 🍴 *Greens fees $$. Cart mandatory. Special policies: reserved for members Fri. after 11:30, weekends all day. Restaurant, driving range.*

Buffalo Creek. This Manatee County–owned course resembling a Scottish links and designed by Lakeland, Florida–based golf architect Ron Garl is in as good condition as most private clubs. It's challenging but playable, with few water-lined fairways or traps in front of the greens. ✉ *8100 Erie Rd., Palmetto 34221,* ☎ *941/776–2611. Yardage: 7,005. Par: 72. USGA rating: 73.1. Total holes: 18.* 🍴 *Greens fees $–$$. Cart optional. Special policies: tee times available 2 days in advance. Restaurant, driving range.*

Innisbrook Hilton Resort. Innisbrook's Copperhead course, generally ranked among Florida's toughest, has several long, dog-leg par-4s. ✉ *U.S. 19, Tarpon Springs 34684,* ☎ *813/942–2000. Yardage: 7,087. Par: 71. USGA rating: 74.4. Total holes: 63.* 🍴 *Greens fees $$$$. Cart mandatory. Special policies: must be a resort guest or a member of a U.S. or Canadian golf club. Restaurant, driving range, accommodations.*

Plantation Golf & Country Club. Local knowledge can be helpful on the Bobcat course: With water on 16 holes and greens not visible from the tee on 12 holes, shot placement and club selection are critical. ✉ *500 Rockley Blvd., Venice 34293,* ☎ *941/493–2000. Yardage: 6,840. Par: 72. USGA rating: 73. Total holes: 36.* 🍴 *Greens fees $$. Cart mandatory. Special policies: reserved for members Oct.–Apr.; tee times available 2 days in advance. Restaurant, driving range, accommodations.*

Plantation Inn & Golf Resort. The Championship Course winds through pines and natural lakes. An assortment of tees makes the course playable for golfers of varying ability levels. ✉ *9301 W. Fort Island Trail, Crystal River 34423,* ☎ *352/795–7211 or 800/632–6262. Yardage: 6,502. Par: 72. USGA rating: 71.6. Total holes: 27.* 🍴 *Greens fees $$. Cart optional off-season. Special policies: tee times available a week in advance, 2 days in advance in Feb. and Mar. Restaurant, driving range, accommodations.*

The Resort at Longboat Key. Water, water everywhere: Amid canals and lagoons, the Islandside Course brings water into play on all but one hole, and play can be especially tough when the wind comes off Sarasota Bay or the Gulf of Mexico. ✉ *301 Gulf of Mexico Dr., Longboat Key 34228,* ☎ *941/383–8821. Yardage: 6,792. Par: 72. USGA rating: 73.8. Total holes: 45.* 🍴 *Greens fees $$$. Cart mandatory. Special policies: must be a resort guest or member; tee times available 3 days in advance. Restaurant, driving range, accommodations.*

Saddlebrook Resort Tampa. The Saddlebrook course, designed by Arnold Palmer, is relatively short, but the premium is on accuracy, with lots of water to avoid. Large undulating greens make four-putting a constant concern. ⊠ *5700 Saddlebrook Way, Wesley Chapel 33543,* ☎ *813/973–1111 or 800/729–8383. Yardage: 6,564. Par: 70. USGA rating: 71. Total holes: 36.* ▦ *Greens fees $$$$. Cart mandatory. Special policies: tee times available 2 months in advance for resort guests. Restaurant, driving range, accommodations.*

Sun 'n Lake Golf Club. The original 18-hole course has a "wilderness" reputation: Deer are often spotted on the fairways, and playing from the rough can feel like playing from a jungle. ⊠ *5223 Sun 'n Lake Blvd., Sebring 33872,* ☎ *941/385–4830. Yardage: 6,731. Par: 72. USGA rating: 72. Total holes: 27.* ▦ *Greens fees $$. Cart mandatory. Special policies: tee times available 6 days in advance; Wed. morning, women members only; Thurs. morning, men members only. Restaurant, driving range, accommodations.*

World Woods Golf Club. The Rolling Oaks course, designed by Tom Fazio, is aptly named. Numerous large trees frame undulating fairways, providing both beauty and challenge. ⊠ *17590 Ponce de Leon Blvd., Brooksville 34614,* ☎ *352/796–5500. Yardage: 6,985. Par: 72. USGA rating: 73.5. Total holes: 48.* ▦ *Greens fees $$$. Cart mandatory. Special policies: tee times available a month in advance. Restaurant, 22-acre practice area with 4-sided driving range, 2-acre putting course.*

Southwest Florida

Cape Coral Golf & Tennis Resort. This course tests those who think themselves expert in sand play. Although not long and not difficult, the course is guarded by more than 100 bunkers. ⊠ *4003 Palm Tree Blvd., Cape Coral 33915,* ☎ *941/542–7879. Yardage: 6,649. Par: 72. USGA rating: 71.6. Total holes: 18.* ▦ *Greens fees $–$$. Cart mandatory. Special policies: tee times available 3 days in advance. Restaurant, driving range, accommodations.*

Eastwood Golf Club. Included on many lists of America's best public courses, Eastwood demands accuracy, with tight fairways, water, and well-bunkered greens. ⊠ *4600 Bruce Herd La., Fort Myers 33905,* ☎ *941/275–4848. Yardage: 6,772. Par: 72. USGA rating: 73.3. Total holes: 18.* ▦ *Greens fees $$. Cart mandatory in season. Driving range.*

Lely Flamingo Island Club. This Robert Trent Jones course was completed in 1991 and was the first of three planned at this resort-in-the-making. Multilevel greens are guarded by a fleet of greedy bunkers, but the wide, rolling fairways generally keep errant drives in play. ⊠ *8004 Lely Resort Blvd., Naples 34113,* ☎ *941/793–2223. Yardage: 7,171. Par: 72. USGA rating: 73.9. Total holes: 36.* ▦ *Greens fees $$$–$$$$. Cart mandatory. Special policies: tee times available 3 days in advance. Restaurant, driving range.*

Naples Beach Hotel & Golf Club. Originally built in 1930, this is one of Florida's oldest courses. Although it is short and flat, the strategic bunkering can make for challenging play. ⊠ *851 Gulf Shore Blvd. N, Naples 34102,* ☎ *941/261–2222 or 800/237–7600. Yardage: 6,497. Par: 72. USGA rating: 71.2. Total holes: 18.* ▦ *Greens fees $$$–$$$$. Cart mandatory. Special policies: tee times available 3 days in advance. Restaurant, driving range, accommodations.*

Pelican's Nest Golf Course. Tom Fazio–designed, the Seminole and Hurricane courses are bordered with swamp and thick vegetation—cypress, pine, oak, and palm trees. The elegant and enormous clubhouse and meticulous groundskeeping make the Pelican's Nest a haven for guests of Naples's luxury resorts. ⊠ *4450 Pelican's Nest Dr. SW, Bonita Springs 34134,* ☎ *941/947–4600. Yardage: 6,972. Par: 72. USGA rating: 74.3. Total holes: 27.* ▦ *Greens fees $$$–$$$$. Cart mandatory. Restaurant, driving range.*

Palm Beach

Boca Raton Resort & Club. It's not so much the resort course as the celebrity aura that serves as an attraction here. When you play this one, you follow in the footsteps (or cart tracks) of Frank Sinatra and Gerald Ford, among others. ✉ *501 E. Camino Real, Boca Raton 33431,* ☎ *561/395–3000 or 800/327–0101. Yardage: 6,523. Par: 71. USGA rating: 71.5. Total holes: 72.* ⛳ *Greens fees $$$$. Cart mandatory. Special policies: must be a resort guest or member; tee times available 5 days in advance. Restaurant, driving range, accommodations.*

Boynton Beach Municipal Golf Course. The rolling terrain of this relatively short public course is unusual around generally flat Palm Beach. ✉ *8020 Jog Rd., Boynton Beach 33437,* ☎ *561/969–2200. Yardage: 6,340. Par: 71. USGA rating: 70.1. Total holes: 27.* ⛳ *Greens fees $$. Cart mandatory until 3. Snack bar, driving range.*

Breakers Hotel Golf Club. The Ocean Course, designed by Donald Ross and among Florida's oldest, compensates for its shortness with tight fairways and small greens. ✉ *1 S. County Rd., Palm Beach 33480,* ☎ *561/655–6611 or 800/833–3141. Yardage: 6,017. Par: 70. USGA rating: 69.3. Total holes: 36.* ⛳ *Greens fees $$$$. Cart mandatory. Special policies: must be a hotel guest or member; free shuttle bus to West Course, 11 mi off-site. Restaurant, driving range, accommodations.*

Emerald Dunes Golf Club. This Tom Fazio–designed course gets official credit as the 1,000th course to open in Florida and was considered one of the best new courses in the United States in 1990. ✉ *2100 Emerald Dunes Dr., West Palm Beach 33411,* ☎ *561/684–4653. Yardage: 7,006. Par: 72. USGA rating: 73.8. Total holes: 18.* ⛳ *Greens fees $$$–$$$$. Cart mandatory. Special policies: tee times available 30 days in advance. Restaurant, driving range.*

Indian River Plantation Beach Resort. This par-61 course is classic Florida—flat, with lots of palms and bunkers, and made tricky by ocean breezes. ✉ *555 N.E. Ocean Blvd., Hutchinson Island, Stuart 34996,* ☎ *561/225–3700 or 800/444–3389. Yardage: 4,048. Par: 61. USGA rating: 57. Total holes: 18.* ⛳ *Greens fees $$. Cart mandatory. Special policies: must be a resort guest or member; tee times available a month in advance for resort guests. Restaurant, driving range, accommodations.*

Palm Beach Polo and Country Club. The Dunes course—the resort's newest—is a Ron Garl/Jerry Pate design with Scottish touches, such as pot bunkers and grass traps. ✉ *13198 Forest Hill Blvd., Wellington 33414,* ☎ *561/798–7000. Yardage: 7,050. Par: 72. USGA rating: 73.9. Total holes: 45.* ⛳ *Greens fees $$$$. Cart mandatory. Special policies: must be a resort guest or member; tee times available 2 days in advance. Restaurant, driving range, accommodations.*

PGA National Resort & Spa. The Champion Course, redesigned by Jack Nicklaus, demands length and accuracy, with water on 17 holes and more than 100 traps. It is the site of the PGA Seniors Championship. ✉ *1000 Ave. of the Champions, Palm Beach Gardens 33418,* ☎ *561/627–1800. Yardage: 7,022. Par: 72. USGA rating: 74.7. Total holes: 90.* ⛳ *Greens fees $$$–$$$$. Cart mandatory. Special policies: must be a resort guest, member, or golf pro; higher greens fees for Champion Course. Restaurant, driving range, accommodations.*

Fort Lauderdale

Bonaventure Country Club. Plenty of trees, water, and bunkers line the East Course. The highlight hole is the par-3 third, where the green fronts a waterfall. ✉ *200 Bonaventure Blvd., Fort Lauderdale 33326,* ☎

954/389–2100. Yardage: 7,011. Par: 72. USGA rating: 74.2. Total holes: 36. ⌨ Greens fees $$$. Cart mandatory. Special policies: tee times available 3 days in advance. Restaurant, driving range, accommodations.
Colony West Country Club. There is water on 14 of the Championship Course's holes. The most interesting hole is the 12th, a par-4 through a cypress forest. ✉ *6800 N.W. 88th Ave., Tamarac 33321, ☎ 954/726–8430. Yardage: 6,864. Par: 71. USGA rating: 73.9. Total holes: 36. ⌨ Greens fees $$. Cart mandatory. Special policies: tee times available 3 days in advance. Restaurant.*
The Oaks Golf & Racquet Club. The Cypress, the most challenging of the three courses, has familiar Florida features: lots of palms and greens well protected by sand and water. ✉ *3701 Oaks Clubhouse Dr., Pompano Beach 33069, ☎ 954/978–1737. Yardage: 6,910. Par: 72. USGA rating: 73.3. Total holes: 54. ⌨ Greens fees $$–$$$. Cart mandatory. Special policies: tee times available a day in advance. Restaurant, driving range, accommodations.*

Miami

Don Shula's Hotel & Golf Club. Large greens and elevated tees—unusual in South Florida—are features of the championship course. For golfers who can't get enough, there's also a par-3 course that's lighted at night. ✉ *7601 Miami Lakes Dr., Miami Lakes 33014, ☎ 305/821–1150. Yardage: 7,055. Par: 72. USGA rating: 73. Total holes: 36. ⌨ Greens fees $$–$$$. Cart optional, $20. Special policies: tee times available a week in advance for members, 3 days in advance for nonmembers. Restaurant, driving range, accommodations.*
Doral Golf Resort and Spa. The 18th hole on the recently renovated Blue Course, nicknamed "the Blue Monster" and venue for the Doral-Ryder Open, rates among the hardest finishing holes on the PGA Tour. Veteran pro Ray Floyd reportedly called it the toughest par-4 in the world. ✉ *4400 N.W. 87th Ave., Doral 33178, ☎ 305/592–2000 or 800/713–6725. Yardage: 7,125. Par: 72. USGA rating: 74.5. Total holes: 81. ⌨ Greens fees $$$–$$$$. Cart optional. Special policies: tee time preference for hotel guests; higher greens fees for Blue Course. Restaurant, driving range, accommodations.*
Links at Key Biscayne. Regularly rated highly among U.S. public courses, this one—the site of the Royal Caribbean Classic on the PGA Seniors Tour—is surrounded by mangrove swamps and inhabited by many bird species and alligators. ✉ *6700 Crandon Blvd., Key Biscayne 33149, ☎ 305/361–9129. Yardage: 7,099. Par: 72. USGA rating: 75.2. Total holes: 18. ⌨ Greens fees $$–$$$. Cart optional after 1. Special policies: tee times available 5 days in advance. Restaurant, driving range.*
Turnberry Isle Resort & Club. The Robert Trent Jones South Course, which has hosted the PGA Seniors Championship, mixes old and new: a double green, similar to those at the Old Course at St. Andrews, Scotland, and a modern island green (on the 18th hole). ✉ *19999 W. Country Club Dr., Aventura 33180, ☎ 305/933–6929. Yardage: 7,003. Par: 72. USGA rating: 73.7. Total holes: 36. ⌨ Greens fees $$$. Cart mandatory. Special policies: must be a hotel guest or member; tee times available 2 days in advance. Restaurant, driving range, accommodations.*

3 Miami and Miami Beach

In the 1980s, a stylized television cop show called Miami Vice *brought notoriety to this southernmost of big Florida cities; in the 1990s the revamped Art Deco District of South Beach put it on the map again. Through all this, the city went from a sleepy enclave of retirees to a vibrant international city with a population that is more than half Latin. Don't miss Coconut Grove, South Florida's oldest settlement. It's chic and casual, full of bistros, cafés, and galleries.*

By Herb Hiller

Updated by
Gary
McKechnie

WHAT MAKES MIAMI DIFFERENT from the rest of the United States is quickly apparent from the air. With the vast Everglades at the western edge and the Atlantic to the east, Miami clings to a ribbon of drained land near the southeastern tip of the country. Still vulnerable to mosquitoes, periodic flooding, and potential devastation by hurricanes, Miami 100 years after its founding is still the wrong place for a city, but it's the right place for an international crossroads. And that's exactly what this hot, humid melting pot has become.

Long before Spain's gold-laden treasure ships passed through the Gulf Stream offshore, the Calusa Indians who lived here had begun to trade with mainland neighbors to the north and island brethren to the south. Repeating this pattern, more than 150 U.S. and multinational companies now locate their Latin American headquarters in Greater Miami. The city has unparalleled airline connections to the Western Hemisphere, its cruise port welcomed 3 million passengers in 1995, and it leads the nation in the number of Edge Act banks. Miami hosts 22 foreign trade offices, 32 binational chambers of commerce, and 52 foreign consulates. No Western Hemisphere city is so universally simpatico.

First-time visitors are always struck by the billboards in Spanish. Initially these seem an affectation, an attempt to promote Miami's exotic international image. But the language and the Latin influence is everywhere. Only after you hear Spanish spoken all around you, or after a computerized elevator announces the floor stops as *primer piso* and *segundo piso,* do you realize that the city *Newsweek* called "America's Casablanca" is really the capital of Latin America. Metro Miami is more than half Latin. Though Cubans make up most of this Spanish-speaking population, there are also significant communities from Colombia, El Salvador, Nicaragua, Panama, Puerto Rico, and Venezuela. The Spanish place-names George Merrick affixed to the streets in Coral Gables in the 1920s—Alhambra, Alcazar, Salzedo—may have been romantic pretense, but today's renamed Avenida Gen. Maximo Gomez and Carlos Arboleya Way are earnest celebrations of a contemporary city's heroes—as is Little Havana's Ronald Reagan Boulevard (renamed after the Gipper had lunch there in 1983). Likewise, balladeers Frank Sinatra and Barbra Streisand have given way in the hearts of Miamians to Julio Iglesias and Gloria Estefan.

In addition to the dominant Spanish-speaking population, Miami is home to some 100,000 Haitians along with Brazilians, Chinese, Germans, Greeks, Iranians, Israelis, Italians, Jamaicans, Lebanese, Malaysians, Russians, and Swedes—all speaking a veritable Babel of tongues. Most either know or are trying to learn English, and communication is eased by speaking slowly and distinctly.

Established Miami has warmed up to its newcomers—a big step forward. Not too long ago metropolitan government enacted an ordinance forbidding essential public information from appearing in Spanish, but in 1993 that restrictive affront was rescinded and resisters have adjusted or moved north. Yesterday's immigrants have become today's citizens, and the nation's most international city now offers a style expressed in its many languages, its world-beat music, and its wealth of exotic restaurants.

Miami has changed fast. Old Miami Beach has been transformed from a run-down geriatric center to South Beach, the deco darling of the world. Between 1980 and 1990, the average age of South Beach residents dropped from 66 to 46, and summer brings more young visitors. Two of every three are male, and three of every four are single. Lincoln Road, once the 5th Avenue of the South and only recently an embarrassing derelict row, has been stunningly brought back to life. On weekends it rivals the pedestrian malls of Cambridge, Lyons, or Munich for crowds and sheer hoi polloi festivity. Next slated for revival is North Beach, as all of Miami Beach becomes a real-world Magic Kingdom, proving it's possible and relatively inexpensive to build community by preserving distinctive architecture rather than by "imagineering" pseudo worlds. (Miamians—especially Miami's immigrant newcomers—still adore Disney, however.)

More changes are in store in this city that seems fueled by caffeine (stop by the window serving station of any Cuban café for a *tinto,* the city's high-test coffee). Not surprisingly, much of the change is taking place in areas hardest hit by Hurricane Andrew in 1992, although nature and contractors have largely restored, and in many cases improved, the natural and man-made beauty of the area. In the Redlands district, the Redlands Conservancy is introducing bicycle trails and B&Bs as a way of preserving South Dade County's agricultural heritage. Coral-rock walls and avocado groves may prove as distinctive in their own way as Art Deco hotels. Additional bike-friendly projects include a planned 200-mi network of trails linking Biscayne and Everglades national parks. For those wanting a quicker pace, Homestead has become a state-of-the-art hub for car racing (☞ Chapter 4).

As a big city, Miami also earns its bad rap. A high percentage of its 2 million citizens live in poverty. It is ranked fourth in the United States for traffic congestion. It ranks first in violent and property crimes and does the worst job of any city in putting and keeping criminals behind bars. Yet some widely publicized crimes against tourists in 1993 led to stepped-up visitor-safety programs. Highway direction signs with red sunburst logos are now installed at ¼-mi intervals on major roads and lead directly to such tourist hot spots as Coconut Grove, Coral Gables, South Beach, and the Port of Miami. Patrol cars bearing the sunburst logo are driven by TOP Cops (Tourist Oriented Police), who cruise heavily touristed areas and add a sense of safety. Identification making rental cars conspicuous to would-be criminals has been removed, and multilingual pamphlets on avoiding crime are widely distributed. The precautions have had a positive impact: From 1992 to 1995, the number of tourist robberies in Greater Miami decreased 72.8%. Despite all the problems and hyped headlines, Miami still has heated allure with a climate, beaches, and international sophistication that few places can match.

Contrary to Orlando's claim to be Hollywood East, it's Miami that's set the stage for the Florida film industry. In recent years, Arnold Schwarzenegger and Jamie Lee Curtis filmed *True Lies* here, Sylvester Stallone and Sharon Stone arrived to film *The Specialist,* Jim Carrey rose to stardom through the Miami-based *Ace Ventura: Pet Detective,* and Robin Williams and Nathan Lane used two Deco buildings on Ocean Drive as their nightclub in *The Birdcage.* All in all, it's a far cry from when Esther Williams used to perform water ballet in Coral Gables's Venetian Pool.

A slew of international celebrities have also moved or purchased homes here: Madonna, Stallone, and k. d. lang, for instance. Four major-league sports franchises call Miami home, along with the Doral-Ryder Open Tournament, the Lipton Championships, and the culture-contributing Miami City Ballet and Florida Grand Opera. On the verge of its centennial year and barely two years after Hurricane Andrew roared through, Miami played host to both the Summit of the Americas and the Super Bowl and will welcome Super Bowl competitors again in 1999. Visitors find in Miami a multicultural metropolis that works and plays with vigor and that welcomes the world to celebrate its diversity.

Pleasures and Pastimes

Beaches

Greater Miami has beaches to fit every style. A sandy, 300-foot-wide beach with several distinct sections extends for 10 mi from the foot of Miami Beach to Haulover Beach Park. Amazingly, it's all man-made. Seriously eroded during the mid-1970s, the beach was restored in a $51.5 million project between 1977 and 1981. Between 23rd and 44th streets, Miami Beach built boardwalks and protective walkways atop a sand dune landscaped with sea oats, sea grape, and other native plants whose roots keep the sand from blowing away.

Biking

Perfect weather and flat terrain make Dade County a popular place for cyclists. Numerous rental shops provide bicycle trail maps as well as bikes, and the county even employs a "bicycle coordinator," whose purpose in life is to share with you the glories of Miami's new bicycle-friendly roads, featuring wide shoulders and mile markers.

Boating

It's not uncommon for traffic to jam at boat ramps, especially on weekend mornings, but the waters are worth the wait. If you have the opportunity to sail, do so. Blue skies, calm seas, and a view of the city skyline make for a pleasurable outing—especially at twilight, when the fabled "moon over Miami" casts a soft glow on the water. Key Biscayne's calm waves and strong breezes are perfect for sailing and windsurfing, and though Dinner Key and the Coconut Grove waterfront remain the center of sailing in Greater Miami, sailboat moorings and rentals are located along other parts of the bay and up the Miami River.

Miami's idle rich prefer attacking the water in sleek and fast "cigarette" boats, but there's plenty of less-powerful powerboating to enjoy as well. Greater Miami has numerous marinas, and dock masters can provide information on marine services you may need. Ask for *Teall's Tides and Guides, Miami-Dade County,* and other nautical publications.

Dining

Miami is the United Nations of dining, serving up dishes native to Spain, Cuba, and Nicaragua as well as China, India, Thailand, Vietnam, and other Asian cultures. Chefs from the tropics combine fresh, natural foods—especially seafood—with classic island-style dishes, creating a new American cuisine that is sometimes called Floribbean.

Golf

From the famed Blue Monster at the Doral Golf Resort and Spa to the scenic Links at Key Biscayne overlooking Biscayne Bay, Greater Miami has more than 30 private and public courses. As with most other sports, the pleasure of golf is enhanced by superb weather.

Lodging

Few urban areas can match Greater Miami's diversity of accommodations. South Beach alone has more than 2,000 rooms, and Miami offers hundreds more hotels, motels, resorts, spas, and B&Bs, with prices ranging from $12 a night in a dormitory-style hostel to $2,000 a night in a luxurious presidential suite. Keep in mind that Miami hoteliers collect roughly 11.5% for city and resort taxes, and many hotels in the South Beach area are inclined to tack on a $5 parking fee. If money is an issue, ask for all charges in advance.

Nightlife

Greater Miami's heaviest concentration of nightspots is on South Beach along Ocean Drive, Washington Avenue, and most recently along Lincoln Road Mall. Other nightlife centers on Little Havana, Coconut Grove, and on the fringes of downtown Miami.

Individual clubs offer jazz, reggae, salsa, various forms of rock, techno-pop, and Top 40 sounds on different nights of the week—most played at a body-thumping, ear-throbbing volume. Some clubs refuse entrance to anyone under 21, others 25, so if that is a concern, call ahead. On South Beach, where the sounds of jazz and reggae spill into the streets, fashion models and photographers frequent the lobby bars of small Art Deco hotels. Throughout Greater Miami, bars and cocktail lounges in larger hotels operate nightly discos, with live weekend entertainment. Many hotels extend their bars into open-air courtyards, where patrons dine and dance under the stars throughout the year. It's a good idea to ask in advance about cover charges; policies change frequently. And be warned: Even the most popular club can fall out of favor quickly. Ask your hotel's concierge or check Friday's *Miami Herald* to find out what's hot and what's just a dying ember.

Scuba Diving and Snorkeling

Though winter diving can be adversely affected when cold fronts come through, causing dive boats to vary their schedules, summer diving conditions in Greater Miami have been compared to those in the Caribbean. Chances are excellent you'll come face to face with a flood of tropical fish. Tons of limestone boulders and more than 65 tankers, trawlers, tugs, and a 727 jet were sunk by the county to create artificial reefs and a habitat for yellow tang, barracudas, nurse sharks, snapper, eels, and grouper. Most dive shops sell a book listing the location of these wrecks. You can also find real reefs, such as Fowey, Triumph, Long, and Emerald, in 10- to 15-foot dives that are perfect for snorkelers and beginning divers. On the edge of the continental shelf, these reefs are ¼ mi from depths greater than 100 feet. Another option is to paddle around the tangled prop roots of the mangrove trees that line the coast, peering at the fish, crabs, and other creatures hiding there.

Shopping

Visitors to Greater Miami are never more than 15 minutes from a major shopping area and the soothing shoosh, shoosh sound of a credit card machine. Today Dade County has more than a dozen major malls, an international free-trade zone, and hundreds of miles of commercial streets lined with stores and small shopping centers that range from the ritzy shops of Bal Harbour to the ethnic offerings of Latin neighborhoods. From children's *vestidos de fiesta* (party dresses) to men's *guayaberas* (a pleated, embroidered tropical shirt), the wealth of Latin merchants and merchandise will convince you that Miami is really a South American *mercado* (market).

No standard store hours exist in Greater Miami, though most malls observe the typical seven-day hours of malls everywhere. Call ahead. When you shop, expect to pay Florida's 6% sales tax (6.5% in Dade County), unless you have the store ship your goods out of state.

Spectator Sports

Greater Miami has franchises in all major-league sports—baseball, basketball, football, and ice hockey—plus top-rated events in boat racing, jai alai, and tennis. Get tickets early. Despite an unfortunate string of Super Bowl losses, Dolphin fans still turn out en masse, as do Heat fans for basketball, Marlin maniacs for baseball, and Panther aficionados for hockey. Generally you can find daily listings of local events in the sports section of the *Miami Herald,* whereas Friday's "Weekend" section carries more detailed schedules and coverage.

Activities of the annual Orange Bowl and Junior Orange Bowl Festival take place from early November to late February. Best known for its King Orange Jamboree Parade and the Federal Express/Orange Bowl Football Classic, the festival also includes two tennis tournaments: the Rolex–Orange Bowl International Tennis Tournament, for top amateur tennis players 18 and under, and an international tournament for players 14 and under. The Junior Orange Bowl Festival is the world's largest youth festival, with more than 20 events between November and January, including sports, cultural, and performing arts activities. The showcase event is the HealthSouth/Junior Orange Bowl Parade, held in downtown Coral Gables.

EXPLORING MIAMI AND MIAMI BEACH

Disney captured Miami's family trade, *Miami Vice* smacked the city upside the head with notoriety, the winds of Hurricane Andrew literally shook its foundation, and South Beach made it a global resort for the turn of the 21st century. Through this, the city went from an enclave of retired northeasterners to the ultimate joyride with a Latin beat. Hardly any part of the city isn't caught up in change. Meanwhile, sightseeing—which used to be pretty much limited to picking fruit off citrus trees and watching alligator wrestling—has become a fun way to glimpse the city at work and at play.

Most visitors to the Greater Miami area don't realize that Miami and Miami Beach are separate cities. Miami, on the mainland, is South Florida's commercial hub. Miami Beach, on 17 islands offshore in Biscayne Bay, is sometimes considered America's Riviera, luring refugees from winter with its warm sunshine; sandy beaches; graceful, shady palms; and ever-rocking nightlife.

Downtown has become the lively hub of the mainland city, now more accessible thanks to the Metromover extension (☞ Getting Around by Train *in* Miami and Miami Beach A to Z, *below*). Other major attractions include Coconut Grove, Little Havana, and the South Beach/Art Deco District, but since these areas are spread out beyond the reach of public transportation, you'll have to drive. Rent a convertible if you can. There's nothing quite like having the wind in your hair as you drive across one of the causeways en route to Miami Beach. (Sunglasses are a must.)

Finding your way around Greater Miami is easy if you know how the numbering system works. Miami is laid out on a grid with four quadrants—northeast, northwest, southeast, and southwest—which meet at Miami Avenue and Flagler Street. Miami Avenue separates east from west, and Flagler Street separates north from south. Avenues and courts run north–south; streets, terraces, and ways run east–west. Roads run diagonally, northwest–southeast.

Many named streets also bear numbers. For example, Unity Boulevard is Northwest and Southwest 27th Avenue, and LeJeune Road is Northwest and Southwest 42nd Avenue. However, named streets that depart markedly from the grid, such as Biscayne Boulevard and Brickell Avenue, have no corresponding numerical designations. Dade County and most other municipalities follow the Miami numbering system.

In Miami Beach, avenues run north–south; streets, east–west. Numbers rise along the beach from south to north and from the Atlantic Ocean in the east to Biscayne Bay in the west.

In Coral Gables, all streets bear names. The town uses the Miami numbering system for north–south addresses but begins counting east–west addresses westward from Douglas Road (Southwest 37th Avenue).

Hialeah has its own grid. Palm Avenue separates east from west; Hialeah Drive separates north from south. Avenues run north–south and streets east–west. Numbered streets and avenues are designated west, east, southeast, southwest, northeast, or northwest.

If all the different names, diagonal highways, one-way avenues, and dead-end streets have you completely confused, don't despair. Just make sure you have a detailed map and adequate directions before heading off, and be prepared to ask directions early and often. But make sure you're in a safe neighborhood or public place when you ask; cabbies and cops are good resources.

Numbers in the text correspond to numbers in the margin and on the Exploring Miami Beach; Exploring Downtown Miami; Exploring Miami, Coral Gables, and Key Biscayne; and Exploring South Dade maps.

Great Itineraries

IF YOU HAVE 3 DAYS

To recuperate from your journey, grab a beach towel and a bottle of suntan lotion, and head for Ocean Drive on South Beach to catch some rays while relaxing on the white sands. Afterward, take a guided or self-guided tour of the Art Deco District to see what all the fuss is about. Keep the evening free to socialize with the oh-so-trendy people who gather at Ocean Drive cafés. The following day, cruise up Collins Avenue to some of the monolithic hotels, such as the Fontainebleau Hilton and Eden Roc; continue north to the swank shops of Bal Harbour; and head back for an evening of shopping, drinking, and outdoor dining at Lincoln Road Mall ⑩. On the third day, wander around Calle Ocho ㉔ in Little Havana, visit Vizcaya Museum and Gardens ㊻, and wrap up the evening a few blocks away in Coconut Grove, enjoying its partylike atmosphere and many nightspots.

IF YOU HAVE 5 DAYS

Follow the suggested three-day itinerary, and add a visit to the beaches of Virginia Key and Key Biscayne. From here you can depart on a diving trip or fishing excursion or learn to windsurf. On the final day, head over to Coral Gables to take in the eye-popping display of 1920s Mediterranean Revival architecture in the city center and the majestic Biltmore Hotel ㉟; then take a dip in the fantastic, thematic Venetian Pool ㉞. That night, indulge in an evening of fine dining at your choice of gourmet restaurants in Coral Gables.

IF YOU HAVE 7 DAYS

A week gives you just enough time to experience fully the multicultural, cosmopolitan, tropical mélange that is Greater Miami and its beaches. With two extra days, see where it all began: Use the Miami Metromover to zip around downtown Miami (if possible, on a tour with historian Dr. Paul George), take the afternoon to shop in the Miami International Arts and Design District ㊹, and in the evening check out the shops and clubs at Bayside Marketplace. The final day can be used to visit South Dade, site of Miami's Metrozoo ㊾ and Monkey Jungle ㊶. Keep the evening free to revisit your favorite nightspots and have a drink with your new pals, Sly and Madonna.

South Beach/Miami Beach

The hub of South Beach (SoBe, to the truly hip) is the 1-sq-mi Art Deco District, fronted on the east by Ocean Drive and on the west by Alton Road. The story of South Beach has become the story of Miami. In the early 1980s, South Beach's vintage hotels were badly run down, catering mostly to infirm retirees. But a group of visionaries led by Barbara Baer Capitman, a spirited New York transplant, saw this collection of buildings as an architectural treasure to be salvaged from a sea of mindless urban renewal. It was, and is, a peerless grouping of Art Deco architecture from the 1920s and 1930s, whose forms and decorative details are drawn from both nature and the streamlined shapes of modern transportation and industrial machinery.

Investors started fixing up the interiors of these hotels and repainting their exteriors with a vibrant pastel palette—a concept borrowed from *Miami Vice*. International bistro operators sensed the potential for a new café society. Fashion photographers and the media took note, and celebrities like singer Gloria Estefan, the late designer Gianni Versace, and record executive Chris Blackwell bought a piece of the action.

As a result, South Beach now holds the distinction of being the nation's first 20th-century district on the National Register of Historic Places, with 650 significant buildings making the roll. But it hasn't all been smooth. Miami officials seem to lack the gene enabling them to appreciate residents who help the city. Barbara Capitman was well into her 60s when she stepped in front of bulldozers ready to tear down the Senator, a Deco hotel. Her reward for helping to save the Deco District and laying the groundwork for a multibillion-dollar tourist trade is a minor side street named in her honor.

More recently, SoBe hoteliers were similarly rewarded for successfully renovating old or abandoned buildings by having their taxes quadrupled—an attempt by the local government to make up for the lack of tax revenues generated in other areas of Dade County. At times it seems political corruption, cronyism, nepotism, shortsightedness, and insensitivity may wind up dissolving the city of Miami. Nevertheless, SoBe continues to roll, and roll it does 24 hours a day. Photographers pose beautiful models for shoots, tanned skaters zip past palm trees, and tourists flock to see what happens in the South's true cosmopolitan city.

SoBe is trendy, it's tropical, and it's a tricky place to find a parking space. From midmorning on, parking is scarce along Ocean Drive. You'll do better on Collins or Washington avenues, the next two streets to the west. Fortunately, there are new parking garages on Collins Avenue at 7th and 13th streets, on Washington Avenue at 12th Street, and west of Washington at 17th Street. Be warned: Tickets are given freely when meters expire, and towing charges are high.

A Good Walk

The stretch of Ocean Drive from 1st to 23rd streets—primarily the 10-block stretch from 5th to 15th streets—has become the most talked-about beachfront in America. A bevy of Art Deco jewels hug the drive, while across the street lies palm-fringed **Lummus Park** ①, whose southern end is a good starting point for a walk. Cross to the west side of Ocean Drive, where there are many sidewalk cafés, and walk north, taking note of the Park Central Hotel, built in 1937 by Deco architect Henry Hohauser, followed closely by the **Beacon Hotel** ②.

At 10th Street, recross Ocean Drive to the beach side and visit the **Art Deco District Welcome Center** ③ in the 1950s-era Oceanfront Auditorium. Here you can rent tapes or hire a guide for a Deco District tour.

Look back across Ocean Drive and take a peek at the wonderful fly-
ing-saucer architecture of the Clevelander, at Number 1020. On the
next block you'll see the late Gianni Versace's Spanish Mediterranean
Amsterdam Palace ④ and the **Victor Hotel** ⑤, yet another fine Deco example. Graceful fluted columns stand guard at the Leslie (Number 1244)
and **The Carlyle** ⑥. A few doors down, you can drop by the happening **Cardozo Hotel** ⑦ and ask to meet the owner—Gloria Estefan.

Walk two blocks west (away from the ocean) on 13th Street to Washington Avenue, where a mix of chic restaurants, avant-garde shops, del-
icatessens, produce markets, and nightclubs have spiced up a once derelict
neighborhood. Turn left on Washington and walk 2½ blocks south to
the **Wolfsonian Foundation Gallery** ⑧, home of a 70,000-plus-item collection of Art Moderne design and Deco-era propaganda arts.

Provided you haven't spent all afternoon in the museum, return north
on Washington Avenue past 14th Street, and turn left on **Espanola
Way** ⑨, a narrow street of Mediterranean-revival buildings, eclectic
shops, and a weekend market. Continue west to Meridian Avenue and
turn right. Three blocks north of Espanola Way is the redesigned **Lincoln Road Mall** ⑩, which is often paired with Ocean Drive as part of
must-see South Beach.

The next main street north of Lincoln Road is 17th Street, and to the
east is the Miami Beach Convention Center. Walk behind the massive
building to the corner of Meridian Avenue and 19th Street to see the
chilling **Holocaust Memorial** ⑪, a monumental record honoring the 6
million Jewish victims of the Holocaust.

Head east and return to Ocean Drive in time to pull up a chair at an
outdoor café, order an espresso, and settle down for an evening of people-watching, SoBe's most popular pastime.

TIMING

To see only the Art Deco buildings on Ocean Drive, allow one hour
minimum. Depending upon your interests, schedule at least five hours
and include a drink or meal at a café and browsing time in the shops
on Ocean Drive, along Espanola Way, and at Lincoln Road Mall.

Start your walking tour as early in the day as possible. In winter the
street becomes crowded as the day wears on, and in summer, afternoon
heat and humidity can be unbearable, wilting even the hardiest soul.

Sights to See

❹ **Amsterdam Palace.** In the early 1980s, before South Beach became the
hotbed of chicness, the late Italian designer Gianni Versace purchased
this run-down Spanish Mediterranean residence, built before the arrival of Deco. Today, the home is an ornate three-story palazzo with
a guest house and a copper dome rooftop observatory and pool that
were added at the expense of a 1950s hotel, the Revere. Its loss and
the razing of the fabled Deco Senator became a rallying point for
preservationists, who like to point out that although they lost a few,
they saved 40. In July 1997, Versace was tragically shot and killed in
front of his home. ⊠ *1114 Ocean Dr.*

❸ **Art Deco District Welcome Center.** Run by the Miami Design Preservation League, this clearinghouse in the Oceanfront Auditorium provides
information about the buildings in the Art Deco District. A well-
stocked gift shop sells 1950s and Art Deco memorabilia, posters, and
books on Miami's history. You can rent audiotapes for a self-guided
tour, join the regular Saturday morning or Thursday evening walking
tours that start here, or take a bicycle tour, all providing detailed his-

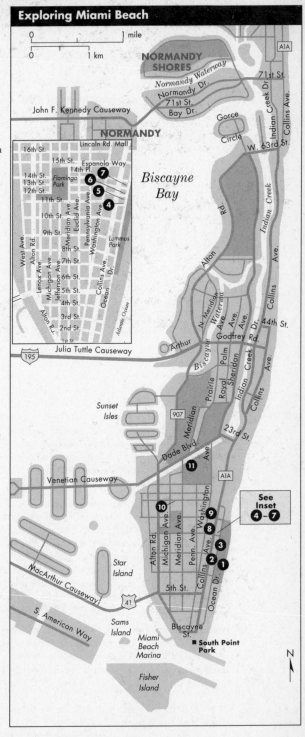

Exploring Miami Beach

tories of the Deco hotels. ⌧ *1001 Ocean Dr., at Barbara Capitman Way,* ☎ *305/531–3484.* ▭ *Free.* ⊙ *Daily 11–6, open later Thurs.–Mon. in season.*

Bass Museum of Art. A diverse collection of European art is the focus of this museum north of SoBe's key sights. Works on display include *The Holy Family,* a painting by Peter Paul Rubens; *The Tournament,* one of several 16th-century Flemish tapestries; and works by Albrecht Dürer and Henri de Toulouse-Lautrec. A project to double the museum's size is expected to begin in mid-1997. ⌧ *2121 Park Ave.,* ☎ *305/673–7530.* ▭ *$5.* ⊙ *Tues.–Sat. 10–5, except 2nd and 4th Wed. of each month 1–9; Sun. 1–5.*

❷ Beacon Hotel. Vertical fluting and racing stripes recall the principles of aerodynamics, a science in its infancy when the Beacon was constructed in 1936. ⌧ *720 Ocean Dr.*

❼ Cardozo Hotel. This classic example of streamlined architecture has a unique facade, first noticed by filmmakers in 1959, when it was used as a setting for the Frank Sinatra film *A Hole in the Head.* Now owned by pop star and Miami icon Gloria Estefan, it's one of SoBe's hottest spots. ⌧ *1300 Ocean Dr.*

❻ The Carlyle. Built in 1941, this is one of the few buildings on Hotel Row that no longer functions as a hotel. Movie fans will recognize it and its neighbor, the Leslie, as the nightclub from *The Birdcage,* starring Robin Williams and Nathan Lane. ⌧ *1250 Ocean Dr.*

❾ Espanola Way. The Mediterranean-revival buildings along this road were constructed in 1925 and frequented through the years by artists and writers. In the 1930s, future bandleader Desi Arnaz strapped on a conga drum and started beating out a rhumba rhythm at a nightclub that is now the Clay Hotel, a youth hostel. Visit this quaint avenue on a Sunday afternoon, when itinerant dealers and craftsmen set up shop to sell everything from garage sale items to handcrafted bongo drums. Between Washington and Drexel avenues, the road has been narrowed to a single lane, and Miami Beach's trademark pink sidewalks have been widened to accommodate sidewalk cafés and shops selling imaginative clothing, jewelry, and art.

★ Fontainebleau Hilton Resort and Towers. For a sense of what Miami was up to during the fabulous '50s, take a drive north to see the finest example of SoBe's grandiose architecture. By the 1950s, smaller Deco-era hotels were passé, and architects like Morris Lapidus got busy designing free-flowing hotels that affirmed the American attitude of "bigger is better." More recently, artist Richard Haas designed a 13,000-square-foot tropical waterfall and foliage mural that reveals how the hotel and its rock-grotto swimming pool would look behind the wall. ⌧ *4441 Collins Ave.,* ☎ *305/538–2000.*

⓫ Holocaust Memorial. The focus of the memorial is a 42-foot-high bronze arm rising from the ground, with sculptured people climbing the arm seeking escape. A memorial wall with victims' names and a meditation garden complement the sculpture. ⌧ *1933–1945 Meridian Ave.,* ☎ *305/538–1663.* ▭ *Free.* ⊙ *Daily 9–9.*

NEED A BREAK?	If your feet are still holding up, head to the **Delano Hotel** (⌧ 1685 Collins Ave.) for a drink. This surrealistic hotel is like a Calvin Klein ad come to life and is generating a buzz among SoBe's fashion models and hepcats.

★ ❿ **Lincoln Road Mall.** A playful, $16 million redesign of this grande dame of Miami Beach spruced up the futuristic 1950s vision of Fontainebleau designer Morris Lapidus and added a grove of 20 towering date palms and five linear pools. Indicative of the road's resurgence is the restoration of dozens of buildings, including a former Jehovah's Witness hall that actor Michael Caine has transformed into a restaurant. The best time to hit the road is on weekend evenings, when cafés are bustling; art galleries, like Romero Britto's Britto Central, schedule openings; street performers take the stage; and bookstores, import shops, and clothing stores are open for late-night purchases.

In the classical four-story Deco gem with friezes at 541–545 Lincoln Road, the **New World Symphony,** a national advanced-training orchestra led by Michael Tilson Thomas, rehearses and performs. To the west toward Biscayne Bay, the street is lined with chic food markets, cafés, and boutiques. Farther west is the **South Florida Art Center,** home to one of the first arts groups to help resurrect the area, and farther still is a black-and-white Deco movie house with a Mediterranean barrel-tile roof, which is now the **Colony Theater.** ✉ *Lincoln Rd. between Collins Ave. and Alton Rd.*

☙ ❶ **Lummus Park.** This palm-shaded oasis on the beach side of Ocean Drive attracts beach-going families with its children's play area. Skaters, too, are drawn to its wide, winding sidewalk. The lush foliage is a pleasing, natural counterpoint to the ultrachic atmosphere just across the street. ✉ *East of Ocean Dr. between 5th and 15th Sts.*

South Pointe Park. From the 50-yard Sunshine Pier, which adjoins the 1-mi-long jetty at the mouth of Government Cut, you can fish while watching huge ships pass. No bait or tackle is available in the park. Other facilities include two observation towers and volleyball courts. ✉ *1 Washington Ave.*

❺ **Victor Hotel.** Despite its intriguing ocean-liner motif, this eight-story structure remains empty—no doubt recovering from the days when Don Johnson shot scenes for *Miami Vice* here. ✉ *1144 Ocean Dr.*

❽ **Wolfsonian Foundation Gallery.** An elegantly renovated 1927 storage facility is now home to the 70,000-plus-item collection of modern design and "propaganda arts" amassed by Miami native Mitchell Wolfson, Jr., a world traveler and connoisseur. Included in the museum's eclectic holdings are 8,000 matchbooks collected by King Farouk. (The name "Wolfsonian," by the way, is intended to echo "Smithsonian.") ✉ *1001 Washington Ave.,* ☎ *305/531–1001,* FAX *305/531–2133.* 🎟 *$5.* ☉ *Tues.–Sat. 11–6, Sun. noon–5.*

Downtown Miami

From a distance you see downtown Miami's future—a 21st-century skyline stroking the clouds with sleek fingers of steel and glass. By day this icon of commerce and technology sparkles in the subtropical sun; at night it basks in the man-made glow of neon and floodlights.

Here staid, suited lawyers and bankers share the sidewalks with Latino merchants wearing open-neck, intricately embroidered shirts called guayaberas. Fruit merchants sell their wares from pushcarts, young European travelers with backpacks stroll the streets, and foreign businesspeople haggle over prices in import-export shops. You hear Arabic, Chinese, Creole, French, German, Hebrew, Hindi, Japanese, Portuguese, Spanish, Swedish, Yiddish, and even a little English now and then. Mostly, however, what's best in the heart of downtown Miami is its Latinization and the sheer energy of Latin shoppers.

Though this metropolis has become one of the great international cities of the Americas, Miami's downtown is sorely neglected. Indeed, Miami teeters on the verge of bankruptcy, and downtown merchants have formed a coalition to disband the city, claiming that for every 30¢ they pay in taxes, they receive only 1¢ of public services. Office workers crowd the area by day, but except for Bayside Marketplace and the Miami Arena, downtown is deserted at night and arena patrons rarely linger. Those who live close to downtown stay at its fringes, as on Claughton Island at the mouth of the Miami River, where a half dozen residential towers have risen to house thousands in the last decade. Visitors, too, spend little time here, since most tourist attractions are in other neighborhoods. Miami's oldest downtown buildings date from the 1920s and 1930s—not very old compared to the historic districts of St. Augustine and Pensacola. But there is a movement afoot to bring a renaissance to downtown. Though nothing has yet been built, a new waterfront arena for the Miami Heat, a performing arts center, and a CocoWalk-style pedestrian mall have been approved and should take shape over the next few years.

Thanks to the Metromover (☞ Getting Around by Train *in* Miami and Miami Beach A to Z, *below*), which has inner and outer loops through downtown plus north and south extensions, this is an excellent tour to take by rail. Attractions are conveniently located within about two blocks of the nearest station. Parking downtown is no less convenient or more expensive than in any city, but the best idea is to leave your car at an outlying Metrorail station and take the train downtown.

A Good Tour
Get off the Metrorail train at Government Center, where the 21-mi elevated Metrorail commuter system connects with Metromover. As you leave the station, notice the **Dade County Courthouse** ⑫, to the east. West on Flagler Street is the **Metro-Dade Cultural Center** ⑬, which contains the city's main art museum, historical museum, and library.

Take the Metromover to the next stop, Ft. Dallas Park, and walk one block south for views from the **Miami Avenue Bridge** ⑭.

At the next Metromover stop, Knight Center, you can transfer to the inner loop and ride one stop to Miami Avenue, a block south of Flagler Street, downtown Miami's commercial spine. As you look at the steel and glass structures, keep in mind that this was one of the first areas of Miami to be carved out of the pine woods and palmetto scrub when Flagler's railroad arrived in 1896. Or you can ride the Metromover spur to the Brickell District. It runs across the Miami River along **Brickell Avenue** ⑮, a southward extension of Southeast 2nd Avenue, where there are architecturally interesting skyscrapers.

The next stop on the outer loop is Bayfront Park, opposite **Claude and Mildred Pepper Bayfront Park** ⑯. South of the park, the lobby of the Hotel Inter-Continental Miami contains *The Spindle*, a huge sculpture by Henry Moore. West of Bayfront Park Station stands the tallest building in Florida, the **First Union Financial Center** ⑰.

As you continue north on the Metromover, take in the fine view of Bayfront Park's greenery, the bay beyond, the Port of Miami in the bay, and Miami Beach across the water. The next Metromover stop, First Street, places you a block north of Flagler Street and the landmark **Gusman Center for the Performing Arts** ⑱, a stunningly beautiful movie palace that now serves as downtown Miami's concert hall.

The College/Bayside Metromover stop serves the downtown campus of **Miami-Dade Community College** ⑲, which has two fine galleries.

As Metromover rounds the curve after College/Bayside Station, look northeast for a view of **Freedom Tower** ⑳, an important milepost in the history of Cuban immigration. (To see the tower up close, walk north from Edcom Station to Northeast 6th Street, then two blocks east to Biscayne Boulevard.) At this point in the loop, a spur curves north to the Omni District.

A two-block walk south from Edcom Station brings you to the **U.S. Courthouse** ㉑, a handsome building with an interesting Depression-era mural. As you round the northwest corner of the loop, at State Plaza/Arena Station, look two blocks north to see the round, squat, windowless, pink **Miami Arena** ㉒.

TIMING

To walk and ride to the various points of interest, allow two hours. If you want to spend additional time eating and shopping at Bayside, allow at least four hours. To include museum visits, allow six hours.

Sights to See

American Police Hall of Fame and Museum. This museum exhibits more than 10,000 law enforcement–related items, including weapons, a jail cell, and an electric chair, as well as a 400-ton marble memorial listing the names of more than 6,000 police officers killed in the line of duty since 1960. ⊠ *3801 Biscayne Blvd.,* ☎ *305/573–0070.* ☞ *$6.* ⊙ *Daily 10–5:30.*

⑮ **Brickell Avenue.** A canyon rimmed by tall buildings, this stretch of street contains the largest concentration of international banking offices in the United States. From the end of the Metromover line you can look south to where several architecturally interesting condominiums rise between Brickell Avenue and Biscayne Bay. Arquitectonica, an internationally prominent architectural firm based in Miami, designed three of these buildings: the **Palace** (⊠ 1541 Brickell Ave.), the **Imperial** (⊠ 1627 Brickell Ave.), and the **Atlantis** (⊠ 2025 Brickell Ave.). Israeli artist Yacov Agam painted the rainbow exterior of **Villa Regina** (⊠ 1581 Brickell Ave.).

⑯ **Claude and Mildred Pepper Bayfront Park.** An oasis among the skyscrapers, this park extends east from busy, palm-lined Biscayne Boulevard to the bay. In the 1920s, it served as an urban landfill, but in 1943, Dade County erected a memorial for casualties of World War II here. Unfortunately, the gesture was premature, and the monument was revised in 1980 to include the names of later victims. Japanese sculptor Isamu Noguchi redesigned the park just before his death in 1989. It now includes a memorial to the *Challenger* astronauts, an amphitheater, and a fountain (usually turned off as a budget-tightening measure) honoring the late Florida congressman Claude Pepper and his wife. ⊠ *Biscayne Blvd. between 2nd and 3rd Sts.*

⑫ **Dade County Courthouse.** Built in 1928, this was once the tallest building south of Washington, DC. It has a pyramid at its peak, where turkey vultures roost in winter. ⊠ *73 W. Flagler St.*

⑰ **First Union Financial Center.** The tallest building in Florida is this 55-story structure. Towering royal palms grace the 1-acre Palm Court plaza beneath the steel-and-glass frame. ⊠ *200 S. Biscayne Blvd.*

⑳ **Freedom Tower.** In the 1960s, this imposing Spanish-baroque structure was used by the Cuban Refugee Center to process more than 500,000 Cubans who entered the United States to flee Fidel Castro's regime. Built in 1925 for the *Miami Daily News,* it was inspired by the Giralda, an 800-year-old bell tower in Seville, Spain. Preservationists were

Exploring Downtown Miami

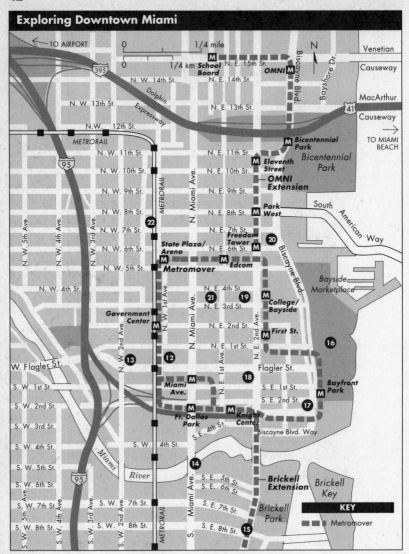

pleased to see the tower restored to its original grandeur in 1988. ⊠ *600 Biscayne Blvd.*

⑱ Gusman Center for the Performing Arts. This ornate former movie palace has been restored as a concert hall. Resembling a Moorish courtyard with twinkling stars in the sky, it hosts performances by the Miami City Ballet and the New World Symphony. ⊠ *174 Flagler St.,* ☎ *305/372–0925.*

★ ⚲ ⑬ Metro-Dade Cultural Center. Containing three important cultural resources, this 3.3-acre complex is one of the focal points of downtown. The city's main art museum, the **Miami Museum of Art,** puts on major touring exhibitions of work by international artists, focusing on work completed since 1850. At the **Historical Museum of Southern Florida,** you can learn about human experience in South Florida from prehistory to the present. The **Main Public Library** contains nearly 4 million holdings and offers art exhibits in the auditorium and second-floor lobby. ⊠ *101 W. Flagler St.,* ☎ *305/375–1700 for art museum,* ☎ *305/375–1492 for historical museum,* ☎ *305/375–2665 for library.* 🎫 *Museums $8.* ☉ *Art museum Tues.–Fri. 10–5, weekends noon–5; historical museum Mon.–Wed. and Fri.–Sat. 10–5, Thurs. 10–9, Sun. noon–5; library Mon.–Wed. and Fri.–Sat. 9–6, Thurs. 9–9, Sun. 1–5.*

㉒ Miami Arena. Home of the NBA's Miami Heat and the NHL's Florida Panthers, the arena also hosts a variety of other sports and entertainment events. ⊠ *701 Arena Blvd.,* ☎ *305/530–4444.*

⑭ Miami Avenue Bridge. This is one of 11 bridges on the Miami River that opens to let ships pass. From the bridge approach, you can watch freighters, tugboats, research vessels, and luxury yachts ply the busy 5-mi waterway.

⑲ Miami-Dade Community College. The campus houses two fine galleries: the third-floor **Centre Gallery,** which hosts various exhibitions, and the fifth-floor **Frances Wolfson Art Gallery,** which houses traveling exhibits of contemporary art. ⊠ *300 N.E. 2nd Ave.,* ☎ *305/237–3278.* 🎫 *Free.* ☉ *Weekdays 10–6.*

㉑ U.S. Courthouse. Made of keystone, the courthouse was erected in 1931 as Miami's main post office. In what was once the second-floor central courtroom is *Law Guides Florida Progress,* a huge Depression-era mural by Denman Fink. Surrounding the central figure of a robed judge are several images that define the Florida of the 1930s: fish vendors, palm trees, beaches, and a Pan Am airplane winging off to Latin America. No cameras or tape recorders are allowed in the building. ⊠ *300 N.E. 1st Ave.* ☉ *Building weekdays 8:30–5, security guards open courtroom on request.*

Little Havana

Nearly 40 years ago the tidal wave of Cubans fleeing the Castro regime flooded into an older neighborhood west of downtown Miami. This area became known as Little Havana. Today, with a million Cubans and other Latins—more than half the metropolitan population—dispersed throughout Greater Miami, Little Havana and neighboring East Little Havana remain magnets for Hispanics and Anglos alike, who come to experience the flavor of traditional Cuban culture. That culture, of course, functions in Spanish. Many Little Havana residents and shopkeepers speak little or no English.

A Good Tour

From downtown go west on Flagler Street across the Miami River to Teddy Roosevelt Avenue (Southwest 17th Avenue), and pause at **Plaza de la Cubanidad** ㉓, on the southwest corner. The plaza's monument is indicative of the prominent role of Cuban history and culture here.

Turn left at Douglas Road (Southwest 37th Avenue), drive south to **Calle Ocho** ㉔ (Southwest 8th Street), and turn left again. You are now on the main commercial thoroughfare of Little Havana. After you cross Unity Boulevard (Southwest 27th Avenue), Calle Ocho becomes a one-way street eastbound through the heart of Little Havana. Parking is more plentiful west of Ronald Reagan Avenue (Southwest 12th Avenue).

At Avenida Luis Muñoz Marín (Southwest 15th Avenue), stop at **Domino Park** ㉕, where elderly Cuban men pass the day with their black-and-white play tiles. The **Brigade 2506 Memorial** ㉖, commemorating the victims of the unsuccessful 1961 Bay of Pigs invasion, stands at Memorial Boulevard (Southwest 13th Avenue). A block south are several other monuments relevant to Cuban history, including a statue of José Martí. Finish the tour by driving five blocks south of Calle Ocho on Ronald Reagan Avenue to the **Cuban Museum of the Americas** ㉗.

TIMING

If the history hidden in the monuments is your only interest, set aside two hours. Allow more time for a strong cup of Cuban coffee on Calle Ocho and a glimpse of Latin culture in the Cuban Museum.

Sights to See

㉖ **Brigade 2506 Memorial.** An eternal flame burns atop a simple stone monument with the inscription: CUBA—A LOS MARTIRES DE LA BRIGADA DE ASALTO ABRIL 17 DE 1961. The monument also bears a shield with the Brigade 2506 emblem, a Cuban flag superimposed on a cross. ⊠ *S.W. 8th St. and S.W. 13th Ave.*

㉔ **Calle Ocho.** Here in Little Havana's commercial heart, experience such Cuban customs as hand-rolled cigars or sandwiches piled with meats and cheeses and topped with hot and mild sauces. Though it all deserves exploring, if time is limited, try the stretch from Southwest 14th to 11th avenues. ⊠ *S.W. 8th St.*

㉗ **Cuban Museum of the Americas.** Created by Cuban exiles to preserve and interpret the cultural heritage of their homeland, the museum has expanded its focus to embrace the entire Hispanic arts community and work produced by young local artists. The collection includes the art of exiles and of artists who continue to live on the island. Other exhibits are drawn from the museum's small permanent collection. ⊠ *1300 S.W. 12th Ave.,* ☎ *305/858–8006.* 🎟 *$3.* ☉ *Tues.–Fri. noon–6, Sat. by appointment.*

㉕ **Domino Park.** Officially known as Maximo Gomez Park, this is a major gathering place for elderly, guayabera-clad Cuban males, who pass the day playing dominoes while arguing anti-Castro politics. A recent addition is a mural of the hemispheric Summit of the Americas, held in Miami in 1994; included are portraits of every leader who took part in the event. ⊠ *S.W. 8th St. and S.W. 15th Ave.* ☉ *Daily 9–6.*

㉓ **Plaza de la Cubinidad.** Redbrick sidewalks surround a fountain and monument with the words of José Martí, a leader in Cuba's struggle for independence from Spain and a hero to Cuban refugees and immigrants in Miami. The quotation, LAS PALMAS SON NOVIAS QUE ESPERAN (The palm trees are girlfriends who will wait), counsels hope and fortitude to the Cubans. ⊠ *W. Flagler St. and S.W. 17th Ave.*

Coral Gables

This planned community of broad boulevards and Spanish Mediterranean architecture justifiably calls itself the City Beautiful—a moniker
it acquired by following the Garden City method of urban planning
in the 1920s. George E. Merrick began selling Coral Gables lots in 1921
and incorporated the city in 1925. He named most of the streets for
Spanish explorers, cities, and provinces and even contracted architects
trained abroad to create themed neighborhood villages, such as American pioneer, Chinese, French city, Dutch South African, and French
Normandy. Like much of Miami, Coral Gables has realized the aesthetic and economic importance of historic preservation and has passed
a Mediterranean design ordinance, rewarding businesses for maintaining or restoring their building's architectural style. Other holdovers
from the '20s are the street signs. Though slightly awkward to read,
the ground-level markers on whitewashed concrete cornerstones are
nevertheless of historical value.

Unfortunately for Merrick, the devastating no-name hurricane of 1926
and the Great Depression prevented him from fulfilling many of his
plans. The city languished until after World War II but then grew
rapidly. Today Coral Gables has a population of about 41,000. In its
bustling downtown, more than 140 multinational companies maintain
headquarters or regional offices, and the University of Miami campus
in the southern part of Coral Gables brings a youthful vibrance.

A Good Tour

From downtown Miami drive south on Southeast 2nd Avenue across
the Miami River, where the street becomes Brickell Avenue. One-half
mile south of the river turn right on Coral Way, which at this point is
Southwest 13th Street. It then turns left under I–95 and becomes
Southwest 3rd Avenue. It continues another mile to a complex five-
point intersection and doglegs right to become Southwest 22nd Street.

Along the Southwest 3rd Avenue and Southwest 22nd Street segments
of Coral Way, banyan trees planted in the median strip in 1929 arch
over the roadway. The banyans end at the Miami–Coral Gables boundary, where Miracle Mile begins. Actually only ½ mi long, this retailing
stretch of Coral Way, from Douglas Road (37th Avenue) to LeJeune
Road (42nd Avenue), is the heart of downtown Coral Gables.

To your right is a 1930s-era movie theater, which was renovated to
serve as the temporary home of the **Miami Youth Museum** ㉘. Notice
the **Colonnade Building** ㉙, before bearing left onto Biltmore Way immediately west of LeJeune Road. At this point you'll see the ornate Spanish Renaissance **Coral Gables City Hall** ㉚ facing Miracle Mile.

Continue west on Biltmore Way to the corner, turn right on Segovia,
left on Coral Way, and right again on Toledo Street to park behind **Coral
Gables Merrick House and Gardens** ㉛, Merrick's boyhood home. As
you leave the parking lot, turn left on Toledo Street and continue to
South Greenway Drive. You'll see the Granada Golf Course, a gorgeously
green nine-hole course amid Coral Gables's largest historic district.

Turn left on South Greenway Drive, follow it to Alhambra Circle, and
turn right. One block ahead on your left, at the intersection of Alhambra
Circle, Greenway Court, and Ferdinand Street, is the restored **Alhambra Water Tower** ㉜, a city landmark dating from 1925.

Now drive south on Alhambra Circle four short blocks to Coral Way.
Turn left and after six blocks turn right on Granada Boulevard. You
are now approaching **De Soto Plaza and Fountain** ㉝. Follow the traf-

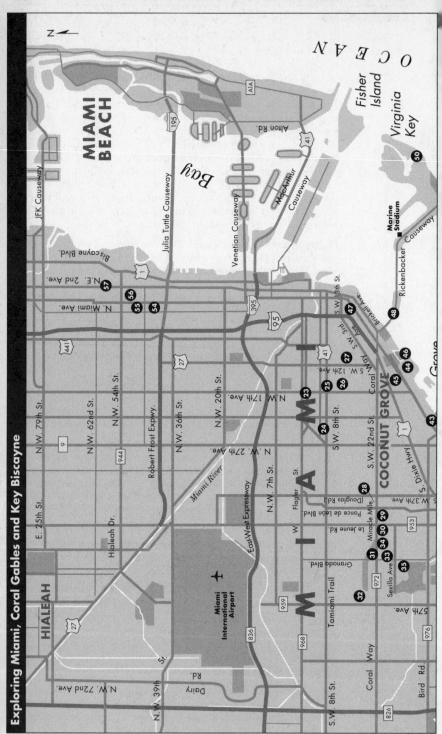

Exploring Miami, Coral Gables and Key Biscayne

OCEAN

Fisher Island

Virginia Key

MIAMI BEACH

Bay

MacArthur Causeway

Marine Stadium

Rickenbacker Causeway

Alton Rd.

Venetian Causeway

Julia Tuttle Causeway

JFK Causeway

Biscayne Blvd.

N.E. 2nd Ave.

N. Miami Ave.

N.W. 54th St.

N.W. 36th St.

N.W. 20th Ave.

N.W. 17th Ave.

N.W. 27th Ave.

N.W. 7th St.

Robert Frost Expwy.

Miami River

East-West Expressway

Flagler St.

Ponce de León Blvd

Douglas Rd.

le Jeune Rd.

Miracle Mile

Granada Blvd.

Sevilla Ave.

S.W. 37th Ave.

S.W. 8th St.

S.W. 22nd St.

S.W. 13th St.

Brickell Ave.

Coral Way N.W. 3rd Ave.

S.W. 12th Ave.

COCONUT GROVE

Grove

S. Dixie Hwy.

Tamiami Trail

Coral Way

S.W. 8th St.

Bird Rd.

57th Ave.

HIALEAH

E. 25th St.

N.W. 79th St.

N.W. 62nd St.

Hialeah Dr.

N.W. 72nd Ave.

N.W. 39th St.

Dairy Rd.

Miami International Airport

MIAMI

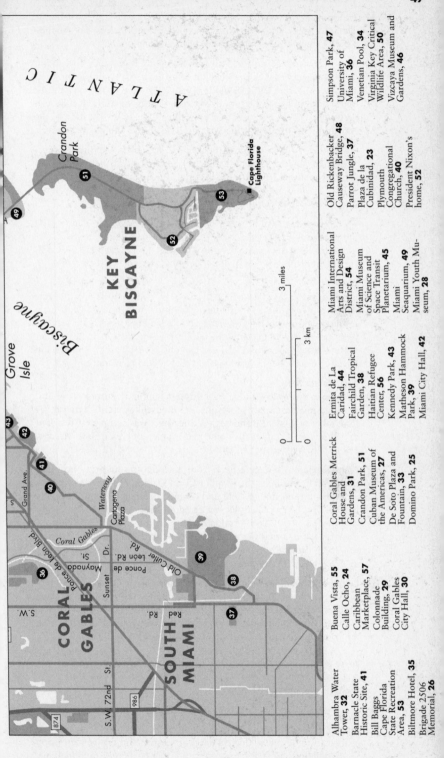

ATLANTIC

Crandon Park

KEY
BISCAYNE

Biscayne

Grove Isle

Cape Florida Lighthouse

Ponce de León Blvd.
Coral Gables
Maynada St.
Old Cutler Rd.
Sunset Dr.
Grand Ave.
Waterway
Cartagena Plaza

CORAL
GABLES

SOUTH
MIAMI

S.W. 72nd St.
Red Rd.
S.W.

874
986

3 miles

3 km

Alhambra Water
Tower, **32**
Barnacle State
Historic Site, **41**
Bill Baggs
Cape Florida
State Recreation
Area, **53**
Biltmore Hotel, **35**
Brigade 2506
Memorial, **26**

Buena Vista, **55**
Calle Ocho, **24**
Caribbean
Marketplace, **57**
Colonnade
Building, **29**
Coral Gables
City Hall, **30**

Coral Gables Merrick
House and
Gardens, **31**
Crandon Park, **51**
Cuban Museum of
the Americas, **27**
De Soto Plaza and
Fountain, **33**
Domino Park, **25**

Ermita de La
Caridad, **44**
Fairchild Tropical
Garden, **38**
Haitian Refugee
Center, **56**
Kennedy Park, **43**
Matheson Hammock
Park, **42**
Miami City Hall, **39**

Miami International
Arts and Design
District, **54**
Miami Museum
of Science and
Space Transit
Planetarium, **45**
Miami
Seaquarium, **49**
Miami Youth Mu-
seum, **28**

Old Rickenbacker
Causeway Bridge, **48**
Parrot Jungle, **37**
Plaza de la
Cubinidad, **23**
Plymouth
Congregational
Church, **40**
President Nixon's
home, **52**

Simpson Park, **47**
University of
Miami, **36**
Venetian Pool, **34**
Virginia Key Critical
Wildlife Area, **50**
Vizcaya Museum and
Gardens, **46**

fic circle almost completely around the fountain to northeast-bound De Soto Boulevard. On your right in the next block is the **Venetian Pool** ㉞, an exotic and unusual public swimming pool.

Return to the De Soto Fountain and follow De Soto Boulevard southwest to the reborn **Biltmore Hotel** ㉟. From the hotel, turn right on Anastasia Avenue, go east to Granada Boulevard, and turn right. Continue south on Granada Boulevard over a bridge across the Coral Gables Waterway, which empties into Biscayne Bay. In the hotel's heyday, Venetian gondolas plied the waterway, bringing guests to a bay-side beach.

At Ponce de León Boulevard turn right. On your left is Metrorail's Stonehengelike concrete structure, and on your right is the main campus of the **University of Miami** ㊱. Turn right at the first stoplight (Stanford Drive) to enter the campus, and park in the lot on your right designated for visitors to the Lowe Art Museum.

If you want to continue on to South Miami, exit the U.M. campus on Stanford Drive, pass under Metrorail, and cross Dixie Highway. Beyond the Burger King on your right, bear right on Maynada Street, and turn right at the next stoplight onto Sunset Drive.

TIMING
Strolling Miracle Mile will only take an hour, unless you plan to shop—and you should—in which case allow four hours. Allow time for a refreshing dip at the Venetian Pool, and plan to spend at least an hour getting acquainted with the Biltmore—longer if you'd like to order a drink and linger poolside. If you can pull yourself away from the lap of luxury, allow an hour to visit the University of Miami campus.

Sights to See

㉜ **Alhambra Water Tower.** In 1925 this city landmark stored water and was clad in a decorative moresque, lighthouselike exterior. After more than 50 years of disuse and neglect, the tower was completely restored in 1993 with a copper-rib dome and multicolor frescoes. ⊠ *Alhambra Circle, Greenway Ct., and Ferdinand St.*

㉟ **Biltmore Hotel.** Bouncing back from dark days as an army hospital, this hotel has become the jewel of Coral Gables. After extensive renovations, it reopened in 1992 and hosted the Summit of the Americas in 1994. Its 16-story tower, like the Freedom Tower in downtown Miami, is a replica of Seville's Giralda Tower. To the west is the Biltmore Country Club, a richly ornamented Beaux Arts–style structure with a superb colonnade and courtyard; it was reincorporated into the hotel in 1989. ⊠ *1200 Anastasia Ave.,* ☎ *305/445–1926.*

㉙ **Colonnade Building.** This restored structure once housed George Merrick's sales office. Its rotunda bears an ornamental frieze and a Spanish-tile roof 75 feet above street level, and the building is now connected to the 13-story Omni Colonnade Hotel and an office building that echoes the rotunda's roofline. ⊠ *133–169 Miracle Mile.*

NEED A BREAK?   Enjoy a rest stop at **Java Centrale** (⊠ 2334 Ponce de León Blvd.), a gourmet coffee café where hot and cold coffees, salads, and sandwiches are served with kindness.

㉚ **Coral Gables City Hall.** This 1928 building has a three-tier tower topped with a clock and a 500-pound bell. A mural by Denman Fink inside the dome ceiling depicts the four seasons and can be seen from the second floor. ⊠ *405 Biltmore Way,* ☎ *305/446–6800,* FAX *305/460–5371.* ⊙ *Weekdays 8–5.*

③ **Coral Gables Merrick House and Gardens.** In 1976 the city of Coral Gables acquired George Merrick's boyhood home. Restored to its 1920s appearance, it contains Merrick family furnishings and artifacts. ⊠ *907 Coral Way,* ☎ *305/460–5361.* ⊞ *House $2, grounds free.* ☉ *House Sun. 2–5, grounds daily 8–sunset.*

③ **De Soto Plaza and Fountain.** Water flows from the mouths of four sculpted faces on a classical column on a pedestal in this Denman Fink–designed fountain from the early 1920s. The closed eyes of the face looking west symbolize the day's end.

✋ **㉘** **Miami Youth Museum.** Housed in temporary facilities on Coral Way, the museum is scheduled to move into a larger space near the Vizcaya Metrorail station in Coconut Grove by late 1998. In the meantime, this lively museum features arts exhibits, hands-on displays, and activities to enhance children's creativity and inspire interest in artistic careers. ⊠ *3301 Coral Way (Miracle Center),* ☎ *305/446–4386.* ⊞ *$4.* ☉ *Weekdays 10–5, weekends 11–6.*

㊱ **University of Miami.** With almost 14,000 full-time, part-time, and noncredit students, U.M. is the largest private research university in the southeast. Walk around campus and visit the **Lowe Art Museum**, which has a permanent collection of 8,000 works that includes Renaissance and Baroque art, American paintings, Latin American art, and Navajo and Pueblo Indian textiles and baskets. The museum also hosts traveling exhibitions. ⊠ *1301 Stanford Dr.,* ☎ *305/284–3535 or 305/284–3536.* ⊞ *$4.* ☉ *Tues.–Sat. 10–5, Sun. noon–5.*

★ ✋ **㉞** **Venetian Pool.** Sculpted from a rock quarry in 1923, this municipal pool remains quite popular, probably due to the themed architecture— a fantasized version of a waterfront Italian village—created by George Merrick's uncle. The pool has earned a place on the National Register of Historical Places and showcases a nice collection of vintage photos depicting 1920s beauty pageants and swank soirees held here long ago. A snack bar, lockers, and showers make this must-see user-friendly as well. ⊠ *2701 De Soto Blvd.,* ☎ *305/460–5356.* ⊞ *$5, free parking across De Soto Blvd.* ☉ *Weekends 10–4:30; plus June–Aug., weekdays 11–7:30; Sept., Oct., Apr., and May, Tues.–Fri. 11:30–5:30; and Nov.–Mar., Tues.–Fri. 10–4:30.*

South Miami

South of Miami and Coral Gables is, not surprisingly, South Miami. A pioneer farm community, it grew into a suburb but retains its small-town charm. Fine old homes and stately trees line Sunset Drive, a city-designated Historic and Scenic Road to and through the town. The local chamber of commerce provides a free, basic map listing u-pick farms and smaller ecotour offerings.

A Good Tour

Drive south from Sunset Drive on Red Road, and turn right just before Killian Drive (Southwest 112th Street) into the 13-acre grounds of **Parrot Jungle** ㊲, one of Greater Miami's oldest and most popular commercial tourist attractions.

From Parrot Jungle follow Red Road ⅓ mi south and turn left on scenic Old Cutler Road, which curves north along the uplands of southern Florida's coastal ridge toward the 83-acre **Fairchild Tropical Garden** ㊳. Just north of the gardens, Old Cutler Road traverses Dade County's lovely **Matheson Hammock Park** ㊴.

TIMING

Most people should allow at least half a day to see these three natural attractions, but dedicated ornithologists and botanists will want to leave a full day. Driving from SoBe should only take 25 minutes—longer during afternoon rush hour.

Sights to See

🕐 ❸❽ **Fairchild Tropical Garden.** Comprising 83 acres, this is the largest tropical botanical garden in the continental United States. Eleven lakes, a rain forest, and lots of flowers, including orchids, mountain roses, bellflowers, coral tree, bougainvillea, and fire trees, make it a garden for the senses. Spicing up the social calendar are garden sales, theatrical performances, moonlight strolls, and symphony concerts. A combination bookstore/gift shop is a popular source for books on gardening and horticulture, ordered by botanists the world over. ✉ *10901 Old Cutler Rd.,* ☎ *305/667–1651.* ✉ *$8.* ⊙ *Daily 9:30–4:30.*

🕐 ❸❾ **Matheson Hammock Park.** In the 1930s, the Civilian Conservation Corps developed this 100-acre tract of upland and mangrove swamp on land donated by a local pioneer, Commodore J. W. Matheson. The park, Dade County's oldest and most scenic, features a bathing beach where the tide flushes a saltwater "atoll" pool through four gates. A 90-slip marina is open, with an additional 162 slips ready in mid-1997. ✉ *9610 Old Cutler Rd.,* ☎ *305/667–3035.* ✉ *Parking for beach and marina $3.50 per car, $8 per car with trailer, $6 per RV; limited free upland parking.* ⊙ *Daily 6–sunset; pool lifeguards winter, daily 8:30–5; summer, daily 7:30–7.*

🕐 ❸❼ **Parrot Jungle.** One of South Florida's original tourist attractions, Parrot Jungle opened in 1936 and is now home to more than 1,100 exotic birds. Many of the parrots, macaws, and cockatoos fly free, and they'll come to you for seeds, which you can purchase from old-fashioned gum-ball machines. Attend a trained-bird show, watch baby birds in training, and pose for the ultimate tourist photo, with colorful macaws perched on your arms. The "jungle" is a natural hammock surrounding a sinkhole. Stroll among orchids and other flowering plants nestled in ferns, bald cypress, and massive live oaks. Other highlights include a playground, petting zoo, cactus garden, primate show, small-wildlife shows, and Flamingo Lake, whose breeding population of 75 Caribbean flamingos was featured on the credits of *Miami Vice.* Plans are in the works to relocate the jungle to Watson Island by late 1998. ✉ *11000 S.W. 57th Ave.,* ☎ *305/666–7834.* ✉ *$12.95.* ⊙ *Daily 9:30–6, last admission 5; café daily 8–6.*

Coconut Grove

South Florida's oldest settlement, the Grove was inhabited as early as 1834 and established by 1873, two decades before Miami. Its early settlers included Bahamian blacks, "Conchs" from Key West, and New England intellectuals. They built a community that attracted artists, writers, and scientists to establish winter homes. By the end of World War I more people listed in *Who's Who* gave addresses in Coconut Grove than any other place in the country.

To this day Coconut Grove reflects its pioneers' eclectic origins. Posh estates mingle with rustic cottages, modest frame homes, and stark modern dwellings, often on the same block. To keep Coconut Grove a village in a jungle, residents lavish affection on exotic plantings while battling to protect remaining native vegetation.

The historic center of the Village of Coconut Grove went through a hippie period in the 1960s, laid-back funkiness in the 1970s, and a teenybopper invasion in the early 1980s. Today the tone is upscale and urban, with a mix of galleries, boutiques, restaurants, bars, and sidewalk cafés. On weekends the Grove is jam-packed. Parking can be a problem, especially on weekend evenings, when police direct traffic and prohibit turns at some intersections to prevent gridlock. Be prepared to walk several blocks from the periphery into the heart of the Grove.

A Good Tour

From downtown Miami follow U.S. 1 south to Grapeland Boulevard (Southwest 27th Avenue), turn left, and drive south to South Bayshore Drive. Turn right and follow this road until it jogs right and becomes McFarlane Road. At the next intersection turn left on Main Highway, which passes through the heart of the Village of Coconut Grove. Before you explore this trendy area, go on to Devon Road and turn right to interesting **Plymouth Congregational Church** ㊵ and its gardens.

Return to Main Highway and head northeast toward the historic Village of Coconut Grove. As you enter the village center, note the Coconut Grove Playhouse to your left and the benches and shelter opposite that mark the entrance to the **Barnacle State Historic Site** ㊶, a pioneer residence built by Commodore Ralph Munroe in 1891.

Leaving the village center, follow McFarlane Road east from its intersection with Grand Avenue and Main Highway. Peacock Park, site of the first hotel in southeast Florida, is on your right. If you turn north at the end of McFarlane Road onto South Bayshore Drive you'll pass the 150,000-square-foot Coconut Grove Convention Center, where antiques, boat, and home shows are held, and Dinner Key Marina, where seabirds soar and sailboats ride at anchor. At the northeast corner of the same lot is the Art Deco **Miami City Hall** ㊷. Continue north on South Bayshore Drive past Kirk Street to **Kennedy Park** ㊸, where you can park your car and walk toward the water.

Drive still further north on South Bayshore Drive. At the entrance to Mercy Hospital, South Bayshore Drive becomes South Miami Avenue, and at the next stoplight turn right on a private road that passes St. Kieran's Church and goes to **Ermita de La Caridad** ㊹.

Another ³⁄₁₀ mi up South Miami Avenue, turn left to reach the **Miami Museum of Science and Space Transit Planetarium** ㊺, a participatory museum with animated displays for all ages. Across South Miami Avenue is the entrance to the don't-miss **Vizcaya Museum and Gardens** ㊻, an estate with an Italian Renaissance–style villa.

Continue north on South Miami Avenue to 17th Road and turn left to get to **Simpson Park** ㊼, where you saunter through a jungle of tropical flora and fauna. You may follow South Miami Avenue the rest of the way downtown or go back two stoplights and turn left to the entrance to the Rickenbacker Causeway and Key Biscayne.

TIMING
Plan on devoting six to eight hours to enjoy Vizcaya, other bay-front sights, and the village's shops, restaurants, and nightlife.

Sights to See

㊶ **Barnacle State Historic Site.** The oldest Miami home still on its original foundation rests in the middle of 5 acres of native hardwood and landscaped lawns surrounded by flashy Coconut Grove. Built by Florida's first snowbird—New Yorker Commodore Ralph Munroe—the home features many original furnishings, a broad sloping roof, and deeply recessed verandas that channel sea breezes into the house. Reservations are essential for groups of eight or more; other visitors should meet the ranger on the porch of the main house. ✉ *3485 Main*

Hwy., ☎ *305/448–9445.* 🎫 *$1.* ☉ *Fri.–Sun. 9–4; tours 10, 11:30, 1, and 2:30, but call ahead.*

NEED A
BREAK?

Cafés at both corners overflow the brick sidewalks around Commodore Plaza. Try the **Green Street Café** (⊠ 3110 Commodore Plaza, ☎ 305/567–0662), on the south side. It features a bar, breakfast until 3, and pastas, pizzas, salads, and sandwiches.

㊹ Ermita de La Caridad (Our Lady of Charity Shrine). This conical building 90 feet high and 80 feet wide overlooks Biscayne Bay, so worshipers face Cuba. A mural above the shrine's altar depicts Cuba's history. ⊠ *3609 S. Miami Ave.,* ☎ *305/854–2404.* ☉ *Daily 9–9.*

㊷ Kennedy Park. From a footbridge over the mouth of a small tidal creek you can enjoy an unobstructed view across Biscayne Bay to Key Biscayne. Film crews often use the park to make commercials and Italian westerns. ⊠ *S. Bayshore Dr.*

㊷ Miami City Hall. Built in 1934 as the terminal for the Pan American Airways seaplane base at Dinner Key, the building retains its nautical-style Art Deco trim. ⊠ *3500 Pan American Dr.,* ☎ *305/250–5357.* ☉ *Weekdays 8–5.*

㊺ Miami Museum of Science and Space Transit Planetarium. This museum is chock-full of hands-on sound, gravity, and electricity displays for children and adults alike. A wildlife center houses native Florida snakes, turtles, tortoises, and birds of prey. Outstanding traveling exhibits appear throughout the year, and virtual reality, life-science demonstrations, and Internet technology are on hand every day. ⊠ *3280 S. Miami Ave.,* ☎ *305/854–4247; planetarium information, 305/854–2222.* 🎫 *Museum $6, planetarium $5, combination $9, laser-light rock-and-roll concert $6.* ☉ *Daily 10–6.*

㊵ Plymouth Congregational Church. Opened in 1917, this handsome coral-rock structure resembles a Mexican mission church. The front door, made of hand-carved walnut and oak with original wrought-iron fittings, came from an early 17th-century monastery in the Pyrenees. Also on the 11-acre grounds are natural sunken gardens; the first schoolhouse in Dade County (one room), which was moved to this property; and the site of the original Coconut Grove waterworks and electric works. ⊠ *3400 Devon Rd.,* ☎ *305/444–6521.* ☉ *Weekdays 9–4:30, Sun. service 10 AM.*

㊼ Simpson Park. Enjoy a fragment of the dense tropical jungle—large gumbo-limbo trees, marlberry, banyans, and black calabash—that once covered the 5 mi from downtown Miami to the Grove. You'll get a glimpse of how things were before the high-rises towered. In summer, mosquitoes are unrelenting. ⊠ *55 S.W. 17th Rd.,* ☎ *305/856–6801.* ☉ *Tues.–Fri. 8–3:30, Sat. 9–5.*

★ **㊻ Vizcaya Museum and Gardens.** Built between 1912 and 1916 by a quarter of Miami's existing labor force, this palace was the winter residence of Chicago industrialist James Deering. Once comprising 180 acres, the grounds now cover a still-substantial 30-acre tract, including a native hammock and more than 10 acres of formal gardens and fountains overlooking Biscayne Bay. The house, open to the public, contains 70 rooms, 34 of which are filled with paintings, sculpture, antique furniture, and other decorative arts dating from the 15th through the 19th centuries and representing the Renaissance, Baroque, Rococo, and Neoclassical styles. So unusual and impressive is Vizcaya, its guest list includes Ronald Reagan, Pope John Paul II, and Queen Elizabeth II.

Guided 45-minute tours are available, and group tours are given by appointment. ⊠ *3251 S. Miami Ave.,* ☎ *305/250–9133.* ⌷ *$10.* ☉ *House and ticket booth daily 9:30–4:30, garden daily 9:30–5:30.*

Virginia Key and Key Biscayne

Government Cut and the Port of Miami separate the city's dense urban fabric from two of its playground islands, Virginia Key and Key Biscayne. Parks occupy much of both keys, providing facilities for golf, tennis, softball, picnicking, and sunbathing, plus uninviting but ecologically valuable stretches of dense mangrove swamp. It was a mixed blessing when Hurricane Andrew hit in 1992. Vegetation and buildings were devastated, but replanting and restorations have made the islands greener and more beautiful.

A Good Tour
To reach Virginia Key and Key Biscayne take the Rickenbacker Causeway ($1 per car) across Biscayne Bay from the mainland at Brickell Avenue and Southwest 26th Road, about 2 mi south of downtown Miami. The causeway links several islands in the bay.

The William M. Powell Bridge rises 75 feet above the water to eliminate the need for a draw span. The panoramic view from the top encompasses the bay, keys, port, and downtown skyscrapers, with Miami Beach and the Atlantic Ocean in the distance. Just south of the Powell Bridge, a stub of the **Old Rickenbacker Causeway Bridge** ㊽, built in 1947, is now a fishing pier with a nice view.

Down the causeway, on Virginia Key, look for the gold dome of the **Miami Seaquarium** ㊾, one of the country's first marine attractions. Opposite the causeway from the Seaquarium, a road leads north to Virginia Key Beach and the adjacent **Virginia Key Critical Wildlife Area** ㊿.

From Virginia Key, the causeway crosses Bear Cut to the north end of Key Biscayne and becomes Crandon Boulevard. The boulevard bisects 1,211-acre **Crandon Park** ⑤, which has a popular Atlantic Ocean beach and nature center. On your right are entrances to the Links at Key Biscayne and the Tennis Center at Crandon Park.

From the traffic circle at the south end of Crandon Park, Crandon Boulevard continues for 2 mi through the developed portion of Key Biscayne. You'll come back that way, but first turn right on Harbor Drive at the first stoplight, go about a mile, and turn right at Matheson Drive to the site of **President Nixon's home** ⑤.

Continue south on Harbor Drive to Mashta Drive; turn left and return to Crandon Boulevard. Then turn right to reach the **Bill Baggs Cape Florida State Recreation Area** ⑤, a 406-acre park containing, among other things, the brick Cape Florida Lighthouse.

Follow Crandon Boulevard back to Crandon Park through Key Biscayne's downtown village, where shops and a 10-acre village green cater mainly to local residents. On your way back to the mainland, pause as you approach the Powell Bridge to admire the Miami skyline. At night the brightly lighted NationsBank Tower looks like a clipper ship running under full sail before the breeze.

TIMING
Set aside the better part of a day for this tour, saving a few late-afternoon hours for Crandon Park and the Cape Florida Lighthouse. Bird-watching at the Virginia Key Critical Wildlife Area can only be done in its three-month season.

Sights to See

53 **Bill Baggs Cape Florida State Recreation Area.** Devastated by Hurricane Andrew, this park at Key Biscayne's southern tip has returned better than ever with new boardwalks, 18 picnic shelters, and a café that serves light lunches. A stroll along the paths and boardwalks provides wonderful views of Miami's dramatic skyline. Also on site are bicycle and skate rentals, a playground, fishing piers, kayak rentals, and, on request, guided tours of the cultural complex and the **Cape Florida Lighthouse,** South Florida's oldest structure. The lighthouse was erected in 1845 to replace an earlier one destroyed in an 1836 Seminole attack, in which the keeper's helper was killed. Climb up 95 feet to visit a replica of the keeper's house. ⊠ *1200 S. Crandon Blvd.,* ☎ *305/361–5811.* ⌦ *$3.25 per vehicle with up to 8 people; $1 per person on bicycle, bus, motorcycle, or foot.* ☉ *Daily 8–sunset.*

51 **Crandon Park.** At the north end of the nice family beach is the **Marjory Stoneman Douglas Biscayne Nature Center.** Explore a variety of natural habitats by taking a tour. ⊠ *4000 Crandon Blvd.,* ☎ *305/361–5421 or 305/642–9600.* ⌦ *Park $3.50 per vehicle, nature center free.* ☉ *Park daily 8–sunset, nature center hours vary.*

NEED A BREAK?   Enjoy that rarity among Miami-area restaurants, a freestanding waterfront dining room, at **Sundays on the Bay** (⊠ 5420 Crandon Blvd., ☎ 305/361–6777). A 60-item brunch is served Sunday 10:30–3:30, and lunch and dinner are served daily.

★ ☁ **49** **Miami Seaquarium.** This popular attraction has six daily shows featuring sea lions, dolphins, and Lolita, a killer whale. (Lolita's tank is small for seaquariums—just three times her length—and some wildlife advocates are trying to get her back to sea.) Exhibits include a shark pool, a 235,000-gallon tropical-reef aquarium, and manatees. Glass-bottom boats take tours of Biscayne Bay. ⊠ *4400 Rickenbacker Causeway,* ☎ *305/361–5705.* ⌦ *$19.95.* ☉ *Daily 9:30–6, last admission 4:30.*

48 **Old Rickenbacker Causeway Bridge.** Here you can watch boat traffic pass through the channel, pelicans and other seabirds soar and dive, and dolphins cavort in the bay. Park at its entrance, about a mile from the tollgate, and walk past anglers tending their lines to the gap where the center draw span across the Intracoastal Waterway was removed. ⊠ *South of Powell Bridge.*

52 **President Nixon's home.** Just as the laid-back village of Key Biscayne has changed since Richard Nixon set up his presidential vacation compound here, so too has a recent owner enlarged and completely changed the house. Nixon was so enamored of his home, he had the Republican National Convention moved from San Diego to Miami in 1972. ⊠ *485 W. Matheson Dr.*

☁ **50** **Virginia Key Critical Wildlife Area.** Plans are in the works to safeguard this 400-acre portion of mangrove-edged island. Residents include reddish egrets, black-bellied plovers, black skimmers, and roseate spoonbills—but you can only see them in May, June, and July. The area is left undisturbed during the other nine months, to make it attractive to migratory shorebirds. Enter at Virginia Key Beach.

Little Haiti

Of some 100,000 Haitians who have settled in South Florida, almost half live in Little Haiti, covering about 200 blocks on Miami's northeast side. More than 400 small Haitian businesses operate here, yet the district's future is uncertain: Immigration from Haiti has virtually ceased, and many Haitians already in Miami question their economic future in this urban enclave. As their fortunes improve, many move out. Still the neighborhood is one of the city's most distinctive.

Once known as Lemon City—a neighborhood of working-class whites—Little Haiti still has many single-family homes from the '20s and '30s, now owned by Haitian families. If you walk or drive along its side streets, you might see Haitian women carrying their burdens atop their heads, as they do on their home island.

For many Haitians, English is a third language, after French and Creole, a French-based patois.

A Good Tour

From downtown Miami, follow Biscayne Boulevard north to Northeast 38th Street; turn left, and drive about ⁹⁄₁₀ mi west, as the street curves and becomes 39th Street. At North Miami Avenue, turn right, and at 40th Street, turn right again onto the main street of the **Miami International Arts and Design District** (54).

Immediately north is the gentrified neighborhood of **Buena Vista** (55), which merges with Little Haiti. A half block east of North Miami Avenue on 54th Street is the tiny storefront office of the **Haitian Refugee Center** (56). Continue north on North Miami Avenue past the former Cuban consulate, an ostentatious Caribbean-Colonial mansion.

North of 85th Street, cross the Little River Canal into El Portal, a tiny suburban village of modest homes, where more than a quarter of the property is now Haitian-owned. Turn right on Northeast 87th Street and right again on Northeast 2nd Avenue. You are now southbound on Little Haiti's tree-lined main commercial street. Between 79th and 45th streets, rows of storefronts in faded pastels reflect a first effort by area merchants to dress up their neighborhood and attract outsiders. The lovely **Caribbean Marketplace** (57) shows the strains of uncertainty in this immigrant community.

TIMING

This tour provides a look at an immigrant community currently in flux. An incredibly depressed section of Miami, it is not very safe at night. Tour during daylight hours.

Sights to See

(55) **Buena Vista.** The area contains some of Miami's oldest dwellings, dating from the dawn of the 20th century through the 1920s land-boom era. Drive the side streets to see elegant Mediterranean-style homes and bungalows with distinctive oolitic limestone trim.

(57) **Caribbean Marketplace.** This building, opened in 1990 by the Haitian Task Force (an economic-development organization), beautifully evokes the Iron Market in Port-au-Prince. Its handful of merchants surrounding a medical clinic sells handmade baskets, Caribbean art and craft items, books, records, and videos. Also unusual is the ice cream, which is made with such tropical fruits as mango, papaya, and coconut. ✉ *5927 N.E. 2nd Ave.*

(56) **Haitian Refugee Center.** A focal point of activity in the Haitian community, the building is decorated with a painting of an uncomprehending Haitian standing in front of the Statue of Liberty, which denies him entry to America. ✉ *119 N.E. 54th St.*

(54) **Miami International Arts and Design District.** Here, near Little Haiti, some 225 wholesale stores, showrooms, and galleries feature interior furnishings, decorative arts, and a rich mix of exclusive and unusual

merchandise. Since 1993 the district has undergone a revival, and there are several new art studios and showrooms. ⊠ *Between N.E. 38th and N.E. 42nd Sts. and between Federal Hwy. and N. Miami Ave.*

BEACHES

Key Biscayne

The beach at **Bill Baggs Cape Florida State Recreation Area** (☞ Virginia Key and Key Biscayne, *above*) is as far south as you can get on the island.

The 3½-mi county beach at **Crandon Park,** popular with families, is rated among the top 10 beaches in North America by many. The sand is soft, and parking is both inexpensive and plentiful. At the north end is an interesting nature center. ⊠ *4000 Crandon Blvd.,* ☎ *305/361–5421 or 305/642–9600.* ▨ *$3.50 per vehicle.* ☉ *Daily 8–sunset.*

Virginia Key Beach, a City of Miami park with a 2-mi stretch of oceanfront, offers shelters, barbecue grills, ball fields, nature trails, and a fishing area. Budget cuts forced an indefinite closing in early 1997. ⊠ *Rickenbacker Causeway,* ☎ *305/361–2749.* ▨ *Parking $2.* ☉ *Daily 9–sunset.*

Miami Beach Area

From **1st to 15th streets,** seniors predominate early in the day. The section from 5th to 15th, known as Lummus Park, lies in the heart of the Deco District. Volleyball, in-line skating along the paved upland path, and a lot of posing go on here, while playgrounds make it popular with families. Along these beaches, officials don't enforce the law against female bathers going topless, so long as everyone behaves with decorum. Gays like the beach between 11th and 13th streets. Sidewalk cafés parallel the entire area, making it easy to come ashore for everything from burgers to quiche. At **23rd Street,** the boardwalk begins, and no skates or bicycles are allowed.

Parlez-vous Français? If you do, you'll feel quite comfortable on the **72nd Street Beach** and from **Surfside to 96th Street.** This stretch of beach is the French Canadian enclave. Many folks here have spent their winters in Miami Beach for years.

Families and those who like things quiet prefer **North Beach** along Ocean Terrace between 73rd and 75th streets. Metered parking is ample right behind the dune and a block behind Collins Avenue along a pleasant, old shopping street. With high prices discouraging developers from SoBe, this area will no doubt see some redevelopment in years to come. However, without the cafés or 300-foot-wide beach to lure tourists, it may never match SoBe's appeal.

At 40 acres, **Oleta River State Recreation Area** is the largest urban park in Florida. It's backed by lush tropical growth rather than hotels. Offered at the park are interpretive talks, group and youth camping, 16 log cabins, kayak and canoe rentals, bicycle trails, and a fishing pier. Popular with outdoor enthusiasts, it also attracts dolphins, osprey, and manatees who arrive for the winter. ⊠ *Collins Ave. between 79th and 87th Sts., Miami Beach; office, Oleta/North Shore GEOpark, 3400 N.E. 163rd St., North Miami Beach,* ☎ *305/919–1846.* ▨ *$3.25 per vehicle with up to 8 people, $1 for pedestrians.* ☉ *Daily 8–6.*

During the winter, wealthy condominium owners cluster from **96th to 103rd streets,** a stretch of prime real estate in tony Bal Harbour. Look close and you may spy Bob Dole sunning himself outside his condo.

If you want the water closer to the upland, try **Haulover Beach Park–Sunny Isles.** Eroded sand was never replaced here, and the strand is mercifully narrow, a plus for older visitors who don't like long marches across hot sand. ⊠ *10800 Collins Ave., Miami,* ☏ *305/947–3525.* ☞ *$3.50 per vehicle.* ☺ *Daily sunrise–sunset.*

DINING

American

Coconut Grove

$ ✕ **Planet Hollywood.** Miami has become a second home for members of Hollywood's A-list, which may explain why Willis, Moore, Stallone, and Schwarzenegger chose it for one of their themed eateries. Not surprisingly, the decor is as if a movie studio warehouse exploded inside the restaurant. The copious memorabilia includes a frozen Stallone packed in ice, from *Demolition Man.* Although you're more likely to see fellow tourists than real celebs, you should walk away satisfied with the service and attention lavished upon you and your food. The fare may seem standard (pizza, pasta, burgers, salads), but the creative preparation places it a few notches above other chains. ⊠ *3390 Mary St.,* ☏ *305/445–7277. AE, D, DC, MC, V.*

Coral Gables

$$$ ✕ **Norman's.** This elegantly casual restaurant, which has won as many awards as it has customers, turns out gourmet cuisine with an edge. Chef Norman Van Aken has created a buzz by perfecting the art of New World cuisine—a combination rooted in Latin, American, Caribbean, and Asian influences. Bold tastes are delivered in every dish, whether it's a simple black-and-white bean soup with sour cream, chorizo, and tortillas or a rum-and-pepper painted grouper on a mango-*habanero mojo* sauce. From the comfortable decor to the staff that never seems harried, even when all seats are filled (usually every minute between opening and closing), Norman's has captured the essence of Miami dining. ⊠ *21 Almeria Ave.,* ☏ *305/446–6767,* ℻ *305/446–7909. AE, DC, MC, V. Closed Sun. No lunch Sat.*

$$ ✕ **Restaurant St. Michel.** The setting is utterly French, the little hotel
★ it's in (☞ Lodging, *below*) is Mediterranean, the town is very Spanish, but the cuisine is American. Stuart Bornstein's window on Coral Gables is a lace-curtained café with sidewalk tables that could be across from a railroad station in Avignon or Bordeaux. A sculpted bust here, a circus poster there, deco chandeliers, and a mirrored, palm frond–shape mosaic all create a whimsical, foreign feel. Lighter dishes include moist couscous chicken and pasta primavera. Among the heartier entrées are a plum, soy, and lemon-glazed fillet of salmon; sesame-coated loin of tuna; and local yellowtail snapper. ⊠ *162 Alcazar Ave.,* ☏ *305/444–1666. AE, DC, MC, V.*

Downtown Miami

$$$$ ✕ **Le Pavillon.** The mahogany, jade marble, and leather appointments
★ of the dining room evoke the conservative air of an English private club. Beautiful floral displays enhance the mood as the attentive staff serves regional American fare from a limited but frequently changing menu, including items low in calories, cholesterol, and sodium. Specialties are char-grilled bluefin tuna fillet, poached yellowtail snapper, panfried corn-fed squab, roasted free-range chicken, spring lamb, and roasted fillet

Miami Area Dining

59

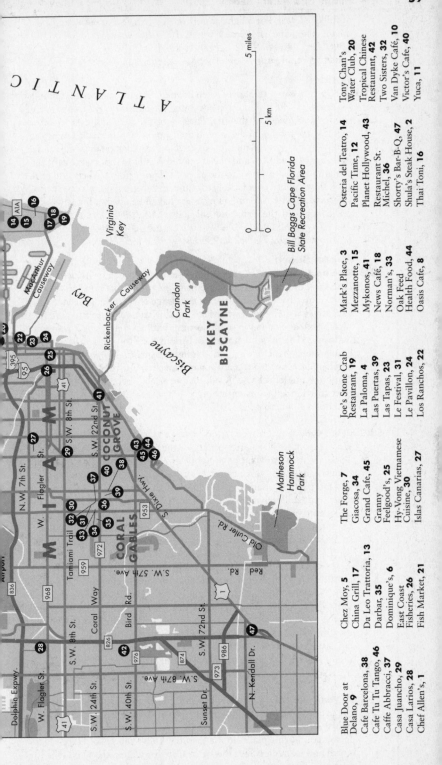

Blue Door at Delano, 9
Cafe Barcelona, 38
Cafe Tu Tu Tango, 46
Caffe Abbracci, 37
Casa Juancho, 29
Casa Larios, 28
Chef Allen's, 1

Chez Moy, 5
China Grill, 17
Da Leo Trattoria, 13
Darbar, 35
Dominique's, 6
East Coast Fisheries, 26
Fish Market, 21

The Forge, 7
Giacosa, 34
Grand Cafe, 45
Granny Feelgood's, 25
Hy-Vong Vietnamese Cuisine, 30
Islas Canarias, 27

Joe's Stone Crab Restaurant, 19
La Paloma, 4
Las Puertas, 39
Las Tapas, 23
Le Festival, 31
Le Pavillon, 24
Los Ranchos, 22

Mark's Place, 3
Mezzanotte, 15
Mykonos, 41
News Café, 18
Norman's, 33
Oak Feed Health Food, 44
Oasis Cafe, 8

Osteria del Teatro, 14
Pacific Time, 12
Planet Hollywood, 43
Restaurant St. Michel, 36
Shorty's Bar-B-Q, 47
Shula's Steak House, 2
Thai Toni, 16

Tony Chan's Water Club, 20
Tropical Chinese Restaurant, 42
Two Sisters, 32
Van Dyke Café, 10
Victor's Cafe, 40
Yuca, 11

of milk-fed veal. For a light dessert try red berry soup with vanilla ice cream. The wine list is extensive. ⊠ *100 Chopin Plaza*, ☎ *305/577–1000, Ext. 4494 or 4462. Jacket required. AE, DC, MC, V. No lunch (except Sun. brunch, noon–3) or Sun. dinner.*

Kendall

$ ✕ **Shorty's Bar-B-Q.** Shorty Allen opened his barbecue restaurant in a log cabin in 1951, and the place has since become a tradition in this suburb southwest of the city. Parents bring their children to show them where mom and dad ate on their honeymoon. Meals are served family-style at long picnic tables. Cowboy hats hang on the walls, along with horns, saddles, and the mounted heads of boar and caribou. Longtime fans are drawn to the barbecued pork ribs, chicken, and pork steak slow-cooked over hickory logs and drenched in Shorty's own warm, spicy sauce, with side orders of tangy baked beans and big chunks of pork, corn on the cob, and coleslaw. ⊠ *9200 S. Dixie Hwy.,* ☎ *305/670–7732;* ⊠ *11575 S.W. 40th St.,* ☎ *305/227–3196;* ⊠ *5989 S. University Dr., Davie,* ☎ *954/680–9900. MC, V.*

Miami Beach

$$$$ **Blue Door at Delano.** A gauzy movie set with a touch of *Alice in Wonderland* (note the giant chess pieces in the pool), this hotel restaurant has the best backyard terrace on the beach to see and be seen. Sadly, executive chef George Fistrovich's food is secondary to the aura; it's high priced and comes in small portions with uneven results. Many appetizers ($14) take advantage of Atlantic seafood, as do the main courses, which include a good balsamic-basted mahimahi with fennel, basil, and oven-dried tomato fumet as well as rack of lamb with olive couscous and feta cheese. A side dish of grilled vegetables is plain-Jane next to whipped yams with honey and spice. Madonna is co-owner. ⊠ *1685 Collins Ave.,* ☎ *305/674–6400. Reservations essential. AE, D, DC, MC, V.*

$$$$ **China Grill.** This crowded, noisy place has no view, but that doesn't detract from its popularity or that of the original China Grill in New York. Contrary to what you might think, Chef Ephraim Kadish turns out not Chinese food but rather "world cuisine," and portions are large and intended for sharing. Crispy duck with caramelized black vinegar sauce and scallion pancakes is a nice surprise, as is pork and beans with green apple and balsamic mojo. Don't miss the broccoli rabe dumpling starter, the wild mushroom pasta entrée, or the flash-fried crispy spinach that shatters when eaten. ⊠ *404 Washington Ave.,* ☎ *305/534–2211. AE, DC, MC, V. No Sat. lunch.*

$ ✕ **News Café.** This is the hippest joint on Ocean Drive. Owners Marc Soyka, who trained on the cosmopolitan beach scene in Tel Aviv, and New Yorker Jeffrey Davis are right on the money. Although there's a bar with 15 stools in back, most visitors prefer sitting outside, where they can feel the salt breeze and gawk at the beautiful people walking by. Offering a little of this and a little of that—bagels, pâtés, chocolate fondue—the café attracts a big crowd all the time, with people coming in around the clock for a snack, a light meal, or an aperitif and, invariably, to indulge in the people parade. ⊠ *800 Ocean Dr.,* ☎ *305/538–6397. AE, DC, MC, V.*

$ ✕ **Van Dyke Café.** Marc Soyka's second restaurant quickly attracted the artsy crowd, just as his News Café draws the fashion crowd. Of course, tourists like it, too. It has the same style menu, but instead of facing south, this place, in the restored 1924 Van Dyke Hotel, faces north and is shadier. Save the News Café for winter, the Van Dyke for summer. Three meals are served, and a 15% gratuity is included. ⊠ *846 Lincoln Rd.,* ☎ *305/534–3600. AE, DC, MC, V.*

North Miami

$$$ ✕ **Mark's Place.** Behind the adobe facade lies a stylish, Deco-detailed
★ dining room, while in the kitchen, owner-chef Mark Militello cooks
contemporary Florida fare in a special oak-burning oven imported from
Genoa. The menu changes nightly, based on the availability of fresh
ingredients (including many organic vegetables). Typical entrées are piz-
zas and pastas (saffron fettucine with Maine lobster, black beans, roast
corn, chilies, tomato, and cilantro, for instance) and, among the spe-
cialties, grilled marinated breast of duck with acorn-squash flan, wilted
greens, and dried-fruit sauce. For dessert there may be warm choco-
late decadence with chocolate sorbet and blackberry *coulis*. Mark also
has a place in Fort Lauderdale, called Mark's Las Olas, and one in Co-
conut Grove, Mark's in the Grove. ⊠ *2286 N.E. 123rd St.,* ☎ *305/893–
6888. AE, DC, MC, V. No lunch.*

North Miami Beach

$$$ ✕ **Chef Allen's.** In this Art Deco world of glass block, neon trim, fresh
★ flowers, and art from the Gallery at Turnberry, your gaze nonetheless
remains riveted on the kitchen. Chef Allen Susser designed it with a
picture window 25 feet wide, so you can watch him create contemporary American masterpieces from a menu that changes nightly. After
a salad of baby greens and warm wild mushrooms or rock-shrimp hash
with roast corn, consider *orecchiette* pasta with sun-dried tomato,
goat cheese, spinach, and toasted pine nuts; swordfish with conch-cit-
rus couscous, macadamia nuts, and lemon; or grilled lamb chops with
eggplant timbale and a three-nut salsa. A favorite dessert is the dou-
ble-chocolate soufflé with lots of nuts. ⊠ *19088 N.E. 29th Ave.,* ☎
305/935–2900. AE, DC, MC, V. Lunch Fri. only.

West Dade

$$–$$$ ✕ **Shula's Steak House.** Steaks, prime rib, and fish (including dolphin)
are almost an afterthought to the icons in this shrine for the NFL-ob-
sessed. Dine in a woody setting with a fireplace, surrounded by memorabilia of retired coach Don Shula's perfect 1972 season with the Miami
Dolphins, including game footballs, assistant coach Howard Schnel-
lenberger's pipe, and a playbook autographed by President Nixon. Also
for Shula fans, there's shula's steak 2, (lowercase borrowed from
espn2), a sports celebrity hangout in Don Shula's Hotel. ⊠ *7601 N.W.
154th St., Miami Lakes,* ☎ *305/820–8102. AE, DC, MC, V.*

Chinese

Downtown Miami

$$ ✕ **Tony Chan's Water Club.** One of a pair of outstanding Chinese
★ restaurants on the mainland, this beautiful dining room just off the lobby
of the high-rise Grand Prix Hotel looks onto a bay-side marina. Filled
with art and chrome, the long room is modern rather than stock Chi-
nese. On the menu of more than 100 appetizers and entrées is minced
quail tossed with bamboo shoots and mushrooms wrapped in lettuce
leaves. Indulge in a seafood spectacular with shrimp, conch, scallops,
fish cake, and crabmeat tossed with broccoli in a bird's nest or pork
chops sprinkled with green pepper in a black bean–garlic sauce. ⊠ *1717
N. Bayshore Dr.,* ☎ *305/374–8888. AE, MC, V.*

South Dade

$–$$ ✕ **Tropical Chinese Restaurant.** The big, lacquer-free room feels as
★ open and busy as a railway station. You'll find unfamiliar items on the
menu—for example, the early spring leaves of snow pea pods sublimely
tender and flavorful. The extensive menu is filled with tofu combinations, poultry, beef, and pork, as well as tender seafood. A dim sum

lunch is served on great carts. In the big open kitchen, 10 chefs prepare everything as if for dignitaries. ⊠ *7991 S.W. 40th St.,* ☎ *305/262–7576 or 305/272–1552. AE, MC, V.*

Continental

Coconut Grove

$$$ ✕ **Grand Cafe.** Understated elegance is the hallmark of this bi-level room
★   with fanlight windows, brass details, pink tablecloths, and floral bouquets. French chef Pascal Oudin's starter specialties include pan-seared Florida crab cake and cherry wood–smoked Chilean salmon. Among entrées, favorites are the baked macadamia-and-ginger-crusted salmon and crusted black-bean seared rare yellowfin tuna. For dessert try the dark-chocolate and praline *crousilliant* (crispy chocolate topped with chocolate mousse and coated with chocolate shavings and sauce). ⊠ *2669 S. Bayshore Dr.,* ☎ *305/858–9600. AE, DC, MC, V.*

$$ ✕ **Cafe Tu Tu Tango.** Local artists set up their easels in the rococo-modern arcades of this eclectic café-lounge on the second story of Coconut Grove's highly popular CocoWalk. You'll be blown away, whether you sit indoors or out. Outside offers some of the best people-watching in the South. Inside, guests graze on chips, dips, breads, and spreads. House specials include frittatas, crab cakes, *picadillo empanadas* (spicy ground beef served with cilantro sour cream), and chicken and shrimp orzo paella, all to be enjoyed with some of the best sangria in the city. ⊠ *3015 Grand Ave. (CocoWalk),* ☎ *305/529–2222. AE, MC, V.*

Miami Beach

$$$ ✕ **The Forge.** Often compared to a museum, this landmark stands behind a facade of 19th-century Parisian mansions, where a forge once stood. Each intimate dining salon has its own historical artifacts, including a chandelier that hung in James Madison's White House. The wine cellar contains 380,000 bottles—including more than 500 dating from 1822 (and costing as much as $35,000) and recorked in 1989 by experts from Domaines Barons de Rothschild. Specialties include Norwegian salmon served over fresh garden vegetables with spinach vinaigrette and free-range Wisconsin duck roasted with black currants. For dessert try the blacksmith pie. This place is a hot party spot on Wednesday nights, and a new private cigar club, the Cuba Club, is very popular with the rich and famous. ⊠ *432 Arthur Godfrey Rd.,* ☎ *305/538–8533. AE, DC, MC, V. No lunch.*

North Miami

$$$ ✕ **La Paloma.** This Swiss Continental restaurant offers a total sensory experience: fine food, impeccable service, and the ambience of an art museum. Since 1977, owners Werner and Maria Staub have displayed the ornate European antiques they've been collecting for decades: Baccarat crystal, Limoges china, Meissen porcelain, and Sèvres clocks. The staff speaks Spanish, French, German, Portuguese, and Arabic. Specialties include fresh local fish and shellfish; Wiener schnitzel; lamb chops coated with bread crumbs, mustard, garlic, and herbs; veal chop with morel sauce; and, for dessert, lemon sherbet with fresh kiwi fruit and vodka. ⊠ *10999 Biscayne Blvd.,* ☎ *305/891–0505. AE, MC, V. No lunch weekends.*

Cuban

Little Havana

$$–$$$ ✕ **Victor's Cafe.** This popular restaurant was inspired by the *casona,* the great house of colonial Cuba. The mood is old Havana, with Cuban art and antiques and a glass-covered fountain courtyard. Owner Victor del Corral, who emigrated from Cuba in 1957, first made his

mark in Manhattan. Now he works with his daughter Sonia Zaldivar and her son Luis. Come on Friday afternoon, when the tapas bar is packed and lunch often lasts to dusk, in Cuban fashion. Entrées come with rice and black beans. Hot appetizers, such as a puff pastry filled with aromatically herbed lump crabmeat or a savory cassava turnover filled with Florida lobster, are enough for a meal. Truly jumbo shrimp are served with yam quenelles in a creamy champagne sauce sprinkled with salmon roe. Romantic music plays nightly. ⌧ *2340 S.W. 32nd Ave.,* ☎ *305/445–1313. AE, MC, V.*

$ ✕ **Islas Canarias.** Since 1976 this has been a gathering place for Cuban poets, pop-music stars, and media personalities. Murals depict a Canary Islands street scene (owner Santiago Garcia's grandfather came from Tenerife). The menu, which includes breakfast, carries such Canary Islands dishes as baked lamb, ham hocks with boiled potatoes, and tortilla *Española* (Spanish omelet with onions and chorizo), as well as Cuban standards like *palomilla* steak and fried kingfish. Don't miss the three superb varieties of homemade chips—potato, malanga, and plantain. ⌧ *285 N.W. 27th Ave.,* ☎ *305/649–0440. D, MC, V.* ⌧ *Coral Way and S.W. 137th Ave., Westchester,* ☎ *305/559–6666. AE, D, MC, V.*

Miami Beach

$$$ ✕ **Yuca.** Top-flight Cuban dining can be had at this bistro-chic restau-
★ rant on renovated Lincoln Road. The name stands for the potatolike staple of Cuban kitchens and is also used to refer to young urban Cuban-Americans. High standards are first evident in the setting and carry over to the food: traditional corn tamale filled with conch and a spicy jalapeño and Creole cheese pesto, the namesake yuca stuffed with *mamacita's* picadillo and dressed in wild mushrooms on a bed of sautéed spinach, and plantain-coated dolphin with a tamarind tartar sauce. Featured desserts include classic Cuban rice pudding in an almond basket and coconut pudding in its coconut. ⌧ *501 Lincoln Rd.,* ☎ *305/532–9822. AE, DC, MC, V.*

West Dade

$ ✕ **Casa Larios.** Yes, South Florida has 1,000 Cuban restaurants, but this one stands out for its consistently excellent food. Chicken soup is golden-yellow, pearly, salty—the perfect elixir. Look for specials like roast pork loin, roasted lamb, *caldo gallego* (white-bean soup with ham and greens), and the Argentine-inspired *churrasco,* a boneless strip steak with *chimichurri* (a cooling sauce of parsley, garlic, onion, and oil). The restaurant is a favorite of the Estefans, who took the concept and helped open Larios on the Beach, on Ocean Drive. ⌧ *7929 N.W. 2nd St.,* ☎ *305/266–5494. AE, MC, V.*

French

Coral Gables

$$$ ✕ **Le Festival.** The canopied entrance to this classical French restau-
rant belies the elegance within, where decor celebrates Parisian *moderne* with etched-glass filigree, posh burgundy, mahogany, and rose-tinted details. A second room, for smokers, is more gilded. Main courses include fillet of grouper in bouillabaisse sauce; stuffed quail with grape and red-wine sauce; milk-fed veal sautéed with mushrooms, grapes, and brandy cream sauce; and chateaubriand for two. Desserts comprise various pastries, mousses, and soufflées. The wine list includes 100 selections, many priced less than $30. ⌧ *2120 Salzedo St.,* ☎ *305/442–8545. Reservations essential for dinner and for lunch parties of 5 or more. AE, D, DC, MC, V. Closed Sun. No lunch Sat.*

Miami Beach

$$ ✕ **Dominique's.** Woodwork and mirrors create an intimate setting for contemporary cuisine at this restaurant in the Alexander Hotel. Dine in either of two enclosed patios, both walled in glass to provide ocean views. The wine list is extensive. Sunday brunch is also served. ⊠ *5225 Collins Ave.,* ☎ *305/865–6500. AE, DC, MC, V.*

Greek

Five Points, Miami

$ ✕ **Mykonos.** This Miami fixture since 1973 brightens the intersection at Five Points in the Roads section of town with a beautiful mural of the Aegean. Inside a sparkling blue-and-white setting is dressed up with Greek travel posters. Specialties include gyro, moussaka, marinated lamb and chicken, calamari and octopus sautéed in wine and onions, and sumptuous Greek salads thick with feta cheese and briny olives. Vegetarian moussaka, eggplant roll, lasagna, and a Greek-style omelet are also on the menu. ⊠ *1201 Coral Way,* ☎ *305/856–3140. AE, DC, MC, V. No lunch Sun.*

Haitian

Little Haiti

$ ✕ **Chez Moy.** At this neighborhood fixture, the music is Haitian, the TV in the corner plays Haitian programs, everyone speaks Creole, and the food is as authentic as on the rue Delmas in Port-au-Prince. You can sit outside on a shaded patio or in a pleasant room with oak tables and high-back chairs. Specialties include *grillot* (pork boiled then fried with spices), fried or boiled fish, stewed goat, and conch with garlic and hot pepper. Try a tropical fruit drink such as sweet sop (also called *anon* or *cachiman*) or sour sop (also called *guanabana* or *corrosol*), blended with milk and sugar, and sweet-potato pie for dessert. ⊠ *1 N.W. 54th St.,* ☎ *305/757–5056. No credit cards.*

Indian

Coral Gables

$$ ✕ **Darbar.** Owner Bobby Nangia's impeccably arranged Darbar (Indian for "Royal Court") is the glory of Miami's Indian restaurants. ★ It's authentic, right down to the portraits of turbaned maharajas. Flavors rise as if in a dance from the *bangan bharta* (eggplant mashed with onions, tomatoes, herbs, and spices and baked in a tandoor). The menu's focus is on northern Indian or frontier cuisine—various kebabs, tandoori platters, and *tikkas* (chicken or lamb marinated in yogurt and spices and cooked tandoori style)—although there are also curries from different regions and *biryani* specialties prepared with basmati rice and garnished with boiled egg, tomato, nuts, and raisins. Everything, including the unusual Indian breads, is cooked to order. ⊠ *276 Alhambra Circle,* ☎ *305/448–9691. AE, DC, MC, V. No lunch Sun.*

Italian

Coral Gables

$$–$$$ ✕ **Caffe Abbracci.** Although the kitchen closes at midnight, the last wave ★ of customers—usually Brazilians—is still partying to flamenco or salsa music on weekends at 2. The setting is graciously deco, with huge bursts of flowers, frosted glass, and fresh roses on white linens; lights above each table are on individual dimmers. After the cold and hot antipasto—various carpaccios, porcini mushrooms, calamari, grilled goat cheese, shrimps, mussels—come festive entrées. Most of the pasta is

made fresh, so consider sampling two or three, maybe with pesto sauce, Gorgonzola, and fresh tomatoes. Room for dessert? Napoleons and tiramisù are made here daily, and there's always a choice of fresh fruit tarts. ⊠ *318 Aragon Ave.,* ☎ *305/441–0700,* FAX *305/442–0061. Reservations essential. AE, DC, MC, V. No lunch weekends.*

$$–$$$ ✕ **Giacosa.** Named for one of Puccini's librettists, this is another of
★ the superbly evocative—and just plain superb—restaurants in Coral Gables. The ambience is wonderfully informed—a thickly carpeted room like a smart Venetian salon, fresh flowers, chair cushions inspired by tapestry. From putting your napkin in your lap to whisking a tower of airy pita bread with olive oil in a carafe to the table, the smooth staff is the standard of competence. Parmesan is freshly grated to the plate. A salad *tricolore* imparts the bitter kiss of arugula; pastas, veals, and fresh seafood are all prepared for peak taste. ⊠ *394 Giralda Ave.,* ☎ *305/445–5858. AE, DC, MC, V. No lunch weekends.*

Miami Beach

$$$ ✕ **Osteria del Teatro.** Thanks to word of mouth, this Northern Ital-
★ ian restaurant is constantly full. Orchids grace the tables in the intimate, gray, gray, and gray room with a low, laced canvas ceiling, deco lamps, and the most refined clink and clatter along Washington Avenue's remarkable restaurant row. You'll start with large, unevenly sliced hunks of homemade bread lightly toasted. Then try an appetizer of grilled portobello mushrooms topped with fontina cheese and served over a bed of arugula with a green peppercorn–brandy sauce, and for the main course, linguine sautéed with chunks of jumbo shrimp, roasted peppers, capers, black olives, fresh diced tomato, and herbs in a tangy garlic–olive oil sauce. ⊠ *1443 Washington Ave.,* ☎ *305/538–7850. AE, DC, MC, V. Closed Tues. No lunch.*

$$ ✕ **Mezzanotte.** Sometime between 6 and 10 PM, the big square room with the square bar transforms from an empty catering hall to a New Year's Eve party. Trendoids call for their capellini with fresh tomato and basil; calamari in clam juice, garlic, and red wine; or scaloppine with mushroom, pepper, and white wine and then top it off with their dolci: fresh napoleon, chocolate mousse, or tiramisù. Chic and intimate, Mezzanotte is known for fine food at moderate prices, but watch out for the coffee at $2.25 a pop! ⊠ *1200 Washington Ave.,* ☎ *305/673– 4343;* ⊠ *3390 Mary St., Coconut Grove,* ☎ *305/448–7677. AE, D, DC, MC, V. No lunch in Miami Beach.*

$–$$ ✕ **Da Leo Trattoria.** Tables from this little restaurant spill across the Lincoln Road Mall, staying full thanks to consistently good food at prices less than half of what trendier places charge. The volume keeps the mood festive and the standards high. You'll be amazed by the art, which covers the walls so completely you might think the canvasses provide structural support. The look is ancient Roman town house (though owner Leonardo Marchini hails from Lucca), with banquettes along one wall and wainscoting along the other. Pastas, fish, veal, and fowl make up most of the entrées. Simpler appetites are satisfied at Da Leo Pizza é Via, directly across the mall. ⊠ *819 Lincoln Rd. Mall,* ☎ *305/674–0350. AE, DC, MC, V. No lunch weekends.*

Mexican

Coral Gables

$$ ✕ **Las Puertas.** Like the rest of Giralda Avenue's restaurant row, this storefront dining room filled with native arts and crafts seems touched by magic. Handsome arches and white tablecloths redeem south-of-the-border cuisine from the limits of quick lunch food. The tastes of several Mexican states are represented. Chicken in green *pipian* sauce (breast grilled and poached in a sauce of ground sesame, pumpkin seeds,

tomatillos, cilantro, and dark green poblanos chiles) hails from Puebla. Yucatán suckling pig comes baked inside banana leaves, and the red snapper from Veracruz is sautéed with capers, tomatoes, and green olives. Of several desserts you've never seen on franchised Mexican menu boards, the best, when available, is the cheesecake of fresh peaches and cream. ⊠ *148 Giralda Ave.,* ☎ *305/442–0708. AE, D, DC, MC, V.*

Natural

Coconut Grove

$ ✗ **Oak Feed Health Food.** If Oak Feed hadn't existed since 1970, someone would build it. The bohemian atmosphere of Coconut Grove is a perfect backdrop for this natural foods grocery store and lunch counter. In addition to a deli and bakery, Oak Feed offers other healthy standards, such as organic produce, vitamins, macrobiotic foods, a juice bar, and cruelty-free cosmetics. ⊠ *2911 Grand Ave.,* ☎ *305/448–7595,* FAX *305/448–4370. AE, MC, V.*

Downtown Miami

$ ✗ **Granny Feelgood's.** "Granny" is a nice gentleman named Irving Fields, who has been catering to health-conscious downtowners for 25 years. Specialties include chicken salad with raisins, apples, and cinnamon; spinach fettucine with pine nuts; grilled tofu; apple crumb cake; and carrot cake. ⊠ *111 N.W. 1st St.,* ☎ *305/579–2104. No credit cards. No breakfast or lunch weekends.*

Miami Beach

$ ✗ **Oasis Cafe.** Fresh flavors and innovative food at budget prices define this quasi–Middle Eastern, quasi-vegetarian spot north of South Beach. As you'd expect, hummus, grape leaves, feta cheese, and kalamata olives figure on the starter menu, but grilled sesame tofu and sautéed garlic spinach are surprising. For entrées, ask for pan-seared turkey chop; roasted vegetable lasagna; penne with turkey, tomato, saffron, and pine nuts; or grilled fresh fish on focaccia. Homemade desserts are luscious. ⊠ *976 41st St.,* ☎ *305/674–7676. AE, D, DC, MC, V.*

Nicaraguan

Downtown Miami

$–$$ ✗ **Los Ranchos.** Owner Carlos Somoza, nephew of Nicaragua's late
★   president Anastasio Somoza, sustains the tradition of Managua's original Los Ranchos by serving Argentine-style beef—lean, grass-fed tenderloin with chimichurri. Nicaragua's own sauces are a tomato-based marinara and the fiery *cebollitas encurtidas,* with jalapeño and pickled onion. Specialties include chorizo and *cuajada con maduro* (skim cheese with fried bananas). Don't look for veggies or brewed decaf, but there is live entertainment. ⊠ *Bayside Marketplace, 401 Biscayne Blvd.,* ☎ *305/375–8188 or 305/375–0666;* ⊠ *125 S.W. 107th Ave., Little Managua,* ☎ *305/221–9367;* ⊠ *Kendall Town & Country, 8505 Mills Dr., Kendall,* ☎ *305/596–5353;* ⊠ *The Falls, 8888 S.W. 136th St., Suite 303, South Miami,* ☎ *305/238–6867;* ⊠ *2728 Ponce de León Blvd., Coral Gables,* ☎ *305/446–0050. AE, DC, MC, V.*

Pacific Rim

Coral Gables

$$ ✗ **Two Sisters.** Competition among Coral Gables restaurants means
★   that food has to be better than fantastic. This restaurant, on the ground floor of the Hyatt Regency, approaches nirvana. Though the mood is understated, the Pacific Rim–inspired dishes add definite pizzazz. Entrées such as wokked tangled shrimp with jungle curry, rice ribbons,

and coconut glaze or jerk marinated snapper with red onion confit and ginger butter might make you consider a vacation in Polynesia. Servers are attentive, and desserts are so delicious you may end up spending the night with Two Sisters. ⊠ *50 Alhambra Plaza,* ☎ *305/441–1234. AE, MC, V.*

Seafood

Downtown Miami

$$–$$$ ✕ **Fish Market.** If fish are truly running scarce in Florida waters, as
★ some claim, the last of what's available should be reserved for this superior dining room tucked in a corner of the Crowne Plaza Miami lobby. The room is as beautiful as the kitchen staff is fluent in seafood's complexities. Modern chrome and comfortable cushions combine in urban sophistication. Though the menu is limited, whatever's fresh is highlighted. Look for seared swordfish with Oriental vinaigrette or pan-roasted Florida lobster tail on mushroom risotto with truffle brandy butter. Chocolate-pecan tart, chocolate Key lime pie, and chocolate-mocha napoleon are among featured desserts. There's free valet parking. ⊠ *Biscayne Blvd. at 16th St.,* ☎ *305/374–4399. AE, D, DC, MC, V. Closed Sun. No lunch Sat.*

$$ ✕ **East Coast Fisheries.** This family-owned restaurant and retail fish
★ market on the Miami River offers fresh Florida seafood from its own 38-boat fleet in the Keys. From tables along the second-floor balcony, watch the cooks prepare your dinner in the open kitchen below. Specialties include a complimentary fish-pâté appetizer, blackened pompano with owner David Swartz's personal herb-and-spice recipe, lightly breaded fried grouper, and a homemade Key lime pie. ⊠ *360 W. Flagler St.,* ☎ *305/372–1300. AE, MC, V. Beer and wine only.*

Miami Beach

$$$ ✕ **Pacific Time.** This cool California-style restaurant is packed nearly
★ every night. The superb eatery, co-owned by chef Jonathan Eismann, has a high blue ceiling and banquettes, accents of mahogany and brass, plank floors, and an open-window kitchen. Entrées include a cedar-roasted salmon, rosemary-roasted chicken, and shiitake mushroom–grilled, dry-aged Colorado beef. Rices, potatoes, and vegetables are à la carte; however, a pre-theater prix fixe dinner ($20), served 6–7 PM, comes with a noodle dish, Szechuan mixed grill, and grilled ginger chicken. Desserts (around $7) include a fresh pear-pecan spring roll. There's an extensive California wine list. Pacific Heights, a new sister restaurant in Coral Gables, is every bit as cool. ⊠ *915 Lincoln Rd.,* ☎ *305/534–5979;* ⊠ *2530 Ponce de León Blvd., Coral Gables,* ☎ *305/461–1774. AE, DC, MC, V.*

$–$$ ✕ **Joe's Stone Crab Restaurant.** "Before SoBe, Joe Be," touts this
★ fourth-generation family restaurant, which reopened in 1996 with a chest-puffing facade on Washington Avenue. You go to wait, people-watch, and finally settle down to an ample à la carte menu. About a ton of stone-crab claws is served daily (except in summer), with drawn butter, lemon wedges, and piquant mustard sauce (recipe available). Popular side orders include salad with a brisk vinaigrette, creamed garlic spinach, french-fried onions, fried green tomatoes, and hash browns. Save room for dessert—Key lime pie or apple pie with a crumb-pecan topping. ⊠ *227 Biscayne St.,* ☎ *305/673–0365; takeout, 305/673–4611; overnight shipping, 800/780–2722. AE, D, DC, MC, V. Closed Sept. 1–Oct. 15. No lunch Sun.–Mon.*

Spanish

Coral Gables

$$ ╳ **Cafe Barcelona.** This room with high ceilings and coral walls is highlighted by gilt-framed art and beautiful, slender ceiling lamps with tiny fluted green shades. The dim glow illuminates the food but little else, yielding an ambience that's part art gallery and part private home. Exceptional food matches the exceptional mood, and in a city where fresh fish has gotten priced off the deep end, entrées here range a good $5 below comparable dishes at first-class restaurants. They do a sea bass in sea salt for two, a traditional codfish with garlic confit, and a grouper in a clay pot with seafood sauce as well as lamb, duck, and several affordable rice dishes, including three types of paella. The *crema Catalana*, a version of flan, is not to be missed. ⊠ *160 Giralda Ave.,* ☎ *305/448–0912. AE, D, DC, MC, V.*

Downtown Miami

$–$$ ╳ **Las Tapas.** Overhung with dried meats and enormous show breads, this popular spot with terra-cotta floors and an open kitchen offers a lot of imaginative creations. Tapas ("little dishes") give you a variety of tastes during a single meal. Specialties include *la tostada* (smoked salmon on melba toast, topped with a dollop of sour cream, baby eels, black caviar, capers, and chopped onion) and *pincho de pollo a la plancha* (grilled chicken brochette marinated in brandy and onions). Also available are soups, salads, sandwiches, and standard-size dinners. ⊠ *Bayside Marketplace, 401 Biscayne Blvd.,* ☎ *305/372–2737. Reservations essential for large parties. AE, D, DC, MC, V.*

Little Havana

$$–$$$ ╳ **Casa Juancho.** This meeting place for the movers and shakers of the
★ Cuban community is also a haven for lovers of fine Spanish regional cuisine. The exterior is marked by *tinajones*, the huge earthen urns of eastern Cuba, but the interior recalls old Castile. Strolling balladeers (university students from Spain) serenade you among brown brick, rough-hewn dark timbers, walls adorned with hooks of smoked meats and colorful Talavera platters. Try the hake prepared in a fish stock with garlic, onions, and white wine flown in from Spain or the *carabineros a la plancha* (jumbo red shrimp with head and shell on, split and grilled). For dessert, the crema Catalana has a delectable crust of burnt caramel atop a rich pastry custard. The house features the largest list of reserved Spanish wines in the States. ⊠ *2436 S.W. 8th St.,* ☎ *305/642–2452. AE, D, DC, MC, V.*

Thai

Miami Beach

$ ╳ **Thai Toni.** Thai silks, bronze Buddhas, dramatic ceiling drapes, private dining alcoves, and two raised platforms with cushions set this exceptional restaurant apart from other trendy eateries in South Beach. The mellow Thai Singha beer complements the spicy jumping squid appetizer with chili paste and hot pepper or the hot, hot pork. Choose from a large variety of inexpensive noodle, fried-rice, and vegetarian dishes or such traditional entrées as beef and broccoli, basil duck, or hot-and-spicy deep-fried whole snapper with basil leaves and mixed vegetables. The homemade lemonade is distinctly tart. ⊠ *890 Washington Ave.,* ☎ *305/538–8424. AE, MC, V. No lunch.*

Vietnamese

Little Havana

$ ✕ **Hy-Vong Vietnamese Cuisine.** Beer-savvy Kathy Manning has in-
★ troduced a half dozen top brews (Double Grimbergen, Moretti, and
Spaten, among them), and magic continues to pour forth from the tiny
kitchen of this plain little restaurant. Come before 7 to avoid a wait.
Favorites include spring rolls (a Vietnamese version of an egg roll, with
ground pork, cellophane noodles, and black mushrooms wrapped in
homemade rice paper), whole fish panfried with *nuoc man* (a garlic-
lime fish sauce), and thinly sliced pork, barbecued with sesame seeds
and fish sauce, served with bean sprouts, rice noodles, and slivers of
carrots, almonds, and peanuts. ⊠ *3458 S.W. 8th St., ☎ 305/446–3674.
No credit cards. Closed Mon. and 2 weeks in Aug. No lunch.*

LODGING

As recently as the 1960s, many hotels in Greater Miami opened only
in winter, to accommodate Yankee snowbirds. Now all hotels stay open
all year. In summer they cater to European and Latin American vacationers, who find Miami congenial despite the heat, humidity, and intense afternoon thunderstorms.

Although some hotels (especially on the mainland) have adopted steady
year-round rates, many still adjust their rates to reflect seasonal demand.
The peak occurs in winter, with a dip in summer (prices are often more
negotiable than rate cards let on). You'll find the best values between
Easter and Memorial Day (a delightful time in Miami but a difficult
time for many people to travel) and in September and October (the height
of hurricane season). At press time The Tides hotel, a Deco landmark
in South Beach, was set to reopen as part of Chris Blackwell's Island
Outpost chain; call 800/688-7678 for information.

Coconut Grove

$$$$ 🏨 **Grand Bay Hotel.** Combining the classical elegance of Greece, a
★ stepped facade that feels vaguely Aztec, a hint of the South, and a brush
of the tropical, this hotel is like no other in South Florida. Guest rooms
are filled with superb touches: a canister of sharpened pencils giving
off an aroma of shaved wood, an antique sideboard that holds house
phones, and matched woods, variously inlaid and fluted. The piano in
814 is tuned when Pavarotti is in residence, but your needs will be met
equally well. Rooms at the northeast corner have the best views, looking out on downtown Miami. Afternoon tea is served. ⊠ *2669 S.
Bayshore Dr., 33133, ☎ 305/858–9600 or 800/327–2788, FAX 305/858–
1532. 132 rooms, 49 suites. Restaurant, bar, lounge, pool, beauty
salon, hot tub, massage, saunas, health club. AE, DC, MC, V.*

$$$$ 🏨 **Mayfair House.** This European-style luxury hotel sits within Mayfair Shops at the Grove, an exclusive open-air shopping mall. Public
areas have Tiffany windows, polished mahogany, marble, imported ce-
ramics and crystal, and an impressive glassed-in elevator. The individually
furnished suites (22 for nonsmokers) have outdoor terraces facing the
street, screened by vegetation and wood latticework. Each has a relatively small Japanese hot tub on the balcony or a Roman tub inside;
50 have antique pianos. One bonus is a rooftop recreation area, but
the miniature lap pool is odd for such a large hotel. Because of the nightclub, Ensign Bitters, ask for a quiet suite. ⊠ *3000 Florida Ave., 33133,
☎ 305/441–0000 or 800/433–4555, FAX 305/447–9173. 183 suites.
Snack bar, pool, sauna, nightclub. AE, D, DC, MC, V.*

Miami Area Lodging

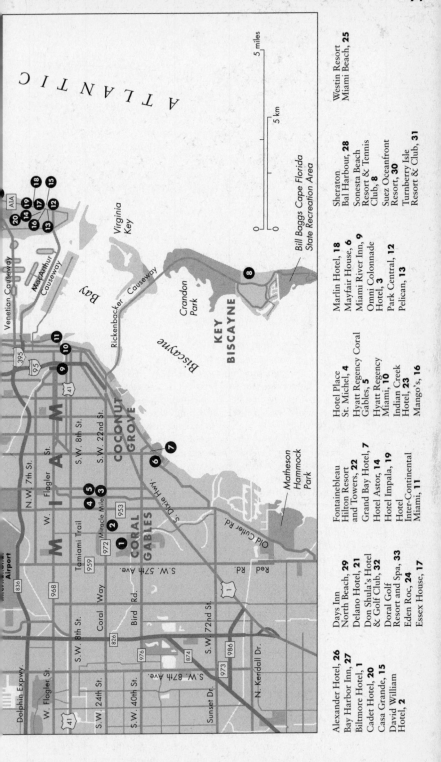

ATLANTIC

Venetian Cswy.

MacArthur
Causeway

Biscayne
Bay

Virginia
Key

Rickenbacker Causeway

Crandon
Park

KEY
BISCAYNE

Biscayne
Bay

Bill Baggs Cape Florida
State Recreation Area

Matheson
Hammock
Park

COCONUT
GROVE

CORAL
GABLES

MIAMI

Miami
Airport

Dolphin Expwy.

5 km

5 miles

Alexander Hotel, 26
Bay Harbor Inn, 27
Biltmore Hotel, 1
Cadet Hotel, 20
Casa Grande, 15
David William
Hotel, 2

Days Inn
North Beach, 29
Delano Hotel, 21
Don Shula's Hotel
& Golf Club, 32
Doral Golf
Resort and Spa, 33
Eden Roc, 24
Essex House, 17

Fontainebleau
Hilton Resort
and Towers, 22
Grand Bay Hotel, 7
Hotel Astor, 14
Hotel Impala, 19
Hotel
Inter-Continental
Miami, 11

Hotel Place
St. Michel, 4
Hyatt Regency Coral
Gables, 5
Hyatt Regency
Miami, 10
Indian Creek
Hotel, 23
Mango's, 16

Marlin Hotel, 18
Mayfair House, 6
Miami River Inn, 9
Omni Colonnade
Hotel, 3
Park Central, 12
Pelican, 13

Sheraton
Bal Harbour, 28
Sonesta Beach
Resort & Tennis
Club, 8
Suez Oceanfront
Resort, 30
Turnberry Isle
Resort & Club, 31

Westin Resort
Miami Beach, 25

Coral Gables

$$$$ ⊡ **Hyatt Regency Coral Gables.** The exterior is overtly Spanish, cour-
★   tesy of tile roofs, white-frame casement windows, and pink stucco, but
interior influences are more subliminal: traces in the headboard design,
a stair-stepped outline at guest information, and fall browns and
blonds. As befits a business hotel, the staff is savvy and helpful and
rooms are designed as alternative offices. An extra $15 buys in-room
fax, computer hookup, free local calls, and a Continental breakfast.
Still the mood is comfortable and residential. A new business center
and meeting facilities are to the side, so vacationers don't feel they're
still in the corporate world. ⊠ *50 Alhambra Plaza, 33134,* ☎ *305/441–
1234,* FAX *305/443–7702. 192 rooms, 50 suites. Restaurant, lounge,
pool, sauna, steam rooms, health club, business services, meeting
rooms. AE, D, DC, MC, V.*

$$$–$$$$ ⊡ **Biltmore Hotel.** Miami's grand boom-time hotel has undergone two
★   renovations since 1986 but still recaptures a bygone era. Now owned
by Coral Gables and operated by Westin, the 1926 Biltmore was the
centerpiece of Merrick's City Beautiful. It rises like a sienna-color
wedding cake in the heart of a residential district. The vaulted lobby
has hand-painted rafters on a twinkling sky-blue background. Large
guest rooms are done in a restrained Moorish style. For $1800 you
can book the Everglades (aka Al Capone) Suite—President Clinton's
room when he's in town. Historical tours are given Sunday at 1:30,
2:30, and 3:30. ⊠ *1200 Anastasia Ave., 33134,* ☎ *305/445–1926 or
800/445–1926,* FAX *305/913–3152. 237 rooms, 38 suites. Restaurant,
café, lounge, pool, sauna, spa, 18-hole golf course, 10 lighted tennis
courts, health club, meeting rooms. AE, DC, MC, V.*

$$$–$$$$ ⊡ **Omni Colonnade Hotel.** The twin 13-story towers of this hotel, of-
★   fice, and shopping complex dominate the heart of Coral Gables, and
architectural details echo the adjoining two-story Corinthian-style ro-
tunda. On display throughout the hotel—only four stories of the build-
ing—are old photos, paintings, and other heirlooms from George
Merrick's family. Oversize rooms come in 26 floor plans and several
styles, each with a sitting area, built-in armoires, and traditional ma-
hogany furnishings. Rooms are ready for modems and fax machines.
The pool, on a 10th-floor terrace, looks south toward Biscayne Bay.
Ask for a room with a private balcony. ⊠ *180 Aragon Ave., 33134,*
☎ *305/441–2600 or 800/533–1337,* FAX *305/445–3929. 157 rooms,
17 bilevel suites. 2 restaurants, pool, 2 saunas, exercise room. AE, D,
DC, MC, V.*

$$$ ⊡ **David William Hotel.** Easily the most affordable of the top Gables
hotels, the 13-story DW (as aficionados call it) was the first high-rise
of Miami's modern era. On the outside it looks as nondescript as a
1960s retirement high-rise. The hotel is solidly built, like a fort, so the
large rooms are very private and very quiet. They have marble baths,
and those facing south (the sunnier exposure) have balconies. Many
have kitchens. The lobby is a bit tacky, with tables outside the elegant
Chez Vendôme, a popular traditional French restaurant. Rooftop cabana rooms are the best bargains. ⊠ *700 Biltmore Way, 33134,* ☎
305/445–7821, FAX *305/445–5585. 116 rooms. Pool. AE, MC, V.*

$$$ ⊡ **Hotel Place St. Michel.** Art-nouveau chandeliers suspended from
★   vaulted ceilings grace the public areas of this intimate hotel in the heart
of downtown. Built in 1926, the historic low rise was restored from
1981 to 1986 and yet again after a 1995 fire. The charming inn is filled
with the scent of fresh flowers, circulated by paddle fans. Each room
has its own dimensions, personality, and imported antiques from En-
gland, Scotland, and France. A complimentary Continental breakfast
is served. ⊠ *162 Alcazar Ave., 33134,* ☎ *305/444–1666 or 800/848–*

4683, FAX *305/529–0074. 24 rooms, 3 suites. Restaurant, lounge. AE, DC, MC, V.*

Downtown Miami

$$$$ ☒ **Hotel Inter-Continental Miami.** From the pool deck, you don't see
★ the ragtag street, only the clean view Miami likes best of itself: the Disneyesque Metromover, Brickell Avenue, the booming port, the beautiful bay, and Key Biscayne. The lobby's marble matches that in *The Spindle,* a sculpture by Henry Moore. With all that marble, the lobby could easily look like a mausoleum, but palms and oversize wicker add softness. Sunlight streams through the atrium from a skylight. Rooms, in grays and beige and dark chintz, are traditional with a Latin flavor. The city's most manorial property, the Inter-Con (as guests call it) is also the most committed to waste reduction and recycling. ☒ *100 Chopin Plaza, 33131,* ☎ *305/577–1000 or 800/327–0200,* FAX *305/577– 0384. 644 rooms, 34 suites. 3 restaurants, lounge, pool, spa, jogging. AE, DC, MC, V.*

$$$$ ☒ **Hyatt Regency Miami.** The blend of leisure and business should position the Hyatt well for the downtown renaissance that began with the opening of the new Miami Avenue Bridge in late 1996. Distinctive public spaces are more colorful than businesslike, and guest rooms are done in unusual avocado, beige, and blond. Rooms yield views of the river or port, and not surprisingly the best ones are from the upper floors. The James L. Knight International Center is accessible without stepping outside, as is the downtown Metromover and its Metrorail connection. ☒ *400 S.E. 2nd Ave., 33131,* ☎ *305/358–1234 or 800/233–1234,* FAX *305/358–0529. 615 rooms, 25 suites. Restaurant, lounge, pool. AE, D, DC, MC, V.*

$$ ☒ **Miami River Inn.** Preservationist Sallye Jude has restored these five 1904 clapboard buildings, the only group of Miami houses left from that period. The inn is an oasis of country hospitality in a working-class neighborhood—one of Miami's safest even if it doesn't look it. Rooms (some with tub only) are filled with antiques. Guests, including many Europeans, receive a free Continental breakfast and can use a fridge. The best rooms look over the river from the second and third floors. Avoid the tiny rooms in Building D with a view of a condo. The city's heart is a 10-minute stroll across the 1st Street Bridge, and José Martí Park, very pretty but lately a haven for homeless, is a few hundred feet away. ☒ *118 S.W. South River Dr., 33130,* ☎ *305/325–0045 or 800/468–3589,* FAX *305/325–9227. 40 rooms (2 with shared bath). Pool. AE, D, DC, MC, V.*

Key Biscayne

$$$$ ☒ **Sonesta Beach Resort & Tennis Club.** Always one of Miami's best,
★ the Sonesta is now more tropical than ever, with reef pastels and stunning sea views, at least from those rooms facing east. Villas are actually three-bedroom homes with full kitchen and screened pool. Don't miss the museum-quality modern art by prominent painters and sculptors, especially Andy Warhol's drawings of rock star Mick Jagger in the hotel's disco bar, Desires. The 750-foot beach, one of Florida's best, has a big variety of recreational facilities. ☒ *350 Ocean Dr., 33149,* ☎ *305/361–2021 or 800/766–3782,* FAX *305/361–3096. 284 rooms, 14 suites, 2 villas. 3 restaurants, bar, snack bar, pool, massage, steam rooms, 9 tennis courts (3 lighted), aerobics, health club, beach, windsurfing, children's program. AE, D, DC, MC, V.*

Miami Beach

$$$$ ★ 🏨 **Alexander Hotel.** Amid the high-rises of the mid-Beach district, this 16-story hotel represents the elegance for which the Beach was once famous. It has immense suites furnished with antiques and reproductions, each with a terrace affording ocean or bay views, each with a living and dining room, kitchen, and two baths. Everything is understated, from the marquetry-paneled and landscaped lobby to the oceanfront dining rooms. Service is of the highest standard and includes twice-daily maid service (on request). ⊠ *5225 Collins Ave., 33140,* ☎ *305/865–6500 or 800/327–6121,* 🖷 *305/341–6553. 158 1- and 2-bedroom suites. Restaurant, coffee shop, 2 pools, spa, beach, boating. AE, D, DC, MC, V.*

$$$$ ★ 🏨 **Casa Grande.** The first of SoBe's new top-flight hotels, this is still the best. The lobby's teak, tile, and recessed lighting create a warm and relaxing look. Luxurious suites capture the fashionable air of Ocean Drive, yet in fine taste and without the invasion of its hectic sounds. Done in teak and mahogany, units have dhurrie rugs, beautiful Indonesian fabrics and artifacts, two-poster beds with ziggurat turns, full electric kitchens with fine European utensils, and large baths—unheard of in the Deco District—adorned with green decorator tiles. Goodies range from a daily newspaper and in-room coffee to fresh flowers, TV/VCR/CD/radio entertainment stations, and evening turndown with Italian chocolates. Book well in advance for peak periods. ⊠ *834 Ocean Dr., 33139,* ☎ *305/672–7003 or 800/688–7678,* 🖷 *305/673–3669. 33 suites. Café, laundry service and dry cleaning, concierge. AE, DC, MC, V.*

$$$$ 🏨 **Delano Hotel.** If Calvin Klein had teamed with Salvador Dali to build a hotel, this weird, wonderful, and a bit snooty property would be it. Tourists marvel at the lobby draped in massive white, billowing drapes as guests mutter about the poor service and loud housekeepers. Apparently this combination (and a $20 million renovation) appeals to female fashion models and men of independent means, who gather beneath cabanas and pose by the pool. Although the standard rooms are a standard size, the stark whiteness of the beds, sheets, desks, and phones makes them appear larger. The gift shop carries magazines you wouldn't want your parents to see. The real appeal here is the surrealism. ⊠ *1685 Collins Ave., 33139,* ☎ *305/672–2000 or 800/555–5001,* 🖷 *305/532–0099. 208 rooms. Restaurant, bar, pool, spa, health club. AE, D, DC, MC, V.*

$$$$ 🏨 **Eden Roc.** Who knows why this grand 1950s hotel designed by Morris Lapidus is overshadowed by the larger, more prominent Fontainebleau? From the moment you enter, its free-flowing lines make it casual and comfortable. A $30-million renovation added new ballrooms and meeting facilities, including a resort yacht for oceangoing meetings. The 55,000-square-foot Spa of Eden usually runs full tilt, while Dolphins coach Jimmy Johnson's beachside sports bar caters to those who prefer lifting weights 16 ounces at a time. Rooms blend a touch of the '50s with casual '90s elegance. ⊠ *4525 Collins Ave., 33140,* ☎ *305/531–0000 or 800/327–8337,* 🖷 *305/674–5555. 346 rooms. 2 restaurants, bar, pool, massage, spa, exercise room, racquetball, meeting rooms. AE, MC, V.*

$$$$ 🏨 **Fontainebleau Hilton Resort and Towers.** This is the Grand Central of area hotels—the busiest, the biggest, and the most ornate. Convention facilities rank second only to the city-owned convention center, and a 30,000-square-foot beachside spa is ideal for self-indulgence. Tower rooms are country in spirit, light and flowery, yet come with traditional amenities and the security of special elevator keys. Other themes vary from the 1950s to contemporary. Even the smallest room is large by most standards. The Continental breakfast is banquetlike, and views extend halfway to the Azores. ✉ *4441 Collins Ave., 33140, ☎ 305/538–2000 or 800/548–8886, ℻ 305/531–9274. 1,146 rooms, 60 suites. 12 restaurants, 4 lounges, 2 pools, saunas, spa, 7 lighted tennis courts, health club, volleyball, beach, windsurfing, boating, parasailing, children's programs, convention center. AE, DC, MC, V.*

\$\$\$\$ ★ 🖪 **Hotel Impala.** One of the nicest inns in the area, the former La Flora is tropical Mediterranean Revival, not Deco. Iron, mahogany, and stone on the inside are in synch with the sporty white-trim ocher exterior. Rooms, among the cleanest in SoBe, are elegant, comfortable, and complete, with a TV/VCR/stereo and stock of CDs and videos. It's all very European, from mineral water and orchids to the Mediterranean-style armoires, wrought-iron furniture, Italian fixtures, heavy ornamental drapery rods, and Spanish surrealist art above white-on-white, triple-sheeted, modified Eastlake sleigh beds. (Not surprisingly, Continental breakfast is included.) Everything from wastebaskets to towels to toilet paper is of exceptional quality. ✉ *1228 Collins Ave., 33139, ☎ 305/673–2021 or 800/646–7252, ℻ 305/673–5984. 17 rooms, 3 suites. Restaurant, lounge. AE, DC, MC, V.*

\$\$\$\$ ★ 🖪 **Marlin Hotel.** The Marlin is so Jamaican that it could be the island's cultural showcase. Fun and funky art complements striking hand-painted furniture, woven grass rugs, batiklike shades, and rattan and mahogany furniture. Every room is different, some with sharp accents of ocher and plum, some with pale sky blue, and some with kitchenettes, but all are completely detailed with VCRs, minibars, and orchid decorations. Even studio suites, with rattan sitting areas, are sizeable; larger suites are like villas. For sunbathing, check out the rooftop deck, and for a nightcap, drop in the brilliant bar that looks like an upscale beach shack. ✉ *1200 Collins Ave., 33139, ☎ 305/673–8770, ℻ 305/673–9609. 11 suites. Bar. AE, D, DC, MC, V.*

\$\$\$\$ 🖪 **Pelican.** Dazzling, brilliant spaces with Deco-inspired frivolity have turned another tired Ocean Drive home for the elderly into pop-eyed digs for the hip. Rooms, with names like Leafforest, Best Whorehouse, People from the 1950s, and Cubarrean, are all different, but all have small sleeping chambers and triple-size bathrooms with outrageous industrial piping. Best Whorehouse envelops you in black silk and thoroughly red flocked wallpaper flecked with gold. Ornaments are bordello extravagant: a heart-shape red velvet chair, hideously aqua night tables, whorish art, and griffins with voluptuous mammaries. Each room comes with its own cylindrical entertainment center. Guests have included JFK, Jr., and Yoko Ono. ✉ *826 Ocean Dr., 33139, ☎ 305/673–3373 or 800/773–5422, ℻ 305/673–3255. 25 units, penthouse. Restaurant, café, concierge. AE, MC, V.*

\$\$\$\$ 🖪 **Sheraton Bal Harbour.** Want to get away from the traffic of SoBe? Go to NoBe. Sensing Miami's resurrection would head north, the owners of this Lapidus-designed hotel gave it a \$52 million face-lift, including a new lush oceanfront garden with waterfalls, a funky neon-laced bistro and bar, upgraded units, and 73,000 square feet of improved meeting space. Rooms offer full or partial views of the city, ocean, or Bal Harbour, and the ritzy Bal Harbour Shops are across the street. Elegant without pretense, the hotel's design is complemented by a staff that has service down to a science. ✉ *9701 Collins Ave., Bal Harbour 33154, ☎ 305/865–7511, ℻ 305/864–2601. 755 rooms, 53 suites. 3 restaurants, piano bar, pool, wading pool, hot tub, massage, sauna, health club, windsurfing, game room, baby-sitting, meeting rooms. AE, D, DC, MC, V.*

\$\$\$\$ ★ 🖪 **Westin Resort Miami Beach.** Of the great Miami Beach hotels, this 18-story glass tower remains a standout. It has the only rooftop restaurant (Alfredo, the Original of Rome), the only rooftop ballroom (with

8,000 twinkling lights), and two presidential suites designed in consultation with the Secret Service. Some of the staff have worked here for 20 or 30 years, and the hotel remembers hospitality as it was before voice mail. Warm-tone guest rooms are filled with nice details: small fridges; three sets of drapes, including blackout curtains; big closets; and bathrooms with high-quality toiletries and a magnifying mirror. Free transportation to Doral Golf Resort and Spa is provided. ⊠ *4833 Collins Ave., 33140,* ☎ *305/532–3600 or 800/223–6725,* 𝔽𝔸𝕏 *305/534–7409. 293 rooms, 127 suites. 3 restaurants, 4 lounges, pool, 2 lighted tennis courts, exercise room, beach, helipad. AE, DC, MC, V.*

$$$–$$$$ 🖼 **Hotel Astor.** How does yet another Deco hotel stand out from the crowd? This hotel does it by double-insulating walls against noise and offering such subtle luxuries as ambient low-voltage lighting, thick towels, paddle fans, and a seductive pool. To cap it off, the festive Gospel Sunday Brunch has diners praising the Lord and giving thanks for delicious culinary creations, such as corn-crusted yellowtail snapper, served in the basement–turned–bright and airy Astor Place Restaurant. The renovation also included expansion of guest rooms and baths and the addition of custom-milled French furniture, Roman shades, muted colors, and sleek sound and video systems. ⊠ *956 Washington Ave., 33139,* ☎ *305/531–8081 or 800/270–4981,* 𝔽𝔸𝕏 *305/531–3193. 42 rooms. Restaurant, bar, pool, massage. AE, MC, V.*

$$$–$$$$ 🖼 **Indian Creek Hotel.** Not as grand as the North Beach behemoths or
★ as hectic as the Ocean Drive offerings, this 1936 Pueblo Deco jewel may just be Miami's most charming and sincere lodge. Owner Marc Levin rescued the inn by adding a cozy dining room with an eclectic and appetizing menu, relandscaping a lush pool and garden, and restoring rooms with Deco furniture, much of it discovered in the basement. Items were cleaned, reupholstered, and put on display, helping the hotel win the Miami Design Preservation League's award for outstanding restoration. Suites have fridges, and safe deposit boxes are available. Stay a while and manager Zammy Migdal and his staff will have you feeling like family. ⊠ *2727 Indian Creek Dr., 33140,* ☎ *305/531–2727,* 𝔽𝔸𝕏 *305/531–5651. 61 rooms. Restaurant, pool, concierge. AE, D, DC, MC, V.*

$$$–$$$$ 🖼 **Park Central.** Across from the glorious beach, this seven-story Deco hotel—painted blue, with wraparound corner windows—makes all the right moves to stay in the forefront of the Art Deco revival. Most of the fashion models visiting town come to this property, which dates from 1937. Black-and-white photos of old beach scenes, hurricanes, and familiar faces attest to its longevity, and board games in the lobby add to its charm. Rooms are decorated with Philippine mahogany furnishings—originals that have been restored. Incorporated in the property, the Imperial Hotel next door has an additional 36 rooms. ⊠ *640 Ocean Dr., 33139,* ☎ *305/538–1611 or 800/727–5236,* 𝔽𝔸𝕏 *305/534–7520. 121 rooms. Bar, pool, exercise room. AE, DC, MC, V.*

$$$ 🖼 **Essex House.** Now painted in cool pastel gray with sulphur-yellow trim, this premier lodging of the Art Deco era was designed by architect Henry Hohauser with an Everglades mural by Earl LaPan. Here are ziggurat arches, hieroglyph-style ironwork, etched-glass panels of flamingos under palms, and 5-foot rose-medallion Chinese urns. Hallways have recessed showcases with original Deco sculptures. The 66 rooms from 1938 are now 60, including petite and grand suites, but many have a generic hotel appearance. Rooms are soundproof from within (otherwise unheard of in 1930s beach properties), and those to the east have extra-thick windows to reduce the band noise from a nearby hotel. Continental breakfast is included. ⊠ *1001 Collins Ave., 33139,* ☎ *305/534–2700 or 800/553–7739,* 𝔽𝔸𝕏 *305/532–3827. 51 rooms, 9 suites. Breakfast room. AE, DC, MC, V.*

$$–$$$ 🏨 **Bay Harbor Inn.** Offering down-home hospitality in the county's most affluent zip code, this inn has two sections and two moods. Town side is a vaguely Georgian 1940 building, the oldest in Bay Harbor Islands. Behind triple sets of French doors under fan windows, the lobby is full of oak desks, hand mills, grandfather clocks, and historical maps. Rooms are antiques-filled, and no two are alike. Along Indian Creek, the former Albert Pick Hotella is shipshape and tropical. Rooms, off loggias surrounded by palms, are mid-century modern with chintz; all face the water. A complimentary Continental breakfast and the *Miami Herald* are provided. The popular Miami Palm restaurant is town side, while the creek-side London Bar serves the best ½-pound burger in the city. ✉ *9660 E. Bay Harbor Dr., Bay Harbor Islands 33154,* ☎ *305/868–4141,* 𝔽𝔸𝕏 *305/867–9094. 25 rooms, 12 suites, penthouse. 2 restaurants, lounge, pool. AE, MC, V.*

$$ 🏨 **Cadet Hotel.** Clark Gable stayed in room 225 when he came for Army Air Corps training in the 1940s. Although this Lincoln Road district lodging doesn't have the glamour to attract stars today, it's still a clean, friendly, and perfectly placed little hotel. Just a few minutes' walk from the Theater of the Performing Arts and the convention center and five minutes from the ocean, it's about half the cost of an Ocean Drive hotel. The other big difference is that the staff doesn't act like it's doing you a favor to let you stay here. Bright without glitz, the Cadet features soft pastels in the lobby, blues and creams in rooms. Ordinary furniture is mixed but not necessarily matched—nor is it crummy. Tiled baths have tubs. A complimentary breakfast is served in the lobby or on the terrace. ✉ *1701 James Ave., 33139,* ☎ *305/672–6688,* 𝔽𝔸𝕏 *305/532–1676. 44 rooms. AE, D, DC, MC, V.*

$$ 🏨 **Mango's.** If you'd rather party than sleep, this two-story hotel in the heart of Ocean Drive may be the place to crash. You can stay up until the bands downstairs blow a fuse and then stumble upstairs for some shut-eye. Any earlier and you'll want to crank up the air-conditioning to drown out the sound of the bands and party people downstairs in Mango's bar. If you're a light sleeper, ask for a back room by the palm garden waterfall. Though units have kitchenettes with usable fridges, no cooking is allowed. Furnishings are basic—a bed, table, and two chairs—and some rooms may have a sofa or easy chair. ✉ *900 Ocean Dr., 33139,* ☎ *305/673–4422,* 𝔽𝔸𝕏 *305/674–0311. 15 rooms. Restaurant, bar. AE, D, DC, MC, V.*

$$ 🏨 **Suez Oceanfront Resort.** Several miles north of Miami Beach in what's known as Motel Row, the carousel-stripe, family-run Suez stands out from the area's fancy but nondescript motels. Look beyond the tacky sphinx icons to the quiet, gardenlike lounge and the landscaped palm courtyard. Rooms have chinois furniture and dazzling color, offsetting generally small spaces. Those in the north wing, with parking lot views, are the smallest and least expensive. Modified American Plan, fridges in all rooms, kitchens in some, free laundry service, and special kids' rates make this an especially good value, popular with Europeans. ✉ *18215 Collins Ave., Sunny Isles 33160,* ☎ *305/932–0661 or 800/327–5278; 800/432–3661 in FL;* 𝔽𝔸𝕏 *305/937–0058. 196 rooms. Restaurant, bar, freshwater and saltwater pools, wading pool, lighted tennis court, shuffleboard, volleyball, beach, playground, laundry service. AE, D, DC, MC, V.*

$–$$ 🏨 **Days Inn North Beach.** Despite talk that it's the next Deco District, North Beach still feels like a neighborhood of retired one-time vacationers. Dating from 1941, this seven-story hotel with modified deco styling used to be the Broadmoor. It was—and still is—the pick of the area, across from a beautiful section of beach backed by grassy dunes. The beach isn't crowded because the neighborhood isn't trendy yet.

Rooms are undistinguished with basic furnishings and fridges, but the lobby is spacious. Restaurant and bar service are provided on the lovely terrace. This is a good choice if you plan to use your room mostly for sleeping. ⊠ *7450 Ocean Terr., 33141,* ☎ *305/866–1631 or 800/325–2525,* FAX *305/868–4617. 95 rooms, 5 suites. Restaurant, bar. AE, D, DC, MC, V.*

North Dade

$$$$ ⊞ **Turnberry Isle Resort & Club.** The finest of the grand resorts, Turnberry
★   sits on 300 superbly landscaped acres by the bay. Choose from the Yacht Club, on the Intracoastal Waterway; the intimate Marina Hotel; a beautiful three-wing Mediterranean-style annex; and the Mizner-style Country Club Hotel. Oversize rooms have light woods and earth tones, large curving terraces, Jacuzzis, honor bar, and safes. The marina has moorings for 117 boats up to 150 feet, and there's a free shuttle to the beach club and the Aventura Mall. ⊠ *19999 W. Country Club Dr., Aventura 33180,* ☎ *305/932–6200 or 800/327–7028,* FAX *305/933–6560. 300 rooms, 40 suites. 7 restaurants, 5 lounges, 4 pools, saunas, spa, steam rooms, 2 golf courses, 24 tennis courts (18 lighted), health club, jogging, racquetball, beach, dive shop, docks, windsurfing, boating, helipad. AE, D, DC, MC, V.*

West Dade

$$$$ ⊞ **Don Shula's Hotel & Golf Club.** This low-rise resort is part of Miami Lakes, a planned town about 14 mi northwest of downtown. Opened in 1962, the golf resort includes a championship course, a lighted executive course, and a golf school. All rooms have balconies, and the decor is English traditional, rich in leather and wood. The hotel, on the other hand, has a typical Florida-tropics look—light pastels and furniture of wicker and light wood. In both locations the best rooms are near the lobby for convenient access; ask to be away from the elevators. ⊠ *6840 Main St., Miami Lakes 33014,* ☎ *305/821–1150 or 800/247–4852,* FAX *305/879–8298. 269 rooms, 32 suites. 5 restaurants, 2 lounges, 2 pools, saunas, steam rooms, 2 golf courses, 9 lighted tennis courts, aerobics, basketball, health club, racquetball, volleyball. AE, D, DC, MC, V.*

$$$$ ⊞ **Doral Golf Resort and Spa.** This 650-acre golf-and-tennis resort has put $30 million into renovating its restaurants, spa, and rooms, adding a lighter tone in eight separate three- and four-story lodges nestled beside golf courses. Dining ranges from a sports bar to an informal trattoria to an elegant seafood restaurant. The famed Blue Monster course has been redesigned, as will the other courses by late 1997. The resort hosts the annual $2 million Doral-Ryder Open Tournament. Beach transportation is provided. ⊠ *4400 N.W. 87th Ave., 33178-2192,* ☎ *305/592–2000 or 800/223–6725,* FAX *305/594–4682. 592 rooms, 102 suites. 4 restaurants, 3 lounges, 4 pools, spa, 5 golf courses, 15 tennis courts (7 lighted), health club, jogging, fishing, bicycles, pro shop. AE, D, DC, MC, V.*

NIGHTLIFE AND THE ARTS

For information on what's happening around town, Greater Miami's English-language daily newspaper, the *Miami Herald,* publishes reliable reviews and comprehensive listings in its "Weekend" section on Friday and in the "Lively Arts" section on Sunday. Call ahead to confirm details. *El Nuevo Herald* is the paper's Spanish version.

If you read Spanish, check **Diario Las Américas,** the area's largest independent Spanish-language paper, for information on the Spanish theater and a smattering of general performing-arts news.

A good source of information on the performing arts and nightspots is the calendar in **Miami Today,** a free weekly newspaper available each Thursday in downtown Miami, Coconut Grove, and Coral Gables. The best, most complete source is the **New Times,** a free weekly distributed throughout Dade County each Wednesday. Various tabloids reporting on Deco District entertainment and society come and go on Miami Beach. **Ocean Drive** out-glosses everything else. **Wire** reports on the gay community.

The free **Greater Miami Calendar of Events** is published twice a year by the Dade County Cultural Affairs Council (✉ 111 N.W. 1st St., Suite 625, 33128, ☎ 305/375–4634).

Real Talk/WTMI (93.1 FM, ☎ 305/856–9393) provides classical concert information in on-air reports three times daily at 7:30 AM and 12:50 and 6:30 PM. Call the station if you miss the report. **WLVE's Entertainment Line** (93.9 FM, ☎ 305/654–9436) gives information on touring groups of all kinds except classical.

The Arts

Miami's performing-arts aficionados will tell you they survive quite nicely, despite the area's historic inability to support a county-based professional symphony orchestra. In recent years this community has begun to write a new chapter in its performing-arts history.

In addition to established music groups, several churches and synagogues run classical-music series with international performers. In theater, Miami offers English-speaking audiences an assortment of professional, collegiate, and amateur productions of musicals, comedy, and drama. Spanish theater also is active.

The not-for-profit **Concert Association of Florida** (✉ 555 17th St., Miami Beach 33139, ☎ 305/532–3491), directed by Judith Drucker, is the South's largest presenter of classical arts, music, and dance.

To order tickets for performing-arts events by telephone, call **Ticketmaster** (☎ 305/358–5885).

Dance

The **Miami City Ballet** (✉ 905 Lincoln Rd., Miami Beach 33139, ☎ 305/532–7713 or 305/532–4880, FAX 305/532–2726) has risen rapidly to international prominence in its relatively short existence. Under the direction of Edward Villella (a principal dancer with the New York City Ballet under George Balanchine), Florida's first major, fully professional, resident ballet company has become a world-class ensemble. The company re-creates the Balanchine repertoire and introduces works of its own during its September–March season. Performances are held at the Jackie Gleason Theater of the Performing Arts; the Broward Center for the Performing Arts; Bailey Concert Hall, also in Broward County; the Raymond F. Kravis Center for the Performing Arts; and the Naples Philharmonic Center for the Arts. Villella narrates children's and works-in-progress programs.

Film

Alliance Film/Video Project (✉ Sterling Building, Suite 119, 927 Lincoln Rd. Mall, Miami Beach 33139, ☎ 305/531–8504) presents cutting-edge international cinema, with special midnight shows.

Screenings of new films from all over the world—including some made here—are held as part of the **Miami Film Festival** (✉ 444 Brickell Ave., Suite 229, Miami 33131, ☎ 305/377–3456). Each year more than 45,000 people descend on the Gusman Center for the Performing Arts for 10 days in late January and early February.

Music

Friends of Chamber Music (✉ 44 W. Flagler St., Miami 33130, ☎ 305/372–2975, FAX 305/381–8734) presents an annual series of chamber concerts by internationally known guest ensembles, such as the Emerson and Guarneri quartets.

Since Greater Miami has no resident symphony orchestra, the **New World Symphony** (✉ 541 Lincoln Rd., Miami Beach 33139, ☎ 305/673–3331 or 305/673–3330), a unique advanced-training orchestra conducted by Michael Tilson Thomas, helps fill the void. Musicians ages 22–30 who have finished their academic studies perform here before moving on to other orchestras. The orchestra began its 10th season, running from October to May, in 1997.

Opera

South Florida's leading company, the **Florida Grand Opera** (✉ 1200 Coral Way, Miami 33145, ☎ 305/854–1643, FAX 305/856–1042) presents five operas each year in the Dade County Auditorium, featuring the Florida Philharmonic Orchestra (James Judd, artistic director). The series brings such luminaries as Placido Domingo and Luciano Pavarotti. (Pavarotti made his American debut with the company in 1965 in *Lucia di Lammermoor.*) Operas are sung in the original language, with English subtitles projected above the stage.

Performing-Arts Centers

What was once a movie theater has become the 465-seat **Colony Theater** (✉ 1040 Lincoln Rd., Miami Beach 33139, ☎ 305/674–1026, FAX 305/534–5026). The city-owned performing-arts center features dance, drama, music, and experimental cinema.

Dade County Auditorium (✉ 2901 W. Flagler St., Miami 33135, ☎ 305/545–3395) satisfies patrons with 2,498 comfortable seats, good sight lines, and acceptable acoustics. Opera, concerts, and touring musicals are usually on the schedule.

If you have the opportunity to attend a concert, ballet, or touring stage production at the **Gusman Center for the Performing Arts** (✉ 174 E. Flagler St., Miami 33131, ☎ 305/372–0925), do so. The 1,739-seat downtown landmark, originally a movie palace, is as far from a mall multiplex as you can get. The stunningly beautiful hall resembles a Moorish courtyard, with twinkling stars and rolling clouds skirting across the ceiling and Roman statues guarding the wings.

Not to be confused with the ornate Gusman theater, **Gusman Concert Hall** (✉ 1314 Miller Dr., Coral Gables 33146, ☎ 305/284–2438, FAX 305/284–6475) is a 600-seat facility on the University of Miami campus. It has good acoustics and plenty of room, but parking is a problem when school is in session.

Acoustics and visibility are perfect for all 2,700 seats in the **Jackie Gleason Theater of the Performing Arts** (TOPA, ✉ 1700 Washington Ave., Miami Beach 33139, ☎ 305/673–7300; box office, ✉ 505 17th St., Miami Beach 33139, ☎ 305/673–8300, FAX 305/538–6810). Renamed for Gleason after his death, it hosts the Broadway Series, with five or six major productions annually; guest artists, such as David Copperfield, Stomp, and Liza Minnelli; and classical-music concerts. In front of the building, the **Walk of the Stars** contains footprints and signatures in concrete of performers who have appeared in the theater since 1984, including Julie Andrews, Leslie Caron, Carol Channing, Edward Villella, and the late George Abbott.

Theater

Actor's Playhouse (✉ 280 Miracle Mile, Coral Gables 33134, ☎ 305/444–9293), a professional Equity company, moved into the renovated 600-seat Miracle Theater, where they still present musicals, comedies, and dramas year-round. They begin presenting children's productions in the Children's Balcony Theatre in 1997.

Built in 1926 as a movie theater, the **Coconut Grove Playhouse** (✉ 3500 Main Hwy., Coconut Grove 33133, ☎ 305/442–4000 or 305/442–2662, FAX 305/444–6437) became a legitimate theater in 1956 and is now owned by the state of Florida. The apricot-hue Spanish-rococo Grove fixture stages tried-and-true Broadway plays and musicals as well as experimental productions in its main theater and cabaret-style Encore Room. It hosted its most popular event in 1996, when David Letterman's road show dropped by for the evening. Parking is $4 during the day, $5 in the evening.

The **Florida Shakespeare Theatre** (✉ 1200 Anastasia Ave., Coral Gables 33134, ☎ 305/446–1116) presents classic and contemporary theater in a 154-seat hall at the Biltmore Hotel. Two Shakespeare productions are given a year.

Gold Coast Theatre Company (✉ 1040 Lincoln Rd., Miami Beach 33140, ☎ 305/538–5500, FAX 305/538–6315) performs October through June in the Colony Theater.

New Theatre (✉ 65 Almeria Ave., Coral Gables 33134, ☎ 305/443–5909, FAX 305/447–1707) is a showcase for contemporary and classical plays.

On the campus of the University of Miami, **Ring Theater** (✉ 1380 Miller Dr., Coral Gables 33124, ☎ 305/284–3355, FAX 305/284–5426) is the 311-seat hall of U.M.'s Department of Theatre Arts. Six plays a year are performed.

SPANISH THEATER

Spanish theater prospers, although many companies have short lives. About 20 Spanish companies perform light comedy, puppetry, vaudeville, and political satire. To locate them, read the Spanish newspapers. When you call, be prepared for a conversation in Spanish—few box-office personnel speak English.

The 255-seat **Teatro de Bellas Artes** (✉ 2173 S.W. 8th St., Miami 33135, ☎ 305/325–0515), on Calle Ocho, presents eight Spanish plays and musicals year-round. Midnight musical follies and female impersonators round out the show-biz lineup.

Nightlife

Bars and Lounges

COCONUT GROVE

Hungry Sailor (✉ 3064½ Grand Ave., ☎ 305/444–9359), with two bars, serves Jamaican-English food, British beer, and music Wednesday to Saturday. **Taurus Steak House** (✉ 3540 Main Hwy., ☎ 305/448–0633) is an unchanging oasis in the trendy Grove. The bar, built of native cypress in 1919, draws an over-30 singles crowd nightly that drifts outside to a patio. A band plays Tuesday through Saturday.

CORAL GABLES

In a building that dates from 1926, **Stuart's Bar-Lounge** (⊠ 162 Al-cazar Ave., ☎ 305/444–1666) was named one of the best new bars of 1987 by *Esquire,* and it's still favored by locals. The style is fostered by beveled mirrors, mahogany paneling, French posters, pictures of old Coral Gables, and art-nouveau lighting. Stuart's is closed Sunday.

MIAMI

Tobacco Road (⊠ 626 S. Miami Ave., ☎ 305/374–1198), opened in 1912, holds Miami's oldest liquor license: 0001! Upstairs, in space oc-cupied by a speakeasy during Prohibition, local and national blues bands perform nightly. There's excellent bar food, a dinner menu, single-malt Scotch, bourbon, and cigars.

MIAMI BEACH

At **Bash** (⊠ 655 Washington Ave., ☎ 305/538–2274), two DJs spin dance music—sometimes reggae, sometimes Latin, plenty of loud disco, and world-beat sounds in the garden, where there are artsy benches. There are bars inside, where it's grottolike, and out, where you can check out the "magical patio." You can also try to join the chic crowd in either of two VIP rooms. **Blue Steel** (⊠ 2895 Collins Ave., ☎ 305/672–1227) is a cool but unpretentious hangout with pool tables, darts, live music, comfy old sofas, and beer paraphernalia. Open-mike night is Friday, and there's a jam on Monday. German *Vogue* liked it so much, they named it the "hippest and hottest" club in SoBe. *Ach du lieber!* **Mac's Club Deuce** (⊠ 222 14th St., ☎ 305/673–9537) is a South Beach gem where top international models pop in to have a drink and shoot some pool. All you get late at night are mini-pizzas, but the pizzazz lasts long. **Marlin Bar** (⊠ 1200 Collins Ave., ☎ 305/673–8770), in SoBe's Marlin Hotel, is Jamaican all the way, thanks to brilliant is-land decor and upbeat Caribbean music. Light meals, such as fried cala-mari, jerked foods, and coconut shrimp, are served.

In a nondescript motel row with nudie bars, baby stores, and bait-and-tackle shops, **Molly Malone's** (⊠ 166 Sunny Isles Blvd., ☎ 305/948–9143) is the only cool, down-to-earth spot that thrives in this neighborhood. The Irish pub, a big local fave, has a traditional Euro-pean look with oak paneling, live Irish music on Friday, and acoustic sounds Saturday. **Rose's Music Bar & Lounge** (⊠ 754 Washington Ave., ☎ 305/532–0228) has the best in local bands from Hendrix-style rock and rap/funk to jazz jams and Afro-Cuban/world beat, with the occasional national act. Though it doesn't take credit cards, there is an ATM. It's open seven nights, but it's packed Wednesday through Saturday.

Discos and Rock Clubs

KEY BISCAYNE

Stefano's of Key Biscayne (⊠ 24 Crandon Blvd., ☎ 305/361–7007) is a northern Italian restaurant with disco. The music is live Tuesday through Sunday, and there's a cover charge Fridays and Saturdays.

MIAMI BEACH

Amnesia (⊠ 136 Collins Ave., ☎ 305/531–5535) feels like a luxuri-ous amphitheater in the tropics, complete with rain forest, what used to be called go-go dancers, and frenzied dancing in the rain when showers pass over the open-air ground-level club. It's open Thurs-day–Sunday. **Bermuda Bar & Grille** (⊠ 3509 N.E. 163rd St., ☎ 305/945–0196) plays LOUD MUSIC for disco dancing. Male bartenders wear knee-length kilts, while female bartenders are in matching minis. The atmosphere and crowd, though, are stylish island casual, and there's a big tropical forest scene, booths you can hide in, and six bars and pool tables. One drawback is there's no draft brew. It's closed Mondays and Tuesdays.

Jazz Club

MIAMI BEACH

MoJazz Cafe (⊠ 928 71st St., ☎ 305/865–2636) combines a local café with real (nonfusion) jazz. It's in the Normandy Isle section—a long-overlooked neighborhood just right for hosting the occasional national name, like Mose Allison, and local talents worthy of national attention, like Ira Sullivan, Little Nicky, and Joe Donato. Highlights include a nightly happy hour, food from the country kitchen, and late-night breakfast. The club opens at 7 Tuesday–Sunday; music plays from 9 to 1, to 2 on Friday and Saturday.

Nightclubs

MIAMI

A reliable standby, **Les Violins Supper Club** (⊠ 1751 Biscayne Blvd., ☎ 305/371–8668) has been owned for decades by the Cachaidora-Currais family, who ran a club and restaurant in Havana. There's a live dance band and a wooden dance floor. The cover charge is $15, and reservations are essential.

MIAMI BEACH

The Fontainebleau Hilton's **Club Tropigala** (⊠ 4441 Collins Ave., ☎ 305/672–7469), lately discovered by such stars as Sylvester Stallone, Madonna, and Elton John, is a four-tier round room. Decorated with orchids, banana leaves, philodendrons, and cascading waterfalls, it feels like a tropical jungle. A 10-piece band plays standards as well as Latin music for dancing on the wooden floor. Reservations are essential, the $15 cover is a must, and gentlemen should wear jackets.

OUTDOOR ACTIVITIES AND SPORTS

In addition to contacting the addresses below directly, you can get tickets to major events from **Ticketmaster** (☎ 305/358–5885).

Auto Racing

Hialeah Speedway, the area's only independent raceway, holds stock-car races on a ⅓-mi asphalt oval in a 5,000-seat stadium. Five divisions of cars run weekly. The Marion Edwards, Jr., Memorial Race for late-model cars is held in November. The speedway is on U.S. 27, ¼ mi east of the Palmetto Expressway (Route 826). ⊠ 3300 W. Okeechobee Rd., Hialeah, ☎ 305/821–6644. ☞ $10, special events $12. ☉ Late Jan.–early Dec., Sat.; gates open at 5, racing 7–11.

Baseball

The Eastern Division **Florida Marlins** (⊠ 2267 N.W. 199th Street, Miami 33056, ☎ 305/626–7400) begin their fifth season in 1997, having made the National League division playoffs in 1996. Home games are played at the former Joe Robbie Stadium, renamed Pro Player Stadium, which is 16 mi northwest of downtown. On game days the Metro-Dade Transit Agency runs buses to the stadium.

Basketball

The **Miami Heat** (⊠ 1 S.E. 3rd Avenue, Miami 33131, ☎ 305/577–4328), Miami's NBA franchise, plays home games November–April at the Miami Arena, a block east of Overtown Metrorail Station.

Biking

A color-coded map outlining roads suitable for bike travel is available for $3.50 from area bike shops and from the **Dade County Bicycle Co-ordinator** (⊠ Metropolitan Planning Organization, 111 N.W. 1st St.,

Suite 910, Miami 33128, ☎ 305/375–4507). For information on dozens of monthly group rides, contact the **Everglades Bicycle Club** (✉ Box 430282, South Miami 33243-0282, ☎ 305/598–3998). As its name implies, **Dade Cycle** (✉ 3216 Grand Ave., Coconut Grove, ☎ 305/444–5997 or 305/443–6075) is one of the many county bike shops that rent cycles. **Gary's Megacycle on the Beach** (✉ 1260 Washington Ave., Miami Beach, ☎ 305/534–3306) is a South Beach rental source.

Boating

The popular **Crandon Park Marina** sells bait and tackle. ✉ *4000 Crandon Blvd., Key Biscayne,* ☎ *305/361–1281.* ☉ *Office 7–6.*

Named for an island where early settlers had picnics, **Dinner Key Marina** is Greater Miami's largest, with 581 moorings at nine piers. There is space for transients and a boat ramp. ✉ *3400 Pan American Dr., Coconut Grove,* ☎ *305/579–6980.* ☉ *Daily 7 AM–11 PM.*

Haulover Marine Center is low on glamour but high on service. It offers a bait-and-tackle shop, marine gas station, and boat launch. ✉ *15000 Collins Ave., Miami Beach,* ☎ *305/945–3934.* ☉ *Bait shop and gas station daily 8–6.*

A "happening" waterfront mecca, **Miami Beach Marina** has restaurants, charters, boat and vehicle rentals, a complete marine hardware store, dive shop and excursions, large grocery store, fuel dock, concierge services, and 400 slips accommodating vessels up to 190 feet. Facilities include air-conditioned rest rooms, washers and dryers, U.S. Customs clearing, and a heated pool. This is the nearest marina to the Deco District, about a 15-minute walk away. ✉ *300 Alton Rd., Miami Beach,* ☎ *305/673–6000,* 𝖥𝖠𝖷 *305/538–1780.* ☉ *Daily 8–6.*

Dog Racing

The Biscayne and Flagler greyhound tracks divide the annual racing calendar. Check with the individual tracks for dates.

At **Biscayne Greyhound Track,** greyhounds chase a mechanical rabbit around illuminated fountains in the track's infield. ✉ *320 N.W. 115th St., near I–95, Miami Shores,* ☎ *954/927–6027.* ⬚ *Table seats and grandstand $1, sports room $2, clubhouse $3, parking 50¢–$2.*

In the middle of Little Havana, **Flagler Greyhound Track** is five minutes east of Miami International Airport, off the Dolphin Expressway (Route 836) and Douglas Road (Northwest 37th Avenue). Closed-circuit TV brings harness-racing action here as well. ✉ *401 N.W. 38th Ct., Miami,* ☎ *305/649–3000.* ⬚ *$1, clubhouse $3, parking 50¢–$2.* ☉ *Racing daily 7:30, plus Tues., Wed., and Sat. 12:30.*

Fishing

Before there was fashion, there was fishing. Deep-sea fishing is still a major draw, and anglers drop a line for sailfish, kingfish, dolphin, snapper, grouper, and tuna. Smaller charter boats can cost $350–$400 for a half day, so you might be better off paying around $25 for passage on a larger fishing boat. Rarely are they filled to capacity. Nearby general stores sell essentials such as fuel, tackle, sunglasses, and beer. Don't let them sell you a fishing license, however; a blanket license should cover all passengers.

Many ocean-fishing charters sail out of **Haulover Marina** (✉ 10800 Collins Ave., Miami Beach), including **Blue Waters Sportfishing Charters** (☎ 305/944–4531), **Kelley Fleet** (☎ 305/945–3801), and *Therapy IV* (☎ 305/945–1578). **Reward Fleet** (✉ 300 Alton Rd., MacArthur Causeway, Miami Beach, ☎ 305/372–9470, 𝖥𝖠𝖷 305/372–1160) operates out of Miami Beach Marina.

Football

Despite the resignation of legendary coach Don Shula, fans keep coming to watch the NFL's **Miami Dolphins**—probably still waiting for a repeat of the 17–0 record of 1972 (a record that still stands). The team plays at the former Joe Robbie Stadium, renamed Pro Player Stadium in honor of a sports apparel company and a $20 million check. The state-of-the-art stadium, which has 75,000 seats and a grass playing surface, is on a 160-acre site 16 mi northwest of downtown Miami, 1 mi south of the Dade–Broward county line and accessible from I–95 and Florida's Turnpike. On game days the Metro-Dade Transit Agency runs buses to the stadium. ⊠ *Pro Player Stadium, 2269 N.W. 199th St., Miami 33056,* ☎ *305/620–2578.* ☉ *Box office weekdays 10–6, also Sat. during season.*

After calling the venerable Orange Bowl home for many years, the **University of Miami Hurricanes** (⊠ 1 Hurricane Dr., Coral Gables 33146, ☎ 305/284–2263), perennial contenders for the top collegiate ranking, are playing their 1997 home games at Pro Player Stadium (☞ *above*) from September to November.

Golf

For information on Miami's private and public golf courses contact the appropriate parks-and-recreation department: City of Miami (☎ 305/575–5256), City of Miami Beach (☎ 305/673–7730), or Metro-Dade County (☎ 305/857–6868).

The 18-hole **Biltmore Golf Course** (⊠ 1210 Anastasia Ave., Coral Gables, ☎ 305/460–5364), known for its scenic layout, has been restored to its original Donald Ross design, circa 1925. The gorgeous hotel makes a scenic backdrop. **Don Shula's Hotel & Golf Club** (⊠ 7601 Miami Lakes Dr., Miami Lakes, ☎ 305/821–1150) has one of the longest championship courses in Miami (7,055 yards), a lighted par-3 course, and a golf school. With four championship and one executive courses, **Doral Golf Resort and Spa** (⊠ 4400 N.W. 87th Ave., Doral, ☎ 305/592–2000 or 800/713–6725) is known for the "Blue Monster" course and the annual Doral-Ryder Open Tournament, with $2 million in prize money. Overlooking the bay, the **Links at Key Biscayne** (⊠ 6700 Crandon Blvd., Key Biscayne, ☎ 305/361–9129) is a top-rated public course. **Normandy Shores Golf Course** (⊠ 2401 Biarritz Dr., Miami Beach, ☎ 305/868–6502) is good for seniors, with modest slopes and average distances. **Presidential Country Club** (⊠ 19650 N.E. 18th Ave., North Miami Beach, ☎ 305/933–5266) offers a nice landscape as well as a snack bar and restaurant. **Turnberry Isle Resort & Club** (⊠ 19999 W. Country Club Dr., Aventura, ☎ 305/933–6929) has 36 holes designed by Robert Trent Jones. **Williams Island California Club** (⊠ 20898 San Simeon Way, North Miami Beach, ☎ 305/651–3590) has an 18-hole course made challenging by a tight front nine and three of the area's toughest finishing holes.

Horse Racing

Calder Race Course, opened in 1971, is Florida's largest glass-enclosed, air-conditioned sports facility. It often has an unusually extended season, from late May to early January, though it's a good idea to call the track for specific starting and wrap-up dates. Calder and Hialeah Park rotate their race dates, so be sure to check with each park to see where the horses are running. Each year between November and early January, Calder holds the Tropical Park Derby for three-year-olds. The track is on the Dade–Broward county line near I–95 and the Hallandale Beach Boulevard exit, ¾ mi from Pro Player Stadium. ⊠ *21001*

N.W. 27th Ave., Miami, ☎ 305/625–1311. ☒ $2, clubhouse $4, parking $1–$3. ☉ Gates open at 11, racing 1–5:30.

A superb setting for Thoroughbred racing, **Hialeah Park** has 228 acres of meticulously landscaped grounds surrounding paddocks, and a clubhouse built in a classic French-Mediterranean style. Since it opened in 1925, Hialeah Park has survived hurricanes and now seems likely to survive even changing demographics, as the racetrack crowd has steadily moved north and east. Although Hialeah tends to get the less prestigious racing dates from March to May, it still draws crowds. The park is open year-round for free sightseeing, during which you can explore the gardens and admire the park's breeding flock of 800 Cuban flamingos. Metrorail's Hialeah Station is on the grounds. ☒ 2200 E. 4th Ave., Hialeah, ☎ 305/885–8000. ☒ Weekdays grandstand $1, clubhouse $2; weekends grandstand $4, clubhouse $4; parking $1–$4. ☉ Gates open at 10:30, racing 1–5:30.

Ice Hockey

The NHL **Florida Panthers** made the playoffs in their inaugural season and were Eastern Conference champs in 1995–96—no mean feat for a city where the only ice you see is in mixed drinks. The team plays at the Miami Arena, a block east of Overtown Metrorail Station, but is scheduled to move to Broward county in 1998. ☒ Miami Arena, 701 Arena Blvd., Miami 33136-4102, ☎ 954/768–1900.

Jai Alai

Built in 1926, the **Miami Jai-Alai Fronton,** a mile east of the airport, is America's oldest fronton. It presents 13 games—14 on Friday and Saturday—some singles, some doubles. This game, invented in the Basque region of northern Spain, is the world's fastest. Jai-alai balls, called *pelotas*, have been clocked at speeds exceeding 170 mph. The game is played in a 176-foot-long court, and players literally climb the walls to catch the ball in a *cesta*—a woven basket—with an attached glove. You can bet on a team to win or on the order in which teams will finish. Dinner is available. ☒ 3500 N.W. 37th Ave., Miami, ☎ 305/633–6400. ☒ $1, reserved seats $3, Courtview Club $5. ☉ Mon., Wed., Fri., and Sat. noon–5 and 7–midnight; Thurs. 7–midnight.

Jogging

Try these recommended jogging routes: in Coconut Grove, along the pedestrian/bicycle path on South Bayshore Drive, cutting over the causeway to Key Biscayne for a longer run; from the south shore of the Miami River, downtown, south along the sidewalks of Brickell Avenue to Bayshore Drive, where you can run alongside the bay; in Miami Beach, along Bay Road (parallel to Alton Road) or on the sidewalk skirting the Atlantic Ocean, opposite the cafés of Ocean Drive; and in Coral Gables, around the Riviera Country Club golf course, just south of the Biltmore Country Club. A good source of running information is the **Miami Runners Club** (☒ 7920 S.W. 40th St., Miami, ☎ 305/227–1500). **Foot Works** (☒ 5724 Sunset Dr., South Miami, ☎ 305/667–9322), a running-shoe store, is a good resource as well.

Scuba Diving

Bubbles Dive Center is an all-purpose dive shop with PADI affiliation. Its boat, *Divers Dream*, is kept on Watson Island on MacArthur Causeway. ☒ 2671 S.W. 27th Ave., Miami, ☎ 305/856–0565. ☉ Weekdays 10–7, Sat. 9–6.

Divers Paradise of Key Biscayne has a complete dive shop and diving-charter service, including equipment rental and scuba instruction, with

PADI affiliation. ✉ *4000 Crandon Blvd., Key Biscayne,* ☎ *305/361–3483.* ⊙ *Weekdays 10–6, weekends 7:30–6.*

The PADI-affiliated **Diving Locker** offers three-day and three-week Professional Diving Instructors Corporation certification courses, wreck and reef dives aboard the *Native Diver,* and full sales, service, and repairs. ✉ *223 Sunny Isles Blvd., North Miami Beach,* ☎ *305/947–6025,* FAX *305/947–2236.* ⊙ *Weekdays 9–9:30, Sat. 8–9:30, Sun. 8–6.*

Tennis

Greater Miami has more than a dozen tennis centers open to the public. Across Dade County, nearly 500 public courts are open to visitors; nonresidents are charged an hourly fee.

Biltmore Tennis Center has 10 hard courts. ✉ *1150 Anastasia Ave., Coral Gables,* ☎ *305/460–5360.* ☞ *Day rate $4.30, night rate $5 per person per hour.* ⊙ *Weekdays 8 AM–9 PM, weekends 8–8.*

Very popular with locals, **Flamingo Tennis Center** has 19 clay courts. ✉ *1000 12th St., Miami Beach,* ☎ *305/673–7761.* ☞ *Day rate $2.67, night rate $3.20 per person per hour.* ⊙ *Weekdays 8 AM–9 PM, weekends 8–8.*

North Shore Tennis Center has 6 clay and 5 hard courts. ✉ *350 73rd St., Miami Beach,* ☎ *305/993–2022.* ☞ *Day rate $2.66, night rate $3.20 per person per hour.* ⊙ *Weekdays 8 AM–9 PM, weekends 8–7.*

The new $18 million, 30-acre **Tennis Center at Crandon Park** is one of America's best. Included are two grass, eight clay, and 17 hard courts. Reservations are required for night play. The only time courts are closed to the public is during the **Lipton Championships** (☎ 305/442–3367), held for 10 days each spring. The tournament is one of the largest in the world in terms of attendance and, with $4.5 million in prize money in 1997, had the fifth-largest purse—enough to attract players like Agassi, Graf, Sampras, and Courier. It's played in a 14,000-seat stadium. ✉ *7300 Crandon Blvd., Key Biscayne,* ☎ *305/365–2300.* ☞ *Laykold courts day rate $3, night rate $5 per person per hour; clay courts $6 per person per hour.* ⊙ *Daily 8 AM–10 PM.*

Windsurfing

New lightweight boards and smaller sails make learning windsurfing easy. The safest and most popular windsurfing area in city waters is south of town at Windsurfer Beach, around Virginia Key and Key Biscayne. Miami Beach's best windsurfing is at 1st Street just north of the Government Cut jetty and at 21st Street. You can also windsurf from Lummus Park at 10th Street and around 3rd, 14th, and 21st streets.

Sailboards Miami, just past the tollbooth for the Rickenbacker Causeway, rents equipment and is the largest windsurfing school in the United States. It offers year-round lessons and a claim to teach anyone within two hours. ✉ *Key Biscayne,* ☎ *305/361–7245.* ☞ *1 hour $20, 10 hours $130, 2-hour lesson $49.* ⊙ *Daily 10–6.*

SHOPPING

Malls

Aventura Mall (✉ 19501 Biscayne Blvd., Aventura, ☎ 305/935–1110), in a northern suburb that became Dade's 28th municipality in 1995, has more than 200 shops anchored by Macy's, Lord & Taylor, JCPenney, Sears, and a Bloomingdale's set to open in late 1997. In a tropical garden setting, **Bal Harbour Shops** (✉ 9700 Collins Ave., Bal

Harbour, ☎ 305/866–0311) is a swank collection of 100 shops and boutiques such as Chanel, Gucci, Cartier, Nina Ricci, Fendi, Bruno Magli, Neiman Marcus, and Florida's largest Saks Fifth Avenue. It was named by fashionable *Elle* magazine as one of the top five shopping collections in the United States. Free buses run twice a day Monday–Saturday from several hotels in Coconut Grove, downtown Miami, and Miami Beach. **Bayside Marketplace** (⊠ 401 Biscayne Blvd., Miami, ☎ 305/577–3344), the 16-acre shopping complex on Biscayne Bay, has 150 specialty shops, entertainment, tour-boat docks, and a food court. It's open late (10 during the week, 11 on Friday and Saturday), but its restaurants stay open even later.

A complex of clapboard, coral-rock, and stucco buildings, **Cauley Square** (⊠ 22400 Old Dixie Hwy., Goulds, ☎ 305/258–3543) was erected in 1907–20 for railroad workers who built and maintained the line to Key West. Although beaten up by Andrew, the stores—primarily crafts and antiques shops—are back in business. **CocoWalk** (⊠ 3015 Grand Ave., Coconut Grove, ☎ 305/441–0777, FAX 305/441–8936) has three floors of nearly 40 specialty shops (Victoria's Secret, the Gap, Banana Republic, among others) that stay open almost as late as the popular restaurants and clubs. A 16-screen theater is also here. If you're ready for an evening of people-watching, this is the place.

The oldest retail mall in the county, **Dadeland** (⊠ 7535 N. Kendall Dr., Miami, ☎ 305/665–6226) is always upgrading. It sits at the south side of town close to the Dadeland North and Dadeland South Metrorail stations. Retailers include Saks Fifth Avenue, JCPenney, Lord & Taylor, more than 175 specialty stores, 17 restaurants, and the largest Burdines, the Limited, and Limited Express in Florida. **The Falls** (⊠ 8888 S.W. 136th St., at U.S. 1, Miami, ☎ 305/255–4570), which derives its name from the several waterfalls inside, is the most upscale mall on the south side of the city. It contains a Macy's as well as another 50 specialty stores, restaurants, and a 12-theater multiplex.

Omni International Mall (⊠ 1601 Biscayne Blvd., Miami, ☎ 305/374–6664) rises vertically alongside the atrium of the Crowne Plaza Miami, whose eye-popping feature is an old-fashioned carousel. Among the 85 shops are a JCPenney, many restaurants, and 10 movie screens. The shortest and most elegant shopping arcade in the metropolis, the **Shops at 550** (⊠ 550 Biltmore Way, Coral Gables) is in the marble halls of the Aztec-like 550 Building.

Outdoor Markets

Coconut Grove Farmers Market (⊠ Grand Ave., 1 block west of MacDonald Ave. [S.W. 32nd Ave.], Coconut Grove), open Saturday 8–2, originated in 1977 and was the first in the Miami area. The **Espanola Way Market** (⊠ Espanola Way, Miami Beach), Sundays noon–9, is one of the city's newest and most entertaining markets. Scattered among the handcrafted items and flea market merchandise, musicians beat out Latin rhythms on bongos, conga drums, steel drums, and guitars. Food vendors sell inexpensive Latin snacks and drinks. Each Saturday morning from mid-January to late March, some 25 produce and plant vendors sell herbs, fruits, fresh-squeezed juices, chutneys, cakes, and muffins at the **Farmers Market at Merrick Park** (⊠ LeJeune Rd. [S.W. 42nd Ave.] and Biltmore Way, Coral Gables). Regular features include gardening workshops, children's activities, and cooking demonstrations offered by Coral Gables's master chefs. More than 500 vendors sell a variety of goods at the **Flagler Dog Track** (⊠ 401 N.W. 38th Ct., Miami), every weekend 9–4. **Lincoln Road Farmers Market** (⊠ Lincoln Rd. between Meridian and Euclid Aves., Miami Beach), open Sundays

November–March, brings about 15 local produce vendors coupled with plant workshops and children's activities.

Shopping Districts

There are 500 garment manufacturers in Miami and Hialeah, and many sell their clothing locally in the **Miami Fashion District** (⊠ 5th Ave. east of I–95, between 25th and 29th Sts., Miami), making Greater Miami the fashion marketplace for the southeastern United States, the Caribbean, and Latin America. Most of the more than 30 factory outlets and discount fashion stores are open Monday–Saturday 9–5. The **Miami International Arts and Design District** (⊠ Between N.E. 38th and N.E. 42nd Sts. and between Federal Hwy. and N. Miami Ave., Miami), also known as 40th Street, is full of showrooms and galleries specializing in interior furnishings and decorative arts. **Miracle Mile** (⊠ Coral Way between 37th and 42nd Aves., Coral Gables) consists of some 160 shops along a wide, tree-lined boulevard. Shops range from posh boutiques to bargain basements, from beauty salons to chain restaurants. As you go west, the quality increases.

Specialty Stores

ANTIQUES

Alhambra Antiques Center (⊠ 3640 Coral Way, Coral Gables ☎ 305/446–1688) is a collection of four antiques dealers that sell high-quality decorative pieces from Europe.

BOOKS

Although it's part of a chain, **Barnes and Noble** (⊠ 152 Miracle Mile, Coral Gables, ☎ 305/446–4152) has managed to preserve the essence of a neighborhood bookstore. Customers can pick a book off the shelf and lounge on a couch without being hassled. A well-stocked magazine and national/international news rack and an espresso bar complete the effect. Greater Miami's best English-language bookstore, **Books & Books, Inc** (⊠ 296 Aragon Ave., Coral Gables, ☎ 305/442–4408; ⊠ Sterling Bldg., 933 Lincoln Rd., Miami Beach, ☎ 305/532–3222) specializes in books on the arts, architecture, Florida, and contemporary and classical literature. At the Coral Gables location, collectors enjoy browsing through the rare-book room upstairs, which doubles as a photography gallery. There are frequent poetry readings and book signings. If being in the Grove prompts you to don a beret, grow a goatee, and sift through a volume of Kerouac, head to **Border's** (⊠ Grand Ave. and Mary St., Coconut Grove, ☎ 305/447–1655). Its 100,000 book titles, 50,000 CDs, and more than 2,000 periodicals and newspapers in 10 languages from 15 different countries make it seem like the southern branch of the Library of Congress.

CHILDREN'S BOOKS AND TOYS

A Kid's Book & Toy Shoppe (⊠ 1895 N.E. Miami Gardens Dr., Skylake Center, North Miami Beach, ☎ 305/937–2665) is an excellent resource on children's books and educational toys. **A Likely Story** (⊠ 5740 Sunset Dr., South Miami, ☎ 305/667–3730) has been helping Miamians choose books and educational toys appropriate to children's interests and stages of development since 1978.

CIGARS

Although Tampa is Florida's true cigar capital, Miami's Latin population is giving it a run for its money. Smoking anything even remotely affiliated with a legendary Cuban has boosted the popularity of Miami cigar stores and the small shops where you can buy cigars straight from the press.

A celebration of Cuban culture, **Babalu** (⊠ 432 Espanola Way, Miami Beach, ☎ 305/538–0679) sells postcards, books, and crafts. To complete the effect, owner Heriberto Sosa has dedicated part of his shop to producing hand-rolled cigars from the petite $3 Palm Gold to the $7 Churchill and $9 Imperial Gold. Although you can also buy a Babalu at Bloomingdale's, it's more fun here. The **Cigar Connection** (⌑ 534 Lincoln Road Mall, Miami Beach, ☎ 305/531–7373, ℻ 305/531–0501) is hoping to capture the trendy tastes of pedestrians strolling on Lincoln Road. Carrying such premium cigars as the Arturo Fuente Opus X and Paul Garmirians, the shop also serves cognac, coffees, and cappuccino. In the heart of Little Havana, **El Credito** (1106 S.W. 8th St., Miami, ☎ 305/858–4162 or 800/726–9481, ℻ 305/858–3810) seems to have been transported from the Cuban capital lock, stock, and stogie. Rows of workers at wooden benches rip through giant tobacco leaves, cut them with rounded blades, wrap them tightly, and press them in vises. Dedicated smokers like Robert DeNiro, Gregory Hines, and George Hamilton have found their way here to pick up a $90 bundle or peruse the *gigantes, supremos,* panatelas, and Churchills available in natural or maduro wrappers.

Havana Ray's (⌑ 3399 Virginia St., Coconut Grove, ☎ 305/446–4003 or 800/732–4427, ℻ 305/558–6512) continues a cigar-making dynasty that began in 1920s Cuba. The Quirantes family's devotion to cigars has resulted in this cozy shop where you can buy cigars and related accouterments. **South Beach News and Tobacco** (⌑ 710 Washington Ave. #9, Miami Beach, ☎ 305/673–3002, ℻ 305/532–1004) has expanded beyond simple cigars to carry imported wines and beers, gourmet espresso and coffee, and international newspapers and magazines. But the real draw is cigars made on premises or imported from the Dominican Republic, Nicaragua, and Honduras.

COLLECTIBLES

Gotta Have It! Collectibles (⌑ 504 Biltmore Way, Coral Gables, ☎ 305/446–5757, ℻ 305/446–6276) will make fans of any kind break out in a cold sweat. Autographed sports jerseys, canceled checks from the estate of Marilyn Monroe, fabulously framed album jackets signed by the four Beatles, and an elaborate autographed montage of all the *Wizard of Oz* stars are among this intriguing shop's museum-quality collectibles. Looking for an Einstein autograph? A Jack Nicklaus–signed scorecard? Look no further. And if they don't have the autograph you desire, fear not—they'll track one down.

DECORATIVE AND GIFT ITEMS

American Details (⌑ 3107 Grand Ave., Coconut Grove, ☎ 305/448–6163) sells colorful, trendy arts and crafts handmade by American artists. Jewelry and handblown glass are popular sellers. The **Indies Company** (⌑ 101 W. Flagler St., Miami, ☎ 305/375–1492), the Historical Museum of Southern Florida's gift shop, offers interesting artifacts reflecting Miami's history, including some inexpensive reproductions. A collection of books on Miami and South Florida is impressive.

JEWELRY

Stones of Venice (⌑ 550 Biltmore Way, Coral Gables, ☎ 305/444–4474), operated by a three-time winner of the DeBeers Diamond Award for jewelry, sells affordable creations. Customers have included Elliott Gould, Pope John Paul II, and film director Barbet Schroeder.

SIDE TRIP

South Dade

Although the population of these suburbs southwest of Dade County's urban core was largely dislocated by Hurricane Andrew in 1992, little damage is evident today. Indeed, FEMA grants and major replanting have made the area better than ever. All attractions—which are especially interesting for kids—have reopened, and a complete exploration of them would probably take two days. Keep an eye open for hand-painted signs announcing agricultural attractions, such as orchid farms, fruit stands, u-pick farms, and horseback riding.

🐚 ❺❽ Aviation enthusiasts touch down at **Weeks Air Museum** to view some 25 planes of WW II vintage. Sadly, Hurricane Andrew destroyed the WW I aircraft, and WW II suffered damage as well. By late 1997, the B-17 Flying Fortress bomber and P-51 Mustang should be back on display. The museum is inside the Tamiami Airport. ✉ *14710 S.W. 128th St.,* ☎ *305/233–5197.* 🎫 *$6.95.* ⊙ *Daily 10–5.*

🐚 ❺❾ One of the only zoos in America in a subtropical environment, the first-class, 290-acre **Metrozoo** is state-of-the-art. Inside the cageless zoo, some 1,000 animals roam on islands surrounded by moats. Major attractions include the Tiger Temple, where white tigers roam, and the African Plains exhibit, where giraffes, ostriches, and zebras graze in a simulated habitat. Paws, a petting zoo for children, features three shows daily; during the Wildlife Show, trained animals demonstrate natural behavior on cue. Kids can touch Florida animals such as alligators and possums at the Ecology Theater. ✉ *12400 Coral Reef Dr. (S.W. 152nd St.),* ☎ *305/251–0401 or 305/251–0400.* 🎫 *$8, 45-min. tram tour $2.* ⊙ *Daily 9:30–5:30, last admission at 4.*

🐚 ❻⓪ Historic railroad cars on display at the **Gold Coast Railroad Museum** include a 1949 *Silver Crescent* dome car and the *Ferdinand Magellan,* the only Pullman car constructed specifically for U.S. presidents. It was used by Franklin Delano Roosevelt, Harry Truman, Dwight Eisenhower, and Ronald Reagan. A train ride is included in the price of admission to the museum, which is next to the zoo. ✉ *12450 Coral Reef Dr. (S.W. 152nd St.),* ☎ *305/253–0063.* 🎫 *$4.* ⊙ *Weekdays 11–3, weekends 11–4.*

🐚 ❻❶ Home to more than 300 monkeys representing 25 species—including orangutans from Borneo and Sumatra and golden lion tamarins from Brazil—**Monkey Jungle** is high on kids' lists of things to do. The park's rain forest trail, damaged in the hurricane, reopened in 1996. Four different performing-monkey shows begin at 10 and run continuously at 30-minute intervals. The walkways of this 30-acre attraction are caged; the monkeys roam free. ✉ *14805 Hainlin Mill Dr. (S.W. 216th St.),* ☎ *305/235–1611.* 🎫 *$11.50.* ⊙ *Daily 9:30–5, last admission at 4.*

❻❷ The 30-acre **Redland Fruit & Spice Park** has been a Dade County treasure since 1944, when it was opened as a 20-acre showcase of tropical fruits and vegetables. Two of the park's three historic buildings were ruined by the hurricane, as well as about half of its trees and plants, but relandscaping has begun and the park has reopened. Plants are now grouped by country of origin and include more than 500 economically important varieties of exotic fruits, herbs, spices, nuts, and poisonous plants from around the world. A sampling reveals 65 types of bananas, 40 varieties of grapes, and 100 kinds of citrus. A gourmet-and-fruit shop offers many varieties of tropical-fruit products, jellies, seeds, aromatic teas, and reference books. ✉ *24801 Redland Rd. (S.W. 187th Ave.),* ☎ *305/247–5727.* 🎫 *$1, guided tour $1.50.* ⊙ *Daily 10–5, tours weekends at 1 and 3.*

🐚 ❻❸ **Coral Castle of Florida** was born when 26-year-old Edward Leedskalnin, a Latvian immigrant, was left at the altar by his 16-year-old fiancée. She went on with her life, while he went off the deep end and began carving a castle out of coral rock. Built between 1920 and 1940,

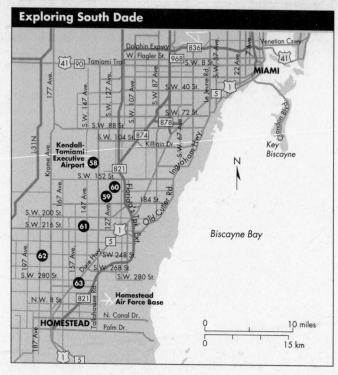

Exploring South Dade

the 3-acre castle is one of South Florida's original tourist attractions. There is a 9-ton gate a child can open (expected to function again in 1997), an accurate working sundial, and a telescope of coral rock aimed at the North Star. ⊠ *28655 S. Dixie Hwy.,* ☎ *305/248–6344.* ⊡ *$7.75.* ⊙ *Daily 9–6.*

MIAMI AND MIAMI BEACH A TO Z

Arriving and Departing

By Boat
If you enter the United States along the Atlantic Coast south of Sebastian Inlet, you must call the **U.S. Customs Service** (☎ 305/536–5263). Customs clears by phone most boats of less than 5 tons, but you may be directed to a marina for inspection.

By Bus
Greyhound (☎ 800/231–2222) buses stop at four terminals in Greater Miami (⊠ 700 Biscayne Blvd., Miami; ⊠ 4111 N.W. 27th St., Miami; ⊠ 16560 N.E. 6th Ave. North Miami; ⊠ 20505 S. Dixie Highway, South Miami) and at Miami International Airport.

By Car
The main highways into Greater Miami from the north are Florida's Turnpike (a toll road) and I–95. From the northwest take I–75 or U.S. 27 into town. From the Everglades, to the west, use the Tamiami Trail (U.S. 41), and from the south use U.S. 1 and the Homestead Extension of Florida's Turnpike.

Continuous reconstruction of I–95 forever slows traffic at one place or another. A three- to four-year repaving project will keep I–95 from operating at peak capacity through most of the decade.

By Plane

Miami International Airport (MIA, ☎ 305/876–7000), 6 mi west of downtown Miami, is the only airport in Greater Miami that provides scheduled service. With a daily average of 1,580 flights, it handled 33.2 million passengers in 1995, more than half of them international travelers. MIA is also the nation's busiest airport for air cargo and third in the world for transporting international freight. Altogether 136 airlines serve 200 cities and five continents with nonstop or one-stop service. MIA has 102 aircraft gates and eight concourses.

Anticipating continued growth, the airport has begun a more than $8 billion expansion program that will require much of the decade to complete. Passengers will mainly notice rebuilt and expanded gate and public areas, which should reduce congestion.

A greatly underused convenience for passengers who have to get from one concourse to another in this long, horseshoe-shape terminal is the Moving Walkway, on the skywalk level, with access points at every concourse. Also available on site is the 230-room **Miami International Airport Hotel** (⊠ Concourse E, upper level, ☎ 305/871–4100), which has the Top of the Port restaurant on the seventh floor and Port Lounge on the eighth. MIA, the first to offer duty-free shops, now boasts 14, carrying liquors, perfumes, electronics, and various designer goods.

Heightened security at MIA has meant that it's suggested you check in 90 minutes before departure for a domestic flight, two hours for an international flight. Services for international travelers include 24-hour multilingual information and paging phones and currency conversion booths throughout the terminal. There is an information booth with a multilingual staff and 24-hour currency exchange at the entrance of Concourse E on the upper level. Other tourist information centers are at the customs exit, Concourse E, lower level (⊗ daily 5 AM–11 PM); customs exit, Concourse B, second level (⊗ daily 11–11); Concourse G, lower level (⊗ daily 11–7); Concourse D, lower level (⊗ daily 11–11); and Satellite Terminal (⊗ daily 11–7).

Airlines that fly into MIA include **ACES** (☎ 305/265–1272), **Aero Costa Rica** (☎ 800/237–6274), **Aeroflot** (☎ 800/995–5555), **Aerolineas Argentinas** (☎ 800/333–0276), **Aeromexico** (☎ 800/237–6639), **AeroPeru** (☎ 800/777–7717), **Air Aruba** (☎ 800/882–7822), **Air Canada** (☎ 800/776–3000), **Air France** (☎ 800/237–2747), **Air Jamaica** (☎ 800/523–5585), **Air South** (☎ 800/247–7688), **Alitalia** (☎ 800/223–5730), **ALM** (☎ 800/327–7230), **American** and **American Eagle** (☎ 800/433–7300), **American TransAir** (☎ 800/225–2995), **APA** (☎ 305/374–1299), **Avensa** (☎ 800/428–3672), **Avianca** (☎ 800/284–2622), **Aviateca** (☎ 800/327–9832), **Bahamasair** (☎ 800/222–4262), **British Airways** (☎ 800/247–9297), **BWIA** (☎ 305/371–2942), **Carnival** (☎ 800/437–2110), **Cayman Airways** (☎ 800/422–9626), **Comair** (☎ 800/354–9822), **Continental** (☎ 800/525–0280), **Copa** (☎ 800/359–2672), **Delta** (☎ 800/221–1212), **El Al** (☎ 800/223–6700), **Faucett** (☎ 800/334–3356), **Finnair** (☎ 800/950–5000), **Gulfstream International** (☎ 800/992–8532), **Guyana Airways** (☎ 800/242–4210), **Iberia** (☎ 800/772–4642), **LAB** (☎ 800/327–7407), **Lacsa** (☎ 800/225–2272), **Lan Chile** (☎ 800/735–5526), **Lauda Air** (☎ 800/645–3880), **LTU** (☎ 800/888–0200), **Lufthansa** (☎ 800/645–3880), **Martinair Holland** (☎ 800/366–4655), **Mexicana** (☎ 800/531–7921), **Northwest** (☎ 800/225–2525), **Paradise Island** (☎ 800/786–7202), **Saeta** (☎ 800/827–2382), **Sahsa** (☎ 800/327–1225), **Servivensa** (☎ 800/428–3672), **South African Airways** (☎ 800/722–9675), **Surinam Airways** (☎ 800/432–1230), **Taca** (☎ 800/535–8780), **Tower Air** (☎

800/348–6937), **Transbrasil** (☎ 800/872–3153), **TWA** (☎ 800/221–2000), **United** (☎ 800/241–6522), **US Airways** and **US Airways Express** (☎ 800/428–4322), **ValuJet** (☎ 800/825–8538), **Varig** (☎ 800/468–2744), **VASP** (☎ 800/732–8277), **Viasa** (☎ 800/468–4272), **Virgin Atlantic** (☎ 800/862–8621), and **Zuliana** (☎ 800/223–8780).

Pan Am Air Bridge (✉ 1000 MacArthur Causeway, Miami, ☎ 305/371–8628 or 800/424–2557, FAX 305/359–5240) is starting over where the original Pan Am began—with seaplane flights. They depart from Watson Island for Bimini, Key West, and the Bahamas, but be warned: They don't offer much room.

BETWEEN THE AIRPORT AND CENTER CITY

By Bus: The county's **Metrobus** (☎ 305/638–6700) still costs $1.25, though equipment has improved. From the airport you can take Bus 7 to downtown (weekdays 5:30 AM–9 PM every 40 minutes; weekends 6:30 AM–7:30 PM every 40 minutes), Bus 37 south to Coral Gables and South Miami (6 AM–11:30 PM every 30 minutes) or north to Hialeah (5:30 AM–11:30 PM every 30 minutes), Bus J south to Coral Gables (6 AM–12:30 AM every 30 minutes) or east to Miami Beach (4:30 AM–11:30 PM every 30 minutes), and Bus 42 to Coconut Grove (5:30 AM–7:20 PM hourly).

By Limousine: Miami, where it seems everyone is on stage, has more than 100 limousine services, though they're frequently in and out of business. If you rely on the Yellow Pages, look for a company with a street address, not just a phone. Offering 24-hour service, **Club Limousine Service** (✉ 11055 Biscayne Blvd., Miami 33161, ☎ 305/893–9850 or 800/824–4820; in FL, 800/325–9834) has shuttle vans as well as limos. One of the oldest companies in town is **Vintage Rolls Royce Limousines of Coral Gables** (✉ 4501 Monserrate St., Coral Gables 33146, ☎ 305/444–7657 or 800/888–7657, FAX 305/661–7402), which operates a 24-hour reservation service and provides chauffeurs for privately owned cars.

By Rental Car: Six rental-car firms—**Avis** (☎ 800/331–1212), **Budget** (☎ 800/527–0700), **Dollar** (☎ 800/800–4000), **Hertz** (☎ 800/654–3131), **National** (☎ 800/227–7368), and **Value** (☎ 800/468–2583)—have booths near the baggage-claim area on MIA's lower level.

By Taxi: Except for the flat-fare trips described below, cabs cost $1.70 per mile plus a $1 toll for trips originating at MIA or the Port of Miami. Approximate fares from MIA include $17 to Coral Gables, $20–$27 to downtown Miami, and $30–$35 to Key Biscayne. Fares to the beaches are $40–$45 to Golden Beach and Sunny Isles, north of Haulover Beach Park; $32 from Surfside through Haulover Beach Park; $27 between 63rd and 87th streets; and $22 from 63rd Street south to the foot of Miami Beach. These fares are per trip, not per passenger, and include tolls and $1 airport surcharge but not tip. The approximate fare between MIA and the Port of Miami is $15.75.

For taxi service to destinations in the immediate vicinity, ask a uniformed county taxi dispatcher to call an **ARTS** (Airport Region Taxi Service) cab for you. These special blue cabs offer a short-haul flat fare in two zones. An inner-zone ride is $5.60; the outer-zone fare is $9. The area of service is north to 36th Street, west to the Palmetto Expressway (77th Avenue), south to Northwest 7th Street, and east to Douglas Road (37th Avenue). Maps are posted in cab windows on both sides.

By Van: SuperShuttle (from MIA, ☎ 305/871–2000; from Broward [Fort Lauderdale], ☎ 954/764–1700; from elsewhere, 800/874–8885) vans transport passengers between MIA and local hotels, the Port of

Miami, and even individual residences on a 24-hour basis. The company's service area extends from Palm Beach to Monroe County (including the Lower Keys). Drivers provide narration en route. Service from MIA is available around the clock, on demand; for the return it's best to make reservations 24 hours in advance, although the firm will try to arrange pickups within Dade County on as little as four hours' notice. The cost from MIA to downtown hotels runs $8–$11. Additional members of a party pay a lower rate for many destinations, and children under four ride free with their parents. There's a pet transport fee of $5 for animals in kennels.

By Train

Amtrak (☎ 800/872–7245) runs three trains daily between New York City and Miami (⊠ 8303 N.W. 37th Ave.; ☎ 305/835–1221 for recorded arrival and departure information; ☎ 800/368–8725 for shipping); the trains make different stops along the way.

Tri-Rail (⊠ 1 River Plaza, 305 S. Andrews Ave., Suite 200, Fort Lauderdale, ☎ 800/874–7245) is Florida's only commuter train system. Daily runs connect Miami with Broward and Palm Beach, stopping at 18 stations along the 70-mi route. Fares are established by zones, with prices ranging from $2 to a high of $9.25 round-trip. Tri-Rail connects with Miami's Metrorail, so you may not have to drive at all.

Getting Around

Greater Miami resembles Los Angeles in its urban sprawl and traffic. You'll need a car to visit many attractions and points of interest. Some are accessible via the public transportation system, run by a department of the county government—the **Metro-Dade Transit Agency,** which consists of 650 **Metrobuses** on 70 routes, the 21-mi **Metrorail** elevated rapid-transit system, and the **Metromover,** an elevated light-rail system. Free maps, schedules, and a "First-Time Rider's Kit" are available. ⊠ *Government Center Station, 111 N.W. 1st St., Miami 33128; Maps by Mail, ☎ 305/654–6586; ☎ 305/638–6700 for route information, weekdays 6 AM–10 PM, weekends 9–5.*

By Bus

Metrobus stops are marked by blue-and-green signs with a bus logo and route information. The frequency of service varies widely, so call in advance to obtain specific schedule information. The fare is $1.25 (exact change), transfers 25¢; 60¢ with 10¢ transfers for people with disabilities, seniors (65 and older), and students. Some express routes carry surcharges of $1.50. Reduced-fare tokens sold 10 for $10 are available from Metropass outlets. Lift-equipped buses for people with disabilities are available on 16 routes, including one from the airport that links up with many routes in Miami Beach as well as Coconut Grove, Coral Gables, Hialeah, and Kendall. All but four of these routes connect with Metrorail (☎ 305/638–6700). Those unable to use regular transit service should call **Special Transportation Services** (☎ 305/263–5400) for information on such services as curb-to-curb van pickup.

By Car

In general, Miami traffic is the same as in any big city, with the same rush hours and the same likelihood that parking garages will be full at peak times. Many drivers who aren't locals and don't know their way around might turn and stop suddenly, or drop off passengers where they shouldn't. Some drivers are short-tempered and will assault those who cut them off or honk their horn.

Motorists need to be careful even when their driving behavior is beyond censure, however, especially in rental cars. Despite the removal of identifying marks, cars piled with luggage or otherwise showing signs that a tourist is at the wheel remain prime targets for thieves. Long-time residents know that reports of crime against tourists are blown way out of proportion by the media and that Miami is more or less as safe for a visitor as any American city its size. The city has also initiated a TOP (Tourist Oriented Police) Cops program to assist tourists with directions and safety. For more safety advice on driving in Miami, *see* Driving *in* the Gold Guide.

By Taxi

One cab "company" stands out immeasurably above the rest. It's actually a consortium of drivers who have banded together to provide good service, in marked contrast to some Miami cabbies, who are rude, unhelpful, unfamiliar with the city, or dishonest, taking advantage of visitors who don't know the area. To plug into this consortium—they don't have a name, simply a number—call the dispatch service (☎ 305/888–4444)—although they can be hard to understand over the phone. If you have to use another company, try to be familiar with your route and destination.

Since 1974 fares have been $1.75 per mile, 25¢ a minute waiting time, with no additional charge for up to five passengers, luggage, or tolls. Taxis can be hailed on the street, although you may not always find one when you need one—it's better to call for a dispatch taxi or have a hotel doorman hail one for you. Some companies with dispatch service are **Central Taxicab Service** (☎ 305/532–5555), **Diamond Cab Company** (☎ 305/545–5555), **Metro Taxicab Company** (☎ 305/888–8888), **Miami-Dade Yellow Cab** (☎ 305/633–0503), **Society Cab Company** (☎ 305/757–5523), **Speedy Cab** (☎ 305/861–9999), **Super Yellow Cab Company** (☎ 305/888–7777), **Tropical Taxicab Company** (☎ 305/945–1025), and **Yellow Cab Company** (☎ 305/444–4444). Many now accept credit cards; inquire when you call.

By Train

Elevated **Metrorail** trains run from downtown Miami north to Hialeah and south along U.S. 1 to Dadeland, daily 5:30 AM–midnight. Trains run every five minutes in peak hours, every 15 minutes at other times. The fare is $1.25. Transfers, which cost 25¢, must be bought at the first station entered. Parking at train stations costs $2.

Metromover has two loops that circle downtown Miami, linking major hotels, office buildings, and shopping areas. The system has been expanded from 2 mi to 4½ mi, including the 1½-mi Omni extension, with six stations to the north, and the 1-mi Brickell extension, with six stations to the south. Service runs daily every 90 seconds, 6 AM–midnight. The fare is 25¢. Transfers to Metrorail are $1.

By Water Taxi

The service, inaugurated in 1987 in Fort Lauderdale, began Miami area operations in 1994 and expanded service between Miami Beach Marina and the Eden Roc in 1995. Canopied boats, 28 feet and longer, connect Miami Beach, Coconut Grove, and Key Biscayne from Bayside Marketplace. Routes cover downtown and Miami Beach hotels and restaurants and the Watson Island airboat station. Taxis operate daily 10 AM–2:30 AM. One-way fares around downtown Miami are $3, longer runs $7. For information, call 954/467–6677.

Contacts and Resources

Doctors and Dentists

Dade County Medical Association (✉ 1501 N.W. North River Dr., Miami, ☎ 305/324–8717) is open weekdays 9–5 for medical referral.

East Coast District Dental Society (✉ 420 S. Dixie Hwy., Suite 2E, Coral Gables, ☎ 305/667–3647) is open weekdays 9–4:30 for dental referral. After hours, stay on the line and a recording will direct you to a dentist. Services include general dentistry, endodontics, periodontics, and oral surgery.

Emergencies

Dial **911** for police or ambulance. You can dial free from pay phones.

AMBULANCE

Randle Eastern Ambulance Service Inc. (✉ 7255 N.W. 19th St., Suite C, Miami 33126, ☎ 305/718–6400) operates at all hours.

HOSPITALS

Miami has 32 hospitals and more than 34,000 health-care professionals. The following hospitals have 24-hour emergency rooms:

In Miami Beach: **Miami Heart Institute** (✉ 4701 N. Meridian Ave., Miami Beach, ☎ 305/672–1111; physician referral, 305/674–3004), **Mt. Sinai Medical Center** (✉ Off Julia Tuttle Causeway, I–195 at 4300 Alton Rd., Miami Beach, ☎ 305/674–2121; emergency, 305/674–2200; physician referral, 305/674–2273), and **South Shore Hospital & Medical Center** (✉ 630 Alton Rd., Miami Beach, ☎ 305/672–2100, ext. 3442).

In the north: **Golden Glades Regional Medical Center** (✉ 17300 N.W. 7th Ave., North Miami, ☎ 305/652–4200). Golden Glades offers physician referral.

In central Miami: **Coral Gables Hospital** (✉ 3100 Douglas Rd., Coral Gables, ☎ 305/445–8461), **Jackson Memorial Medical Center** (✉ 1611 N.W. 12th Ave., near Dolphin Expressway, Miami, ☎ 305/585–1111; emergency, 305/585–6901; physician referral, 305/547–5757), **Mercy Hospital** (✉ 3663 S. Miami Ave., Coconut Grove, ☎ 305/854–4400; emergency, 305/285–2171; physician referral, 305/285–2929), and **Pan American Hospital** (✉ 5959 N.W. 7th St., Miami, ☎ 305/264–1000; emergency, 305/264–6125; physician referral, 305/264–5118).

In the south: **Baptist Hospital of Miami** (✉ 8900 N. Kendall Dr., Miami, ☎ 305/596–1960; emergency, 305/596–6556; physician referral, 305/596–6557) and **South Miami Hospital** (6200 S.W. 73rd St., South Miami, ☎ 305/661–4611; emergency, 305/662–8181; physician referral, 305/633–2255).

LATE-NIGHT PHARMACIES

Eckerd Drugs (✉ 1825 Miami Gardens Dr. NE, at 185th St., North Miami Beach, ☎ 305/932–5740) is open until midnight. The following are open 24 hours: **Eckerd Drugs** (✉ 9031 S.W. 107th Ave., Miami, ☎ 305/274–6776) and **Walgreens** (✉ 500–B W. 49th St., Palm Springs Mall, Hialeah, ☎ 305/557–5468; ✉ 12295 Biscayne Blvd., North Miami, ☎ 305/893–6860; ✉ 5731 Bird Rd., Miami, ☎ 305/666–0757; ✉ 1845 Alton Rd., Miami Beach, ☎ 305/531–8868; ✉ 791 N.E. 167th St., North Miami Beach, ☎ 305/652–7332).

Guided Tours

AIR TOURS

Air Tours of Miami (✉ 1470 N.E. 123rd St., Suite 602, Miami, ☎ 305/893–5874) flies over Miami, the Everglades, and nearby waters in a one-hour sightseeing tour on a Piper Seneca II six-seater. Tours depart from Opa-Locka Airport (ask for directions) and cost $75 per person (three-adult minimum). Reservations are required.

BOAT TOURS

Heritage of Miami II offers sightseeing cruises on board a two-masted, 85-foot topsail schooner. Tours start and end at **Bayside Marketplace** (✉ 401 Biscayne Blvd., ☎ 305/442–9697). One-hour sails cost $7 per person, and two-hour sails are $12. Tours loop through lower Biscayne Bay with views of the Vizcaya Museum and Gardens, movie-star homes, Cape Florida Lighthouse, the Port of Miami, and several residential islands.

Island Queen, Island Lady, and *Pink Lady* are 150-passenger double-decker tour boats docked at **Bayside Marketplace** (✉ 401 Biscayne Blvd., ☎ 305/379–5119). They go on daily 90-minute narrated tours of the Port of Miami and Millionaires' Row, costing $12.

HISTORIC TOURS

Art Deco District Tour (✉ 1001 Ocean Dr., Bin L, Miami Beach 33139, ☎ 305/672–2014), operated by the Miami Design Preservation League, is a 90-minute guided walking tour departing from the league's welcome center at the Oceanfront Auditorium at 10:30 AM Saturday and 6:30 PM Thursday. Private group tours can be arranged with advance notice. A two-hour bike tour leaves from the **Miami Beach Bike Center** (✉ 601 5th St., Miami Beach, ☎ 305/673–2055) at 10:30 on the first and third Sundays of the month. The walking tour costs $6; the bike tour is $10 with a rental bike, $5 with your own bike. You can go at your own pace with a self-guided $5 audio tour, which takes roughly an hour. The league also sells the *Art Deco District Guide,* a book of six detailed walking or driving tours of the Art Deco District, for $10.

Deco Tours Miami Beach (✉ 420 Lincoln Rd., Suite 412, Miami Beach, ☎ 305/531–4465) offers walking tours of the Art Deco District. These 90-minute tours, which cost $15, depart from various locations and take in Lincoln Road, Washington Avenue, Espanola Way, Ocean Drive, Lummus Park, and the Art Deco Welcome Center. Tours of the city are conducted in vans and buses.

Professor Paul George (✉ 1345 S.W. 14th St., Miami, ☎ 305/858–6021), a history professor at Miami-Dade Community College and past president of the Florida Historical Society, leads a variety of walking tours as well as boat tours and tours that make use of Metrorail and Metromover. Pick from tours covering downtown, historic neighborhoods, cemeteries, Coconut Grove, and the Miami River. They start Saturday at 10 and Sunday at 11 at various locations, depending on the tour, and generally last about 2½ hours. Call for each weekend's schedule and for additional tours by appointment. The fee is $15.

RICKSHAW TOURS

Majestic Rickshaw (✉ 75 N.E. 156 St., Biscayne Gardens) has two-person rickshaws along Main Highway in Coconut Grove's Village Center, nightly 8 PM–2 AM. You can take a 10-minute ride through Coconut Grove or a 20-minute lovers' moonlight ride to Biscayne Bay.

Services for People with Hearing Impairments

Fire, police, medical, rescue (TDD, ☎ 305/595–4749; voice, ☎ 305/595–6263 or 911).

Operator and directory assistance (TDD ☎ 800/855–1155).

Deaf Services of Miami (✉ 9100 S. Dadeland Blvd., Suite 104, Miami 33156; TDD, ☎ 305/668–3323; voice, ☎ 305/668–4407; 24-hour hot line, ☎ 305/668–4693; 24-hour emergency numerical pager for interpreters, ☎ 305/806–6090).

Florida Relay Service (TDD, ☎ 800/955–8771; voice, ☎ 800/955–8770).

Visitor Information

Greater Miami Convention & Visitors Bureau (✉ 701 Brickell Ave., Suite 2700, Miami 33131, ☎ 305/539–3063 or 800/283–2707). Satellite tourist information centers are at Bayside Marketplace (✉ 401 Biscayne Blvd., Miami 33132, ☎ 305/539–2980), **Miami Beach Chamber of Commerce, and South Dade Visitor Information Center** (✉ 160 U.S. 1, Florida City 33034, ☎ 305/245–9180 or 800/388–9669, FAX 305/247–4335).

Coconut Grove Chamber of Commerce (✉ 2820 McFarlane Rd., Coconut Grove 33133, ☎ 305/444–7270, FAX 305/444–2498). **Coral Gables Chamber of Commerce** (✉ 50 Aragon Ave., Coral Gables 33134, ☎ 305/446–1657, FAX 305/446–9900). **Florida Gold Coast Chamber of Commerce** (✉ 1100 Kane Concourse, Suite 210, Bay Harbor Islands 33154, ☎ 305/866–6020) serves the beach communities of Bal Harbour, Bay Harbor Islands, Golden Beach, North Bay Village, Sunny Isles, and Surfside. **Greater Miami Chamber of Commerce** (✉ 1601 Biscayne Blvd., Miami 33132, ☎ 305/350–7700, FAX 305/374–6902). **Greater South Dade/South Miami Chamber of Commerce** (✉ 6410 S.W. 80th St., South Miami 33143-4602, ☎ 305/661–1621, FAX 305/666–0508). **Key Biscayne Chamber of Commerce** (✉ Key Biscayne Bank Bldg., 95 W. McIntyre St., Key Biscayne 33149, ☎ 305/361–5207). **Miami Beach Chamber of Commerce** (✉ 1920 Meridian Ave., Miami Beach 33139, ☎ 305/672–1270, FAX 305/538–4336). **North Miami Chamber of Commerce** (✉ 13100 W. Dixie Hwy., North Miami 33181, ☎ 305/891–7811, FAX 305/893–8522). **Surfside Tourist Board** (✉ 9301 Collins Ave., Surfside 33154, ☎ 305/864–0722 or 800/327–4557, FAX 305/861–1302).

4 The Everglades

Created in 1947, this national park in the southernmost extremity of the peninsula preserves a portion of the slow-moving "River of Grass"—a 50-mi-wide stream flowing through marshy grassland en route to Florida Bay. Biscayne National Park, nearby, is the largest national park with living coral reefs within the continental United States.

Updated by
Diane P.
Marshall

THE ONLY METROPOLITAN AREA in the United States with two national parks in its backyard is Miami. Everglades National Park, created in 1947, was meant to preserve the slow-moving "River of Grass"—a freshwater river 50 mi wide but only 6 inches deep, flowing from Lake Okeechobee through marshy grassland into Florida Bay. Along the Tamiami Trail (U.S. 41), marshes of cattails extend as far as the eye can see, interspersed only with hammocks or tree islands of bald cypress and mahogany, while overhead southern bald eagles make circles in the sky. A wide variety of trees and flowers, including ferns, orchids, and bromeliads, share the brackish waters with otters, turtles, marsh rabbits, and, occasionally, that gentle giant, the West Indian manatee. Not so gentle, though, is the saw grass. Deceptively graceful, these tall, willowy sedges have small sharp teeth on the edges of their leaves.

Biscayne National Park, established as a national monument in 1968 and 12 years later expanded and designated a national park, is the nation's largest marine park and the largest national park within the continental United States with living coral reefs. A small portion of the park's almost 274 sq mi consists of mainland coast and outlying islands, but 96% is under water, much of it in Biscayne Bay. The islands contain lush, heavily wooded forests with an abundance of ferns and native palm trees. Of particular interest are the mangroves and their tangled masses of stiltlike roots and stems that thicken the shorelines. These "walking trees," as locals sometimes call them, have striking curved prop roots, which arch down from the trunk, while aerial roots drop from branches. Mangroves reproduce by dropping propagules, which look like 6- to 12-inch-long green cigars and eventually sprout roots of their own. These trees draw freshwater from saltwater and create a coastal nursery capable of sustaining all types of marine life.

Unfortunately, Miami's backyard is being threatened by suburban sprawl and agriculture. What results is competition among environmental, agricultural, and developmental interests—for government money and control of this unique region's future.

The biggest issue is water. Originally, alternating floods and dry periods maintained wildlife habitat and regulated the water flowing into Florida Bay. The brackish seasonal flux sustained a remarkably vigorous bay, including the most productive shrimp beds in American waters, with thriving mangrove thickets and coral reefs at its Atlantic edge. The system nurtured sea life and attracted anglers and divers. Starting in the 1930s, however, a giant flood-control system began diverting water to canals running to the gulf and the ocean. As you travel Florida's north–south routes, you cross this network of canals symbolized by a smiling alligator representing the South Florida Water Management District, ironically known as "Protector of the Everglades."

The unfortunate side effect of flood control has been devastation of the wilderness. Park visitors decry diminished bird counts (a 90% reduction over 50 years); the black bear has been eliminated, and the Florida panther nears extinction. Exotic plants once imported to drain the Everglades and feral pigs released for hunting are crowding out indigenous species. In 1996, the nonprofit group American Rivers again ranked the Everglades among the most threatened rivers of North America. Meanwhile the loss of freshwater has made Florida Bay more salty, devastating breeding grounds and creating dead zones where pea-green algae has replaced sea grasses and sponges.

Even while the ecosystem continues to fade, new policies, still largely on paper, hold promise. Some 40% of what is commonly called Big Cypress Swamp was established as Big Cypress National Preserve in 1974 to protect the watershed of Everglades National Park. More recently, tourism and fishing industries, preservationists, and aggressive park management have pushed for improvement. Federal and state governments are now working together to push environmental protection toward the top of water-management goals. Congressional appropriations to study restoration of the Everglades have increased. The state has acquired the Frog Pond, some 1,800 acres of critical farmland east of the Everglades, in order to allow more natural flooding. Passage of the Everglades Forever Act mandates creation of 40,000 acres of filtration marshes to remove harmful nutrients before they enter the protected wetlands. Within the next decade, farming must sharply reduce its phosphorus runoff, and the U.S. Army Corps of Engineers, which maintains Florida's flood-control system, proposes restoring a more natural flow of water into the Everglades and its related systems. Although the future of the natural system hangs uncertainly in this time of transition, these are certainly promising signs.

Pleasures and Pastimes

Biking and Hiking

In the Everglades, there are several nice places to ride and hike. The Shark Valley Loop Road (15 mi round-trip) makes a good bike trip. "Foot and Canoe Trails of the Flamingo Area," a leaflet, lists others. A vast network of almost 200 mi of bicycle and hiking trails is under development along the banks of flood-control canals. Inquire about water levels and insect conditions before you go, and plan accordingly, stocking up on insect repellent, sunscreen, and water, as necessary.

Boating and Canoeing

One of the best ways to experience the Everglades is by boat, and almost all of Biscayne National Park is accessible only by water. Boat rentals are available in both parks.

In the Everglades, the 99-mi inland Wilderness Trail between Flamingo and Everglades City is open to motorboats as well as canoes, although powerboats may have trouble navigating the route above Whitewater Bay. Flat-water canoeing is best in winter, when temperatures are moderate, rainfall is minimal, and mosquitoes are tolerable. You don't need a permit for day trips, but tell someone where you're going and when you expect to return. Getting lost is easy, and spending the night without proper gear can be unpleasant, if not dangerous.

On the Gulf Coast, you can explore the nooks, crannies, and mangrove islands of Chokoloskee Bay, as well as many rivers near Everglades City. The Turner River Trail, a good day trip, passes through mangrove, dwarf cypress, coastal prairie, and freshwater slough ecosystems of Everglades National Park and Big Cypress National Preserve.

Dining

With a few exceptions, the dining experience on the north, south, and east sides of the Everglades centers on low-key mom-and-pop places that serve hearty home-style food and small eateries specializing in local fare: seafood, conch, alligator, turtle, and frogs' legs. Restaurants run by Native Americans add another dimension, serving local favorites as well as catfish, Indian fry bread (a flour-and-water dough), pumpkin bread, and Indian burgers (ground beef browned, rolled in fry-bread dough, and deep-fried) and tacos (fry bread with chili, lettuce, tomato, and shredded Cheddar cheese on top). Restaurants in Everglades City, to the west, appear to operate with a "captive audience" philosophy: Prices run high, service is mediocre, and food preparation is uninspired. The closest good restaurants are in Naples, 35 mi northwest.

Although both Everglades and Biscayne national parks are wilderness areas, there are restaurants within a short drive. Most are between Miami and Shark Valley along the Tamiami Trail (U.S. 41), in the Homestead–Florida City area, in Everglades City, and in the Florida Keys along the Overseas Highway (U.S. 1). The only food service in either park is at Flamingo, in the Everglades, but many of the independent restaurants will pack picnics. (You can also find fast-food establishments on the Tamiami Trail east of Krome Avenue and along U.S. 1 in Homestead–Florida City.)

Fishing

Largemouth bass are plentiful in freshwater ponds, while snapper, redfish, and sea trout are caught in Florida Bay. The mangrove shallows of the Ten Thousand Islands, along the gulf, yield tarpon and snook. Whitewater Bay is also a favorite spot. Note: The state has issued health advisories for sea bass, largemouth bass, and other freshwater fish, especially those caught in the canals along the Tamiami Trail, due to high mercury content. Signs are posted throughout the park, and consumption should be limited.

Lodging

Homestead–Florida City, southwest of Miami, has become a bedroom community for both parks. Here you'll find well-kept, older properties. Along U.S. 1 and Krome Avenue, several chains have opened in recent years. Prices tend to be somewhat lower than in Greater Miami. There are also a few lodgings closer to the Everglades, off U.S. 41. On the Everglades City front, the choices are low-key motels, friendly bed-and-breakfasts, and a few independent hotels.

Shopping

For the sheer fun as well as the bargain, stop in at any of the local farms where you can pick your own produce. The harvest season runs November–April and you can expect to find strawberries for $2 a pound, corn at $1.25 a dozen, and tomatoes for 50¢ a pound. Fresh mangos, papayas, and other tropical fruits are a great buy. Look for signs—in season they're everywhere among the fields. You can also buy fresh-picked produce at roadside stands. Souvenirs worth considering include Native American crafts, especially dolls and colorful patchwork clothing, and an artistic Clyde Butcher photograph.

Exploring the Everglades

The southern tip of the Florida peninsula is largely taken up by Everglades National Park, but land access to it is primarily by two roads: The main park road traverses the southern Everglades from the gateway towns of Homestead and Florida City to the outpost of Flamingo, on Florida Bay. In the northern Everglades, you can take the Tamiami Trail (U.S. 41) from the Greater Miami area in the east to the western park entrance in Everglades City. In far southeastern Florida, Biscayne National Park lies almost completely offshore. As a result, most of the sports and recreational opportunities in both national parks are based on water, the study of nature, or both, so even on land, be prepared to get a bit damp on the region's marshy trails.

Though relatively compact, as compared with the national parks of the West, these parks still require a bit of time to see. The narrow, two-lane roads through the Everglades make for long travel, whereas it's the necessity of sightseeing by boat that takes time at Biscayne.

Numbers in the text correspond to numbers in the margin and on The Everglades and Biscayne National Parks map.

Great Itineraries

IF YOU HAVE 1 DAY

You'll have to make a choice—the Everglades or Biscayne. If you want quiet and nature, go with the Everglades. If you're interested in boating or underwater flora and fauna, Biscayne is your best bet. Either way, you'll experience a little of what's left of the "real" Florida.

For a day in Everglades National Park, begin in Homestead ⑫, near the entrance to the park, for a visit to historic Old Town Hall. Continue to Florida City ⑬, gateway to the park and site of a museum on Florida pioneer life. Head to the Main Visitor Center ① for an overview of the park and its ecosystems, and continue to the Royal Palm Visitor Center ② for a look at several unique plant systems. Then go to Flamingo ③, where you can rent a boat or take a tour of Florida Bay.

If Biscayne is your preference, begin at Convoy Point ⑭ for an orientation before forsaking dry land. Sign up for a snorkel or dive trip or an outing on a glass-bottom boat, or explore an offshore island.

IF YOU HAVE 3 DAYS

With three days, you can explore both the northern and southern Everglades as well as Biscayne National Park. Start in the north by driving west along the Tamiami Trail, stopping at Everglades Safari Park ④ for an airboat ride; at Shark Valley ⑥ for a tram tour, walk, or bicycle trip; at the Miccosukee Indian Village ⑦ for lunch; at the Big Cypress Gallery to see Clyde Butcher's photographs; and then at the Ochopee post office ⑨, before ending in 🏨 **Everglades City** ⑪, home of the Gulf Coast Visitor Center. From here you can visit historic Smallwood's Store on Chokoloskee Island and watch the sunset. Day two is for exploring the south. Return east on the Tamiami Trail to Homestead ⑫, pausing at Everglades Air Tours to take a sightseeing trip before following the one-day Everglades itinerary above and overnighting in 🏨 **Florida City** ⑬. Biscayne National Park is the subject of day three. If you plan to scuba or take the glass-bottom boat, get an early start. You can explore the visitor center at Convoy Point ⑭ when you return and finish your day checking out sights in Florida City and Homestead. Snorkel trips leave later, giving you time to see Florida City and Homestead, have lunch, and learn about the park's ecosystem at the visitor center first. Be warned that though you can fly and then scuba dive, you can't dive and then fly within 24 hours. So if you're flying out, reverse the days' sequence accordingly.

IF YOU HAVE 5 DAYS

Follow day one above, spending the night in 🏨 **Everglades City** ⑪. Begin the second day with a canoe, kayak, or boat tour of the Ten Thousand Islands. In the late afternoon take a walk on the boardwalk at Fakahatchee Strand State Preserve ⑩ to see rare epiphytic orchids or on a 2½-mi trail at the Big Cypress National Preserve. Drive east to Coopertown, and take a nighttime airboat tour with Ray Cramer. Spend the night in 🏨 **Florida City** ⑬. Day three is spent at Biscayne National Park, then sightseeing in Homestead and Florida City as suggested above. Begin day four at Everglades Air Tours in Homestead ⑫; then browse the antiques shops along Krome Avenue, before picking up a picnic lunch and seeing some of South Dade's other nearby attractions. On day five, augment your picnic lunch with goodies from the remarkable fruit stand Robert is Here, before heading to the southern portion of Everglades National Park, as described above.

When to Tour the Everglades

Winter is the best time to visit Everglades National Park. Temperatures and mosquito activity are low to moderate, low water levels concentrate the resident wildlife around sloughs that retain water all year, and migratory birds swell the avian population. Winter is also the busiest time in the park. Make reservations and expect crowds at Flamingo, the Main Visitor Center, and Royal Palm.

In spring the weather turns hot and rainy, and tours and facilities are less crowded. Migratory birds depart, and you must look harder to see wildlife. Be careful with campfires and matches; this is when the wild-fire-prone saw grass prairies and pinelands are most vulnerable.

Summer brings intense sun and billowing clouds unleashing torrents of rain almost every afternoon. Save your outdoor activities for early or late in the day to avoid the rain and the sun's strongest rays, and use a sunscreen. Water levels rise and wildlife disperses. Mosquitoes hatch, swarm, and descend on you in voracious clouds. (Carrying mosquito repellent is a good idea at any time of year, but it's a necessity in summer.) Although the power of a summer storm over the marshlands is something to behold, basically it's a good time to stay away. Europeans constitute 80% of the summer visitors.

In mid-October, the first cold front usually sweeps through. The rains diminish, water levels start to fall, and the ground begins to dry out. Wildlife moves toward the sloughs. Flocks of migratory birds and tourists swoop in, and the cycle of seasons begins once more.

Even if you're not lodging in Everglades National Park, try to stay until dusk, when dozens of bird species feed around the ponds and trails. While shining a flashlight over the water in marshy areas, look for two yellowish-red reflections above the surface—telltale alligator signs.

EVERGLADES NATIONAL PARK

11 mi southwest of Homestead, 45 mi southwest of Miami International Airport.

The best way to experience the real Everglades is to get your feet wet, like paddling a canoe into the River of Grass to stay in a backcountry campsite. Most visitors won't do that, however. Luckily, there are several ways to see the wonders of the park with dry feet. Take a boat tour in Everglades City or Flamingo, ride the tram at Shark Valley, or walk the boardwalks along the main park road. And there's more to see than natural beauty. Miccosukee Indians operate a range of attractions and restaurants worthy of a stop.

Coverage below begins in the southern Everglades, followed by the northern Everglades, starting in the east and ending in Everglades City.

The Main Park Road

The main park road (Route 9336) travels from the Main Visitor Center to Flamingo, across a section of the park's eight distinct ecosystems: hardwood hammock, freshwater prairie, pineland, freshwater slough, cypress, coastal prairie, mangrove, and marine/estuarine. Highlights of the trip include a dwarf cypress forest, the ecotone (transition zone) between saw grass and mangrove forest, and a wealth of wading birds at Mrazek and Coot Bay ponds. Boardwalks, looped trails, several short spurs, and observation platforms allow you to stay dry.

❶ The new, expanded **Main Visitor Center,** at park headquarters, opened in December 1996 with a wide range of interactive exhibits and films. Stand in a simulated blind and peer through a spyglass to watch birds in the wild; though it's actually a film, the quality is so good, you'll think you're outside. Move on to a bank of telephones to hear differing viewpoints on the Great Water Debate. There's a 15-minute film on the park, two movies on hurricanes, and a 45-minute wildlife film for children. Computer monitors present a schedule of daily ranger-led activities park-wide. In the Everglades Discovery Shop you can browse through lots of neat nature, science, and kid's stuff. Park fees cover all park entrances for seven days. The Main Visitor Center provides information on the entire park. ⊠ *11 mi west of Homestead on Rte. 9336,* ☎ *305/242–7700.* 🖼 *Park $10 per car, $5 per person on foot or bicycle, $5 per motorcycle.* ⊗ *Daily 8–5.*

❷ The **Royal Palm Visitor Center** is a must for anyone who wants to experience the real Everglades. You can stroll along the Anhinga Trail boardwalk or follow the Gumbo Limbo Trail through a hardwood hammock. The visitor center has an interpretive display, a bookstore, and vending machines. ⊠ *4 mi west of Main Visitor Center on Rte. 9336.* ☎ *305/242–7700.* ⊗ *Daily 8–5.*

Flamingo

❸ *38 mi southwest of Main Visitor Center.*

Here at the far end of the main road you'll find a cluster of buildings containing a visitor center, lodge, restaurant and lounge, gift shop, marina, and bicycle rentals, plus an adjacent campground. Tour boats narrated by interpretive guides, fishing expeditions of Florida Bay, and canoe and kayak trips all leave from here. Nearby is Eco Pond, one of the most popular wildlife observation areas.

The **Flamingo Visitor Center** provides an interactive display and has natural history exhibits in the Florida Bay Museum. Check the schedule for ranger-led activities, such as naturalist discussions, evening programs in the campground amphitheater, and hikes along area trails. ☎ *305/242–7700.* ⊗ *Daily 8–4.*

Dining and Lodging

$$ ✕ **Flamingo Restaurant.** The grand view, convivial lounge, and casual style are great. Big picture windows on the visitor center's second floor overlook Florida Bay, revealing soaring eagles, gulls, pelicans, terns, and vultures. Dine at low tide to see birds flock to the sandbar just offshore. Less satisfying is the food itself. Look for pastas and a few grills. Service is limited to buffets in summer, though the marina store snack bar is open all year for pizza, sandwiches, and salads, or order a picnic basket for lunch. ⊠ *Flamingo Lodge, 1 Flamingo Lodge Hwy.,* ☎ *941/695–3101. AE, D, DC, MC, V.*

$$ 🏨 **Flamingo Lodge Marina & Outpost Resort.** This simple low-rise motel is the only lodging inside the park. Accommodations are basic but well kept, and an amiable staff helps you adjust to bellowing alligators, roaming raccoons, and ibis grazing on the lawn. Rooms have contemporary furniture, floral bedspreads, and art prints of bird life, and though they face Florida Bay, they don't necessarily overlook it. Bathrooms are tiny. Cottages, in a wooded area on the margin of a coastal prairie, have kitchenettes and accommodate four or six people. Reservations are essential in winter. ⊠ *1 Flamingo Lodge Hwy., 33034,* ☎ *941/695–3101 or 800/600–3813. 101 rooms, 24 cottages. Restaurant, lounge, snack bar, pool, coin laundry. AE, D, DC, MC, V.*

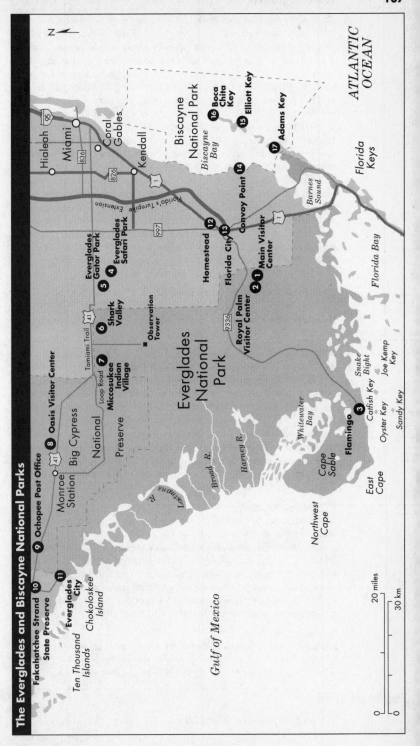

The Everglades and Biscayne National Parks

ATLANTIC OCEAN

Miami
Hialeah
Coral Gables
Kendall
95
836
826
1

Florida's Turnpike Extension
997
41 Tamiami Trail

Biscayne National Park
Biscayne Bay
16 Boca Chita Key
15 Elliott Key
17 Adams Key
14 Convoy Point
Barnes Sound
Florida Keys
Florida Bay

12 Homestead
13 Florida City
Main Visitor Center
2 1 Royal Palm Visitor Center
9336
Everglades Gator Park
5 4 Everglades Safari Park
6 Shark Valley
Observation Tower
7 Miccosukee Indian Village
Loop Road

8 Oasis Visitor Center
Big Cypress National Preserve
Monroe Station
9 Ochopee Post Office
41

10 Fakahatchee Strand State Preserve
11 Everglades City
Ten Thousand Islands
Chokoloskee Island

Everglades National Park

Gulf of Mexico

Northwest Cape
East Cape
Cape Sable
Flamingo 3
Whitewater Bay
Harney R.
Broad R.
Lostmans R.
Snake Bight
Catfish Key
Oyster Key
Sandy Key
Joe Kemp Key

20 miles
30 km

N

$ ⚠ **Everglades National Park.** Deep in the park are 48 backcountry sites, many inland and some on the beach. Two are accessible by land, the others by canoe; 15 have chickees (raised wooden platforms with thatch roofs). All have chemical toilets. Several are within an easy day's canoeing of Flamingo; five are closer to Everglades City. Carry your food, water, and supplies in; carry out all trash. You'll need a free, site-specific permit, available on a first-come, first-served basis from the Flamingo or Gulf Coast Visitor Center (☞ Contacts and Resources *in* Everglades A to Z, *below,* for both). In addition, there are three de-veloped campgrounds and group campsites with drinking water, sewage dump station, and rest rooms. **Long Pine Key** has 108 drive-up sites; **Flamingo** has 235 drive-up sites, 60 walk-in sites, and cold showers; and **Chekika** has 20 drive-up sites, warm showers, and swimming fa-cilities. For Long Pine Key and Flamingo, you can make reservations up to five months in advance for December 15–April 30 through a ser-vice called **Destinet.** In May–October sites are available on a first-come, first-served basis, as they are at Chekika year-round; come early to get a good site, especially in winter. Pets are allowed. ☎ *Destinet: 800/365–2267.* 🖃 *Backcountry sites free; developed sites June–Aug. free, Sept.–May $14, groups $28.* ☉ *Destinet: daily 10–7.*

Outdoor Activities and Sports

BIKING

Flamingo Lodge Marina & Outpost Resort (☎ 941/695–3101) rents bikes for $14 a day, $8 per half day, or $3 an hour.

BOATING

The marina at **Flamingo Lodge Marina & Outpost Resort** (☎ 941/695–3101) rents 10 power skiffs for $80 per day, $60 a half day, and $20 per hour as well as fully furnished and outfitted houseboats that sleep six. Rates (two-day minimum) run $475 without air-conditioning for two days, $575 with air-conditioning for two days. Several private boats are also available for charter. There are two ramps, one for Florida Bay, the other for Whitewater Bay and the backcountry. The hoist across the plug dam separating Florida Bay from the Buttonwood Canal can take boats up to 26 feet long. A small store sells food, camping sup-plies, bait and tackle, propane, and fuel.

CANOEING AND KAYAKING

The Everglades has six well-marked canoe trails in the Flamingo area, including the southern end of the 99-mi Wilderness Trail from Ever-glades City to Flamingo. **Flamingo Lodge Marina & Outpost Resort** (☎ 941/695–3101) rents canoes in two sizes: small (up to two paddlers) and family size (up to four). Small canoes rent for $27 per day, $22 per half day (four hours), and $8 per hour; family size run $40, $30, and $12. Single-person kayaks cost $43 per day, $27 per half day, and $11 per hour; doubles rent for $54, $38, and $16.

FISHING

Flamingo Lodge Marina & Outpost Resort (☎ 941/695–3101) helps arrange charter fishing trips for two to six persons. The cost is $265 a day for up to two people, $25 each additional person.

Tamiami Trail

141 mi from Miami to Fort Myers.

In 1915, when officials decided to build an east–west highway linking Miami to Fort Myers and continuing north to Tampa, someone sug-gested calling it the Tamiami Trail. The name stuck. It wasn't until 1928 that the road became a reality, cutting through the Everglades and altering the natural flow of water and the lives of the Miccosukee Indians who eked out a living fishing, hunting, and frogging here.

Today, the traffic screams through Everglades National Park, Big Cypress National Preserve, and Fakahatchee Strand State Preserve. The landscape is surprisingly varied, changing from hardwood hammocks to pinelands, then abruptly to tall cypress trees dripping with Spanish moss and back to coastal prairie. Those who slow to take in the scenery can see alligators sunning themselves along the banks of roadside canals and in the shallow waters, hundreds of waterbirds, chickee huts, people fishing, Native American villages, and airboats parked at roadside enterprises. Several sights are even worth a stop.

Businesses along the trail give their addresses either in the distance from Krome Avenue, Florida's Turnpike, and Miami on the east coast or Fort Myers and Naples on the west coast or by mile marker. Between Miami and Fort Myers, the road goes by several names, including Tamiami Trail, U.S. 41, and, at the Miami end, Southwest 8th Street.

❹ Attractions at **Everglades Safari Park** include a jungle trail, an educational alligator show and wrestling demonstration, a wildlife museum, airboat rides (included in admission), and a restaurant and gift shop. Climb the observation platform and take in the beauty of the Glades. ✉ *26700 Tamiami Trail, 9 mi west of Krome Ave.,* ☎ *305/226–6923 or 305/223–3804,* 𝐅𝐀𝐗 *305/554–5666.* ☞ *$15.* ◷ *Daily 8:30–5.*

❺ At **Everglades Gator Park,** you can hold a baby alligator while friends snap a photo, squirm in a "reptilium" of venomous and nonpoisonous native snakes, or learn about Native Americans of the Everglades through a reproduction of a Miccosukee village. The park also features airboat tours, fishing charters, and RV campsites as well as a gift shop and restaurant. ✉ *24050 Tamiami Trail, 12 mi west of Florida's Turnpike,* ☎ *305/559–2255 or 800/559–2205.* ☞ *Free, tours $12.* ◷ *Daily 10–5, tours 9–5.*

❻ Though **Shark Valley** is the national park's north entrance, no roads here lead to other parts of the park. The only route is a paved 15-mi loop; at the half-way point there's a concrete observation tower built by an oil company in the early 1940s on the site of a test well. Climb the wide ramp that spirals skyward 50 feet and look down at alligators sunbathing and birds stalking fish in the shallow waters. Everything as far as the eye can see is the vast River of Grass. To reach the tower, you can walk, bicycle, or take a tram tour. Along the way, expect to see all kinds of waterbirds as well as alligators warming themselves along the banks and on the road (most quickly move out of the way). Just behind the bike rental area, a short boardwalk trail meanders through the saw grass. A small visitor center features rotating exhibits, a bookstore, and park rangers ready to answer questions. ✉ *23.5 mi west of Florida's Turnpike,* ☎ *305/221–8776.* ☞ *Park $8 per car, $4 per person on foot, bicycle, or motorcycle.* ◷ *Visitor center daily 8:30–5:30.*

❼ At the **Miccosukee Indian Village,** Miccosukee families prepare food and make crafts, on sale at the cultural center. Informative alligator-wrestling shows as well as airboat rides and a restaurant are other attractions. The Everglades Music & Craft Festival falls on a July weekend, and the weeklong Indian Arts Festival is in late December. ✉ *Just west of Shark Valley entrance, 25 mi west of Florida's Turnpike,* ☎ *305/223–8380.* ☞ *$5, rides $7.* ◷ *Daily 9–5.*

❽ Pause at the **Oasis Visitor Center** to learn about the national park's northern neighbor, the **Big Cypress National Preserve.** Through the 1950s and early 1960s, the world's largest cypress-logging industry prospered in the Big Cypress Swamp. The industry died out in the 1960s, and the government began buying parcels. Today part of the swamp, which encompasses more than 729,000 acres, has become this national preserve. Its variegated pattern of wet prairies, ponds, marshes, sloughs, and strands provides a sanctuary for a variety of wildlife, but because of a politically dictated policy of balanced land use—"use without abuse"—the watery wilderness is devoted to research and recreation as well as preservation. Unlike most national parks, for example, the preserve allows hunting, off-road vehicle (airboat, swamp buggy) use by permit, and cattle grazing. The 8-mi Turner River Canoe Trail begins here and crosses through Everglades National Park before ending in Chokoloskee Bay, near Everglades City. Hikers can join the Florida National Scenic Trail, which runs north–south through the preserve for 31 mi. Seven primitive campsites are available on a first-come, first-served basis. ⊠ *50 mi west of Miami, 20 mi west of Shark Valley,* ☎ *941/695–4111.* ⚐ *Free.* ⊙ *Daily 8:30–4:30.*

9 The tiny **Ochopee post office** is the smallest post office in North America. Buy a picture postcard of the little one-room shack and mail it to a friend, thereby helping to keep this picturesque spot in business. ⊠ *Ochopee, 50 mi west of Miami, just east of Rte. 29,* ☎ *941/695–4131.* ⊙ *Weekdays 9:30–noon and 12:30–4, Sat. 9:30–11:30.*

10 The ½-mi boardwalk at the **Fakahatchee Strand State Preserve** affords an opportunity to see rare plants, bald cypress, and North America's largest stand of native royal palms and largest concentration and variety of epiphytic orchids. ⊠ *Rte. 29 and Tamiami Trail; ranger station 3 mi north of Tamiami Trail on Rte. 29, Box 548, Copeland 33926,* ☎ *941/695–4593.* ⊙ *Daily 8–sunset.*

Dining and Lodging

$ ✕ **Coopertown Restaurant.** A nearby roadside sign proclaims, "Coopertown: Population 8," a perfect introduction to this rustic eatery just into the Everglades west of Miami. Around for more than a half century, it's full of Old Florida style—alligator skulls, stuffed alligator heads, and gator accessories. Try the alligator and frogs' legs, breaded and deep-fried; they're available for breakfast, lunch, or dinner. ⊠ *22700 S.W. 8th St., Miami,* ☎ *305/226–6048. MC, V. Beer only.*

$ ✕ **Miccosukee Restaurant.** Murals depict Native American women cooking and men engaged in a powwow in this restaurant at the Miccosukee Indian Village. Favorites are catfish and frogs' legs breaded and deep-fried, Indian fry bread, pumpkin bread, and Indian burgers and tacos. Breakfast is also served. ⊠ *25 mi west of Florida's Turnpike,* ☎ *305/223–8380 ext. 332. MC, V.*

$ ✕ **Pit Bar-B-Q.** The intense aroma of barbecue and blackjack-oak smoke will overwork your salivary glands. Order at the counter; then pick up your food when called. Specialties include barbecued chicken and ribs with a tangy sauce, french fries, cole slaw, and a fried biscuit as well as catfish and frogs' legs deep-fried in vegetable oil. ⊠ *16400 S.W. 8th St., Miami,* ☎ *305/226–2272. AE, MC, V.*

$ ⚠ **Everglades Gator Park** is popular with the RV set because besides airboats and Everglades attractions, the park has full hookups for as many as 80 RVs. You can rent a campsite by the night, week, or month or just store your RV. ⊠ *24050 S.W. 8th St., Miami (mailing address: 13800 S.W. 8th St., Box 107, Miami 33184),* ☎ *305/559–2255 or 800/559–2205.* ⚐ *$25 per night, $100 per week. MC, V.*

Outdoor Activities and Sports

BIKING

Shark Valley Tram Tours (✉ Shark Valley, ☎ 305/221–8455) rents bikes daily 9–4 (last rental at 3) for $3.25 per hour.

Shopping

Clyde Butcher does for the River of Grass what Ansel Adams did for the West, and you can check out his stunning photographs at his **Big Cypress Gallery** (✉ 52388 Tamiami Trail, 37 mi west of Miami, ☎ 941/695–2428). Working with large-format black-and-white film, Butcher captures every blade of grass, barb of feather, and flicker of light. At the **Miccosukee Indian Village** (✉ Just west of Shark Valley entrance, 25 mi west of Florida's Turnpike, ☎ 305/223–8380), you can buy some of the most unusual crafts in South Florida, including beadwork, moccasins, dolls, pottery, baskets, and patchwork fabric and clothes. With ethnic clothing very fashionable, it's not surprising that patchwork skirts, dresses, and vests made here have appeared in major women's magazines.

Everglades City

⓫ *35 mi southeast of Naples, 83 mi west of Miami.*

The western gateway to Everglades National Park, this community, just off the Tamiami Trail, has been around since the late 19th century. Its biggest draw is the park and the canoe, airboat, fishing, and bird-watching excursions you can take within it. The annual Seafood Festival, held the first weekend of February, attracts 60,000–75,000 visitors to eat seafood, hear nonstop music, and buy crafts. The rest of the year, dining out is a big disappointment. Still, you have to eat someplace.

The **Gulf Coast Visitor Center,** at the Everglades' western entrance, offers interpretive exhibits about local flora and fauna. Backcountry campers can pick up the required free permits, and for those in need of a little more guidance, there are ranger-led boat trips. The center offers access to the Ten Thousand Islands region along the Gulf of Mexico, but there are no roads from here to other sections of the park. ✉ *Rte. 29,* ☎ *941/695–3311.* ◻ *Park free.* ◷ *Mid-Nov.–mid-Apr., daily 7–5:30; reduced hours mid-April–mid-Nov.*

On the banks of the Barron River, the **Rod and Gun Club** (✉ 200 Riverside Dr., ☎ 941/695–2101) is a vestige of Florida's cracker glory days, when imperial developer Barron Collier greeted U.S. presidents, Barrymores, and Gypsy Rose Lee for days of leisurely fishing. Most of them flew to the private landing strip; in the evenings they dined on one of Collier's big catches, prepared by a chef who once worked for Kaiser Wilhelm. Sit on the screened porch, have a beer, and watch the yachts and fishing boats go by.

OFF THE
BEATEN PATH

SMALLWOOD'S STORE – This restored old trading post dates from 1906. Ted Smallwood pioneered this last American frontier and built a 3,000-square-foot pine store raised on pilings in Chokoloskee Bay. Smallwood's granddaughter Lynn McMillin reopened it in 1989, after it had been closed several years, and installed a small gift shop and museum chockablock with original goods from the store; historic photographs; Indian clothing, furs, and hides; area memorabilia; and an exhibit on such loners as Ed Watson, who allegedly killed the outlaw Belle Starr, and was himself killed just outside the store. On the third Saturday in March, a festival celebrates the nearly 100-year relationship the store has had with local Native Americans. ✉ *360 Mamie St., Chokoloskee*

Island, ☎ *941/695-2989.* 🎫 *$2.50.* ⊙ *Dec.–May, daily 10–5; May–Nov., daily 10–4.*

Dining and Lodging

$ ✕ **Ivey House Restaurant.** Home-style meals are served every night at 6. (Call for a reservation by 4 if you're not a guest of the hotel.) The nightly changing menu features a mix of meat and vegetarian selections. For $11.95 you can dine on barbecued chicken with potatoes, vegetable, salad, pineapple upside-down cake, and coffee or tea, and on Mexican night the fare is chicken fajitas, tortillas, beans, rice, flan, and coffee or tea. ⊠ *107 Camellia St.,* ☎ *941/695–3299,* 📠 *941/695–4155. MC, V. Closed May–Oct.*

$ ✕ **Oar House Restaurant.** With wood paneling, picnic table–style booths, and a mishmash of fishing and Glades decor, the first full-service eatery in town has the ambience of a diner. The menu features a blend of seafood and such local specialties as frogs' legs, turtle, conch, and gator. To its credit, the service is friendly, prices are very reasonable, the food is fried in canola and corn oil, and most dishes can be grilled or broiled if you prefer. It's open for breakfast, and there are lounges both in the restaurant and in a separate building behind. ⊠ *305 Collier Ave.,* ☎ *941/695–3535. D, MC, V.*

$ ✕ **Susie's Station.** Though it was built just a few years ago, you'd swear this place dates from Everglades City's heyday. The vintage mood is created by a white-balustered screened porch, gas station memorabilia, an 1898 horse-drawn oil tanker, antiques on all the walls, and replica '20s lamps strung over booths set with beige cloths. Car buffs stop just to see the refurbished antique cars and truck. As for the food, Biss Williams serves seafood, including stone crabs in season and a cold seafood plate with lobster salad; steaks; and pizzas. The best buy is the nightly dinner special—maybe lasagna, baked chicken, or Salisbury steak. The homemade Key lime pie sells out daily. Takeout and drive-through service are available. ⊠ *103 S.W. Copeland Ave.,* ☎ *941/695–2002. No credit cards.*

$$ 🏨 **Rod and Gun Club.** With a veranda, dark cypress fixtures, and a nautical theme, this landmark inn is like a time-warp trip back to the '20s, when wealthy hunters, anglers, and yachting parties from all over the world came to Florida for the winter season. The old guest rooms above the restaurant and bar aren't open anymore, but you can stay in comfortable cottages (no phone, however). The food is more than passable. Breakfast, lunch, and dinner are still served in the original dining room or on the wide veranda, and, as in Collier's day, if you catch a "keeper," the chef will prepare it for your dinner. ⊠ *200 Riverside Dr., Box 190, 34139,* ☎ *941/695–2101. 17 rooms. Restaurant, lounge, pool, tennis courts, fishing. No credit cards.*

$–$$ 🏨 **On the Banks of the Everglades.** Built in 1923, this lodging takes its name from the building it occupies, the former Bank of Everglades. Patty Flick Richards and her father, Bob Flick, did all the restoration and decoration, creating three spacious rooms, two suites, and three efficiencies with queen- or king-size beds and stylish coordinating linens, wall coverings, and draperies. Suites and efficiencies have private baths and kitchens; rooms share a women's or men's bath. Amenities include hair dryers and in-room ironing boards. At night you can snack on popcorn and watch movies in the parlor. A breakfast of baked goods, cereal, fresh fruit, juices, and coffee and tea is served in the bank's vault. There is no smoking. ⊠ *201 W. Broadway, Box 455, 34139,* ☎ *941/695–3151 or 888/431–1977,* 📠 *941/695–3335. 8 units (3 share baths). AE, D, MC, V.*

$ 🏠 **Ivey House B&B.** This clean, friendly bargain is run by the folks who operate North American Canoe Tours, David and Sandee Harraden. Guests are well-educated, well-traveled, and in tune, as evidenced by the new annex, whose rooms have modem connections so "guests can hook up their laptop computers to stay in touch with their families." In the evening people talk about adventures and do jigsaw puzzles in the big living room, and there's chatter over breakfast, too. Because of the dearth of good local restaurants, many guests eat here. Family-style dinners ($10–$15) often end with homemade apple pie. The shotgun-style cracker house was a boardinghouse for workers building the Tamiami Trail. ✉ *107 Camellia St., 34139,* ☎ *941/695–3299,* FAX *941/695–4155. 30 rooms (10 share baths), 1 2-bedroom cottage. Bicycles, recreation room, library. MC, V. Closed May–Oct.*

Outdoor Activities and Sports

BIKING

North American Canoe Tours (✉ Ivey House, 107 Camellia St., ☎ 941/695–4666, FAX 941/695–4155) rents bikes for $3 per hour, $15 per day (free for Ivey House guests).

CANOEING AND KAYAKING

Everglades National Park Boat Tours (✉ Gulf Coast Visitor Center, ☎ 941/695–2591; in FL, 800/445–7724) rents 17-foot Grumman canoes for day and overnight use. Rates are $21 per day, $17 for a half day. Car shuttle service is provided for canoeists paddling the Wilderness Trail, and travelers with disabilities can be accommodated. **North American Canoe Tours** (✉ Ivey House, 107 Camellia St., ☎ 941/695–4666, FAX 941/695–4155) is an established source for canoes, sea kayaks, and guided Everglades trips (November–April). Canoes cost $20 the first day, $18 for every day after. Kayaks are $35–$55 per day. Car shuttles for canoeists paddling the Wilderness Trail are $135 with NACT canoe or $200 with your own, plus the $10 park entrance fee.

GATEWAY TOWNS

The farm towns of Homestead and Florida City, flanked by Everglades National Park on the west and Biscayne National Park to the east, provide the closest visitor facilities to the parks. (The area's better restaurants are in Homestead, but the best lodgings are in Florida City.) The towns date from early in the century, when Henry Flagler extended his railroad to Key West but soon decided that farming would do more for rail revenues than ferrying passengers. Devastated in 1992 by Hurricane Andrew, both towns have fully recovered.

Homestead

🄬 *30 mi southwest of Miami.*

When Hurricane Andrew tore across South Florida with winds approaching 200 mph, it ripped apart lives and the small community of Homestead. Led by its mayor, the city seized the opportunity to rebuild itself stronger and better, redefining its role as the "Gateway to the Keys" and attracting major hotel chains, shopping centers, a new sports complex, and residential development. The historic downtown area has become a preservation-driven Main Street city. Krome Avenue (Route 997), which cuts through the city's heart, is lined with restaurants and antiques shops, drawing people from around South Florida.

West of Krome Avenue, miles of fields grow tomatoes, corn, strawberries, beans, and squash. Some are harvested commercially. Others have

U-PICK signs, inviting families to harvest their own. Stands that sell farm-fresh produce abound.

In addition to its agricultural legacy, the town has an eclectic flavor, attributable to its population mix: descendants of pioneer crackers, Hispanic growers, and farm workers as well as latter-day northern retirees. Until Hurricane Andrew, the military also had a huge presence. Homestead Air Force Base is slated to become a civil air facility with commercial development in a few years. Today it serves as home to several military reserve units.

In the downstairs lobby of the **Old Town Hall,** a restored 1917 landmark that houses the chamber of commerce, you can view a historic photo collection depicting life in the Homestead and Florida City area from 1904 to 1950. The exhibit is part of a 1,200-picture collection belonging to the Florida Pioneer Museum Association. More of the collection is displayed in the windows of the historic Seminole Theater Building, now a storefront, across the street, and in the Florida Pioneer Museum (☞ Florida City, *below*). ⊠ *43 N. Krome Ave.,* ☎ *305/247–2332.* ✲ *Tues.–Fri. 9–5.*

To find out about more area attractions, *see* the South Dade side trip *in* Chapter 3.

Beach

With a saltwater atoll pool that's flushed by tidal action, **Homestead Bayfront Park,** adjacent to Biscayne National Park, is popular among local families as well as anglers and boaters. Highlights include a playground, ramps for people with disabilities (including a ramp that leads into the swimming area), a picnic pavilion with grills of various sizes, showers, and rest rooms. ⊠ *9698 S.W. 328th St.,* ☎ *305/230–3034.* ▨ *$3.50 per passenger vehicle, $8 per vehicle with boat.* ✲ *Sunrise–sunset.*

Dining

$ ✕ **El Toro Taco.** The Hernandez family came to the United States from
★   San Luis Potosí, Mexico, to pick crops. In 1976 they opened what has become an area institution, where they make their own salt-free tortillas and nacho chips with Texas corn ground on site. The cilantro-dominated salsa is mild; if you like more fire on your tongue, ask for a side dish of minced jalapeño peppers to mix in. Specialties include *chile rellenos* (green peppers stuffed with ground beef and topped with cheese) and chicken fajitas. It's also open for breakfast. ⊠ *1 S. Krome Ave.,* ☎ *305/245–8182. D, MC, V. BYOB.*

$ ✕ **Potlikker's.** This Southern country-style restaurant takes its name from the broth—pot liquor—left over from the boiling of greens. The food is simple home cooking, service is attentive, and prices are attractive. A dinner of soup or salad, entrée with two vegetables, and roll or corn bread costs $6.99–$10.99. Specialties include a lemon-pepper chicken breast with lemon sauce, roast turkey with homemade dressing, and at least 11 different vegetables. Barbecued chicken is fall-off-the-bone tender, but the sauce is only so-so. The slightly spicy conch gumbo is thick with rice and chunks of conch and fresh vegetables. Tuesday is all-you-can-eat catfish night; on Friday you can stuff yourself with fried shrimp. For dessert, try a peach or berry cobbler or the 4-inch-tall Key lime pie. ⊠ *591 Washington Ave.,* ☎ *305/248–0835. AE, MC, V.*

$ ✕ **Tiffany's.** This country-French cottage with shops and a restaurant under a big banyan tree looks like a converted pioneer house with its high-pitched roof and lattice. Teaberry-color tables, satinlike floral place mats, marble-effect floor tiles, fresh flowers on each table, and lots of country items make for a very quaint atmosphere. Featured entrées include hot crab meat au gratin and asparagus supreme (rolled in ham with hollandaise sauce). Homemade desserts are to die for: a very tall carrot cake, strawberry whipped-cream cake, and a harvest pie with double crust that has layers of apples, cranberries, walnuts, raisins, and a caramel topping. There's also a Sunday brunch. ⊠ *22 N.E. 15th St.,* ☎ *305/246–0022. MC, V. Closed Mon. No dinner.*

Outdoor Activities and Sports

AUTO RACING

The **Metro-Dade Homestead Motorsports Complex** (⊠ 1 Speedway Blvd., 33035, ☎ 305/230–7223) is a state-of-the-art facility with an 8-degree banked-turn track resembling the Indianapolis Motor Speedway. The 1.5-mi oval is the key element of the 2.21-mi road course. A schedule of year-round manufacturer and race-team testing, club racing, and other events is highlighted by the Marlboro Grand Prix of Miami presented by Toyota (PPG CART World Series), the Florida Dodge Dealers 400 (NASCAR Craftsman Truck Series), and the season-ending Jiffy Lube Miami 300 (NASCAR Busch Series).

BOATING

Black Point Park is a 155-acre Metro-Dade County park with a hurricane-safe harbor. Though there's no beach, there are picnic tables, a bait shop, boat ramp, large barbecue grill, restaurant, canoe rentals, and rest rooms. ⊠ *24777 S.W. 87th Ave., Miami,* ☎ *305/258–3500.* ⊙ *Office daily 8:30–5 (later in summer), park daily 6–sunset.*

Boaters give high ratings to the facilities at **Homestead Bayfront Park,** just 5 mi south of Black Point Park. The 173-slip marina has a ramp, dock, bait-and-tackle shop, fuel station, ice, dry storage, and boat hoist, which can handle vessels up to 25 feet long with lifting rings. The park also has a tidal swimming area and concessions. ⊠ *9698 S.W. 328th St.,* ☎ *305/230–3033.* ▣ *$3.50 per passenger vehicle, $8 per vehicle with boat, $10 hoist.* ⊙ *Sunrise–sunset.*

SKYDIVING

Skydive Miami offers jumps above Homestead General Aviation Airport. All first jumps start with an hour of classroom instruction, leading to a flight to altitude and a tandem dive with an instructor. ⊠ *Homestead General Aviation Airport, 28730 S.W. 217th Ave.,* ☎ *305/759–3483; in South FL, 800/759–3483;* FAX *305/245–6160.* ▣ *$139.* ⊙ *Jumps weekends 7–sunset with 1-hour notice for more than 2 people, weekdays by appointment with 24 hours notice.*

Shopping

In addition to Homestead Boulevard (U.S. 1) and Campbell Drive (Southwest 312th Street and Northeast 8th Street), **Krome Avenue** is popular for shopping. In the heart of old Homestead, it has a brick sidewalk and many antiques stores.

Florida City

⑬ *2 mi southwest of Homestead.*

Florida's Turnpike ends in this southernmost town on the peninsula, spilling thousands onto U.S. 1 and eventually west to Everglades National Park, east to Biscayne National Park, or south to the Florida Keys. As the last civilization before 18 mi of mangroves and water, this stretch of U.S. 1 is lined with fast-food eateries, service stations, hotels, bars, dive shops, and restaurants.

Like Homestead, Florida City has roots planted in agriculture, as evidenced by hundreds of acres of farmland west of Krome Avenue and a huge farmers' market that processes produce to be shipped around the country.

A former station agent's house, the **Florida Pioneer Museum** was rebuilt from its original plans after Hurricane Andrew destroyed it. You can pore over a collection of articles from daily life that evokes the area's homestead period, on the last frontier of mainland America. Items recall a time when Henry Flagler's railroad vaulted the development of the Florida Keys all the way to Key West, and Homestead and Florida City were briefly the take-charge supply outposts. A caboose outside, which dates from the days of the old Florida East Coast Railway station, is one of a few wooden cars left in the country. ⌧ *826 N. Krome Ave.,* ☎ *305/246–9531.* ☉ *Daily 1–5.*

Dining and Lodging

$$ ✕ **Mutineer Restaurant.** Former Sheraton Hotels builder Allan Bennett created this upscale roadside restaurant with an indoor-outdoor fish and duck pond in 1980, back when Florida City was barely on the map. Etched glass divides the bi-level dining rooms, where striped velvet chairs, stained glass, and a few portholes set the scene; in the lounge are an aquarium and nautical antiques, including a crow's nest with stuffed crow, a gold parrot, and a treasure chest. The big menu offers 18 seafood entrées plus another half dozen daily seafood specials, as well as game, ribs, and steaks. Favorites include barbecued baby-back ribs, whole Dungeness crab, and snapper Oscar (topped with crab and asparagus). There's live music Thursday through Saturday evenings. ⌧ *11 S.E. 1st Ave. (U.S. 1 and Palm Dr.),* ☎ *305/245–3377. AE, D, DC, MC, V.*

$–$$ ✕ **Richard Accursio's Capri Restaurant and King Richard's Room.** One
★ of the oldest family-run restaurants in Dade County—since 1958—this is where locals dine out. (The Rotary Club meets each Wednesday at noon.) Specialties include pizza with light, crunchy crusts and ample toppings; mild, meaty conch chowder; mussels in garlic or marinara sauce; Caesar salad with lots of cheese and anchovies; antipasto with a homemade vinaigrette; ricotta-stuffed pasta shells in tomato sauce; yellowtail snapper française; and Key lime pie with plenty of real Key lime juice. More than a half-dozen early-bird entrées are offered 4:30–6:30 for $8.95, including soup or salad and potato or spaghetti. ⌧ *935 N. Krome Ave.,* ☎ *305/247–1544. AE, MC, V.*

$ ✕ **Farmers' Market Restaurant.** Although it's in the farmers' market and serves fresh vegetables, this restaurant's specialty is seafood. A family of fishermen runs the place, so fish and shellfish are only hours from the sea. Catering to the fishing and farming crowd, it opens at 5:30, serving pancakes, jumbo eggs, and fluffy omelettes with home fries or grits. The lunch menu has shrimp, fish, and conch baskets, as well as burgers, salads, and sandwiches. As at most Southern restaurants, fish tends to come fried, but you can ask for it broiled or grilled. ⌧ *300 N. Krome Ave.,* ☎ *305/242–0008. No credit cards.*

$$ ⊞ **Best Western Gateway to the Keys.** This two-story motel sits well back from the highway and contains such amenities as full closets, a heat lamp in the bathroom, and complimentary Continental breakfast. Standard rooms have two queen or one king bed. More expensive rooms come with wet bar, refrigerator, microwave, and coffeemaker. Otherwise it's a standard modern motel with floral prints and twin reading lamps. ⌧ *1 Strano Blvd., 33034,* ☎ *305/246–5100,* FAX *305/242–0056. 114 units. Pool, spa, coin laundry, dry cleaning. AE, D, DC, MC, V.*

$$ ⊞ **Hampton Inn.** This two-story motel just off the highway has good clean rooms (including a post–Hurricane Andrew wing) and public-friendly policies, including free Continental breakfast, local calls, and movie channels. All rooms have at least two upholstered chairs, twin

reading lamps, and a desk and chair. Units are color-coordinated and carpeted. Baths have tub-showers. ⊠ *124 E. Palm Dr., 33034,* ☎ *305/247–8833 or 800/426–7866,* ℻ *305/247–6456. 123 units. Pool. AE, D, DC, MC, V.*

Shopping
Florida Keys Factory Shops (⊠ 250 E. Palm Dr.) has 50 discount stores plus a small food court. **Robert Is Here** (⊠ 19900 Palm Dr. [S.W. 344th St.], ☎ 305/246–1592), a remarkable fruit stand, sells vegetables, fresh-fruit milk shakes, 10 flavors of honey, more than 100 flavors of jams and jellies, fresh juices, salad dressings, and, seasonally, some 40 kinds of tropical fruits, including carambola, litchi, egg fruit, monstera, sapodilla, soursop, sugar apple, and tamarind. The stand started in 1960, when 7-year-old Robert sat at this spot selling his father's bumper crop of cucumbers. Now Robert ships around the world, and everything is first quality. Seconds are given to needy area families. Kids love to look through the glass of an observation bee hive, count the 50 land tortoises, and talk to Fred, the family's green-winged macaw.

BISCAYNE NATIONAL PARK

Occupying 180,000 acres along the southern portion of Biscayne Bay, south of Miami and north of the Florida Keys, this national park is 96% underwater, and its altitude ranges from 4 feet above sea level to 10 fathoms, or 60 feet, below. Contained within it are four distinct zones formed during the Ice Age, some 10,000 years ago. From shore to sea, they are mangrove forest along the coast, Biscayne Bay, the undeveloped upper Florida keys, and coral reefs.

Mangroves line the mainland shore much as they do elsewhere in South Florida. Biscayne Bay, like Florida Bay, functions as a lobster sanctuary and a nursery for fish, sponges, and crabs. Manatees and sea turtles frequent its warm, shallow waters. Lamentably, this bay, too, is under assault from forces similar to those in its southern neighbor.

To the east, about 8 mi off the coast, lie 44 tiny keys, stretching 18 nautical mi north–south and accessible only by boat. There is no commercial transportation between the mainland and the islands, and only a handful can be visited: Elliott, Boca Chita, Adams, and Sands keys. The rest either are wildlife refuges, are too small, or have rocky shores or waters too shallow for boats. It's best to explore the keys between December and April, when the mosquito population is relatively quiescent.

Another 3 mi east of the keys, in the ocean, lies the park's main attraction—the northernmost section of Florida's living tropical coral reefs. Some are the size of a student's desk, others as large as a football field. You can take a glass-bottom boat ride to see this underwater wonderland, but you really have to snorkel or scuba dive to appreciate it fully. A diverse population of colorful fish—angelfish, gobies, grunts, parrot fish, pork fish, wrasses, and many more—flits through the reefs. Unfortunately, the coral is frequently harmed by boat anchors and commercial ships that run off course. At the park's boundary, the continental shelf runs 60 feet deep; farther east, the shelf falls rapidly away to a depth of 400 feet at the edge of the Gulf Stream.

More than 170 species of birds have been seen around the park. Though all of the keys offer excellent birding opportunities, Jones Lagoon, south of Adams Key, between Old Rhodes Key and Totten Key, is one of the best. It's approachable only by nonmotorized craft.

It took nearly five years for the park to recover from Hurricane Andrew. Most of the damage was limited to man-made structures and vegetation, and the reefs were relatively unharmed. In fact, scientists now believe the hurricane may actually have helped regenerate them. As with much post-Andrew construction, a new visitor center and other facilities are bigger and better than before.

Convoy Point

⑭ *9 mi east of Florida City, 30 mi south of downtown Miami.*

Reminiscent of area pioneer homes, the new **Convoy Point Visitor Center** is a wooden building with a metal roof and wide veranda from which you can look out across mangroves and Biscayne Bay and see the Miami skyline. At the entrance, a tile mosaic depicts the park's four major ecosystems. Inside, a museum, aquariums, hands-on exhibits, dioramas, and videos explore the systems in depth. Among the facilities are a weather station that forecasts reef conditions, a 50-seat auditorium, the park's concessioner, rest rooms with showers, a ranger information area, and bookstore. A short trail and boardwalk lead to a jetty and launch ramp. This is the only area of the park accessible without a boat. ⊠ *S.W. 328th St., Homestead,* ☎ *305/230–7275.* ⊠ *Free.* ☉ *Park daily 8–sunset; visitor center weekdays 8:30–4:30 (5:30 June–Aug.), weekends 8:30–5.*

Outdoor Activities and Sports

CANOEING

Biscayne National Underwater Park, Inc. (⊠ Convoy Point Visitor Center, ☎ 305/230–1100, FAX 305/230–1120), the park's official concessioner, has a dozen canoes for rent on a first-come, first-served basis. Prices are $7 an hour, $20 for four hours.

SCUBA DIVING AND SNORKELING

Biscayne National Underwater Park, Inc. (⊠ Convoy Point Visitor Center, Box 1270, Homestead 33090, ☎ 305/230–1100, FAX 305/230–1120) rents and sells equipment and conducts snorkel and dive trips aboard the 45-foot *Boca Chita*. Snorkel trips ($27.95) leave daily at 1:30 and include mask, fins, snorkel, and vest. Two-tank scuba trips, which leave at 8:30 on Wednesday, Saturday, and Sunday (daily during busy periods) cost $34.50, complete gear rental is $37, and instruction is available. Trips include 1¼ hours on reefs and wrecks. Reservations are recommended, especially December–February. Arrive 45 minutes before departure.

Elliott Key

⑮ *9 mi east of Convoy Point.*

This key, accessible only by boat (on your own or by special arrangement with the concessioner), has a rebuilt boardwalk made from recycled plastic and two nature trails with a variety of tropical plant life, including native gumbo-limbo, mahogany, and satin leaf trees. Take an informal, ranger-led nature walk, or walk its 7-mi length on your own along a rough path through the hammock that's locally referred to as the "spite highway," after developers bulldozed it before the park was created. Videos shown at the ranger station describe the island. Facilities include rest rooms, fresh water, showers (cold), grills, and a campground. Pets are allowed on a leash but not on trails.

Beach

A 30-foot-wide sandy beach about a mile north of the harbor on the west (bay) side of the key is the only one in the national park. Boaters like to anchor off it to swim. For day use only, it has picnic areas and a short trail that follows the shore and cuts through the hammock.

Lodging

$ 🏕 **Biscayne National Park.** Elliott Key has 40 primitive campsites, for which there are neither fees nor reservations. Just bring plenty of insect repellent. The park concessioner runs boats to the key periodically to drop off campers ($21 round-trip) because there is no regular ferry service or boat rental. However, there is a new $15 per night charge for docking private vessels.

Boca Chita Key

16   *10 mi northeast of Convoy Point.*

This island was once owned by Mark C. Honeywell, former president of Minneapolis's Honeywell Company. Most of the historical structures damaged by Hurricane Andrew have been repaired and stabilized, and revegetation, harbor repair, and rest room construction are complete. There is no fresh water, but grills and campsites (details similar to Elliott Key) are available. Access is by private boat only. No pets are allowed.

Adams Key

17   *9 mi southeast of Convoy Point.*

This small key, a stone's throw off the western tip of Elliott Key, is open for day use and has picnic areas, rest rooms, dockage, and a short trail that runs along the shore and through a hardwood hammock. Access is by private boat.

EVERGLADES A TO Z

Arriving and Departing

By Boat

If you're entering the United States by boat, you must phone **U.S. Customs** (☎ 800/432–1216) either from a marine phone or on first arriving ashore. At their discretion, customs agents will direct you to Dodge Island Seaport (Miami), will otherwise rendezvous with you, or will clear you by phone.

By Car

From Miami, the main highways to the area are U.S. 1, the Homestead Extension of Florida's Turnpike, and Krome Avenue (Rte. 997 [old U.S. 27]).

By Plane

Miami International Airport (MIA) is 34 mi from Homestead and 83 mi from Flamingo in Everglades National Park.

BETWEEN THE AIRPORT AND TOWNS

Airporter (☎ 800/830–3413) runs shuttle buses three times daily off-season, four times daily in winter, that stop at the Hampton Inn in Florida City on their way between MIA and the Florida Keys. Shuttle service, which takes about an hour, runs 6:10 AM–5:20 PM from Florida City, 7:30 AM–6 PM from the airport. Reserve in advance. Pickups can be arranged for all baggage-claim areas. The cost is $20 one-way.

Greyhound Lines (☎ 800/231–2222) buses from MIA to the Keys make a stop in Homestead (⌧ 5 N.E. 3rd Rd., ☎ 305/247–2040) three times a day. Buses leave from Concourse E, Lower Level and cost $6 one-way, $12 round-trip.

SuperShuttle (☎ 305/871–2000) operates 11-passenger air-conditioned vans to Homestead. Service from MIA is available around the clock, on demand; booths are located outside most luggage areas on the lower level. For the return to MIA, reserve 24 hours in advance. The cost is $41 for the first person, $12 for each additional person at the same address.

Getting Around

By Boat

Bring aboard the proper *NOAA Nautical Charts* before you cast off to explore park waters. The charts run $15–$15.95 at many marine stores in South Florida, at the Convoy Point Visitor Center in Biscayne National Park, and at Flamingo Marina in the Everglades.

The annual *Waterway Guide* (southern regional edition) is widely used by boaters. Bookstores all over South Florida sell it, or you can order it directly from the publisher (⊠ Intertec Publishing, Book Department, 6151 Powers Ferry Rd., Atlanta, GA 30339, ☎ 800/233–3359) for $33.95 plus $3 shipping and handling.

By Car

To reach Everglades National Park's Main Visitor Center and Flamingo, head west on Route 9336 in Florida City, and follow signs. From Homestead, the Main Visitor Center is 11 mi; Flamingo is 49 mi.

To get to the south end of Everglades National Park in the Florida Keys, take U.S. 1 south from Homestead. It's 27 mi to the Key Largo Ranger Station (⊠ Between Mile Markers 98 and 99, BS, Overseas Hwy.), which is not always staffed but has maps and information. From here the park is only accessible by boat.

The north entrance of Everglades National Park at Shark Valley is reached by taking the Tamiami Trail about 20 mi west of Krome Avenue.

To reach the west entrance of Everglades National Park at the Gulf Coast Visitor Center in Everglades City, take Route 29 south from the Tamiami Trail.

To reach Biscayne National Park from Homestead, take U.S. 1 or Krome Avenue to Lucy Street (Southeast 8th St.), and turn east. Lucy Street becomes North Canal Drive (Southwest 328th St.). Follow signs for about 8 mi to the park headquarters.

By Taxi

Cab companies servicing the area include **Action Express Taxi** (☎ 305/743–6800) and **South Dade Taxi** (☎ 305/256–4444).

Contacts and Resources

Car Rentals

Agencies in the area include **A&A Auto Rental** (⊠ 30005 S. Dixie Hwy., Homestead 33030, ☎ 305/246–0974), **Budget Rent a Car** (⊠ 29949 S. Dixie Hwy., Homestead 33030, ☎ 305/246–1000), and **Enterprise Rent-a-Car** (⊠ 30428 S. Dixie Hwy., Homestead 33030, ☎ 305/246–2056 or 800/325–8007).

Emergencies

Dial **911** for police, fire, or ambulance. If you are a TTY caller, tap the space bar or use a voice announcer to identify yourself. In the national parks, rangers answer police, fire, and medical emergencies: **Bis-**

cayne (☎ 305/247−7272) or **Everglades** (☎ 305/247−7272). **Florida Marine Patrol** (☎ 305/795−2145), a division of the Florida Department of Natural Resources, maintains a 24-hour telephone service for reporting boating emergencies and natural-resource violations. **Miami Beach Coast Guard Base** (✉ 100 MacArthur Causeway, Miami Beach, ☎ 305/535−4300 or 305/535−4314) responds to local marine emergencies and reports of navigation hazards. The base broadcasts on VHF-FM Channel 16. The National Weather Service supplies local forecasts through its **National Hurricane Center** (✉ Florida International University, 11691 S.W. 17th St., Miami, ☎ 305/229−4470).

HOSPITALS

Hospital emergency line (☎ 305/596−6556). **SMH Homestead Hospital** (✉ 160 N.W. 13th St., Homestead, ☎ 305/248−3232; physician referral, ☎ 305/633−2255 or 305/596−6557).

Guided Tours

The National Park Service organizes a variety of free programs, typically focusing on native wildlife, plants, and park history. At Biscayne National Park, for example, rangers give informal tours of Elliott and Boca Chita keys, which you can arrange in advance, depending on ranger availability. Contact the respective visitor centers for details.

AIRBOAT TOURS

In Everglades City, **Florida Boat Tours** (✉ 200 Rte. 29, ☎ 941/695−4400; 800/282−9194 in FL) runs 30- to 40-minute backcountry tours aboard custom-designed jet airboats. The cost is $12.95. **Swampland Airboat Tours** (✉ Box 476, Copeland 34137, ☎ 941/695−2740) offers custom tours of the Everglades or the Big Cypress National Preserve. The cost is $60 per hour for two or $25 per hour per person for three to six. Reservations are required. **Wooten's Everglades** (✉ Wooten's Alligator Farm, Tamiami Trail, ☎ 941/695−2781 or 800/282−2781) runs airboat and swamp-buggy tours through the Everglades. (Swamp buggies are giant tractorlike vehicles with oversize rubber wheels.) Tours of approximately 30 minutes cost $12.50.

Southwest of Florida City near the entrance to Everglades National Park, **Everglades Alligator Farm** (✉ 40351 S.W. 192nd Ave., ☎ 305/247−2628 or 800/644−9711) runs a 4-mi, 30-minute tour of the River of Grass with departures 20 minutes after the hour. The tour ($12.50) includes free hourly alligator and wildlife shows, or you can take in the show only ($7). No reservations are necessary.

From the Shark Valley area, **Buffalo Tiger's Florida Everglades Airboat Ride** (✉ 12 mi west of Krome Ave., 20 mi west of Miami city limits on Tamiami Trail, ☎ 305/559−5250) is led by a former chairman of the Miccosukee tribe. The 35- to 40-minute trip through the Everglades includes a stop at an old Native American camp. Tours cost $10 and operate Monday through Thursday and Saturday 10−sunset and Sunday 11−sunset. Reservations are not required. **Coopertown Airboat Ride** (✉ 5 mi west of Krome Ave. on Tamiami Trail, ☎ 305/226−6048) operates the oldest airboat rides in the Everglades (since 1945). The 30- to 35-minute tour visits two hammocks and alligator holes. The charge is $10, with a $24 minimum for the boat. **Everglades Gator Park** (✉ 12 mi west of Florida's Turnpike on Tamiami Trail, ☎ 305/559−2255 or 800/559−2205) offers 45-minute narrated airboat tours ($12). **Everglades Safari Park** (✉ 26700 Tamiami Trail, 9 mi west of Krome Ave., ☎ 305/226−6923 or 305/223−3804, FAX 305/554−5666) runs 40-minute airboat rides for $15. The **Miccosukee Indian Village** (✉ 25 mi west of Florida's Turnpike on Tamiami Trail, ☎ 305/223−8380) offers 30-minute airboat rides ($7) in addition to its other attractions.

Ray Cramer's Everglades Airboat Tours, Inc. (✉ Coopertown (mailing address: 1307 Almay St., Key Largo 33037), ☎ 305/852–5339) conducts airboat trips accommodating six to 12, for $42.60 per person. Ray Cramer spent his youth fishing, frogging, and hunting in the Everglades with his father and friends. Though daytime trips are offered, a better option is the tour that departs an hour before sundown so you can see birds and fish in daylight and alligators, raccoons, and other nocturnal animals when night falls.

AIR TOURS

Everglades Air Tours (✉ Homestead General Aviation Airport, 28790 S.W. 217th Ave., Homestead, ☎ 305/247–7757) gives bird's-eye tours of the Everglades and Florida Bay that last 30 minutes and cost $35 per person, with a two-passenger minimum.

BOAT TOURS

Tours at Biscayne National Park are now run by people-friendly **Biscayne National Underwater Park, Inc.** (✉ Convoy Point, east end of North Canal Dr. [S.W. 328th St.], Box 1270, Homestead 33090, ☎ 305/230–1100, FAX 305/230–1120). Daily trips (at 10, with a second trip at 1 during high season, according to demand) explore the park's living coral reefs 10 mi offshore on *Reef Rover IV,* a 53-foot glass-bottom boat that carries up to 48 passengers. On days when the weather is unsuitable for reef viewing, an alternative two-hour, ranger-led, interpretive tour visits Elliott Key. Reservations are recommended, especially in summer. The cost is $19.95, and you should arrive at least 45 minutes before departure.

Everglades National Park Boat Tours (✉ Gulf Coast Visitor Center, Everglades City, ☎ 941/695–2591; 800/445–7724 in FL) operates three separate tours ($13–$16) through the Ten Thousand Islands region and can accommodate large numbers. (The two biggest boats have drink concessions.) Trips that stop on Sandfly Island include a 30-minute, ranger-led tour of the island's flora and fauna. **Majestic Everglades Excursions** (✉ Box 241, Everglades City 34139, ☎ 941/695–2777) are led by exceptionally well-informed guides Frank and Georgia Garrett. The 3½- to 4-hour ecotours, on a 24-foot boat with a covered deck, take in Everglades National Park and the Ten Thousand Islands. Narration focuses on the region's unique flora and fauna and its colorful early residents. Departing from Glades Haven, just shy of a mile south of the circle in Everglades City, tours are limited to six passengers and include brunch or afternoon snacks. The cost is $65.

CANOE AND KAYAK TOURS

North American Canoe Tours (✉ Ivey House, 107 Camellia St., Box 5038, Everglades City 34139, ☎ 941/695–3299, FAX 941/695–4155) leads one-day to five-night Everglades tours November through April. Highlights include bird and gator sightings, mangrove forests, no-man's-land beaches, relics of the hideouts of infamous and just plain reclusive characters, and spectacular sunsets. Included in the cost of extended tours ($450–$750) are canoes, all necessary equipment, a guide, meals, and lodging for the first and last nights at the Ivey House B&B. Day trips cost $40–$60, and one-day bicycling and hiking tours are also offered.

TRAM TOURS

Starting at the Shark Valley visitor center, **Shark Valley Tram Tours** (✉ Box 1739, Tamiami Station, Miami 33144, ☎ 305/221–8455) follows a 15-mi loop road into the interior, stopping at a 50-foot observation tower especially good for viewing gators in winter. Two-hour narrated tours depart hourly 9–4 and cost $8. Reservations are recommended December–March.

Visitor Information

Big Cypress National Preserve (✉ HCR61, Box 11, Ochopee 33943, ☎ 941/695–4111). **Biscayne National Park:** Convoy Point Visitor Center (✉ 9700 S.W. 328th St., Box 1369, Homestead 33090-1369, ☎ 305/230–7275). **Everglades City Chamber of Commerce** (✉ Rte. 29 and Tamiami Trail, Everglades City 33929, ☎ 941/695–3941). **Everglades National Park:** Main Visitor Center (✉ 40001 Rte. 9336, Homestead 33034-6733, ☎ 305/242–7700), Gulf Coast Visitor Center (✉ Rte. 29, Everglades City 34139, ☎ 941/695–3311), Flamingo Visitor Center (✉ 1 Flamingo Lodge Hwy., Flamingo 33034-6798, ☎ 941/695–2945). **Greater Homestead–Florida City Chamber of Commerce** (✉ 43 N. Krome Ave., Homestead 33030, ☎ 305/247–2332 or 888/352–4891). **Tropical Everglades Visitor Association** (✉ 160 U.S. 1, Florida City 33034, ☎ 305/245–9180 or 800/388–9669, FAX 305/247–4335).

5 Fort Lauderdale and Broward County

Once known for its wild spring breaks, this southern Florida city on the east coast is newly chic. Just as the beach has renewed itself, so has downtown— with revitalized nightlife and an emerging cultural arts district.

By Herb Hiller

Updated by
Alan Macher

WHEN YOU THINK OF FORT LAUDERDALE, do you conjure up an image of: (a) scenic inland waterways dotted with million-dollar homes, (b) thousands of rowdy college students letting loose on spring break, or (c) a revitalized city with people-friendly beach access, a growing arts and culture district, and a bustling downtown with new restaurants and a reenergized nightlife scene?

Today's answer is *c*. True, tour boats ply the waterways as they did when, in the years after World War II, sleepy Fort Lauderdale promoted itself as the "Venice of America" and the nation's yachting capital. A few college students still show up for spring break, but it's a far cry from the hordes that once came. In 1960, the narrator of the film *Where the Boys Are* described how 20,000 students swarmed to these peaceful shores during spring break and "turned night into day and a small corner of heaven into a sizable chunk of bedlam." By 1985, the 20,000 had mushroomed to 350,000. Hotel owners complained of 12 students to a room, the beachfront was littered with souvenir outlets and tacky bars, and drug trafficking was a major problem. So city leaders put in place policies and restrictions designed to encourage students to go elsewhere. And they did.

Now a dozen years later, the city has been totally transformed into a leading warm-weather vacation destination. This remarkable turnaround has resulted from major investments by both private and public sectors. More than $1.5 billion in new projects are to be completed by 2000, including a major airport expansion and new attractions. Fort Lauderdale has clearly become a city with a mission.

Take Las Olas Boulevard, whose emergence has been credited with creating a whole new identity for Fort Lauderdale. Though it was already famous for its trendy shops, now the sidewalks aren't rolled up when the sun goes down. Nearly two dozen restaurants have sprung up, and on weekend evenings hundreds of strollers tour the boulevard, taking in the food, the jazz bands, and the scene. On-street parking on weekends has slowed traffic, and the street has a village atmosphere. Two new entertainment, shopping, and restaurant centers have extended the boulevard's reach: At the eastern end, at the beach, is the 17-story Beach Place, and at the western end is Brickell Station, an even larger complex with a 24-screen movie theater and a half-dozen more restaurants.

Farther west, along New River, is evidence of Fort Lauderdale's cultural renaissance: a new arts and entertainment district and its crown jewel, the Broward Center for the Performing Arts. Still farther west, the county enters major-league sports with a new $212 million arena for the NHL's Florida Panthers, in Sunrise.

Of course, what makes Fort Lauderdale and Broward County a major draw for visitors are the beaches. Fort Lauderdale's 2-mi stretch of unobstructed beachfront has been enhanced even further with a sparkling new look designed for the pleasure of pedestrians rather than cars.

Tying this all together is a transportation system that is relatively hassle-free, unusual in congested South Florida. A new expressway system, including the long-awaited widening of I–95, connects the city and suburbs and even provides a direct route to the airport and Port Everglades. For slower and more scenic rides, you can take the trolley, or to really see this canal-laced city, cruise aboard the water taxi.

None of this was envisioned by Napoleon Bonaparte Broward, Florida's governor from 1905 to 1909, for whom the county was named. His drainage schemes opened much of the marshy Everglades region for farming, ranching, and settlement (in retrospect an environmental disaster). Fort Lauderdale's first known white settler, Charles Lewis, established a plantation along the New River in 1793. But it was for Major William Lauderdale, who built a fort at the river's mouth in 1838 during the Seminole Indian wars, that the city was named.

Incorporated in 1911, with just 175 residents, Fort Lauderdale grew rapidly during the Florida boom of the 1920s. Today its population is 150,000, and its suburbs keep growing—1.3 million live in the county. New homes, offices, and shopping centers have filled in the gaps between older communities along the coastal ridge. Now they're marching west along I–75, I–595, and Route 869 (the Sawgrass Expressway). Broward County is blessed with near-ideal weather, with some 3,000 hours of sunshine a year. The average temperature is 66°F–77°F in winter, 84°F in summer. Once a home for retirees, the county today attracts younger, working-age families. It's always been a sane and pleasant place to live. Now it's also becoming one of Florida's most diverse and dynamic places to vacation.

Pleasures and Pastimes

The Arts
Taking in the arts is a favorite part of any trip to Fort Lauderdale. During the past 20 years, the city has made a massive financial commitment, resulting in an arts district whose centerpiece, the Broward Center for the Performing Arts, is complemented by many galleries and museums.

Beaches
Broward County's beachfront extends for miles without interruption, although the character of the communities behind the beach changes. For example, in Hallandale, the beach is backed by towering condominiums; in Hollywood, by motels and the hoi polloi Broadwalk; and just north of there—blessedly—there's nothing at all.

Cruises
Superb facilities and ease of transportation (the airport is practically next door) have made Port Everglades one of the world's busiest cruise ports, second only to the Port of Miami in terms of passenger traffic. During the busy winter season, more than 30 ships dock at Port Everglades, most offering three- and seven-day cruises to the Caribbean. Several lines also offer day cruises to the Bahamas. The port is a favorite shore leave spot for U.S. Navy and foreign naval ships, and public tours are often available when these ships are in port.

Dining
Food critics in dining and travel magazines agree that the Greater Fort Lauderdale area offers some of the finest and most varied dining of any U.S. city its size. You can pick from the cuisines of Asia, Europe, or Central, South, or (naturally) North America and enjoy more than just the food. The ambiance, wine, service, and decor can be as varied as the language spoken, and memorable, too.

Fishing
Four main types of fishing are available in Broward County: bottom or drift-boat fishing from party boats, deep-sea fishing for large sport fish on charters, angling for freshwater game fish, and dropping a line off a pier. For bottom fishing, party boats typically charge between $20 and $22 per person for up to four hours, including rod, reel, and bait. For charters, a half day for as many as six people runs up to $325, six-hour charters up to $495, and full-day charters (eight hours) up to $595.

Skipper and crew, plus bait and tackle, are included. Split parties can be arranged at a cost of about $85 per person for a full day.

Several Broward towns—Dania, Lauderdale-by-the-Sea, Pompano Beach, and Deerfield Beach—have fishing piers that draw anglers for pompano, amber jack, bluefish, snapper, blue runners, snook, mackerel, and Florida lobsters.

Golf
More than 50 courses green the landscape in metro Fort Lauderdale, including famous championship links. Most area courses are inland, in the suburbs west of the city, and there are some great bargains. Off-season (May–October) greens fees range from $15 to $45, peak-season (November–April) charges run $35 to $75. Fees can be trimmed by working through Next Day Golf, a local service, and many hotels offer golf packages.

Horse Racing
If you want to catch a race or place a bet, visit Hallandale's Gulfstream Park Race Track, which features Thoroughbred racing including the Florida Derby, or Pompano Harness Track.

Lodging
In Fort Lauderdale, Pompano Beach, and the Hollywood-Hallandale area, dozens of hotels open onto Atlantic beaches. In Fort Lauderdale, however, lodgings are mostly limited to the upland side of beach roads and in much of Hollywood to the upland side of the Broadwalk, leaving the beaches open. Lodgings range from economy motels—notably those along much of the Hollywood beachfront and in the non-ocean-front areas of Fort Lauderdale—to a few opulent beachfront and canal-front resorts in Fort Lauderdale. Good choices are found, too, in Lauderdale-by-the-Sea, a small northern suburb graced with an accessible cultural life and high standards.

An innovative Superior Small Lodging program, set up by the Greater Fort Lauderdale Convention & Visitors Bureau, has led to substantial upgrading of many smaller properties, without appreciable elevation of their usually modest rates.

Wherever you stay, reservations are a good idea. Tourists from the northern United States and Canada fill the hotels from Thanksgiving through Easter. In summer, southerners and Europeans create a second season that's almost as busy.

Scuba Diving
Good diving can be enjoyed within 20 minutes of shore. Among the most popular of the county's 80 dive sites is the 2-mi-wide, 23-mi-long Fort Lauderdale Reef, the product of Florida's most successful artificial reef–building program. More than a dozen houseboats, ships, and oil platforms have been sunk in depths of 10 to 150 feet to provide a habitat for fish and other marine life, as well as to help stabilize beaches. The most famous sunken ship is the 200-foot German freighter *Mercedes,* which was blown onto Palm Beach socialite Mollie Wilmot's pool terrace in a violent Thanksgiving storm in 1984; the ship is now underwater a mile off Fort Lauderdale beach.

Shopping
Fort Lauderdale offers two kinds of shopping—in individual shops and boutiques along Las Olas Boulevard and Route A1A, on the beach, and at that ubiquitous American institution—the mall, several of which are in western suburbs.

Exploring Fort Lauderdale and Broward County

Though most activity centers on Fort Lauderdale, there's plenty to see in other parts of Broward County, to the north, south, and, increasingly, west.

The metro area is laid out in a basic grid system, and only the hundreds of canals and waterways interrupt the straight-line path of the streets and roads. Nomenclature is important here. Streets, roads, courts, and drives run east–west. Avenues, terraces, and ways run north–south. Boulevards can run any which way. Las Olas Boulevard is one of the most important east-west thoroughfares, whereas Route A1A—referred to as Atlantic Boulevard and Ocean Boulevard along some stretches—runs along the north-south oceanfront. These names can be confusing to visitors, as there are separate streets called Atlantic and Ocean in Hollywood and Pompano Beach.

The boulevards, those that are paved and those made of water, give Fort Lauderdale its distinct character. Honeycombed with more than 260 mi of navigable waterways, the city is home port for about 40,000 privately owned boats. You won't see the gondolas you'd find in Venice, but you will see just about every other type of craft imaginable docked beside the thousands of homes and businesses that each have a little piece of waterfront. Visitors can tour the canals via the city's water-taxi system, made up of small motor launches that provide transportation and quick, narrated tours. Larger, multideck touring vessels and motorboat rentals for self-guided tours are other options. The Intracoastal Waterway, a massive canal that parallels Route A1A, is the nautical equivalent of an interstate highway. It runs north–south through the metro area and provides easy access to neighboring beach communities; Deerfield Beach and Pompano Beach lie to the north and Dania and Hollywood lie to the south. All are within a 15-mi radius of the city center.

Great Itineraries

Since most Broward County sights are relatively close to each other, it's easy to pack a lot into very little time, but you will probably need a car. You can catch a lot of the history, the museums, and the shops and bistros in Fort Lauderdale's downtown area and along Las Olas Boulevard, and then if you feel like hitting the beach, just take a 10-minute drive east to the intersection of Las Olas and A1A and you're there. Many of the neighboring suburbs, with attractions of their own, are just north or south of Fort Lauderdale. As a result, you can hit most of the high points in 3 days, and with 7 to 10 days, you can see virtually all of Broward's mainstream charms.

Numbers in the text correspond to numbers in the margin and on the Broward County and Fort Lauderdale maps.

IF YOU HAVE 3 DAYS

With a bigger concentration of hotels, restaurants, and sights to see than its suburban neighbors, ⊺ **Fort Lauderdale** ①–⑪ makes a logical base of operations for any visit. On your first day there, see the downtown area, especially Las Olas Boulevard between Southeast 6th and Southeast 11th avenues. After enjoying lunch at a sidewalk café, head for the nearby Arts and Science District and the downtown Riverwalk ⑤, which you can see at a leisurely pace in half a day. On your second day, spend at least some time at the beach, shopping when the hot sun drives you off the sand. Tour the canals on the third day, either on a rented boat from one of the various marinas along Route

A1A, or via the water taxi or a sightseeing boat, both of which can be boarded all along the Intracoastal Waterway.

IF YOU HAVE 5 DAYS

With additional time, you can see more of the beach and the arts district and still work in some outdoor sports—and you'll be more able to rearrange your plans depending on the weather. On the first day, visit the Arts and Science District and the downtown Riverwalk ⑤. Set aside the next day for an offshore adventure, perhaps a deep-sea fishing charter or a dive trip to the Fort Lauderdale Reef. On the third day, shop, dine, and relax along the Fort Lauderdale beachfront ⑨, and at the end of the day, sneak a peak at the Hillsboro Light, at Lighthouse Point ⑱. Another good day can be spent at the Hugh Taylor Birch State Recreation Area. Enjoy your fifth day in Hollywood ⑳, perhaps combining time on the Broadwalk with a visit to the Anne Kolb Nature Center at West Lake Park.

IF YOU HAVE 7 DAYS

With a full week, you have time for a wider variety of attractions, fitting in beach time around other activities. In fact, enjoy any of the county's public beach areas on your first day. The second day can be spent in another favorite pastime—shopping, either at chic shops or one of the malls. On the next day, tour the canals on a sightseeing boat or water taxi. Then shop and dine along Las Olas Boulevard. The fourth day might be devoted to the many museums in downtown Fort Lauderdale and the fifth to an airboat ride at Sawgrass Recreation Park ⑭, at the edge of the Everglades. Fort Lauderdale offers plenty of facilities for outdoor recreation; spend day six fishing and picnicking on one of the area's many piers or playing a round at a top golf course. Set aside the seventh day for Hollywood ⑳, where you can stroll along the scenic Broadwalk, or walk through the aviary at Flamingo Gardens, in Davie ㉒, before relaxing in peaceful Hollywood North Beach Park.

When to Tour Fort Lauderdale and Broward County

Tourists visit the area all year long, choosing to come in winter or summer depending on interests, hobbies, and the climate where they live. The winter season, about Thanksgiving through March, still sees the biggest influx of visitors and "snowbirds"—seasonal residents who show up when the snow starts to fly up north. Concert, art, and show seasons are at their height then, and restaurants and highways all show the stress of crowds, Americans and Europeans alike.

Summer has its own fans. Waits at even the most popular restaurants are likely to be reasonable or even nonexistent, but though few services close in the summer, some may establish slightly shorter hours than during the peak season. Summer is the rainy season; the tropics-style rain arrives about midafternoon and is usually gone in an hour. When downpours hit, however, driving can be treacherous.

For golfers, almost anytime is great for playing. Just like everywhere else, waits for tee times are longer on weekends year-round.

Remember that sun can cause real scorching burns all year long, especially at midday, marking the tourist from the experienced resident or vacationer. You might want to plan your beach time for morning and late afternoon and go sightseeing or shopping in between.

FORT LAUDERDALE

Like some southeast Florida neighbors, Fort Lauderdale has been revitalizing itself for several years. What's unusual in a state where gaudy tourist zones stand aloof from workaday downtowns is that the city exhibits consistency at both ends of the 2-mi Las Olas corridor. The sparkling look results from a decision to thoroughly improve both beachfront and downtown, as opposed to focusing design attention in town and letting the beach fall prey to development solely by T-shirt retailers. Matching the downtown's new arts district, cafés, and boutiques is an equally inventive beach area with its own share of cafés and shops facing an undeveloped shoreline.

Downtown

The jewel of the downtown area along the New River is a new arts and entertainment district. Pricey tickets are available for Broadway shows at the riverfront Broward Center for the Performing Arts. Clustered within a five-minute walk are the Museum of Discovery and Science, the expanding Fort Lauderdale Historical Museum, and the Museum of Art. Restaurants, sidewalk cafés, delis, and blues, folk, jazz, reggae, and rock clubs flourish. Brickell Station, along several blocks once owned by pioneers William and Mary Brickell, opens its multi-story entertainment stages, restaurants, and shops in 1998.

Tying this district together is the Riverwalk, which extends 1 mi along the New River's north bank and ½ mi along the south. Tropical gardens with benches and interpretive displays fringe the walk on one side, boat landings on the other. East along Riverwalk is Stranahan House, and a block away, Las Olas attractions begin. Tropical landscaping and trees separate the traffic lanes in some blocks, setting off fine shops, restaurants, and popular nightspots. From here it's five minutes by car or 30 minutes by water taxi back to the beach.

A Good Tour

Start on Southeast 6th Avenue at Las Olas Boulevard, where you'll find **Stranahan House** ①, a turn-of-the-century structure that's now a museum. Between Southeast 6th and 11th avenues, Las Olas has Spanish-Colonial buildings housing high-fashion boutiques, jewelry shops, and art galleries. If you drive east, you'll cross into the Isles, Fort Lauderdale's most prestigious neighborhood, where homes line canals with large yachts beside the seawalls.

Return west on Las Olas to Andrews Avenue, turn right, and park in one of the municipal garages so you can walk around downtown Fort Lauderdale. First stop is the **Museum of Art** ②, which has a major collection of works from the CoBrA (Copenhagen, Brussels, and Amsterdam) movement. Walk one block north to the **Broward County Main Library** ③ to see works from Broward's Art in Public Places program.

Go west on Southeast 2nd Street to Southwest 2nd Avenue, turn left, and stop at the **Fort Lauderdale Historical Museum** ④, which surveys the city's not-so-recent history. Just to the south is the palm-lined **Riverwalk** ⑤, a good place for a leisurely stroll. Head north toward a cluster of new facilities collectively known as the Arts and Science District. The district contains the outdoor Esplanade, whose exhibits include a hands-on display of the science and history of navigation, and the major science attraction, the **Museum of Discovery and Science** ⑥. The adjacent Broward Center for the Performing Arts, a massive glass-and-concrete structure by the river, opened in 1991.

Finally, go west along Las Olas Boulevard to Southwest 7th Avenue and the entrance to **Sailboat Bend** ⑦. You can return to the start of the tour by traveling east along Las Olas Boulevard.

TIMING

Depending on how long you like to linger in museums and how many hours you want to spend in the quaint shops on Las Olas Boulevard, you can spend anything from half a day to an entire day on this tour.

Sights to See

3 Broward County Main Library. This distinctive building was designed by Marcel Breuer. Works on display from Broward's Art in Public Places program include a painting by Yaacov Agam; a wood construction by Marc Beauregard; an outdoor, aluminum-and-steel sculpture by Dale Eldred; and ceramic tile by Ivan Chermayeff. (Art in Public Places displays more than 200 works—painting, sculpture, photographs, weaving—by nationally renowned and Florida artists. Pieces can be found at 13 major sites, including the main bus terminal and the airport.) Productions from theater to poetry readings are presented in a 300-seat auditorium. ⊠ *100 S. Andrews Ave.,* ☎ *954/357–7444 or 954/357–7457 for self-guided Art in Public Places walking tour brochure.* ☜ *Free.* ⊙ *Mon.–Thurs. 9–9, Fri. and Sat. 9–5, Sun. noon–5:30.*

4 Fort Lauderdale Historical Museum. In 1996 this museum expanded into several historic buildings, including the King-Cromartie House and the New River Inn. The complex surveys city history from the Seminole era to World War II. A model in the lobby depicts old Fort Lauderdale. There's also a research library and bookstore. ⊠ *219 S.W. 2nd Ave.,* ☎ *954/463–4431.* ☜ *$2.* ⊙ *Tues.–Fri. 10–4.*

★ 2 Museum of Art. Housed in an Edward Larrabee Barnes–designed building that's considered an architectural masterpiece, this museum has Florida's largest art exhibition space. The impressive permanent collection features 20th-century European and American art, including works by Picasso, Calder, Moore, Dali, Rivers, Warhol, and Stella, as well as a notable collection of works by celebrated Ashcan School artist William Glackens. Opened in 1986, the museum launched a revitalization of the downtown district and nearby Riverwalk area. ⊠ *1 E. Las Olas Blvd.,* ☎ *954/763–6464.* ☜ *$6.* ⊙ *Tues.–Thurs. and Sat. 10–5, Fri. 10–8, Sun. noon–5.*

★ ☙ 6 Museum of Discovery and Science. Forget those old, cheesy 3D movies. The new IMAX theater—converted to 3D in a $2.5 million project—uses the latest film technology; regularly changing features shown on a five-story screen will astound you. The museum also features interactive exhibits on ecology, health, and outer space. Many displays focus on the local environment, including a replica of an oak forest complete with mosses, lichens, and air plants, which grow without soil. Another unusual exhibit offers a cutaway of an Indian shell mound. For a sunny respite from the labyrinth of indoor displays, check out the exhibits on the Esplanade. ⊠ *401 S.W. 2nd St.,* ☎ *954/467–6637 for museum or 954/463–4629 for IMAX.* ☜ *Museum $6, IMAX $5, both $8.* ⊙ *Weekdays 10–5, Sat. 10–8:30, Sun. noon–5.*

★ 5 Riverwalk. This lovely, paved promenade on the north bank of the New River is great for entertainment as well as views. On the first Sunday of every month a jazz brunch attracts visitors. The walk is being extended 2 mi on both sides of the beautiful urban stream, connecting the facilities of the Arts and Science District.

7 Sailboat Bend. Between Las Olas and the river, as well as just across the river, lies a neighborhood with much of the character of Old Town in Key West and historic Coconut Grove in Miami. No shops or services are located here.

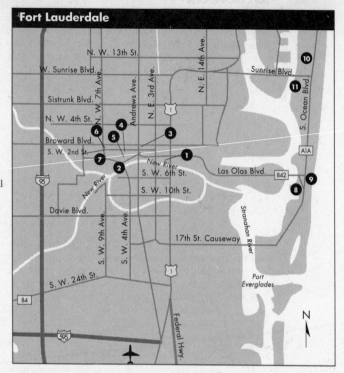

Fort Lauderdale

● **Stranahan House.** The oldest standing structure in the city was once the home of pioneer businessman Frank Stranahan. Stranahan arrived in 1892 and, with his wife, Ivy, befriended the Seminole Indians, traded with them, and taught them "new ways." In 1901 he built a store and later made it his home. Now it's a museum with many of his original furnishings on display. ⊠ *1 Stranahan Pl. (S.E. 6th Ave. at Las Olas Blvd.),* ☎ *954/524–4736.* ⚏ *$5.* ⊗ *Wed.–Sat. 10–4, Sun. 1–4.*

The Beach

No trip to the Fort Lauderdale area would be complete without breathing in the salt air and feeling the sand against your skin. Fort Lauderdale's beachfront offers the best of all possible worlds, with easy access to restaurants and shops. For 2 mi beginning just north of the new welcome center and the big Radisson Bahia Mar Beach Resort, strollers and café goers along Route A1A enjoy clear views, typically across rows of colorful beach umbrellas, to the sea and ships passing in and out of nearby Port Everglades. Those on the beach can look back on an exceptionally graceful promenade.

Pedestrians rank ahead of cars in Fort Lauderdale. Broad walkways line both sides of the shore road, and traffic has been trimmed to two gently curving northbound lanes, where in-line skaters dance alongside the slow-moving cars. On the beach side, a low masonry wall, which serves as an extended bench, edges the promenade. At night, the wall is wrapped in ribbons of fiber-optic color. On the west (inland) side of the street, the 17-story Beach Place residential, retail, and entertainment complex opened in late 1996, two blocks north of Las Olas. Otherwise there are mostly low-rise hotels plus a defining row of smart cafés, bars, and shops that seem to have sprung up overnight.

The most crowded portion of beach is between Las Olas and Sunrise boulevards. This is the onetime "strip" famed from *Where the Boys Are* and the era of spring-break madness, now but a memory. Parking is readily available, often at parking meters.

North of the redesigned beachfront are another 2 mi of open and natural coastal landscape. Much of the way parallels the Hugh Taylor Birch State Recreation Area, which preserves a patch of primeval Florida.

A Good Tour

Go east on Southeast 17th Street across the Brooks Memorial Causeway over the Intracoastal Waterway and bear left onto Seabreeze Boulevard (Route A1A). You will pass through a neighborhood of older homes set in lush vegetation before emerging at the south end of Fort Lauderdale's beachfront strip. On your left is the newly renovated Radisson Bahia Mar Beach Resort, where novelist John McDonald's fictional hero, Travis McGee, is honored with a plaque at marina slip F-18, where he docked his houseboat. Three blocks north, visit the **International Swimming Hall of Fame Museum and Aquatic Complex** ⑧, which celebrates its 33rd anniversary in 1998. As you approach Las Olas Boulevard, you will see the lyrical new styling that has given a distinctly European flavor to the **Fort Lauderdale beachfront** ⑨.

Turn left off Route A1A at Sunrise Boulevard, then right into **Hugh Taylor Birch State Recreation Area** ⑩, where many outdoor activities can be enjoyed amid picturesque flora and fauna. Cross Sunrise Boulevard and visit the **Bonnet House** ⑪ to marvel at both the mansion and the surrounding subtropical 35-acre estate.

TIMING

The beach is all about recreation and leisure. To enjoy it as it's meant to be, allow at least a day to loll about or rent a fishing boat.

Sights to See

★ ⑪ **Bonnet House.** A 35-acre oasis in the heart of the beach area, this subtropical estate is a tribute to the history of old South Florida. The charming mansion was the winter residence of Frederic and Evelyn Bartlett, artists whose personal touches and small surprises are evident throughout. Whether you're interested in architecture, artwork, or the natural environment, this is a special place. ⊠ *900 N. Birch Rd.,* ☎ *954/563–5393.* ⊠ *$9.* ☉ *Wed.–Fri. 10–2, weekends noon–2.*

★ ⑨ **Fort Lauderdale beachfront.** A wave theme unifies the setting—from the low, white wave wall between the beach and widened beachfront promenade to the widened and bricked inner promenade in front of shops, restaurants, and hotels. Alone among Florida's major beachfront communities, Fort Lauderdale's beach remains open and uncluttered. More than ever, the boulevard is worth promenading.

⑩ **Hugh Taylor Birch State Recreation Area.** Amid the tropical greenery of this 180-acre park you can stroll along a nature trail, visit the Birch House Museum, picnic, play volleyball, pitch horseshoes, and paddle a rented canoe. ⊠ *3109 E. Sunrise Blvd.,* ☎ *954/564–4521.* ⊠ *$3.25 per vehicle with up to 8 people.* ☉ *Daily 8–sunset; ranger-guided nature walks Fri. at 10:30.*

★ ⑧ **International Swimming Hall of Fame Museum and Aquatic Complex.** This monument to underwater accomplishments has two 10-lane, 50-meter pools and an exhibition building featuring photos, medals, and other souvenirs from major swimming events around the world, as well as a theater that shows films of onetime swimming stars Johnny Weissmuller and Esther Williams. ⊠ *1 Hall of Fame Dr.,* ☎ *954/462–6536 for museum or 954/468–1580 for pool.* ⊠ *$3 museum, $3 pool.* ☉

*Museum and pro shop daily 9–7; pool weekdays 8–4 and 6–8, week-
ends 8–4; closed mid-Dec.–mid-Jan.*

Dining

American

$$$ ✕ **Burt & Jack's.** At the far end and most scenic lookout of Port Ev-
erglades, this local favorite has been operated by veteran restaurateur
Jack Jackson and actor Burt Reynolds since 1984. Behind the heavy
mission doors and bougainvillea, guests are presented with Maine lob-
ster, steaks, and chops, and the waitstaff displays the main ingredients
in the raw before orders are taken. The two-story gallery of hacienda-
like dining rooms surrounded by glass has views of both Port Ever-
glades and John U. Lloyd Beach State Recreation Area. Come for
cocktails in early evening on Saturday or Sunday and watch the cruise
ships steam out. The dining area is no-smoking. ✉ *Berth 23, Port Ev-
erglades,* ☎ *954/522–2878 or 954/525–5225. Jacket required. AE,
D, DC, MC, V. No lunch.*

$$$ ✕ **Mark's Las Olas.** Mark's is an expansion of Mark's Cafe in North
★ Dade with chef Mark Militello in command. Entrées change daily, but
typical choices include Gulf shrimp, dolphin, yellowtail snapper,
grouper, swordfish, Florida lobster, and callaloo (a West Indian spinach),
chayote (cho-cho on Mark's menu), ginger, jicama, and plantain, all
brilliantly presented and combined in sauces that tend to be low fat.
Pastas and full-size dinner pizzas are thoughtful offerings. Metallic fin-
ishes bounce the hubbub around the room. ✉ *1032 E. Las Olas Blvd.,*
☎ *954/463–1000. AE, DC, MC, V.*

Continental

$$$ ✕ **Down Under.** This elegant dining room in a gracious old house has
★ nothing to do with Australia. The name refers to the location, below
a bridge approach at the edge of the Intracoastal Waterway. The
gourmet cuisine includes Florida farm-raised striped bass with fennel
and broth, spinach flan, tomato strips, and potatoes; a classic duck con-
fit with crunchy red cabbage, roasted new potatoes, and truffle sauce;
and many grilled meats, such as a hot and spicy Jamaican jerked roast
pork tenderloin with Calvados apples, a trio of lamb chops, and steak
au poivre. Desserts include raspberry tiramisù and a Grand Marnier
sabayon with fresh berries. ✉ *3000 E. Oakland Park Blvd.,* ☎
954/563–4123. AE, D, DC, MC, V.

$$$ ✕ **Primavera.** Northern Italian food is the specialty at this lovely find
in the middle of an ordinary shopping plaza. Elegant floral arrange-
ments enhance the fine dining experience. In addition to interesting pasta
and risotto entrées, there is a wide variety of creative fish, poultry, veal,
and beef dinners. One of the chef's favorites is veal chop Boscaiola (with
shallots, wild mushrooms, and bordelaise sauce). Primavera is renowned
for its spectacular assortment of both appetizers and desserts. ✉ *830
E. Oakland Park Blvd.,* ☎ *954/564–6363. AE, D, DC, MC, V.*

$$$ ✕ **Sheffield's.** You might expect dishes like beef Wellington,
chateaubriand, and rack of lamb at this formal oceanfront restaurant
in Fort Lauderdale's most upscale luxury hotel, but skillful prepara-
tion keeps them from becoming Continental clichés. An extensive
seafood selection includes salmon, grouper, swordfish, tuna, tilapia,
red snapper, dolphin, and lobster; all can be ordered sautéed, grilled,
blackened, poached, or broiled. A curried mango glaze and fresh raisin
butter are two of the excellent toppings you can choose from, and the
symphony of shellfish, made with lobster, shrimp, and scallops, is ex-
cellent eating. ✉ *Marriott's Harbor Beach Resort, 3030 Holiday Dr.,*
☎ *954/525–4000. AE, D, DC, MC, V.*

$$ ★ **Mistral.** This dining room, surrounded by tropical art and pottery, rates high in both taste and looks. The kitchen staff turns out hearty pastas, such as a *primavera* redolent with garlic and herbs and *tagliolini* (an angel-hair pasta) with prosciutto, pine nuts, and tomato. Other favorites are grilled shrimp and black-bean cakes as well as pan-seared dolphin. Pizzas, big salads, and a strong selection of affordable wines, including by the glass, are also served. As part of a novelty dinner you can board a train replica for a progressive dinner that includes Mistral's two sister restaurants: Evangeline, just down the oceanfront walk, and Sage, in town. ⊠ *201 Rte. A1A,* ☎ *954/463–4900. AE, D, DC, MC, V.*

Creole

$$$ ✕ **Evangeline.** Set inside and out on the ocean drive just south of its sister restaurant Mistral, Evangeline celebrates Acadian Louisiana in decor and food. The mood is created by paneled wainscoting and plank floors—a tankard and tavern look—highlighted by verse from Longfellow's legendary poem inscribed along the turn of the ceiling. Traditional favorites include smoked rabbit gumbo with andouille sausage, a crawfish Caesar salad, jambalaya (clams, mussels, shrimp, and chicken andouille with a Creole sauce), sautéed alligator in a meunière sauce topped with flash-fried oysters, and crisp roasted duckling with poached plums and prunelle brandy. There's music nightly, and a Dixieland band plays weekends, including Sunday afternoon. ⊠ *211 Rte. A1A,* ☎ *954/522–7001. AE, D, DC, MC, V.*

French

$$ ✕ **French Quarter.** This 1920 building, formerly a Red Cross headquarters, sits on a quiet street, just off bustling Las Olas Boulevard. The French-style architecture has a touch of New Orleans style, and the food captures both Creole and traditional French elements. Interior rooms are small and intimate, watched over by the friendly, excellent waitstaff. Among the favorites are shrimp *maison* (large shrimp sautéed with carrots and mushrooms in beurre blanc), bouillabaisse, crab cakes, and escargot appetizers. French baking is done on site, and fresh bread and all pastry desserts are made daily. A fixed-price three-course, pre-theater dinner ($18.95) is served until 6:30. ⊠ *215 S.E. 8th Ave.,* ☎ *954/463–8000. AE, MC, V. Closed Sun.*

$$ ✕ **La Coquille.** Although this country-French restaurant sits at the edge of busy Sunrise Boulevard, it seems worlds away thanks to French doors, pastel coral and green, faux open beams, and a tropical garden. The friendly and helpful service comes with a delightful French accent, and the cuisine is equally authentic: Dubonnet and vermouth cassis aperitifs are a prelude to seared sea scallops with spring vegetables, honey-glazed duckling with lingonberry sauce and wild rice, sweetbreads in a morel and truffle sauce, or veal with shallots and sweet bell peppers. There's always a soufflé among the desserts and a multicourse dinner special most nights. ⊠ *1619 E. Sunrise Blvd.,* ☎ *954/467–3030. AE, MC, V. Closed Mon. No lunch Sat.–Thurs.*

$ ✕ **Sage.** This joyous, country-French café has a country-American setting: exposed brick walls, captain's chairs, lace curtains, and baskets of dried grains and flowers. The menu is a happy mix of affordable quiches and pâtés, salads, main-course specialties, and dessert crepes. Entrées include coq au vin, beef bourguignon, *cassoulet à l'Armagnac* (layers of duck and garlic sausage with white beans), and a platter of fresh vegetables that's a veritable garden of legumes. Early-bird dinners (weekdays 4:30–6) feature four courses for $12.50. There are good selections of beers and wines by the glass. ⊠ *2378 N. Federal Hwy.,* ☎ *954/565–2299. AE, D, MC, V.*

$ ✕ **Studio One French Bistro.** More like an art gallery—intimate, black-
★ and-white, mirrored—this restaurant serves up bountiful portions at
ridiculously low prices. Food is thoughtfully presented, from high-gluten
breads through a dozen or so appetizers, dinner-size salads, and entrées that include a grilled salmon in puff pastry with lobster sauce,
Camembert-stuffed chicken breast with French cranberry sauce, and
crispy roasted duckling with vanilla sauce. For dessert try the mildly
sweet custard apple tart. Chef Bernard Asendorf now has charge of
the kitchen, and his wife, Roberta, carries on the tradition of greeting
by name the locals who return time and again, often bringing out-of-
town guests. ⊠ *2447 E. Sunrise Blvd.,* ☎ *954/565–2052. AE, DC,
MC, V. Closed Mon. mid-May–mid-Dec. No lunch.*

Seafood

$$ ✕ **Rustic Inn Crabhouse.** Wayne McDonald started with a cozy one-
room roadhouse in 1955, when this was a remote service road just west
of the little airport. Now, the plain, rustic place is huge. Steamed crabs
seasoned with garlic and herbs, spices, and oil are eaten with mallets
on tables covered with newspapers; peel-and-eat shrimp are served ei-
ther with garlic and butter or spiced and steamed with Old Bay sea-
soning. The big menu includes other seafood items as well. Pies and
cheesecakes are offered for dessert. ⊠ *4331 Ravenswood Rd.,* ☎
954/584–1637. AE, D, DC, MC, V.

$$ ✕ **Shirttail Charlie's.** Diners look out on the New River from the outdoor deck or upstairs dining room of this restaurant, named for a
yesteryear Seminole Indian who wore his shirttails out. A free 30- to
40-minute after-dinner cruise on *Shirttail Charlie's Express* chugs up-
river past an alleged Al Capone speakeasy or across the river to and
from the Broward Center. Charlie's is built to look old, with a 1920s
tile floor that leans toward the water. Florida-style seafood includes
conch served four ways, crab balls, blackened tuna with Dijon mustard sauce, crunchy coconut shrimp with a not-too-sweet piña colada
sauce, and three fresh catches nightly. The Key lime pie is superbly tart.
⊠ *400 S.W. 3rd Ave.,* ☎ *954/463–3474. AE, D, MC, V.*

Lodging

On the Beach

$$$$ 🏨 **Lago Mar Resort Hotel & Club.** No sooner had Walter Banks opened
★ a new wing in 1993 than he turned to renovating older hotel rooms,
adding suitelike areas, balconies, and new furniture. The sprawling Lago
Mar has been owned by the Banks family since the early 1950s. The
lobby is luxurious, with fanlight surrounds, a coquina-rock fireplace,
and an eye-popping saltwater aquarium behind the registration desk.
Allamanda trellises and bougainvillea plantings edge the swimming lagoon, and guests have use of the broadest beach in the city. Lago Mar
is less a big resort than a small town—and, in its way, a slice of Old
Florida. ⊠ *1700 S. Ocean La., 33316,* ☎ *954/523–6511 or 800/524–
6627,* ℻ *954/524–6627. 32 rooms, 123 1-bedroom suites, 15 2-bed-
room suites. 4 restaurants, 2 pools, miniature golf, 4 tennis courts,
shuffleboard, volleyball. AE, DC, MC, V.*

$$$$ 🏨 **Marriott's Harbor Beach Resort.** If you look down from the upper
stories (14 in all) at night, this 16-acre property south of the big public beach shimmers like a jewel. Spacious guest rooms are done in tropical colors, lively floral prints, rattan, wicker, and wood. Each has a
balcony facing the ocean or the Intracoastal Waterway, and there are
in-room minibars. Sheffield's is one of the city's top restaurants. No
other hotel gives you so many options. ⊠ *3030 Holiday Dr., 33316,*
☎ *954/525–4000 or 800/228–6543,* ℻ *954/766–6152. 588 rooms,*

36 suites. 5 restaurants, 3 lounges, pool, massage, saunas, 5 tennis courts, health club, beach, windsurfing, boating, parasailing, children's program (ages 5–12). AE, DC, MC, V.

$$$ ☎ **Bahia Cabana Beach Resort.** *Boating Magazine* ranks the waterfront bar and restaurant here among the world's 10 best, but it's far enough from guest rooms so that nightly entertainment is not disturbing. A video bar yields a sweeping view of the marina. Rooms are spread among five buildings furnished in tropical-casual style. Those in the 500 building are more motel-like and overlook the parking lot, but rates here are lowest. ⊠ *3001 Harbor Dr., 33316,* ☎ *954/524–1555 or 800/922–3008; in FL, 800/232–2437;* FAX *954/764–5951. 52 rooms, 37 efficiencies, 10 suites. Restaurant, 2 bars, café, 3 pools, hot tub, saunas, shuffleboard. AE, D, DC, MC, V.*

$$$ ☎ **Lauderdale Colonial.** This 1950 resort motel, consisting of two
★ two-story buildings with good overhangs, occupies a prime location, right where the New River empties into the Intracoastal Waterway, 600 yards from the beach. The setting keeps it from feeling commercial, and the views are spectacular. Every unit—motel rooms, efficiencies, and one- and two-bedroom apartments—has a water view, and the best have full views. Most are large, done in tropical rattan and mock French provincial: whites, pastels, chintz, and stripes. Even the small motel rooms are desirable, since space is used well. Motel rooms have a coffeepot and small refrigerator, whereas other units have full kitchens. ⊠ *3049 Harbor Dr., 33316–2491,* ☎ *954/525–3676,* FAX *954/463–3787. 14 units. Pool, dock, fishing, coin laundry. MC, V.*

$$ ☎ **Nina Lee Motel.** This is typical of the modest, affordable 1950s-style lodgings that can be found within a block or two of the ocean along the Fort Lauderdale shore. Be prepared for plain rooms—homey and clean, but not tiny, with at least a toaster, coffeepot, and refrigerator; efficiencies have gas kitchens, large closets, and tub-showers. The pool is set in a garden, and the entire property is just removed enough from the beach causeway to be quiet. ⊠ *3048 Harbor Dr., 33316,* ☎ *954/524–1568. 14 units. Pool. MC, V.*

Downtown and Beach Causeways

$$$$ ☎ **Hyatt Regency Pier Sixty-Six.** The trademark of this high-rise re-
★ sort located on the Intracoastal Waterway is its rooftop Pier Top Lounge, which revolves every 66 minutes and is reached by an exterior elevator. The 17-story tower dominates a 22-acre spread that includes the Spa LXVI. Tower and lanai lodgings are tops from the ground up. In the early evening, guests try to perch at the Pelican Bar; at 6:06 a cannon is fired, and anybody around the bar gets a drink on the house. When you want to swim in the ocean, hail the water taxi at the resort's dock for a three-minute trip to the beach. ⊠ *2301 S. 17th St., 33316,* ☎ *954/525–6666 or 800/327–3796,* FAX *954/728–3541. 380 rooms, 8 suites. 3 restaurants, 3 lounges, pool, hot tub, spa, 2 tennis courts, dock, snorkeling, boating, parasailing, waterskiing, fishing. AE, D, MC, V.*

$$$ ☎ **Banyan Marina Apartments.** French doors have been added to guest
★ quarters, further fine-tuning these already outstanding waterfront apartments on a residential island just off Las Olas Boulevard. Imaginative landscaping includes a walkway through the upper branches of a banyan tree. Luxurious units with leather sofas, springy carpets, real potted plants, sheer curtains, custom drapes, high-quality art, and jalousies for sweeping the breeze in make these apartments as comfortable as any first-class hotel—but for half the price. Also included are a full kitchen, dining area, beautiful gardens, dockage for eight yachts, and exemplary housekeeping. ⊠ *111 Isle of Venice, 33301,* ☎ *954/524–*

4430, FAX 954/764–4870. *10 rooms, 1 efficiency, 4 1-bedroom apartments, 2 2-bedroom apartments. Pool. MC, V.*

$$$ ⊞ **Riverside Hotel.** This six-story hotel was built in 1936 and has been steadily upgraded. A sidewalk café fronts Bob Jenny's tropical murals, one of which is a New Orleans–style work that stretches across 725 square feet of the hotel's facade. Old Fort Lauderdale photos grace the hallways, and rooms are outfitted distinctively, with antique oak furnishings, framed French prints, and European-style baths. The poolside bar in back offers a great view of the New River, as do the best guest rooms; the least desirable are the 36 series, from which you can hear the elevator. No-smoking rooms are available. An attentive staff includes many who have been with the hotel for two decades or more. ⊠ *620 E. Las Olas Blvd., 33301,* ☎ *954/467–0671 or 800/325–3280,* FAX *954/462–2148. 103 rooms, 7 suites. 2 restaurants, bar, pool, volleyball, dock. AE, DC, MC, V.*

Nightlife and the Arts

For the most complete weekly listing of events, read the **"Showtime!"** entertainment insert and events calendar in the Friday *Fort Lauderdale News/Sun Sentinel.* **"Weekend"** in the Friday edition of the *Herald,* the Broward edition of the *Miami Herald,* carries listings of area happenings. The weekly **XS** is principally an entertainment and dining paper with a relic "underground" look. A 24-hour **Arts & Entertainment Hotline** (☎ 954/357–5700) provides updates on art, attractions, children's events, dance, festivals, films, literature, museums, music, opera, and theater.

Tickets are sold at individual box offices and through **Ticketmaster** (☎ 954/523–3309). (There is a service charge.)

The Arts

Broward Center for the Performing Arts (⊠ 201 S.W. 5th Ave., ☎ 954/462–0222) is the waterfront centerpiece of Fort Lauderdale's new cultural arts district. More than 500 events a year are scheduled at the 2,700-seat architectural masterpiece, including Broadway musicals, plays, dance, symphony and opera, rock, film, lectures, comedy, and children's theater.

Nightlife

BARS AND LOUNGES

Baja Beach Club (⊠ Coral Ridge Mall, 3200 N. Federal Hwy., ☎ 954/561–2432) offers trendy entertainment: karaoke, lip sync, virtual reality, performing bartenders, temporary tatoos—plus a 40-foot free buffet. **Cheers** (⊠ 941 E. Cypress Creek Rd., ☎ 954/771–6337) is a woody nightspot with two bars and a dance floor. Every night has something special. **O'Hara's Pub & Sidewalk Cafe** (⊠ 722 E. Las Olas Blvd., ☎ 954/524–1764) features live jazz and blues nightly. It's packed for TGIF, though usually by the end of each day the trendy crowd spills onto this prettiest of downtown streets. The **Parrot Lounge** (⊠ 911 Sunrise La., ☎ 954/563–1493) is a loony feast for the eyes, with a casual, friendly, local crowd. Fifteen TVs and frequent sing-alongs add to the fun. A jukebox jams all night. **Squeeze** (⊠ 2 S. New River Dr., ☎ 954/522–2151) welcomes a wide-ranging clientele—hard-core new-wavers to yuppie types.

COMEDY CLUB

ComedySportz (⊠ 1432 N. Federal Hwy., ☎ 954/565–1369) has an innovative approach to comedy. Laugh improvisation contests, Thursday through Sunday starting at 8:30, feature teams competing in response to audience suggestions.

COUNTRY-AND-WESTERN CLUB
Desperado (⊠ 2520 S. Miami Rd., ☎ 954/463–2855) offers a mechanical bull and free line-dance lessons. The club is open Wednesday through Sunday.

Outdoor Activities and Sports

Baseball
From mid-February to March, the **Baltimore Orioles** (⊠ Fort Lauderdale Stadium, N.W. 12th Ave., ☎ 954/776-1921) are in spring training.

Biking
Some of the most popular routes are Route A1A and Bayview Drive, especially early in the morning before traffic builds, and a 7-mi bike path that parallels Route 84 and the New River and leads to Markham Park, which has mountain-bike trails. For a free bicycle map, contact **County Bicycle Coordinator** (⊠ 115 S. Andrews Ave., 33301, ☎ 954/357–6661). Most area bike shops also have cycling maps.

Fishing
If you're interested in a saltwater charter, check out the **Radisson Bahia Mar Beach Resort** (⊠ 801 Seabreeze Blvd., ☎ 954/764–2233). **Captain Bill's** (⊠ South dock, Radisson Bahia Mar Beach Resort, 801 Seabreeze Blvd., ☎ 954/467–3855) offers bottom fishing.

Rugby
The **Fort Lauderdale Knights** play September through April on the green at Croissant Park. ⊠ S.W. 17th St. at 2nd Ave., ☎ 954/561–5263. ☎ Free. ☼ Games Sat. at 2.

Scuba Diving and Snorkeling
Lauderdale Diver (⊠ 1334 S.E. 17th St. Causeway, ☎ 954/467–2822 or 800/654–2073), which is PADI affiliated, arranges dive charters throughout the county. Dive trips typically last four hours. Nonpackage reef trips are open to divers for $38; scuba gear is extra.

Pro Dive (⊠ Radisson Bahia Mar Beach Resort, 801 Seabreeze Blvd., ☎ 954/761–3413 or 800/772–3483), a PADI five-star facility, is the area's oldest diving operation and offers packages with Radisson Bahia Mar Beach Resort, from where its 60-foot boat departs. Snorkelers can go out for $25 on the four-hour dive trip or $20 on the two-hour snorkeling trip, which includes snorkel equipment but not scuba gear. Scuba divers pay $35 using their own gear or $85 with all rentals included.

Tennis
With 21 courts, 18 of them clay and 14 lighted, **Holiday Park Tennis Center** is Fort Lauderdale's largest public tennis facility. Chris Evert, one of the game's greatest players, learned the sport here under the watchful eye of her father, James Evert, who continues here as the tennis professional. ⊠ 701 N.E. 12th Ave., ☎ 954/761–5378. ☎ $4 per person per hour. ☼ Weekdays 8 AM–9:15 PM, weekends 8–7.

Shopping

Boutiques
If only for a stroll and some window-shopping, don't miss the **Shops of Las Olas** (⊠ 1 block off New River east of U.S. 1). The city's best boutiques plus top restaurants (many affordable) and art galleries line a beautifully landscaped street.

Mall

With a convenient in-town location just west of the Intracoastal Waterway, the split-level **Galleria Mall** (⊠ 2414 E. Sunrise Blvd.) contains more than 1 million square feet of space. It's anchored by Neiman-Marcus, Lord & Taylor, Dillards, and Saks Fifth Avenue and features 150 world-class specialty stores with an emphasis on fashion and sporting goods.

Side Trips

The Western Suburbs and Beyond

West of Fort Lauderdale is an ever-growing mass of suburbs flowing one into the other. They're home to most of the city's golf courses as well as some attractions and large malls. As you head farther west, the terrain becomes more Everglades-like, and you'll occasionally see an alligator sunning itself on a canal bank. No matter how dedicated developers are to building over this natural resource, the Everglades keeps trying to assert itself. Waterbirds, fish, and other creatures are found in canals and lakes, even man-made ones, throughout the western areas.

☝ ⑫ Thousands of caterpillars representing as many as 150 species pupate and emerge as butterflies in the walk-through laboratory that is **Butterfly World,** on 3 acres inside Tradewinds Park. A screened aviary called North American Butterflies is reserved for native species. Tropical Rain Forest is a 30-foot-high construction with observation decks, waterfalls, ponds, and tunnels, where colorful butterflies flit and shift about. ⊠ 3600 W. Sample Rd., Coconut Creek, ☎ 954/977–4400. ☞ $9.95. ☉ Mon.–Sat. 9–5, Sun. 1–5.

☝ ⑬ At the **Young at Art Children's Museum,** kids can work in paint, graphics, sculpture, and crafts according to themes that change three times a year. Then they take their masterpieces home with them. ⊠ 801 S. University Dr., in Fountains Shoppes, Plantation, ☎ 954/424–0085. ☞ $3. ☉ Tues.–Sat. 11–5, Sun. noon–5.

⑭ To understand and enjoy the Everglades, take an airboat ride at **Sawgrass Recreation Park.** You'll probably see all sorts of plants and wildlife, such as birds, alligators, turtles, snakes, and fish. Included in the entrance fee along with the airboat ride is admission to an Everglades nature exhibit, a native Seminole Indian village, and exhibits about alligators, other reptiles, and birds of prey. A souvenir and gift shop, food service, and an RV park with hookups are also at the park. ⊠ U.S. 27 north of I-595, ☎ 954/426–2474. ☞ $13.85. ☉ Daily 6–6, airboat rides 8–5.

⑮ The 30-acre **Everglades Holiday Park** provides a good glimpse of the Everglades. Here you can take an airboat tour, look at an 18th-century-style Native American village, or watch an alligator-wrestling show. A souvenir shop, TJ's Grill, a convenience store, and a campground with RV hookups and a tent are all on site. ⊠ 21940 Griffin Rd., ☎ 954/434–8111. ☞ Free, $12.50 airboat tour. ☉ Daily 9–5.

THE ARTS

Sunrise Musical Theatre (⊠ 5555 N.W. 95th Ave., Sunrise, ☎ 954/741–7300) is a newly refurbished 4,000-seat theater, featuring everything from ballet to top-name pop, rock, and country artists.

LODGING

$$$$ 🏨 **Registry Resort & Spa Fort Lauderdale.** As its name suggests, this resort offers the luxury, amenities, and facilities of a resort with the health-consciousness of a spa. Spacious guest rooms and suites are done

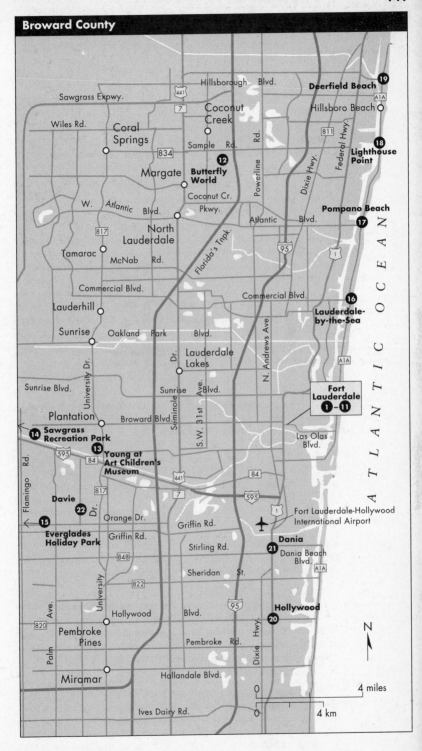

Broward County

Hillsborough Blvd.

Deerfield Beach 19

Sawgrass Expwy.

441

7

Hillsboro Beach

Coconut Creek

Wiles Rd.

Coral Springs

811

Lighthouse Point 18

Sample Rd.

Federal Hwy.

834

Margate

Butterfly World 12

Powerline Rd.

Dixie Hwy.

Coconut Cr. Pkwy.

Pompano Beach 17

W. Atlantic Blvd.

Atlantic Blvd.

I-95

North Lauderdale

817

1

Tamarac

McNab Rd.

Commercial Blvd.

Commercial Blvd.

16

Lauderhill

Lauderdale-by-the-Sea

Sunrise

Oakland Park Blvd.

A1A

N. Andrews Ave.

University Dr.

Lauderdale Lakes

Sunrise Blvd.

Sunrise Blvd.

Seminole Dr.

S.W. 31st Ave.

Fort Lauderdale 1 – 11

Plantation

Broward Blvd.

Las Olas Blvd.

Sawgrass Recreation Park 14

595

84

Young at Art Children's Museum 13

441

84

Flamingo Rd.

817

7

595

Davie 22

1

Dr.

Orange Dr.

Griffin Rd.

Fort Lauderdale-Hollywood International Airport

15

Everglades Holiday Park

Griffin Rd.

Griffin Rd.

848

Dania 21

Stirling Rd.

Dania Beach Blvd.

A1A

University

822

Sheridan St.

I-95

820

Hollywood Blvd.

Dixie Hwy.

Hollywood 20

Pembroke Pines

Palm Ave.

Pembroke Rd.

Miramar

Hallandale Blvd.

N

ATLANTIC OCEAN

0 4 miles

0 4 km

in tropical colors with rattan seating and overlook a lake or golf course. Oversize baths have dressing areas. In the morning, complimentary caffeine-free herbal teas are offered; in the afternoon it's fresh fruit. The staff nutritionist follows American Heart Association and American Cancer Society guidelines and can accommodate macrobiotic and vegetarian diets. Also on site, and open to the public, is a full-service beauty salon. The resort offers combination spa-tennis and spa-golf packages. ⊠ *250 Racquet Club Rd., 33326,* ☎ *954/389–3300 or 800/327–8090,* FAX *954/384–0563. 493 units. 4 restaurants, 2 lounges, 5 pools, beauty salon, spa, 2 golf courses, 24 tennis courts, bowling, horseback riding, roller-skating rink, shops. AE, D, MC, V.*

OUTDOOR ACTIVITIES AND SPORTS

Fishing. The marina at **Everglades Holiday Park** (⊠ 21940 Griffin Rd., ☎ 954/434–8111) caters to freshwater fishing. For $47.50 for five hours, you can rent a 14-foot johnboat (with a 9.9-horsepower Yamaha outboard) that carries up to four people. A rod and reel rent for $9 a day, and bait is extra. For two people, a fishing guide for a half day (four hours) is $110; for a full day (eight hours), $170. A third person adds $25 for a half day, $50 for a full day. You can also buy a freshwater fishing license (mandatory) here; a seven-day nonresident license is $16.50. Freshwater fishing with a guide out of **Sawgrass Recreation Park** (⊠ U.S. 27 north of I–595, ☎ 954/426–2474) costs $145 for two people for half a day, $195 for a full day. Resident and nonresident fishing licenses and live bait are available.

Golf. Next Day Golf (☎ 954/772–2582) provides access, at no extra fee, to private courses normally limited to members and arranges bookings up to 12 months in advance—a big advantage for golfers planning trips during the busy winter months. **Bonaventure Country Club** (⊠ 200 Bonaventure Blvd., ☎ 954/389–2100) has 36 holes. **Broken Woods Country Club** (⊠ 9000 Sample Rd., Coral Springs, ☎ 954/752–2270) has 18 holes. **Colony West Country Club** (⊠ 6800 N.W. 88th Ave., Tamarac, ☎ 954/726–8430) offers play on 36 holes. Just west of Florida's Turnpike, the **Inverrary Country Club** (⊠ 3840 Inverrary Blvd., Lauderhill, ☎ 954/733–7550) has 18 holes. **Jacaranda Golf Club** (⊠ 9200 W. Broward Blvd., Plantation, ☎ 954/472–5855) has 18 holes to play. **Sabal Palms Golf Course** (⊠ 5101 W. Commercial Blvd., Tamarac, ☎ 954/731–2600) has 18 holes. **Sunrise Country Club** (⊠ 7400 N.W. 24th Pl., Sunrise, ☎ 954/742–4333) provides 18 holes.

Ice Hockey. A new $212 million arena is being built in Sunrise for the Florida Panthers, who currently play at the Miami Arena. The Panthers' new home will be ready for the 1998–99 season.

SHOPPING

Broward's shopping extravaganza, **Fashion Mall at Plantation** (⊠ University Dr. north of Broward Blvd., Plantation) is a jewel of a mall. The three-level complex includes such department stores as Macy's, Lord & Taylor, and Burdines; a Sheraton Suites Hotel; and more than 100 specialty shops. In addition to a diverse food court, the Brasserie Max restaurant offers gourmet dining.

Containing more than 270 stores, the huge (2 million square feet) **Sawgrass Mills Mall** (⊠ Flamingo Rd. and Sunrise Blvd., Sunrise) is a destination in itself. Travelers and locals alike come for the shopping, restaurants, food courts, entertainment, and great prices, and the place teems on weekends and holidays. Shops, many of which are outlets, include Neiman-Marcus, Loehmann's, JCPenney, Ann Taylor, Alfred Angelo Bridal, Levi's, TJ Maxx, Donna Karan, Saks Fifth Avenue, and Kenneth Cole.

NORTH ON SCENIC A1A

North of Fort Lauderdale's Birch Recreation Area, Route A1A edges back from the beach through the section known as the Galt Ocean Mile, and a succession of ocean-side communities line up against the sea. Traffic can line up, too, as it passes through a changing pattern of beach-blocking high-rises and modest family vacation towns and back again. Here and there a scenic lighthouse or park punctuates the landscape, while other attractions and recreational opportunities are found inland.

Lauderdale-by-the-Sea

⑯ *5 mi north of Fort Lauderdale.*

Tucked just north of Fort Lauderdale's northern boundary, this low-rise family resort town bans construction of more than three stories. You can drive along lawn-divided El Mar Drive, lined with garden-style motels a block east of Route A1A. In actuality, however, you don't need a car in Lauderdale-by-the-Sea. Dozens of good restaurants and shops are in close proximity to hotels and the beach.

Where Commercial Boulevard meets the ocean, you can walk out onto **Anglin's Fishing Pier,** stretching 875 feet into the Atlantic. Here you can fish, stop in at any of the popular restaurants clustered around the seafront plaza, or just soak up the scene.

Dining and Lodging

$$ ✕ **Sea Watch.** It's back from the road and easy to miss, but after more than 20 years, this nautical-theme restaurant right on Lauderdale-by-the-Sea's beach stays packed during lunch and dinner. Waits can be as long as 30 minutes, but time passes quickly in the sumptuous upstairs lounge with comfy sofas and high-back rattan chairs. The menu has all the right appetizers: oysters Rockefeller, Gulf shrimp, clams casino, and Bahamian conch fritters. Typical daily specials might be sautéed yellowtail snapper, oat-crusted with roasted red bell pepper sauce and basil, or a charbroiled dolphin fillet marinated with soy sauce, garlic, black pepper, and lemon juice. Desserts include a cappuccino brownie and strawberries Romanoff. Good early-bird specials are offered off season. ⊠ *6002 N. Ocean Blvd. (Rte. A1A), Fort Lauderdale,* ☎ *954/781–2200. AE, MC, V.*

$ ✕ **Aruba Beach Cafe.** This is your best bet at the pier. A big beachside barn of a place—very casual, always crowded, always fun—it serves large portions of Caribbean conch chowder, Cuban black-bean soup, fresh tropical salads, burgers, sandwiches, and seafood. ⊠ *1 E. Commercial Blvd.,* ☎ *954/776–0001. AE, D, DC, MC, V.*

$$$–$$$$ ☷ **Tropic Seas Resort Inn.** It's only a block off A1A, but it's a million-dollar location—directly on the beach, two blocks from municipal tennis courts. Built in the 1950s, units are plain but clean and comfortable, with tropical rattan furniture and ceiling fans. Managers Sandy and Larry Lynch tend to the largely repeat, family-oriented clientele. The complimentary Sunday brunch and weekly wiener roast and rum swizzle party are good opportunities to mingle with other guests. ⊠ *4616 El Mar Dr., 33308,* ☎ *954/772–2555 or 800/952–9581,* ℻ *954/771–5711. 16 rooms, 6 efficiencies, 7 apartments. Pool, beach. AE, D, DC, MC, V.*

$$$ ☷ **Pier Pointe Resort.** Built in the 1950s, this oceanfront resort one block off the main street (Route A1A) and one block from the fishing pier is reminiscent of the Gold Coast 40 years ago. The aqua canopied entry opens onto two- and three-story buildings set among brick pathways on cabbage-palm lawns. The wood pool deck is set off by sea grapes and rope-strung bollards. Rooms are plain and comfortable and have balconies; most have a kitchen. There's a complimentary barbecue on Wednesday. ⊠ *4320 El Mar Dr., 33308,* ☎ *954/776–5121 or 800/331–6384,* FAX *954/491–9084. 40 suites, 31 efficiencies, 27 apartments. 3 pools, volleyball, beach, coin laundry. AE, D, DC, MC, V.*

$–$$ ☷ **Blue Seas.** Bubbly innkeeper Cristie Furth runs this one- and two-story motel with her husband, Marc, and small as it is, they keep investing their future in it. Lattice fencing and gardens of cactus and impatiens were added in front for more privacy around the brick patio and garden-set pool. Guest quarters feature kitchenettes, terra-cotta tiles, bright Haitian and Peruvian art, and generally Tex-Mex and Danish furnishings, whose woody textures work well together. Hand-made painted shutters and indoor plants add to the look. This remains an excellent buy in a quiet resort area just a block from the beach. ⊠ *4525 El Mar Dr., 33308,* ☎ *954/772–3336. 13 units. Pool, coin laundry. MC, V.*

Outdoor Activities and Sports
FISHING
Anglin's Fishing Pier (☎ 954/491–9403) is open for fishing 24 hours a day. Fishing is $3 for adults and $2 for children up to 12, tackle rental is an additional $10 (plus $10 deposit), and bait averages $2.

Pompano Beach

⓱ *3 mi north of Lauderdale-by-the-Sea.*

As Route A1A enters this town directly north of Lauderdale-by-the-Sea, the high-rise procession begins again. Sportfishing is big in Pompano Beach, as its name implies, but there's more to beachside attractions than the popular Fisherman's Wharf. Behind a low coral rock wall, Alsdorf Park extends north and south of the wharf along the road and beach.

Dining and Lodging
$$$ ✕ **Cafe Maxx.** New-wave epicurean dining had its South Florida start
★ here in the early 1980s, and Cafe Maxx remains popular among regional food lovers. The setting is ordinary, in a little strip of stores, but inside there's a holiday glow year-round. Chef Oliver Saucy demonstrates ritual devotion to the preparation of fine cuisine. The menu changes nightly but always showcases foods from the tropics: jumbo stone crab claws with honey-lime mustard sauce and black-bean and banana pepper chili with Florida avocado. Desserts, too, reflect a tropical theme, from praline macadamia mousse over chocolate cake with butterscotch sauce to candied ginger with pears poached in muscatel and sun-dried cherry ice cream. More than 200 wines are offered by the bottle, another 20 by the glass. ⊠ *2601 E. Atlantic Blvd.,* ☎ *954/782–0606. AE, D, DC, MC, V. No lunch.*

$$$$ ☷ **Palm-Aire Spa Resort.** This 750-acre health, fitness, and stress-reduction spa offers exercise activities, personal treatments, and calorie-controlled meals. Separate men's and women's pavilions have private sunken Roman baths, Swiss showers, and some of the most experienced hands in the massage business. There are 166 spacious rooms and 18 golf villas with private terraces. All have separate dressing rooms and some have two baths. You can have use of the spa for $125 for a half day or $225 for the whole day, including lunch; special spa programs include massage, facial, and fitness classes. The resort is 15 minutes from downtown. ⊠ *2601 Palm-Aire Dr. N, 33069,* ☎ *954/972–3300* *or 800/272–5624. 184 units. Restaurant, pools, hot tubs, massage, saunas, spa, steam rooms, 3 golf courses, 37 tennis courts, aerobics, exercise room, racquetball, squash. AE, D, MC, V.*

Outdoor Activities and Sports

FISHING

Fisherman's Wharf (☎ 954/943–1488) extends 1,080 feet into the Atlantic. The cost is $2.65 for adults, $1.06 for children under 10; rod-and-reel rental is $10.07 (including admission and initial bait).

For bottom fishing, try **Fish City Pride** (✉ Fish City Marina, 2621 N. Riverside Dr., ☎ 954/781–1211). You can arrange for a saltwater charter boat through the **Hillsboro Inlet Marina** (✉ 2629 N. Riverside Dr., ☎ 954/943–8222).

GOLF

Crystal Lake South Course (✉ 3800 Crystal Lake Dr., ☎ 954/943–2902) has 18 holes. **The Oaks Golf & Racquet Club** (✉ 3701 Oaks Clubhouse Dr., ☎ 954/978–1737) has 54 holes.

HORSE RACING

Pompano Harness Track, Florida's only harness track, features world-class trotters and pacers during its October–August meet. The Top o' the Park restaurant overlooks the finish line. ✉ 1800 S.W. 3rd St., ☎ 954/972–2000. 🎫 Grandstand $1, clubhouse $2. ⊙ Racing Mon., Wed., Fri., and Sat. 7:30.

Shopping

The old Pompano Fashion Square has been reborn as **Pompano Square** (✉ 2001 N. Federal Hwy.) and now features a tropical motif. This comfortably sized city mall has 110 shops, four department stores, and a few places for food.

Lighthouse Point

⑱ *2 mi north of Pompano Beach.*

The big attraction here is the view across Hillsboro Inlet to **Hillsboro Light,** the brightest light in the Southeast. Mariners have used this landmark for decades. From the ocean, you can see the light almost halfway to the Bahamas. Although the lighthouse is on private property and is inaccessible to the public, it's well worth a peek.

Dining

$$$ ✕ **Cafe Arugula.** Chef Dick Cingolani draws upon the culinary tradi-
★   tions of warm climates from Italy to the American Southwest. The decor, too, blends Southwestern with Mediterranean looks—a row of mauve velvet booths beneath steamboat-wheel windows surrounds an entire wall of chili peppers, corn, cactus, and garlic cloves. A frequently changing menu may include succulent fresh hogfish with capers and shaved almonds over fettuccine or a free-range loin of venison with juniper–wild mushroom sauce, quesadilla, and stir-fried vegetables. ✉ 3110 N. Federal Hwy., ☎ 954/785–7732. AE, D, DC, MC, V. No lunch.

$$–$$$ ✕ **Cap's Place.** On an island that was once a bootlegger's haunt, this
★   seafood restaurant is reached by launch and has served such luminaries as Winston Churchill, FDR, and John F. Kennedy. "Cap" was Captain Theodore Knight, born in 1871, who, with partner-in-crime Al Hasis, floated a derelict barge to the area in the 1920s. Today the rustic restaurant, built on the barge, is run by descendants of Hasis. Baked wahoo steaks are lightly glazed and meaty, the long-cut french fries arouse gluttony, hot and flaky rolls are baked fresh several times a night, and tangy lime pie is a great finishing touch. Turn east off Federal High-

way onto Northeast 24th Street (two blocks north of Pompano Square); follow the double yellow line to the launch. ⊠ *Cap's Dock, 2765 N.E. 28th Ct.,* ☎ *954/941–0418. AE, MC, V. No lunch.*

En Route   To the north, Route A1A traverses the so-called Hillsboro Mile (actually more than 2 mi), which not many years ago was one of Florida's outstanding residential corridors—a millionaire's row. Changes in zoning laws, however, have altered it; except for sections in the south and north, the island seems destined to sink under the weight of its massive condominiums. The road runs along a narrow strip of land between the Intracoastal Waterway and the ocean, with bougainvillea and oleanders edging the way and yachts docked along both banks. In winter, the traffic often creeps at a snail's pace, as vacationers and retirees gawk at the views.

Deerfield Beach

⑲   *3½ mi north of Lighthouse Point.*

The highlight here is **Deerfield Island Park,** which can only be reached by boat. This 8½-acre island, officially designated an urban wilderness area, resulted from the dredging of the Intracoastal Waterway and from construction of the Royal Palm Canal. It's a paradise of coastal hammock, or tree islands, and its mangrove swamp provides a critical habitat for gopher tortoises, gray foxes, raccoons, and armadillos. ⊠ *1 Deerfield Island; boat landing at Riverview Restaurant, Riverview Rd.,* ☎ *954/360–1320.* ☎ *Free.* ☉ *Wed. and Sat. 8:15–sunset.*

Dining and Lodging

$$ ✕ **Brooks.** This is one of the city's better restaurants, thanks to a
★   French perfectionist, Bernard Perron. Meals are served in a series of rooms filled with replicas of Old Masters, cut glass, antiques, and tapestry-like floral wallpapers, though the shedlike dining room still feels very Florida. Fresh ingredients go into distinctly Floridian cuisine. Main courses include red snapper in papillotte, broiled fillet of pompano with seasoned root vegetables, and a sweet lemongrass linguine with bok choy and julienne of crisp vegetables. Desserts include pecan pie with banana ice cream, a filo purse filled with chocolate ganache and strawberries, and rum-basted bananas with coconut ice cream and toasted macadamia nuts. ⊠ *500 S. Federal Hwy.,* ☎ *954/427–9302. AE, D, MC, V.*

$$$–$$$$ 🏨 **Ocean Terrace Suites.** This four-story motel is in one of the quieter sections of north Broward, just south of the Palm Beach county line, across the narrow shore road from the beach. Large units—efficiencies and one- and three-bedroom apartments—all have big balconies overlooking the sea. Colors are from shore washed to bright; pink and green pastels tint the bedrooms. The furniture is rattan, and units are clean and neat. Art is throwaway, flowers are artificial, and materials are bargain quality. Still, for size, location, and price this is a good buy. An outdoor barbecue grill is available. ⊠ *2080 E. Hillsboro Blvd., 33441,* ☎ *954/427–8400,* FAX *954/427–0555. 30 units. Pool. AE, D, DC, MC, V.*

$$$–$$$$ 🏨 **Royal Flamingo Villas.** This small community of houselike villas, built in the 1970s, reaches from the Intracoastal Waterway to the sea. The roomy and comfortable one- and two-bedroom villas are all condominium owned, so they're fully furnished the way owners want them. All are so quiet that you hear only the soft click of ceiling fans and kitchen clocks. The development is wisely set back a bit from the beach, which is eroding but enjoyable at low tide. Lawns are so lushly

landscaped you might trip. If you don't need lavish public facilities, this is your upscale choice at a reasonable price. ⊠ *1225 Hillsboro Mile (Rte. A1A), Hillsboro Beach 33062,* ☎ *954/427–0669, 954/427–0660, or 800/241–2477,* FAX *954/427–6110. 40 villas. Pool, putting green, shuffleboard, beach, dock, boating, coin laundry. D, MC, V.*

$$–$$$ ⊞ **Carriage House Resort Motel.** This clean and tidy motel sits one block from the ocean. Run by a French-American couple, the two-story, black-shuttered, white, Colonial-style motel is actually two buildings connected by a second-story sundeck. Steady improvements have been made to the facility, including the addition of Bahama beds that feel and look like sofas. Kitchenettes are equipped with good-quality utensils. Rooms are self-contained and quiet and have walk-in closets and room safes. ⊠ *250 S. Ocean Blvd., 33441,* ☎ *954/427–7670,* FAX *954/428–4790. 6 rooms, 14 efficiencies, 10 apartments. Pool, shuffleboard, coin laundry. AE, MC, V.*

Outdoor Activities and Sports

GOLF
Off Hillsborough Boulevard, west of I–95, **Deer Creek Golf Club** (⊠ 2801 Country Club Blvd., ☎ 954/421–5550) has 18 holes.

SOUTH BROWARD

From Hollywood's Broadwalk, a 27-foot-wide thoroughfare paralleling 2 mi of palm-fringed beach, to the western reaches of Old West–flavored Davie, this region has a personality all its own. South Broward's roots are in early Florida settlements. Thus far it has avoided some of the glitz and glamour of its neighbors to the north and south, and folks here like it that way. Still, there's plenty to see and do—excellent restaurants in every price range, world-class pari-mutuels, and a new focus on the arts.

Hollywood

🕚 *7 mi south of Fort Lauderdale.*

This 70-year-old oceanfront community has virtually nothing in common with its West Coast namesake, though it does feel like a Los Angeles County beach town. With trendy shops, an occasional surfer or two, and young people on Rollerblades, it could easily be in California, if it weren't 15 minutes south of downtown Fort Lauderdale. And this small town is diverse. It has everything from a classic beachfront area to a full-fledged Indian reservation.

In 1921 Joseph W. Young, a California real estate developer, began developing the community of Hollywood from the woody flatlands. Reminders of the glory days of the Young era remain in places like Young Circle (the junction of U.S. 1 and Hollywood Boulevard) and the Hollywood Beach Resort Hotel, opened by Young in 1922 and now a timeshare with some units available for short-term stays.

The **Art and Culture Center of Hollywood** is a visual and performing arts center with an art reference library, outdoor sculpture garden, arts school, and museum store. It's just east of Young Circle. ⊠ *1650 Harrison St.,* ☎ *954/921–3274.* 🎟 *Wed.–Sat. $3, Sun. $5 (including classical or jazz concert); donations welcome Tues.* 🕐 *Tues.–Sat. 10–4, Sun. 1–4.*

With the Intracoastal Waterway to its west and the beach and ocean to the east, the 2.2-mi paved promenade known as the **Broadwalk** has been popular with pedestrians and cyclists since 1924. Expect to hear

French spoken along this scenic stretch, especially during the winter; Hollywood Beach has been a favorite winter getaway for Québecois ever since Joseph Young hired French-Canadians to work here in the 1920s.

Hollywood North Beach Park is at the northern end of the Broadwalk. No high-rises overpower the scene, nothing hip or chic, just a laid-back old-fashioned place for enjoying the sun, sand, and sea. ⊠ *Rte. A1A and Sheridan St.,* ☎ *954/926–2444.* ☞ *Free; parking $5 until 2, $3 after.* ⊙ *Daily 8–6.*

Comprising 1,400 acres at the Intracoastal Waterway, **West Lake Park** is one of Florida's largest urban nature facilities, providing a wide range of recreational activities. You can rent a canoe, kayak, or boat with an electric motor (no fossil fuels are allowed in the park) or take the 40-minute environmental boat tour. Extensive boardwalks traverse a mangrove community, where endangered and threatened species abound. A 65-foot observation tower allows views of the entire park. More than $1 million in exhibits are on display at the **Anne Kolb Nature Center,** named after the late county commissioner who was a leading environmental advocate. A great place to take youngsters, the center's exhibit hall features 27 interactive displays, an ecology room, and a tri-level aquarium. ⊠ *1200 Sheridan St.,* ☎ *954/926–2410.* ☞ *Weekends and holidays $1, weekdays free; exhibit hall $3.* ⊙ *8–6.*

At the edge of Hollywood lies **Seminole Native Village,** a reservation where Seminole Indians both sell their arts and crafts and run a high-stakes bingo parlor and low-stakes poker tables. ⊠ *4150 N. Rte. 7,* ☎ *954/961–5140 or 954/961–3220.* ⊙ *Daily 9–5.*

In addition to displaying a collection of artifacts from the Seminoles and other tribes, Joe Dan and Virginia Osceola sell contemporary Native American arts and crafts at the **Anhinga Indian Museum and Art Gallery.** It's just across the street from the Seminole Native Village, though that technically puts it over the Fort Lauderdale border. ⊠ *5791 S. Rte. 7, Fort Lauderdale,* ☎ *954/581–0416.* ⊙ *Daily 9–5.*

Dining and Lodging

$$$ ✕ **Martha's.** While upstairs is more informal, the downstairs is dressy—tables adorned with orchid buds, fanned napery, etched-glass dividers, brass, rosewood, and an outdoor patio surrounded by a wild floral mural. Piano music accompanies dinner downstairs, and later a band plays for dancing, setting a supper-club mood. Both floors offer similar menus, however—chiefly Florida seafoods: flaky dolphin in a court bouillon; shrimp dipped in a piña colada batter, rolled in coconut, and pan-fried with orange mustard sauce; and snapper prepared 17 ways. For dessert, try sorbet and vanilla and chocolate ice cream topped with meringue and hot fudge brandy sauce. ⊠ *6024 N. Ocean Dr.,* ☎ *954/923–5444. Reservations essential. AE, D, DC, MC, V.*

$$ ✕ **Las Brisas.** There's a wonderful bistro atmosphere at this small and cozy restaurant with Mexican tiles and blue-and-white checked tablecloths beneath paddle fans. Right next to the beach, Las Brisas offers eating inside or out, and food is Argentine with an Italian flair. Antipasto salads are prepared for two; the roasted vegetables are crunchy and flavorful. A small pot sits on each table filled with *chimichurri* (a paste made of oregano, parsley, olive oil, salt, garlic, and crushed pepper) for spreading on steaks. Grilled or deep-fried fish are favorites, as are pork chops, chicken, and pasta entrées. Desserts include a rum cake, a flan like *mamacita* used to make, and a *dulce con leche* (a sweet milk pudding). The wine list is predominantly Argentine. ⊠ *600 N. Surf Rd.,* ☎ *954/923–1500. AE, MC, V. Closed Mon. No lunch.*

$–$$ ✕ **Sushi Blues Cafe.** First-class Japanese food, accompanied by live music Thursday through Saturday evenings, is served up in a cubicle setting that's so jammed you wonder where this hip group goes by day. Chef Yozo Masuda prepares conventional and macrobiotic-influenced dishes that range from a variety of sushi and rolls (California, tuna, and the "Yozo roll" with snapper, flying-fish eggs, asparagus, and Japanese mayonnaise) to steamed veggies with tofu and steamed snapper with miso sauce. Also available are a few wines by the glass or bottle, a selection of Japanese beers, and some very un-Japanese desserts—fried banana and Swiss chocolate mousse cake. ⊠ *1836 S. Young Circle,* ☎ *954/929–9560. No credit cards. Closed Sun. No lunch.*

$ ✕ **Istanbul.** The owners of this Turkish delight take pride in preparing everything from scratch: hummus, tabouli, *adana* kebab (partially grilled, chopped lamb on skewers on a bed of yogurt-soaked pita squares, oven-finished with hot butter sauce), pizza, salads, soups, and filo pie fingers filled with spinach, chicken, or meat. At lunch, blue-suited attorney-types dine alongside beachgoers. You should also consider getting takeout. After all, how often can you lounge on the beach with a reasonably priced Turkish picnic? ⊠ *707 N. Broadwalk,* ☎ *954/921–1263. No credit cards.*

$ ✕ **Le Tub.** Formerly a Sunoco gas station, this place is now a quirky waterside saloon with a seeming affection for claw-foot bathtubs. Hand-painted tubs are everywhere—under ficus, sea grape, and palm trees. The eatery is highly favored by locals for affordable food: mostly shrimp, burgers, and barbecue. ⊠ *1100 N. Ocean Dr.,* ☎ *954/921–9425. No credit cards.*

$$–$$$ ▥ **Sea Downs.** This three-story lodging directly on the Broadwalk is a good choice for efficiency or apartment living (one-bedroom apartments can be joined to make two-bedroom units). Views vary from full on the beach to rear-of-the-house prospects of neighborhood motels. Luck of the draw determines what you get. All units are comfortably done in chintz, however, with blinds, not drapes. Kitchens are fully equipped and most units have tub-showers and closets. Every room has a ceiling fan, air-conditioning, TV, and phone. Housekeeping is provided once a week. In between, guests receive fresh towels daily and sheets on request, but they make their own beds. ⊠ *2900 N. Surf Rd., 33019-3704,* ☎ *954/923–4968,* ℻ *954/923–8747. 5 efficiencies, 8 1-bedroom apartments. Pool. No credit cards.*

$$ ▥ **Driftwood on the Ocean.** This attractive late-'50s-era resort motel faces the beach at the secluded south end of Surf Road. The setting is what draws guests, but attention to maintenance and frequent refurbishing are what make it a value. Most units have a kitchen, one-bedroom apartments have a daybed, and standard rooms have a queen-size Murphy bed. All have balconies. ⊠ *2101 S. Surf Rd., 33019,* ☎ *954/923–9528,* ℻ *954/922–1062. 10 rooms, 39 efficiencies. Pool, shuffleboard, beach, bicycles, coin laundry. AE, MC, V.*

$$ ▥ **Maison Harrison.** This house is reflective of the 1920s and 1930s, when developer Joseph Young planned and built Hollywood. In fact, the building originally housed Young's salesmen. Rooms are complete, if a little overdone. Here and there a closet or bathroom-cabinet door doesn't quite close, or unplugged screw holes remain where a towel rack once hung. Furnishings are mostly traditional, with much upholstery and Oriental-style rugs. An expanded Continental breakfast is included. This is a good option for those who want neither a sterile motel nor that sense of obligation that sometimes comes with doting hosts. ⊠ *1504 Harrison St., 33020,* ☎ *954/922–7319. 4 rooms. No credit cards.*

$$
★ 🖼 **Manta Ray Inn.** Canadians Donna and Dwayne Boucher run this exemplary two-story lodging on the beach and have kept the place immaculate and the rates affordable. Dating from the 1940s, the inn offers the casual, comfortable beachfront that vacations in Hollywood are famous for. Nothing's fussy—white spaces with burgundy trim and rattan furniture—and everything's included. Kitchens are equipped with pots, pans, and mini-appliances that make housekeeping convenient. All apartments have full closets, and all except for two-bedroom units with stalls have tub-showers. Grills are available. ⊠ 1715 S. Surf Rd., 33019, ☎ 954/921–9666, 𝐅𝐀𝐗 954/929–8220. 12 units. Beach. No credit cards.

Outdoor Activities and Sports

BIKING

The 2-mi **Broadwalk,** which has its own bike path, is popular with cyclists.

DOG RACING

Hollywood Greyhound Track has dog-racing action during its December–April season. There is a clubhouse dining room. ⊠ 831 N. Federal Hwy., Hallandale, ☎ 954/454–9400. 🎫 Box seats 50¢–$1, grandstand $1, clubhouse $2. ☼ Racing Tues., Thurs., Sat. 12:30 and 7:30; Sun., Mon., Wed., and Fri. 7:30.

FISHING

Sea Leg's III (⊠ 5400 N. Ocean Dr., ☎ 954/923–2109) runs drift-fishing trips from 8 to 12:30 and 1:30 to 6, at a cost of $23, and bottom-fishing trips from 7 PM to midnight, for $25. Both trips include fishing gear.

GOLF

The **Diplomat Resort & Country Club** (⊠ 501 Diplomat Pkwy., Hallandale, ☎ 954/457–2082), with 18 holes, is south of town. The course at **Emerald Hills** (⊠ 4100 Hills Dr., ☎ 954/961–4000) has 18 holes.

HORSE RACING

Gulfstream Park Race Track is the winter home of some of the nation's top Thoroughbreds. The park greatly improved its facilities during the past few years: Admission costs have been lowered, time between races shortened, and the paddock ring elevated for better viewing by fans. The season is capped by the $500,000 Florida Derby, which always features Kentucky Derby hopefuls. Racing is held January through mid-March. ⊠ 901 S. Federal Hwy., Hallandale, ☎ 954/454–7000. 🎫 $3, including parking and program, clubhouse $5 plus $2 for reserved seat or $1.75 for grandstand. ☼ Racing Wed.–Mon. at 1.

Dania

㉑ *3 mi north of Hollywood, 4 mi south of Fort Lauderdale.*

This town at the south edge of Fort Lauderdale is probably best known for its antiques dealers, but there are other attractions as well.

Graves Museum of Archaeology & Natural History, a little-known treasure, has the goal of becoming the "Smithsonian of the South." Its wide-ranging collections feature everything from pre-Columbian art and Greco-Roman materials to underwater artifacts from St. Thomas harbor and a 9,000-square-foot dinosaur hall. Also on display are a 3-ton quartz crystal and dioramas on Tequesta Indian life and jaguar habitat. Monthly lectures, conferences, field trips, and a summer archaeological camp are offered. The museum bookstore is one of the best in Florida. ⊠ *481 S. Federal Hwy.,* ☎ *954/925–7770,* ᴼᴬˣ *954/925–7064.* 🎫 *$5.* ⊙ *Tues.–Wed., Fri., and Sat. 10–4; Thurs. 10–8; Sun. 1–4.*

★ The **John U. Lloyd Beach State Recreation Area** is a pleasant plot of land with a pine-shaded beach and a jetty pier where you can fish. It also has good views to the north toward Palm Beach County and south to Miami Beach. From the road, look west across the waterway to the deep-water freighters and cruise ships in Port Everglades. ⊠ *6503 N. Ocean Dr.,* ☎ *954/923–2833.* 🎫 *$3.25 per vehicle with up to 8 people.* ⊙ *Daily 8–sunset.*

Outdoor Activities and Sports

FISHING

The 920-foot **Dania Pier** (☎ *954/927–0640*) is open around the clock. Fishing is $3 for adults (including parking), tackle rental is $6, bait is about $2, and spectators pay $1.

JAI ALAI

Dania Jai-Alai Palace has one of the fastest games on the planet. Games are held year-round. ⊠ *301 E. Dania Beach Blvd.,* ☎ *954/428–7766.* 🎫 *$1, reserved seats $1.50–$7. Games Tues., Thurs., and Sat. noon and 7:15; Wed. and Fri. 7:15; closed Wed. in June.*

Shopping

More than 75 **antiques** dealers line Federal Highway (U.S. 1), ½ mi south of the Fort Lauderdale airport and ½ mi north of Hollywood. Take the Stirling Road or Griffin Road East exits off I–95.

Davie

22 *4 mi west of Dania.*

This town's horse farms and estates are the closest thing to the Old West in South Florida. Folks in Western wear ride their fine horses through downtown and order up takeout at "ride-through" windows. Davie's most famous activity is an authentic rodeo every Thursday night. For information, call the Davie Chamber of Commerce.

Gators, crocodiles, river otters, and birds of prey can be seen at **Flamingo Gardens,** as can a 23,000-square foot walk-through aviary, a plant house, and an Everglades museum in the pioneer Wray Home. Admission includes a half-hour guided tram ride through a citrus grove and wetlands area. ⊠ *3750 Flamingo Rd.,* ☎ *954/473–2955.* 🎫 *$8.* ⊙ *Daily 10–6.*

Dining

$$ ✕ **Armadillo Cafe.** Eve Montella and Kevin McCarthy have created a
★ restaurant whose Southwestern theme, casual decor, and award-winning food make it worth the drive from anywhere in Broward County. It has been named to best-restaurant lists in local and national publications, and visitors from around the world have feasted on its Southwestern-style South Florida seafood. Though some exotic dishes are prepared, everything is served in a creative and fun atmosphere. ⊠ *4630 S.W. 6th Ave.,* ☎ *954/791–5104. AE, D, DC, MC, V.*

Nightlife and the Arts

THE ARTS

Bailey Concert Hall (⊠ Central Campus of Broward Community College, 3501 S.W. Davie Rd., ☎ 954/475–6884) is a popular place for classical music concerts, dance, drama, and other performing arts activities, especially October–April.

Uncle Funny's Comedy Club (⊠ 9160 Rte. 84, ☎ 954/474–5653) has national and local comics in two shows Friday and Saturday.

Outdoor Activities and Sports
Bicycle enthusiasts can ride at the **Brian Piccolo Park velodrome** (⊠ Sheridan St. and N.W. 101st Ave., Cooper City), south of Davie.

Rolling Hills (⊠ 3501 Rolling Hills Circle, ☎ 954/475–3010) has 27 holes.

FORT LAUDERDALE AND BROWARD COUNTY A TO Z

Arriving and Departing

By Bus
Greyhound Lines (☎ 800/231–2222) buses stop in Fort Lauderdale (⊠ 515 N.E. 3rd St., ☎ 954/764–6551).

By Car
Access to Broward County from the north or south is via Florida's Turnpike, I–95, U.S. 1, or U.S. 441. I–75 (Alligator Alley) connects Broward with Florida's west coast and runs parallel to Route 84 within the county.

By Plane
Fort Lauderdale–Hollywood International Airport (FLHIA) (☎ 954/359–6100), 4 mi south of downtown Fort Lauderdale and just off U.S. 1, is becoming one of Florida's busiest—more than 11 million arrivals and departures a year, a figure that's expected to triple within 20 years. With the addition of Laker Airways service to London, British travelers are now the largest group of Europeans flying here, and when Southwest Airlines selected FLHIA as its South Florida hub, domestic passenger travel also increased. Scheduled airlines include **Air Jamaica** (☎ 800/523–5585), **American** (☎ 800/433–7300), **Bahamasair** (☎ 800/260–2699), **Carnival Air Lines** (☎ 800/824–7386), **Comair** (☎ 800/354–9822), **Continental** (☎ 800/525–0280), **Delta** (☎ 800/221–1212), **Icelandair** (☎ 954/359–2735), **Island Express** (☎ 954-359-0380), **Laker** (☎ 888/525–3724), **Martinair** (☎ 800/366–4655), **Midway** (☎ 800/446–4392), **Midwest Express** (☎ 800/452–2022), **Northwest** (☎ 800/225–2525), **Pan Am** (☎ 800/424–2557), **Southwest** (☎ 800/435–9792), **TWA** (☎ 800/221–2000), **United** (☎ 800/241–6522), **US Airways** (☎ 800/428–4322), and **Valujet** (☎ 800/825–8538).

Broward Transit (☎ 954/357–8400) operates bus route No. 1 between the airport and its main terminal at Broward Boulevard and Northwest 1st Avenue, in the center of Fort Lauderdale. Service from the airport begins daily at 5:30 AM; the last bus from the downtown terminal to the airport leaves at 9:50 PM. The fare is $1 (50¢ for seniors). **Gray Line** (☎ 954/561–8886) provides limousine service to all parts of Broward County. Fares to most Fort Lauderdale beach hotels are in the $6–$10 range.

Rental-car agencies in the airport include **Avis** (☎ 954/359–3255), **Budget** (☎ 954/359–4700), **Dollar** (☎ 954/359–7800), **Hertz** (☎ 954/359–5281), and **National** (☎ 954/359–8303). In season you'll pay about

$120–$130 by the week; the collision-damage waiver adds about $11 per day.

By Train

Amtrak (☎ 800/872–7245) provides daily service to the Fort Lauderdale station (✉ 200 S.W. 21st Terr., ☎ 954/463–8251) as well as to the other Broward County stops, Hollywood and Deerfield Beach.

Tri-Rail (☎ 954/728–8445) operates train service daily, 5 AM–11 PM (more limited on weekends) through coastal Broward, Dade, and Palm Beach counties. There are six Broward stations west of I–95: Hillsboro Boulevard in Deerfield Beach, Cypress Creek, Fort Lauderdale, Fort Lauderdale Airport, Sheridan Street in Hollywood, and Hollywood Boulevard.

Getting Around

By Boat

Water Taxi (☎ 954/467–6677) provides service along the Intracoastal Waterway between Port Everglades and Commercial Boulevard 10 AM–1 AM and between Atlantic Boulevard in Pompano Beach and Hillsboro Boulevard in Deerfield Beach noon–midnight. Boats stop at more than 30 restaurants, hotels, shops, and nightclubs; the fare is $7 one-way, $12 round-trip, and $15 for an all-day pass. Children under 12 accompanied by an adult pay half fare.

By Bus and Trolley

Broward County Mass Transit (☎ 954/357–8400) bus service covers the entire county. The fare is $1, plus 15¢ for a transfer. Service on all beach routes starts before 6 AM and continues past 10 PM except on Sunday. Call for route information. Special seven-day tourist passes, which cost $8, are good for unlimited use on all county buses. These are available at some hotels, at Broward County libraries, and at the main bus terminal (✉ Broward Blvd. at N.W. 1st Ave., Fort Lauderdale).

Supplementary bus and trolley services include the expanding free **Downtown Trolley** (☎ 954/761–3543), which operates weekdays 7:30–5:30 on the Red Line (Courthouse Line) and 11:30–2:30 on the Green (Arts & Science to Las Olas) and Blue (Las Olas to Courthouse) lines. The wait is rarely more than 10 minutes. The lines connect major tourist sites in the Arts and Science District, offices, banks, and government and academic buildings to water taxi stops along the Riverwalk and to the main bus terminal. Along the beach, the **Wave Line Trolley** (☎ 954/527–5600) costs $1 and operates daily every hour 10:15–8:15 except half-hourly 4:45–6:15. It runs along Route A1A from the Galleria Mall on Sunrise Boulevard in the north to close by the Hyatt Regency Pier Sixty-Six in the south.

By Car

Except during rush hour, Broward County is a fairly easy place to drive. East–west I–595 runs from westernmost Broward County and links I–75 with I–95 and U.S. 1, providing handy access to Fort Lauderdale–Hollywood International Airport. The scenic but slow Route A1A generally parallels the beach.

By Taxi

It's difficult to hail a cab on the street. Sometimes you can pick one up at a major hotel. Otherwise, phone ahead. Fares are not cheap; meters run at a rate of $2.45 for the first mile and $1.75 for each additional mile; waiting time is 25¢ per minute. The major company serving the area is **Yellow Cab** (☎ 954/565–5400).

Contacts and Resources

Emergencies

Dial **911** for police or ambulance.

Florida Poison Information Center (☎ 800/282–3171).

HOSPITALS

The following hospitals have a 24-hour emergency room: **Broward General Medical Center** (✉ 1600 S. Andrews Ave., Fort Lauderdale, ☎ 954/355–4400; physician referral, ☎ 954/355–4888), **Coral Springs Medical Center** (✉ 3999 Coral Hills Dr., Coral Springs, ☎ 954/344–3000; physician referral, ☎ 954/355–4888), **Florida Medical Center South** (✉ 6701 W. Sunrise Blvd., Plantation, ☎ 954/581–7800; physician referral, ☎ 954/730–2700), **Hollywood Medical Center** (✉ 3600 Washington St., Hollywood, ☎ 954/985–6274; physician referral, ☎ 800/237–8701), **Holy Cross Hospital** (✉ 4725 N. Federal Hwy., Fort Lauderdale, ☎ 954/492–5753; physician referral, ☎ 954/776–3223), **Imperial Point Medical Center** (✉ 6401 N. Federal Hwy., Fort Lauderdale, ☎ 954/776–8500; physician referral, ☎ 954/355–4888), **North Broward Medical Center** (✉ 201 E. Sample Rd., Pompano Beach, ☎ 954/941–8300; physician referral, ☎ 954/355–4888), and **Plantation General Hospital** (✉ 401 N.W. 42nd Ave., Plantation, ☎ 954/797–6470; physician referral, ☎ 954/587–5010).

LATE-NIGHT PHARMACIES

The following are open 24 hours: **Eckerd Drug** (✉ 1385 S.E. 17th St., Fort Lauderdale, ☎ 954/525–8173; 1701 E. Commercial Blvd., Fort Lauderdale, ☎ 954/771–0660; 154 University Dr., Pembroke Pines, ☎ 954/432–5510) and **Walgreen** (✉ 2855 Stirling Rd., Fort Lauderdale, ☎ 954/981–1104; 5001 N. Dixie Hwy., Oakland Park, ☎ 954/772–4206; 289 S. Federal Hwy., Deerfield Beach, ☎ 954/481–2993).

Guided Tours

Carrie B. (✉ Riverwalk at S.E. 5th Ave., Fort Lauderdale, ☎ 954/768–9920), a 300-passenger day cruiser, gives 90-minute tours up the New River and Intracoastal Waterway.

Jungle Queen III and IV (✉ Radisson Bahia Mar Beach Resort, 801 Seabreeze Blvd., Fort Lauderdale, ☎ 954/462–5596) are 175-passenger and 538-passenger tour boats that take day and night cruises up the New River, through the heart of Fort Lauderdale. The sightseeing cruises at 10 and 2 cost $9.95, whereas the evening dinner cruise costs $22.95. You can also take a daylong trip to Miami's Bayside Marketplace ($13.95), on Biscayne Bay, for shopping and sightseeing.

Las Olas Horse and Carriage (✉ 600 S.E. 4th St., Fort Lauderdale, ☎ 954/763–7393) operates in-town tours and transportation to and from the performing arts center.

Professional Diving Charters (✉ Radisson Bahia Mar Beach Resort, 801 Seabreeze Blvd., Fort Lauderdale, ☎ 954/467–6030) operates the 60-foot glass-bottom boat *Pro Diver II*. On Tuesday through Saturday mornings and Sunday afternoon, two-hour sightseeing trips take in offshore reefs, and snorkeling can be arranged.

School of Environmental Education (✉ 2514 Hollywood Blvd., Suite 400, Box 222145, Hollywood 33020-2145, ☎ 954/371–6399 or 800/498–8129), a not-for-profit organization, conducts dry-land field trips throughout South Florida and one-day, overnight, and longer boat tours as part of its program. Unaccompanied children can sometimes be accommodated at lower cost in undersubscribed school trips, on both land and water. Call in advance for availability.

Walking Tours (✉ 219 S.W. 2nd Ave., Fort Lauderdale, ☎ 954/463–4431), cosponsored by the Fort Lauderdale Historical Society, trace the New River by foot.

Visitor Information

Chamber of Commerce of Greater Fort Lauderdale (✉ 512 N.E. 3rd Ave., Fort Lauderdale 33301, ☎ 954/462–6000). **Davie/Cooper City Chamber of Commerce** (✉ 4185 Davie Rd., Davie 33314, ☎ 954/581–0790). **Greater Deerfield Beach Chamber of Commerce** (✉ 1601 E. Hillsboro Blvd., Deerfield Beach 33441, ☎ 954/427–1050). **Greater Fort Lauderdale Convention & Visitors Bureau** (✉ 200 E. Las Olas Blvd., Suite 1500, Fort Lauderdale 33301, ☎ 954/765–4466 or 800/227–8669). **Hollywood Chamber of Commerce** (✉ 2410 Hollywood Blvd., Hollywood 33019, ☎ 954/923–4000). **Lauderdale-by-the-Sea Chamber of Commerce** (✉ 4201 N. Ocean Dr., Lauderdale-by-the-Sea 33308, ☎ 954/776–1000). **Pompano Beach Chamber of Commerce** (✉ 2200 E. Atlantic Blvd., Pompano Beach 33062, ☎ 954/941–2940). **Visitors Information Center** (✉ 600 Seabreeze Blvd., Fort Lauderdale), on the beach three blocks south of Las Olas Boulevard.

6 Palm Beach and the Treasure Coast

Golden beaches are a standard feature of the shoreline of this part of Florida, from the Gold Coast of wealthy Palm Beach, the land of power shopping and pricey dining, north along the Treasure Coast of rustic Martin, St. Lucie, and Indian River counties, dotted with nature preserves and small towns with thriving arts communities. Inland there's not much to do except fish, but it's some of the best fishing in the world.

THIS SECTION OF ATLANTIC COAST defies categorization. Though it's easy to affix labels—the stretch from Palm Beach to Boca Raton is considered the northern reaches of the Gold Coast (which, in its entirety, extends all the way to Miami), while north of Palm Beach is called the Treasure Coast—individual communities have their own personalities. Here you'll find the center-stage glitziness of Palm Beach and the low-key quiet of Hutchinson Island. The unifying attraction is compelling—golden beaches bordered by luxuriant palms.

By Herb Hiller

Updated by
Pamela
Acheson

The focus of the region is indisputably Palm Beach. While tourists may go to Delray Beach or Jupiter Island or scores of other towns to catch some rays and feel sand between their toes, most stop in Palm Beach for a completely different pastime: gawking. The gold on this stretch of coast is the kind you put in a vault, and for a century now, the island town has been a hotbed of conspicuous consumption. Palm Beach is the richest city, per capita, in Florida and would easily compete for honors with places like Monaco and Malibu as the most affluent community in the world. It has long been the winter address for families with names like Rockefeller, Vanderbilt, Kennedy, and Trump.

It all started with Henry Morrison Flagler, co-founder of Standard Oil, who, in addition to bringing the railroad to Florida in the 1890s, brought his own view of civilization. The poor and middle-class fishermen and laborers who inhabited the place in the pre-Flagler era were moved a mile west or so to West Palm Beach. Still a proletariat cousin, West Palm is home to those who serve Flagler's successors on the island today.

The town of Palm Beach represents only 1% of the land area in Palm Beach County, however. The rest is given over to classic Florida beach towns, citrus farms, malls, and to the west, Lake Okeechobee, the largest lake in Florida and one of the country's hot spots for bass-fishing devotees. The arts also flourish here. In town after town, you will find a profusion of museums, galleries, theaters, and groups committed to historic preservation.

Also worth exploring is the Treasure Coast, which encompasses the northernmost part of Palm Beach County plus Martin, St. Lucie, and Indian River counties. Although late to develop, the Treasure Coast now has its share of malls and beachfront condominiums, and yet much of its shoreline is laid-back and peaceful. Martin and Indian River counties are known for their high environmental standards (though not St. Lucie County in between). Inland is largely devoted to citrus production and cattle ranching in rangelands of pine-and-palmetto scrub.

Along the coast, the broad tidal lagoon called the Indian River separates the barrier islands from the mainland. In addition to sheltering boaters on the Intracoastal Waterway and playing nursery for many saltwater game fish, it's a natural radiator, keeping frost away from the tender orange and grapefruit trees that grow near its banks. Sea turtles come ashore at night from April to August to lay their eggs on the beaches.

Pleasures and Pastimes

Beaches

Half the towns in the area include the word "beach" in their name, and for good reason. Here are miles of golden strands—some relatively remote and uncrowded, some buzzing with activity, and all blessed with the kind of blue-green waters you just won't find farther north. Among the least crowded are those at Hobe Sound National Wildlife Refuge and Fort Pierce Inlet State Recreation Area. Boca Raton's three beaches are among the most popular.

Canoeing

Plenty of good canoeing opportunities are available in this area, including organized trips down the Sebastian River and through the Pelican Island and Arthur R. Marshall–Loxahatchee National wildlife refuges.

Dining

Not surprisingly, several elegant establishments offer Continental and nouvelle cuisine that stacks up well among foodies, but the area also has good casual dining in waterfront watering holes that serve up a mean fried grouper. Just an hour west, on Lake Okeechobee, you can dine on panfried catfish a few hundred yards from where it was caught. Lower-priced "early-bird" menus, a Florida hallmark, are offered by most restaurants.

Fishing

Within a 50-mi radius of Palm Beach, you'll find virtually every form of fishing except, of course, ice fishing. If it involves a hook and a line, you can do it here—year-round. Charter a boat for deep-sea fishing out of towns from Boca Raton to Sebastian Inlet. West of Vero Beach, there's tremendous marsh fishing for catfish, bass, and perch. Lake Okeechobee is one of the world's bass-fishing capitals.

Golf

Palm Beach County is to golf what Saudi Arabia is to oil. For openers, there's the Professional Golfing Association (PGA) headquarters at the PGA National Resort & Spa in Palm Beach Gardens (a mere five golf courses are located there). In all, there are nearly 150 public, private, and semiprivate golf courses in Palm Beach County. A Golf-A-Round program, in which more than 100 hotels participate, lets you play at one of 10 courses each day, with no greens fees.

Hiking and Walking

You'll never find a wider variety of hiking environments than in the Palm Beach County area. If you want to go uptown, try a walking tour of Worth Avenue. At the other end of the spectrum, venture west to Lake Okeechobee and take a walk through the Everglades. Numerous hiking trails can also be found at wildlife preserves dotting the Gold Coast's barrier islands.

Lodging

Though resort prices in Palm Beach and Boca Raton hover at the high end of the scale, you can find inexpensive rooms at smaller establishments that aren't on the beach. Other towns in this part of Florida offer a greater range of reasonably priced, casual establishments where the owners don't mind a little sand on the floor; prices drop precipitously as you move inland toward Lake Okeechobee. To get the best for less, particularly in winter months, book far in advance.

Polo

Polo, a sport for the ultrarich, has an egalitarian side. Many matches are free and open to the public. Palm Beach County is home to four polo organizations, providing good opportunities to catch a match or two of this unusual sport.

Shopping

A quarter mile of the most expensive stores in America cluster on Worth Avenue, which is comparable to Rodeo Drive in Beverly Hills as an upscale shopper's nirvana. But there's also plenty of middle-American shopping nearby, including the likes of the Palm Beach Mall and the Manufacturers Outlet Center. You can browse in art galleries and antiques shops in Vero Beach, Delray Beach, and Boca Raton's Mizner Park.

Water Sports

The 47 mi of Atlantic shoreline in Palm Beach County offer some great opportunities for getting on or in the water. Sailboats, fishing boats, and large and small powerboats are available for rent, with or without a licensed captain. Numerous vendors along the Intracoastal Waterway rent Jet Skis as well as outboard-powered runabouts that you can drive yourself.

Exploring Palm Beach and the Treasure Coast

The center of most any visit to the area is Palm Beach proper (and it certainly is!). Not only is it within an hour's drive of most of the region but its Gatsby-era architecture, stunning mansions, and highbrow shopping make it unlike any other place in Florida. From there you can head in any of three directions: south along the Gold Coast toward Boca Raton, north to the mainland and barrier-island treasures of the Treasure Coast, or west for some inland delights.

Great Itineraries

Tucked into an island 12 mi long and about ¼ mi wide, Palm Beach is easy to cover thoroughly in just a day or two. If you have several days, you can take in a lot of varied sights, exploring everything from galleries to subtropical wildlife preserves, and with a week, you'll easily be able to see the whole area. Of course you could just do what a lot of visitors prefer—laze around soaking up the rays and the atmosphere.

Numbers in the text correspond to numbers in the margin and on the Palm Beach and West Palm Beach and the Gold Coast and Treasure Coast maps.

IF YOU HAVE 3 DAYS

With a short amount of time, make ⊡ **Palm Beach** ①–⑨ your base. On the first day, start in the middle of downtown, Worth Avenue ⑦, to do some window shopping and gallery browsing. After you've refreshed yourself with a très-chic bistro lunch, head for that other must-see on even the shortest itinerary: the Henry Morrison Flagler Museum ⑤. Your second day is for the beach; two good options are Lantana Public Beach, which has great food concessions, and Oceanfront Park. Spend the better part of your last day exploring attractions you wouldn't expect to find in South Florida, such as the Morikami Museum and Japanese Gardens in nearby Delray Beach ㉗. Trite as it may sound, it's like a one-day visit to Japan.

IF YOU HAVE 5 DAYS

With five days you can be more contemplative at the galleries and museums, more leisurely at the beaches, and have time for more serendipitous exploring. Stay in ⊡ **Palm Beach** ①–⑨ for two nights. The first day, visit the Henry Morrison Flagler Museum ⑤ and the luxury hotel known as The Breakers ③, another Flagler legacy. Then head to Worth Avenues ⑦ for a leisurely lunch and an afternoon of window shopping. On the second day, drive over to West Palm Beach ⑩–⑳ and the Norton Gallery of Art ⑪, which has an extensive collection of 19th-century French Impressionists. On day three, choose between making an overnight visit to ⊡ **Lake Okeechobee** ㊱–㊶, the bass-fishing capital of the world, and staying in Palm Beach another night and driving a half hour to explore the Arthur R. Marshall–Loxahatchee National

Wildlife Refuge. Head south to ⚅ **Boca Raton** ㉘ on the fourth day, and check into a beachfront hotel before spending the rest of the afternoon wandering through Mizner Park's shops. On your fifth day, meander through the Boca Raton Museum of Art in the morning and get some sun at South Beach Park after lunch.

IF YOU HAVE 7 DAYS

With an entire week, you can see the Gold and Treasure coasts thoroughly, with time left to fit in such recreational pursuits as taking sailboard or croquet lessons, going deep-sea fishing, or jet skiing. Stay two nights in ⚅ **Palm Beach** ①–⑨, spending your first day taking in its best sights, mentioned above. On day two, rent a bicycle and follow the 10-mi path along Lake Worth, providing a great look at the backyards of many of Palm Beach's big mansions. Drive north on day three, across the Jerry Thomas Bridge to Singer Island and the John D. MacArthur Beach State Park. Spend the third night farther north, on ⚅ **Hutchinson Island** ㉜, and relax the next morning on the beach in front of your hotel. On your way back south, explore Stuart ㉛ and its tiny but interesting historic downtown area, and pause at the Arthur R. Marshall–Loxahatchee National Wildlife Refuge before ending up in ⚅ **Boca Raton** ㉘, for three nights at a beachfront hotel. Split day five between shopping at Mizner Park and beaching it at South Beach Park. Day six is for cultural attractions: the Boca Raton Museum of Art followed by the galleries and interesting Japanese museum in Delray Beach ㉗. If you have time on your last day, take in one of Boca Raton's other two beaches, Spanish River and Red Reef parks.

When to Tour Palm Beach and the Treasure Coast

The weather is optimum November through May, but the trade-off is that facilities are more crowded and prices are somewhat higher. In summer you'll need a tolerance for heat and humidity if you want to spend time outside; also watch for frequent afternoon downpours. If you're set on watching the sea turtles come ashore to nest, make sure to visit between late April and August, and remember that nesting occurs at night. No matter when you visit, bring insect repellent if you plan outdoor outings.

THE PALM BEACHES

The star of the Palm Beaches is, of course, glitzy Palm Beach, whose island setting comes with an ocean beach. Across the inland waterway is the booming and bustling small city of West Palm Beach, and just north is Palm Beach Gardens, a largely residential spot with many inexpensive motels. On the southern tip of Singer Island, Palm Beach Shores is Palm Beach's poor relation to the north.

Palm Beach

78 mi north of Miami.

Setting the tone in this incredibly wealthy town is the baroque architecture of developer Addison Mizner, who began building homes, stores, and public buildings here in the 1920s and whose Moorish-gothic style has influenced virtually all the landmarks of the community. Thanks to Mizner and those influenced by him, Palm Beach has a kind of neo-Camelot look. You can get a taste of what the town is all about when you squeeze into a parking place on Worth Avenue, among the Mercedes and Bentleys, and head to its boutiques to rub Versace-covered shoulders with shoppers whose credit card limits likely exceed the gross national product of Liechtenstein.

Away from downtown, along County Road and Ocean Boulevard (the shore road, also designated as Route A1A), are Palm Beach's other defining landmarks: mansions. In some parts, they're fronted by thick 20-foot hedgerows and topped by the seemingly de rigueur barrel-tile roofs. The low wall that separates the dune-top shore road from the sea hides a badly eroded beach in many places. Here and there where the strand deepens a bit, homes are built directly on the beach.

❶ A road cut about 25 feet deep through a ridge of reddish-brown sandstone and oolite limestone, the small **Canyon of Palm Beach** (⊠ Lake Way Rd.) gives you a brief feeling of being in the desert Southwest.

❷ Spanish-style architecture defines the exterior of the **Palm Beach Post Office** (⊠ 95 N. County Rd., ☎ 561/832-1867). Inside murals depict Seminole Indians in the Everglades and stately royal and coconut palms.

★ ❸ Originally built by Henry Flagler in 1895 and rebuilt by his descendants after a fire in 1925, **The Breakers** (⊠ 1 S. County Rd., ☎ 561/655–6611) was one of the starting points of Florida tourism. The luxury hotel resembles an ornate Italian Renaissance palace and was renovated to the tune of $150 million not long ago. Walk into the lobby and take a look at the painted, arched ceilings hung with crystal chandeliers, and peek into the ornate Florentine Dining Room with its 15th-century Flemish tapestries.

❹ The Spanish-gothic Episcopal church **Bethesda-by-the-Sea** was built in 1927 by the first Protestant congregation in southeast Florida. Next to it are the formal, ornamental **Cluett Memorial Gardens.** ⊠ *141 S. County Rd.,* ☎ *561/655–4554.* ☉ *Church and gardens daily 8–5; services Sept.–May, Sun. 8, 9, and 11, and June–Aug., Sun. 8 and 10; call for weekday schedule.*

★ ❺ The opulence of Florida's Gilded Age is still apparent at Whitehall, the palatial 73-room mansion Henry Flagler had built in 1901 for his third wife, Mary Lily Kenan, and now home to the **Henry Morrison Flagler Museum.** Then-famous architects John Carrère and Thomas Hastings were instructed to spare no expense in creating the finest home they could imagine. They did as they were told, and Whitehall rivals some of the fine palaces of Europe. In 1960, Flagler's granddaughter, Jean Flagler Matthews, bought the building and made it a museum. On display are many of the original furnishings, an art collection, a 1,200-pipe organ, and exhibits on the history of the Florida East Coast Railway. Flagler's personal railroad car, "The Rambler," is parked behind the building. A tour by well-informed guides takes about an hour. ⊠ *1 Whitehall Way,* ☎ *561/655–2833.* ☉ *$7.* ☉ *Tues.–Sat. 10–5, Sun. noon–5.*

❻ In addition to presenting cultural events, the **Society of the Four Arts,** a privately endowed arts and educational institution, incorporates an exhibition hall, library, 13 distinct gardens, and the Philip Hulitar Sculpture Garden. ⊠ *Four Arts Plaza,* ☎ *561/655–7226.* ☞ *$3.* ☉ *Galleries Mon.–Sat. 10–5, also Sun. 2–5 Dec.–mid-Apr.; library, children's library, and gardens weekdays 10–5, also Sat. 9–1 Nov.–May.*

★ ❼ The ¼-mi-long **Worth Avenue** (⊠ Between Cocoanut Row and S. Ocean Blvd.) is synonymous with posh, pricey shopping. A stroll amid the Moorish architecture of its scores of top-drawer shops—Cartier, Charles Jourdan, and Giorgio Armani, to name a few—gives you a taste of what the good life must be like.

❽ Perhaps no Palm Beach mansion represents the town's ongoing generations of flashbulb fame better than **El Solano** (⊠ 721 S. County Rd.).

Palm Beach and West Palm Beach

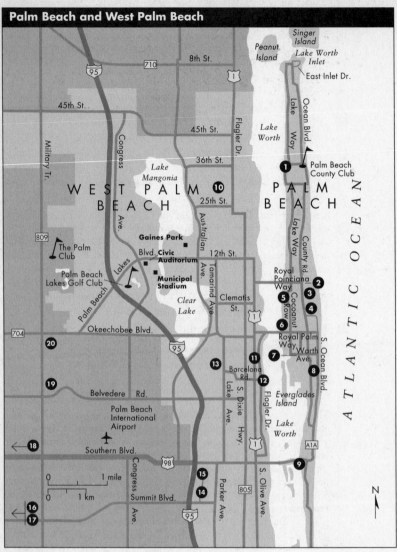

The Spanish-style home was built by Addison Mizner for himself in 1925. Mizner then sold it to Harold Vanderbilt, and the property made the rounds of socialites, photo shoots, and expansions until it was bought by John Lennon and Yoko Ono 10 months before Lennon's death. Now owned by a banking executive, El Solano is not open to the public.

⑨ Still one of the grandest of homes along Ocean Boulevard, **Mar-A-Lago** (⊠ 1100 S. Ocean Blvd.) has Italianate towers silhouetted against the sky. The former estate of breakfast-food heiress Marjorie Meriweather Post, it has more recently been owned by real-estate magnate Donald Trump, who first turned it into a membership club and now plans to subdivide the property, which curves for ⅓ mi along the road.

Beaches

Parking meters along Ocean Boulevard between Worth Avenue and Royal Palm Way signify Palm Beach's only stretch of beach with convenient public access. South of Worth Avenue, small **Mid-Town Beach** is especially popular because it is so close to town. ⊠ *400 S. Ocean Blvd., no phone.* ⊠ *Parking 25¢ for 15 min.* ⊙ *Daily 8–6.*

Besides the ubiquitous beautiful beach, some picnic tables, and grills, **Phipps Ocean Park** has a Palm Beach County landmark in the **Little Red Schoolhouse.** Dating from 1886, it was the first schoolhouse in what was then Dade County. ⊠ *2145 S. Ocean Blvd.* ⊠ *Parking 25¢ for 20 min.* ⊙ *Mon.–Sat. 8–6.*

Dining and Lodging

$$$–$$$$ ✕ **Café L'Europe.** This is one of the most popular and elegant restau-
★ rants in Palm Beach. Sumptuous oak paneling, dim lighting, and elaborate flower bouquets set the mood. Ladies-who-lunch can enjoy spa cuisine, while evening guests dine expensively on specialty pastas, such as spinach, shiitake mushroom, and mascarpone ravioli with pignoli-hazelnut butter; seafood dishes, like potato-crusted Florida snapper with shaved baby fennel and beurre blanc; or Cornish hen, rack of lamb, or black Angus filet. Apple pancake with lingonberries is the signature dessert. A pianist plays nightly at the casual, less expensive Bistro Room. ⊠ *331 S. County Rd.,* ☎ *561/655–4020. Reservations essential. Jacket required. AE, DC, MC, V. No lunch Sun.*

$$$ ✕ **Amici.** Night after night a steady stream of six-figure automobiles
★ pulls into the valet parking spot of this new place to be seen. Inside, the lighting is dim, and tables are close together but never empty. The northern Italian menu features such house specialties as antipasti of cold marinated and grilled vegetables, rigatoni with spicy tomato sauce and Italian sausage, penne with fresh tomatoes and garlic, grilled veal chops, risottos, and a long list of pizzas cooked in the wood-burning oven. There are nightly pasta and fresh-fish specials as well. If you want to avoid the crowds, stop by for a late lunch. ⊠ *228 S. County Rd.,* ☎ *561/832–0201. Reservations essential. AE, D, DC, MC, V.*

$$$ ✕ **Bice Ristorante.** This dining establishment is so thoroughly Italian that it's easy to be disappointed when the parking attendant speaks to you in English. Brilliant flower arrangements and lots of brass accent a dark beige-and-yellow color scheme. Aromas of basil, chives, and oregano fill the air as waiters bring out the divine home-baked focaccia accompanying such house favorites as *Robespierre alla moda della bice* (sliced steak topped with arugula salad) and *costoletta di vitello impanata alla milanese* (breaded veal cutlet with a tomato salad). The name is short for Beatrice, mother of Roberto Ruggeri, who founded the original in Milan in 1926 and has opened branches here and in other smart places since then. ⊠ *313¼ Worth Ave.,* ☎ *561/835–1600. Jacket required. AE, DC, MC, V.*

$$$ ✕ **Jo's.** With 150 seats and a full bar, pastel, latticed, and mirrored French restaurant occupies a prominent corner on South County Road. Chef Richard Kline, son of the owner, Jo, holds sway in the kitchen. Look for the three-soup sampler (lobster bisque, green pea soup, and beef consommé) as well as osso buco and boned half roast duckling with orange—always moist but never rare. For dessert try the tarte tatin (upside-down apple pie) or fresh raspberries. ⊠ *375 S. County Rd.,* ☎ *561/659-6776. AE, MC, V.*

$$ ✕ **Chuck & Harold's.** Ivana Trump, Larry Holmes, Brooke Shields, and Michael Bolton are among the celebrities who have eaten at this combination power-lunch bar, sidewalk café, and jazz/big band garden, which is popular day and night. Locals who want to be part of the scenery and tourists hot to people-watch catch a seat and linger in the outdoor café, next to pots of red and white begonias mounted on the sidewalk rail. Specialties include conch chowder, terrific hamburgers, an onion-crunchy gazpacho, and tangy Key lime pie. A big blackboard lists daily specials and celebrity birthdays. ⊠ *207 Royal Poinciana Way,* ☎ *561/659–1440. AE, DC, MC, V.*

$$ ✕ **Dempsey's.** This New York–style Irish pub under the palms comes complete with paisley table covers, plaid café curtains, burgundy banquettes, horse prints, and antique coach lanterns. When major sports events are on the big TV, this place is always packed, noisy, and as electric as a frenzied Friday at the stock exchange. Along with much socializing, people enjoy Maine lobster, fresh seafood, chicken hash Dempsey (with a dash of Scotch), and Welsh rarebit, followed by hot apple pie. ⊠ *50 Cocoanut Row,* ☎ *561/835–0400. AE, MC, V.*

$$ ✕ **Ta-boó.** Dressed in gorgeous pinks, greens, and florals, the spaces
★ of this Worth Avenue landmark are divided into discreet salons: One resembles a courtyard, another an elegant living room with a fireplace, and a third a skylit gazebo. The Tiki Tiki bar makes an elegant salon for the neighborhood crowd. Appetizers range from a very proletariat nachos grande with chili to Beluga caviar; dinners include chicken and arugula from the grill, prime rib, steaks, frogs' legs, and main course salads. White pizza with goat and mozzarella cheeses, pesto, and sweet roasted red peppers is a favorite. Drop in late at night during the season and you're bound to spot a famous face or two. ⊠ *221 Worth Ave.,* ☎ *561/835–3500. AE, MC, V.*

$ ✕ **TooJay's.** New York deli food served in a bright California-style setting—what could be more Florida? The menu at this spot, one of nine TooJay's in the Sunshine State, includes matzoh ball soup, corned beef on rye, and a killer cake made with five kinds of chocolate and topped with whipped cream. A salami-on-rye sandwich layered with onions, Muenster cheese, coleslaw, and Russian dressing is a house favorite. On the High Holidays look for carrot tzimmes (a sweet vegetable compote), brisket, and roast chicken. Wisecracking waitresses keep the pace fast. ⊠ *313 Royal Poinciana Plaza,* ☎ *561/659-7232. AE, DC, MC, V. Beer and wine only.*

$$$$ ⊞ **Brazilian Court.** Spread out over half a block, the yellow-stucco Spanish-style facade with a red tile roof reminds you of this hotel's 1931 origins. Rooms are brilliantly floral—in yellows, blues, and greens—with theatrical bed canopies, white-lattice patterns on carpets, and sunshiny pane windows. Bathroom shelf space is tight, but at least you can line up your toiletries on marble. Closets are big enough for people who once brought trunks for the entire season. (Some still do.) French doors, polished wood floors, bay windows, loggias, cherub fountains, and chintz garden umbrellas beneath royal palms create a lyrical style. Classical music plays as you enter. ⊠ *301 Australian Ave., 33480,* ☎

561/655-7740 or 800/552-0335; in Canada, 800/228-6852; FAX *561/655-0801. 128 rooms, 6 suites. 2 restaurants, bar, pool. AE, D, DC, MC, V.*

$$$$
★ ⊞ **The Breakers.** Dating from 1926 and enlarged in 1969, this opulent seven-story Italian Renaissance–style resort sprawls over 140 splendidly manicured acres. Cupids frolic in the Florentine fountain at the main entrance, while majestic ceiling vaults and frescoes grace the lobby. Balancing formality with casualness, the hotel no longer *requires* men to wear jackets and ties after 7 PM. A $75 million renovation modernized the resort and enhanced its elegance without sacrificing old-world luxury. Many rooms have been enlarged, and all have been redecorated. ⊠ *1 S. County Rd., 33480,* ☎ *561/655–6611 or 800/833–3141,* FAX *561/659–8403. 572 rooms, 48 suites. 5 restaurants, 2 lounges, pool, saunas, 2 golf courses, 20 tennis courts, croquet, health club, jogging, shuffleboard, beach, boating, children's programs. AE, D, DC, MC, V.*

$$$$
★ ⊞ **The Colony.** What distinguishes this legendary pale, pale yellow Georgian-style hotel only steps from Worth Avenue is its attentive staff that is youthful yet experienced. There's a buzz of competence and a true desire to please, evinced by the policy of relaxing the dress code in summer. Cool and classical guest rooms have fluted blond cabinetry and matching draperies and bedcovers in deep floral prints. As in many older hotels, bathrooms are small. "The scene" for glitterati after charity balls at The Breakers, this is where Roxanne Pulitzer retreated after her infamous seven-week marriage in 1992. ⊠ *155 Hammon Ave., 33480,* ☎ *561/655–5430 or 800/521–5525,* FAX *561/832–7318. 63 rooms, 36 suites and apartments, 7 villas, 3 penthouses. Restaurant, lounge, pool, spa. AE, D, DC, MC, V.*

$$$$
★ ⊞ **Four Seasons Ocean Grand.** This 6-acre property at the south end of town is coolly elegant but warm in detail. Marble, art, fanlight windows, swagged drapes, chintz, and palms create a serene atmosphere. On weekend evenings year-round, piano music accompanies cocktails in the Living Room lounge. On some weekend nights in season, jazz groups perform, and there are classical recitals on Sunday afternoons. Although its name suggests grandeur, this four-story hotel with a long beach is more like a small jewel. Spacious rooms, each with private balcony, are furnished in Palm Beach finery with muted natural tones and teal, mauve, and salmon accents. ⊠ *2800 S. Ocean Blvd., 33480,* ☎ *561/582–2800 or 800/432–2335,* FAX *561/547–1557. 210 rooms and suites. 2 restaurants, lounge, pool, saunas, 3 tennis courts, health club, beach. AE, D, DC, MC, V.*

$$$–$$$$
★ ⊞ **Plaza Inn.** This three-story hotel, deco-designed from the 1930s, operates B&B style; a full breakfast is included. The pool, gardens, and piano bar have the intimate charm of a trysting place for the likes of Cary Grant and Katharine Hepburn. Inn owner Ajit Asrani is a retired Indian Army officer who raises show horses and polo ponies. The courteous staff and location in the heart of Palm Beach are pluses, and the uncluttered, individually decorated rooms with phone and refrigerator provide a welcome change from other B&Bs. So, too, does the appealing courtyard with waterfalls and a pool. ⊠ *215 Brazilian Ave., 33480,* ☎ *561/832–8666 or 800/233–2632,* FAX *561/835–8776. 50 rooms and suites. Lounge, pool, hot tub. AE, MC, V.*

$$$
⊞ **Palm Beach Historic Inn.** Longtime hoteliers Harry and Barbara Kehr manage this delightfully unexpected inn in the heart of downtown. The setting, tucked between Town Hall and a seaside residential block, combines town and vacationland. B&B touches include flowers, wine and fruit, snacks, seasonal turndown, tea and cookies in rooms, and a generous Continental breakfast. Guest rooms tend to the frilly

with lots of lace, ribbons, and scalloped edges. Most are furnished with Victorian antiques and reproductions (some out of old mansions, others more secondhand than authentic) and chiffon wall drapings above the bed. A 1944 Coke machine still supplies an 8-ounce bottle for a dime. Bath towels are as thick as parkas. ⊠ *365 S. County Rd., 33480,* ☎ *561/832–4009,* FAX *561/832–6255. 9 rooms, 4 suites. Library. AE, D, DC, MC, V.*

$$–$$$ 🏨 **Palm Beach Sea Lord Hotel.** If you don't need glamour or brand names, and you're not the B&B type, this garden-style hideaway is for you. Choose from accommodations that overlook Lake Worth, the pool, or the ocean; the reasonably priced café adds to the at-home, comfy feeling and attracts repeat customers. Units are plain but not cheap in season and come with carpet, at least one comfortable chair, small or large refrigerator, and tropical print fabrics. ⊠ *2315 S. Ocean Blvd., 33480,* ☎ FAX *561/582–1461. 19 rooms, 11 apartments, 6 efficiencies. Restaurant, pool, beach. D, MC, V.*

Nightlife and the Arts

THE ARTS

The Royal Poinciana Playhouse (⊠ 70 Royal Poinciana Plaza, ☎ 561/659–3310) presents seven productions each year between December and April. **Society of the Four Arts** (⊠ Four Arts Plaza, ☎ 561/655–7226) offers concerts, lectures, and Friday films December–March. Movie tickets can be purchased at time of showing; other tickets may be obtained a week in advance.

NIGHTLIFE

Cheek-to-cheek dancers head to **The Colony** (⊠ 155 Hammon Ave., ☎ 561/655–5430) for a spin around the dance floor. A trio plays Thursday, Friday, and Saturday nights. As the weekend dinner crowd thins out, late-night party-seekers fill up **Ta-boó** (⊠ 221 Worth Ave., ☎ 561/835–3500), where a DJ keeps everyone on their feet.

Outdoor Activities and Sports

BIKING

Bicycling is an excellent way to get a good look at Palm Beach, which is as small and flat as the top of a billiard table (and just as green). The wonderful, 10-mi, palm-fringed **Palm Beach Bicycle Trail** (⊠ Parallel to Lake Way) skirts the backyards of many palatial mansions and the edge of Lake Worth. Just a block from the bike trail, the **Palm Beach Trail Bicycle Shop** (⊠ 223 Sunrise Ave., ☎ 561/659–4583) rents bikes by the hour or day.

DOG RACING

Since 1932, the hounds have been racing year-round at the 4,300-seat **Palm Beach Kennel Club.** There are also simulcasts of jai alai and horse racing, as well as wagering on live and televised sports. ⊠ *1111 N. Congress Ave., 33409,* ☎ *561/683–2222.* 🎫 *50¢, terrace level $1, parking free.* ☉ *Racing Mon. 12:30; Wed., Thurs., and Sat. 12:30 and 7:30; Fri. 7:30; Sun. 1; simulcasts Mon. and Fri. noon and Tues. 12:30.*

GOLF

Breakers Hotel Golf Club (⊠ 1 S. County Rd., ☎ 561/655–6611 or 800/833–3141) has 36 holes. **Palm Beach Par 3** (⊠ 2345 S. Ocean Blvd., ☎ 561/547–0598) has 18 holes, including four on the Atlantic and three on the inland waterway.

Shopping

One of the world's showcases for high-quality shopping, **Worth Avenue** runs ¼-mi east–west across Palm Beach, from the beach to Lake Worth. The street has more than 250 shops, and many upscale stores

(Cartier, Gucci, Hermès, Pierre Deux, Saks Fifth Avenue, and Van Cleef & Arpels) are represented, their merchandise appealing to the discerning tastes of the Palm Beach clientele. The six blocks of **South County Road** north of Worth Avenue also have appealing stores. For specialty items (out-of-town newspapers and health foods), try the shops along the north side of **Royal Poinciana Way.**

West Palm Beach

2 mi west of Palm Beach.

Long considered Palm Beach's impoverished cousin, West Palm is economically vibrant in its own right. Far larger than its upper-crust neighbor to the east, it has become the cultural, entertainment, and business center of the county and of the region to the north. Sparkling government buildings like the mammoth $124 million Palm Beach County Judicial Center and Courthouse and the State Administrative Building exemplify the health of the city's corporate life, and facilities such as the $60 million Kravis Center for the Performing Arts attest to the strength of the arts and entertainment community. The historic preservation movement has yielded an attractive downtown area. Along beautifully landscaped Clematis Street, you'll find boutiques, good restaurants, and exuberant nightlife that mimics that of South Beach. There's a free downtown shuttle by day and free on-street parking at night and on weekends.

🔟 The 1920s-era **Old Northwood Historic District** (⊠ West of Flagler Dr. between 26th and 35th Sts.), on the National Register of Historic Places, hosts special events and Sunday walking tours (☞ Guided Tours *in* Palm Beach and the Treasure Coast A to Z, *below*).

★ ⑪ Constructed in 1941 by steel magnate Ralph H. Norton, the **Norton Gallery of Art** boasts an extensive permanent collection of 19th- and 20th-century American and European paintings with special emphasis on 19th-century French Impressionists. There are also Chinese bronze and jade sculptures, a sublime outdoor patio with sculptures on display in a tropical garden, and a library housing more than 3,000 art books and periodicals. Nine new galleries showcase traveling exhibits as well as art from the permanent collection. ⊠ *1451 S. Olive Ave.,* ☎ *561/832–5194.* ☜ *$5.* ☉ *Tues.–Sat. 10–5, Sun. 1–5.*

⑫ The **Ann Norton Sculpture Gardens,** a monument to the late American sculptor Ann Weaver Norton, second wife of Norton Gallery founder Ralph H. Norton, consist of charming 3-acre grounds displaying seven granite figures and six brick megaliths. Plantings were designed by Norton, an environmentalist, to attract native bird life. ⊠ *253 Barcelona Rd.,* ☎ *561/832–5328.* ☜ *$3.* ☉ *Tues.–Sat. 10–4 (call ahead; schedule is not always observed) or by appointment.*

⑬ Built by the WPA in 1939, the **Armory Arts Center** is now a complete visual arts center. Its gallery hosts rotating exhibitions, and classes are held throughout the year. ⊠ *1703 S. Lake Ave.,* ☎ *561/832–1776.* ☜ *Free.* ☉ *Weekdays 9–5, Sun. 10–2.*

⊙ ⑭ Head to the **Dreher Park Zoo** for a look at Florida panthers, red kangaroos, and Bengal tigers. This wild kingdom is a 22-acre complex with more than 500 animals representing more than 100 species. Also of note are a nature trail, an Australian Outback exhibit, and a children's zoo. ⊠ *1301 Summit Blvd.,* ☎ *561/533–0887 or 561/547–9453.* ☜ *$6, boat rides $1.* ☉ *Daily 9–5 (until 7 on spring and summer weekends), boat rides every 15 min.*

You'll find hands-on exhibits, aquarium displays with touch tanks, planetarium shows, and a chance to observe the heavens Friday night through the most powerful telescope in South Florida (weather permitting) at the **South Florida Science Museum.** ⊠ *4801 Dreher Trail N,* ☎ *561/832–1988.* ☞ *$5; planetarium $1.75 extra, laser show $2 extra.* ⊙ *Sat.–Thurs. 10–5, Fri. 10–10.*

The **Pine Jog Environmental Education Center** is 150 acres of mostly undisturbed Florida pine flatwoods. There are now two self-guided ½-mi trails, and formal landscaping around the five one-story buildings features an array of native plants. Dioramas and displays show native ecosystems. Trails are reserved for the classes that are given here during the week but are open to the public on Sunday. ⊠ *6301 Summit Blvd.,* ☎ *561/686–6600.* ☞ *Free.* ⊙ *Sun. 2–5.*

At the popular **Okeeheelee Nature Center,** you can explore 5 mi of trails through 90 acres of native pine flatwoods and wetlands. A spacious visitor center/gift shop has hands-on exhibits. ⊠ *7715 Forest Hill Blvd.,* ☎ *561/233–1400.* ☞ *Free.* ⊙ *Visitor center Tues.–Fri. 1–4:45, Sat. 8:15–4:45; trails open daily.*

Drive (with car windows closed) on 8 mi of paved roads through **Lion Country Safari,** a 500-acre cageless zoo where 1,000 wild animals roam. Lions, elephants, white rhinoceroses, giraffes, zebras, antelopes, chimpanzees, and ostriches are among those in residence. ⊠ *Southern Blvd. W,* ☎ *561/793–1084.* ☞ *$13.95, car rental $6 per hour.* ⊙ *Daily 9:30–5:30.*

Take advantage of balmy weather at **Mounts Horticultural Learning Center,** where you can walk among tropical and subtropical plants. Free tours are given. ⊠ *531 N. Military Trail,* ☎ *561/233–1749.* ☞ *Free.* ⊙ *Mon.–Sat. 8:30–5, Sun. 1–5; tours Sat. 11, Sun. 2:30.*

The **Puppetry Arts Center** provides shows and educational programs from the home of the Gold Coast Puppet Guild. ⊠ *Cross County Mall, 4356 Okeechobee Blvd. and Military Trail,* ☎ *561/687–3280.* ☞ *Shows $2.50.* ⊙ *Call for schedule.*

Dining and Lodging

$$–$$$ ✕ **Basil's Neighborhood Café.** This informal restaurant is named for a fictitious gentleman—more or less the establishment's mascot—who in turn was named after the herb, which the chef uses frequently and adroitly. Start with the swamp cabbage salad (hearts of palm with an oil-and-basil sauce) before tackling the basil-touched main dishes, such as chicken breasts stuffed with cheese, walnuts, and spinach and covered with lemon-basil sauce. Basil mania stops short of dessert, but the chocolate-topped hazelnut cake does fine on its own. ⊠ *771 Village Blvd.,* ☎ *561/687–3801. AE, DC, MC, V. Closed Mon. June–Dec.*

$–$$ ✕ **Comeau Bar & Grill.** Everybody still calls it Roxy's (including the staff), its name from 1934 until it moved into an art deco downtown high-rise's lobby in 1989. Outside there are tables under the canopy; inside, behind the authentic old saloon, is a clubby, pecky cypress-paneled room that serves no-surprise, all-American food: steaks, shrimp, chicken, duck, some pastas, and Caesar and Greek salads. Try the Roxy Burger—a combination of veal and beef herbed and spiced. ⊠ *319–323 Clematis St.,* ☎ *561/833–2402 or 561/833–1003. AE, MC, V. No dinner Sun.*

$$$$ ☷ **Palm Beach Polo and Country Club.** Spacious, privately owned studios, one- and two-bedroom villas, and condominiums are available for daily, weekly, or monthly rental in this exclusive 2,200-acre resort, where World Cup and USPA Gold Cup tournaments are hosted. Each residence is furnished according to the resort's quality standards. Still, styles range from stagily backlit and modern to Ozzie and Harriet plaids and bulky rattan. Specify any preferences for decor or proximity to a particular sport—polo, tennis, or golf—when reserving. All units have kitchens and a range of amenities. ⊠ *11809 Polo Club Rd., Wellington 33414, ☏ 561/798–7000 or 800/327–4204. 100 villas and condominiums. 5 dining rooms, 10 pools, sauna, 2 18-hole and 1 9-hole golf courses, 24 tennis courts, croquet, horseback riding, racquetball, squash. AE, DC, MC, V.*

$$ 🏠 **West Palm Beach Bed & Breakfast.** More informal and Key West–like than most of Old Northwood, this cottage-style B&B has a clump of rare paroutis palms out front. All rooms are vividly colored, but the splashy poolside carriage house and the brightly striped cottage with the fruity fabrics and Peter Max–style posters are where you want to be. The parlor has a delightful montage of work by Florida's favorite painter of hotel art, Eileen Seitz. ⊠ *419 32nd St., 33407, ☏ 561/848–4064 or 800/736–4064, ℻ 561/842–1688. 2 rooms, carriage house, cottage. Pool. AE, MC, V.*

$–$$ 🏠 **Hibiscus House.** Few Florida B&B hosts work harder at hospital-
★ ity and at looking after their neighborhood than Raleigh Hill and Colin Rayner. As proof, since the inn opened in the late 1980s, 11 sets of guests have bought houses in Old Northwood, which is listed on the National Register of Historic Places thanks to Hill and Rayner's ef-forts. Their Cape Cod–style B&B is full of the antiques Hill has col-lected during decades of in-demand interior designing: a 150-year-old four-square piano, a gorgeous green and cane planter chair, and Louis XV pieces in the living room. Outstanding, too, is the land-scaped, tropical pool-patio area. Both Hill and Rayner are informed about the best—and most affordable—dining in the area. ⊠ *501 30th St., 33407, ☏ 561/863–5633 or 800/203–4927. 8 rooms. Pool. AE, DC, MC, V.*

Nightlife and the Arts

THE ARTS

Part of the treasury of arts attractions is the **Raymond F. Kravis Cen-ter for the Performing Arts** (⊠ 701 Okeechobee Blvd., ☏ 561/832–7469), a $60 million, 2,200-seat, glass, copper, and marble showcase occupying the highest ground in West Palm Beach. Its 250-seat **Rinker Playhouse** includes a space for children's programming, family pro-ductions, and other special events. Some 300 performances of drama, dance, and music—everything from gospel and bluegrass to jazz and classical—are scheduled each year.

Palm Beach Opera (⊠ 415 S. Olive Ave., 33401, ☏ 561/833–7888) stages four productions each winter at the Kravis Center. **Quest The-atre** (⊠ 444 24th St., 33407, ☏ 561/832–9328) showcases African-American productions in its own performance hall and on tour throughout the county. **Carefree Theatre** (⊠ 2000 S. Dixie Hwy., 33401, ☏ 561/833–7305) is Palm Beach County's premier showcase of foreign and art films.

NIGHTLIFE

Respectable Street Cafe (⊠ 518 Clematis St., ☏ 561/832–9999) ex-plodes in high energy like an indoor Woodstock. It's open until 4 AM Wednesday–Saturday (Thursday nights feature the best in underground alternative sound) and for special concerts on other days. **Underground Coffeeworks** (⊠ 105 S. Narcissus Ave., ☏ 561/835–4792), a retro '60s spot, has "something different going on" (usually live music) Tues-day–Saturday.

Outdoor Activities and Sports

BASEBALL

The **Atlanta Braves and Montreal Expos** (⊠ 1610 Palm Beach Lakes Blvd., ☎ 561/683–6012) both train at Municipal Stadium, also home of the Class A Palm Beach Expos of the Florida State League.

GOLF

The plush **Emerald Dunes Golf Club** (⊠ 2100 Emerald Dunes Dr., ☎ 561/684–4653) has 18 holes of golf. **Palm Beach Polo and Country Club** (⊠ 13198 Forest Hill Blvd., Wellington, ☎ 561/798–7000 or 800/327–4204) has 45 holes with an excellent overall layout.

Shopping

Good as the malls are, they're sterile compared to the in-the-midst-of-things excitement—the mix of food, art, performance, landscaping, and retailing—that has renewed downtown West Palm around **Clematis Street.** Shopping per se is still the weakest part of the mix, but waterview parks, outdoor performing areas, and attractive plantings and lighting—including fanciful palm tree sculptures—add to the pleasure of browsing and window shopping. For those single-mindedly bent on mall shopping, the **Palm Beach Mall** (⊠ Palm Beach Lakes Blvd. at I–95) has a Burdines, JCPenney, Lord & Taylor, and Sears.

Palm Beach Shores

㉑ *7 mi north of Palm Beach.*

This residential town rimmed by mom-and-pop motels is at the southern tip of Singer Island, across Lake Worth Inlet from Palm Beach. To get between the two, however, you must cross over to the mainland before returning to the beach. The main attraction of this unpretentious middle-class community is its affordable beachfront lodging. By staying here you get Palm Beach's weather and ocean views without its pretense and price.

OFF THE BEATEN PATH

JOHN D. MACARTHUR BEACH STATE PARK – Here you will find almost 2 mi of beach, good fishing and shelling, and one of the finest examples of subtropical coastal habitat remaining in southeast Florida. Visit the **William T. Kirby Nature Center,** which has exhibits on the coastal environment, or take an interpretive walk to a mangrove estuary along the upper reaches of Lake Worth. ⊠ 10900 Rte. A1A, North Palm Beach, ☎ 561/624–6950 for office or 561/624–6952 for nature center. 🖾 $3.25 per vehicle with up to 8 people. ☉ 8–sunset; nature center Wed.–Mon. 9–5.

LOGGERHEAD PARK MARINE LIFE CENTER OF JUNO BEACH – Established by Eleanor N. Fletcher, "the turtle lady of Juno Beach," the center focuses on the natural history of sea turtles. Also on view are displays of coastal natural history, sharks, whales, and shells. ⊠ 1200 U.S. 1 (entrance on west side of park), Juno Beach, ☎ 561/627–8280. 🖾 Donations welcome. ☉ Tues.–Sat. 10–4, Sun. noon–3.

Dining and Lodging

$$ ✕ **The Galley.** Don't overlook this open-air waterfront restaurant. After a hot day of mansion-gawking or beach-bumming, there's no better place to chill out. The blender seems to run nonstop, churning out tropical drinks like piña coladas and Goombay Smashes. Old Florida favorites like grouper and conch chowder are mainstays, but there are also a few highbrow entrées (this is Palm Beach County, after all), such as lobster tail or baby sea scallops sautéed in garlic and lemon butter.

Gold Coast and Treasure Coast

This is also a good spot for breakfast. ⊠ *98 Lake Dr.,* ☎ *561/848–1492. MC, V. No dinner Mon. and Tues.*

$$–$$$ ⬚ **Sailfish Marina.** This long-established, one-story motel has a ma-
★   rina with 94 deep-water slips and 15 rooms and efficiencies that open
to landscaped grounds. None are directly on the water, but units 9–
11 have ocean views across the blacktop drive. Rooms have peaked
ceilings, carpeting, king or twin beds, and stall showers; many have
ceiling fans. Much of the art is original, traded with artists who display in an informal show on the dock every Thursday night. From the
seawall, you can see fish through the clear inlet water. The motel's staff
is informed and helpful, the proprietors as promotional as they are
friendly. There are no in-room phones, but several pay phones are on
the property and messages are taken. ⊠ *98 Lake Dr., 33404,* ☎
561/844–1724 or 800/446–4577, 𝖥𝖠𝖷 *561/848–9684. 15 units. Restaurant, bar, grocery, pool, dock. AE, MC, V.*

Palm Beach Gardens

❷❷   *5 mi north of West Palm Beach, 10 mi northwest of Palm Beach.*

About 15 minutes northwest of Palm Beach is this relaxed, upscale residential community widely known for its high-profile golf complex,
the PGA National Resort & Spa. Although the town is not on the beach,
the ocean is just a 15-minute drive away.

Dining and Lodging

$$ ✕ **Arezzo.** The pungent smell of fresh garlic tips you off that the food's
★   the thing at this outstanding Tuscan grill at the PGA National Resort
& Spa. In this unusually relaxed, upscale resort setting, you can dine
in shorts or in jacket and tie. Families are attracted by the affordable
prices (as well as the food), so romantics might be tempted to pass Arezzo
up. Their loss. Dishes include the usual variety of chicken, veal, fish,
and steaks, but there are a dozen pastas and almost as many pizzas.
Specialties include rigatoni *alla Bolognese* (with ground veal, marinara
sauce, and Parmesan). The decor, too, has the right idea: an herb gar-
den in the center of the room, slate floors, upholstered banquettes to
satisfy the upscale mood, and butcher paper over yellow table covers
to establish the light side. ⊠ *400 Ave. of the Champions,* ☎ *561/627–
2000. AE, MC, V. No lunch. Closed Mon.*

$$ ✕ **River House.** People keep returning to this waterfront restaurant for
the large portions of straightforward American fare; the big salad bar
and fresh, slice-it-yourself breads; the competent service; and, thanks
to the animated buzz of a rewarded local clientele, the feeling that you've
come to the right place. Choices include seafoods (always with a daily
catch), steaks, chops, and seafood/steak combo platters. Booths and
freestanding tables are surrounded by lots of blond wood, high ceilings, and nautical art under glass. The wait on Saturday nights in season can be up to 45 minutes. Reserve one of the 20 upstairs tables,
available weekends only; the upstairs is a little more formal and doesn't
have a salad bar (bread comes from below), but it does possess a
cathedral ceiling. ⊠ *2373 PGA Blvd.,* ☎ *561/694–1198. AE, MC, V.
No lunch.*

$$$$ ⬚ **PGA National Resort & Spa.** Outstanding mission-style rooms are
decorated in deep, almost somber florals, and the rest of the resort is
equally richly detailed, from lavish landscaping to limitless sports facilities to excellent dining. The spa is housed in a building styled after
a Mediterranean fishing village. Its six outdoor therapy pools, dubbed
"Waters of the World," are joined by a collection of imported mineral

salt pools; there are 22 private treatments. Golf courses and croquet courts are adorned with 25,000 flowering plants amid a 240-acre nature preserve. Two-bedroom, two-bath cottages with fully equipped kitchens and no-smoking rooms are available, too. ⊠ *400 Ave. of the Champions, 33418,* ☎ *561/627–2000 or 800/633–9150. 275 rooms, 60 suites, 85 cottages. 6 restaurants, lake, pool, hot tubs, saunas, spa, 5 golf courses, 19 tennis courts, croquet, racquetball, boating. AE, D, DC, MC, V.*

Nightlife
Irish Times (⊠ 9920 Alternate A1A, Promenade Shopping Plaza, ☎ 561/624–1504) is a four-leaf-clover find, featuring a microbrewery. There are live music and live Irish acts Wednesday through Saturday.

Outdoor Activities and Sports
AUTO RACING
Weekly ¼-mi drag racing; monthly 2¼-mi, 10-turn road racing; and monthly AMA motorcycle road racing take place year-round at the **Moroso Motorsports Park** (⊠ 17047 Beeline Hwy., Box 31907, 33420, ☎ 561/622–1400).

GOLF
PGA National Resort & Spa (⊠ 1000 Ave. of the Champions, ☎ 561/627–1800) offers a reputedly tough 90 holes.

Shopping
The Gardens mall (⊠ 3101 PGA Blvd.) contains the standards if you want to make sure you're not missing out on anything at home: Bloomingdale's, Burdines, Macy's, Saks Fifth Avenue, and Sears.

SOUTH TO BOCA RATON

Strung together by Route A1A, the towns between Palm Beach and Boca Raton are notable for their variety. Though the glamour of Palm Beach has rubbed off on many towns, there are pockets of modesty and unpretentiousness alongside the well-established high and mighty. In one town you might find a cluster of sophisticated art galleries and fancy eateries, whereas the very next town could have a few hamburger stands and mom-and-pop "everything" stores.

Lake Worth
㉓ *2 mi south of West Palm Beach.*

Tourists are mainly interested in this mainland town for its inexpensive lodging in close proximity to Palm Beach, which is accessible via a nearby bridge.

The Arts
Klein Dance Company (⊠ 3208 2nd Ave. N, No. 10, 33461, ☎ 561/586–1889) is a nationally acclaimed, world-touring, professional troupe that also gives local performances.

Beach
Lake Worth Municipal Park, also known as Casino Park, has a beach, Olympic-size swimming pool, fishing pier, picnic areas, shuffleboard, restaurants, and shops. ⊠ *Rte. A1A at end of Lake Worth Bridge,* ☎ *561/533–7367.* ☞ *Pool $2; parking 25¢ for 15 min.* ☉ *Daily 9–4:45.*

Dining and Lodging
$ ✕ **John G's.** About the only time the line lets up is when the restaurant closes at 3 PM. The menu is as big as the crowd: big fruit platters,

sandwich-board superstars, grilled burgers, seafood, and eggs every which way, including a United Nations of ethnic omelets. Breakfast is served until 11. ⊠ *Lake Worth Casino,* ☎ *561/585–9860. No credit cards. No dinner.*

$–$$ 🏨 **Holiday House.** Standing out from its motel strip, a five-minute walk
★   from the heart of town, is this uncommercial-looking lodging with bougainvillea-entwined balconies and rich tropical gardens. The motel rooms, efficiencies, and one-bedroom apartments live up to expectations. Located in two adjacent two-story buildings dating from the late 1940s, but kept up nicely, each is warmly furnished, clean, and fitted out with refrigerator and microwave. Maid service is provided weekly for efficiencies and apartments (one-week stay minimum) and daily for rooms. ⊠ *320 N. Federal Hwy., 33460,* ☎ *561/582–3561,* ᴲᴬˣ *561/582– 3561. 30 units. Pool, coin laundry. MC, V.*

$–$$ 🏨 **New Sun Gate Motel.** Each room is dedicated to a famous movie star of a bygone era—Cary Grant, Rita Hayworth, James Dean—in this simple establishment near downtown. Units are decorated in art deco style, and some have microwaves. ⊠ *901 S. Federal Hwy., 33460,* ☎ *561/588–8110,* ᴲᴬˣ *561/588–8041. 31 rooms. Restaurant, pool, coin laundry. AE, MC, V.*

Outdoor Activities and Sports

POLO

Gulfstream Polo Club, the oldest club in the Palm Beach area, began in the 1920s and plays medium-goal polo (for teams with handicaps of 8–16 goals). There are six polo fields. ⊠ *4550 Polo Rd.,* ☎ *561/965–2057.* 🎫 *Free.* ⊗ *Games Dec.–Apr.*

Lantana

㉔ *2 mi south of Lake Worth.*

Like Lake Worth, Lantana has inexpensive lodging and a bridge connecting the town to Palm Beach's barrier island. It's just a bit farther away from Palm Beach. A closer island neighbor is **Manalapan,** a tiny residential community with a luxury beach resort.

Beach

Lantana Public Beach has one of the best food concessions around. You'll find fresh fish on weekends and breakfast and lunch specials every day outdoors under beach umbrellas. ⊠ *100 N. Ocean Ave., no phone.* 🎫 *Parking 25¢ for 15 min.* ⊗ *Daily 9–4:45.*

Dining and Lodging

$$ ✕ **Old House.** Overlooking the Intracoastal Waterway, the 1889 Lyman House has grown in spurts over the years and is now a patchwork of shedlike spaces. Partners Wayne Cordero and Captain Bob Hoddinott have turned it into an informal Old Florida seafood house that serves not only local seafood but also, incongruously, Baltimore steamed crab—the specialty. Although there's air-conditioning, dining is still open-air most evenings and in cooler weather. ⊠ *300 E. Ocean Ave.,* ☎ *561/533–5220. AE, MC, V.*

$$$$ 🏨 **Ritz-Carlton, Palm Beach.** Despite its name, this hotel is actually in
★   Manalapan, halfway between Palm Beach and Delray. The bisque-color, triple-tower landmark may look like the work of Addison Mizner, but in fact it was built in 1991. Dominating the lobby is a huge, double-sided marble fireplace, foreshadowing the luxury of the guest rooms' marble tubs and upholstered furniture. Most rooms have ocean views,

and oceanfront rooms have balconies. Not to be outdone by the fabulous beaches, a large pool and courtyard area has more than 100 coconut palms. Bikes and scuba and snorkeling equipment can be rented. ⊠ *100 S. Ocean Blvd., Manalapan 33462,* ☎ *561/533–6000 or 800/241–3333,* FAX *561/588–4555. 5 restaurants, pool, beauty salon, massage, sauna, spa, steam room, 7 tennis courts, bicycles. AE, D, DC, MC, V.*

$ 🏨 **Super 8 Motel.** There's nothing special about this sprawling, one-story motel except the price—a real bargain, considering the proximity to Palm Beach. Efficiencies and rooms (some with refrigerators) are clean but basically furnished. ⊠ *1255 Hypoluxo Rd., 33462,* ☎ *561/585–3970,* FAX *561/586–3028. 129 rooms, 11 efficiencies. Pool, coin laundry. AE, DC, MC, V.*

Outdoor Activities and Sports

FISHING

B-Love Fleet (⊠ 314 E. Ocean Ave., ☎ 561/588–7612) offers three deep-sea fishing excursions daily: 8–noon, 1–5, and 7–11. No reservations are needed; just show up 30 minutes before the boat is scheduled to leave. The cost is $22 per person.

Boynton Beach

㉕ *3 mi south of Lantana.*

This town is far enough from Palm Beach to have kept its laid-back, low-key atmosphere. Its two parts, on the mainland and the barrier island, are connected by a causeway.

Knollwood Groves dates from the 1930s, when it was planted by the partners of the "Amos & Andy" radio show. You can take a 30-minute, 30-acre tram tour through the orange groves and a processing plant and visit the **Hallpatee Seminole Indian Village,** where there's an alligator exhibit and crafts shop. During the busy season, special guest Martin Twofeather gives a weekly one-hour alligator-handling show. ⊠ *8053 Lawrence Rd.,* ☎ *561/734–4800.* 🎫 *Tour $1, show $5.* ☉ *Daily 8:30–5:30, show Sat. at 2.*

OFF THE BEATEN PATH

ARTHUR R. MARSHALL–LOXAHATCHEE NATIONAL WILDLIFE REFUGE – The most robust part of the Everglades, this 221-square-mi refuge is one of three huge water-retention areas that account for much of the Everglades outside of the national park. These areas are managed less to protect natural resources, however, than to prevent flooding to the south. Start from the visitor center, where there are two walking trails: a boardwalk through a dense cypress swamp and a marsh trail to a 20-foot-high observation tower overlooking a pond. There is also a 5½-mi canoe trail, recommended for more-experienced canoeists because it's rather overgrown. Wildlife viewing is good year-round, and you can fish for bass and panfish. ⊠ *10119 Lee Rd., off U.S. 441 between Boynton Beach Blvd. (Rte. 804) and Atlantic Ave. (Rte. 806), west of Boynton Beach,* ☎ *561/734-8303.* 🎫 *$4 per vehicle, $1 per pedestrian.* ☉ *Daily 6–sunset, visitor center weekdays 8–4, weekends 8–4:30.*

Beach

Oceanfront Park has a boardwalk, concessions, grills, a jogging trail, and playground. Parking is expensive if you're not a Boynton resident. ⊠ *Ocean Ave. at Rte. A1A, no phone.* 🎫 *Parking $10 per day in winter, $5 per day rest of year.* ☉ *Daily 9–midnight.*

Outdoor Activities and Sports

FISHING

You can fish the canal at the **Arthur R. Marshall–Loxahatchee National Wildlife Refuge** (☎ 561/734–8303). There's a boat ramp, and the waters are decently productive, but bring your own equipment.

GOLF

Boynton Beach Municipal Golf Course (⊠ 8020 Jog Rd., ☎ 561/969–2200) has 27 holes.

Gulf Stream

㉖ *2 mi south of Boynton Beach.*

This beautiful little beachfront community was also touched by Mizner. As you pass the bougainvillea-topped walls of the Gulf Stream Club, a private police officer may stop traffic for a golfer to cross.

Lodging

$$ 🏨 **Riviera Palms Motel.** Hans and Herter Grannemann have owned this small, two-story motel dating from the 1950s since 1978. It has two primary virtues: It's clean and it's well located. Across Route A1A from mid-rise apartment houses on the water, it has three wings surrounding a grassy front yard and heated pool. Rooms are done in Danish modern and a blue, brown, and tan color scheme; all have at least a refrigerator but no phone. ⊠ *3960 N. Ocean Blvd., 33483,* ☎ *561/276–3032. 17 rooms, efficiencies, and suites. Pool. No credit cards.*

Delray Beach

㉗ *2 mi south of Gulf Stream.*

What began as an artists' retreat and a small settlement of Japanese farmers is now a sophisticated beach town with a successful local historic preservation movement. Atlantic Avenue, the main drag, has been transformed into a 1-mi-long stretch of palm-dotted brick sidewalks, almost entirely lined with stores, art galleries, and dining establishments. Running east–west and ending at the beach, it's a pleasant place for a stroll day or night. Another lovely pedestrian way begins at the edge of town, across Northeast 8th Street (George Bush Boulevard), along the big broad swimming beach that extends north and south of Atlantic Avenue.

The chief landmark along Atlantic Avenue is the Mediterranean-revival **Colony Hotel** (⊠ 525 E. Atlantic Ave., ☎ 561/276–4123), still open only for the winter season as it has been for more than 60 years.

The **Old School Square Cultural Arts Center,** just off Atlantic Avenue, houses several museums in restored school buildings dating from 1913 and 1926. The **Cornell Museum of Art & History** offers an ever-changing array of art exhibits. ⊠ *51 N. Swinton Ave.,* ☎ *561/243–7922.* 🎫 *Donations welcome.* ☉ *Tues.–Sat. 11–4, Sun. 1–4.*

Cason Cottage, a restored Victorian-style home that dates from about 1915, now serves as offices of the Delray Beach Historical Society. The house is filled with relics of the Victorian era, including an old pipe organ donated by descendants of one of the original families to settle Delray Beach. Periodic displays celebrate the town's architectural evolution. The cottage is a block north of the cultural center. ⊠ *5 N.E. 1st St.,* ☎ *561/243–0223.* 🎫 *Free.* ☉ *Tues.–Fri. 11–4.*

★ Florida seems an odd place for the **Morikami Museum and Japanese Gardens.** At this 200-acre cultural and recreational facility, a display in a building modeled after a Japanese imperial villa recalls the Yamato Colony, an agricultural community of Japanese settlers who came to Florida in 1905. Gardens include the only known collection of bonsai Florida plants. There are also programs and exhibits in a lakeside museum and theater as well as a nature trail, picnic pavilions, a library and audiovisual center, and snack bar. ⊠ *4000 Morikami Park Rd.,* ☎ *561/495–0233.* ⊡ *$4.25, free Sun. 10–noon.* ☉ *Park daily sunrise–sunset, museum Tues.–Sun. 10–5.*

Beach
The **Municipal Beach** (⊠ Atlantic Ave. at Rte. A1A) has a boat ramp and volleyball court.

Dining and Lodging

$–$$ ✕ **Blue Anchor.** Unbelievably, this pub was actually shipped from England, where it stood for 150 years as the old Blue Anchor Pub in London's historic Chancery Lane. There it was a regular watering hole for many famous Englishmen, including Winston Churchill. The Delray Beach incarnation still cooks up authentic British pub fare: ploughman's lunch (a chunk of Cheddar or Stilton cheese, a chunk of bread, and English pickled onions), steak-and-kidney pie, fish-and-chips, and bangers (sausage) and mash, to name just a few. You can also get delicious hamburgers, sandwiches, and salads. The dessert menu includes an English sherry trifle and a Bailey's Irish Cream pie. English beers and ales are available on tap and in the bottle. ⊠ *804 E. Atlantic Ave.,* ☎ *561/272–7272. AE, MC, V.*

$–$$ ✕ **Boston's on the Beach.** Often a restaurant that's facing a beach relies on its location to fill the place up and doesn't worry enough about the food. Not so with Boston's, which is just across the street from the public beach. As you might expect from the name, you'll find good New England clam chowder and several lobster dishes, as well as fresh fish grilled, fried, or prepared just about any other way. All this is presented in an ultra-informal setting. Tables are old and wooden, and walls are decorated with traffic signs and other conversation-stoppers, most notably paraphernalia from the Boston Bruins, New England Patriots, and Boston Red Sox, including a veritable shrine to Ted Williams. After dark the place becomes a casual club with live music. ⊠ *40 S. Ocean Blvd. (Rte. A1A),* ☎ *561/278–3364. AE, MC, V.*

$$$–$$$$ 🏨 **Seagate Hotel & Beach Club.** One of the best garden hotels in Palm Beach County, this property offers value, comfort, style, and personal attention. The one-bedroom suite is all chintz and rattan, with many upholstered pieces. All suites have at least kitchenettes; the less expensive studios have compact facilities behind foldaway doors. You can dress up and dine in a smart little mahogany- and lattice-trimmed beachfront salon or have the same Continental fare in casual attire in the equally stylish bar. Guests enjoy privileges at the private beach club. ⊠ *400 S. Ocean Blvd., 33483,* ☎ *561/276–2421 or 800/233–3581. 70 1- and 2-bedroom suites. Restaurant, lounge, freshwater and saltwater pools, beach. AE, DC, MC, V.*

$$–$$$$ 🏨 **Harbor House.** These white, two-story, 1950s buildings have a privileged location in a quiet residential enclave three blocks east of U.S. 1 and across from the Delray Marina. In addition to two tiny motel rooms, there are 23 efficiencies and one- and two-bedroom apartments with kitchens and a mix of seating generally done in white, beige, tan, and blue. Everything retains a 1950s look, but carpets and upholstery are replaced before they look tired. In a nice touch, matching fabrics are changed by the season: solid blue in summer, blue florals in winter. ⊠ *124 Marine Way, 33483,* ☎ *561/276–4221. 25 units. Pool, shuffleboard, coin laundry. MC, V.*

$$–$$$$ **Sea Breeze of Delray Beach.** Considering its prime location—opposite the Gulfstream Bath & Tennis Club, across from the beach—this is an exceptional buy. The one- and two-story buildings are set around beautiful lawns. Each of the studios and one- or two-bedroom apartments has a kitchen; updated ones have microwaves. Furnishings include lots of floral prints, brocaded pieces, and French provincial reproductions, which create a comfortable, beachy look. Though it dates from the 1950s and kitchenware is mismatched, the place remains beautifully maintained and clean. There is twice-weekly maid service off-season. ✉ 820 N. Ocean Blvd., 33483, ☎ 561/276–7496. 23 units. Pool, shuffleboard, coin laundry. MC, V.

Nightlife and the Arts

THE ARTS

The **Crest Theater** (✉ 51 N. Swinton Ave., ☎ 561/243–7922), in the Old School Square Cultural Arts Center, presents productions in dance, music, and theater.

NIGHTLIFE

Back Room Blues Lounge (✉ 303 W. Atlantic Ave., ☎ 561/243–9110), behind Westside Liquors, has comedy night on Wednesday and live bands Thursday–Saturday. **Boston's on the Beach** (✉ 40 S. Ocean Blvd., ☎ 561/278–3364) presents live reggae music Monday and rock and roll Tuesday–Sunday.

Outdoor Activities and Sports

BIKING

There is a bicycle path in Barwick Park and a special oceanfront lane along Route A1A. **Rich Wagen's Bicycle Shop** (✉ 217 E. Atlantic Ave., ☎ 561/276–4234) rents bikes by the hour or day.

SCUBA DIVING AND SNORKELING

Scuba and snorkeling equipment can be rented from longtime family-owned **Force E** (✉ 660 Linton Blvd., ☎ 561/276–0666). It has PADI affiliation, provides instruction at all levels, and offers charters.

TENNIS

Each winter the **Delray Beach Tennis Center** (✉ 201 W. Atlantic Ave., ☎ 561/243–7380) hosts a professional women's tournament that attracts players like Steffi Graf. The center is also a great place to practice or learn; it has 14 clay courts and five hard courts and offers individual lessons and clinics.

WATER SPORTS

Lake Ida Park (✉ 2929 Lake Ida Rd., ☎ 561/964–4420) is an excellent place to water-ski, whether you're a beginner or a veteran. The park has a boat ramp, slalom course, and trick ski course.

Shopping

The recently beautified **Atlantic Avenue** is a showcase for art galleries, shops, and restaurants. In addition to serving lunch and a traditional afternoon tea, the charmingly old-fashioned **Sundy House** (✉ 106 S. Swinton Ave., ☎ 561/278–2163 or 561/272–3720) sells antiques and gifts in the former home of onetime Flagler foreman and first Delray mayor John Shaw Sundy. The structure's beautiful gardens and five gingerbread gables complement Delray's finest wraparound porch.

Boca Raton

28 6 mi south of Delray Beach.

This upscale town at the south end of Palm Beach County, 30 minutes south of Palm Beach, has a lot in common with its ritzy cousin. For one thing, both reflect the unmistakable architectural presence of Addison Mizner, their principal developer in the mid-1920s. Mizner Park, an important Boca Raton shopping district, bears his name.

Built in 1925 as the headquarters of the Mizner Development Corporation, the structure at **2 East El Camino Real** (☎ 561/391–9800) is a good example of Mizner's characteristic Spanish-revival architectural style, with its wrought-iron grills and handmade tiles. It now houses an excellent Italian restaurant, Addison's Flavors of Italy.

☾ Championed by *Beetle Bailey* cartoonist Mort Walker, the **International Museum of Cartoon Art** moved to Boca Raton from New York State. It showcases more than 160,000 pieces of art created over two centuries by more than 1,000 artists from more than 50 countries—everything from turn-of-the-century Buster Brown cartoons to the *Road Runner* to Charles Schulz's *Peanuts.* ✉ *201 Plaza Real,* ☎ *561/391–2200.* ✇ *$6.* ☉ *Tues.–Sat. 11–5, Sun. noon–5.*

Containing whimsical metal sculptures on the lawn, the **Boca Raton Museum of Art** is a must. The permanent collection includes works by Picasso, Degas, Matisse, Klee, and Modigliani as well as notable pre-Columbian art. ✉ *801 W. Palmetto Park Rd.,* ☎ *561/392–2500.* ✇ *$3.* ☉ *Weekdays 10–4, weekends noon–4.*

The residential area behind the Boca Raton Museum of Art is known as **Old Floresta.** Developed by Addison Mizner starting in 1925 and landscaped with many varieties of palms and cycads, it includes houses that are mainly in a Mediterranean style, many with upper balconies supported by exposed wood columns.

☾ A big draw for kids, the **Gumbo Limbo Nature Center** has four huge saltwater sea tanks and a long boardwalk through dense forest with a 50-foot tower you can climb to overlook the tree canopy. In the spring and early summer, staff members lead nighttime turtle walks to see nesting females come ashore and lay their eggs. ✉ *1801 N. Ocean Blvd.,* ☎ *561/338–1473.* ✇ *Donations welcome; turtle tours $3 (tickets must be obtained in advance).* ☉ *Mon.–Sat. 9–4, Sun. noon–4; turtle tours late May–mid-July, Mon.–Thurs. 9 PM–midnight.*

The Arts
Caldwell Theatre Company (✉ 7873 N. Federal Hwy., ☎ 561/241–7432), an Equity regional theater, hosts the multimedia Mizner Festival each April and May and stages four productions each winter. **Jan McArt's Royal Palm Dinner Theatre** (✉ 303 S.E. Mizner Blvd., Royal Palm Plaza, ☎ 561/392–3755 or 800/841–6765), an Equity theater, presents five or six musicals a year.

Beaches
Red Reef Park (✉ 1400 N. Rte. A1A) offers a beach and playground plus picnic tables and grills. Popular **South Beach Park** (✉ 400 N. Rte. A1A) has a concession stand. In addition to its beach, **Spanish River Park** (✉ 3001 N. Rte. A1A) has picnic tables, grills, and a large playground.

Dining and Lodging
$$$–$$$$　✕ **Addison's Flavors of Italy.** Architecture buffs would be sated just by the building, which is a painstakingly restored old office building designed and built by Addison Mizner in 1925 to house the Mizner Development Corporation. But there are plenty of culinary attractions in this northern Italian restaurant, most notably veal piccata and rigatoni with salmon, tomatoes, and cream. Locals love the courtyard, shaded by massive banyan trees, as a setting for wedding receptions

and other galas. The rich and extensive Sunday brunch is a tradition. ⊠ *2 E. Camino Real,* ☎ *561/391–9800. AE, D, DC, MC, V.*

$$$–$$$$ ✕ **La Vieille Maison.** This French restaurant remains one of the tem-
★ ples of haute cuisine along the Gold Coast. Featuring a stunning courtyard, it occupies a 1920s-era dwelling believed to be an Addison Mizner design. Closets and cubbyholes have been transformed into intimate private dining rooms. Fixed-price, à la carte, Temptations, and Grand menus are available, and all feature Provençal dishes, including *soupe au pistou* (vegetable soup with basil and Parmesan cheese) and roast rabbit with artichokes, green olives, and walnut gnocchi. Health-conscious selections are available on all menus. Dessert choices include flourless chocolate cake, a napoleon with candied walnuts, and cinnamon-poached pears. ⊠ *770 E. Palmetto Park Rd.,* ☎ *561/391–6701 or 561/737–5677. AE, D, DC, MC, V. Closed early July–Aug.*

$$$ ✕ **Gazebo Café.** The locals who patronize this popular restaurant know where it is, even though there is no sign. You'll have to look a little harder. (It's near the Barnett Bank Hyde Park Plaza, a block north of Spanish River Boulevard.) Once you find the place, take your seat near the open kitchen, where chef Paul Sellas (co-owner with his mother, Kathleen) and his staff perform a gastronomic ballet. The main dining room can be noisy; you may prefer the smaller back dining room. Specialties include fresh lump crabmeat glazed with excellent Mornay sauce on a marinated artichoke bottom, a robust bouillabaisse that includes Maine lobster, and raspberries with a Grand Marnier–sabayon sauce. ⊠ *4199 N. Federal Hwy.,* ☎ *561/744–0605. AE, D, DC, MC, V. Closed Sun. mid-May–Dec.*

$$$ ✕ **Maxaluna Tuscan Grill.** Virtually the neighborhood restaurant of
★ choice for affluent Bocans, this 150-seat shrine to nuovo Italian gastronomy is as hard to find as the Gazebo Café. With its beautiful landscaping, the setting—the courtyard of Crocker Center, an office park and shopping mall—is as artful as the modern art hanging from the walls. Inside, orchids rise from slender bud vases, and halogen lights drop from colorful ceiling panels suspended from a black roof. Tables zigzag across natural wood floors, and at the rear, past the polished aluminum bar and brick walls, chefs in the open kitchen work in Italian bicycle caps. Lighthearted in style, Maxaluna's is serious about food. Diners exult in chef Pierre Viau's pastas and risottos. There's a large selection of wines by the glass. ⊠ *Crocker Center, 5050 Town Center Circle,* ☎ *561/391–7177. AE, D, DC, MC, V. No lunch weekends.*

$ ✕ **Tom's Place.** "This place is a blessing from God," says the sign over the fireplace, and after braving the long lines and sampling the superb menu you will add an "Amen!" That's in between mouthfuls of Tom Wright's soul food—sauce-slathered ribs, pork-chop sandwiches, chicken cooked in peppery mustard sauce over hickory and oak, sweet-potato pie. Buy a bottle or two of Tom's barbecue sauce ($2.25 a pint) just as Lou Rawls, Ben Vereen, Sugar Ray Leonard, and a rush of NFL players have before you. ⊠ *7251 N. Federal Hwy.,* ☎ *561/997–0920. MC, V. Closed Sun., also Mon. May–mid-Nov.*

$$$$ ▢ **Boca Raton Resort & Club.** Addison Mizner built the Mediterranean-
★ style Cloister Inn here in 1926; it has been added to several times since to create this sprawling, elegant resort, which counts a golf school run by Dave Pelz among its facilities. Rooms in the Cloister tend to be small and warmly traditional; those in the 27-story Tower are in a similar style but larger, while rooms in the Beach Club are light, airy, and contemporary. The concierge staff speaks at least 12 languages. Rates during the winter season don't include meals, but you can pay extra for

MAP (including breakfast and dinner). ✉ *501 E*
0825, ☎ *561/395–3000 or 800/327–0101. 9/*
rooms, and golf villas. 7 restaurants, 3 lounge
34 tennis courts, basketball, 3 health clubs, b
DC, MC, V.

Outdoor Activities and Sports

BIKING

Plenty of bike trails and quiet streets make for pleasant pedaling in the
area; for current information, contact the city of Boca Raton's **Bicycle
Coordinator** (☎ 561/393–7797).

BOATING

If you ever wanted the thrill of blasting across the water at up to 80
mph, check out **Air and Sea Charters** (✉ 490 E. Palmetto Park Rd.,
Suite 330, ☎ 561/368–3566). For $80 per person (four-person min-
imum), you can spend a wild-eyed hour holding on to your life vest
aboard an 800-horsepower offshore racing boat. For a more leisurely
trip, go for Air and Sea's 55-foot catamaran or 45-foot sailboat.

GOLF

Two championship courses and a golf school are available at **Boca Raton
Resort & Club** (✉ 501 E. Camino Real, ☎ 561/395–3000 or 800/327–
0101).

POLO

Royal Palm Polo, founded in 1959 by Oklahoma oilman John T. Oxley
and now home to the $100,000 International Gold Cup Tournament,
has seven polo fields within two stadiums. ✉ *6300 Old Clint Moore
Rd.,* ☎ *561/994–1876.* ⬛ *$6, box seats $10–$25.* ⊙ *Games Jan.–Apr.,
Sun. 1 and 3.*

SCUBA DIVING AND SNORKELING

Information about dive trips, as well as rental scuba and snorkeling
equipment, can be obtained at **Force E** (✉ 877 E. Palmetto Park Rd.,
☎ 561/368–0555).

Shopping

Mizner Park (✉ Federal Hwy. between Palmetto Park Rd. and Glades
Rd.) is a distinctive 30-acre shopping village with apartments and
town houses among the gardenlike spaces. Some three dozen retail stores
include the excellent Liberties Fine Books & Music, a Jacobson's specialty department store, seven restaurants with sidewalk cafés, and eight
movie screens. **Town Center** (✉ 6000 W. Glades Rd.) combines a business park with ritzy shopping and great dining. Major retailers include
Bloomingdale's, Burdines, Lord & Taylor, Saks Fifth Avenue, and
Sears—201 stores and restaurants in all.

THE TREASURE COAST

From south to north, the Treasure Coast encompasses the top end of
Palm Beach County plus Martin, St. Lucie, and Indian River counties.
Though dotted with towns, this section of coastline is one of Florida's
quietest. Most towns are small and laid-back, and there's lots of undeveloped land between them. Vero is the region's most sophisticated
town and the one place you'll find clusters of fine dining establishments
and upscale shops. The beaches along here are sought out by nesting
sea turtles; you can join locally organized watches, which go out to
view the turtles laying their eggs in the sand between April and August.

㉙ *14 mi north of Palm Beach.*

This little town is located on one of the few parts of the east coast of Florida that does not have an island in front of it. Beaches here are part of the mainland, and Route A1A runs for almost 4 mi along the beachfront dunes, offering a great ocean view.

Take a look at how life once was in the **Dubois Home,** a modest pioneer home dating from 1898. Sitting atop an ancient Jeaga Indian mound 20 feet high and looking onto Jupiter Inlet, it features Cape Cod as well as "cracker" design. Even if you arrive when the house is closed, surrounding **Dubois Park** is worth the visit for its lovely beaches and swimming lagoons. ⊠ *Dubois Rd., no phone.* ☎ *Donations welcome.* ⊙ *Wed. 1–4.*

Permanent exhibits at the **Florida History Center and Museum** review not only modern-day development along the Loxahatchee River, but also shipwrecks, railroads, and Seminole, steamboat-era, and pioneer history. ⊠ *805 N. U.S. 1, Burt Reynolds Park,* ☎ *561/747–6639.* ☎ *$4.* ⊙ *Tues.–Sat. 10–4, Sun. 1–5.*

☙ **Burt Reynolds Ranch and Film Studio Tours** is a 160-acre working horse ranch owned by the famous actor. You can take a 1½-hour tour by air-conditioned bus, with stops that include movie sets, a chapel, tree house, petting farm, and wherever filming may be in progress. It's 2 mi west of I–95 at Exit 59-B. ⊠ *16133 Jupiter Farms Rd.,* ☎ *561/747–5390.* ☎ *Tour $10, petting farm free.* ⊙ *Daily 10–4:30.*

Beach

Carlin Park (⊠ *400 Rte. A1A*) provides beachfront picnic pavilions, hiking trails, a baseball diamond, playground, six tennis courts, and fishing sites. The Park Galley, serving snacks and burgers, is usually open daily 9–5.

Dining and Lodging

\$\$–\$\$\$ ✕ **Charley's Crab.** The grand view across the Jupiter River complements
★ the soaring ceiling and striking interior architecture of this marina-side restaurant. You'll have great water views whether you choose to dine inside or out, and if you eat after dark, you can watch the searching beam of the historic Jupiter Light House. Come here for expertly prepared seafood, including outstanding pasta choices: *pagliara* with scallops, fish, shrimp, mussels, spinach, garlic, and olive oil; fettuccine *verde* with lobster, sun-dried tomatoes, fresh basil, and goat cheese; and shrimp and tortellini boursin with cream sauce and tomatoes. Consider also such fresh fish as citrus-marinated halibut with black-bean basmati rice and pineapple relish. Other branches of Charley's are in Boca Raton, Deerfield Beach, Fort Lauderdale, Palm Beach, and Stuart. ⊠ *1000 N. U.S. 1,* ☎ *561/744–4710. AE, D, DC, MC, V.*

\$\$–\$\$\$ ✕ **Sinclairs Ocean Grill & Rotisserie.** Located in the Jupiter Beach Resort, this popular spot, where you can dine inside or on the terrace, looks out over the ocean. The menu features a daily selection of fresh locally caught fish, which you can have grilled, blackened, baked, or fried. Landlubbers can choose thick juicy steaks (filet mignon is the house specialty) and a variety of chicken dishes, plus pastas and salads. Sunday brunch is a big draw. ⊠ *5 N. Rte. A1A,* ☎ *561/746–2551. AE, MC, V.*

\$ ✕ **Lighthouse Restaurant.** Low prices match the plain decor in this coffee shop–style building, but the menu and cuisine are a delightful surprise. You can get chicken breast stuffed with sausage and fresh vegetables, burgundy beef stew, and king crab cakes, and a full-time pastry chef is at work, too. The same people-pleasing formula has been employed for more than 60 years: round-the-clock service (except 10 PM Sunday–6 AM Monday) and a menu that changes daily to take advantage of the best market buys. Those looking for something less "stick-to-the-ribs" can order one of the affordable "lite dinners." ⊠ *1510 U.S. 1,* ☎ *561/746–4811. D, DC, MC, V.*

$$$$ 🏨 **Jupiter Beach Resort.** Management can say without equivocation that this is the best beachfront resort in Jupiter—of course, it's the only beachfront resort in Jupiter. Nevertheless, this unpretentious, elegant hotel would bear up well even against Palm Beach properties. Most guest rooms have balconies, the restaurant is worth staying in for, and the resort takes full advantage of its location. In season, sign up for the turtle watch, when you can see newly hatched turtles make their way to the water for the first time. Snorkeling and scuba equipment are available for rent. ⊠ *5 N. Rte. A1A, 33477,* ☎ *561/746–2511 or 800/228–8810,* FAX *561/747–3304. 187 rooms, 28 suites. Restaurant, 4 lounges, pool, tennis court, beach, dive shop, recreation room, children's programs, coin laundry, business services.*

Outdoor Activities and Sports

CANOEING

Canoe Outfitters of Florida (⊠ 4100 W. Indiantown Rd., ☎ 561/746–7053) runs trips along 8 mi of the Loxahatchee River, Florida's only designated wild and scenic river. Canoe rental for two people, with drop off and pickup, costs $28 plus tax. You can also just paddle around for an hour.

GOLF

The **Indian Creek Golf Club,** (⊠ 1800 Central Blvd., ☎ 561/747–6262) has 18 holes of varying difficulty. **Jupiter Dunes Golf Club** (⊠ 401 Rte. A1A, ☎ 561/746–6654) has 18 holes and a putting green.

Jupiter Island and Hobe Sound

30 *5 mi north of Jupiter.*

Northeast across the Jupiter Inlet from Jupiter is the southern tip of Jupiter Island, which includes a carefully planned community of the same name. Here estates often retreat from the road behind screens of vegetation, while at the north end of the island, turtles come to nest in a wildlife refuge. To the west, on the mainland, is the little community of Hobe Sound.

The **Jupiter Inlet Lighthouse,** a redbrick Coast Guard navigational beacon, has operated here since 1866. Tours of the 105-foot-tall local landmark are given every half hour, and there is also a small museum. ⊠ *Rte. 707, Jupiter Island,* ☎ *561/747–8330.* 🎟 *Tour $5.* ⊙ *Sun.–Wed. 10–4, last tour 3:30.*

Within **Blowing Rocks Preserve,** a 73-acre Nature Conservancy holding, you'll find plant communities native to beachfront dune, coastal strand (the landward side of the dunes), mangrove, and hammock (tropical hardwood forest). The best time to visit is when high tides and strong offshore winds coincide, causing the sea to blow spectacularly through holes in the eroded outcropping. Park in the lot; police ticket cars parked along the road. ⊠ *Rte. 707, Jupiter Island,* ☎ *561/744–6668.* 🎟 *$3 donation.* ⊙ *Daily 6–5.*

The **Hobe Sound National Wildlife Refuge** actually consists of two tracts: 232 acres of sand pine and scrub oak forest in Hobe Sound and 735 acres of coastal sand dune and mangrove swamp on Jupiter Island. Trails are open to the public in both places. Turtles nest and shells wash ashore on the 3½-mi beach, which has been severely eroded by high tides and strong winds; during winter high tides only a sliver remains. ⊠ *13640 S.E. Federal Hwy., Hobe Sound,* ☎ *561/546–6141;* ⊠ *Beach Rd., off Rte. 707, Jupiter Island.* ⊡ *$4 per vehicle.* ☉ *Daily sunrise–sunset.*

Though located on the Hobe Sound National Wildlife Refuge, the appealing **Hobe Sound Nature Center** is an independent organization. Its museum, which has baby alligators, baby crocodiles, and a scary-looking tarantula, is a child's delight. Interpretive exhibits focus on the environment, and a ½-mi trail winds through a forest of sand pine and scrub oak—one of Florida's most unusual and endangered plant communities. A classroom program on environmental issues is for preschool-age children to adults. ⊠ *13640 S.E. Federal Hwy., Hobe Sound,* ☎ *561/546–2067.* ⊡ *Free.* ☉ *Trail daily sunrise–sunset, nature center weekdays 9–11 and 1–3, call for Sat. hours; group tours by appointment.*

Once you've gotten to the **Jonathan Dickinson State Park,** follow signs to Hobe Mountain. An ancient dune topped with a tower, it yields a panoramic view across the park's 10,285 acres of varied terrain, as well as the Intracoastal Waterway. The Loxahatchee River, part of the federal government's wild and scenic rivers program, cuts through the park and harbors manatees in winter and alligators year-round. Among amenities here are bicycle and hiking trails, a campground, and a snack bar. ⊠ *16450 S.E. Federal Hwy., Hobe Sound,* ☎ *561/546–2771.* ⊡ *$3.25 per vehicle with up to 8 people.* ☉ *Daily 8–sunset.*

Outdoor Activities and Sports

CANOEING

Jonathan Dickinson's River Tours (⊠ Jonathan Dickinson State Park, ☎ 561/746–1466) rents canoes for use around the park.

Stuart

③① *7 mi north of Hobe Sound.*

This compact little town on a peninsula that juts out into the St. Lucie River has a remarkable amount of river shoreline for its size as well as a charming historic district. The ocean is about 5 mi east.

Strict architectural and zoning standards guide civic renewal projects in **historic downtown Stuart,** which now claims eight antiques shops, nine restaurants, and more than 50 specialty shops within a two-block area. The old courthouse has become the **Cultural Court House Center** (⊠ 80 E. Ocean Blvd., ☎ 561/288–2542), which features art exhibits. The George W. Parks General Store is now the **Stuart Heritage Museum** (⊠ 101 S.W. Flagler Ave., ☎ 561/220–4600). On the National Register of Historic Places, the **Lyric Theatre** (⊠ 59 S.W. Flagler Ave., ☎ 561/220–1942) has been revived for performing and community events; a gazebo features free music performances. For information on downtown, contact the **Stuart Main Street Office** (⊠ 151 S.W. Flagler Ave., 34994, ☎ 561/286–2848).

Dining and Lodging

$$ ✕ **The Ashley.** Since expanding in 1993, this restaurant has more tables, more art, and more plants than before. However, it still has elements of the old bank that was robbed three times early in the century by the Ashley Gang (hence the name). The big outdoor mural in the French Impressionist style was paid for by downtown revivalists, whose names are duly inscribed on wall plaques inside. The Continental

menu appeals with lots of salads, fresh fish, and pastas. Crowds head to the lounge for a popular happy hour. ⊠ *61 S.W. Osceola St.,* ☎ *561/221–9476. AE, MC, V. Closed Mon. in off-season.*

$$ ✕ **Jolly Sailor Pub.** In an old historic-district bank building, this eatery is owned by a retired 27-year British Merchant Navy veteran, which may account for the endless ship paraphernalia. A veritable Cunard museum, it has a model of the *Brittania,* prints of 19th-century side-wheelers, and a big bar painting of the *QE2.* There's a wonderful brass-railed wood bar, a dartboard, and such pub grub as fish-and-chips, cottage pie, and bangers and mash, with Guinness and Double Diamond ales on tap. You can also get hamburgers and salads. ⊠ *1 S.W. Osceola St.,* ☎ *561/221–1111. AE, MC, V.*

$$–$$$ 🏨 **HarborFront.** On a quiet site that slopes to the St. Lucie River, this
★ B&B combines an unusual mix of accommodations and imaginative extras, including picnic baskets and conciergelike custom planning. Rooms and cottages are cozy and eclectic, ranging from a spacious chintz-covered suite to a cozy apartment with full kitchen, from rooms that are tweedy and dark to those that are airy and bright with a private deck. Furnishings mix wicker and antiques. From hammocks in the yard you can watch pelicans and herons, or take a full- or half-day sail on the 33-foot sailboat that's tied up to the dock. ⊠ *310 Atlanta Ave., 34994,* ☎ *561/288–7289. 8 apartments, cottages, suites, rooms. Dock, boating. MC, V.*

$$ 🏨 **The Homeplace.** The house was built in 1913 by pioneer Sam Matthews, who contracted much of the early town construction for railroad developer Henry Flagler. Jean Bell has restored the house to its early look, down to hardwood floors and fluffy pillows. Fern-filled dining and sunrooms, full of chintz-covered cushioned wicker, overlook a pool and patio. A full breakfast is included. ⊠ *501 Akron Ave., 34994,* ☎ *561/220–9148. 4 rooms. Pool, hot tub. MC, V.*

Outdoor Activities and Sports

FISHING

Deep-sea charters are available at the **Sailfish Marina** (⊠ 3565 S.E. St. Lucie Blvd., ☎ 561/283–1122).

Shopping

More than 60 restaurants and shops featuring antiques, art, and fashions have opened along **Osceola Street** in the restored downtown, with hardly a vacancy.

Hutchinson Island (Jensen Beach)

32 *5 mi northeast of Stuart.*

Unusual care limits development here and prevents the commercial crowding found to the north and south, although there are some high-rises here and there along the shore. The small town of Jensen Beach, part of which is in the central part of the island, actually stretches across both sides of the Indian River. Citrus farmers and fishermen still play a big role in the community, giving the area a down-to-earth feel. Its most notable population is that of the sea turtles; in summer more than 6,000 turtles come to nest along the town's Atlantic beach.

Built in 1875, the **House of Refuge Museum** is the only remaining building of nine such structures erected by the U.S. Life Saving Service (a predecessor of the Coast Guard) to aid stranded sailors. Exhibits include antique lifesaving equipment, maps, artifacts from nearby wrecks, and boat-making tools. ⊠ *301 S.E. MacArthur Blvd.,* ☎ *561/225–1875.* 🎫 *$2.* ☉ *Tues.–Sun. 11–4.*

The pastel-pink **Elliott Museum** was built in 1961 in honor of Sterling Elliott, inventor of an early automated addressing machine and a four-wheel bicycle. The museum features antique automobiles, dolls and toys, and fixtures from an early general store, blacksmith shop, and apothecary shop. ⊠ *825 N.E. Ocean Blvd.,* ☎ *561/225–1961.* ⊡ *$4.* ☉ *Daily 11–4.*

Run by the Florida Oceanographic Society, the **Coastal Science Center** consists of a coastal hardwood hammock and mangrove forest. Expansion has yielded a visitor center, a science center with interpretive exhibits on coastal science and environmental issues, and a ½-mi interpretive boardwalk. There are also plans for an aquarium, an auditorium, research laboratory, and permanent library. Guided nature walks are offered. ⊠ *890 N.E. Ocean Blvd.,* ☎ *561/225–0505.* ⊡ *$3.50.* ☉ *Science and visitor centers Mon.–Sat. 10–5, boardwalk Mon.–Sat. 10–4, nature walks Mon.–Sat. 10:30 and by request.*

Beach

Bathtub Beach (⊠ MacArthur Blvd., off Rte. A1A), at the north end of the Indian River Plantation Beach Resort, is ideal for children because the waters are shallow for about 300 feet offshore and usually calm. At low tide, bathers can walk to the reef. Facilities include rest rooms and showers.

Dining and Lodging

$$-$$$ ✕ **11 Maple Street.** This 16-table restaurant is as good as it gets on
★ the Treasure Coast. Run by Margee and Mike Perrin, it offers a Continental menu that changes nightly. The soft recorded jazz and the earnest, friendly staff satisfy as fully as the brilliant food served in ample portions. Appetizers might include walnut bread with melted fontina cheese or sautéed conch with balsamic vinegar; among entrées are salmon with leeks, lobster, and blue-crab cake, and porcini mushroom risotto. For dessert, look out for cherry clafouti (like a bread pudding) and white-chocolate custard with blackberry sauce. ⊠ *3224 Maple Ave.,* ☎ *561/334–7714. Reservations essential. MC, V. Closed Mon. and Tues. No lunch.*

$$ ✕ **Conchy Joe's.** This classic Florida stilt house full of antique fish mounts, gator hides, and snakeskins dates from the late 1920s—but Conchy Joe's, like a hermit crab sliding into a new shell, only moved up from West Palm Beach in 1983. Under a huge Seminole-built chickee (raised wood platform) with a palm through the roof, you find a super-casual atmosphere and the freshest Florida seafoods from a menu that changes daily. Staples, however, are the grouper marsala, broiled sea scallop, and fried cracked conch. Try the rum drinks with names like Goombay Smash and Bahama Mama, while listening to steel-band calypso Thursday–Sunday. Happy hour is 3–6 daily and during all NFL games. ⊠ *3945 N. Indian River Dr.,* ☎ *561/334–1130. AE, D, MC, V.*

$$ ✕ **Scalawags.** The look is plantation tropical—coach lanterns, gingerbread, wicker, slow-motion paddle fans—but the top-notch buffets are aimed at today's resort guests. Standouts are the all-you-can-eat Wednesday evening seafood buffet, with jumbo shrimp, Alaskan crab legs, clams on the half shell, marinated salmon, and fresh catch. As if that weren't enough, there's also the Friday prime rib buffet with traditional Yorkshire pudding and baked potato station. A regular menu with a big selection of fish, shellfish, and grills, plus a big salad bar, is also offered. The main dining room in this second-floor restaurant at the Indian River Plantation overlooks the Indian River; there is also a private 20-seat wine room and a terrace that looks out on the marina. ⊠ *555 N.E. Ocean Blvd.,* ☎ *561/225–6818. AE, DC, MC, V.*

$ ╳ **The Emporium.** Indian River Plantation's coffee shop is an old-fashioned soda fountain and grill that also serves hearty breakfasts. Specialties include eggs Benedict, omelets, deli sandwiches, and salads. ⊠ *555 N.E. Ocean Blvd.,* ☏ *561/225–3700. AE, DC, MC, V.*

$$$$ 🏨 **Indian River Plantation Beach Resort.** Longtime Florida visitors rec-
★ ognize this residential-sports complex as one of a kind among full-service resorts. Its oceanfront setting in the assuredly warm subtropics is just the beginning; with an unpretentious style, the resort fits well on Hutchinson Island. Three buildings have rooms and suites available for shorter stays, and there are also rentals in new condominiums, mostly designed with bright island themes, abundant latticework, and balconies. ⊠ *555 N.E. Ocean Blvd., Hutchinson Island, Stuart 34996,* ☏ *561/225–6990 or 800/947–2148. 326 rooms and suites, 150 condominiums. 5 restaurants, bar, 4 pools, spa, 2 golf courses, 13 tennis courts, boating. AE, DC, MC, V.*

$$–$$$ 🏨 **Hutchinson Inn.** Sandwiched among the high-rises, this modest and affordable two-story motel from the mid-1970s has the feel of a B&B thanks to pretty canopies and bracketing. An expanded Continental breakfast is served in the well-appointed lobby, and you can borrow a book or a stack of magazines to take to your room, where homemade cookies are delivered in the evenings. On Saturday there's a noon barbecue. Rooms range from small but comfortable to fully equipped efficiencies and seafront suites with private balconies. ⊠ *9750 S. Ocean Dr., 34957,* ☏ *561/229–2000,* FAX *561/229–8875. 21 units. Pool, tennis court, beach. MC, V.*

Outdoor Activities and Sports

BASEBALL

The **New York Mets** (⊠ 525 N.W. Peacock Blvd., Port St. Lucie, ☏ 561/871–2115) train at the St. Lucie County Sport Complex, in Port St. Lucie.

GOLF

Indian River Plantation Beach Resort (⊠ 555 N.E. Ocean Blvd., ☏ 561/225–3700 or 800/444–3389) has 18 holes.

Fort Pierce

③③ *11 mi north of Stuart.*

This community, about an hour north of Palm Beach, has a distinctive rural feel, focusing on ranching and citrus farming rather than tourism. It has several worthwhile stops for visitors, including those easily seen while following Route 707.

Once a reservoir, 550-acre **Savannahs Recreation Area** has been returned to its natural state. Today the semiwilderness has campsites, a petting zoo, botanical garden, boat ramps, and trails. ⊠ *1400 E. Midway Rd.,* ☏ *561/464–7855.* 🎫 *$1 per vehicle.* ☉ *Daily 8 AM–9 PM.*

At the **Heathcote Botanical Gardens,** a self-guided tour takes in a palm walk, Japanese garden, and subtropical foliage. ⊠ *210 Savannah Rd.,* ☏ *561/464–4672.* 🎫 *$2.50.* ☉ *Tues.–Sat. 9–5, also Sun. 1–5 Nov.–Apr.*

As the home of the Treasure Coast Art Association, the **A. E. "Bean" Backus Gallery** displays the works of Florida's foremost landscape artist. The gallery also mounts changing exhibits and offers exceptional buys on work by local artists. ⊠ *500 N. Indian River Dr.,* ☏ *561/465–0630.* 🎫 *Donations welcome.* ☉ *Tues.–Sun. 1–5.*

Highlights at the **St. Lucie County Historical Museum** include historic photos, early 20th-century memorabilia, vintage farm tools, a restored 1919 American La France fire engine, replicas of a general store and the old Fort Pierce railroad station, and the restored 1905 Gardner House. ✉ *414 Seaway Dr.,* ☎ *561/468–1795.* ⌨ *$2.* ☉ *Tues.–Sat. 10–4, Sun. noon–4.*

The 340-acre **Fort Pierce Inlet State Recreation Area** contains sand dunes and a coastal hammock. The park offers swimming, surfing, picnicking, hiking, and a self-guiding nature trail. ✉ *905 Shorewinds Dr.,* ☎ *561/468–3985.* ⌨ *$3.25 per vehicle with up to 8 people.* ☉ *Daily 8– sunset.*

The **UDT-Seal Museum** commemorates the site where more than 3,000 Navy frogmen trained during World War II. Weapons and equipment are on view, and exhibits depict the history of the UDTs (Underwater Demolition Teams). Numerous patrol boats and vehicles are displayed outdoors. ✉ *3300 N. Rte. A1A,* ☎ *561/595–1570.* ⌨ *$2.* ☉ *Tues.–Sat. 10–4, Sun. noon–4.*

Accessible only by footbridge, the **Jack Island Wildlife Refuge** contains 4⅓ mi of trails. The 1½-mi Marsh Rabbit Trail across the island traverses a mangrove swamp to a 30-foot observation tower overlooking the Indian River. ✉ *Rte. A1A,* ☎ *561/468–3985.* ⌨ *Free.* ☉ *Daily 8–sunset.*

The **Harbor Branch Oceanographic Institution** is an internationally recognized, diversified research and teaching facility that offers a glimpse into the high-tech world of marine research. Its fleet of research vessels—particularly its two submersibles—operates around the world for NASA, NOAA, and NATO, among other contractors. Visitors can take a 90-minute tour of the 500-acre facility, including aquariums of sea life indigenous to the Indian River Lagoon, exhibits of marine technology, and other learning facilities. There are also lifelike and whimsical bronze sculptures created by founder J. Seward Johnson, Jr. and a gift shop with imaginative, sea-related items. ✉ *5600 Old Dixie Hwy.,* ☎ *561/465–2400.* ⌨ *$5.* ☉ *Tours Mon.–Sat. 10, noon, and 2.*

Dining and Lodging

$$ ✕ **Mangrove Mattie's.** Since its opening in the late 1980s, this upscale but rustic spot on Fort Pierce Inlet has provided dazzling waterfront views and imaginative nautical decor with delicious seafood. Dine outdoors on the terrace or inside in the cool air-conditioning, and try the coconut-fried shrimp or the chicken and scampi. Or come by during happy hour (weekdays 5–8) for a free buffet of snacks. ✉ *1640 Seaway Dr.,* ☎ *561/466–1044. AE, D, DC, MC, V.*

$ ✕ **Theo Thudpucker's Raw Bar.** Businesspeople dressed for work mingle here with people fresh from the beach wearing shorts. On squally days everyone piles in off the jetty. Specialties include oyster stew, smoked fish spread, conch salad and conch fritters, fresh catfish, and alligator tail. ✉ *2025 Seaway Dr. (South Jetty),* ☎ *561/465–1078. No credit cards.*

$$–$$$ ▥ **Harbor Light Inn.** The pick of the pack of lodgings lining the Fort Pierce Inlet along Seaway Drive is this modern, nautical, blue-trimmed motel. Spacious units on two floors feature kitchen or wet bar and routine but well-cared-for furnishings. Half of the rooms have a waterfront porch or balcony. In addition to the motel units there is a set of four apartments across the street (off the water), where in-season weekly rates are $350. ✉ *1156–1160 Seaway Dr., 34949,* ☎ *561/468–*

3555 or 800/433–0004. 21 units. Pool, fishing, coin laundry. AE, D, DC, MC, V.

$$ 🏠 **Mellon Patch Inn.** This little B&B has an excellent location—across the shore road from a beach park, at the end of a canal leading to the Indian River Lagoon. One side of the canal has a bank of attractive new homes; the other has the Jack Island Wildlife Refuge. Images of split-open melons permeate the house—on pillows, crafts, and candies on night tables. Each of the guest rooms has imaginative accessories, art, and upholstery appropriate to its individual theme. The cathedral-ceiling living room features a wood-burning fireplace, and full breakfast is included. ✉ *3601 N. Rte. A1A, North Hutchinson Island 34949,* ☎ *561/461–5231. 4 rooms. MC, V.*

Outdoor Activities and Sports

FISHING

For charter boats and fishing guides, try the **Dockside Inn** (✉ 1152 Seaway Dr., ☎ 561/461–4824).

JAI ALAI

Fort Pierce Jai Alai operates seasonally for live jai alai and year-round for off-track betting on horse-racing simulcasts. ✉ *1750 S. Kings Hwy., off Okeechobee Rd.,* ☎ *561/464–7500 or 800/524–2524.* 🎟 *$1.* ☉ *Games Jan.–Apr., Wed. and Sat. 12:30 and 7, Thurs. and Fri. 7, Sun. 1; call to double-check schedule; simulcasts Wed.–Mon. noon and 7.*

SCUBA DIVING

Some 200 yards from shore and ¼ mi north of the UDT-Seal Museum on North Hutchinson Island, the **Urca de Lima Underwater Archaeological Preserve** features the remains of a flat-bottom, round-bellied storeship. Once part of a treasure fleet bound for Spain, it was destroyed by hurricane. Dive boats can be chartered through the **Dockside Inn** (✉ 1152 Seaway Dr., ☎ 561/461–4824).

Shopping

One of Florida's best discount malls, the **Manufacturer's Outlet Center** (✉ Rte. 70, off I–95 at Exit 65) contains 41 stores offering such brand names as American Tourister, Jonathan Logan, Aileen, Polly Flinders, Van Heusen, London Fog, Levi Strauss, and Geoffrey Beene.

En Route To reach Vero Beach, you have two options—Route A1A, along the coast, or Route 605 (often called Old Dixie Highway), on the mainland. As you approach Vero on the latter, you'll pass through an ungussied landscape of small farms and residential areas—a very relaxing experience.

Vero Beach

③④ *12 mi north of Fort Pierce.*

There's a tranquility to this Indian River County seat, an affluent town with a strong commitment to the environment and the arts. Retirees make up about half of the winter population. In the exclusive Riomar Bay area of town, "canopy roads" are shaded by massive live oaks, and a popular cluster of restaurants and shops is just off the beach.

At the **Indian River Citrus Museum,** photos, farm tools, and videos tell about when oxen hauled the citrus crop to the railroads, when family fruit stands dotted the roadsides, and when gorgeous packing labels made every crate arriving up north an enticement to visit the Sunshine State. You can also book free citrus tours in actual groves. ✉ *2140*

14th Ave., ☎ *561/770–2263.* 🎟 *Donations welcome.* ⊗ *Tues.–Sat.*
10–4, Sun. 1–4.

In Riverside Park's Civic Arts Center, the **Center for the Arts** presents
a full schedule of exhibitions, art movies, lectures, workshops, and other
events, with a focus on Florida artists. ⊠ *3001 Riverside Park Dr.,* ☎
561/231–0707. 🎟 *Free.* ⊗ *Fri.–Wed. 10–4:30, Thurs. 10–8.*

In addition to a wet lab containing aquariums filled with Indian River
Lagoon life, the outstanding 51-acre **Environmental Learning Center**
has a 600-foot boardwalk through mangrove shoreline and a 1-mi canoe
trail. The center is on the north edge of Vero Beach, on Wabasso Island, but it's a pretty drive and worth the trip. ⊠ *255 Live Oak Dr.,*
☎ *561/589–5050.* 🎟 *Free.* ⊗ *Weekdays 9–5, weekends 1–4.*

The Arts

The **Civic Arts Center** (⊠ Riverside Park), a cluster of cultural facilities, includes the **Riverside Theatre** (⊠ 3250 Riverside Park Dr., ☎
561/231–6990), which stages six productions each season in its 633-
seat performance hall; the **Agnes Wahlstrom Youth Playhouse** (⊠
3280 Riverside Park Dr., ☎ 561/234–8052), which mounts children's
productions; and the **Center for the Arts** (⊠ 3001 Riverside Park Dr.,
☎ 561/231–0707), which presents art movies and lectures in addition
to its other offerings. **Riverside Children's Theatre** (⊠ 3280 Riverside
Park Dr., ☎ 561/234–8052) offers series of professional touring and
local productions, as well as acting workshops at the Agnes Wahlstrom
Youth Playhouse.

Beaches

All along the east edge of town there are beach-access parks with
boardwalks and steps bridging the foredune. Admission is free, and
the parks are open daily 7 AM–10 PM. **Humiston Park** (⊠ Ocean Dr.
below Beachland Blvd.) has a large children's play area and picnic tables and is across the street from shops.

Dining and Lodging

$$ ✕ **Black Pearl.** This intimate restaurant with pink and green art deco
furnishings offers entrées that emphasize fresh local ingredients. Spe-
cialties include chilled leek-and-watercress soup, local fish in parch-
ment paper, and panfried veal with local shrimp and vermouth. **Pearl's
Bistro** (⊠ 54 Royal Palm Blvd., ☎ 561/778–2950), a more casual and
less expensive sister restaurant, serves Caribbean-style food for lunch
and dinner. ⊠ *1409 Rte. A1A,* ☎ *561/234–4426. AE, MC, V. No lunch
weekends.*

$$ ✕ **Ocean Grill.** Opened by Waldo Sexton as a hamburger shack in 1938,
★ the Ocean Grill is now furnished with Tiffany lamps, wrought-iron chan-
deliers, and Beanie Backus paintings of pirates and Seminole Indians.
The menu includes black-bean soup, jumbo lump crabmeat salad, and
at least three kinds of fish every day. The house drink, the Leaping Limey,
a curious blend of vodka, blue curaçao, and lemon, commemorates the
1894 wreck of the *Breconshire* that occurred just offshore and from
which 34 British sailors escaped. The bar looks over the water. ⊠ *1050
Sexton Plaza (Beachland Blvd. east of Ocean Dr.),* ☎ *561/231–5409.
AE, D, DC, MC, V. Closed 2 weeks following Labor Day. No lunch
weekends.*

$$$$ 🏨 **Disney's Vero Beach Resort.** Built on 71 oceanfront acres, this
sprawling vacation getaway that operates both as a time-share and a
hotel is the classiest resort in Vero Beach. The main four-story building, three freestanding villas, and six beach cottages are nestled among
tropical greenery. Buildings are painted in pale pastels and sport steeply

pitched gables, and many units have balconies. Bright interiors feature rattan furniture and tile floors. ✉ *9235 Rte. A1A, 32963,* ☎ *561/234–2000. 175 units. 2 restaurants, lounge, pool, wading pool, tennis courts, basketball, bicycles, game room. AE, D, DC, MC, V.*

$$$$ 🏨 **Doubletree Guest Suites.** Built in 1986 and taken over by Doubletree in 1996, this five-story rose-color stucco hotel on Ocean Drive provides easy access to specialty shops and boutiques. One- and two-bedroom suites have patios opening onto a pool or balconies and excellent ocean views. ✉ *3500 Ocean Dr., 32963,* ☎ *561/231–5666. 55 suites. Bar, 2 pools, wading pool, hot tub. AE, D, DC, MC, V.*

$$–$$$ 🏨 **Islander Resort.** The aqua-and-white-trim Islander has a snoozy Key West style that contrasts stylishly with the smart shops across from the beach along Ocean Drive. Jigsaw-cut brackets and balusters and beach umbrellas dress up the pool. All rooms feature white wicker, paddle fans hung from vaulted ceilings, and fresh flowers. It's just right for beachside Vero. ✉ *3101 Ocean Dr., 32963,* ☎ *561/231–4431 or 800/952–5886. 16 rooms, 1 efficiency. Pool. AE, DC, MC, V.*

Outdoor Activities and Sports

BASEBALL

The **Los Angeles Dodgers** (✉ 4101 26th St., ☎ 561/569–4900) train at Dodgertown, actually in Vero Beach.

Shopping

Along **Ocean Drive** near Beachland Boulevard, a specialty shopping area includes art galleries, antiques shops, and upscale clothing stores.

Sebastian

③⑤   *7 mi north of Vero Beach.*

One of only a few sparsely populated areas on Florida's east coast, this little fishing village has as remote a feeling as you'll find anywhere between Jacksonville and Miami Beach. That remoteness adds to the appeal of the recreation area around Sebastian Inlet, where you can walk for miles along quiet beaches.

The **McLarty Museum,** designated a National Historical Landmark, features displays dedicated to the 1715 hurricane that sank a fleet of Spanish treasure ships. ✉ *13180 N. Rte. A1A,* ☎ *561/589–2147.* 🎫 *$1.* ⊙ *Daily 10–4:30.*

You've really come upon hidden loot when you step into **Mel Fisher's Treasure Museum.** You can view some of the recovery from the Spanish treasure ship *Atocha* and its sister ships of the 1715 fleet. Fisher operates a similar museum in Key West. ✉ *1322 U.S. 1,* ☎ *561/589–9874.* 🎫 *$5.* ⊙ *Mon.–Sat. 10–5, Sun. noon–5.*

Because of the highly productive fishing waters of Sebastian Inlet, at the northern end of Orchid Island, the 587-acre **Sebastian Inlet State Recreation Area** is the best-attended park in the Florida state system. On both sides of the high bridge that spans the inlet, the recreation area attracts plenty of anglers as well as those eager to see the spectacular views from the bridge. A concession stand on the north side of the inlet sells short-order food, rents various craft, and has an apparel and surf shop. A boat ramp is available. Not far away along the sea is a dune area that's part of the **Archie Carr National Wildlife Refuge,** a haven for sea turtles and other protected Florida wildlife. ✉ *9700 S. Rte. A1A, Melbourne Beach,* ☎ *561/984–4852.* 🎫 *Free.* ⊙ *Bait and tackle shop daily 7:30–6, concession stand daily 8–5.*

Beaches

Just to the north and south of **Sebastian Inlet** are fine sandy beaches, known for having the best waves in the state.

Dining and Lodging

$–$$ ✕ **Capt. Hiram's.** This family-friendly restaurant on the Indian River Lagoon is easygoing, fanciful, and fun—definitely not purposefully hip. "Neckties," as the sign says, "are prohibited." Other than molded-plastic tables, the place is "real"—full of wood booths, stained glass, umbrellas on the open deck, and ceiling fans. Don't miss Capt. Hiram's Sandbar, where kids can play while parents enjoy a drink at stools set in an outdoor shower or a beached boat. Choose among seafood brochette, New York strip steak, fresh catch, and lots of other seafood dishes as well as raw-bar items. The full bar has a weekday happy hour and free hot hors d'oeuvres Fridays 5–6. There's nightly entertainment in season. ⊠ *1606 N. Indian River Dr.,* ☎ *561/589–4345. AE, D, MC, V.*

$–$$ ✕ **Hurricane Harbor.** Built in 1927 as a garage and used during Prohibition as a smugglers' den, Hurricane Harbor now draws a year-round crowd of retirees and locals. Guests love the waterfront window seats on stormy nights, when sizable waves break outside in the Indian River Lagoon. The menu features seafood, steaks, and grills, along with lighter fare. On Friday and Saturday nights the Antique Dining Room is opened, with linen, stained glass, and a huge antique breakfront. There's also live music nightly. ⊠ *1540 Indian River Dr.,* ☎ *561/589– 1773. AE, D, MC, V. Closed Mon.*

$–$$ 🛏 **Captain's Quarters.** The four units—three overlooking the Indian River Lagoon and the marina at Capt. Hiram's restaurant and one two-room suite—are all Key West cute. Painted in bright colors with matching fabrics, the rooms have pine and white wicker furniture and pine plank floors with grass rugs. The adequate bathrooms have large stall showers. Glass doors open to a plank porch, but the porches are all within sight of each other. ⊠ *1606 Indian River Dr., 32958,* ☎ *561/589–4345. 3 rooms, 1 suite. Restaurant. AE, D, MC, V.*

$–$$ 🛏 **Davis House Inn.** Vero native Steve Wild modeled his two-story inn after the clubhouse at Augusta National, and, perhaps surprisingly, it fits right in with Sebastian's fishing-town look. Wide overhung roofs shade wraparound porches. In a companion house that Steve calls the Gathering Room, he serves a complimentary expanded Continental breakfast. Rooms are huge—virtual suites, with large sitting areas— though somewhat underfurnished. Overall, it's a terrific value. ⊠ *607 Davis St., 32958,* ☎ *561/589–4114. 12 efficiencies. Bicycles. MC, V.*

Outdoor Activities and Sports

CANOEING AND KAYAKING

Bill Rogers Outdoor Adventures (⊠ 1541 DeWitt La., ☎ 561/564–9600) outfits canoe trips down the Sebastian River, along Indian River Lagoon, through Pelican Island Wildlife Refuge, as well as more distant locations. The concession stand at **Sebastian Inlet State Recreation Area** (⊠ 9700 S. Rte. A1A, Melbourne Beach, ☎ 561/984–4852) rents canoes, kayaks, and paddleboats.

FISHING

The best inlet fishing in the region is at **Sebastian Inlet State Recreation Area** (⊠ 9700 S. Rte. A1A, Melbourne Beach), where the catch includes bluefish, flounder, jack, redfish, sea trout, snapper, snook, and Spanish mackerel. For deep-sea fishing try *Miss Sebastian* (⊠ Sembler Dock, ½ block north of Capt. Hiram's restaurant, ☎ 561/589–3275); $25 for a half day covers rod, reel, and bait. **Sebastian Inlet Marina at**

Capt. Hiram's (⊠ 1606 Indian River Dr., ☎ 561/589–4345) offers half- and full-day fishing charters.

The **Sailboard School** (⊠ 9125 U.S. 1, ☎ 561/589–2671 or 800/253–6573, FAX 561/589–7963) provides year-round one-day, weekend, and five-day programs of sailboarding instruction, including boards, for $120 a day, $575 for five days.

LAKE OKEECHOBEE

Rimming the western shore of Palm Beach County, this second-largest freshwater lake in the United States is girdled by 120 mi of roads; yet for almost its entire circumference, it remains hidden from sight. It is Lake Okeechobee—the Seminole's Big Water—heart of the great Everglades watershed.

The lake measures 730 square mi—roughly 33 mi north–south and 30 mi east–west—with an average natural depth of only 10 feet (flood control brings the figure up to 12 feet and deeper). Six major lock systems and 32 separate water-control structures manage the water. These combine with a 1,400-mi grid of canals and levees to form the essential plumbing of the 16,000-sq-mi Central and Southern Florida Flood Control District, which extends from just south of Orlando to Everglades National Park.

All the headlines about the troubled Everglades have their source in the flood-control system that for half a century has contained Lake Okeechobee within its 30-foot-high levee, a great grassy berm officially called the Herbert Hoover Dike and locally known as "the wall." Outside the wall, small towns depend for their livelihoods on raising the sugarcane, beef and dairy cows, and, more recently, citrus that flood control makes possible. Maintained jointly by a state flood-control agency and the U.S. Army Corps of Engineers, the system of drainage canals dates from the late 19th century, when a bankrupt Florida contracted with a wealthy Philadelphian, Hamilton Disston, to drain the Everglades for agriculture. The end result, however, is that by curtailing the natural water flow, Lake Okeechobee does serious damage to the Everglades ecosystem. Water pollution caused by fertilizer runoff from nearby farms is also a constant concern.

On top of the wall is the Lake Okeechobee Scenic Trail. Stretching north and south atop the levee, this coarse track has been integrated into the Florida National Scenic Trail. The dike trail is the focus of one of the most ambitious recreational trail developments in the United States. Although the route can be hiked or ridden on mountain bikes, some $8 million in improvements, to be completed before 2000, will smooth the surface and provide shelters and interpretive materials.

Inside the wall, on the big lake itself, fisherfolk come from everywhere for reputably the best bass fishing in North America. As such, the lake region is the antithesis of Palm Beach—as important to blue-collar culture as Palm Beach is to the starched-collar group. While Palm Beach is alive with polo and croquet matches, bass-fishing zealots fill up the trailer camps along the lake shores.

This propensity for fish naturally shows up on local menus. In particular, no menu is without catfish, and not just any catfish—fried catfish. You can try to get it broiled or steamed, but waitresses may let you know they'd rather not pass that order on to the kitchen. It's delicious however it's cooked.

The Okeechobee region makes for one-of-a-kind touring and outdoor recreation that can occupy days at a time for anyone interested in exploring an unadvertised Florida. Or you can tour the region in a single (but exhausting) day.

Towns are discussed in a clockwise fashion, starting with Belle Glade, at the southeastern end of the lake.

Belle Glade

36 *46 mi west of Palm Beach on U.S. 98/441.*

The motto of this town is "Her soil is her fortune," for Belle Glade is the eastern hub of the 700,000-acre Everglades Agricultural Area, the crescent of farmlands lying south and east of the lake.

Grouped together in Belle Glade's **Municipal Complex** are the public library and the **Lawrence E. Will Museum**, both with materials on the town's history. Out front on the lawn is a Ferenc Verga sculpture of a family fleeing from the wall of water that poured from the lake in the catastrophic hurricane of 1928. More than 2,000 people lost their lives and 15,000 families were left homeless by the torrential flood. ⊠ *530 Main St.,* ☎ *561/996–3453.* ▧ *Free.* ☉ *Mon., Tues., and Fri. 9–4; Wed. and Sat. 9–1; Thurs. 9–8.*

The **Zora Neale Hurston Roof Garden Museum** is dedicated to the renowned writer, one of whose best-known works, *Their Eyes Were Watching God,* includes a fictional account of the terrible 1928 hurricane. You can view a collection of Hurston's research and writings, as well as a history of the African-American experience around Lake Okeechobee. ⊠ *Glades Pioneer Park, 866 Rte. 715,* ☎ *561/996–2161,* ▧ *Free.* ☉ *Tues.–Fri. 10–4.*

OFF THE **LAKE HARBOR** – West of Belle Glade on U.S. 27 is what's left of a
BEATEN PATH promising lake town. Today the tiny community is home to massive locks, where you can see water-flow control for the Miami Canal at work. You can also look at the restored Lock No. 1, which dates from 1919.

The Arts
The **Dolly Hand Cultural Arts Center** (⊠ 1977 College Dr., ☎ 561/992–6160), on the Palm Beach Community College Glades Campus, presents a winter series of seven or eight productions.

Dining and Lodging
$ ✕ **Dino's Restaurant.** Downtown Belle Glade's best, this faux-Tudor pizza house with Leatherette booths and lyre-back chairs features subs, steaks, dogs, burgers, pastas, and salads. It's open for three meals a day. ⊠ 1100 N. Main St., ☎ 561/996–1901. AE, D, DC, MC, V.

$ ✕ **Drawbridge Cafe.** A big-windowed country-club dining room is to one side; the Rusty Anchor Lounge, with pool table, jukebox, and TV, is to the other. There are buffets for midweek luncheons and weekend breakfasts plus nightly specials: If you haven't had your fill of catfish yet, come on Wednesday. ⊠ Torry Island Rd., ☎ 561/992–9370. MC, V.

$ ▥ **Okeechobee Inn.** Rooms in this simple two-story L-shape motel, 2 mi west of Belle Glade, are furnished in green floral prints. Large windows let in plenty of light. All rooms have balconies that overlook the pool, and fishing and boat ramps are just a mile away. ⊠ 265 N. U.S.

27, South Bay, 33493, ☎ *561/996–6517. 115 rooms. Pool, playground. MC, V.*

$ 🏕 **Belle Glade Marina Campground.** Just a few miles north of downtown Belle Glade, just offshore in Lake Okeechobee, is Torry Island. Campsites have water and electrical hookups; some have sewer hookups and docking facilities. ✉ *Torry Island, 33493,* ☎ *561/996–6322. 350 campsites. Horseshoes, shuffleboard, dock, picnic area. MC, V.*

Outdoor Activities and Sports

FISHING

In addition to operating the bridge to Torry Island (the last remaining swing bridge in Florida, it is cranked open and closed by hand, swinging at right angles to the road), brothers Charles and Gordon Corbin run **Slim's Fish Camp** (✉ Torry Island, ☎ 561/996–3844). Here you'll find a complete tackle shop, guides, camping facilities, fully equipped bass boats, and even the name of a good taxidermist to mount your trophy. **J-Mark Fish Camp** (✉ Torry Island, ☎ 561/996–5357) provides fully equipped bass boats, fishing guides, tackle, bait, and licenses.

GOLF

Belle Glade Municipal Country Club (✉ Torry Island Rd., ☎ 561/996–6605) has an 18-hole golf course and restaurant open to the public.

Clewiston

③⑦ *20 mi northwest of Belle Glade.*

"The sweetest town in America" is also the most prosperous lake town thanks to the resident headquarters of the **United States Sugar Corporation** (✉ 111 Ponce DeLeon Ave., ☎ 941/983–8121), on the west side of the crescent-shape Civic Park. As the largest employer and tax-revenue source, the company effectively governs Clewiston. Its style reflects an enlightened paternalism that dates from 1931, when an investment group of General Motors principals took over the Southern Sugar Company, which had failed with the onset of the Depression. To the park's north is the **Public Library** (✉ 120 W. Osceola Ave., ☎ 941/983–1493), and to the east is the **Clewiston Inn,** a landmark for its antebellum architecture, restaurant, and lounge. As you enter town on U.S. 27, otherwise known as the Sugarland Highway, you'll come to several marinas, stores offering freshwater fishing equipment, and condominium-motels along a canal in the lee of the dike.

The **Clewiston Museum** details the history of the city with stories not only of sugar and of the Herbert Hoover Dike construction, but also of a ramie crop grown here to make rayon, of World War II RAF pilots who trained at the Clewiston airfield, and of a German POW camp. ✉ *112 S. Commercio St.,* ☎ *941/983–1493.* 🎫 *Free.* 🕐 *Tues.–Fri. 10–4.*

Dining and Lodging

$ ✕ **Colonial Dining Room.** This Clewiston Inn's restaurant has ladderback chairs, chandeliers, and fanlight windows, and though the food is good, the attitude's not fancy. Southern regional and Continental dishes—chicken, pork, steak, and the ubiquitous catfish—are served. ✉ *108 Royal Palm Ave. at U.S. 27,* ☎ *941/983–8151. MC, V.*

$ ✕ **Old South Bar-B-Q Ranch.** Curiosity about the piles of cornball signs that lead here ("Y'all be shore'n stop in t'help pay for theez dern signs") pull in half a million visitors a year. Displays of pioneer home and farm relics, Confederate money, and stagey versions of legendary moments in Western lore make it a great spot for kids. There are wagon wheels behind the picnic tables, and servers sport Western wear. The chow is lots of barbecue, catfish, hush puppies, and corn on the cob. ⊠ *602 E. Sugarland Hwy.,* ☎ *941/983–7756. D, MC, V.*

$–$$ 🖼 **Clewiston Inn.** This classic antebellum-style country hotel in the heart of town was built in 1938. Its cypress-panel lobby, wood-burning fireplace, Colonial Dining Room, and Everglades Lounge with a wraparound Everglades mural are standouts. Rooms are pleasant but basic, with reproduction furniture. Still it's worth a stay to soak up the lore and take advantage of the excellent value (full breakfast included). A pool is across the street in the park. ⊠ *108 Royal Palm Ave. at U.S. 27, 33440,* ☎ *941/983–8151 or 800/749–4466,* 🆃🆇 *941/983–4602. 48 rooms, 5 suites. Restaurant, lounge, lighted tennis courts, jogging. AE, D, DC, MC, V.*

Outdoor Activities and Sports
GOLF

Clewiston Country Club (⊠ 1 Golf View Rd., ☎ 941/983–8641) has an 18-hole course and restaurant open to the public.

Moore Haven

③⑧ *18 mi northwest of Clewiston.*

With a population under 2,000, Moore Haven is the seat of the proportionally small Glades County. Sugar-cane farming and cattle ranching account for most private-sector jobs here. On U.S. 27, just before town, the four-laner narrows and crosses a drawbridge over the Caloosahatchee River, which along with the St. Lucie Canal (on the opposite side of the lake) and the lake constitute the fully navigable, 152-mi Okeechobee Waterway, linking the Atlantic with the gulf. The prominent downtown landmark is the **Lone Cypress,** a tree that has guided explorers to this spot on the lake since early Seminole times.

Shopping
Lundy's Hardware (⊠ 35 Ave. J, ☎ 941/946–0833) is the genuine article. In business since 1919, it's a catchall general store, although the only food it carries is for livestock.

OFF THE   **CYPRESS KNEE MUSEUM** – This attraction about 16 mi outside Moore
BEATEN PATH   Haven is a bit run down now (the owners are quite old), but it's still worth a visit. In the museum are hundreds of cypress knees—the knotty, gnarled protuberances that sprout mysteriously from the bases of some cypress trees and grow to resemble all manner of people and things. Specimens resemble dogs, bears, ballet dancers' feet, an anteater, Joseph Stalin, and Franklin D. Roosevelt. There's also a beautiful, ¼-mi walk into a cypress swamp. The spindly hand-carved road signs, with such sayings as LADY, IF HE WON'T STOP, HIT HIM ON THE HEAD WITH A SHOE, that once directed visitors to the entrance are now in the museum. ⊠ ¼ mi north of Rte. 29 on U.S. 27, Palmdale, ☎ 941/675-2951. 🖼 Donations welcome. ☉ Daily 8–sunset.

GATORAMA – To take a good long gander at a variety of gator species and sizes smiling toothily, come see the more than 1,000 alligators and assorted crocodiles that cohabit here. Since the attraction is also a commercial gator farm, you'll see how the "mink" of the leather trade is raised for profit. ⊠ 3 mi south of Rte. 29 on U.S. 27, Palmdale, ☎ 941/675-0623. 🖼 $4.50. ☉ Daily 8–6.

En Route   Route 78 curves along most of the western shore of Lake Okeechobee, and sugar gives way to cattle as the road turns to the northeast across

Fisheating Creek. You'll pass Lakeport and the huge ranch that is the Brighton Seminole Indian Reservation before approaching the town of Okeechobee. The closer you get to Okeechobee County, the more RV parks and fishing camps you'll see along the roadside and canal bank.

Okeechobee

39 *37 mi northeast of Moore Haven.*

Long before this town near the top of the lake was settled, the vicinity was made immortal by the Battle of Okeechobee. On Christmas day, 1837, General Zachary Taylor's forces defeated a Seminole force led by Chiefs Alligator, Sam Jones, and Wildcat. The battle effectively ended large-scale Seminole conflict, though resistance continued for almost 20 more years. (A historical marker commemorating the battle is about 6½ mi outside of town on U.S. 441.)

The region came to prominence more peacefully in 1915, when the Florida East Coast Railway arrived and the town was formally laid out as an agricultural center. Citrus production has outgrown cattle ranching as the principal economy, while dairying, though still important, is diminishing as the state acquires land in its efforts to reduce water pollution.

Okeechobee's downtown is distinctive for its wide, grass-malled, east–west main street. Stop to look at the graceful, Mediterranean revival **Okeechobee County Courthouse** (⊠ N.W. 2nd St., ☎ 941/763–6441).

OFF THE BEATEN PATH

BRIGHTON SEMINOLE INDIAN RESERVATION – Get your chips ready. One of the region's largest ranches—35,000 acres—the Brighton reservation (⊠ Off Rte. 721) also features bingo Monday–Friday nights. For information, contact the **Seminole Tribe of Florida, Inc.** (⊠ Culture Educational Center, Rte. 6, Box 585, 34974, ☎ 941/763–7501, 941/467–6857, or 941/467–9998).

Beach

At a pivotal corner of the lake near Okeechobee, a modest **public beach** (⊠ Rte. 78 and U.S. 441) rims the north shore. Access to the beach and a fishing pier is via a short cutoff over the dike.

Dining and Lodging

$–$$ ★ ✕ **Lightsey's.** The pick of the lake, this beautiful lodgelike restaurant at the Okee-Tantie Recreation Area started closer to town as a fish company with four tables in a corner. Now everybody comes out here. You can get most items fried, steamed, broiled, or grilled. The freshest are the catfish, cooter (freshwater turtle), frogs' legs, and gator. ⊠ *10430 Rte. 78 W,* ☎ *941/763–4276. MC, V. Beer and wine only.*

$ ✕ **Calusa Lodge Restaurant.** Some places call themselves rustic, but this is the real thing. Everybody's here, from locals griping about the Corps of Engineers' plan to remove part of the dike to Seminoles to cyclists. Weekend breakfast buffets and all-you-can-eat catfish dinners are popular. There is live entertainment in the lounge on weekends. You gotta be here if you're in town. ⊠ *Rtes. 78 and 721, Lakeport,* ☎ *941/946–1900. MC, V.*

$ ★ ▥ **Okeechobee Days Inn Pier II.** This modern two-story motel on the rim canal has a five-story observation tower for looking over the levee to the lake. Large, clean, motel-plain rooms are well maintained. Out back there's a 600-foot fishing pier and Oyster Bar, one of the best hangouts on the lake for shooting a game of pool or watching a game on TV. It attracts a good mix of locals and out-of-towners. ⊠ *2200 S.E. U.S. 441, 34974,* ☎ *941/763–8003 or 800/874–3744,* FAX *941/763–2245. 89 rooms. Lounge, fishing. AE, D, DC, MC, V.*

$ ⚠ **Okee-Tantie Recreation Area.** In addition to its recreational facilities, the park offers 215 RV sites, 38 tent sites, picnic areas, rest rooms, showers, Lightsey's restaurant, and a shop from which you can buy groceries and sandwiches. ⊠ *10430 Rte. 78 W, 34974,* ☎ *941/763–2622. MC, V.*

Outdoor Activities and Sports

BIKING
Euler's Cycling & Fitness (⊠ 50 S.E. U.S. 441, ☎ 941/357–0458) is the only source for bicycle rentals and repairs on the lake.

FISHING
Since the **Okee-Tantie Recreation Area** (⊠ 10430 Rte. 78 W, ☎ 941/763–2622) has direct access to the lake, it's a popular place for fishing. There are two public boat ramps, fish-cleaning stations, a marina, picnic areas and a restaurant, a playground, rest rooms, showers, and a bait shop (☎ 941/763–9645) that stocks groceries.

En Route   East of Okeechobee, U.S. 441 becomes an especially beautiful rural road as it follows the eastern shore of the lake. There are several unforgettable views of a vast calm blue lake bordered by brilliant green grass. Just before the ghost town of Port Mayaca, the road rises up onto a grand span across the St. Lucie Waterway. The bridge is wide enough for you to pull to the far right and gather in the spectacular view of the lake to the west. Alternately, you can take a cutoff road just before the span and drive to the top of the levee for an almost equal view.

Indiantown

40 *31 mi southeast of Okeechobee on Rte. 710 and 11 mi east of Port Mayaca on Rte. 76.*

Somewhat set back from the lake, Indiantown is the western hub of Martin County, noteworthy for citrus production, cattle ranching, and timbering. The town reached its apex in 1927, when the Seaboard Airline Railroad briefly established its southern headquarters and a model town here. Today it's a good place to stop when visiting the nearby Barley Barber Swamp.

The Florida Power and Light Company's Martin Power Plant maintains the **Barley Barber Swamp,** a 400-acre freshwater cypress swamp preserve. A 5,800-foot-long boardwalk enables you to walk through this vestige of what near-coastal Florida was largely like before the vast water-control efforts began in the 19th century. Dozens of birds, reptiles, and mammals inhabit these wetlands and lowlands with an outstanding reserve of bald cypress trees, land and swamp growth, and slow-flowing, coffee-color water. Reservations are required at least one week in advance for tours. In addition, during certain times of the year there are manatee and turtle walks. Call for schedules. ⊠ *Rte. 710,* ☎ *800/552–8440.* ◻ *Free.* ◷ *Tours Fri.–Wed. 8:30 and 12:30.*

Lodging

$ ▦ **Seminole Country Inn.** This two-story, Mediterranean revival inn,
★ once the southern headquarters of the Seaboard Airline Railroad, was restored by longtime Indiantown patriarch, the late Holman Wall. It's now being run for the second time (other innkeepers didn't get it right) by his daughter, Jonnie Wall Williams, a fifth-generation native, who

is devoted to the inn's restoration. Rooms are done in country ruffles and prints, with full carpeting and comfy beds. There are rocking chairs on the porch, Indiantown memorabilia in the lobby, a sitting area on the second floor, and good local art throughout. ✉ *15885 S.W. Warfield Blvd., 34956,* ☎ *561/597–3777. 21 rooms. 2 restaurants, pool. AE, D, MC, V.*

En Route   Going south on U.S. 441 toward the sliver of town called Canal Point, you'll find yourself back in serious sugar country. Almost 80% of Florida's sugarcane production takes place in this area.

Pahokee

④   *11 mi southwest of Port Mayaca.*

Pahokee means "grassy waters" in the Seminole language, and it's possible to drive up onto the levee here and look out across the lake spreading like an ocean to the horizon. Though the town of nearly 7,000 may share a county with Palm Beach, its rural style twangs a world away. The town depends almost entirely on sugar, and two giant mills are located here.

For a look back into the sugar-centric past, check out the **Pahokee Historical Museum** (✉ 115 E. Main St., ☎ 516/924–5579), located in the chamber of commerce. The **Bank of Pahokee** (✉ 800 S. Main St., ☎ 561/924–5272) has a series of Everglades murals.

The Arts

The **Prince Theater** (✉ 231 E. Main St., ☎ 561/924–5534), a restored 1939 art deco movie house, is now used as a performance center.

Dining

$ ✕ **Pam's Seafood & Deli.** This erstwhile downtown favorite is run by Jimmy and Georgia Jones, whose motto is "You buy. We fry." Their rationale: "The kitchen isn't big enough anyway for a grill." A block from city hall, the place is bright with vinyl and a lot of shell art. Anybody you want to meet shows up. ✉ *149 S. Lake Ave.,* ☎ *561/924–7231. No credit cards. Closed Sun.*

Outdoor Activities and Sports

FISHING

After seeing them in all the local restaurants, try to catch your own catfish at the **Pahokee Marina & Campground** (✉ 171 N. Lake Ave., ☎ 561/924–7832).

PALM BEACH AND THE TREASURE COAST A TO Z

Arriving and Departing

By Bus

Greyhound Lines (☎ 800/231–2222) buses arrive at the station in West Palm Beach (✉ 100 Banyan Blvd., ☎ 561/833–8534).

By Car

I–95 runs north–south, linking West Palm Beach with Miami and Fort Lauderdale to the south and with Daytona, Jacksonville, and the rest of the Atlantic Coast to the north. To get to central Palm Beach, exit at Belvedere Road or Okeechobee Boulevard. Florida's Turnpike runs up from Miami through West Palm Beach before angling northwest to reach Orlando.

By Plane

Palm Beach International Airport (PBIA) (✉ Congress Ave. and Belvedere Rd., West Palm Beach, ☎ 561/471–7400) is served by **Air Canada** (☎ 800/776–3000), **American/American Eagle** (☎ 800/433–7300), **American Trans-Air** (☎ 800/225–2995), **Canadian Holidays** (☎ 800/661–8881), **Carnival Airlines** (☎ 800/824–7386), **Comair** (☎ 800/354–9822), **Continental** (☎ 800/525–0280), **Delta** (☎ 800/221–1212), **KIWI Intl. Airlines** (☎ 800/538–5494), **Northwest** (☎ 800/225–2525), **Paradise Island** (☎ 800/432–8807), **Republic Air Travel** (☎ 800/233–0225), **TWA** (☎ 800/221–2000), **United** (☎ 800/241–6522), and **US Airways/US Airways Express** (☎ 800/428–4322).

BETWEEN THE AIRPORT AND THE TOWNS

Rte. 10 of **Tri-Rail Commuter Bus Service** (☎ 800/874–7245) runs from the airport to Tri-Rail's nearby Palm Beach Airport station daily. **Co-Tran** (☞ Getting Around by Bus, *below*) Rte. 4-S operates from the airport to downtown West Palm Beach every two hours at 35 minutes after the hour from 7:35 AM until 5:35 PM. The fare is $1.

Palm Beach Transportation (☎ 561/689–4222) provides taxi and limousine service from PBIA. Reserve at least a day in advance for a limousine. The lowest fares are $1.50 per mile, with the meter starting at $1.25. Depending on your destination, a flat rate (from PBIA only) may save money. Wheelchair-accessible vehicles are available.

By Train

Amtrak (☎ 800/872–7245) connects West Palm Beach (✉ 201 S. Tamarind Ave., ☎ 561/832–6169) with cities along Florida's east coast and the Northeast daily and via the *Sunset Limited* to New Orleans and Los Angeles three times weekly. Included in Amtrak's service is transport from West Palm Beach to Okeechobee (✉ 801 N. Parrott Ave.; station unmanned).

Getting Around

The **Downtown Transfer Facility** (✉ Banyan Blvd. and Clearlake Dr., West Palm Beach), off Australian Avenue at the western entrance to downtown, links the downtown shuttle, Amtrak, Tri-Rail (the commuter line of Dade, Broward, and Palm Beach counties), CoTran (the county bus system), Greyhound, and taxis.

By Bus

CoTran (Palm Beach County Transportation Authority) buses require exact change. The cost is $1.50, $1 for students, seniors, and people with disabilities (with reduced-fare ID); transfers are 20¢. Service operates 5 AM–8:30 PM, though pickups on most routes are 5:30 AM–7 PM. For details, call 561/233–1111 (Palm Beach) or 561/930–5123 (Boca Raton–Delray Beach).

Palmtran (☎ 561/833–8873) is a shuttle system that provides free transportation around downtown West Palm Beach, weekdays 6:30 AM–7:30 PM.

By Car

U.S. 1 threads north–south along the coast, connecting most coastal communities, while the more scenic Route A1A ventures out onto the barrier islands. The interstate, I–95, runs parallel to U.S. 1 a bit farther inland.

A nonstop four-lane route, Okeechobee Boulevard, carries traffic from west of downtown West Palm Beach, near the Amtrak station in the airport district, directly to the Flagler Memorial Bridge and into Palm

Beach. Flagler Drive will be turned over for pedestrian use before the end of the decade.

The best way to get to Lake Okeechobee from West Palm is to drive west on Southern Boulevard from I–95, past the cutoff road to Lion Country Safari. From there, the boulevard is designated U.S. 98/441.

By Taxi
Palm Beach Transportation (☎ 561/689–4222) has a single number serving several cab companies. Meters start at $1.25, and the charge is $1.25 per mile within West Palm Beach city limits; if the trip at any point leaves the city limits, the fare is $1.50 per mile. Some cabs may charge more. Waiting time is 25¢ per 75 seconds.

By Train
Tri-Rail (☎ 305/728–8445 or 800/874–7245), the commuter rail system, has six stations in Palm Beach County (13 stops altogether between West Palm Beach and Miami). The round-trip fare is $5, $2.50 for students and seniors.

Contacts and Resources

Emergencies
Dial **911** for police or ambulance.

HOSPITALS
The following hospitals have 24-hour emergency rooms: **Good Samaritan Hospital** (⊠ Flagler Dr. and Palm Beach Lakes Blvd., West Palm Beach, ☎ 561/655–5511; physician referral, ☎ 561/650–6240), **JFK Medical Center** (⊠ 5301 S. Congress Ave., Atlantis, ☎ 561/965–7300; physician referral, ☎ 561/642–3628), **Palm Beaches Medical Center** (⊠ 2201 45th St., West Palm Beach, ☎ 561/881–2670; physician referral, ☎ 561/881–2661), **Palm Beach Regional Hospital** (⊠ 2829 10th Ave. N, Lake Worth, ☎ 561/967–7800; physician referral, ☎ 800/237–6644), and **St. Mary's Hospital** (⊠ 901 45th St., West Palm Beach, ☎ 561/844–6300; physician referral, ☎ 561/881–2929).

LATE-NIGHT PHARMACIES
Eckerd Drug (⊠ 3343 S. Congress Ave., Palm Springs, ☎ 561/965–3367) and **Walgreen Drugs** (⊠ 1688 S. Congress Ave., Palm Springs, ☎ 561/968–8211; ⊠ 7561 N. Federal Hwy., Boca Raton, ☎ 561/241–9802; ⊠ 1634 S. Federal Hwy., Boynton Beach, ☎ 561/737–1260; ⊠ 1208 Royal Palm Beach Blvd., Royal Palm Beach, ☎ 561/798–9048; ⊠ 6370 Indiantown Rd., Jupiter, ☎ 561/744–6822; ⊠ 20 E. 30th St., Riviera Beach, ☎ 561/848–6464).

Guided Tours
AIRBOAT TOURS
J-Mark Fish Camp (☎ 561/996–5357), on Torry Island, offers 45- to 60-minute airboat rides for $20 per person, with a minimum of two people and a maximum of six; 90- to 120-minute rides for $30 per person include a look at an active eagle's nest. **Loxahatchee Everglades Tours** (☎ 561/482–6107) operates year-round from west of Boca Raton through the marshes between the built-up coast and Lake Okeechobee.

BOAT TOURS
Capt. Doug's (☎ 561/589–2329) offers three-hour lunch and dinner cruises from Sebastian along the Indian River on board a 35-foot sloop. Cost is $100 per couple including meal, tips, beer, and wine. In the Okeechobee area, **Capt. J P Boat Cruises** (☎ 941/946–3306), based at the Moore Haven marina, operates tours on the lake and rim canal from mid-November to mid-April. **Jonathan Dickinson's**

River Tours (☎ 561/746–1466) runs two-hour guided riverboat cruises from Jonathan Dickinson State Park in Hobe Sound daily at 9, 11, 1, and 3 and once a month, at the full moon, at 7. The cost is $10. *The Manatee Queen* (☎ 561/744–2191), a 49-passenger catamaran, offers day and evening cruises on the Intracoastal Waterway and into the cypress swamps of Jonathan Dickinson State Park, November–May.

Ramblin' Rose Riverboat (☎ 561/243–0686) operates luncheon, dinner-dance, and Sunday brunch cruises from Delray Beach along the Intracoastal Waterway. *The Spirit of St. Joseph* (☎ 561/467–2628) offers seven lunch and dinner cruises weekly on the Indian River, leaving from alongside the St. Lucie County Historical Museum, November–April. *Star of Palm Beach* (☎ 561/842–0882) runs year-round from Singer Island, each day offering one dinner-dance and three sightseeing cruises on the Intracoastal Waterway. **Water Taxi Scenic Cruises** (☎ 561/775–2628), in Palm Beach, offers several different daily tours in a 16-person launch designed to let you get a close-up look at the mansions of the rich and famous. The southern tour includes the mansions of Palm Beach, while the northern tour includes the North Palm Beach Canal. There's also a one-hour BYOB sunset cruise. Departures are from Sailfish Marina and Riviera Beach Marina.

ENVIRONMENTAL TOURS

Contact the **Audubon Society of the Everglades** (☎ 561/588–6908) for field trips and nature walks. **Swampland Tours** (☎ 941/467–4411), on Lake Okeechobee, operates interpretive boat tours through the National Audubon Society Wildlife Sanctuary.

HISTORIC TOURS

The **Boca Raton Historical Society** (✉ 71 N. Federal Hwy., Boca Raton, ☎ 561/395–6766) offers afternoon tours of the Boca Raton Resort & Club on Tuesday year-round and to other South Florida sites. The **Fort Pierce Historical Society** (✉ 131 Main St., Fort Pierce, ☎ 561/466–3880) gives walking tours of the town's historic section, past buildings built by early settlers. The **Indian River County Historical Society** (✉ 2336 14th Ave., Vero Beach, ☎ 561/778–3435) conducts walking tours of downtown Vero on Wednesdays at 11 and 1 (by reservation). **Old Northwood Historic District Tours** (✉ 501 30th St., West Palm Beach, ☎ 561/863–5633) leads two-hour walking tours that include visits to historic home interiors. They leave Sundays at 2, and a $5 donation is requested.

Visitor Information

Belle Glade Chamber of Commerce (✉ 540 S. Main St., Belle Glade 33430, ☎ 561/996–2745). **Chamber of Commerce of the Palm Beaches** (✉ 401 N. Flagler Dr., West Palm Beach 33401, ☎ 561/833–3711). **Clewiston Chamber of Commerce** (✉ 544 W. Sugarland Hwy., Clewiston 33440, ☎ 941/983–7979). **Glades County Chamber of Commerce** (✉ U.S. 27 and 10th St., Moore Haven 33471, ☎ 941/946–0440). **Indian River County Tourist Council** (✉ 1216 21st St., Box 2947, Vero Beach 32961, ☎ 561/567–3491). **Indiantown Chamber of Commerce** (✉ 15518 S.W. Osceola St., Indiantown 34956, ☎ 561/597–2184). **Okeechobee County Chamber of Commerce** (✉ 55 S. Parrott Ave., Okeechobee 34974, ☎ 941/763–6464). **Pahokee Chamber of Commerce** (✉ 115 E. Main St., Pahokee 33476, ☎ 561/924–5579). **Palm Beach Chamber of Commerce** (✉ 45 Cocoanut Row, Palm Beach 33480, ☎ 561/655–3282). **Palm Beach County Convention & Visitors Bureau** (✉ 1555 Palm Beach Lakes Blvd., Suite 204, West Palm Beach 33401, ☎ 561/471–3995). **St. Lucie County Tourist Development Council** (✉ 2300

Virginia Ave., Fort Pierce 34982, ☎ 561/462–1535 or 800/344–8443). **Stuart/Martin County Chamber of Commerce** (✉ 1650 S. Kanner Hwy., Stuart 34994, ☎ 561/287–1088). For more information on the Okeechobee area, contact the **U.S. Army Corps of Engineers** (✉ South Florida Operations Office, 525 Ridgelawn Rd., Clewiston 33440-5399, ☎ 941/983–8101).

7 The Florida Keys

This slender necklace of landfalls off the southern tip of Florida is strung together by a 110-mi-long highway. The Keys have two faces: one, a wilderness of flowering jungles and shimmering seas amid mangrove-fringed islands dangling toward the tropics; the other, a traffic jam with a view of billboards, shopping centers, and trailer courts. Embrace the best of the Keys by enjoying the deep-sea fishing, the first-class snorkeling and diving, and the colorful community of Key West.

By Herb Hiller

Updated by
Diane P.
Marshall

THE FLORIDA KEYS ARE A WILDERNESS of flowering jungles and shimmering seas, a jade necklace of mangrove-fringed islands dangling toward the tropics. The Florida Keys are also a 110-mi traffic jam lined with garish billboards, hamburger stands, shopping centers, motels, and trailer courts. Unfortunately, in the Keys you can't have one without the other. A river of tourist traffic gushes along U.S. 1 (also called the Overseas Highway), the main artery between Key Largo and Key West. Residents of Monroe County live by diverting that river's flow of green dollars to their own pockets. In the process, the fragile beauty of the Keys—or at least the 45 that are inhabited and linked to the mainland by 43 bridges—has paid the environmental price.

Despite designation as "an area of critical state concern" in 1975 and a subsequent state-mandated development slowdown, rapid growth has continued and the Keys' natural resources are still in peril. In 1990, Congress established the Florida Keys National Marine Sanctuary, covering 2,800 square nautical miles of coastal waters. Adjacent to the Keys landmass are spectacular, unique, and nationally significant marine environments, including sea grass meadows, mangrove islands, and extensive living coral reefs. These fragile environments support rich and diverse biological communities possessing extensive conservation, recreational, commercial, ecological, historical, research, educational, and aesthetic values. In late 1996, a comprehensive management plan was put into place.

The Florida Keys National Marine Sanctuary and Protection Act, which includes a new marine zoning concept that would reserve 6% of the waters as "no harvest" zones, is intended to protect the coral reefs and restore worsening water quality. But problems continue. Increased salinity in Florida Bay causes large areas of sea grass to die and drift in mats out of the bay. These mats then block sunlight from reaching the reefs, stifling their growth and threatening both the Keys' recreational diving economy and tourism in general.

Also posing a potential threat to the Keys and their charm is the four-laning of U.S. 1 between the mainland and the islands. Increased tourism, population, and traffic seem inevitable, as does the eventual widening of the rest of U.S. 1 throughout the Keys, prompting many to ask if a trip to paradise will still be worth it.

For now, however, take pleasure as you drive down U.S. 1 along the islands. Most days you can gaze over the silvery blue and green Atlantic and its still-living reef, with Florida Bay, the Gulf of Mexico, and the backcountry on your right. (The Keys extend east–west from the mainland.) At a few points, the ocean and gulf are as much as 10 mi apart. In most places, however, they are within 1–4 mi, and on the narrowest landfill islands, they are separated only by the road.

The Overseas Highway varies from a frustrating traffic-clogged trap to a mystical pathway skimming the sea. More islands than you can remember appear. Follow the green mile markers along the road, and even if you lose track of island names, you cannot get lost.

Things to do and see are everywhere, but first you have to remind yourself to get off the highway. Once you do, rent a boat and find a secluded anchorage and fish, swim, or marvel at the sun, sea, and sky. In the Atlantic, you can dive to spectacular coral reefs or pursue dolphin, blue marlin, and other deep-water game fish. Along the Florida Bay coastline you can seek out the bonefish, snapper, snook, and tarpon that lurk in the grass flats and in the shallow, winding channels of the backcountry.

Along the reefs and among the islands are more than 600 kinds of fish. Diminutive deer and pale raccoons, related to but distinct from their mainland cousins, inhabit the Lower Keys. And throughout the islands you'll find such exotic West Indian plants as Jamaica dogwood, pigeon plum, poisonwood, satin leaf, and silver and thatch palms, as well as tropical birds, including the great white heron, mangrove cuckoo, roseate spoonbill, and white-crowned pigeon. Mangroves, with their gracefully bowed prop roots, appear to march out to sea. Day by day they busily add more keys to the archipelago.

Another Keys attraction is the weather: In the winter it's typically 10° warmer than on the mainland; in the summer it's usually 10° cooler. The Keys also get substantially less rain, around 30 inches annually compared to 55–60 inches in Miami and the Everglades. Most of the rain falls in quick downpours on summer afternoons, except in June, September, and October, when tropical storms can dump rain for two to four days. In winter, continental cold fronts occasionally stall over the Keys, dragging overnight temperatures down to the 40s.

The Keys were only sparsely populated until the early 20th century. In 1905, however, railroad magnate Henry Flagler began building the extension of his Florida railroad south from Homestead to Key West. His goal was to establish a rail link to the steamships that sailed between Key West and Havana, just 90 mi across the Straits of Florida. The railroad arrived at Key West in 1912 and remained a lifeline of commerce until the Labor Day hurricane of 1935 washed out much of its roadbed. For three years thereafter, the only way in and out of Key West was by boat. The Overseas Highway, built over the railroad's old roadbeds and bridges, was completed in 1938, and many sections and bridges have recently been widened or replaced.

Pleasures and Pastimes

The Arts

The Keys are more than warm weather and luminous scenery—a vigorous and sophisticated artistic community flourishes here. Key West alone currently claims among its residents several dozen full-time writers and hundreds of painters and craftspeople. Arts organizations in the Keys sponsor many special events—some lasting only a weekend, others spanning an entire season.

Biking

Cyclists are now able to ride all but a tiny portion of the bike path that runs along the Overseas Highway from MM 106 south to the Seven Mile Bridge. The state plans to extend the route throughout the Keys.

Boating

If it floats, local marinas rent it. For up-close exploration of the mangroves and near-shore islands in Florida Bay, nothing beats a kayak or canoe. You can paddle within a few feet of a flock of birds without disturbing them. Visiting the backcountry islands and inlets of Everglades National Park requires a shallow-draft boat: A 14- to 17-foot skiff with a 40- to 50-horsepower outboard is sufficient. For diving the reef or fishing on the open ocean, you'll need a larger boat with greater horsepower. Houseboats are ideal for cruising the Keys.

Only experienced sailors should attempt to navigate Florida Bay with deep-keeled sailboats, which are better suited for the Gulf of Mexico and ocean side. On the other hand, small, shallow-draft, single-hulled sailboats and catamarans are ideal for either side. Personal water vehicles, such as Wave Runners and Jet Skis, rent by the half hour or hour. Flat, stable pontoon boats are a good choice for anyone with seasickness. Those interested in experiencing the reef without getting wet can take a glass-bottom boat trip.

Dining

A number of talented young chefs have settled in the Keys, contributing to the area's image as one of the nation's points of culinary interest. Restaurants' menus, rum-based fruit beverages, and music reflect the Keys' tropical climate and the proximity to Cuba and other Caribbean islands. Better restaurants serve imaginative and tantalizing fusion cuisine that draws on traditions from all over the world; Florida citrus, seafood, and tropical fruits figure prominently.

The queen conch is an endangered species, so any conch you get has come fresh-frozen from the Bahamas, Belize, or the Caribbean. However, Florida lobster and stone crab should be local and fresh from August to March. Also keep an eye out for authentic Key lime pie. The real McCoy has a yellow custard in a graham-cracker crust with a meringue top and tastes like nothing else.

Restaurants may close for a two- to four-week vacation during the slow season—between mid-September and mid-November. Check local newspapers or call ahead, especially if driving any distance.

Fishing

These sun-bathed waters are home to 100 species of game fish as well as lobster, shrimp, and crabs. Flats fishing and backcountry fishing are Keys specialties. In flats fishing, a guide poles a shallow-draft outboard boat through the shallow, sandy-bottomed waters while sighting for bonefish and snook to be caught on light tackle, spin, and fly. Backcountry fishing may include flats fishing or fishing in the channels and basins around islands in Florida Bay. Charter boats fish the reef and Gulf Stream for deep-sea fish like tuna, dolphin (not the mammal), marlin, sailfish, and shark. Party boats, which can be crowded, carry up to 50 people to fish the reefs for grouper, kingfish, and snapper. Some operators boast a guarantee or "no fish, no pay" policy.

Nary a month goes by without a fishing tournament. Pick up the "Official Florida Keys Fishing Tournament Guide" from a tourist office for a schedule.

Lodging

Accommodations are as varied as they are plentiful. The majority of lodgings outside Key West are in small waterfront resorts, whose efficiency and one- or two-bedroom units are decorated in tropical colors. They offer dockage and either provide or will arrange boating, diving, and fishing excursions. In high season, expect to pay $65–$165 for an efficiency (in low season, $45–$145). In Key West you'll find historic cottages, restored turn-of-the-century Conch (pronounced "conk") houses, and large resorts. Throughout the Keys, campground and RV park rates with electricity and water run $22–$48.

Some properties require two- or three-day minimum stays during holidays and on weekends in high season. Conversely, discounts are given for midweek, weekly, and monthly stays, and rates can drop 20%–40% April–June and September–October. Ask about reduced rates during especially slow periods. Keep in mind that salty winds and soil play havoc with anything man-made, and constant maintenance is a must; inspect your accommodations before checking in.

Scuba Diving and Snorkeling

Diving in the Keys is spectacular. In shallow and deep water with visibility up to 120 feet, you can explore sea canyons and mountains covered with waving sea plumes, brain and star coral, historic shipwrecks, and sunken submarines. The colors of the coral are surpassed only by the brilliance of the fish that live around it. There's no best season for diving, but occasional storms in June, September, and October cloud the waters and make seas rough.

You can dive the reefs with scuba, snuba, or snorkeling gear, using your own boat, renting a boat, or booking a tour with a dive shop. (Most shops also rent underwater still and video cameras or will film your dive.) Key Largo has more dive shops per square mile than anywhere else in the world. Tours depart two or three times a day, stopping at two sites on each trip. The first trip of the day is usually the best. It's less crowded—vacationers like to sleep in—and visibility is better before the wind picks up in the afternoon. There's also night diving.

If your time is limited and you want to scuba dive but are not certified, take an introductory resort course. Though it doesn't result in certification, it allows you to scuba with an instructor in the afternoon following morning classroom and pool instruction.

Nearly all of the waters surrounding the Keys are part of the Florida Keys National Marine Sanctuary and thus are protected. Signs, brochures, tour guides, and marine enforcement agents remind visitors that the reef is fragile and shouldn't be touched.

Shopping

Keys shopping is an unexpected pleasure. Boutique shelves runneth over with the best names in resort wear. Galleries showcase internationally recognized and up-and-coming artists. Dive and boating shops sell the latest in fashionable and functional sports clothing and equipment, and tackle shops carry an enviable selection of fishing gear. Traditional Keys goods include jewelry fashioned out of coins and artifacts from shipwrecks; local food, like Key lime pie, conch chowder, and fresh seafood; hand-rolled cigars; fine art with marine themes; and hand-painted tropical fabrics.

Sunset Watching

With virtually no distracting air pollution or obstructive high-rises in the Keys, sunsets are a pure, unadulterated spectacle that each evening attracts thousands of tourists and locals to waterfront parks, piers, restaurants, bars, and resorts throughout the Keys.

Exploring the Florida Keys

Finding your way around the Keys isn't hard once you understand the unique address system. Many addresses are simply given as a mile marker (MM) number. The markers themselves are small green rectangular signs along the side of the Overseas Highway (U.S. 1). They begin with MM 126 a mile south of Florida City and end with MM 0 on the corner of Fleming and Whitehead streets in Key West. Keys residents use the abbreviation BS for the bay side of U.S. 1 and OS for the ocean side.

The Keys are divided into four areas: the Upper Keys, from Key Largo to the Long Key Channel (MM 106–65) and Ocean Reef and North Key Largo, off Card Sound Road and Route 905, respectively; the Middle Keys, from Conch Key through Marathon to the south side of the Seven Mile Bridge, including Pigeon Key (MM 65–40); the Lower Keys, from Little Duck Key south through Big Coppitt Key (MM 40–9); and Key West, from Stock Island through Key West (MM 9–0). The Keys don't end with the highway, however; they stretch another 70 mi west of Key West to the Dry Tortugas.

Numbers in the text correspond to numbers in the margin and on the Florida Keys and Key West maps.

Great Itineraries

IF YOU HAVE 3 DAYS

You can fly and then dive, but if you dive you can't fly for 24 hours, so spend your first morning diving or snorkeling at John Pennekamp Coral Reef State Park in ⊞ **Key Largo** ②. If you aren't certified, take a resort course, and you'll be exploring the reefs by afternoon. Afterwards, breeze through the park's visitor center. The rest of the afternoon can be whiled away either lounging around a pool or beach or visiting the Maritime Museum of the Florida Keys. Dinner or cocktails at a bay-side restaurant or bar will give you your first look at a fabulous Keys sunset. On day two, get an early start to savor the breathtaking views on the way to Key West. Along the way, make stops at the natural history museum that's part of the Museums of Crane Point Hammock, in Marathon ⑧, and Bahia Honda State Park, on Bahia Honda Key ⑨, where you can stretch your legs on a forest trail or snorkel on an offshore reef. Once in ⊞ **Key West** ⑬–㉞, you can watch the sunset before dining at one of the island's first-class restaurants. Spend the next morning exploring beaches or taking a walking or trolley tour of Old Town before driving back to the mainland.

IF YOU HAVE 4 DAYS

Spend the first day as you would above, overnighting in ⊞ **Key Largo** ②. Start the second day by renting a kayak and exploring the mangroves and small islands of Florida Bay or take an ecotour of the islands in Everglades National Park. In the afternoon, stop by the Florida Keys Wild Bird Rehabilitation Center before driving down to ⊞ **Islamorada** ④. Pause to read the inscription on the Hurricane Monument, and before day's end, make plans for the next day's fishing. After an early dinner on day three—perhaps at one of the many restaurants that will prepare your catch for you—set off for ⊞ **Key West** ⑬–㉞, and spend the last day as you would above.

IF YOU HAVE 7 DAYS

Spend your first three days as you would in the four-day itinerary, but stay the third night in ⊞ **Islamorada** ④. In the morning catch a boat to Lignumvitae Key State Botanical Site, before heading to ⊞ **Marathon** ⑧, where you can visit the natural history museum that's part of the Museums of Crane Point Hammock and walk or take a train across the Old Seven Mile Bridge to Pigeon Key. The next stop is just 10 mi away at Bahia Honda State Park, on ⊞ **Bahia Honda Key** ⑨. Take a walk on a wilderness trail, go snorkeling on an offshore reef, wriggle your toes in the beach's soft sand, and spend the night in a waterfront cabin, letting the waves lull you to sleep. Your sixth day starts with either a half day of fabulous snorkeling or diving at Looe Key National Marine Sanctuary or a visit to the National Key Deer Refuge, on Big Pine Key ⑩. Then continue on to ⊞ **Key West** ⑬–㉞, and get in a little sightseeing before watching the sunset. The next morning take a walking, bicycling, or trolley tour of town or catch a ferry or seaplane to Dry Tortugas National Park before heading home.

When to Tour the Florida Keys

High season in the Keys is mid-December through March, and traffic on the Overseas Highway is inevitably heavy. From November to the middle of December, crowds are thinner and the weather is superlative. Summer, which is hot and humid, is becoming a second high season, especially among families and Europeans. Key West's annual Fantasy Fest is the last week in October; if you plan to attend this popular event, reserve at least six months in advance. Rooms are also scarce the first few weekends of lobster season, which starts in August.

THE UPPER KEYS

The tropical coral reef tract that runs a few miles off the seaward coast accounts for most of the Upper Keys' reputation. This is a diving heaven, thanks to scores of diving options, accessible islands and dive sites, and an established tourism infrastructure.

Yet while diving is king here, fishing and nature tours draw an enviable number of tourists. Within 1½ mi of the bay coast lie the islands of Everglades National Park; here naturalists lead ecotours to see one of the world's only saltwater forests, endangered manatees, dolphin, roseate spoonbills, and tropical bird rookeries. Though the number of birds has dwindled since John James Audubon captured their beauty on a visit to the Keys, bird-watchers won't be disappointed. At sunset, flocks take to the skies, and in spring and autumn, migrating birds add their numbers. Tarpon and bonefish teem in the shallow waters surrounding the islands, providing food for birds and a challenge to light-tackle fishermen. These same crystal-clear waters attract kayakers, windsurfers, sailors, and powerboaters.

Dining in the Upper Keys used to be, with one or two exceptions, ho hum. However, within the last five years, half a dozen fine restaurants have opened and are thriving on repeat local customers and word-of-mouth tourist business.

Key Largo

56 mi south of Miami International Airport.

The first Key reachable by car, 30-mi-long Key Largo—named Cayo Largo (long key) by the Spanish—is also the largest island in the chain. Comprising three areas—North Key Largo, Key Largo, and Tavernier—it runs northeast–southwest between Lake Surprise and Tavernier Creek, at MM 95. Most businesses are on the four-lane divided highway (U.S. 1) that runs down the middle, but away from the overdevelopment and generally suburban landscape you can find many areas of pristine wilderness.

❶ One such area is **North Key Largo,** which still contains a wide tract of virgin hardwood hammock and mangrove as well as a crocodile sanctuary. To reach North Key Largo, take Card Sound Road just south of Florida City or, from within the Keys, take Route 905 north.

At the **Crocodile Lakes National Wildlife Refuge** (✉ Card Sound Rd. [Rte. 905A], North Key Largo, ☎ 305/872–2239), 300–500 crocodiles make up the largest concentration of these shy reptiles in North America. The refuge is closed to visitors because of the habitat's critical nature, but in winter you can use binoculars to see crocodiles sunning on the banks farthest from the road. Don't leave the road's shoulder, however, as you could disturb tern nests or aggravate rattlesnakes.

The 2,005-acre **Key Largo Hammocks State Botanical Site** is the largest remaining stand of the vast West Indian tropical hardwood hammock and mangrove wetland that once covered most of the Keys' upland areas. Among the site's 84 species of protected plants and animals are the endangered American crocodile and the Key Largo wood rat. Concrete skeletons of defunct developments remain but are slowly disappear-

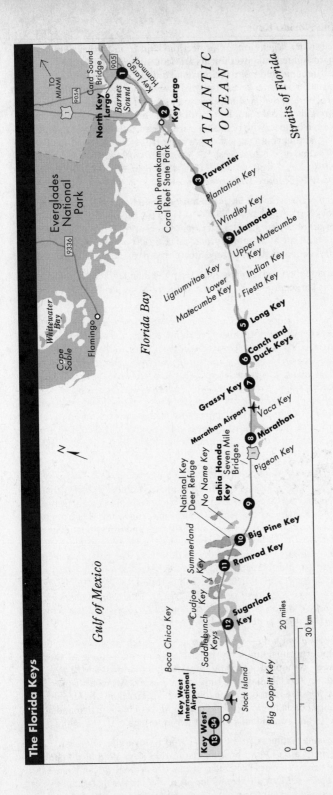

The Florida Keys

ing under vegetation. To protect the land from further development, state and federal governments are acquiring as much of the hammock as they can, and visitor centers and additional nature trails are anticipated. You can take a self-guided tour by picking up an informational brochure at the park entrance and looking for the numbered boulders along the paved road. Better still are the biweekly tours led by Ranger Joseph Nemec, who points out rare species, tells humorous nature stories, and encourages visitors to taste fruits of native plants. Pets are welcome on a 6-foot leash. ⊠ *1 mi north of U.S. 1 on Rte. 905, OS, North Key Largo,* ☎ *305/451–7008 or 305/451–1202.* ▣ *Free.* ⊙ *Daily 8–5, tours Thurs. and Sun. 10.*

The architecture of **St. Justin Martyr Catholic Church** (⊠ MM 105.5, BS, North Key Largo, ☎ 305/451–1316) evokes the colors and materials of the Keys. Among its art are a beautiful fresco of the Last Supper and an altar table formed of a 5,000-pound mass of Carrara marble quarried in Tuscany. Stop at the parish office for the key.

Taking the Overseas Highway from the mainland lands you closer to **②** **Key Largo** proper, abounding with shopping centers, chain restaurants, and, of course, dive shops.

The small but earnest, not-for-profit **Maritime Museum of the Florida Keys** depicts the local history of shipwrecks and salvage efforts through retrieved treasures, reconstructed wreck sites, and artifacts in various stages of preservation. Some of the more notable exhibits have come from a fleet of treasure ships wrecked by a hurricane in 1715. A new bottle exhibit, the first of its kind, tells Keys history using some of the museum's more than 200 salvaged bottles, dating from as early as the 1600s. The museum is a labor of love, and its primary purpose is preservation, as demonstrated by the two years it took to clean and preserve the large anchor at the entrance. ⊠ *MM 102.5, BS,* ☎ *305/451– 6444.* ▣ *$5.* ⊙ *Mon.–Wed., Fri., Sat. 10–5; Sun. noon–5.*

★ **John Pennekamp Coral Reef State Park** encompasses 78 square mi of coral reefs, sea-grass beds, and mangrove swamps. Its reefs contain 40 of the 52 species of coral in the Atlantic Reef System and more than 650 varieties of fish, and the diving and snorkeling here are famous. A concessioner rents canoes and sailboats and offers boat trips to the reef. Even a landlubber can appreciate the superb interpretive aquarium, exhibits, and video in the visitor center. The park also includes a nature trail through a mangrove forest, two man-made beaches, picnic shelters, a snack bar, and a campground. ⊠ *MM 102.5, OS, Box 487, 33037,* ☎ *305/451–1202.* ▣ *$2 for 1 person, $4 per vehicle for 2–8 people plus 50¢ per person county surcharge; $2 per vehicle an hour before closing.* ⊙ *Daily 8–sunset.*

The *African Queen*—the steam-powered workboat on which Katharine Hepburn and Humphrey Bogart rode in their movie of the same name—is moored at the **Key Largo Harbor Marina** (⊠ MM 99.7, OS), next to the Holiday Inn Key Largo Resort. Also on display is the *Thayer IV*, a 22-foot mahogany Chris Craft used by Ms. Hepburn and Henry Fonda in *On Golden Pond*. Both vessels are in demand at boat shows and occasionally vacate their moorings.

③ The southernmost part of Key Largo is **Tavernier.** Woodcarver and teacher Laura Quinn brought the **Florida Keys Wild Bird Rehabilitation Center** here in 1991, and nowhere else in the Keys can you see birds so close up. Many are kept for life because of injuries that can't be healed, whereas others are brought for rehabilitation and then set free. At any time the residents can include ospreys, hawks, pelicans, cormorants, terns, and herons of various types. A short nature trail runs into the mangrove forest (bring bug spray), and a video explains the center's mission. ⊠ *MM 93.6, BS, Tavernier,* ☎ *305/852–4486.* ▣ *Donations welcome.* ☉ *Daily sunrise–sunset.*

Harry Harris County Park (⊠ MM 93, OS, Burton Dr., Tavernier, ☎ 305/295–4385 or 888/227–8136) has play equipment, a small swimming lagoon, a boat ramp, ball fields, barbecue grills, and rest rooms. Though the turnoff is clearly marked on the Overseas Highway, the road to the ocean is circuitous.

Dining and Lodging

$$ ✕ **The Fish House.** Behind the screened, diner-style facade are an amus-
★   ing Keys mural and display cases filled with the freshest catches, which are then baked, blackened, broiled, fried, sautéed, steamed, or stewed as if every night were the finals of a seafood competition. (In fact, there are many such competitions, and the Fish House is often the winner.) The dining room—festooned with nets and fishy Christmas ornaments—is as redolent of the Keys as a Bogart movie. Generous portions come with corn on the cob, new potatoes, and coleslaw; the Key lime pie is homemade. You can't beat the fast service and great eats. ⊠ *MM 102.4, OS,* ☎ *305/451–4665. AE, D, MC, V. Closed mid-Sept.–early Oct.*

$–$$ ✕ **Anthony's Italian Restaurant & Lounge.** The portly proprietor greets guests at the door or their tables, making sure they are enjoying his hospitality. There's little to be concerned about; the food, faithful to Italian tradition, speaks for itself. The solid kitchen serves veal, chicken, and home-style pasta dishes in a comfortable setting. Spicy mussels marinara are so good you'll want an order to go. ⊠ *MM 97.6, in the median,* ☎ *305/853–1177. AE, D, MC, V.*

$–$$ ✕ **Cafe Largo.** Soothing jazz plays in this intimate bistro-style restau-
★   rant. Dinner starts with a basket of foccacia bread and garlic rolls. Next choose one of the chef's specials; you won't be disappointed. The chicken garlic—two thin breast cutlets lightly coated and sautéed, then covered in a light sauce of garlic and rosemary—is divine. The penne with shrimp and broccoli has tender shrimp, al dente broccoli, and a hint of garlic. A more than ample wine list, international beers, Italian bottled waters, and, of course, espresso and cappuccino are offered, and the dessert list is short but sweet. The same owners run the waterfront Bayside Grille, directly behind it. ⊠ *MM 99.5, BS,* ☎ *305/451–4885. AE, MC, V. No lunch.*

$–$$ ✕ **Crack'd Conch.** For serious beer connoisseurs, there isn't a better choice than this seafood restaurant. The food's good, the staff loves to tease customers, and more than 100 different imported and domestic brews are poured along with seafood sandwiches and entrées like fried alligator and blackened fish. As you might guess, conch figures prominently in salads, sandwiches, or just plain fried. Portions are big, but you can get takeout. ⊠ *MM 105, OS,* ☎ *305/451–0732. AE, D, MC, V. Closed Wed.*

$–$$ ✕ **Frank Keys Cafe.** Although on U.S. 1, this Continental restaurant
★   in the middle of a natural hardwood hammock is hidden behind trees except at night, when little white lights in the branches mark the spot. The wooden, Victorian-style house has a deep porch for dining alfresco. Chef-owner Frank Graves III and executive chef Mark Dixon do wonderful things with fresh fish. The pan-sautéed catch is washed in egg, lightly coated, then given a kiss of sherry. Opt for the famous pasta *la roma*, a seductive dish of penne with slices of filet mignon covered in a light sauce. For dessert, the blueberry crunch à la mode is nonpareil. ⊠ *MM 100, OS,* ☎ *305/453–0310. AE, MC, V. Closed Tues. and Wed.*

$ ✕ **Alabama Jack's.** In 1953 Alabama Jack Stratham opened his seafood restaurant on two barges in an old fishing community 13 mi southeast of Homestead. The spot, something of a no-man's-land, belongs to the Keys in spirit thanks to the Card Sound toll bridge. Regular customers include Keys fixtures, Sunday cyclists, local retirees, boaters, and anyone else fond of country dancing and clapping for cloggers. There's a live band on weekends. You can also admire tropical birds in nearby mangroves and the occasional crocodile in the canal. Though Jack is gone, owner Phyllis Sague has kept the favorites, including peppery crab cakes, crispy-chewy conch fritters, crunchy breaded shrimp, and homemade tartar sauce. The completely open-air place closes by 7 or 7:30 because that's when the skeeters come out. ⊠ *58000 Card Sound Rd., Card Sound,* ☎ *305/248–8741. No credit cards.*

$ ✕ **Harriette's Restaurant.** This eatery is thick with down-home personality. Owner Harriette Mattson takes the trouble to know many of her guests by name and remember what they eat. Wisecracking waitresses will tell you that the three-egg omelet usually has six eggs because Harriette has a heavy hand. Harriette's is famous for breakfast: steak and eggs with hash browns or grits and toast and jelly for $6.95, or old-fashioned hotcakes with whipped butter and syrup and sausage or bacon for $3.75. A Keys mural, a little paneling, and some carpet touch things up, but a homey style, punctuated with local crafts and photos on consignment, pervades. ⊠ *MM 95.7, BS,* ☎ *305/852–8689. No credit cards. No dinner.*

$ ✕ **Mrs. Mac's Kitchen.** Hundreds of beer cans, beer bottles, and expired license plates from all over the world decorate the walls of this wood-paneled, screened, open-air restaurant. At breakfast and lunch, the counter and booths fill up early with locals. Regular nightly specials are worth the stop: meat loaf on Monday, Italian on Wednesday, and seafood Thursday–Saturday. The chili is always good, and the beer of the month is $1.50 a bottle. ⊠ *MM 99.4, BS,* ☎ *305/451–3722. No credit cards. Closed Sun.*

$$$$ ⊡ **Jules' Undersea Lodge.** In the "not for everyone" category, this novel accommodation caters to well-finned visitors who want a total Keys diving experience. The hotel, a former underwater research lab, is five fathoms (30 feet) below the surface. Hence to be one of the six guests, you have to be a certified diver or take the hotel's three-hour introductory course (an additional $75). Rooms have a shower, telephone, VCR and stereo (no TV), and galley. The lodge is popular with honeymooners. Rates include breakfast, dinner, snacks, beverages, and diving gear. Because of the length of stay underwater, once back on terra firma, you can't fly or make deep dives for 24 hours. ⊠ *MM 103.2, OS, 51 Shoreland Dr., 33037,* ☎ *305/451–2353,* FAX *305/451–4789. 2 bedrooms, sleeps up to 6. Dining room. AE, D, MC, V.*

$$$$ ⊡ **Marriott's Key Largo Bay Beach Resort.** This 17-acre bay-side resort's five lemon-yellow, grill-balconied, and spire-topped stories are sliced between highway and bay and give off an air of warm indolent days. The facilities are as good as the guest rooms, which feature chintz, rattan, paddle fans, and balconies. (From some you can watch the sunset sweep across the bay.) A European health spa and wave pool opened in 1997. ⊠ *MM 103.8, BS, 103800 Overseas Hwy., 33037,* ☎ *305/453–0000 or 800/932–9332,* FAX *305/453–0093. 153 rooms, 20 2-bedroom suites, 6 3-bedroom suites, 1 penthouse suite. Restaurant, 3 bars, pool, beauty salon, hot tub, massage, beach, dive shop, fishing, meeting rooms. AE, D, DC, MC, V.*

$$$$ ⊡ **Sheraton Key Largo Resort.** This pink and turquoise gem is tucked
★   away in a hardwood hammock. A $3 million upgrade is evident from the lush landscaping to the new waterfront restaurant, Chez Roux. Fourth-floor bay-side rooms afford marvelous water views, whereas units on the first three floors overlook the woods, except the 230, 330,

and 430 series, which face the parking lot. All rooms are spacious and comfortable, with new tropical decor. Lighted nature trails and boardwalks wind through the woods to a beach. Two pools, one for adults only, are separated by a coral rock wall and waterfall. ⊠ *MM 96.9, BS, 97000 Overseas Hwy., 33037,* ☎ *305/852–5553 or 800/826–1006,* FAX *305/852–8669. 190 rooms, 10 suites. 2 restaurants, 2 bar/grills, lounge, 2 pools, hot tub, 2 tennis courts, beach, dock, windsurfing, boating, fishing. AE, D, DC, MC, V.*

$$$ 🏨 **Holiday Inn Key Largo Resort and Marina.** New owners have been busy refurbishing, so that even though this place, the closest resort to Pennekamp Reef, is a Holiday Inn, it's outfitted with Keys pride. Chintz and Keys-themed art accent guest rooms, while good sense has brought a new kids' playroom with an imaginative mural and convenient buffet meal service off the lobby to accommodate families. Former owner James W. Hendricks still docks the *African Queen* at the adjacent Key Largo Harbor Marina much of the time. ⊠ *MM 99.7, OS, 99701 Overseas Hwy., 33037,* ☎ *305/451–2121 or 800/843–5397,* FAX *305/451–5592. 32 rooms. Restaurant, 2 pools, hot tub, boating. AE, D, DC, MC, V.*

$$$ 🏨 **Marina Del Mar Resort and Marina.** This two-to-four-story resort on a deep-water marina caters to sailors and divers. Heavy use doesn't show, as owner Scott Marr renovates rooms year-round. Units have original watercolors by Keys artist Mary Boggs, as well as refrigerators. Suites 502–504 have kitchens (as do studios) and plenty of room for groups. There's live entertainment nightly in the restaurant and bar, a free Continental breakfast in the lobby, and spectacular sunrise and sunset views from the fourth-floor observation deck. ⊠ *MM 100, OS, 527 Caribbean Dr., 33037,* ☎ *305/451–4107 or 800/451–3483,* FAX *305/451–1891. 52 rooms, 8 suites, 16 studios. Restaurant, bar, pool, 2 tennis courts, exercise room, boating, fishing. AE, D, DC, MC, V.*

$$–$$$$ 🏨 **Frank's Key Haven Resort.** In a quiet neighborhood under a canopy of graceful, towering gumbo-limbo trees, this lodge, made of beams from Flagler's railroad tracks and imported German concrete, was built in the 1930s to withstand hurricane-force winds. The original owner ran bird-watching tours, and though the enlarged property still offers ecotours, it now caters more to divers. The resort has its own dive boat, waterfront, and training pool and offers diving certification as well as diving/lodging packages that include night dives. Screened porches have racks for dive equipment. Rooms vary from one-room efficiencies to one- and two-bedroom apartments and family units. A lounge has a TV and half-kitchen. ⊠ *MM 92, BS, 198 Harborview Dr., Tavernier 33070,* ☎ *305/852–3017 or 800/765–5397,* FAX *305/852–3880. 13 units. Pool, 2 docks. MC, V.*

$$–$$$$ 🏨 **Kona Kai Resort.** A narrow sidewalk winds between beautifully land-
★ scaped cottages to a sandy beach and marina. The garden alone, featuring fruits and rare and native plants, makes this one of the best places to stay in the Keys, but owners Joe and Ronnie Harris go further. They redecorated with beautiful tropical furnishings, added special toiletries made from fruits and flowers, and personally cater to their guests. Studios and one- and two-bedroom suites with full kitchens are spacious and light-filled. Beachfront hammocks and a pool make it easy to while away the day, but there's plenty for those who want more activity. Try a paddleboat or kayak, or visit the new art gallery, with works by South Florida artists. ⊠ *MM 97.8, BS, 97802 Overseas Hwy., 33037,* ☎ *305/852–7200 or 800/365–7829. 11 units. Pool, tennis courts, basketball, volleyball, beach, dock. AE, DC, MC, V.*

$$–$$$ 🏨 **Largo Lodge.** No two rooms are the same in this 1950s-vintage re-
★ sort, but all are cozy and fully equipped with kitchens, rattan furniture, and screened porches but no phones. The prettiest palm alley you've ever

seen sets the mood, while tropical gardens with more palms, sea grapes, and orchids surround the guest cottages. There's 200 feet of bay frontage. Late in the day, wild ducks, pelicans, herons, and other birds come looking for a handout from longtime owner Harriet "Hat" Stokes. If you want a top-value tropical hideaway not too far down the Keys, this is it. ⊠ *MM 101.5, BS, 101740 Overseas Hwy., 33037, ☎ 305/451–0424 or 800/468–4378. 6 apartments, 1 efficiency. Pool, beach, dock. MC, V.*

$–$$ 🏠 **Popp's Motel.** For 45 years and four generations, Popp family members have welcomed guests to this small and private motel. Rooms are just yards from a sandy beach, and you can take part in activities galore or relax in a hammock while the kids play on swings. One- and two-bedroom units have complete kitchens, whereas efficiencies have kitchenettes. Though the place is clean and has been updated several times, dark wood paneling and terrazzo floors in some rooms reveal their age. Other than that, it's a gem of a resort. ⊠ *MM 95.5, BS, 95500 Overseas Hwy., 33037, ☎ 305/451–2353, FAX 305/852–5200. 10 units. Picnic area, hot tub, beach, dock, playground. AE, MC, V.*

$ ⚠ **America Outdoors.** Reserve early if you want to camp here, especially around holidays and from January to mid-March. A waterfront location and woodsy setting, security, boat ramps and rentals, a sandy beach, store, bait shop, bathhouse, and an adult recreation center make it popular with snowbirds and South Floridians, who come back year after year and weekend after weekend. It's also very clean, orderly, and well-managed. Rates are the same for tents and RVs year-round: $33 for water and electric, $38 for full hookups ($45 on the beach). ⊠ *MM 97.5, BS, 97450 Overseas Hwy., 33037, ☎ 305/852–8054. 154 sites. Beach, dock, boating, fishing, coin laundry, recreation room. AE, D, MC, V.*

Nightlife

The semiweekly *Keynoter* (Wednesday and Saturday), weekly *Reporter* (Thursday), and Friday to Sunday editions of the *Miami Herald* are the best sources of information on entertainment and nightlife.

Breezers Tiki Bar (⊠ MM 103.8, BS, ☎ 305/453–0000), in Marriott's Key Largo Bay Beach Resort, is popular with the smartly coiffed crowd. Office workers join guests for cocktails to toast the sun going down. Scenes from the classic 1948 Bogart-Bacall flick *Key Largo* were shot in the **Caribbean Club** (⊠ MM 104, BS, ☎ 305/451–9970), now plastered with memorabilia of Bogart films. It draws a hairy-faced, down-home group to shoot the breeze while shooting pool but is friendlier than you might imagine. It also has postcard-perfect sunsets. **Coconuts** (⊠ MM 100, OS, 528 Caribbean Dr., ☎ 305/453–9794), in the Marina Del Mar Resort, has nightly entertainment year-round. The cabana bar and waterfront terrace of the **Italian Fisherman** (⊠ MM 104, BS, ☎ 305/451–4471) are ideal spots to watch the sunset while nibbling snacks and sipping drinks. It's big with families.

Outdoor Activities and Sports

BIKING

Equipment Locker Sport & Cycle (⊠ Tradewinds Plaza, MM 101, OS, ☎ 305/453–0140) rents mountain bikes and single-speed adult and children's bikes. Cruisers go for $10 a day, $50 a week; mountain bikes are $15 a day, $75 a week. No helmets are available.

FISHING

Sailors Choice (⊠ MM 99.7, OS, ☎ 305/451–1802 or 305/451–0041) runs two party boats daily plus a night trip on Friday and Saturday. The ultramodern 60-foot, 49-passenger boat with an air-conditioned cabin leaves from the Holiday Inn docks.

SCUBA DIVING AND SNORKELING

Key Largo National Marine Sanctuary (⌧ Box 1083, 33037, ☎ 305/451–1644) protects 103 sq mi of coral reef from the eastern boundary of John Pennekamp Coral Reef State Park (also a great dive site), 3 mi off Key Largo, to a depth of 300 feet some 8 mi offshore. Managed by NOAA (National Oceanic and Atmospheric Administration), the sanctuary includes Elbow, French, and Molasses reefs; the 1852 Carysfort Lighthouse and its surrounding reefs; Grecian Rocks; Key Largo Rocks; the torpedoed World War II freighter *Benwood;* and the 9-foot **Christ of the Deep** statue, a popular dive destination.

The Keys' newest water attraction, **Aquaworld** (⌧ MM 100, BS, ☎ 305/453–3907 or 800/595–2746) is an import from Australia's Great Barrier Reef. Four times a day the *Reef Express,* a fast water taxi, whisks you to one of three coral reefs in the Key Largo National Marine Sanctuary. Once there, you can spend the day snorkeling or sunbathing on the *Reef Adventure,* a party boat outfitted with a snorkel equipment center, snack bar, lockers, music, and a gift shop. Those who prefer to stay dry can see the reef aboard the *Sub See Explorer,* an air-conditioned 47-passenger semisubmersible craft with a large picture window at each seat. A lively narration and identification cards introduce the underwater world. On request, visitors can take a shuttle to John Pennekamp Coral Reef State Park. The $49 price includes all transportation and snorkel equipment.

Like other dive outfits, **American Diving Headquarters** (⌧ MM 105.5, BS, ☎ 305/451–0037) offers certification and dive tours. Unlike others, however, its tours are on request, not a schedule, and a Water-Tight Guarantee ensures you'll get your money's worth. The staff is concerned about guests and the environment, the latter evidenced by a new reef ecology and fish identification course. Before getting your toes wet, you listen to lectures and watch slide presentations, enabling you to get more out of the dive experience. The cost is $50 for a two-tank dive with tank and weight rental, $75 if you need everything.

Captain Slate's Atlantis Dive Center (⌧ MM 106.5, OS, 51 Garden Cove Dr., ☎ 305/451–3020 or 800/331–3483) is a full-service dive shop (NAUI, PADI, SSI, and YMCA certified) that also performs underwater weddings. **Coral Reef Park Co.** (⌧ John Pennekamp Coral Reef State Park, MM 102.5, OS, ☎ 305/451–1621) offers scuba and snorkeling tours of the park. **Quiescence Diving Service, Inc.** (⌧ MM 103.5, BS, ☎ 305/451–2440) sets itself apart in two ways: It limits groups to six to ensure personal attention and offers twilight dives an hour before sundown, the time when sea creatures are most active. Two day and night dives are also available.

WATER SPORTS

Coral Reef Park Co. (⌧ John Pennekamp Coral Reef State Park, MM 102.5, OS, ☎ 305/451–1621) rents boats and equipment for sailing, canoeing, and windsurfing. You can rent a canoe or a one- or two-person sea kayak, even camping equipment, from **Florida Bay Outfitters** (⌧ MM 104, BS, ☎ 305/451–3018). Real pros, they match the right equipment to the right skill level, so even novices feel confident paddling off. Rentals are by the hour, half day, or day.

Islamorada

❹ *MM 90.5–70.*

Early settlers named Islamorada after their schooner, the *Island Home,* but to make the name more romantic, they translated it into Spanish—

"Isla Morada." The local chamber of commerce prefers to say it means "the purple isles." Early maps show Islamorada as only Upper Matecumbe Key. Historians refer to it as the group of islands between Tavernier Creek at MM 90 and Fiesta Key at MM 70, including Plantation Key, Upper Matecumbe Key, Lower Matecumbe Key, Craig Key, and Fiesta Key. In addition, two islands—Indian Key in the Atlantic Ocean and Lignumvitae Key in Florida Bay—belong to the group.

For nearly 100 years, seasoned anglers have recognized these sun-bathed waters as home to a huge variety of game fish (100 species) as well as lobster, shrimp, and crabs. The rich, the famous, the powerful have all fished here, including Lou Gehrig, Ted Williams, and presidents Hoover, Truman, Carter, and Bush. More than 150 backcountry guides and 400 offshore captains operate out of this 20-mi stretch.

Activities abound throughout the year, ranging from a dozen fishing tournaments to arts festivals and historic reenactments. During September and October, Heritage Days feature free lectures on Islamorada history, a golf tournament, and the Indian Key Festival. Holiday Isle Resort sponsors boating, fishing, car, and golf tournaments, as well as numerous bikini and body-building contests.

Between 1885 and 1915, settlers earned good livings growing pineapples on **Plantation Key** (MM 90.5–86), using black Bahamian workers to plant and harvest their crops. The plantations are gone, replaced by a dense concentration of homes and businesses.

At 16 feet above sea level, **Windley Key** (MM 86–84) is the highest point in the Keys. Originally two islets, the area was first inhabited by Native Americans, who left middens and other remains, and then by settlers, who farmed and fished here in the mid-1800s and called the islets the Umbrella Keys. The Florida East Coast Railway bought the land from homesteaders in 1908, filled in the narrow inlet between the two islands, and changed the name. They quarried rock for the rail bed and bridge approaches in the Keys—the same rock used in many historic South Florida structures, including Miami's Vizcaya and the Hurricane Monument on Upper Matecumbe. Though the Quarry Station stop was destroyed in the 1935 hurricane, quarrying continued until the 1960s. Today, a few resorts and attractions occupy the island.

When the Florida East Coast Railway drilled, dynamited, and carved Windley Key's limestone bed, it exposed the once-living fossilized coral reef that was laid down about 125,000 years ago, now visible at the **Windley Key Fossil Reef State Geologic Site.** Five trails lead to old quarrying equipment and cutting pits, where you can stand within a petrified reef and take rubbings of beautifully fossilized brain coral and sea ferns. Volunteers give tours once a month, but you can sign out a brochure and gate key at Long Key State Recreation Area (☞ Long Key, *below*) and follow a self-guided tour. ⊠ *MM 85.5, BS,* ☎ *305/664–4815.* ☜ *Free.* ☉ *Tours 3rd Sat. of month 9 and 11.*

At the **Theater of the Sea,** 12 dolphins, two sea lions, and an extensive collection of tropical fish swim in the pits of a 1907 Windley Key railroad quarry, whose huge blasted holes are now filled with seawater. Allow at least two hours to attend the dolphin and sea-lion shows and visit all the exhibits, which include an injured birds of prey display, a "bottomless" boat ride, touch tank, a pool where sharks are fed by a trainer, and a 300-gallon "living reef" aquarium with invertebrates and small reef fishes. For an additional fee, you can even swim with dolphins for 30 minutes, after a 30-minute orientation. ⊠

MM 84.5, OS, Box 407, 33036, ☎ 305/664–2431. ✑ $14; swim with dolphins $80, reservations required with 50% deposit; video or still photos $70 (inquire at concession). ◷ *Daily 9:30–4.*

Upper Matecumbe Key (MM 84–79) was one of the earliest in the Upper Keys to be permanently settled. Homesteaders were so successful at growing pineapples and limes in the rocky soil that at one time the island had the largest U.S. pineapple crop; however, Cuban pineapples and the hurricane of 1935 killed the industry. Today life centers on fishing and tourism, and the island is lively with homes, charter fishing boats, bait shops, restaurants, stores, nightclubs, marinas, nurseries, and offices.

Somewhere In Time is a small, unlikely combination museum and antiques and jewelry shop crowded with hundreds of interesting artifacts. Nearly every inch of wall and counter space is filled with objects salvaged from merchant, slave, and military ships that plied Florida's waters. There are coins from the *Atocha,* rare ceramic containers, original 18th-century maps, cannon, solid silver bars, slave artifacts, religious medallions, rare bottles, a pirate flag, and a corny diorama of two English women who were pirates. The owner tells marvelous stories about the objects' provenance. ✉ *MM 82.8, OS,* ☎ *305/664–9699.* ◷ *Daily 9–5.*

Home to the local chamber of commerce, a **red train caboose** sits at the site where the Florida East Coast Railway had a station and living quarters, before they washed away with the hurricane of 1935. Artifacts ranging from dishes and flatware to uniform buttons and medicine bottles were excavated and are on display in the caboose. A new museum and chamber building are being built on the site. ✉ *MM 82.5, BS.* ✑ *Free.* ◷ *Weekdays 9–5, weekends 9–2.*

A bronze marker explains that the small **Pioneer Cemetery** (✉ MM 82, OS), on the grounds of Cheeca Lodge, holds the remains of 50 Anglo-Bahamian Conchs—descendants of the Russells, Pinders, and Parkers—who organized the first community on Matecumbe Key in the mid-1800s. Before the 1935 hurricane, the land also held the Matecumbe United Methodist Church, the key's first house of worship. Of its 112 parishioners, only 35 survived the storm. The rebuilt church (✉ MM 82.5, OS) still stands.

Beside the highway, the **Hurricane Monument** (✉ MM 81.6, OS) marks the mass grave of 423 victims of the 1935 Labor Day hurricane. Many of those who perished were World War I veterans who had been working on the Overseas Highway and died when a tidal surge overturned a train sent to evacuate them. The 65-foot by 20-foot art deco–style monument, built of Keys coral limestone with a ceramic map of the Keys, depicts wind-driven waves and palms bowing before the storm's fury. Note that the trees bend in the wrong direction.

OFF THE
BEATEN PATH

INDIAN KEY STATE HISTORIC SITE – Off the coast of the Matecumbe islands, small Indian Key—only 10½ acres—was inhabited by Native Americans for several thousand years before Europeans arrived, as archaeological excavations here show. The islet was a county-seat town and base for early 19th-century shipwreck salvagers, known as wreckers, until an Indian attack wiped out the settlement in 1840. Dr. Henry Perrine, a noted botanist, was killed in the raid. Today you can see his plants overgrowing the town's ruins. Though no guide is available, trails and sites are marked. On the first weekend in October, the Indian Key Festival celebrates the key's heritage with reenactments of the attack and of daily life. The island is reachable only by boat, either your own or a rental. The official concessioner is Robbie's Marina (☞ *below*). ✉ *MM 78.5, OS, Box 1052, 33036,* ☎ *305/664–4815.*

LIGNUMVITAE KEY STATE BOTANICAL SITE – A virgin hardwood forest still cloaks this 280-acre bay-side island, punctuated by the home and gardens that chemical magnate William Matheson built as a private retreat in 1919. Access is only by boat, and Robbie's Marina (☞ *below*) is the official concessioner. Even with your own boat, you need to reserve a guided tour with a ranger, from whom you can request a list of native and well-naturalized plants. To make a reservation, contact Long Key State Recreation Area (☞ Long Key, *below*). ✉ *MM 78.5, BS, Box 1052, 33036,* ☎ *305/664–4815.* 🎫 *Free.* ☉ *Tours Thurs.–Mon. at 10 and 2.*

Though tarpon are known for the exciting fight they put up when hooked, you'd never know it judging by the 50 or so prehistoric-looking specimens that gather around the docks at **Robbie's Marina,** on Lower Matecumbe Key. These fish—some as long as 5 feet—literally eat out of the hands of children who buy a $2 bucket of bait fish. Both kids and adults enjoy watching them. ✉ *MM 77.5, BS,* ☎ *305/664–9814 or 305/664–4196.* 🎫 *Dock access $1.* ☉ *Daily 8–5:30.*

Beaches

Anne's Beach (✉ MM 73.5, OS, ☎ 305/295–4385 or 888/227–8136), on Lower Matecumbe Key, has a ½-mi elevated wooden boardwalk that meanders through a natural wetland hammock. Covered picnic areas along the boardwalk provide a place to rest and enjoy the view. Rest rooms are at the north end.

Tucked away behind the Islamorada library is a small beach on a creek at Upper Matecumbe's **Islamorada County Park** (✉ MM 81.5, BS, ☎ 305/295–4385 or 888/227–8136). The water isn't very deep, but it is crystal clear. Currents are swift, making swimming unsuitable for young children, but they can enjoy the playground as well as picnic tables, grassy areas, and rest rooms.

On weekends, locals and frequent visitors with boats head for the **Sand Bar** (✉ MM 84, OS), a long narrow strip of sand off Holiday Isle that is almost exposed at low tide. As many as 200–300 people—some with dogs—come to sunbathe on partially submerged lawn chairs, play Frisbee, or just people-watch as a parade of tanned men and women, some topless, wade past in the knee-deep ocean. From the shore, they appear to be walking on water. A palm frond–lined pontoon boat serves as a mobile restaurant-cum-store.

Dining and Lodging

$$–$$$ ✗ **Grove Park Cafe.** French doors on a renovated Conch house, lace
   ★ tablecloths, artwork, crafts, and sky-blue walls with wispy white clouds give this place a light, airy feel. Nibble on triangles of freshly baked foccacia bread set in a pool of olive oil and balsamic vinegar while looking over the bistro-style menu. Caribbean conch chowder followed by grilled vegetable antipasto with couscous will satisfy any appetite. The Grove Park crab cake served as a salad on mixed greens or as a sandwich on foccacia bread is outstanding. For dinner, try steamed mussels in a white wine and garlic broth or the yellowtail Tropicale (a fillet of local yellowtail snapper encrusted, sautéed, and served with a fresh mango-and-papaya salsa). The herbs and some of the fruits are grown on the property. ✉ *MM 81.7, OS, 81701 Old Hwy.,* ☎ *305/664–0116,* FAX *305/664–2309. AE, D, MC, V. Closed Wed.*

$$ ✕ **Marker 88.** The best seats in chef-owner Andre Mueller's main din-
★ ing room catch the last glimmers of sunset. After that, the lighting gets
a little dim (romantic, some might contend). Hostesses recite a lengthy
list of daily specials and offer a wine list with more than 200 entries.
You can get a good steak or veal chop here, but seafood is the spe-
cialty. Try the robust conch chowder, salad Trevisana (radicchio, leaf
lettuce, Belgian endive, watercress, and sweet-and-sour dill dressing—
former President Bush's favorite), sautéed conch, grouper Rangoon (with
papaya, banana, and pineapple in a cinnamon and currant jelly sauce),
Key lime pie, and Key lime baked Alaska. ✉ *MM 88, BS,* ☎ *305/852–
9315. AE, D, DC, MC, V. Closed Mon. No lunch.*

$$ ✕ **Mimi's Island Deli.** Mornings start with three basic omelets or bagels
and sour cream, but lunch at this unassuming deli is reserved for in-
ventive soups, salads, and sandwiches. Try a meat loaf club sandwich,
an authentically pressed Cuban sandwich, or Mimi's take on a traditional Caesar, with an eggless mayonnaise-base dressing and anchovies
on request. Sample the desserts: The homemade peach cobbler is tart,
the apple crisp sweet and crunchy. Phone in the night before for a fisherman's lunch box, which you can pick up the next morning after 5:30.
✉ *MM 84, OS, 84341 Old Hwy.,* ☎ *305/664–4333. No credit cards.
No dinner.*

$$ ✕ **Papa Joe's Landmark Restaurant.** The decor—captain's chairs,
mounted fish, fish buoys, and driftwood strung year-round with Christ-
mas lights—never gets ahead of the first-rate food at this 1937 restau-
rant with an upper-level, over-the-water tiki bar. You can savor succulent
dolphin and fresh green beans and carrots al dente. For dessert dive
into Key lime cake or pie or peanut-butter pie. Here, you can still have
your catch cooked (but not cleaned): $8.95 up to 1 pound per person
fried, broiled, or sautéed; $10.95 for other styles, including meunière,
blackened, coconut-dipped, Cajun, amandine, or Oscar (sautéed,
topped with béarnaise sauce, crabmeat, and asparagus). An early-bird
menu served 4–6 is priced at $7.95–$9.95. ✉ *MM 79.7, BS,* ☎
305/664–8756. AE, MC, V. Closed Tues. and mid-Dec.

$$ ✕ **Squid Row.** This roadside eatery may look like just another cute,
★ affordable food stop on the way to Key West, but it's attitude-free and
serves the freshest fish you haven't caught yourself, courtesy of the
seafood wholesalers who own it. Grouper comes grilled, divinely flaky,
or in bread crumbs and sautéed, served with citrus butter. Service is
friendly and prompt, and the wait staff can talk about the specials without theatrics. They'll brew a fresh pot of coffee and volunteer to wrap
what's left of the flavorful, airy banana bread that comes at the start
of the meal but is best as dessert. There's also a bar with happy hour
4–7. ✉ *MM 81.9, OS,* ☎ *305/664–9865. AE, D, DC, MC, V.*

$–$$ ✕ **Manny & Isa's.** Fewer than a dozen tables are squeezed into the sim-
ple room, but forget the lack of ambience. Come for the always perfect Cuban and Spanish cuisine. The regular menu is split between
traditional Cuban dishes and local seafood, and there are several fish,
chicken, and pork chop specials, all served with salad and Cuban
bread. Succulent fish fingers served with black beans and rice will set
you back only $8.95. Manny's Key lime pies are legendary. On any
evening you can watch a parade of customers coming in to get them
takeout, and speaking of takeout, many people call ahead for meals
to go, to avoid lines on weekends and in high season. ✉ *MM 81.6,
OS, 81610 Old Hwy.,* ☎ *305/664–5019. AE, D, MC, V. Closed Tues.
and mid-Oct.–mid.-Nov.*

$–$$ ✕ **Old Tavernier Restaurant.** Eat indoors or step through the French
★ doors to eat outside on the balcony. In either location, the Italian specialties come out divine. The flavor of the supple and succulent fried

calamari appetizer is enhanced by herbs and spices. At $24.95, the lamb chops are one of the priciest items on the menu. That does not deter regulars, who often arrive early to put in their orders before the chops are sold out. ⊠ *MM 90.3, OS,* ☎ *305/852–6012. AE, MC, V.*

$ ✕ **Islamorada Fish Company.** When the sun starts to set, this very casual place is one of the prettiest spots in the Keys to have dinner. Small umbrella-covered tables and family-style, awning-covered picnic benches are arranged inches from the water, overlooking several islets and the calm waters of Florida Bay. At the fish market's dock, boats unload the fresh catch, which minutes later is served fried, grilled, blackened, or broiled by casually clad waitresses. The food is good, satisfying, and simple. There's wine, and the beer, sodas, and pink lemonade are served icy cold. ⊠ *MM 81.5, BS,* ☎ *305/664–9271. MC, V.*

$$$$ ⛫ **Cheeca Lodge.** This 27-acre, low-rise resort amid tranquil fish-filled lagoons and gardens on Upper Matecumbe Key is the leader in green activism. Biodegradable products are used, most things are recycled, Jet Skis and other noisemakers are banned, the golf course was reengineered to use less water, and Camp Cheeca makes learning about the environment fun. Rooms feature tropical colors, British colonial–style furniture, intriguing hand-painted mirror frames, and surreal artwork. Suites have kitchens and screened balconies; fourth-floor rooms in the main lodge have ocean or bay views. A new concessioner offers eco-tours and water excursions. ⊠ *MM 82, OS, Box 527, 33036,* ☎ *305/664–4651 or 800/327–2888,* 𝙵𝙰𝚇 *305/664–2893. 139 rooms, 64 suites. 2 restaurants, lounge, 2 pools, saltwater tidal pool, 9-hole golf course, 6 lighted tennis courts, boating, parasailing, fishing, children's programs, playground. AE, D, DC, MC, V.*

$$$$ ⛫ **The Moorings.** This one-time coconut plantation on 18 acres—still
★   free of cluttering "profit centers"—is one of the finest places to stay in the Keys. Tucked in a tropical forest, one-, two-, and three-bedroom cottages are furnished with wicker and artistic African fabrics and have pristine white kitchens. Peaked roofs rise behind French doors, lighting is soft, and there are many exquisite touches from thick towels to extra-deep cushiony bedcovers. The beach has 1,100 feet of sea frontage, a scattering of Adirondack chairs and hammocks, and a dock you can swim from (no Jet Skis allowed). A new waterfront café is called Morada Bay. ⊠ *MM 81.6, OS, 123 Beach Rd., 33036,* ☎ *305/664–4708,* 𝙵𝙰𝚇 *305/664–4242. 18 cottages. Pool, tennis court, beach, dock. MC, V.*

$$$–$$$$ ⛫ **Caloosa Cove.** Set back from the road and landscaped with native and tropical plants, this 10-acre ocean-side time-share resort on Lower Matecumbe Key feels like it's away from the world. Condominiums have the kitchen conveniences of home, two baths, and either one or two balconies, almost all of which have water views. Some suites have a den with sofa bed, and decor is fresh, crisp, and tropical. Also available are a wide sandy beach, 40-slip marina, bait and tackle shop, and barbecues. The best rooms are 126, 127, 226, and 227. Rentals are by the day, week, or month. ⊠ *MM 73.8, OS, 73801 Overseas Hwy., 33036,* ☎ *305/664–8811. 30 units. Restaurant, bar, pool, tennis, basketball, shuffleboard, beach, dock, bicycles, game room. MC, V.*

$$–$$$ ⛫ **Ragged Edge Resort.** Two-story buildings are covered with rustic planks at this grassy little ocean-side establishment, ¼ mi off U.S. 1. Rooms feature pine paneling, chintz, and a tile bath suite, and most have kitchens with irons. Most downstairs units have screened porches, whereas upper units have large decks, more windows, and beam ceilings. Though the place feels expensive, it's surprisingly affordable due to a lack of staff and extras (like in-room phones). Amenities take the form of a thatch-roof observation tower, picnic areas with barbecue

pits, and free coaster-brake bikes. There's not much of a beach, but you can swim off the dock—a virtual rookery when boats don't disturb the pelicans, herons, anhingas, and terns. ✉ *MM 86.5, OS, 243 Treasure Harbor Rd., 33036, ☎ 305/852–5389. 10 units. Pool, shuffleboard, dock, bicycles. MC, V.*

Nightlife

Holiday Isle Beach Resorts & Marina (✉ MM 84, OS, ☎ 305/664–2321) is the liveliest spot in the Upper Keys. Weekends, especially during spring break and holidays, the resort's three entertainment areas are mobbed, primarily with the under-30 set, whose IDs are carefully scrutinized. Live bands play everything from reggae to heavy metal. Back behind the larger-than-life mermaid is the Keys-easy, over-the-water cabana bar the **Lorelei** (✉ MM 82, BS, ☎ 305/664–4656). Live nightly sounds are mostly reggae and light rock.

Outdoor Activities and Sports

BIKING

Pete's Bike Shop (✉ MM 82.9, BS, ☎ 305/451–1910) rents adult, children's, and tandem bikes—single-speed bicycles with coaster brakes and multispeed mountain bikes. Helmets and locks are included in the price: $10 a day, $50 a week. Repairs are available.

BOATING

To experience the Keys as they were before the highway intruded, rent a houseboat from **Houseboat Vacations of the Florida Keys** (✉ MM 85.9, BS, 85944 Overseas Hwy., 33036, ☎ 305/664–4009), operated by the Florida Keys Sailing School. The 40- and 42-foot boats accommodate six people and come fully outfitted with safety equipment and necessities—except food—as well as an AM/FM cassette stereo. You can rent by the day, with a two-day minimum; a week costs $860—$1,070. **Robbie's Boat Rentals & Charters** (✉ MM 77.5, BS, 77520 Overseas Hwy., 33036, ☎ 305/664–9814 or 305/664–4196) rents a 14-foot skiff with a 25-horsepower outboard (the smallest you can charter) for $25 an hour, $60 for four hours, and $80 for the day. Boats up to 27 feet are also available. Other than clothes and food, Pam and Pete Anderson of **Treasure Harbor Marine** (✉ MM 86.5, OS, 200 Treasure Harbor Dr., 33036, ☎ 305/852–2458 or 800/352–2628, FAX 305/852–5743) provide everything you'll need for a vacation at sea—linens, safety gear, and, best of all, advice on where to find the best beaches, marinas, and lobster sites. Bareboat or crewed, boats include a 19-foot Cape Dory, 41-foot custom-built ketch, 35-foot Mainship, and 35-foot Chenhwa trawler, as well as Morgans, Watkins, and Hunters. Most business is repeat customers. Marina facilities are basic—water and electric—and dockage is only $1 a foot.

FISHING

The 65-foot deluxe party boat *Gulf Lady* (✉ Bud 'n' Mary's Marina, MM 79.8, OS, ☎ 305/664–2628 or 305/664–2451) operates full-day and night fishing trips. Party boats can be crowded, so call about loads in advance. For almost 40 years, Captain Ken Knudsen of the *Hubba Hubba* (✉ Bud 'n' Mary's Marina, MM 79.8, OS, ☎ 305/664–9281) has fished the waters around Islamorada, first taking out guests at his family's hotel when he was 12, later as a licensed backcountry guide. His expertise earned him ranking as one of the top 10 guides in Florida by national fishing magazines, and he fishes what he knows best: bonefish, permit, and tarpon. Unlike most guides, he offers four-hour sunset trips for tarpon ($275) and sunrise trips for bonefish ($175), as well as half- ($250) and full-day ($350) outings. Prices are for two anglers, $50 extra for a third. Tackle and bait are included. On *Tag 'Em* (✉ Holiday Isle Marina, MM 84, OS, ☎ 305/852–8797 or 305/664–2321 ext. 642), Captain John Magursky runs one of the best charters in the Keys. The crew is refreshingly knowledgeable, clean, friendly, and hardworking, whether they're doing light tackle and fly-fishing or going after deep-sea game fish like dolphin, sailfish, tuna, or marlin. The 40-foot vessel has a four-chair cockpit and well-maintained custom tackle. For off-shore and reef fishing, half- and full-day trips ($400 and $600, respectively, for four anglers) include everything but food and beverages.

SCUBA DIVING AND SNORKELING

About a mile off the western tip of Indian Key, the **San Pedro Underwater Archaeological Preserve** (⊠ MM 78.5, OS, ☎ 305/664–4815) is a 90-foot by 30-foot underwater park in 18 feet of water. A sand pocket surrounded by turtle grass and coral heads is home to the *San Pedro,* part of a Spanish treasure fleet wrecked by a hurricane in 1733. After salvage efforts left very little other than a pile of ballast stones intact, seven cannon replicas, an anchor, and a plaque were added for interest. You can get here only by boat; buoys allow you to tie up without damaging the site. For more information, contact Long Key State Recreation Area (☞ Long Key, *below*).

Florida Keys Dive Center (⊠ MM 90.5, OS, Box 391, Tavernier 33070, ☎ 305/852–4599 or 800/433–8946) organizes dives from John Pennekamp Coral Reef State Park to Alligator Light. The center has two Coast Guard–approved dive boats, offers scuba training, and is one of few Keys dive centers to offer Nitrox, mixed gas, diving. At **Holiday Isle Dive Center** (⊠ MM 84, OS, 84001 Overseas Hwy., 33036, ☎ 305/664–4145), you can benefit from the experienced crew of the *Captain Scuba.* Instructor Mari Magursky, recent PADI Award of Excellence recipient, offers all levels of PADI and NAUI certification, from basic open water to assistant instructor. Departing at 9 and 1, trips take in two dive sites along 14 mi between Conch and Alligator reefs as well as the wreck of the *Eagle.* The center also supports a full dive shop. For more than 15 years, **Lady Cyana Divers** (⊠ MM 85.9, BS, Box 1157, 33036, ☎ 305/664–8717 or 800/221–8717), a PADI five-star training resort, has operated dives on deep and shallow wrecks and reefs between Molasses and Alligator reefs. The 40-, 45-, and 50-foot boats provide everything a diver needs, including full bathrooms.

TENNIS

The four clay and two hard courts at **Islamorada Tennis Club** (⊠ MM 76.8, BS, ☎ 305/664–5340) are busiest December–March, and reservations are essential to play between 9 and 11. It's popular partly because it's cheap ($7 an hour) and partly because it's well run. Amenities include tension stringing, ball machines, private lessons, a pro shop, night games, and partner pairing.

Shopping

Two Miami teachers knocked down walls, added a coffee bar, and turned the once tiny **Cover to Cover Books** (⊠ MM 90.1, OS, 90130 Old Hwy., ☎ 305/852–1415, FAX 305/852–1650) into one of the best bookstores in the Keys. They also sell gifts and jewelry and hold book signings and readings for kids. There is an extensive selection of books, cards, and maps on Florida and the Keys. **H. T. Chittum & Co.** (⊠ MM 82.7, OS, ☎ 305/664–4421) carries informal clothing from Timberland and Nautica, specialty knives, and smart ready-to-wear. There are branches in Marathon (⊠ MM 48.5, OS, ☎ 305/743–4171) and Key West (⊠ 725 Duval St., ☎ 305/292–9002). At **Island Silver & Spice** (⊠ MM 82, OS, ☎ 305/664–2714), the first floor is devoted to women's and men's resort wear, a large jewelry section with high-end Swiss watches and marine-theme jewelry, tropical housewares, cards, and toys and games. Climb the wooden stairway to the second floor to browse through tropical bedding and bath goods and a sale section.

A 20-year-old crafts village set in a tropical garden of native plants and orchids, **Rain Barrel** (⊠ MM 86.7, BS, ☎ 305/852–3084) represents works by numerous local and national artists and has eight resident artists in separate studios. On the third weekend in March, the largest arts show in the Keys takes place here; some 20,000 visitors view the work of 100 artists and listen to live jazz. Some of the country's best outdoor artists—Kendall Van Sant, Chet Reneson, Millard Wells, and Don Ray among them—are represented at the **Redbone Gallery** (⊠ MM 81, OS, 200 Industrial Dr., ☎ 305/664–2002 or 800/999–7332). The gallery is closed weekends. At **Treasure Village** (⊠ MM 86.7, OS, 86729 Old Hwy., ☎ 305/852–0511), salvage master Art McKee ran McKee's Treasure Museum in the 1950s. An enormous fabricated lobster by artist Richard Blaes stands in front of the center, where a dozen crafts and specialty shops plus the excellent little Made to Order eat-in and carryout restaurant operate. George Hommell Jr., who's served as fishing guide to President George Bush, General Norman Schwarzkopf, and numerous celebrities, opened **World Wide Sportsman** (⊠ MM 81.5, BS, ☎ 305/664–4615) in 1967. Though he has since sold it, he continues to manage the new two-level center, which sells everything a marine angler could want. In addition, it has a women's department, small gourmet food section, and 60-slip marina and hosts fishing seminars and tournaments.

Long Key

❺ *MM 70–65.5.*

This island is best known for the **Long Key State Recreation Area.** On the main, ocean side, the Golden Orb Trail leads onto a boardwalk through a mangrove swamp alongside a lagoon, where herons and other waterbirds congregate in winter. The park also has a campground, picnic area, rest rooms and showers, a canoe trail through a tidal lagoon, and a not-very-sandy beach fronting a broad expanse of shallow grass flats. Bring a mask and snorkel to observe the marine life in this rich nursery area. Across the road, near a historical marker partially obscured by foliage, is the **Layton Nature Trail** (⊠ MM 67.7, BS), named after Del Layton, who incorporated the city of Layton in 1963 and served as its mayor. The clearly marked trail, which takes 20–30 minutes to walk, leads through tropical hardwood forest to a rocky Florida Bay shoreline overlooking shallow grass flats. A marker relates the history of the Long Key Viaduct, the first major bridge on the rail line, and the exclusive Long Key Fishing Camp, which Henry Flagler established nearby in 1906 and which attracted famous and wealthy sportsmen. Zane Grey, the noted western novelist and conservationist, was its first president. (He had a cottage at MM 68.) The camp was washed away in the 1935 hurricane and never rebuilt. For Grey's efforts, the creek running near the recreation area was named for him. ⊠ *MM 67.5, OS, Box 776, 33001,* ☎ *305/664–4815.* ⊠ *$2 for 1 person, $4 per vehicle for 2–8 people plus 50¢ per person county surcharge; canoe rental $2.14 per hour; Layton Nature Trail free.* ⊙ *Daily 8–sunset.*

Dining and Lodging

$ ✕ **Little Italy.** The hearty Italian and seafood dishes here are a great value. Lunches like fried fish fingers, snapper amandine, baked grouper, lasagna, and a 21-shrimp basket run $4.50–$6.95 including salad, french fries, and bread. Dinner selections are equally tasty and well priced—chicken, seafood, veal, and steak for $8.50–$13.95. Don't miss the rich, dreamy hot chocolate pecan pie. A children's menu is available. ⊠ *MM 68.5, BS,* ☎ *305/664–4472. AE, D, MC, V.*

$$–$$$ 🏨 **Lime Tree Bay Resort Motel.** This popular 2½-acre hideaway has attractive wicker- and rattan-furnished guest rooms, tropical art, and cottages with kitchens. A boat-rental hut, little beach, nice landscaping, beautiful pool deck, hammocks, a gazebo, and covered walkway complete the look. The best units are the cottages out back (no bay views) and four deluxe rooms upstairs, which have cathedral ceilings and skylights. The upstairs Tree House, the best bet for two couples traveling together, has a palm tree growing through its private deck and a divine canvas sling chair. You can swim and snorkel in the shallow grass flats offshore. ⊠ *MM 68.5, BS, Box 839, Layton 33001,* ☎ *305/664–4740 or 800/723–4519,* ☏ *305/664–0750. 29 rooms. Restaurant, picnic area, pool, hot tub, tennis court, horseshoes, shuffleboard, beach, boating. AE, D, DC, MC, V.*

Outdoor Activities and Sports
BOATING AND FISHING

Captain Kevin (⊠ MM 68.5, BS, ☎ 305/664–0750) arranges for backcountry fishing guides and operates recreational watercraft from Lime Tree Bay Resort.

En Route   As you cross Long Key Channel, look beside you at the old **Long Key Viaduct.** The second-longest bridge on the former rail line, this 2-milong structure has 222 reinforced-concrete arches.

THE MIDDLE KEYS

Stretching from Conch Key to the far side of the Seven-Mile Bridge, the Middle Keys contain U.S. 1's most impressive stretch, MM 65–40, bracketed by the Keys' two longest bridges—Long Key Bridge and Seven Mile Bridge, both historic landmarks. Activity centers on the town of Marathon, the Keys' third-largest metropolitan area.

Fishing and diving are the main attractions. There are 50 prime diving sites, including 25-foot-deep Sombrero Reef, marked by a 140-foot lighthouse. Should a diving accident occur, the Middle Keys are the safest place to be, since the Keys' only hyperbaric recompression chamber is based here. In both bay and ocean, the deep-water fishing is superb at places like the Marathon West Hump, whose depth ranges from 500 to more than 1,000 feet. Anglers successfully fish from a half-dozen bridges, including Long Key Bridge, the old Seven Mile Bridge, and both ends of Toms Harbor.

There are many beaches and natural areas in the Middle Keys, including the northern end of the Great White Heron National Wildlife Refuge (☞ Big Pine Key *in* the Lower Keys, *below*), which starts just northwest of Marathon.

Conch and Duck Keys

❻ *MM 63–61.*

This stretch of islands is rustic. Fishing dominates the economy, and many residents are descendants of immigrants from the mainland South. Across a causeway from Conch Key, a tiny fishing and retirement village, lies Duck Key, an upscale community and resort.

In case you want to see the world.

At American Express, we're here to make your journey a smooth one. So we have over 1,700 travel service locations in over 120 countries ready to help. What else would you expect from the world's largest travel agency?

do more®

Travel

In case you want to be welcomed there.

We're here to see that you're always welcomed at establishments everywhere. That's why millions of people carry the American Express® Card – for peace of mind, confidence, and security, around the world or just around the corner.

do more

Cards

In case you're running low.

We're here to help with more than 118,000 Express Cash locations around the world. In order to enroll, just call American Express before you start your vacation.

do more

Express Cash

And just in case.

We're here with American Express® Travelers Cheques and Cheques *for Two*.® They're the safest way to carry money on your vacation and the surest way to get a refund, practically anywhere, anytime.

Another way we help you...

do more ®

**Travelers
Cheques**

Dining and Lodging

$$ ✕ **Watersedge.** A collection of historic photos on the walls depicts the railroad era, the development of Duck Key, and many of the notables who have visited this eatery at the Hawk's Cay Resort. You can dine indoors or under the dockside canopy. Dinners include soup and a 40-item salad bar. Specialties range from homemade garlic bread, Swiss onion soup, Florida stone crab claws (in season), and steaks to mud pie and coffee ice-cream pie. ✉ *MM 61, OS, Duck Key,* ☎ *305/743–7000. AE, D, DC, MC, V. No lunch.*

$$$$ ⊞ **Hawk's Cay Resort.** Morris Lapidus, architect of Miami Beach's Fontainebleau Hilton, designed this rambling West Indies–style resort, which opened in 1959. Over the years it has entertained film stars and politicians, who come to relax and be pampered by a friendly, low-key staff. Decor features wicker, a sea-green-and-salmon color scheme, and contemporary artwork. Many rooms face the water, and two-bedroom marina villas are available. Guests can use a nearby golf course, take a dive trip, or swim in the smooth saltwater lagoon. Dolphin Discovery is a new interactive, in-the-water educational program. ✉ *MM 61, OS, 33050,* ☎ *305/743–7000 or 800/432–2242,* ℻ *305/743–5215. 160 rooms, 16 suites, 22 villas. 4 restaurants, 2 lounges, pool, 8 tennis courts, health club, boating, fishing, video games, children's programs. AE, D, DC, MC, V.*

$$$–$$$$ ⊞ **Conch Key Cottages.** This happy hideout on its own island slightly larger than a tot's sandbox and bridged by a pebbly causeway has a castaway, live-and-let-live mood. Allamanda, bougainvillea, and hibiscus jiggle colorfully, and the beach curves around a mangrove-edged cove. Lattice-trimmed cottages with kitchens, some with two bedrooms, rise up on pilings, old-fashioned in Dade County pine. Cool tile floors, hammocks, and furnishings of reed, rattan, and wicker create an island look. Three cottages face the beach. Though not on the water, the small honeymoon cottage is very charming. If you need a coffee fix, bring your own to prepare, as the closest source is 1½ mi away. At night, highway noise can be distracting. ✉ *MM 62.3, OS, R.R. 1, Box 424, Marathon 33050,* ☎ *305/289–1377 or 800/330–1577,* ℻ *305/743–8207. 12 units. Pool, beach. D, MC, V.*

Grassy Key

❼ *MM 60–57.*

Local lore has it that this sleepy little key was named not for its vegetation—mostly native trees and shrubs—but for an early settler. It's primarily inhabited by a few families who operate small fishing camps and motels.

A 35-foot-long concrete sculpture of the dolphin Theresa and her offspring Nat stands outside the **Dolphin Research Center,** the former home of Milton Santini, creator of the original *Flipper* movie. It's now home to a colony of about 15 dolphins. A not-for-profit organization offers a half-day program called Dolph*Insight*, which teaches dolphin biology and human–dolphin communications and allows you to touch the dolphins out of the water. A 2½-hour instruction-education program aptly called Dolphin Encounter enables you to do just that for 20 minutes. ✉ *MM 59, BS, Box 522875, Marathon Shores 33052,* ☎ *305/289–1121.* ▧ *$9.50, DolphInsight $75, Dolphin Encounter $90.* ☼ *Daily 9–4. Walking tours Wed.–Sun. 10, 11, 12:30, 2, and 3:30. Children 5–12 must swim with accompanying, paying adult. Reserve for Dolphin Encounter after 1st day of any month for next month (for example, Mar. 1 for Apr.).*

Dining

$ ✕ **Grassy Key Dairy Bar.** Tables, counters, and even white shirts in the kitchen are now found at this ever-improving little landmark that dates from 1959. It's marked by Dairy Queen–style concrete ice-cream cones near the road. Locals and construction workers stop here for quick lunches. Owner-chefs George and Johnny Eigner are proud of their fresh-daily homemade bread, soups and chowders, and fresh seafood and fresh-cut beef. ⊠ *MM 58.5, OS,* ☎ *305/743–3816. No credit cards. Closed Sun. and Mon. No lunch Sat.*

En Route   Driving along the next string of narrow keys, you'll see little but mangroves until you reach Key Colony Beach, a booming upscale development. These keys are breeding and nesting grounds for the now-protected loggerhead and green hawksbill turtles, once harvested for their shells and for soup.

Marathon

❽   *MM 53–47.5.*

This laid-back community is the commercial hub of the Middle Keys. It's on Vaca Key, or Key Vaca, which gets its name from the Spanish word *vaca* (cow), probably because manatees (a.k.a. sea cows) were abundant in these waters in the 18th century.

Commercial fishing—still a big local industry—began here in the early 1800s. Pirates, salvers, fishermen, spongers, and later farmers eked out a living, traveling by boat between islands. About half the population were blacks, who burned charcoal for a living. According to local lore, Marathon was renamed after a 1906 hurricane, when a worker commented that it was a marathon task to rebuild the railway across the 6-mi island.

The railroad brought businesses and a hotel, and today Marathon is a bustling town by Keys standards, thanks to an airport, seven resorts of 60 or more rooms, a concert series that brings national talent, and a golf course. Yet the town remains laid-back. Fishing, diving, and boating are the primary attractions, and the rocky and mangrove-fringed shoreline has plenty of natural appeal.

★   The small **Museums of Crane Point Hammock**—part of a 63-acre tract that includes the last known undisturbed thatch-palm hammock—is owned by the Florida Keys Land Trust, a private, nonprofit conservation group. In the **Museum of Natural History of the Florida Keys,** behind a stunning bronze-and-copper door crafted by Roy Butler of Plantation, are a few dioramas, a shell exhibit, and displays on Keys geology, wildlife, and cultural history. Also here is the **Florida Keys Children's Museum,** which has iguanas, fish, and a pirate dress-up room. Outside, on the 1-mi indigenous loop trail, you can visit the remnants of a Bahamian village, site of the restored **George Adderly House,** the oldest surviving example of Conch-style architecture outside Key West. From November to Easter, docent-led tours, included in the price, are available; bring good walking shoes and bug repellent. ⊠ *MM 50.5, BS, 5550 Overseas Hwy., Box 536, 33050,* ☎ *305/743–9100.* ☜ *$7.50.* ☉ *Mon.–Sat. 9–5, Sun. noon–5; tours weekdays 10, 11, 1:30, 2:30 (call to confirm).*

OFF THE   **PIGEON KEY –** This small patch of land under the Seven Mile Bridge was
BEATEN PATH   once the site of a railroad work camp and, later, of a bar and restaurant, a park, and government administration building. In 1993 the nonprofit Pigeon Key Foundation leased this National Historic District from

Monroe County and started developing it as a center focusing on Florida Keys culture. Its first project was the restoration of the old railroad work-camp buildings, the earliest of which dates from 1908. A museum recalling the history of the railroad and the Keys is taking shape, too. A 28-minute video chronicles the life and projects of railroad baron Henry M. Flagler. To reach the island, you can either take the shuttle, which departs from the depot on Knight's Key (⊠ MM 47), or walk across a 2-mi stretch of the Old Seven Mile Bridge. Families bring picnics and stay the day. ⊠ MM 45, OS, Box 500130, Pigeon Key 33050, ☎ 305/289–0025, FAX 305/289–1065. ☞ $2; shuttle and admission, $4. ☉ Shuttle Tues.–Sun. 10–5.

Beach

Sombrero Beach has separate areas for swimmers, jet boats, and windsurfers, as well as a grassy park with barbecue grills, picnic kiosks, showers, rest rooms, a baseball diamond, large playground, and volleyball court. The park is accessible for travelers with disabilities. Turn left at the traffic light in Marathon, and follow signs to the end. ⊠ MM 50, OS, Sombrero Rd., ☎ 305/295–4385 or 888/227–8136. ☞ Free. ☉ Daily 8–sunset.

Dining and Lodging

$$ ✕ **Kelsey's.** This eatery at the Faro Blanco Marine Resort is hung with boat paddles inscribed by charter-boat captains and other frequent diners. Entrées are served with fresh-toasted baguettes prepared here daily. You can bring your own cleaned and filleted catch for the chef to prepare. Desserts may include banana pecan pie, white-chocolate mousse, macadamia pie, and Key lime cheesecake. ⊠ MM 48.5, BS, ☎ 305/743–9018. AE, D, MC, V. Closed Mon. No lunch.

$ ✕ **Herbie's.** A local favorite for lunch and dinner since the 1940s, Herbie's has three small rooms, including a screened outdoor room, with two counters. Specialties include spicy conch chowder with chunks of tomato and crisp conch fritters with homemade horseradish sauce. ⊠ MM 50.5, BS, ☎ 305/743–6373. No credit cards. Closed Sun. and 1 month in fall (usually Sept.).

$ ✕ **7 Mile Grill.** The walls of this open-air diner built in 1954 at the
★ Marathon end of Seven Mile Bridge are lined with beer cans, mounted fish, sponges, and signs describing individual menu items. The prompt, friendly service rivals the great food at breakfast, lunch, and dinner. Favorites include fresh-squeezed orange juice, a cauliflower and broccoli omelet, conch chowder, fresh fish sandwiches, and foot-long chili dogs. Don't pass up the authentic Key lime pie or, for a change, the peanut-butter pie, served near frozen in a chocolaty shell. ⊠ MM 47, BS, ☎ 305/743–4481. No credit cards. Closed Wed., Thurs., and at owner's discretion Aug.–Sept.

$$–$$$$ 🏨 **Banana Bay Resort & Marina.** Situated among fruit trees and other native and tropical plants—including bananas, of course—this 10-acre resort is ideal for active vacationers. It has the largest freshwater pool in the Keys, a marina with boat ramp, and Adirondack-style chairs on a wide sandy beach, and arrangements can be made for fishing, sailing, and diving. The crowd is a mix of vacationers, conventioneers, and marina guests. Rooms, decorated in a Caribbean plantation style, have either one king or two double beds and are loaded with amenities. Rates include Continental breakfast. ⊠ MM 49.5, BS, 4590 Overseas Hwy., 33050, ☎ 305/743–3500 or 800/226–2621, FAX 305/743–2670. 60 units. Pool, 2 tennis courts, exercise room, beach, dock. AE, D, DC, MC, V.

$$–$$$$ 🏨 **Faro Blanco Marine Resort.** One of the oldest resorts in the Keys, Faro Blanco has built up a loyal following of repeat guests, thanks to service that's first-rate without being fussy. The property stretches on both sides of the highway, and guest rooms, most with kitchens, are found in cottages; houseboats; three-bedroom, two-bath condominiums; and two lighthouse apartments, one of which sprawls over three floors. A full-service marina and marine repair shop meet boaters' needs, and diving and fishing charters can be arranged. Pets are allowed. ⊠ *MM 48.2, BS and OS, 1996 Overseas Hwy., 33050,* ☎ *305/743–9018 or 800/759–3276,* ℻ *305/743–2918. 86 units. 4 restaurants, pool, dock, boating, bicycles. AE, D, MC, V.*

$$–$$$ 🏨 **Coral Lagoon.** Surrounded by lush landscaping on a short, deep-water canal, these charming pastel-color duplex cottages each have a hammock on a private sundeck, a kitchen, and king or twin beds and a sofa bed. Units also have central air, ceiling fans, videocassette players ($1 tape rental), wall safes, and hair dryers, and you can take advantage of complimentary morning coffee, tennis rackets, fishing equipment, dockage, and barbecues. For a fee, you can also enjoy admission to a private beach club, charter fishing, and scuba and snorkel trips arranged through the Diving Site, a dive shop that also offers certification. Pets are accepted. ⊠ *MM 53.5, OS, 12399 Overseas Hwy., 33050,* ☎ *305/289–0121,* ℻ *305/289–0195. 18 units. Pool, tennis court, dive shop, dock, library. AE, D, MC, V.*

$–$$ 🏨 **Valhalla Beach Resort Motel.** People come back year after year to this unpretentious Crawl Key motel with the waterfront location of a posh resort. This year's guests will be treated to remodeled units with new tile floors. Other highlights are a sandy beach, lush palm trees that rustle in the wind, and plenty of peace and quiet. Bruce Schofield is the second-generation proprietor of this 1950s-era plain-Jane place. Clean and straightforward, with rattan and laminate furniture and fridges in the rooms, it's excellent for families because of the safe, shallow beaches. Barbecue grills get lots of use. Since it's far off the highway, there's no traffic noise, but take care not to miss the sign. ⊠ *MM 56.5, OS, Ocean Dr., Crawl Key, Rte. 2, Box 115, 33050,* ☎ *305/289–0616. 4 rooms, 8 efficiencies. Beach, dock. No credit cards.*

Outdoor Activities and Sports

BIKING

The Marathon area is popular with cyclists. Some of the best paths include those along Aviation Boulevard on the bay side of Marathon Airport, the four-lane section of the Overseas Highway through Marathon, Sadowski Causeway to Key Colony Beach, Sombrero Beach Road to the public beach, and the roads on Boot Key (⊠ Across a bridge on 20th St., OS). There's easy cycling at the south end of Marathon, where a 1-mi off-road path connects to the 2 mi of the Old Seven Mile Bridge that go to Pigeon Key.

Equipment Locker Sport & Cycle (⊠ MM 53, BS, ☎ 305/289–1670) rents cruisers and mountain bikes for adults and children.

BOATING

Captain Pip's (⊠ MM 47.5, BS, 1410 Overseas Hwy., 33050, ☎ 305/743–4403) rents 20-foot or larger motor-equipped boats.

FISHING

A pair of 65-footers, **Marathon Lady** and **Marathon Lady III** (⊠ MM 53, OS, at 117th St., 33050, ☎ 305/743–5580) go on half- and full-day fishing charters from the Vaca Cut Bridge, north of Marathon.

GOLF

Key Colony Beach Par 3 (⊠ MM 53.5, OS, 8th St., Key Colony Beach, ☎ 305/289–1533), a nine-hole course near Marathon, charges $6.50 for nine holes, $4.50 for each additional nine, $2 per person for club rental, and $1 for a pull cart. The beauty of this course is that there are no tee times and no rush. Play from 7:30 to dusk. A little golf shop meets basic golf needs.

SCUBA DIVING AND SNORKELING

Hall's Diving Center and Career Institute (⊠ MM 48.5, BS, 1994 Overseas Hwy., 33050, ☎ 305/743–5929 or 800/331–4255), next to Faro Blanco Resort, runs trips to Looe Key, Sombrero Reef, Delta Shoal, Content Key, Coffins Patch, and the 110-foot wreck *Thunderbolt*.

Shopping

The owner of **Enchanted Elephant Gift Shop & Museum** (⊠ MM 54, OS, Quay Shopping Village, ☎ 305/289–0646) has a thing for pachyderms. First she started collecting them (her collection is on display), then she started selling, and now she heads an elephant collectors' club. She also carries other nature-themed items, most under $50. **Food for Thought** (⊠ MM 51, BS, Gulfside Village, ☎ 305/743–3297) is a bookstore and natural-foods store with a good selection of Florida titles. **Martha's Caribbean Cupboard & Dangerous John Hubert's Hot Sauces & Cigars** (⊠ MM 54, OS, Quay Shopping Village, ☎ 305/743–9299 or 888/476–6566) is an adventure, partly due to the merchandise and partly due to its outgoing owner, John Hubert. One section holds colorful Caribbean-style kitchenware and arts and crafts; another has locally made and imported hot sauces, other condiments, and Keys and Caribbean cookbooks. A third section features cigars, imported from the Caribbean, Latin America, Europe, and, by special request, almost anyplace else.

En Route To cross the broad expanse of water separating the Middle and Lower keys, you'll travel over the **Seven Mile Bridge,** actually 6.79 mi long. Believed to be the world's longest segmental bridge, it has 39 expansion joints separating its cement sections. Each April, runners gather in Marathon for the annual Seven Mile Bridge Run. You can look across at what remains of the **Old Seven Mile Bridge,** an engineering marvel in its day that's now on the National Register of Historic Places. It rested on a record 546 concrete piers. No private cars are allowed on the bridge today, but locals like to ride bikes on it to watch the sunset and to reach Pigeon Key.

THE LOWER KEYS

In truth, the Lower Keys include Key West, but since it's covered in its own section and is as different from the rest of the Lower Keys as peanut butter is to jelly, this section comprises just the limestone keys between MM 37 and MM 9. From Bahia Honda Key south, islands are clustered, smaller, and more numerous, a result of ancient tidal waters flowing between the Florida Straits and the gulf. Here you're more likely to see birds and mangroves than other tourists; more refuges, beaches, and campgrounds than museums, restaurants, and hotels. Many of these keys are not traversed by the highway, nor are there many man-made structures. Instead there are pine trees and palm trees, abandoned homesteads and groves, left when the roadway was rerouted in 1938.

The islands are made up of two types of limestone, both more dense than the highly permeable Key Largo limestone of the Upper Keys. As a result, freshwater pools rather than percolates, forming watering holes that support Key deer, alligators, fish, snakes, Lower Keys rabbits, raccoons, migratory ducks, Key cotton and silver rice rats, pines, saw palmettos, silver palms, grasses, and ferns. (Many of these animals and plants can be seen in the National Key Deer Refuge on Big Pine Key.)

Nature was generous with her beauty in the Lower Keys. They're home to both Looe Key National Marine Sanctuary, arguably the most beautiful coral reef tract in the Keys, and Bahia Honda State Park, considered by many one of the best beaches in the world.

Bahia Honda Key

9   *MM 38–36.*

Bahia Honda translates from Spanish as "deep bay," a good description of local waters. The government owns most of the island, which is devoted to 524-acre **Bahia Honda State Park.** The Silver Palm Trail leads through a dense tropical forest where you can see rare West Indian plants, including the Geiger tree, sea lavender, Key spider lily, bay cedar, thatch and silver palms, and several species found nowhere else in the Keys: the West Indies yellow satinwood, Catesbaea, Jamaica morning glory, and wild dilly. The park also contains the Keys' only natural sandy beach of notable size. Even more unusual is that it extends on both gulf and ocean sides and has deep water close to shore. The park includes a campground, cabins, a snack bar, marina, and dive shop. You can get a panoramic view of the island from what's left of the railroad—the Bahia Honda Bridge. ⊠ *MM 37, OS, 36850 Overseas Hwy., 33043,* ☎ *305/872–2353.* ⌷ *$2 for 1 person, $4 per vehicle for 2–8 people plus 50¢ per person county surcharge; $2 per vehicle an hour before closing.* ☉ *Daily 8–sunset.*

Lodging

$$–$$$ 🏨 **Bahia Honda State Park.** Views from the six bay-front cabin units on stilts are spectacular. Each is completely furnished (no TV or radio); has two bedrooms, full kitchen, and bath; and sleeps eight. The best bet to reserve one is to call at 8 AM 60 calendar days before your planned visit. The park also has 80 campsites, suitable for motor homes and tents. ⊠ *MM 37, OS, 36850 Overseas Hwy., 33043,* ☎ *305/872–2353. 3 duplex cabins. MC, V.*

Outdoor Activities and Sports

Bahia Honda Dive Shop (⊠ MM 37, OS, ☎ 305/872–3210), the concessioner at Bahia Honda State Park, operates offshore-reef snorkel trips, scuba trips, and boat rentals. Two-hour snorkel trips ($22) leave daily at 10 and 2 (one trip at 1, October–November) and include an hour on the reef. Rental craft range from a 20-foot pontoon boat and 22-foot center console fishing/dive boat to kayaks. Sunset cruises depart daily, except October–November.

Big Pine Key

10   *MM 32–30.*

Known for its concentration of Key deer, this island is the site of the 2,300-acre **National Key Deer Refuge.** The sanctuary was established in 1954 to protect the dwindling population of Key deer, a subspecies of the Virginia white-tailed deer. These deer once ranged throughout the Lower and Middle keys, but hunting, habitat destruction, and a growing human population have caused their numbers to decline to 250–300. The best place to see Key deer in the refuge is along Key Deer Boulevard (Route 940), which leads onto No Name Key, a sparsely populated island just east of Big Pine Key. You can get out of your car to walk around, but close all doors and windows to keep raccoons from wandering in. Deer may turn up along the road at any time of day—especially in early morning and late afternoon. Admire their beauty, but feeding them is against the law. The **Blue Hole**, a sinkhole left over from railroad days, is the largest body of freshwater in the Keys. From the observation platform and walking trail, you might see alligators, birds, turtles, Key deer, and other wildlife. The well-marked trail in nearby **Watson's Hammock,** named after Jack Watson, an environmentalist and the refuge's first warden, is one of the most accessible places to see an unspoiled hardwood hammock and subtropical foliage. ⊠ *Headquarters, MM 30, BS,* ☎ *305/872–2239.* 🖼 *Free.* ☉ *Daily sunrise–sunset; headquarters weekdays 8–5.*

OFF THE
BEATEN PATH

GREAT WHITE HERON NATIONAL WILDLIFE REFUGE – Stretching from northwest of Marathon to Key West, the refuge encompasses small bayward islands known as the backcountry. The only real way to get here is by kayak, canoe, or shallow-draft boat, but it's worth the effort. Chances are you'll see a vast assortment of local and migratory birds—including some rare and endangered species—up close. ⊠ *Box 430510, 33043-0510,* ☎ *305/872-2239.*

Dining and Lodging

$ ✕ **Island Reef Restaurant.** Built in the Flagler era, this Keys-perfect cottage-style foodery has counter seats, tables covered with bright beneath-the-sea-blue prints, and outdoor tables—outdoor rest rooms, too. Nightly specials, which start at $10 and don't run much higher, come with soup or salad; potato; vegetable; rolls and scones; homemade pie, pudding, or ice cream; and tea or coffee. Entrées include seafood, steaks, veal, and Spanish dishes, such as paella. It's open for breakfast. ⊠ *MM 31.3, BS,* ☎ *305/872–2170. AE, D, MC, V.*

$$–$$$ 🖼 **The Barnacle.** This bed-and-breakfast is one of three under separate ownership within a mile of each other, all built on stilts. Tim and Jane Marquis, owners of a dive shop in Louisiana, bought the Barnacle and moved down to run it in 1995. There are two rooms in the main house, both on the second floor; one in a cottage; and another, below the house, that opens to the beach. Each has its own kitchen. Guest rooms are large, and those in the main house adjoin an atrium, where a hot tub sits in a beautiful garden overlooking sea and sky. Furnishings, collected from around the world, are colorful and whimsical. The stained-glass windows are very impressive. ⊠ *MM 33, OS, 1557 Long Beach Dr., 33043,* ☎ *305/872–3298. 4 rooms. Hot tub, beach, dock, boating, bicycles. MC, V.*

$$–$$$ 🖼 **Casa Grande.** Run by Kathleen Threlkeld, this oceanfront B&B next to the Barnacle has a white sandy beach along a rocky, shallow shoreline. It's markedly Mediterranean, with a massive Spanish door and mainly contemporary furnishings. Spacious guest rooms have color TVs, small refrigerators, air-conditioning, carpeting, and high open-beam ceilings with paddle fans. Here, too, there is a screened, second-story atrium facing the sea. Guests cozy up to the sitting room fireplace and get to know one another on cool nights. ⊠ *MM 33, OS, Long Beach Dr., Box 378, 33043,* ☎ *305/872–2878. 3 rooms. Hot tub, beach, dock, boating, bicycles. No credit cards.*

$$ 🖼 **Deer Run.** The most casual of the local B&Bs, this lodging is populated by lots of animals: cats, caged birds, and a herd of deer, which forages along the beach and lush seafront gardens. Like her fellow innkeepers, longtime Big Pine resident Sue Abbott is caring and informed, well settled, and hospitable. Two downstairs units (one with a sea view) occupy part of a onetime garage. The upstairs unit looks out on the sea through trees and mulched pathways. Guests have use of a living room, screened porch, hammocks, a grill, and water toys. Like its neighbors,

Deer Run is a great value. Smoking and children are not welcomed. ✉ *MM 33, OS, 1985 Long Beach Dr., Box 431, 33043,* ☎ *305/872–2015,* FAX *305/872–2842. 3 rooms. Hot tub, beach, bicycles. No credit cards.*

$-$$ ☆ **Big Pine Key Fishing Lodge.** At $88, the five lodge rooms at this fam-
★   ily-oriented lodge and campground are one of the Keys' best buys. They
feature tile floors, wicker furniture, louvered and screened windows,
doors that allow sea breezes to blow through, king beds, a second-bed-
room loft, vaulted ceilings, and half kitchens. A skywalk joins them
with the new pool and deck. Other units are either spic-and-span mobile homes or efficiencies. Immaculately clean white tile lines the spacious bathhouse for campers. Separate game and recreation rooms have
TVs, a bar, and other amusements, and there is dockage along a 735-
foot canal. A three-day minimum is required. ✉ *MM 33, OS, Box
430513, 33043,* ☎ *305/872–2351,* FAX *305/872–3868. 16 rooms,
158 campsites. Pool, dock, Ping-Pong, billiards, game room, recreation
room, video games. MC, V.*

Outdoor Activities and Sports

BIKING

A good 10 mi of paved and unpaved roads run from MM 30.3, BS,
along Wilder Road, across the bridge to No Name Key, and along Key
Deer Boulevard into the National Key Deer Refuge. You might see some
Key deer. Stay off the trails that lead into wetlands, where fat tires can
do damage.

In addition to selling and repairing bikes, **Big Pine Bicycle Center** (✉
MM 30, OS, ☎ 305/872–0130) rents old-fashioned single-speed, fat-
tired cruisers for adults and children. Helmets are included.

FISHING

Strike Zone Charters (✉ MM 29.5, BS, 29675 Overseas Hwy., 33043,
☎ 305/872–9863 or 800/654–9560), run by Captain Larry Threlkeld,
offers fishing charters on air-conditioned boats at $300 for a half day,
$500 for a full day. In addition, sightseeing trips can include time to
fish, as well as bait and tackle.

SCUBA DIVING

Containing reefs where the Keys' northern margin drops off into the
gulf, Great White Heron National Wildlife Refuge and the National
Key Deer Refuge attract fewer divers than the better-known Atlantic
reefs. A favorite gulf spot for local divers is the **Content Key** (✉ MM
30), 5 mi offshore.

Ramrod Key

⓫ *MM 27.*

Primarily a base for divers headed for Looe Key National Marine
Sanctuary, 5 mi away, the key derives its name from a ship that wrecked
on nearby reefs in the early 1800s. The undeveloped backcountry is
at your back door, making this an ideal location for fishing and kayaking, too. Nearby **Little Torch Key** provides accommodations.

Lodging

$$$$ ☆ **Little Palm Island.** The lobby sits blandly beside U.S. 1 on Little Torch
★   Key, but the resort dazzles 3 mi offshore on a palm-fringed island at
the western edge of the Newfound Harbor Keys. Close by the water,
14 thatch-roof villas on stilts each have two suites with Mexican-tile
baths, Jacuzzis, mosquito netting–draped beds, Mexican and Guatemalan
wicker and rattan furniture, minibars, and safes. A third-floor suite on
a houseboat adds to the mix. The only phone sits in a dolled-up former outhouse, and there's no TV. Instead, indulge in a fountain-fed

pool or some terrific snorkeling, diving, and fishing. In the middle of Coupon Bight State Aquatic Preserve, the island is the closest land to Looe Key. The food draws yachtfolk from all over, who tie up at the marina come dinnertime. ✉ *MM 28.5, OS, 28500 Overseas Hwy., Summerland Key 33042,* ☎ *305/872–2524 or 800/343–8567,* FAX *305/872–4843. 30 suites. Restaurant, bar, pool, sauna, exercise room, beach, fishing, boating. AE, D, DC, MC, V.*

$–$$$$ 🏨 **Parmer's Place.** Each holiday the Parmers send out 15,000 Christmas cards to former guests, many of whom return year after year to stay in the pastel-color, family-style waterfront cottages and rooms spread over 5 landscaped acres. Most rooms have a deck or balcony; all have cable and a full or half kitchen; and none have a telephone. While there is no beach swimming, docks, a large pool, and kayak and PWC rentals provide plenty of opportunities to enjoy the water. Complimentary Continental breakfast is served outside in a small garden. Guests may dine together or take trays back to their rooms. ✉ *MM 29, BS, 565 Barry Ave., Little Torch Key 33043,* ☎ *305/872–2157,* FAX *305/872–2014. 16 rooms, 12 suites, 10 efficiencies, 2 apartments. Pool, dock, jet skiing. AE, D, MC, V.*

Outdoor Activities and Sports

FISHING

Scandia-Tomi (✉ MM 25, BS, Summerland Chevron Station, Summerland Key, ☎ 305/745–8633 or 800/257–0978), under Captain Bill Hjorth, takes up to six passengers on varied fishing trips.

SCUBA DIVING AND SNORKELING

Named for the H.M.S. *Looe,* a British warship wrecked in 1744, **Looe Key National Marine Sanctuary** (✉ MM 27.5, OS, 216 Ann St., Key West 33040, ☎ 305/292–0311) contains a 5.3-sq-nautical-mi reef 5 mi off Ramrod Key. Perhaps the most beautiful and diverse coral community in the region, it has large stands of elk-horn coral on its eastern margin, immense purple sea fans, and abundant populations of sponges and sea urchins. On its seaward side, it has an almost-vertical drop-off to depths of 50–90 feet. Both snorkelers and divers will find the sanctuary a quiet place to observe reef life, except in July, when the annual Underwater Music Festival pays homage to Looe Key's beauty and promotes reef awareness with six hours of music broadcast via underwater speakers. Dive shops and private charters transport hundreds of divers to "hear" the spectacle, which includes Caribbean, classical, jazz, new age, and, of course, Jimmy Buffett.

Looe Key Dive Center (✉ MM 27.5, OS, Box 509, Summerland Key 33042, ☎ 305/872–2215 ext. 2 or 800/942–5397 ext. 2), the closest dive shop to Looe Key, offers two-day and overnight dive packages. It's part of the full-service Looe Key Reef Resort, which, not surprisingly, caters to divers. The dive boat, a 45-foot Corinthian catamaran, is docked within 100 feet of the hotel, whose guests have free use of tanks, weights, and snorkeling equipment. Captain Bill Hjorth of the ***Scandia-Tomi*** (✉ MM 25, BS, Summerland Chevron Station, Summerland Key 33042, ☎ 305/745–8633 or 800/257–0978) takes divers and snorkelers to Looe Key. **Strike Zone Charters** (✉ MM 29.5, BS, 29675 Overseas Hwy., Big Pine Key 33043, ☎ 305/872–9863 or 800/654–9560) offers regular trips to two sites on Looe Key.

En Route   The huge object that looks like a white whale floating over Cudjoe Key (MM 23–21) is not a figment of your imagination. It's Fat Albert, a radar balloon that monitors local air and water traffic.

Sugarloaf Key

⑫ *MM 20–17.*

This key has a history of failed enterprises. In the early 1900s, Chase, Florida, was a thriving sponging community of whites and blacks. However, due to lack of funds and the outbreak of World War I, the industry collapsed, and little remains of the town. The land was next sold to R. C. Perky, who renamed the town Perky. His three ventures—revival of the sponge business, operation of a luxury resort, and eradication of mosquitoes—all failed. Plagued by mosquitoes, Perky erected a 35-foot tower and imported hundreds of bats. The bats flew away, but the mosquitoes remained. Today the **bat tower** (⊠ *MM 17*), sometimes called Perky's folly, is a historic landmark.

Dining

$$ ✕ **Mangrove Mama's.** This rambling open-air, lattice-front Conch structure, a remnant from 1919, has a wooden deck out back, furnished with plastic tables and chairs amid palms and banana plants. Along with some unlikely dishes like a vegetarian dinner plate and steamed brown rice, the fare includes fresh fish, seafood, some decent beers, and rave-worthy Key lime pie. Concrete floors, Keys art, a Tennessee oak bar, and lights twinkling in the banana trees at night contribute to a tropical ambience. The bar is popular with locals, and music is loud, perhaps to cover the road noise. Avoid the fish tempura; it's heavy and greasy. ⊠ *MM 20, BS,* ☎ *305/745–3030. MC, V.*

$$ ✕ **Raimondo's Club 800.** Mussels are delicately steamed in a pesto broth for the hot *cozze alla Genovese* appetizer. For a light meal, try a large salad: *tricolore* salad with arugula, endive, and radicchio or *insalata francesca*, in which tangy gorgonzola accents sun-dried tomatoes, artichoke hearts, and greens. A juicy rack of lamb has more than a hint of rosemary, and fresh local snapper is the heart of *dentice livornese* (covered in capers, black olives, and fresh tomatoes). ⊠ *MM 21, OS, 457 Drost Dr., Cudjoe Key,* ☎ *305/745–9999. AE, D, MC, V.*

Outdoor Activities and Sports

BIKING

Here are miles of roads with little traffic. Routes 939 and 939A leave the Overseas Highway on the ocean side at MM 20 (Mangrove Mama's) and loop back at MM 17 (Sugar Loaf Lodge). Peaceful Old State Road 4A is lined with mangroves and provides views of the opalescent Atlantic. The road crosses a small channel onto Upper Sugarloaf Key and dead-ends at Sugarloaf Boulevard.

KEY WEST

MM 4–0.

In April 1982 the U.S. Border Patrol threw a roadblock across the Overseas Highway just south of Florida City to catch drug runners and illegal aliens. Traffic backed up for miles as Border Patrol agents searched vehicles and demanded that the occupants prove U.S. citizenship. City officials in Key West, outraged at being treated like foreigners by the federal government, staged a mock secession and formed their own "nation," the so-called Conch Republic. They hoisted a flag and distributed mock border passes, visas, and Conch currency. The embarrassed Border Patrol dismantled its roadblock, and now an annual festival recalls the secessionists' victory.

The episode exemplifies Key West's odd station in Florida affairs. Situated 150 mi from Miami and just 90 mi from Havana, this tropical island city has always maintained its strong sense of detachment, even after it was connected to the rest of the United States—by the railroad in 1912 and by the Overseas Highway in 1938.

The U.S. government acquired Key West from Spain in 1821 along with the rest of Florida. The Spanish had named the island Cayo Hueso (Bone Key) after the Native American skeletons they found on its shores. In 1823 Uncle Sam sent Commodore David S. Porter to chase pirates away.

For three decades, the primary industry in Key West was "wrecking"—rescuing people and salvaging cargo from ships that foundered on the nearby reefs. According to some reports, when pickings were lean, the wreckers hung out lights to lure ships aground. Their business declined after 1849, when the federal government began building lighthouses.

In 1845 the army started construction of Fort Taylor, which held Key West for the Union during the Civil War. After the war, an influx of Cuban dissidents unhappy with Spain's rule brought the cigar industry here. Fishing, shrimping, and sponge-gathering became important industries, and a pineapple-canning factory opened. Major military installations were established during the Spanish-American War and World War I. Through much of the 19th century and into the second decade of the 20th, Key West was Florida's wealthiest city in per-capita terms.

In 1929 the local economy began to unravel. Modern ships no longer needed to provision in Key West, cigar-making moved to Tampa, Hawaii dominated the pineapple industry, and the sponges succumbed to a blight. Then the Depression hit, and the military moved out. By 1934 half the population was on relief. The city defaulted on its bond payments, and the Federal Emergency Relief Administration took over the city and county governments.

Federal officials began promoting Key West as a tourist destination. They attracted 40,000 visitors during the 1934–35 winter season. Then the 1935 Labor Day hurricane struck the Middle Keys, sparing Key West but wiping out the railroad and the tourist trade. For three years, until the Overseas Highway opened, the only way in and out of town was by boat.

Ever since, Key West's fortunes have waxed and waned with the vagaries of world affairs. An important naval center during World War II and the Korean conflict, the island remains a strategic listening post on the doorstep of Fidel Castro's Cuba. It was during the '60s that the fringes of society began moving here and in the mid-'70s that gay guest houses began opening in rapid succession. Whatever tension between gays and straights existed then, nearly none is apparent today.

Key West reflects a diverse population: native "Conchs" (white Key Westers, many of whom trace their ancestry to the Bahamas), fresh-water Conchs (longtime residents who migrated from somewhere else years ago), gays (who now make up at least 20% of Key West's citizenry), black Bahamians (descendants of those who worked the railroads and burned charcoal), Hispanics (primarily Cuban immigrants), recent refugees from the urban sprawl of Miami and Fort Lauderdale, transient navy and air force personnel, students waiting tables, and a miscellaneous assortment of vagabonds, drifters, and dropouts in search of refuge at the end of the road.

Whereas the rest of the Keys is more oriented to nature and the outdoors, Key West has more of a city feel. Few open spaces remain, as promoters continue to foster fine restaurants, galleries, shops, and museums to interpret the city's intriguing past. As a tourist destination, Key West has a lot to sell—superb frost-free weather with an average temperature of 79°F, quaint 19th-century architecture, and a laid-back lifestyle. There's also a growing calendar of artistic and cultural events and a lengthening list of annual festivals—including the Conch Republic Celebration in April, Hemingway Days in July, and a Halloween Fantasy Fest (big with gays and straights alike) that rivals the New Orleans Mardi Gras. Few cities of its size—a mere 2 mi by 4 mi—offer the joie de vivre of this one.

Yet as elsewhere when preservation has successfully revived once-tired towns, next have come those unmindful of style, eager for a buck. Duval Street is becoming show biz—an open-air mall of T-shirt shops and tour shills. Mass marketers directing the town's tourism have attracted cruise ships, which dwarf the town's skyline, and Duval Street floods with day-trippers who gawk at the earringed hippies with dogs in their bike baskets and the otherwise oddball lot of locals. You can still find fun, but the best advice is to come sooner rather than later.

Old Town

The heart of Key West, this historic area runs from White Street west to the waterfront. Beginning in 1822, wharves, warehouses, chandleries, ship-repair facilities, and eventually in 1891 the U.S. Customs House sprang up around the deep harbor to accommodate the navy's large ships and other sailing vessels. Wealthy wreckers, merchants, and sea captains built lavish houses near the bustling waterfront. A remarkable number of these fine Victorian and pre-Victorian structures have been restored to their original grandeur and now serve as homes, guest houses, and museums. These, along with the dwellings of famous writers, artists, and politicians who've come to Key West over the past 175 years, are among the area's approximately 3,000 historic structures. Old Town also has the city's finest restaurants and hotels, lively street life, and popular nightspots.

A Good Tour

To cover a lot of sights, take the Old Town Trolley, which lets you get off and reboard a later trolley, or the Conch Tour Train. Old Town is also very manageable on foot, bicycle, or moped, but be warned that the tour below covers a lot of ground. You'll want to either pick and choose from it or break it into two days. Or pick up a copy of one of several self-guided tours on the area.

Start at the **Southernmost Point** ⑬, on the corner of South and Whitehead streets. Continue north on Whitehead to **Hemingway House** ⑭, the author's former home, and then cross the street and climb to the top of the **Lighthouse Museum** ⑮ for a spectacular view. Follow Whitehead north to Angela Street and turn right. At Margaret Street, the **City Cemetery** ⑯ has above-ground vaults and unusual headstone inscriptions. Head north on Margaret to Southard Street, turn left, then right onto Simonton Street. Halfway up the block, Free School Lane is occupied by **Nancy Forrester's Secret Garden** ⑰. After touring this tropical haven, return west on Southard to Duval Street and turn right, where you can view the lovely tiles and woodwork in the **San Carlos Institute** ⑱ and then cross the street to admire the facade of the 1934 **Strand Theater** ⑲. Return again to Southard Street, turn right, and follow it through Truman Annex to **Ft. Zachary Taylor State Historic Site** ⑳; after viewing the fort, you can take a dip at the beach.

Head back to Simonton and Eaton streets, where you can admire the antiques in the circa 1860 **Donkey Milk House** ㉑. (A $15 ticket covers admission to four historic houses: Donkey Milk House, Audubon House, Heritage House Museum, and the Duval Street Wreckers Museum.) Then head north on Simonton and take a left on Caroline Street, where you can climb to the widow's walk on the top of **Curry Mansion** ㉒. A left on Duval Street puts you in front of the **Duval Street Wreckers Museum** ㉓, Key West's oldest house. **Heritage House Museum** ㉔ is just west of Duval on Caroline Street. Continue west into Truman Annex to see the **Harry S Truman Little White House Museum** ㉕, President Truman's vacation residence. Return east on Caroline, and turn left on Whitehead to visit the **Audubon House** ㉖, honoring the artist/naturalist. Follow Whitehead north to Greene Street, and turn left to see the salvaged sea treasures of the **Mel Fisher Maritime Heritage Society Museum** ㉗. At Whitehead's northern end is the **Key West Aquarium** ㉘. Then follow the crowds to Mallory Square, behind the aquarium, to watch Key West's nightly sunset spectacle. For dinner, head east on Caroline Street to **Key West Bight** ㉙, where there are numerous restaurants and bars.

TIMING

Allow two full days to see all the Old Town museums and homes, especially with a little shopping thrown in. For a narrated trip on the tour train or trolley, budget 1½ hours to ride the loop without getting off, an entire day if you plan to get off and on at some of the sights and restaurants.

Sights to See

㉖ **Audubon House and Gardens.** This three-story dwelling built in the mid-1840s commemorates ornithologist John James Audubon's 1832 visit to Key West. On display are several rooms of period antiques, a children's room, and a large collection of Audubon engravings. Admission includes an audiotape for the self-guided tour of the first floor (proceed on your own through the upper stories) and the tropical gardens, complemented by an informational booklet and signs that identify the rare indigenous plants and trees you'll see. ⊠ *205 Whitehead St.,* ☎ *305/294–2116.* 🎫 *$7.50.* ۞ *Daily 9:30–5.*

★ ⑯ **City Cemetery.** Clustered near a flagpole resembling a ship's mast are the graves of 22 sailors killed in the sinking of the battleship U.S.S. *Maine,* and there are interesting headstones to be found as well. Volunteers from the Historic Florida Keys Preservation Board lead 90-minute tours from the sexton's office. Brochures are available there, too. ⊠ *Margaret and Angela St.,* ☎ *305/292–6718.* 🎫 *Free, tour donation $5.* ۞ *Sunrise–6 PM, tours Tues. and Thurs. 9:30.*

㉒ **Curry Mansion.** This 22-room home built in 1899 for Milton Curry, the son of Florida's first millionaire, is an adaptation of a Parisian town house. It has Key West's only widow's walk open to the public. The owners have restored most of the house and turned it into a winning B&B. Take an unhurried self-guided tour; a brochure describes the home's history and contents. ⊠ *511 Caroline St.,* ☎ *305/294–5349.* 🎫 *$5.* ۞ *Daily 10–5.*

㉑ **Donkey Milk House.** This classic Key West revival house was built around 1866 by prominent businessman and U.S. marshal Peter "Dynamite" Williams, a hero of the great fire of 1886. Antiques and artifacts fill its two balconied floors. The house, with a veranda off every room, has won several restoration awards. ⊠ *613 Eaton St.,* ☎ *305/296–1866.* 🎫 *$5.* ۞ *Daily 10–5.*

㉓ **Duval Street Wreckers Museum.** Built in 1829 and alleged to be the oldest house in South Florida, the museum was originally home to Francis Watlington, a sea captain and wrecker. He was also a Florida state

Key West

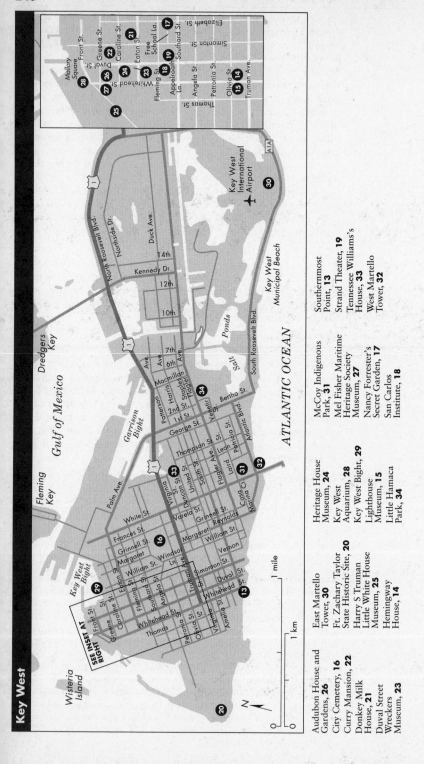

Audubon House and
Gardens, **26**
City Cemetery, **16**
Curry Mansion, **22**
Donkey Milk
House, **21**
Duval Street
Wreckers
Museum, **23**

East Martello
Tower, **30**
Ft. Zachary Taylor
State Historic Site, **20**
Harry S Truman
Little White House
Museum, **25**
Hemingway
House, **14**

Heritage House
Museum, **24**
Key West
Aquarium, **28**
Key West Bight, **29**
Lighthouse
Museum, **15**
Little Hamaca
Park, **34**

McCoy Indigenous
Park, **31**
Mel Fisher Maritime
Heritage Society
Museum, **27**
Nancy Forrester's
Secret Garden, **17**
San Carlos
Institute, **18**

Southernmost
Point, **13**
Strand Theater, **19**
Tennessee Williams's
House, **33**
West Martello
Tower, **32**

senator but resigned to serve in the Confederate navy during the Civil War. Six rooms are now open, furnished with 18th- and 19th-century antiques and providing exhibits on the wrecking industry of the 1800s. In an upstairs bedroom, an eight-room dollhouse of Conch design is outfitted with tiny early 19th-century furniture. ⊠ *322 Duval St.,* ☎ *305/294–9502.* ☞ *$4.* ☉ *Daily 10–4.*

⑳ Ft. Zachary Taylor State Historic Site. Built between 1845 and 1866, this fort served as a base for the Union blockade of Confederate shipping during the Civil War. (More than 1,500 Confederate vessels were detained in Key West's harbor.) Today it's a fort within a fort. A new moat suggests how the fort originally looked when it was surrounded by water, and a 30-minute tour is included in the admission price. Because of an artificial reef, snorkeling is excellent here, except when the wind blows south–southwest and muddies the water. ⊠ *End of Southard St., through Truman Annex,* ☎ *305/292–6713.* ☞ *$2.50 per person for first 2 people in vehicle plus 50¢ each additional up to 8, $1.50 per pedestrian or bicyclist.* ☉ *Daily 8–sunset, tours noon and 2.*

㉕ Harry S Truman Little White House Museum. On the grounds of **Truman Annex**, a 103-acre former military parade grounds and barracks, the home served as a winter White House for Presidents Truman, Eisenhower, and Kennedy. It has been restored to its post–World War II glory and contains displays of Truman family memorabilia as well as changing exhibits that range from circa-1951 Truman fashion to the Eisenhower Room's presidential photos. Part of the grounds have been converted into a Victorian-style commercial residential development. ⊠ *111 Front St.,* ☎ *305/294–9911.* ☞ *$7.* ☉ *Daily 9–5, grounds 8–sunset.*

★ ⑭ Hemingway House. Hemingway bought this house in 1931 and wrote about 70% of his life's work here, including *For Whom the Bell Tolls* and *The Old Man and the Sea.* It is now a museum dedicated to the novelist's life and work. Built in 1851, this two-story Spanish colonial dwelling was the first house in Key West to have running water and a fireplace. Three months after Hemingway died in 1961, local jeweler Bernice Dickson bought the house and two years later opened it as a museum. Of special interest are the huge bed with a headboard made from a 17th-century Spanish monastery gate, a ceramic cat by Pablo Picasso (a gift to Hemingway from the artist), the hand-blown Venetian glass chandelier in the dining room, and the pool. The museum staff gives guided tours rich with anecdotes about Hemingway and his family and feeds the more than 50 feline habitants, descendants of Hemingway's own 50 cats. Tours begin every 10 minutes and take 25–30 minutes; then you're free to explore on your own. ⊠ *907 Whitehead St.,* ☎ *305/294–1575.* ☞ *$6.50.* ☉ *Daily 9–5.*

㉔ Heritage House Museum. The former residence of Jessie Porter Newton, grand dame of Old Town preservation, this Caribbean-colonial house dates from the 1830s, when it was home to ship's captain George Carey. Among its original furnishings are antiques and seafaring artifacts from 19th-century China. Out back in beautiful gardens is a cottage that was often occupied by poet Robert Frost; here recordings of his poetry can be heard. ⊠ *410 Caroline St.,* ☎ *305/296–3573.* ☞ *$6.* ☉ *Mon.–Sat. 10–5, Sun. 1–5, last tour 4:30.*

☝ ㉘ Key West Aquarium. Hundreds of brightly colored tropical fish and other fascinating sea creatures from Key West waters make their home here. A touch tank enables you to handle starfish, sea cucumbers, horseshoe and hermit crabs, even horse and queen conchs—living totems of the Conch Republic. Built in 1934 by the Works Progress

Administration as the world's first open-air aquarium, the building has been enclosed for all-weather viewing, though an outdoor area with a small Atlantic shores exhibit, including red mangroves, remains. Guided tours include shark feedings. ⊠ *1 Whitehead St.,* ☎ *305/296–2051.* ⌨ *$7.* ☉ *Daily 10–6, tours 11, 1, 3, and 4:30.*

㉙ Key West Bight. Also known as Harbor Walk, this site was formerly the Singleton Shrimp Fleet and Ice & Fish House. It is the last funky area of Old Key West. In the area are numerous charter boats, classic old yachts, and the Waterfront Market.

⑮ Lighthouse Museum. Behind a spic-and-span white picket fence is this 92-foot lighthouse built in 1847 and an adjacent 1887 clapboard house, where the keeper lived. You can climb 88 steps to the top of the lighthouse for a glimpse of the sizable Fresnel lens, installed at a cost of $1 million in the 1860s; a spectacular view of the island town awaits you as well. On display in the keeper's quarters are vintage photographs, ship models, nautical charts, and lighthouse artifacts from all along the Key reefs. ⊠ *938 Whitehead St.,* ☎ *305/294–0012.* ⌨ *$5.* ☉ *Daily 9:30–5, last admission 4:30.*

㉗ Mel Fisher Maritime Heritage Society Museum. Gold and silver bars, coins, jewelry, and other artifacts recovered in 1985 from the Spanish treasure ships *Nuestra Señora de Atocha* and *Santa Margarita* are displayed here. The two galleons foundered in a hurricane in 1622 near the Marquesas Keys, 40 mi west of Key West. In the museum you can lift a gold bar weighing 6.3 Troy pounds and see a 77.76-carat natural emerald crystal worth almost $250,000. ⊠ *200 Greene St.,* ☎ *305/294–2633.* ⌨ *$6.50.* ☉ *Daily 9:30–5, last video 4:30.*

⑰ Nancy Forrester's Secret Garden. Nancy Forrester has devoted 25 years to creating one of the most beautiful tropical gardens in the world. Horticulturalists, botanists, and garden lovers come away smiling after winding their away under the canopy of rare palms and cycads; along trails lined with ferns, bromeliads, and bright gingers and heliconias; and past towering native gumbo-limbos strewn with hanging orchids and twining vines. Many brides and grooms have exchanged their vows here. The secret within this secret is a restored cottage with vintage hardware and furnishings, and an art gallery features botanical prints. ⊠ *1 Free School La.,* ☎ *305/294–0015.* ⌨ *$5.* ☉ *Daily 10–5, later in summer.*

⑱ San Carlos Institute. This Cuban-American heritage center houses a museum and research library focusing on the history of Key West and of 19th- and 20th-century Cuban exiles. The institute was founded in 1871 by Cuban immigrants. Cuban patriot Jose Martí delivered many famous speeches from the balcony of the auditorium, and opera star Enrico Caruso sang in the Opera House, which reportedly has the best acoustics of any concert hall in the South. On weekends you can watch the almost hour-long documentary *Nostalgia Cubano,* about Cuba from the 1930s to 1950s. ⊠ *516 Duval St.,* ☎ *305/294–3887.* ⌨ *$3.* ☉ *Tues.–Fri. 11–5, Sat. 11–9, Sun. 11–6.*

⑬ Southernmost Point. A huge concrete marker wrongly proclaims this spot to be the southernmost point in the United States. Most tourists snapping pictures of each other in front of the marker are oblivious to Key West's real southernmost point, on a nearby navy base off limits to civilians but visible through the fence to your right.

✋ ⑲ Strand Theater. Pause to admire the colorful marquee and ornamental facade of this edifice, built in 1918 by Cuban craftsmen. After a period as a movie theater and a music hall, the Strand is now the Odditorium, one of a chain of Ripley's Believe It or Not museums, displaying weird and eccentric artifacts. ⊠ *527 Duval St.,* ☎ *305/293–9686.* ☞ *$9.95.* ⊘ *Sun.–Thurs. 10–11, Fri. and Sat. 10–midnight.*

New Town

The area east of White Street to Cow Key Channel is called New Town, part of which was created with dredged fill. The island would have continued growing this way had the Army Corps of Engineers not determined in the early 1970s that it was detrimental to the reef. The Overseas Highway splits as it enters Key West. The southern fork becomes South Roosevelt Boulevard (Route A1A), whereas along the north shore, North Roosevelt Boulevard (U.S. 1) passes the Key West Welcome Center, new shopping centers, chain hotels, fast-food eateries, and Palm Avenue, which leads to Charter Boat Row, U.S. Navy facilities, and Old Town.

A Good Tour

The best way to take in New Town's sights is by car or moped. Take South Roosevelt Boulevard from the island's entrance, passing Houseboat Row—a community of unusual houseboats whose residents have included famous authors and artists—before stopping at **East Martello Tower** ㉚, near the airport. Continue past the Riggs Wildlife Refuge salt ponds, stop at Smathers Beach for a dip, and then go to the end of South Roosevelt Boulevard, which turns into Atlantic Boulevard. At White Street, there are three worthwhile stops: **McCoy Indigenous Park** ㉛, **West Martello Tower** ㉜, and Higgs Beach. Follow White north, and turn right on Duncan, stopping at **Tennessee Williams's House** ㉝. Turn right on Leon Street, left on Flagler, and right on Government Road for a picnic or stroll through **Little Hamaca Park** ㉞.

TIMING

Allow two to three hours for brief stops at each attraction. If your interest lies in art, gardens, or Civil War history, you'll need half a day. Throw in time at the beach, and you can make a full day of it.

Sights to See

★ ㉚ **East Martello Tower.** Relics of the U.S.S. *Maine* are housed here, as is a museum operated by the Key West Art and Historical Society. The collection includes Stanley Papio's "junk art" sculptures, Cuban folk artist Mario Sanchez's chiseled and painted wood carvings of historic Key West street scenes, memorabilia from movies shot in the Keys, a Cuban refugee raft, and books by many of the 60-some famous writers (including seven Pulitzer Prize winners) who have lived in Key West. Thematic exhibits present a history of the city and the Keys. A circular 48-step staircase in the central tower leads to a platform overlooking the airport and surrounding waters. ⊠ *3501 S. Roosevelt Blvd.,* ☎ *305/296–3913,* ℻ *305/296–6206.* ☞ *$5.* ⊘ *Daily 9:30–5, last admission 4.*

㉞ **Little Hamaca Park.** This area, a vestige of old Key West and for years a wildlife sanctuary, was saved from condo development in 1991 and turned into a park. A boardwalk leads into the natural area. Nearby are the salt ponds where early residents evaporated seawater to collect salt. (Even when the park is open, the gates aren't necessarily. Cyclists lift their bikes over.) ⊠ *Government Rd. off Flagler Ave.* ☞ *Free.* ⊘ *Daily 7–sunset.*

㉛ **McCoy Indigenous Park.** The park contains more than 100 species of trees and shrubs; the largest collection of native tropical plants in the Florida Keys, including many fruit-bearing trees; migrating songbirds spring and fall; and many species of colorful butterflies. ⊠ *Atlantic Blvd. and White St.,* ☎ *305/292–8157.* 🎦 *Free.* ☉ *Weekdays 7–4.*

㉝ Tennessee Williams's House. This modest two-story, red-shuttered Bahamian-style cottage behind a white picket fence was the playwright's home from 1949 until his death in 1983. After years of neglect, the house was purchased in 1992 and fixed up by a couple named Paradise. The house is not open to the public. ⊠ *1431 Duncan St.*

㉜ West Martello Tower. This fort was built in 1861 and used as a lookout during the Spanish-American War. Within its walls the Key West Garden Club maintains an art gallery and tropical garden. ⊠ *Atlantic Blvd. and White St.,* ☎ *305/294–3210.* 🎦 *Donations welcome.* ☉ *Wed.–Sun. 9:30–3:15.*

Beaches

Almost all of the beaches are man-made, with sand imported from the U.S. mainland or the Bahamas. Public beaches are open daily 7 AM–11 PM, and admission is free. Tip: If you go out swimming anywhere in the Keys, wear an old pair of tennis shoes to protect your feet against the coral strewn along the ocean floor.

Atlantic Shores Resort (⊠ 510 South St.) is a clothing optional area. **Dog Beach** (⊠ Vernon and Waddell Sts.) is the only beach in Key West where dogs are allowed. **Ft. Zachary Taylor State Historic Site** (⊠ End of Southard St.) has several hundred yards of beach near the western end of Key West, and an adjoining picnic area has barbecue grills in a stand of Australian pines. Snorkeling is good except when winds blow from the south–southwest. This beach is relatively uncrowded and attracts more locals than tourists; nude bathing is not allowed. A Monroe County park, **Higgs Memorial Beach** (⊠ Near end of White St.) is a popular sunbathing spot. A nearby grove of Australian pines provides shade, and the West Martello Tower provides shelter should a storm suddenly sweep in. **Simonton Street Beach** (⊠ North end of Simonton St.), facing the gulf, is a great place to watch boat traffic in the harbor. Parking, however, is difficult. **Smathers Beach** (⊠ S. Roosevelt Blvd.) features almost 2 mi of sand. Trucks along the road rent rafts, Windsurfers, and other beach "toys." On the Atlantic, **South Beach** (⊠ Foot of Duval St.), a.k.a. City Beach, is popular with tourists at nearby motels. It has limited parking and a nearby buffet-type restaurant, the South Beach Seafood and Raw Bar.

Dining

American

$$ ✕ **Pepe's Cafe and Steak House.** Judges, police officers, carpenters, and anglers rub elbows at breakfast in their habitual seats, at tables or dark pine booths under a jumbo paddle fan. Face the street or dine outdoors under a huge rubber tree if you're put off by the naked-lady art on the back wall. Pepe's was established downtown in 1909 (which makes it the oldest eating house in the Keys) and moved here in 1962. Specials change nightly: barbecued chicken, pork tenderloin, ribs, steak, fresh fish, potato salad, red or black beans, and corn bread on Sunday; meat loaf on Monday; seafood Tuesday and Wednesday; a traditional Thanksgiving every Thursday; prime rib on Saturday; and filet mignon daily. ⊠ *806 Caroline St.,* ☎ *305/294–7192. D, MC, V.*

$ ✕ **Sunset Pier Bar.** When the crowds get too thick on the Mallory Dock at sunset, you can thin your way out 200 feet offshore behind the Ocean Key House. A limited menu offers crispy conch fritters, potato salad, shrimp, and jumbo Hebrew National hot dogs. Live island music is featured nightly. If you prefer your sunsets with a dash of serenity, look elsewhere. ⊠ *0 Duval St.,* ☎ *305/296–7701. AE, D, DC, MC, V.*

Asian

$$ ✕ **Dim Sum.** In a sophisticated little Oriental kiosk in gardenlike Key
★ Lime Square, splendid Far Eastern cookery is notable for its variety if not its subtlety. Ask for dishes light on the sauces, and you'll enjoy the food as well as the captivating atmosphere. The intimate restaurant has a high-peak bamboo roof, bamboo dividers, batik covers under glass, and Oriental art. The culinary mix includes vegetarian dishes, noodles, Chinese sausage or shrimp, and Delights Exotica (sweet-and-sour grouper, cashew chicken, and roast duck stir-fried with lily flowers and black mushrooms). Korean dishes have been added, and the *Kalbi* (short ribs marinated in a Korean-style sauce) is becoming a favorite. There's a good selection of beer and wine. ⊠ *613½ Duval St. [rear],* ☎ *305/294–6230. AE, D, DC, MC, V.*

Cuban

$ ✕ **El Siboney.** This sprawling, three-room, family-style restaurant serves traditional Cuban food, including a well-seasoned black-bean soup. Specials include beef stew Monday, pepper steak Tuesday, chicken fricassee Wednesday, chicken and rice Friday, and oxtail stew on Saturday. Always available are roast pork, cassava, paella, and *palomilla* steak. Popular with locals, sí, but enough tourists pass through that you'll fit right in even if you have to ask what a "Siboney" is. (Answer: A Cuban Indian tribe.) ⊠ *900 Catherine St.,* ☎ *305/296–4184. No credit cards. Closed 2 wks in June.*

Floribbean

$$$ ✕ **Cafe Marquesa.** This intimate restaurant with attentive service and
★ superb food is a felicitous counterpart to the small Marquesa Hotel. It's a mellow place with bluesy ballads in the background and an open kitchen viewed through a trompe l'oeil pantry mural. Ten or so entrées are featured nightly, and all-star regional ingredients—mango relish with grilled boneless quail and veal and pork *boudin* sausage, coconut milk in the Caribbean shrimp chowder with sweet potatoes, and perhaps a little tropical fruit chutney with the grilled tamarind-glazed pork tenderloin. Some low-fat options are featured. Desserts are quite the contrary: a plum cardamom cake with fresh whipped cream, crème brûlée, and warm apple crisp with caramel sauce. There's also a fine selection of wines and a choice of microbrewery beers. ⊠ *600 Fleming St.,* ☎ *305/292–1244. AE, DC, MC, V. No lunch.*

$ ✕ **Blue Heaven.** The inspired remake of an old blue-on-blue clap-
★ board, Greek-revival house with peach and yellow trim was once a bordello where Hemingway refereed boxing matches and customers watched cockfights. There's still a rooster graveyard out back, as well as a water tower hauled here in the 1920s. Upstairs is an art gallery (check out the zebra-stripe bikes), and downstairs are affordable fresh eats, in both the house and big leafy yard. There are five nightly specials and a good mix of natural and West Indian foods. Top it off with Banana Heaven (banana bread, bananas flamed with spiced rum, and vanilla ice cream). Three meals are served six days a week; Sunday there's a to-die-for brunch and hammered-dulcimer music. Expect a line; everybody knows how good this is. ⊠ *729 Thomas St.,* ☎ *305/296–8666. Reservations not accepted. D, MC, V.*

International

$$$ ✕ **Louie's Backyard.** Key West paintings and pastels adorn this oceanfront institution, where you dine outside under the mahoe tree. Chef de cuisine Doug Shook shares Louie's limelight with lunch chef Annette Foley and sous chef Rich DesRoches. The changing menu might

include roasted rack of Australian lamb with huckleberry port, whipped sweet potatoes, and fried root vegetable strips; grouper with Thai peanut sauce; and stir-fried Asian vegetables. End with Louie's lime tart or the irresistible chocolate terrine Grand Marnier with crème anglaise. ⊠ *700 Waddell Ave.,* ☎ *305/294–1061. AE, DC, MC, V.*

Italian

$–$$ ✕ **Mangia Mangia.** Fresh homemade pasta comes alfredo, marinara,
★ meaty, or with pesto, either in the twinkly brick garden with its spec-imen palms or in the nicely dressed-up old-house dining room. One of the best restaurants in Key West—and one of its best values—Mangia Mangia is run by Elliot and Naomi Baron, ex–Chicago restaurateurs who found Key West's warmth and laid-back style irresistible. Every-thing that comes out of the open kitchen is outstanding, especially the pasta, made-on-the-premises Key lime pie, and Mississippi mud pie. The wine list with more than 350 selections, the largest in Monroe County, contains a good selection under $20. ⊠ *900 Southard St.,* ☎ *305/294–2469. AE, MC, V. No lunch.*

Seafood

$ ✕ **Half Shell Raw Bar.** "Eat It Raw" is the motto, and even off-season the oyster bar keeps shucking. You eat at shellacked picnic tables in an open-air building with life buoys, a mounted dolphin, and old li-cense plates overhead and a view of the deep-sea fishing fleet outside. Classic signs offer homage to Keys' passions. Reads one: FISHING IS NOT A MATTER OF LIFE AND DEATH. IT'S MORE IMPORTANT THAN THAT. Spe-cials, chalked on the blackboard, may include broiled dolphin sand-wich or linguine seafood marinara. Whatever it is, it's fresh. ⊠ *Land's End Marina, 231 Margaret St.,* ☎ *305/294–7496. D, MC, V.*

$ **Original Conch Fritters.** For $5 you can get six (a dozen for $9) of what may be the Keys' most authentic conch fritters at this strictly stand-up eatery, previously a Cuban snack stand from the '30s. Current owners flaunt their buttermilk and peanut oil recipe. Aficionados say it's the conch that counts. ⊠ *1 Whitehead St.,* ☎ *305/294–4849. No credit cards. Reservations not accepted.*

Tropical French

$$$ ✕ **Cafe des Artistes.** Dining at this intimate restaurant is so good that
★ guests in T-shirts and shorts don't even blanch at a $100 check for two. It was once part of a hotel building constructed in 1935 by C. E. Alfeld, Al Capone's bookkeeper. The look is studiously unhip with its rough stucco walls, old-fashioned lights, and a knotty-pine ceiling. Haitian paintings and Keys scenes by local artists dress the walls. You dine in two indoor rooms or on a rooftop deck beneath a sapodilla tree. Chef Andrew Berman presents a French interpretation of tropi-cal cuisine, using fresh local seafood and produce and light sauces. The wine list is strong on both French and California labels. ⊠ *1007 Si-monton St.,* ☎ *305/294–7100. AE, MC, V. No lunch.*

Lodging

Condo

$$$–$$$$ ▦ **Hyatt Sunset Harbor Resort.** You'd have to be on one of the big cruise ships to have a room any closer to the water; 80% of the balconied units overlook the lushly landscaped pool, deck, and Key West Har-bor. Bright tropical colors inside offset the white island-style exterior. Units come in one- and two-level suites with one or two bedrooms, all of which can be joined to form larger units. As time-share rentals, they have every comfort of home, including full kitchens and minibars. ⊠ *200 Sunset La., 33040,* ☎ *305/292–2001,* FAX *800/926–4447. 40 condominiums. Pool, hot tub. AE, MC, V.*

Guest Houses

$$$$ ▣ **Curry Mansion Inn.** Careful dedication to detail by Key West architect
★   Thomas Pope and much care by owners Al and Edith Amsterdam have
made the annex rooms exceptionally comfortable, even if not as detailed as the now rarely used rooms in the circa-1899 main house. Each
room has a different tropical pastel color scheme; all have wicker furnishings and quilts. Rooms 1 and 8, honeymoon suites, feature canopy
beds and balconies. Eight suites are at the restored James House; 306
and 308 face south and have beautiful morning light. There's complimentary Continental breakfast and happy hour with an open bar and
live piano music; guests also enjoy beach privileges at Pier House
Beach Club and Casa Marina. A wheelchair lift is available. ⊠ *511–*
512 Caroline St., 33040, ☎ *305/294–5349 or 800/253–3466,* ℻
305/294–4093. 18 rooms, 10 suites. Pool. AE, D, DC, MC, V.

$$$$ ▣ **Island City House.** This guest house is actually three buildings: the
vintage-1880s Island City House, with a widow's walk; Arch House,
a former carriage house; and a 1970s reconstruction of a cigar factory.
Arch House features a dramatic carriage entry that opens into a lush
courtyard, and though all its suites front on busy Eaton Street, bedrooms in only numbers 5 and 6 actually face it. Units in Cigar House
are largest, those in Island City House the best decorated. Floors are
pine, and ceiling fans and antiques abound. Guests share a private tropical garden and are given free Continental breakfasts. Children are welcome—a rarity in Old Town guest houses. ⊠ *411 William St., 33040,*
☎ *305/294–5702 or 800/634–8230,* ℻ *305/294–1289. 24 suites. Pool,*
hot tub, bicycles. AE, D, DC, MC, V.

$$$$ ▣ **Paradise Inn.** Renovated cigar-makers' cottages and authentically
★   reproduced Bahamian-style houses with sundecks and balconies stand
amid a lush tropical garden with a pool, lily pond, and whirlpool, light-
years away from the hubbub of Key West. The only sound disturbing
the perfect quiet is the trickling of water from the pool's fountain. Inside, light streams through French doors onto fine earth-tone fabrics.
Gracious appointments include phones and whirlpools in marble bathrooms, plush robes, polished oak floors, armoires, complimentary
fresh breakfast pastries from Louie's Backyard, room safes, and minibars. Suite 205 and the Poinciana Cottage are gilded lilies. One suite
is designed for travelers with disabilities. ⊠ *819 Simonton St., 33040,*
☎ *305/293–8007 or 800/888–9648,* ℻ *305/293–0807. 3 cottages,*
15 suites. Pool, hot tub, concierge. AE, D, DC, MC, V.

$$$–$$$$ ▣ **Heron House.** With four separate buildings centered on a pool, all
slightly different but all Key West–style, Heron House feels like an old
town within Old Town. A high coral fence, brilliantly splashed with
spotlights at night, surrounds the compound (just a block off Duval
Street but quieter by a mile). Neither antiques nor frills are owner Fred
Geibelt's thing. Superb detailing is. Most units feature a complete wall
of exquisitely laid wood (parquet, chevron pattern, herringbone), en-
tries with French doors, and bathrooms of polished granite. Some
have floor-to-ceiling panels of mirrored glass and/or an oversize
whirlpool. An expanded Continental breakfast is included. ⊠ *512 Si-*
monton St., 33040, ☎ *305/294–9227,* ℻ *305/294–5692. 23 rooms.*
Pool. AE, DC, MC, V.

$$$–$$$$ ▣ **Watson House.** This small guest house with many amenities com-
★   bines utmost privacy with Duval Street convenience: It's a block from
the bustle but miles from the hassle. Ed Czaplicki, with partner Joe Beres,
has restored the house to its 1860s Bahamian look, which guests find
caressingly soothing once they get past the busy lobby doubling as Ed's
real estate office. French doors and gingerbread trim dress up the pris-
tine yellow-and-white exterior. The deco Cabana Suite, by the two-tier

pool gardens, and the contemporary second-floor William Suite, have full kitchens. The Susan Room is charmingly furnished in white wicker. ✉ *525 Simonton St., 33040,* ☎ *305/294–6712 or 800/621–9405,* FAX *305/294–7501. 3 suites. Pool, hot tub. AE, MC, V.*

$$–$$$$ ⊡ **Popular House/Key West Bed & Breakfast.** Unlike so many prissy
★ hotels that wall the world out, Jody Carlson brings Key West in. Doors stay open all day. Local art—large splashy canvases, a mural in the style of Gauguin—hangs on the walls, and tropical gardens and music set the mood. Jody offers both inexpensive rooms with shared bath and luxury rooms, reasoning that budget travelers deserve the same good local style as the rich. Low-end rooms burst with bright yellows and reds; the hand-painted dressers will make you laugh out loud. Spacious third-floor rooms, though, are best (and most expensive), decorated with a paler palette and brilliantly original furniture. The Continental breakfast is lavish. ✉ *415 William St., 33040,* ☎ *305/296–7274 or 800/438–6155. 8 rooms (5 with shared baths). Hot tub, sauna. AE, D, DC, MC, V*

$$–$$$ ⊡ **The Colony Exclusive Cottages.** Separating this romantic hideaway
★ from the chaos of Duval Street two blocks away is an authentic Conch-style residential neighborhood. In 1985 owners Didier Moritz and Irwin Mayer converted two ramshackle Conch homes into the first of nine luxury units. Many units have cathedral ceilings and skylights; most have a living room, dining area, kitchen, and wooden deck—in a secluded tropical garden; and all have a supply of coffee and tea. Big on what's best for the guest, Didier and Irwin see to it that every new arrival is greeted with a large welcome basket with wine, cheese, cookies, crackers, and coffee. ✉ *714 Olivia St., 33040,* ☎ *305/294–6691. 9 units. Pool. MC, V.*

$$–$$$ ⊡ **Frances Street Bottle Inn.** With established inns going more and more for the luxury trade, this wonderful B&B is a refreshing change. Owners Bob and Kady Elkins look after guests as if they were all favorite cousins. The two-story Conch house dates from the 1890s, and the clean and tidy rooms are all pale, with plain furniture, paddle fans, and air-conditioning that's virtually silent. Dedicated to conservation, the Elkins have installed low-flow toilets and shower heads, and they compost and recycle. A downstairs bedroom opens to a porch-patio, three upstairs rooms have a balcony, and even the two least-expensive rooms have two exposures. The house's name comes from the antique bottles that Bob, a commercial spear fisherman, collects. Continental breakfast is included. ✉ *535 Frances St., 33040,* ☎ *305/294–8530 or 800/294–8530. 7 rooms. Hot tub. AE, MC, V.*

Hostel

$ ⊡ **Hostelling International–Key West.** This financial oasis in a sea of
★ expensive hotels gets high marks for location, comfort, friendliness, amenities, and good value. It is two blocks from the beach in Old Town, yet costs only $14.50 for members of Hostelling International–American Youth Hostels, $17.85 for nonmembers. During holidays add another 75¢. Dinner and breakfast cost $2 each. When you're not snorkeling or scuba diving at a reduced rate, you can rent bicycles, write letters in the outdoor courtyard, or enjoy a barbecue. There is free transportation from the Greyhound station. ✉ *718 South St., 33040,* ☎ *305/296–5719,* FAX *305/296–0672. 86 beds in dorm-style rooms share baths. Bicycles, billiards, game room, video games, library, coin laundry. D, MC, V.*

Hotels

$$$$ ⊡ **Hyatt Key West.** Given the imaginative adaptation of traditional Old Town architecture, this compound comes off a winner. Three four-story buildings are shoehorned into a tight waterfront site. Rooms have

Hyatt flair, many with irregular shapes, high tongue-in-groove wainscoting, and a generally good blend of muted and bold colors. In a city where water pressure is notoriously low, the showers at the Hyatt flow with knock-down force. ⊠ *601 Front St., 33040,* ☎ *305/296–9900,* FAX *305/292–1038. 120 rooms, 4 full suites, 4 minisuites. 3 restaurants, 2 bars, pool, hot tub, massage, exercise room, beach, boating, fishing, bicycles. AE, D, DC, MC, V.*

$$$$ 🏨 **La Concha Holiday Inn.** This seven-story Art Deco hotel in the heart of downtown is the city's tallest building and a great spot for watching the Fantasy Fest parade. Dating from 1926, it still has its original louvered room doors, light fixtures, and floral trim on the archways. The lobby's polished floor of pink, mauve, and green marble and a conversation pit with comfortable chairs are among the details beloved by La Concha's guests. Large rooms are outfitted with 1920s-era antiques, lace curtains, and big closets. You can enjoy the sunset from the Top, a lounge that overlooks the entire island, Atlantic Ocean, and Gulf of Mexico. No-smoking rooms are available, and the staff is friendly. ⊠ *430 Duval St., 33040,* ☎ *305/296–2991, 800/745–2191, or 800/465–4329,* FAX *305/294–3283. 158 rooms, 2 suites. Restaurant, 3 bars, pool, bicycles. AE, D, DC, MC, V.*

$$$$ 🏨 **Marquesa Hotel.** This coolly elegant, restored 1884 home is Key West's
★ finest lodging. Guests (typically shoeless in Marquesa robes) relax among richly landscaped pools and gardens against a backdrop of brick steps rising to the villalike suites on the property's perimeter. Elegant rooms contain eclectic antique and reproduction furnishings, dotted Swiss curtains, and botanical print fabrics. The lobby resembles a Victorian parlor, with antique furniture, Audubon prints, flowers, and wonderful photos of early Key West, including one of Harry Truman in a convertible. Tea is offered poolside 11:30–6. Although the clientele is mostly straight, the hotel is very gay-friendly. ⊠ *600 Fleming St., 33040,* ☎ *305/292–1919 or 800/869–4631,* FAX *305/294–2121. 27 rooms. Restaurant, 2 pools. AE, DC, MC, V.*

$$$$ 🏨 **Marriott's Casa Marina Resort.** Flagler's heirs built 13-acre La Casa Marina in 1921 at the end of the Florida East Coast Railway line. The entire resort revolves around an outdoor patio and lawn facing the ocean. The rich, luxurious lobby has a beam ceiling, polished Dade County pine floor, and wicker furniture; guest rooms are decorated in mauve and green pastels and Key West scenes. Among the best rooms are the two-bedroom loft suites with balconies facing the ocean and the lanai rooms on the ground floor of the main building, which have French doors opening onto the lawn. Rooms for nonsmokers are available. ⊠ *1500 Reynolds St., 33040,* ☎ *305/296–3535,* FAX *305/296–4633. 248 rooms, 63 suites. 2 restaurants, bar, 2 pools, massage, sauna, 3 tennis courts, exercise room, health club, boating, jet skiing, fishing, bicycles, children's programs. AE, D, DC, MC, V.*

$$$$ 🏨 **Pier House.** This is Key West's catbird seat—just off the intersection
★ tion of Duval and Front streets and an easy walk from Mallory Square and downtown. Since the 1930s, when David Wolkowsky began restoring and expanding this once-modest lodging, the Pier House has defined Key West's festive ambience. Weathered-gray buildings, including an original Conch house, flank a courtyard of tall coconut palms and hibiscus blossoms. Most rooms are smaller than in newer hotels, except in the Caribbean Spa section, which has hardwood floors, two-poster plantation beds, and some baths that convert to steam rooms or have whirlpools. Gather with locals at the Beach Club's thatch-roof tiki bar, or have a massage, aromatherapy, or facial in the fitness center. ⊠ *1 Duval St., 33040,* ☎ *305/296–4600 or 800/327–8340,* FAX *305/296–7569. 129 rooms, 13 suites. 3 restaurants, 4 bars, pool, massage, health club, beach. AE, D, DC, MC, V.*

$$$–$$$$ ★   🏨 **Best Western Key Ambassador Inn.** Even though rooms are decorated in typical motel style, there is a cheerful spirit with bright appointments and ample room. The grounds—7 acres bordered by salt ponds—are well cared for, and the pool looks over the Atlantic a couple of hundred feet away across Roosevelt Boulevard. Each room has a balcony and most offer ocean and pool views. A complimentary Continental breakfast is included, and a free newspaper is delivered to rooms weekdays. ✉ *3755 S. Roosevelt Blvd., 33040,* ☎ *305/296–3500 or 800/432–4315,* FAX *305/296–9961. 100 rooms. Bar, snack bar, pool, shuffleboard, coin laundry. AE, D, DC, MC, V.*

$$$–$$$$ 🏨 **Cuban Club Suites.** Originally built to house cigar makers, the "club" was rebuilt as a luxury hotel after a 1983 fire. Eight fully equipped town-house units, 900–1,900 square feet, have either two bedrooms and two baths or one bedroom and 1½ baths. Grouped in two buildings that feel like an exclusive apartment complex, they have king four-poster beds, queen-size sofa beds, wing chairs, cathedral ceilings, full kitchens, tile counters and floors, and washers and dryers. Wide balconies overlook the excitement of Duval Street. Casa de Luces, the club's poor cousin next door, is less elegant but has many winning characteristics. Guests have pool and beach privileges at the Marriott Reach, and pets are allowed. ✉ *1108 Duval St. (lobby at 422 Amelia St.), 33040,* ☎ *305/296–0465 or 800/432–4849,* FAX *305/293–7669. 8 suites. AE, MC, V.*

Motels

$$$ 🏨 **Harborside Motel & Marina.** The appeal of this ordinary motel is its affordability and its safe, pleasant location between a quiet street and Garrison Bight (the charter boat harbor), between Old Town and New Town. Units are boxy, clean, and basic, with little patios, ceramic-tile floors, phones, and basic color cable TV. Three stationary houseboats each sleep four. ✉ *903 Eisenhower Dr., 33040,* ☎ *305/294–2780,* FAX *305/292–1473. 14 efficiencies. Pool, coin laundry. AE, D, DC, MC, V.*

$$$ 🏨 **Southwinds.** A short walk from Old Town, this pastel, 1940s-style motel has mature tropical plantings, all nicely set back from the street a block from the beach. Rooms have basic furnishings. It's as good as you'll find at the price, and though rates have gone up, they drop if demand gets slack. On-premises parking is available, as are wheelchair-accessible accommodations. ✉ *1321 Simonton St., 33040,* ☎ *305/296–2215. 13 rooms, 5 efficiencies. Pool, coin laundry. AE, D, DC, MC, V.*

Nightlife and the Arts

The Arts

Red Barn Theater (✉ 319 Duval St. [rear], ☎ 305/296–9911), a professional, small theater, performs dramas, comedies, and musicals, including plays by new playwrights. **Tennessee Williams Fine Arts Center** (✉ Florida Keys Community College, 5901 College Rd., ☎ 305/296–9081 ext. 5), on Stock Island, presents chamber music, dance, jazz concerts, and dramatic and musical plays with national and international stars, as well as other performing-arts events, November–April. **Waterfront Playhouse** (✉ Mallory Sq., ☎ 305/294–5015) is a mid-1850s wrecker's warehouse that was converted into a 185-seat, non-Equity community theater presenting comedy and drama November–May.

Nightlife

BARS AND LOUNGES

Capt. Tony's Saloon (✉ 428 Greene St., ☎ 305/294–1838) is a landmark bar, owned until 1988 by a legend in his own right, Captain Tony

Tarracino—a former bootlegger, smuggler, mercenary, gunrunner, gambler, raconteur, and Key West mayor. The building dates from 1851, when it was first used as a morgue and ice house; later it was Key West's first telegraph station. The bar was the original Sloppy Joe's from 1933 to 1937. Hemingway was a regular, and Jimmy Buffett got his start here. Live country and rhythm and blues set the scene nowadays, and the rum-based house drink, the Pirates' Punch, still wows those brave enough to try it. Pause for a libation at the open-air **Green Parrot Bar** (⊠ 601 Whitehead St., at Southard St., ☎ 305/294–6133). Built in 1890, the bar is said to be Key West's oldest, a sometimes-rowdy saloon where locals outnumber the tourists, especially on weekends when bands play. **Margaritaville Cafe** (⊠ 500 Duval St., ☎ 305/292–1435) is owned by former Key West resident and recording star Jimmy Buffett, who has been known to perform here. The drink of choice is, of course, a margarita. There's live music nightly.

Called "the last little piece of Old Key West," **Schooner Wharf Bar** (⊠ 202 William St., ☎ 305/292–9520) is a laid-back waterside tiki hut where the town's waiters and waitresses hang out. You can hear live music weekends (and sometimes at other times) in the warehouse space next door. **Sloppy Joe's** (⊠ 201 Duval St., ☎ 305/294–5717) is the successor to a famous speakeasy named for its founder, Captain Joe Russell. Ernest Hemingway liked to gamble in a partitioned club room in back. Decorated with Hemingway memorabilia and marine flags, the bar is popular with tourists and is full and noisy all the time. Live entertainment plays daily, noon–2 AM. The **Top Lounge** (⊠ 430 Duval St., ☎ 305/296–2991) is on the seventh floor of the La Concha Holiday Inn and is one of the best places to view the sunset. (**Celebrities,** on the ground floor, presents nightly entertainment and serves food.)

DISCOS

Key West regulars knew it as the Copa, a wild and popular gay disco, but it's returned as **Epoch** (⊠ 623 Duval St., ☎ 305/296–8521). The well-mixed crowd is new, but they're still wild and eager to party. There are two floors, five bars, and a lounge overlooking the dance floor. House dancers set the tone as hip local spinmaster DJ Hunter grooves the tunes. In the Pier House, **Havana Docks Lounge** (⊠ 1 Duval St., ☎ 305/296–4600), a high-energy disco, is popular with young locals and visitors. The deck is a good place to watch the sun set when Mallory Square gets too crowded.

Outdoor Activities and Sports

Biking

Key West is a cycling town, but if you aren't accustomed to so many bikes, ride carefully. Paved road surfaces are poor, so it's best to ride a fat-tired Conch cruiser. Some hotels rent bikes to guests; others will refer you to a nearby shop and reserve a bike for you.

Keys Moped & Scooter (⊠ 523 Truman Ave., ☎ 305/294–0399) rents beach cruisers with large baskets as well as mopeds and scooters. Rates are the lowest in Key West. Look for the huge American flag on the roof. **Moped Hospital** (⊠ 601 Truman Ave., ☎ 305/296–3344) supplies balloon-tire bikes with yellow safety baskets, as well as mopeds, tandem mopeds, and scooters for adults and children. Helmets are no charge.

Fishing

Though more known for diving, **Captain's Corner** (⊠ 511-A Greene St., 30040, ☎ 305/296–8865) also runs fishing charters. As first mate for his mother, Vicki (☞ Guided Tours *in* Florida Keys A to Z, *below*), **Captain Steven Impallomeni** learned the backcountry. Now he works as a flats-fishing guide on the *Gallopin' Ghost*. Charters leave from Murray's Marina (⊠ MM5, Stock Island, ☎ 305/292–9837). **Key West Bait and Tackle** (⊠ 201 Margaret St., ☎ 305/292–1961) carries just that.

Golf

Key West Resort Golf Course (⊠ 6450 E. College Rd., ☎ 305/294–5232) is an 18-hole course on the bay side of Stock Island. Nonresident fees are $70 for 18 holes (cart included) in season.

Scuba Diving

Captain's Corner (⊠ 511-A Greene St., 30040, ☎ 305/296–8865), a PADI five star–rated shop, provides dive classes in several languages. All captains are licensed dive masters. A 60-foot dive boat, *Sea Eagle*, departs twice daily. Reservations are accepted for regular reef and wreck diving, spear and lobster fishing, and archaeological and treasure hunting.

Shopping

Key West contains dozens of characterless T-shirt shops, but some art galleries and curiosity shops have lots worth toting home.

Art and Crafts

The oldest private art gallery in Key West, **Gingerbread Square Gallery** (⊠ 1207 Duval St., ☎ 305/296–8900) represents mainly Keys artists who have attained national and international prominence. **Haitian Art Co.** (⊠ 600 Frances St., ☎ 305/296–8932) sells the original colorful iron, wood, and ceramic works of 200 or so Haitian artists. **Lucky Street Gallery** (⊠ 919 Duval St., ☎ 305/294–3973) shows tropical contemporary crafts, blown glass, wood carvings, and other art for hanging and mounting. **Pelican Poop** (⊠ 314 Simonton St., ☎ 305/296–3887) sells Haitian and Ecuadorean art around a lush, tropical courtyard garden with a gorgeous aqua pool. (Hemingway once lived in the apartments out back, called Casa Antigua.) **Plantation Pottery** (⊠ 521 Fleming St., ☎ 305/294–3143) is not to be missed for its original, never-commercial pottery. Potters Charles Pearson and Timothy Roeder are **Whitehead St. Pottery** (⊠ 1011 Whitehead St., ☎ 305/294–5067), where they display their porcelain stoneware and raku-fired vessels.

Books and Periodicals

The Red Doors Building, a restored 1868 house that was once a brothel, contains several interesting shops, including one of the best bookstores in town, **Caroline Street Books** (⊠ 800 Caroline St., ☎ 305/294–3931). The bookstore has a large selection of books by or about local authors (Hemingway, Tennessee Williams, Robert Frost, etc.), as well as a range of gay and lesbian books and magazines. **Key West Island Bookstore** (⊠ 513 Fleming St., ☎ 305/294–2904) is the literary bookstore of the large Key West writers' community. **L. Valladares & Son** (⊠ 1200 Duval St., ☎ 305/296–5032), a fourth-generation newsstand, sells more than 4,000 periodicals and 3,000 paperback books along with state, national, and international papers.

Clothing and Fabrics

Inter Arts (⊠ 506 Southard St., ☎ 305/296–4081) is stocked with textiles to wear, display, walk on, and keep you cool in bed. **Key West Hand Print Fashions and Fabrics** (⊠ 201 Simonton St., ☎ 305/294–9535 or 800/866–0333), since 1964, is noted for its vibrant tropical prints, yard goods, and resort wear for men, women, and children. It's in the

Curry Warehouse, a brick building erected in 1878 to store tobacco. **Tikal Trading Co.** (✉ 129 Duval St., ☎ 305/296–4463) sells its own line of women's clothing of handwoven Guatemalan cotton and knit tropical prints.

Food and Drink

Take time, even if you're not buying, to enjoy the smells at **Baby's Place Coffee Bar** (✉ 1111 Duval St., ☎ 305/292–3739 or 800/523–2326), the "southernmost coffee roasters." Dozens of varieties of beans plus fresh-baked pastries are for sale. **Fausto's Food Palace** (✉ 522 Fleming St., ☎ 305/296–5663; ✉ 1105 White St., ☎ 305/294–5221) may be under a roof, but it's a market in the traditional town-square sense. Since 1926, Fausto's has been the spot to catch up on the week's gossip and to chill out in summer—it has the heaviest air-conditioning in town. **Waterfront Market** (✉ 201 William St., ☎ 305/294–8418 or 305/296–0778) purveys health and gourmet foods, deli items, produce, salads, cold beer, and wine. If you're there, be sure to check out the bulletin board. There's a fish market (☎ 305/296–0778) in the same building.

Gifts and Souvenirs

Like a parody of Duval Street T-shirt shops, the hole-in-the-wall **Art Attack** (✉ 606 Duval St., ☎ 305/294–7131) throws in every icon and trinket anyone nostalgic for the days of peace and love might fancy: beads, necklaces, medallions, yin-yang banners, harmony bells, and of course Dead and psychedelic T-shirts. **Fast Buck Freddie's** (✉ 500 Duval St., ☎ 305/294–2007) sells imaginative items you'd never dream of, including battery-operated alligators that eat Muenster cheese, banana leaf–shape furniture, fish-shape flatware, and every flamingo item imaginable. In a town with a gazillion T-shirt shops, **Last Flight Out** (✉ 706A Duval St., ☎ 305/294–8008) stands out for its selection of classic namesake T's, specialty clothing, and gifts that appeal to aviation types as well as those reaching for the stars. A survivor of Key West's seafaring days, **Perkins & Son Chandlery** (✉ 901 Fleming St., ☎ 305/294–7635), redolent of pine tar and kerosene, offers one of the largest selections of used marine gear in the Keys, as well as nautical antiques, books, outdoor clothing, and collectibles.

Health and Beauty

Key West Aloe (✉ 524 Front St., ☎ 305/294–5592 or 800/445–2563) was founded in a garage in 1971; today it produces some 300 perfume, sunscreen, and skin-care products for men and women. You can also visit the factory store (✉ Greene and Simonton Sts.).

Side Trip

Dry Tortugas National Park

This sanctuary for thousands of birds, 70 mi off the shores of Key West, consists of seven small islands. Its main facility is the long-deactivated Ft. Jefferson, where Dr. Samuel Mudd was imprisoned for his alleged role in Lincoln's assassination. For information and a list of authorized charter boats, seaplanes, and water taxis, contact **Everglades National Park** (✉ 40001 Rte. 9336, Homestead 33034-6733, ☎ 305/242–7700).

A three-hour journey to the park aboard the 100-foot *Yankee Freedom* of the **Yankee Fleet Dry Tortugas National Park Ferry** includes a full breakfast. On arrival a naturalist leads a 45-minute guided tour, followed by lunch and a free afternoon for swimming, snorkeling, and exploring. ✉ *Lands End Marina, 251 Margaret St., Key West 33050,*

☎ 305/294–7009 or 800/634–0939. ☎ $79, lunch $5. ☉ Trips daily in season last 8 AM–7 PM.

THE FLORIDA KEYS A TO Z

Arriving and Departing

By Airport Shuttle

One-way shuttle fares from Miami International Airport (MIA) to the Upper Keys range from $45 first person ($30 each additional) on **Miami Airport Limo Service** (☎ 305/852–9533) to $78 first passenger ($15 each additional) on the **SuperShuttle** (☎ 305/871–2000). To go farther into the Keys, you must book an entire van (up to 11 passengers), which costs $250 to Marathon, $350 to Key West. Super Shuttle requests 24-hour advance notice for transportation back to the airport. **Airporter** (☎ 305/852–3413 or 800/830–3413) operates scheduled van and bus service from MIA's baggage areas to wherever you want to go in Key Largo ($30) and Islamorada ($33). Reservations are required. With 24-hour notice, **Upper Keys Transportation** (☎ 305/453–0100 or 800/749–5397) meets arriving flights; one-hour notice is needed for departures. Fares are $45 for one person, $70 for two (8 AM–6 PM, added charge other times) to Key Largo; $115 for one, $125 for two to Marathon.

By Boat

Boaters can travel to Key West either along the Intracoastal Waterway (5-foot draft limitation) through Card, Barnes, and Blackwater sounds and into Florida Bay or along the deeper Atlantic Ocean route through Hawk Channel, a buoyed passage. Refer to NOAA Nautical Chart No. 11451 for Miami to Marathon and Florida Bay, Nos. 11445 and 11441 for Marathon to Dry Tortugas. The Keys are full of marinas that welcome transient visitors, but they don't have enough slips for everyone. Make reservations in advance, and ask about channel and dockage depth—many marinas are quite shallow.

Coast Guard Group Key West (✉ Key West 33040, ☎ 305/292–8727) provides 24-hour monitoring of VHF-FM Channel 16. Safety and weather information is broadcast at 7 AM and 5 PM Eastern Standard Time on VHF-FM Channel 16 and 22A. There are three stations in the Keys: Islamorada (☎ 305/664–4404), Marathon (☎ 305/743–6778), and Key West (☎ 305/292–8856).

Key West Excursions (☎ 941/263–3900) runs ferry service to Key West from Naples and Marco Island on a 112-foot powered catamaran, the *Friendship V*. Daily departures from Naples at 7:30 AM and Marco Island at 8:45 reach Key West by 12:15. The same-day round-trip fare is $99, including Continental breakfast and dinner. Similar service is available to Fort Myers Beach.

By Bus

Almost as fast as a shuttle and a fraction of the price, **Greyhound Lines** (☎ 800/231–2222) provides service three times a day between MIA (departing from Concourse E, Lower Level) and stops throughout the Keys and on request.

By Car

From MIA, follow signs to Coral Gables and Key West, which put you on Lejeune Road, then Route 836 west. Take the Florida's Turnpike Extension south (toll road), which ends at Florida City and connects to U.S. 1. Tolls from the airport run approximately $1.25. The alternative from Florida City is Card Sound Road (Route 905A), which has a bridge toll of $1.75. Continue to the only stop sign, and turn right on Route 905, which rejoins U.S. 1 31 mi from Florida City.

Avoid flying into Key West and driving back to Miami; there are substantial drop-off charges for leaving a Key West car in Miami.

By Plane

Service between **Key West International Airport** (⊠ S. Roosevelt Blvd., Key West, ☎ 305/296–5439 or 305/296–7223) and Miami, Fort Lauderdale/Hollywood, Naples, Orlando, and Tampa is provided by **American Eagle** (☎ 800/433–7300), **Cape Air** (☎ 800/352–0714), **Comair** (☎ 800/354–9822), **Gulfstream International Airlines** (☎ 800/992–8532), and **US Airways/US Airways Express** (☎ 800/428–4322). **Marathon Airport** (⊠ MM 52, BS, Marathon, ☎ 305/743–2155) connects to Miami via American Eagle, to Tampa via USAir Express.

Getting Around

Chambers of commerce, marinas, and dive shops offer **Teall's Guides**, land and nautical charts that pinpoint popular fishing and diving areas. A complete set can also be purchased for $7.95, postage included, from 111 Saguaro Lane, Marathon 33050, ☎ 305/743–3942.

By Bus

The City of Key West Department of Transportation (☎ 305/292–8165) operates two bus routes: Mallory Square (counterclockwise around the island) and Old Town (clockwise around the island). The fare is 75¢ (exact change).

By Car

In Key West's Old Town, parking is scarce and costly ($1.50 per hour at Mallory Square). Use a taxi, bicycle, or moped to get around, or walk. Elsewhere in the Keys, a car is crucial. Gas costs more than on the mainland, so fill your tank in Miami and top it off in Florida City.

Except for four-lane sections through Key Largo, Tavernier, Marathon, Bahia Honda State Park, Boca Chica Key, and Stock Island, the Overseas Highway is narrow and crowded (especially weekends). Expect delays behind RVs, trucks, cars towing boats, and rubbernecking tourists.

The best Keys road map, published by the Homestead/Florida City Chamber of Commerce, can be obtained for $2 from the **Tropical Everglades Visitor Center** (⊠ 160 U.S. 1, Florida City 33034, ☎ 305/245–9180 or 800/388–9669).

By Limousine

Paradise Transportation Service, Inc. (⊠ 3134 Northside Dr., ☎ 305/293–3010) operates in Key West.

By Taxi

In the Upper Keys (MM 94–74), **Island Taxi** (☎ 305/664–8181) charges $4 for the first 2 mi and $1.50 each additional mile for up to two adults and any accompanying children; extra adults pay $1 per mile. In the Middle Keys, **Cheapo Taxi** (☎ 305/743–7420) rates are $1 for pickup and $1 per mile. Drops beyond MM 61 and MM 40 are $1.50 a mile. Four cab companies operate around the clock in Key West: **Five Sixes Cabs** (☎ 305/296–6666), **Florida Keys Taxi Dispatch** (☎ 305/296–1800), **Maxi-Taxi Sun Cab System** (☎ 305/296–7777), and **Yellow Cabs of Key West** (☎ 305/294–2227). The fare for two or more from the Key West Airport to New Town is $5 per person with a cap of $15; to Old Town it's $6 and $20. Otherwise meters register $1.40

to start, 35¢ for each ⅓ mi, and 35¢ for every 50 seconds of waiting time.

Contacts and Resources

Car Rentals

Avis (☎ 305/743–5428 or 800/831–2847), **Budget** (☎ 305/743–3998 or 800/527–0700), and **Value** (☎ 305/743–6100 or 800/468–2583) serve Marathon Airport. Key West's airport has booths for **Avis** (☎ 305/296–8744), **Budget** (☎ 305/294–8868), **Dollar** (☎ 305/296–9921 or 800/800–4000), **Hertz** (☎ 305/294–1039 or 800/654–3131), and **Value** (☎ 305/296–7733). **Tropical Rent-A-Car** (✉ 1300 Duval St., Key West, ☎ 305/294–8136) is based in the city center. **Enterprise Rent-A-Car** (☎ 800/325–8007) has offices in Key Largo, Marathon, Islamorada, and Key West. **Thrifty Car Rental** has locations in Tavernier (✉ MM91.8, OS, ☎ 305/852–6088) and Key West (✉ 3820 N. Roosevelt Blvd., ☎ 305/295–9777).

Emergencies

Dial **911** for police, fire, or ambulance. If you are a TTY caller, tap the space bar or use a voice announcer to identify yourself. **Florida Marine Patrol** (✉ MM 48, BS, 2796 Overseas Hwy., Suite 100, State Regional Service Center, Marathon 33050, ☎ 305/289–2320; after 5 PM, ☎ 800/342–5367) maintains a 24-hour telephone service to handle reports of boating emergencies and natural-resource violations. **Coast Guard Group Key West** (☎ 305/295–9700) responds to local marine emergencies and reports of navigation hazards.

HOSPITALS

The following hospitals have 24-hour emergency rooms: **Fishermen's Hospital** (✉ MM 48.7, OS, Marathon, ☎ 305/743–5533); **Florida Keys Hyperbaric Center** (✉ MM 54, OS, Suite 101, Marathon, ☎ 305/743–9891), for diving accidents; **Lower Florida Keys Health System** (✉ MM 5, BS, 5900 College Rd., Stock Island, ☎ 305/294–5531 or 800/233–3119); and **Mariners Hospital** (✉ MM 88.5, BS, 50 High Point Rd., Plantation Key, ☎ 305/852–4418).

LATE-NIGHT PHARMACIES

The Keys have no 24-hour pharmacies. Hospital pharmacists will help with emergencies after regular retail business hours.

Guided Tours

AIR TOURS

Island Aeroplane Tours (✉ 3469 S. Roosevelt Blvd., Key West Airport, Key West 33040, ☎ 305/294–8687) flies up to two passengers in an open-cockpit biplane. Tours range from a quick six- to eight-minute overview of Key West ($50 for two) to a 50-minute look at the offshore reefs ($200 for two).

BIKE TOURS

The **Key West Nature Bike Tour** (✉ Truman Ave. and Simonton St., Key West, ☎ 305/296–3344) departs from Moped Hospital (✉ 601 Truman Ave.) on Sunday at 10:30 and Tuesday–Saturday at 9 and 3. The cost is $15 with your own bike, $3 more to rent one.

BOAT TOURS

Adventure Charters (✉ 6810 Front St., Key West 33040, ☎ 305/296–0362) operates tours on the 42-foot catamaran *Island Fantasea* for a maximum of 12 passengers. Trips range from a half day into the backcountry to daylong and overnight sojourns. **Coral Reef Park Co.** (✉ John Pennekamp Coral Reef State Park, MM 102.5, OS, Key Largo, ☎ 305/451–1621) runs sailing trips on a 38-foot catamaran as well as glass-bottom boat tours. **Everglades Safari Tours** (✉ Box 3343, Key Largo 33037, ☎ 305/451–4540 or 800/959–0742) operates daily 60-minute champagne sunset tours year-round on pontoon boats ($15 per person) and a variety of custom tours. Trips leave from the Quay Restaurant docks (✉ MM 102, BS). **Gale Force Eco-tours** (✉ Rte. 2, Box 669-F, Summerland Key 33042, ☎ 305/745–2868) runs tours into the Great White Heron National Wildlife refuge aboard the *Gale Force,* a 24-foot skiff with a viewing tower. Departing from T. J.'s Sugarshack Marina (✉ MM 17, BS), next to Sugar Loaf Lodge, four-hour trips cost $45 per person for two to six people; seven-hour tours for two people cost $175, $50 each additional person. All tours include free snorkel gear, instruction, snacks, beverages, and sometimes walking tours and beach time.

Key Largo Princess (✉ MM 99.7, OS, 99701 Overseas Hwy., Key Largo 33037, ☎ 305/451–4655) offers two-hour glass-bottom boat trips and sunset cruises on a luxury 70-foot motor yacht with a 280-square-foot glass viewing area, departing from the Holiday Inn docks. **M/V Discovery** (✉ Land's End Marina, 251 Margaret St., Key West 33040, ☎ 305/293–0099, FAX 305/293–0199) and the 65-foot *Pride of Key West* (✉ 2 Duval St., Key West 33040, ☎ 305/296–6293 or FAX 305/294–8704) are glass-bottom boats. **Strike Zone Charters** (✉ MM 29.5, BS, 29675 Overseas Hwy., Big Pine Key 33043, ☎ 305/872–9863 or 800/654–9560), run by Lower Keys native Captain Larry Threlkeld, offers glass-bottom boat excursions into the backcountry and to Looe Key. On the five-hour Island Excursion ($45), nature and Keys history are emphasized. Besides close encounters with birds, sea life, and vegetation, there's a barbecue on an island. Snorkel and fishing equipment, food, and drinks are included.

Victoria Impallomeni, noted wilderness guide and authority on the ecology of Florida Bay, invites nature lovers aboard the *Imp II,* a 22-foot Aquasport, for four-hour half-day ($300) and seven-hour full-day ($400) ecotours. While island-hopping, you visit underwater gardens, natural shoreline, and mangrove habitats. Everything is supplied except the picnic. Tours depart from Murray's Marina (✉ MM 5, Stock Island, ☎ 305/294–9731). *Wolf* (✉ Schooner Wharf, Key West Seaport, end of Greene St., Key West 33040, ☎ 305/296–9653) is Key West's tall ship and the flagship of the Conch Republic. The 74-foot, 44-passenger topsail schooner operates day cruises as well as sunset and starlight cruises with live music.

CANOE AND KAYAK TOURS

Adventure Charters (✉ 6810 Front St., Key West 33040, ☎ 305/296–0362) offers half-day kayak trips ($35), departing at 9 and 2, and full-day trips ($100), which include snorkeling, fishing, a grilled lunch, and drinks. The folks at **Florida Bay Outfitters** (✉ MM 104, BS, 104050 Overseas Hwy., Key Largo 33037, ☎ 305/451–3018) know Keys waters well. You can take a one- to seven-day canoe or kayak tour to the Everglades or Lignumvitae or Indian Key, or a night trip to neighboring islands. **Mosquito Coast Island Outfitters and Kayak Guides** (✉ 1107 Duval St., Key West 33040, ☎ 305/294–7178) runs full-day, guided sea-kayak natural-history tours around the mangrove islands just east of Key West. The $45-a-day charge covers transportation and supplies, including snorkeling gear. **Reflections Kayak Nature Tours** (✉ MM 28.5, OS/BS, Box 430861, Big Pine Key 33043, ☎ 305/872–2896), based at Parmer's Place B&B on Little Torch Key, operates daily trips into the Great White Heron National Wildlife Refuge and Everglades National Park. Tours last about three hours, and $45 covers granola bars, fresh fruit, raisins, spring water, a bird-identification sheet, and the use of waterproof binoculars; snorkeling gear (optional) is extra. Six-hour tours ($80) also include lunch.

ORIENTATION TOURS

The **Conch Tour Train** (☎ 305/294–5161) is a 90-minute, narrated tour of Key West, traveling 14 mi through Old Town and around the island. Board at Mallory Square and Roosevelt Boulevard (just north of the Quality Inn) depots every half hour (9:30–4:30 from Mallory Square, later at other stops). The cost is $14. **Old Town Trolley** (⊠ 1910 N. Roosevelt Blvd., Key West, ☎ 305/296–6688) operates 12 trackless trolley-style buses, departing Mallory Square and Roosevelt Boulevard depots every 30 minutes (9–4:30 from Mallory Square, later at other stops), for 90-minute, narrated tours of Key West. The smaller trolleys go places the train won't fit. You may disembark at any of 14 stops and reboard a later trolley. The cost is $15.

WALKING TOURS

The **Historic Florida Keys Preservation Board** (⊠ 510 Greene St., Old City Hall, Key West 33040, ☎ 305/292–6718) publishes a free pamphlet and map to the **Cuban Heritage Trail,** whose 36 sites demonstrate Key West's close connection to Cuba. Also available are the annotated map **Key West, Tropical Island with a Colorful Past,** about the historic district, and a brochure and map to the Key West cemetery. A walking tour of the cemetery is led Tuesday and Thursday at 9:30. Sharon Wells of **Island City Strolls** (☎ 305/294–8380 or 305/293–0255) knows plenty about Key West. State historian in Key West for nearly 20 years and owner of a historic preservation consulting firm, she has authored many works, including the interesting magazine-size guide, **"The Walking and Biking Guide to Historic Key West,"** available free at Key West bookstores. If that whets your appetite, sign on for one of her personalized walking tours, including "Architectural Strolls," "Nancy's Secret Garden: A Rainforest Stroll," "Bike Tours," and "Historic Military Sites." Tours cost $10–$15 and last one–two hours.

"Pelican Path" is a free walking guide to Key West published by the Old Island Restoration Foundation. The tour discusses the history and architecture of 43 structures along 25 blocks of 12 Old Town streets. Pick up a copy at the chamber of commerce. **Writers' Walk,** a one-hour guided tour sponsored by the Key West Literary Seminar (☎ 305/293–9291), visits the residences of prominent Key West authors, including Frost, Hemingway, and Williams. Tours leave at 10:30, on Saturday from the Heritage House Museum (⊠ 410 Caroline St.) and on Sunday from in front of Hemingway House (⊠ 907 Whitehead St.). Tickets ($10) must be purchased in advance from the Heritage House Museum or Key West Island Bookstore (⊠ 513 Fleming St.).

Lodging Reservations

Key West Vacation Rentals (⊠ 525 Simonton St., Key West 33040, ☎ 305/292–7997 or 800/621–9405, FAX 305/294–7501) lists historic cottages, homes, and condominiums for rent. **Property Management of Key West, Inc.** (⊠ 1213 Truman Ave., Key West 33040, ☎ 305/296–7744) offers lease and rental service for condominiums, town houses, and private homes.

Publications

The best of the publications covering Key West is *Solares Hill,* (⊠ 330-B Julia St., Key West 33040, ☎ 305/294–3602, FAX 305/294–1699). The monthly is witty, controversial, and tough on environmental issues and gets the best arts and entertainment advertising. The best weekday source of information on Key West is the *Key West Citizen* (⊠ 3420 Northside Dr., Key West 33040, ☎ 305/294–6641), which also publishes a Sunday edition. For the Upper and Middle Keys, turn to the semiweekly *The Keynoter,* a Knight-Ridder publication. The *Free Press* covers the same area once a week. The *Miami Herald* publishes a Keys edition with good daily listings of local events. The monthly *Southern Exposure* is a good source for gay and lesbian travelers.

Visitor Information

Florida Keys & Key West Visitors Bureau (⊠ 402 Wall St., Key West 33040, ☎ 800/352–5397). **Greater Key West Chamber of Commerce (mainstream)** (⊠ 402 Wall St., Key West 33040, ☎ 305/294–2587 or 800/527–8539, FAX 305/294–7806). **Islamorada Chamber of Commerce** (⊠ MM 82.5, BS, Box 915, Islamorada 33036, ☎ 305/664–4503 or 800/322–5397). **Key Largo Chamber of Commerce** (⊠ MM 106, BS, 106000 Overseas Hwy., Key Largo 33037, ☎ 305/451–1414 or 800/822–1088). **Key West Business Guild (gay)** (⊠ Box 1208, Key West 33041, ☎ 305/294–4603 or 800/535–7797). **Lower Keys Chamber of Commerce** (⊠ MM 31, OS, Box 430511, Big Pine Key 33043, ☎ 305/872–2411 or 800/872–3722, FAX 305/872–0752). **Marathon Chamber of Commerce & Visitor Center** (⊠ MM 53.5, BS, 12222 Overseas Hwy., Marathon 33050, ☎ 305/743–5417 or 800/842–9580).

8 Walt Disney World® and the Orlando Area

When Walt Disney chose 28,000 acres in central Florida as the site of his eastern Disneyland, he forever changed the face of a cattle-and-citrus town called Orlando. Over the years those who followed Walt have expanded his empire. But today there is plenty of competition as the big companies play the corporate equivalent of keeping up with the Joneses. It's easy to spend weeks here—and there isn't an ocean-pounded beach in sight.

LONG BEFORE "IT'S A SMALL WORLD" echoed through the palmetto scrub, other theme parks tempted visitors away from the beaches into the scruffy interior of central Florida. I–4 hadn't even been built when Dick and Julie Pope created Cypress Gardens, which holds the record as the region's oldest continuously running attraction—it celebrated 60 years in 1997. But when Walt Disney World (WDW) opened with the Magic Kingdom as its centerpiece on October 1, 1971, and was immediately successful, the central Florida theme-park scene became big business. Sea World filled its tanks two years later. WDW debuted Epcot in 1982 and Disney–MGM Studios Theme Park in 1989; Universal Studios answered the latter's challenge one year later. Things continue to evolve as Disney's Animal Kingdom, an animal-theme park, opens in 1998, and Universal targets the evening crowd with the CityWalk entertainment complex.

The problem for visitors with tight schedules or slim wallets is that each park is worth a visit. The Magic Kingdom, Epcot, and Sea World are not to be missed. Of the two movie parks, Universal Studios and Disney–MGM Studios, the former is probably more spectacular. Cypress Gardens is a 60-minute drive through the dusty remnants of the region's citrus groves.

It is easy to forget that this ever-expanding fantasy world grew up around a sleepy farming town founded as a military outpost, Fort Gatlin, in 1838. Though not on any major waterway, Orlando was surrounded by small spring-fed lakes, and transplanted northerners planted sprawling oak trees to vary the landscape of palmetto scrub and citrus groves. Most of the tourist development is in southwest Orlando, along the I–4 corridor south of Florida's Turnpike. Orlando itself has become a center of international business, and north of downtown are several handsome, prosperous suburbs, most notably Winter Park, which retains its white-gloves-at-tea Southern charm.

Pleasures and Pastimes

Boating
Orlando is truly a boater's paradise. The Orlando area has one of the highest concentration of lakes—both large and small—of anywhere in the continental United States. If you decide to tow your boat along, you won't be disappointed. On the other hand, rentals are easily available.

You can even take advantage of the huge network of lakes and rivers that run right through Disney property by renting any manner of powerboat or Jet Ski at the various Disney resorts. Another, often overlooked possibility is one of the best: Pack a picnic, rent a low-speed pontoon boat for a few hours, and take a ride up a few lazy rivers at your own pace. It's a great way to unwind after you've been on Mr. Toad's Wild Ride one too many times.

Dining
If they batter it, fry it, microwave it, torture it under a heat lamp until it's ready to sign a confession, and serve it with a side of fries, you can find it in central Florida. Cruise down International Drive or U.S. 192 and you'll probably be convinced that some obscure federal law mandates that any franchise restaurant company doing business in the United States has to have at least one outlet in Orlando. Not all the franchises are burger barns, however, and even those that are try to put their best foot forward in Orlando, where food is consumed by

millions of international visitors. The McDonald's on International Drive, for example, is the largest in the nation. Restaurateurs build monuments here, so you'll ask "Hey, why don't they have one of these in our town?" This fiercely competitive dining market even brings out the best from the hometown eateries that predate Disney. The result is that dining choices in Orlando are like entertainment choices. There's simply more than you can sample on any one trip.

Because of the large, international tourist trade and the community's own increasing sophistication, Orlando eateries don't end with fast food. The whole spectrum is available, from the very simplest mom-and-pops to basic ethnic eateries to elaborate restaurants serving excellent food, beautifully presented in lovely surroundings.

Golf

Orlando has been a mecca for professional golfers for decades. Some of the greats, like Arnold Palmer, have established winter homes in the city, and some hometown Orlando boys, like Payne Stewart, have made it to national acclaim. Not surprisingly, the city offers some of the best golfing anywhere, including courses designed by PGA pros and by the elite of professional golf course designers, such as Pete Dye, Tom Fazio, and Robert Trent Jones.

Lodging

The sheer variety of accommodations around Orlando will make your head spin faster than after riding in a Mad Tea Party teacup. Resorts, hotels, motels, B&Bs, campgrounds; on Disney property or off; owned by Disney or not: It's all here. For those who want total immersion in the WDW experience, Disney offers elaborate resorts with themes that span both the years and the globe. For those who just want a relatively cheap place to crash, there are plenty of mom-and-pop and chain motels at a little distance from the main attractions. Moreover, many of these properties have programs and facilities for children that range from good to fabulous.

Shopping

It's only fitting that the world's number-one tourist destination should offer excellent shopping. It wasn't always thus, however. Recent years have seen a building bonanza of both retail stores and factory outlets. Every year, it seems, a new mall opens. In late 1996, locals were thrilled by the opening of the brand-new West Oaks mall as well as the area's first Saks Fifth Avenue (at the Florida Mall).

For shopping with a more eclectic feel, the tony shops and bistros of Winter Park's Park Avenue are a must. This elegant little street is home to a number of boutiques as well as the usual assortment of chains: the Gap, Banana Republic, et. al. But the real charms here are the shops tucked away in the area's tiny nooks and crannies.

Walking

For a culture that's car-centered, this might seem a rather odd pastime, but rest assured, there's plenty in Orlando to explore on foot. Downtown Orlando itself is home to Lake Eola, which just a few short years ago was a haven for the city's transients. Now spiffed up and renovated, there's a walkway around the lake's circumference that invites strolling. A delightful playground anchors one end of the park. Just a few steps away from downtown's tourist meccas are delightful residential neighborhoods with brick-paved streets and live oaks literally dripping with Spanish moss.

EXPLORING WALT DISNEY WORLD AND THE ORLANDO AREA

Most visitors spend the majority of their time at the theme parks, largely concentrated southwest of Orlando proper. But Orlando and its upscale neighbor to the north, Winter Park, contain some natural and cultural attractions it would be a shame to miss.

Numbers in the text correspond to numbers in the margin and on the Orlando Area map.

Great Itineraries

IF YOU HAVE 3 DAYS

No stay in the area would be complete without visiting the Magic Kingdom ①. A full three-day trip would include that bit of Disney magic, plus a trip to Epcot ②. Catch the fireworks one night and spend the other night at one of the local dinner show extravaganzas. Finish out your sojourn with a day up the road at Universal Studios ⑨. Choose lodging inside 🏨 **Walt Disney World** to make the most of your stay.

IF YOU HAVE 5 DAYS

Spend the first two days at Walt Disney World, visiting the Magic Kingdom ① and Epcot ②, followed by evenings at Pleasure Island and Church Street Station. The third day should be for Universal Studios ⑨, the fourth for Sea World ⑧. End your day at Universal by dining at the Hard Rock Café; then spend the rest of the night around your hotel pool. On your fourth evening, take in a dinner show, perhaps Sea World's luau. A slow-paced final day will give everyone a chance to unwind before heading home, so, on the fifth day, venture into Winter Park; take a leisurely boat tour, visit the Charles Hosmer Morse Museum ㉔, and stop by the Orlando Museum of Art ⑳. If you have younger children, consider the Orlando Science Center ㉑ for its great interactive activities. Lodging at 🏨 **Walt Disney World** or on 🏨 **International Drive** in Orlando is most convenient.

IF YOU HAVE 10 DAYS

You'll have time to see *all* the theme parks, but pacing is key. So that go-go Orlando tourism scene doesn't wear you down, intersperse theme park outings with some low-key sightseeing or shopping. Start with the Magic Kingdom ①, staying late the first night for the fireworks. The second day, tackle WDW's Epcot ②, and hit Pleasure Island that evening. Set aside the third day for a visit to slower-paced Sea World ⑧, making luau reservations when you enter the park. On your fourth day, it's back to Disney—either Blizzard Beach ④ or Typhoon Lagoon ⑥. Return to the Magic Kingdom and the other WDW parks on your fifth and sixth days, hitting the attractions you missed or taking one more spin on those you loved. Have a dinner at Planet Hollywood, and either take in a late movie at the Pleasure Island cinemas or stroll along International Drive. On day seven, a day of (relative) rest, enjoy a boat tour through Winter Park and visit the Orlando Science Center ㉑ and Orlando Museum of Art ⑳ at Loch Haven Park, which has lovely grassy areas good for a picnic. In late afternoon, walk around Church Street Station, visit Terror on Church Street ㉒, and have dinner. On your eighth day, drive out to Cypress Gardens ⑩ or Splendid China ⑪, and catch a dinner show in the evening. Reserve day nine for Universal Studios ⑨. Your last day can be spent hitting a mall or outlet stores for some last-minute shopping, or revisit your favorite theme park. Leave time to clean up back at the hotel and have a bon voyage dinner at a restaurant outside Walt Disney World, to ease your return to real life.

264

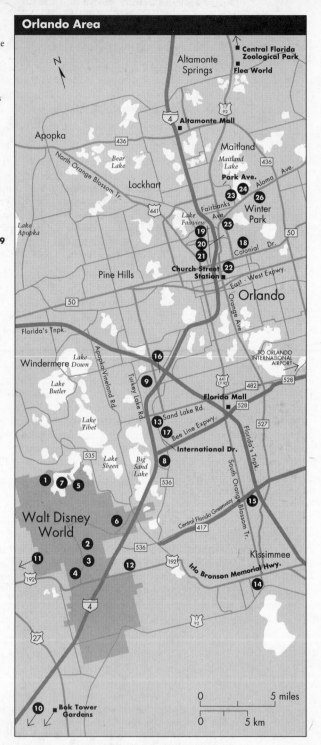

Since you'll be jumping around the area on this one, no lodging is more convenient than any other.

When to Tour Walt Disney World and the Orlando Area

That the Orlando area is an obvious destination for vacationing families has a few important corollaries. If you're traveling without youngsters, try to avoid school holiday periods. If you have preschoolers, follow the same course; crowds can overwhelm small fry. If you're traveling with children of varying ages and those in school are good students, consider taking the kids out of school so that you can visit during a less-congested period. If your children cannot afford to miss school, try to vacation in late May or early June, as soon as the school year ends, or visit at Thanksgiving, which is not as busy as other holidays. Try to avoid the period around July 4 and the Christmas season, especially if you're bringing small children. Although the parks are completely staffed up and feature many special activities and beautiful decorations, the crowds can be overwhelming.

DISNEY THEME PARKS

No doubt about it, the Disney parks have a special magic. You probably know lots about the Magic Kingdom (which is something like California's Disneyland), Epcot, and Disney–MGM Studios, and you'll be hearing more about WDW's new major theme park, Disney's Animal Kingdom, open by mid-1998. But there are also three wonderful water parks—River Country (the oldest), Typhoon Lagoon, and Blizzard Beach. Discovery Island, in the middle of one of the several lakes on Disney property, displays birds and other small animals and makes a pleasant break during a day in the larger theme parks.

Ratings

Every visitor leaves the Magic Kingdom, Epcot, and Disney–MGM Studios with a different opinion about what was "the best." Some attractions get raves from all visitors, whereas others are enjoyed most by young children or older travelers. To take this into account, our descriptions rate each attraction with ★, ★★, or ★★★, depending on the strength of its appeal to the visitor group noted by the italics preceding the stars.

Magic Kingdom

❶ *Take the Magic Kingdom–U.S. 192 exit off I–4; from there it's 4 mi along Disney's main entrance road and another mi to the parking lot; be prepared for serious traffic.*

For most people, the Magic Kingdom *is* Walt Disney World. Certainly it is both the heart and soul of the Disney empire. The Magic Kingdom is comparable to California's Disneyland; it was the first Disney outpost in Florida when it opened in 1971, and it is the park that traveled, with modifications, to France and Japan. For a park that wields such worldwide influence, the Magic Kingdom is surprisingly small: At barely 98 acres, it is the tiniest of Walt Disney World's Big Four. However, the unofficial theme song—"It's a Small World After All"— doesn't hold true when it comes to the Magic Kingdom's attractions. Packed into seven different "lands" are nearly 50 major crowd pleasers, and that's not counting all the ancillary attractions: shops, eateries, live entertainment, cartoon characters, fireworks, parades, and, of course, the sheer pleasure of strolling through the beautifully landscaped and manicured grounds.

The park is laid out on a north–south axis, with Cinderella Castle at the epicenter and the various lands surrounding it in a broad circle. Upon passing through the entrance gates, you immediately discover yourself in **Town Square,** a central connection point that directly segues into **Main Street,** a boulevard filled with Victorian-style stores and dining spots. Main Street runs due north and ends at the Hub, a large tree-lined circle, known as Central Plaza, in front of Cinderella Castle. Rope Drop, the ceremonial stampede that kicks off each day, occurs at various points along Main Street and the Hub.

As you move clockwise from the Hub, the Magic Kingdom's various lands begin with **Adventureland, Frontierland,** and **Liberty Square.** Next, **Fantasyland** is directly behind Cinderella Castle—in the Castle's courtyard, as it were. **Mickey's Toontown Fair** is set off the upper right-hand corner—that's northeast, for geography buffs—of Fantasyland. And **Tomorrowland,** directly to the right of the Hub, rounds out the circle.

Main Street

With its pastel Victorian-style buildings, antique automobiles "oohga-oohga"-ing as they stop to offer you a lift, sparkling sidewalks, and atmosphere of what one writer has called "almost hysterical joy," Main Street is more than a mere conduit to the other enchantments of the Magic Kingdom. It is where the spell is first cast.

Although attractions with a capital "A" are minimal on Main Street, there are plenty of inducements to spend more than the 40 minutes most visitors usually take. The stores that most of the structures contain range from the Main Street Athletic Shop, which sells a variety of "Team Mickey" clothing, to the Harmony Barber Shop, where you can have yourself shorn; from a milliner's emporium stocking Cat-in-the-Hat fantasies to Disneyana Collectibles, a bright yellow, Victorian-style gingerbread building that's a trivia buff's delight, featuring animation art and other memorabilia. All sorts of snacks and souvenirs are on sale. If the weather looks threatening, head for the Emporium to purchase those signature mouse-eared umbrellas and bright yellow ponchos with Mickey emblazoned on the back.

City Hall. This is information central, where you can pick up maps and guidebooks and inquire about all things Disney.

Main Street Cinema. Six screens run continuous vintage Disney cartoons in cool, air-conditioned quiet. It's a great opportunity to see the genius of Walt Disney and to meet the endearing little mouse that brought Disney so much fame. *Audience: All ages. Rating:* ★★

Walt Disney World Railroad. Step right up to the elevated platform above the Magic Kingdom's entrance for a ride into living history. The 1½-mi track runs along the perimeter of the Magic Kingdom, through the woods, and past Tom Sawyer Island and other attractions; stops are in Frontierland and Mickey's Toontown Fair. It's a great introduction to the layout of the park and a much-welcome relief for tired feet and dragging legs. *Audience: All ages. Rating:* ★

Adventureland

From the scrubbed brick, manicured lawns, and meticulously pruned trees of the Central Plaza, an artfully dilapidated wooden bridge leads to Adventureland, Disney's version of jungle fever. The landscape artists went wild here: South African Cape honeysuckle droops; Brazilian bougainvillea drapes; Mexican flame vines cling; spider plants clone; and three different varieties of palm trees sway, all creating a seemingly spontaneous mess.

Enchanted Tiki Birds. Don't expect much when your preshow host is a mechanical toucan called Claude Birdbrain. Inside the blessedly air-

Walt Disney World

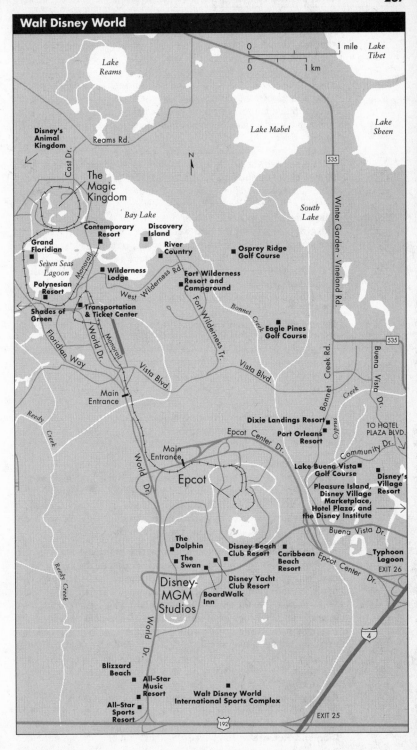

Lake Tibet

Lake Reams

Lake Mabel

Lake Sheen

Disney's Animal Kingdom

Reams Rd.

Cast Dr.

535

The Magic Kingdom

South Lake

Bay Lake

Contemporary Resort

Discovery Island

Osprey Ridge Golf Course

River Country

Grand Floridian

Seven Seas Lagoon

Wilderness Lodge

Fort Wilderness Resort and Campground

Bonnet Creek

Winter Garden - Vineland Rd.

Polynesian Resort

West Wilderness Rd.

Eagle Pines Golf Course

Fort Wilderness Tr.

535

Shades of Green

Transportation & Ticket Center

Monorail

World Dr.

Bonnet Creek Rd.

Buena Vista Dr.

Floridian Way

Vista Blvd.

Vista Blvd.

Cyprus Creek

Reedy Creek

Main Entrance

Dixie Landings Resort

TO HOTEL PLAZA DR.

Epcot Center Dr.

Port Orleans Resort

Community Dr.

Main Entrance

Lake Buena Vista Golf Course

Disney's Village Resort

Epcot

Pleasure Island, Disney Village Marketplace, Hotel Plaza, and the Disney Institute

World Dr.

Buena Vista Dr.

The Dolphin

Disney Beach Club Resort

The Swan

Caribbean Beach Resort

Typhoon Lagoon

EXIT 26

Disney-MGM Studios

Disney Yacht Club Resort

Epcot Center Dr.

BoardWalk Inn

Reedy Creek

I-4

World Dr.

Blizzard Beach

All-Star Music Resort

All-Star Sports Resort

Walt Disney World International Sports Complex

EXIT 25

192

EXIT 25

0 ___ 1 mile

0 ___ 1 km

N

conditioned Polynesian longhouse that houses the birds, the avian intelligence quotient doesn't improve markedly. "Tropical Serenade" is sung and whistled by hundreds of Audio-Animatronics figures: exotic birds, swaying flowers, and Tiki god statues with blinking red eyes. *Audience: All ages. Rating:* ★

Jungle Cruise. During this ride, you cruise through three continents and along four rivers: the Congo, the Nile, the Mekong, and the Amazon. The canopied launches pack in visitors tighter than sardines, the safari-suited guides make a point of checking their pistols, and the *Irrawady Irma* or *Mongala Millie* is off for another "perilous" journey. The guide's spiel is surprisingly funny, with just the right blend of cornball humor and the gently snide. *Audience: All ages. Rating:* ★★★

Pirates of the Caribbean. This boat ride is Disney at its best: memorable vignettes, incredible detail, a gripping story, and catchy music whose relentless "Yo-Ho!"-ing can only be eradicated by "It's a Small World." One of the pirate's "Avast, ye scurvy scum!" is the sort of greeting your kids will proclaim for the next week—which gives you an idea of the ride's impact. Emerging from a pitch-black time tunnel, you're literally in the middle of a furious battle. A pirate ship, cannons blazing, is attacking a stone fortress. Cannonballs splash into the water just off your bows, and Audio-Animatronics pirates hoist the Jolly Roger while brave soldiers scurry to defend the fort—to no avail. *Audience: All ages. Rating:* ★★★

Swiss Family Robinson Treehouse. Based on the classic novel by Johann Wyss about the adventures of a family shipwrecked on the way to America, the treehouse shows what you can do with a big banyan and a lot of imagination. The rooms are furnished with patchwork quilts and mahogany furniture. Disney detail abounds: The kitchen sink is made of a giant clamshell; the boys' room, strewn with clothing, has two hammocks instead of beds; and an ingenious system of rain barrels and bamboo pipes provides running water in every room. *Audience: All ages; toddlers unsteady on their feet may have trouble with the stairs. Rating:* ★★

Frontierland

Frontierland, in the northwest quadrant of the Magic Kingdom, invokes the American frontier. The period seems to be the latter half of the 19th century, and the West is being won by Disney staffers dressed in checked shirts, leather vests, cowboy hats, and brightly colored neckerchiefs. Banjo and fiddle music twang from tree to tree.

Big Thunder Mountain Railroad. As any true roller-coaster lover can tell you, this three-minute ride is a tame one; despite the posted warnings, you won't stagger off, you won't throw up, and you won't vow never to subject yourself to the experience again. The thrills are there, however, thanks to the intricate details and stunning scenery along every inch of the 2,780-foot-long wooden track. Set in gold-rush days, the runaway train rushes and rattles past 20 Audio-Animatronics figures—including donkeys, chickens, a goat, and a grizzled old miner surprised in his bathtub. *Audience: All but young children. No pregnant women or guests with back, neck, or leg braces; minimum height 40". Rating:* ★★★

Country Bear Jamboree. In this stage show, wisecracking, cornpone Audio-Animatronics bears joke, sing, and play country music and 1950s rock and roll. *Audience: All ages. Rating:* ★★★

Diamond Horseshoe Jamboree. "Knock, knock." "Who's there?" "Ya." "Ya who?" "Yaaahooo!" And they're off, with another rip-roaring, raucous, corny, nonstop, high-kicking, elbow-jabbing, song-and-dance-and-fiddling show staged in a re-creation of an Old West saloon. *Audience: All but young children. Rating:* ★★

Splash Mountain. At Rope Drop, the hordes hoof it to this incredibly popular log-flume ride. Based on the animated sequences in Disney's 1946 film *Song of the South,* it features Audio-Animatronics creations of Brer Rabbit, Brer Bear, Brer Fox, and a menagerie of Brer beasts (including Brer Frog and a Heckle-and-Jeckle duo of Brer Crows). You get one heart-stopping pause at the top—just long enough to grab the safety bar—and then the boat plummets down the world's longest and sharpest flume drop right into a gigantic briar patch. *Audience: All but very young children. No pregnant women or guests with back, neck, or leg braces; minimum height 44".* *Rating:* ★★★

Tom Sawyer Island. The 6-mi-long island—actually two islands connected by an old-fashioned swing bridge—is a natural playground, all hills and trees and rocks and shrubs. Other guidebooks suggest that parents sit this one out on the porch of Aunt Polly's Landing, sipping lemonade; we say, why let the kids have all the fun? Most of the attractions are on the main island. These include the mystery cave, an almost-pitch-black labyrinth where the wind wails in a truly spooky fashion; Injun Joe's cave, all pointy stalactites and stalagmites and endowed with lots of columns and crevices from which to jump out and startle younger sisters and brothers; Harper's Mill, an old-fashioned grist mill; and, in a clearing at the top of the hill, a rustic playground. *Audience: All ages. Rating:* ★★

Liberty Square

The weathered siding gives way to neat clapboard and solid brick, the mesquite and cactus are replaced by stately oaks and masses of azalea, and the rough-and-tumble Western frontier gently slides into Colonial America. Liberty Square picks up where Frontierland leaves off, continuing around the shore of Rivers of America and forming the western boundary of Fantasyland.

Hall of Presidents. This multimedia tribute to the Constitution caused quite a sensation when it opened, because it was here that the first refinements of the Audio-Animatronics system of computerized robots could be seen. Now surpassed by Epcot's American Adventure, it's still well worth attending, as much for the spacious, air-conditioned theater as for the two-part show. It starts with a film, narrated by writer Maya Angelou, that discusses the Constitution as the codification of the spirit that founded America. The second half is a roll call of all 42 U.S. presidents. Each chief executive rises and responds with a nod—even those who blatantly attempted to subvert the Constitution. The detail is lifelike, right down to the brace on Franklin Delano Roosevelt's leg. *Audience: Older children and adults. Rating:* ★★

Haunted Mansion. Part walk-through, part ride on a "doom buggy," this eight-minute buggy ride is scary but not terrifying, and the special effects are phenomenal. Catch the glowing bats' eyes on the wallpaper; the strategically placed gusts of damp, cold air; the wacky inscriptions on the tombstones; and the spectral xylophone player. One of the all-time best. *Audience: All but young children. Rating:* ★★★

Liberty Square Riverboat. A real old-fashioned steamboat, the *Liberty Belle,* is authentic, from its calliope whistle and the gingerbread trim on its three decks to the boilers that produce the steam that drives the big rear paddle wheel. The trip is slow and not exactly thrilling, but it's a relaxing break for all concerned. *Audience: All ages. Rating:* ★

Mike Fink Keel Boats. They're short and dumpy and you have to sit on a bench, wedged tightly between fellow visitors. *Audience: All ages. Rating:* ★

Fantasyland

Many of the rides here are for children, and the lines move slowly. If you're traveling without young kids, skip this area, with the possible exception of Cinderella's Golden Carrousel.

Cinderella Castle. At 180 feet, this castle is more than 100 feet taller than Disneyland's Sleeping Beauty Castle, and, with its elongated towers and lacy fretwork, immeasurably more graceful.

Cinderella's Golden Carrousel. The whirling, musical heart of Fantasyland—and maybe even of the entire Magic Kingdom—is the antique Cinderella's Golden Carrousel. It has 90 prancing horses, each one completely different. The rich notes of the band organ—no calliope here—play favorite tunes from Disney movies. *Audience: All ages. Rating:* ★★★

Dumbo, the Flying Elephant. Jolly Dumbos fly around a central column, each pachyderm packing a couple of kids and a parent. A joystick controls each Dumbo's vertical motion, making him ascend or descend at will. Doesn't sound like much? It's one of Fantasyland's best rides. Just ask any mom or dad towing a toddler, or the littl'uns themselves. Alas, the ears do not flap. *Audience: Young children and the young at heart. Rating:* ★

It's a Small World. Visiting Walt Disney World and not stopping here—why, the idea is practically un-American. Moving somewhat slower than a snail, barges inch through several barnlike rooms, each crammed with musical moppets dressed in various national costumes and madly singing the theme song, "It's a Small World After All." But somehow by the time you reach the end of the 11-minute ride, you're grinning and humming, too—as has been the case with almost everyone who's ever heard them since it debuted at the 1964–65 New York World's Fair. *Audience: All ages. Rating:* ★★

Legend of the Lion King. Unlike many of Magic Kingdom stage shows, this one showcases "humanimals," Disneyspeak for bigger-than-life-size figures that are manipulated by human "animateers" hidden from audience view. (The adult Simba, for instance, is nearly 8 feet tall.) The preshow consists of the "Circle of Life" overture from the film. *Audience: All ages. Rating:* ★★★

Mad Tea Party. In this ride based on the 1951 Disney film about a girl named Alice in Wonderland, you hop into oversize, pastel-color teacups and whirl for two minutes around a giant platter. If the centrifugal force hasn't shaken you up too much, check out the soused mouse that pops out of the teapot centerpiece. *Audience: All ages. Rating:* ★

Mr. Toad's Wild Ride. Based on the 1949 Disney release *The Adventures of Ichabod and Mr. Toad,* itself derived from Kenneth Grahame's classic children's novel, *The Wind in the Willows,* this attraction puts you in the jump seat of the speed-loving amphibian's flivver for a jolting, jarring three-minute jaunt through the English countryside. *Audience: All ages. Rating:* ★★

Peter Pan's Flight. Here you board two-person magic sailing ships with brightly striped sails that catch the wind and soar into the skies above London en route to Never Land. Adults will especially enjoy the dreamy views of London by moonlight. *Audience: All ages. Rating:* ★★

Skyway to Tomorrowland. This cable car takes off on its one-way aerial trip to Tomorrowland from an enchanted attic perched above the trees in a far corner of Fantasyland not far from It's a Small World. Can anyone say "photo opportunity"? *Audience: All ages. Rating:* ★

Snow White's Adventures. What was for many years an unremittingly scary, three-minute, indoor spook-house ride, whose dwarfs might as well have been named Anxious and Fearful, has reopened as a kinder, gentler attraction. Now with six-passenger cars and more like a miniversion of the movie, the ride has been tempered. There's still the evil queen, her nose wart, and her cackle, and the trip is still packed with scary moments, but the Prince and Snow White have joined the cast, and there's an honest-to-goodness kiss followed by a happily ever-after ending, which might even have you heigh-ho-ing on your way out. *Audience: All ages; toddlers may be scared. Rating:* ★★

Mickey's Toontown Fair

For a company that owes its fame to a certain endearing, big-eared little fellow, Walt Disney World is astonishingly mouse-free. Until, that is, you arrive here, a concentrated dose of adulation built in 1988 and originally named Mickey's Birthdayland to celebrate the Mouse's Big Six-O. Due to its popularity with the small-fry set, it was retained year after year under the appellation Mickey's Starland. The area is now an official Magic Kingdom "land." The 3-acre niche set off to the side of Fantasyland is like a scene from a cartoon, and everything is child size. Its pastel houses are positively Lilliputian, with miniature driveways, toy-size picket fences, and signs scribbled with finger paint. The best way to arrive is on the Walt Disney World Railroad, the old-fashioned choo-choo that also stops at Main Street and Frontierland.

Goofy's Wiseacres Farm. Traditional red barns and farm buildings form the nucleus here. The real attraction is **The Barnstormer,** a kid-sized roller coaster that's housed in a 1920s crop-dusting biplane. *Audience: Young children. Rating:* ★★

Mickey's Country House. This slightly goofy architectural creation is right in the heart of Toontown Fairgrounds. Inside, a radio in the living room is "tooned" to scores from Mickey's favorite football team, Duckburg University, while his clothes are neatly arranged in his bedroom beside Mickey's baby pictures and a photo of Minnie. *Audience: All ages, although teens may be put off by the terminal cuteness. Rating:* ★★

Minnie's Country House. A peek inside this baby blue and pink house reveals Minnie's lively lifestyle. In addition to her duties as editor of *Minnie's Cartoon Country Living* magazine, the mousy Martha Stewart also quilts, paints, and gardens. *Audience: All ages, although teens may be put off by the terminal cuteness. Rating:* ★★

Toon Park. Another play area, this spongy green meadow is filled with foam topiary in the shapes of goats, cows, pigs, and horses. Kids can jump and hop on interactive lily pads to hear animal topiaries moo, bleat, and whinny. *Audience: Young children, mainly. Rating:* ★★

Toontown Hall of Fame. Check out the blue-ribbon winning entries from the Toontown Fair.

Tomorrowland

The stark, antiseptic future that Disney Imagineers seemed to be forecasting with their original design had become embarrassingly inaccurate by the mid-'90s. Its huge expanses of concrete, its plain white walls trying so hard to be sleek, and its outdated rides said more about Eisenhower-era aesthetics (or lack thereof) than third-millennium progress.

To revitalize what had become the least appealing area of the Magic Kingdom, Disney artists and architects created new facades, restaurants, and shops for an energized Future City, which is more similar in mood to the themed villages of the other lands. And this time around the creators showed that they had learned their lesson: Rather than predict a tomorrow destined for obsolescence, they focused instead on "the future that never was"—the future envisioned by sci-fi writers and moviemakers in the 1920s and 1930s, when space flight, laser beams, and home computers belonged in the world of fiction, not fact.

Alien Encounter. The story here is that you've entered a convention center of the future to watch a test of a new teleportation system, whereupon an attempt to transport the CEO of the device's manufacturer, an alien corporation called XS-Tech, fails. The catastrophic result is a close encounter with a frightening alien creature. Despite a disappointing lack of truly special effects, this is one of the Magic Kingdom's most popular attractions. *Audience: All but young children. Rating:* ★★

AstroOrbiter. The superstructure of revolving planets has come to symbolize the new Tomorrowland as much as Dumbo represents Fantasyland. Despite the spiffy new look, though, the ride is still just the old Starjets, something like Dumbo for grown-ups but with Buck Rogers-style vehicles rather than elephants. You can control the altitude if not the velocity. *Audience: All ages. Rating:* ★★

Carousel of Progress. This 20-minute show in a revolving theater, first seen at the 1964–65 World's Fair and updated many times since then, traces the impact of technological progress from the turn of this century into the near future. In each decade, an Audio-Animatronics family sings the praises of the new gadgets that technology has wrought. The preshow, on overhead video monitors, details the design of the original carousel and features Walt Disney himself singing the theme song, "There's a Great Big Beautiful Tomorrow"—very fitting for the new Tomorrowland. *Audience: All ages. Rating:* ★

Grand Prix Raceway. Be prepared for instant addiction among kids: brightly colored Mark VII model gasoline-powered cars swerve around the four 2,260-foot tracks with much vroom-vroom-vrooming. But there's way too much waiting. *Audience: Older children (minimum height 52" to drive; be sure to check your youngster's height before lining up). Rating:* ★

Skyway to Fantasyland. You can pick up the brightly colored cable cars right outside Space Mountain for the commute to the far western end of Fantasyland. The silence aloft is quite pleasant after the hubbub on the ground. *Audience: All ages. Rating:* ★

Space Mountain. Its needlelike spires and 180-foot-high, gleaming white concrete cone are a Magic Kingdom icon. Inside you'll find a roller coaster that may well be the world's most imaginative. The ride only lasts two minutes and 38 seconds and attains a top speed of a mere 28 mph, but the devious twists and drops, and the fact that it's all in the dark so that you can never see where you're going, make it seem twice as long and four times as thrilling. Try and grab the very front car. *Audience: All but young children. No pregnant women or guests with back, neck, or leg braces; minimum height 44". Rating:* ★★★

Take Flight. That there's almost never a wait here should put your suspicions on red alert. It's in the same building complex as the Timekeeper, and, in fact, the entrances can be easily confused—Take Flight is farther along and to the right. This ride takes a look at the adventure and romance of flying. The idea is cute, but the execution—surprising given Disney's experience with special effects—falls far short of thrilling. *Audience: All ages. Rating:* ★

Timekeeper. Disney Imagineers have pulled out the stops for this attraction in the Metropolis Science Centre. Combining CircleVision 360 filmmaking with Audio-Animatronics figures, it takes you on a time-traveling adventure to the past and into the future. Don't plan on a relaxing voyage, however; there are no seats in the theater—only lean rails, which veterans of the Epcot film circuit can tell you all about. Hosted by Timekeeper, a C-3PO clone whose frenetic personality is provided by Robin Williams, and Nine-Eye, a slightly frazzled droid, the trip introduces you to famous inventors and visionaries of the machine age. *Audience: All ages. Rating:* ★★

Tomorrowland Transit Authority (TTA). All aboard for a nice, leisurely ride around the perimeter of Tomorrowland, circling the AstroOrbiter and eventually gliding through the middle of Space Mountain. Like the old WEDway People Mover, of which this is a redo, the TTA is smooth and noiseless, thanks to an electromagnetic linear induction motor that has no moving parts, uses little power, and emits no pollutants. It's Disney's look at the future of mass transit. *Audience: All ages. Rating:* ★

Entertainment

Beginning at 3 every day, the 30-minute-long **Daily Parade** proceeds down Main Street through Frontierland; there are floats, balloons, cartoon characters, dancers, singers (usually lip-synching to music played over the PA system), and much waving and cheering. It's pleasant and young children love it. Really thrilling is **SpectroMagic,** an incredible 30-minute nighttime extravaganza of twinkle-lighted floats, sequined costumes, sparkling decorations, and sparkling trees. **Fantasy in the Sky** is the Magic Kingdom fireworks display. Heralded by a dimming of all the lights along Main Street, a single spotlight illuminates the top turret of the Cinderella Castle and—poof!—Tinker Bell emerges in a shower of pixie dust to fly over the treetops and the crowds. Her disappearance signals the start of the fireworks. It's a great show and well worth waiting around for.

Epcot

❷ *Take the Epcot–Disney Village exit off I–4.*

Walt Disney World was created because of Walt Disney's dream of EPCOT, an "Experimental Prototype Community of Tomorrow." Disney envisioned a future in which nations coexisted in peace and harmony, reaping the miraculous harvest of technological achievement. He suggested the idea as early as October 1966, saying, "EPCOT will be an experimental prototype community of tomorrow that will take its cue from the new ideas and new technologies that are now emerging from the creative centers of American industry." The permanent community that he envisioned has not yet come to be. Instead, we have Epcot (the "Center" was dropped from the park's name in 1994)—which opened in 1982, 16 years after Disney's death—a showcase, ostensibly, for the concepts that would be incorporated into the Epcots of the future.

Epcot is that rare paradox—an educational theme park—and a very successful one, too. Although rides have been added over the years to amuse young 'uns, the thrills are mostly in the mind. Consequently, because it helps to have a well-developed intelligence that one can exercise, Epcot is best for older children and adults.

The two parts of Epcot are separated by the 40-acre World Showcase Lagoon. The northern half, comprising Future World, is where the monorail drops you off and is considered the official entrance. The southern half, at whose International Gateway the trams from the Dolphin and Swan hotels and Disney's Beach and Yacht clubs and BoardWalk Inn drop you off, comprises World Showcase.

Future World

Future World is made up of two concentric circles of pavilions. The inner core is composed of the Spaceship Earth geosphere and, just beyond it, the Innoventions exhibit and Innoventions Plaza. The large Fountain of Nations serves as a dividing point between the inner core and the pavilions beyond.

Seven pavilions compose the outer ring of the circle. On the east side they are, in order, Universe of Energy, Wonders of Life, Horizons, and Test Track. With the exception of the Wonders of Life, the pavilions present a single, self-contained ride and an occasional post-ride show-case; a visit rarely takes more than 30 minutes, but it depends on how long you spend in the post-ride area. On the west side there's the Living Seas, the Land, and Journey into Imagination. Like the Wonders of Life, these blockbuster exhibits contain both rides and interactive displays; count on spending at least 1½ hours per pavilion—and wanting to stay longer.

Horizons. This pavilion is a relentlessly optimistic look at the once and future future. After being enjoined to "live your dreams," you ride a tram past visions of the future, where former great minds imagine what the world might have been like in 100 years or so. The tram then moves past a series of tableaux of life in a future space colony. The Omega Centuri tableau, portraying a free-floating space colony, prefigures virtual reality, with its games of zero-gravity basketball and simulated outdoor sports. *Audience: All ages. Note that this pavilion may be closed for renovation during the time you visit. Rating:* ★★

Innoventions. Repeat visitors will remember this attraction as Communicore East and West. Live stage demonstrations, interactive hands-on displays, and exhibits highlight new technology that affects daily living. Each major exhibition area is presented by a leading manufacturer. **Innoventions East** will appeal more strongly to adults, with manufacturers such as General Electric, Hammacher Schlemmer, and Honeywell displaying products for the home of the not-too-distant future. There's also a hands-on display of Apple computer software that will keep your kids entertained—provided they can get to a PC. **Innoventions West** features an enormous display of Sega toys and games. You'll be hard-pressed to pull the kids out of here. *Audience: All ages, although young children will tend to be bored. Rating:* ★★

Journey into Imagination. *Honey, I Shrunk the Audience* is one of the most popular attractions in Epcot. This 3-D adventure utilizes the futuristic "shrinking" technologies demonstrated in two hit films that starred Rick Moranis. Just be prepared to laugh and scream your head off, courtesy of the special in-theater effects, moving seats, and 3-D film technology. Don't miss this one. *Audience: All but very young children. Rating:* ★★★

No other theme park has anything that compares with Journey into Imagination's **Image Works,** an electronic fun house crammed with interactive games and wizardry that will give your imagination a real workout. *Audience: All ages. Rating:* ★★★

The stars of the **Journey into Imagination Ride** are a jolly, red-headed, full-bearded, professorial type called Dreamfinder and his sidekick, the ever-inquisitive, pop-eyed purple dragon, Figment. They guide you on the dreamy exploration of how creativity works. *Audience: All ages. Rating:* ★★★

The Land. Shaped like an intergalactic greenhouse, the enormous sky-lighted The Land pavilion dedicates 6 acres and a host of different attractions to everyone's favorite topic: food. You can easily spend two hours exploring here.

The main event is a boat ride called **Celebrate the Land,** piloted by an informative, overalls-clad guide. You cruise through three biomes—rain forest, desert, and prairie ecological communities—and into an experimental greenhouse that demonstrates how food sources may be grown in the future, not only on the planet but also in outer space. *Audience: Teens and adults. Rating:* ★★★

Circle of Life is a film featuring three stars of *The Lion King*—Simba the lion, Timon the meerkat, and Pumbaa the waddling warthog—in an enlightening and powerful message about protecting the world's environment for all living things. *Audience: All ages, although some toddlers may nap. Rating:* ★★

Food Rocks is a rowdy concert in which recognizable rock-and-roll performers take the shape of favorite foods and sing about the joys of nutrition. *Audience: Children. Rating:* ★

Guided **Greenhouse Tours** of the greenhouses and aquacell areas in the Land cover the same topics as the boat ride but in much more detail—and you have the chance to ask questions. Reservations are essential. *Audience: Adults and budding horticulturists. Rating:* ★★

Living Seas. On Epcot's western outer ring is the first satellite pavilion, Living Seas, a favorite among children. Epcot is known for its imaginative fountains; the one at Living Seas flings surf in a never-ending wave against a rock garden beneath the stylized marquee. Time and technology have caught up with the 5.7-million-gallon aquarium at the pavilion's core—thrilling when it first opened—so that what was once revolutionary has now been equaled by top aquariums around the country and at Sea World. Still, the three-minute **Caribbean Coral Reef Ride** encircling the acrylic tank may be too short. Sometimes you'll catch sight of a diver, testing out the latest scuba equipment, surrounded by a cloud of parrot fish. After the reef ride, you may want to circumnavigate the tank at your own speed on an upper level, pointing out barracudas, stingrays, parrot fish, sea turtles, and even sharks, before exploring the two levels of **Sea Base Alpha**, a prototype undersea research facility that is a typical Epcot playground. *Audience: All but young children. Rating:* ★★★

Spaceship Earth. Balanced like a giant golf ball waiting for some celestial being to tee off, the multifaceted silver geosphere of Spaceship Earth is to Epcot what the Cinderella Castle is to the Magic Kingdom. Everyone likes to gawk at the golf ball, but here are some truly jaw-dropping facts: It weighs 1 million pounds, measures 164 feet in diameter and 180 feet in height—aha! you say, it's not really a sphere!

Spaceship Earth ride explores human progress and the continuing search for better forms of communication. Scripted by science fiction writer Ray Bradbury and narrated by Jeremy Irons (who replaced Walter Cronkite as the disembodied voice of the past, present, and future), the journey begins in the darkest tunnels of time. It then proceeds through history and ends poised on the edge of the future, including a dramatic look at a "virtual reality" classroom. Special effects, animated sets, and audience-enclosing laser beams are used to create the experience. *Audience: All ages, but persons who experience anxiety in dark, narrow, or enclosed spaces should not ride. Rating:* ★★★

Test Track. This small-scale version of a General Motors test track was introduced to Epcot in mid-1997. The main draw is the ride itself, billed as "the longest and fastest ride in Disney World history." You get into a six-passenger Test Track vehicle and take a heart-pounding ride through seven different tests: hill climbing, suspension, brakes, environmental, handling, barriers, and, finally, high speed. *Audience: All but young children.*

Universe of Energy. The first of the pavilions on the left, or east, side of Future World occupies a large, lopsided pyramid, sheathed in thousands of mirrors, which serve as solar collectors to power the ride and films within. One of the most technologically complex shows at Epcot, the exhibit combines a ride, three films, the largest Audio-Animatronics animals ever built, 250 prehistoric trees, and enough cold, damp fog to make you think you've been transported to the inside of a defrosting refrigerator. *Audience: All ages. Rating:* ★★★

Wonders of Life. A towering statue of a DNA double helix stands outside the gold-crowned dome of one of the most popular wonders of Epcot. The attraction takes an amusing but serious and educational look at health, fitness, and modern lifestyles.

Walt Disney World's first flight simulator—**Body Wars**—takes visitors on a bumpy platelet-to-platelet ride through the human circulatory system. *Audience: All but young children. No pregnant women or guests with neck, back, or heart problems or motion sickness. Rating:* ★★★.

The theater housing **Cranium Command** seats 200 at a shot. Combining a fast-paced movie with an elaborate set, this engaging show looks at how the cranium manages to make the heart, the uptight left brain, the laid-back right brain, the stomach, and an ever-alert adrenal gland all work together as their host, a 12-year-old boy, suffers the slings and arrows of a typical day. *Audience: All ages. Rating:* ★★★

The **Fitness Fairground,** an educational playground that teaches both adults and children about good health, takes up much of Wonders of Life. There are games in which you can test your golf and tennis prowess, pedal around the world on a stationary bicycle while watching an ever-changing view on video, and guess your stress level at an interactive computer terminal. *Audience: All ages. Rating:* ★★

World Showcase

The 40-acre World Showcase Lagoon is 1⅓ mi around, but in that space, you circumnavigate the globe, or at least explore it, in pavilions representing 11 different countries in Europe, Asia, North Africa, and the Americas. In these, native food, entertainment, art and handicrafts, and usually a multimedia presentation showcase the culture and people; architecture and landscaping re-create well-known landmarks.

American Adventure. The pavilion's superlative attraction is a 100-yard dash through history called the **American Adventure.** To the music of a piece called the "Golden Dream," performed by the Philadelphia Orchestra, it combines evocative sets, the world's largest rear-projection screen (72 feet wide), enormous movable stages, and 35 Audio-Animatronics players, which are some of the most lifelike ever created. *Audience: All ages. Rating:* ★★★

While waiting for the American Adventure show to begin, be sure to read the quotes on the walls of the **Hall of Presidents.** They include thought-provoking comments from Wendell Wilkie, Jane Addams, Charles Lindbergh, and Ayn Rand. Directly opposite the pavilion, on the edge of the lagoon, is the **American Gardens Theatre,** the venue for concerts and shows of the Yankee Doodle Dandy variety.

Canada. "Oh, it's just our Canadian outdoors," said a typically modest native guide upon being asked the model for the striking rocky chasm and tumbling waterfall that represent just one of the high points of Canada. The top attraction is the CircleVision film *O'Canada!* And that's just what you'll say after the stunning opening shot of the Royal Canadian Mounted Police literally surrounding you as they circle the screen. *Audience: All ages, although no strollers permitted and toddlers have to be held aloft to see. Rating:* ★★★

China. A shimmering red-and-gold, three-tiered replica of Beijing's Temple of Heaven towers over a serene Chinese garden, an art gallery displaying treasures from the People's Republic, a spacious emporium devoted to Chinese goods, and two restaurants. The **Wonders of China,** a sensational panorama of the land and people, is dramatically portrayed on a 360° CircleVision screen. *Audience: All ages, although no strollers permitted and small children have to be held aloft to see. Rating:* ★★★

France. You don't need the scaled-down model of the Eiffel Tower to tell you that you've arrived in France, specifically Paris. There's the poignant accordion music wafting out of concealed speakers, the trim sycamores pruned in the French style to develop signature knots at the end of each branch, and the delicious aromas surrounding the Boulangerie Pâtisserie bakeshop. The intimate Palais du Cinema, inspired by the royal theater at Fontainebleau, screens the film *Impressions de France,* an homage to the glories of the country. Shown on five screens spanning 200° in an air-conditioned, sit-down theater, the film takes you to vineyards at harvesttime, Paris on Bastille Day, the Alps, Versailles, Normandy's Mont-St-Michel, and the stunning châteaus of the Loire Valley. *Audience: Adults. Rating:* ★★★

Germany. This jovial make-believe village distills the best folk architecture from all over that country. You'll hear the hourly chimes from the specially designed glockenspiel on the clock tower, musical toots and tweets from multitudinous cuckoo clocks, folk tunes from the spinning dolls and lambs sold at Der Teddybär, and the satisfied grunts of hungry visitors chowing down on hearty German cooking. Other than the four-times-a-day oompah band show in the Biergarten restaurant, Germany doesn't offer any specific entertainment, but it does boast the most shops of any pavilion. *Audience: Adults and older children. Rating:* ★★

Italy. The star here is the Piazza San Marco, complete with a re-creation of Venice's Doge's Palace that's accurate right down to the gold leaf on the ringlets of the angel perched 100 feet atop the Campanile, gondolas tethered to a seawall stained with age, and Romanesque columns, Byzantine mosaics, Gothic arches, and stone walls that have all been carefully "antiqued" to look historic. *Audience: Adults and older children. Rating:* ★★

Japan. A brilliant vermilion torii gate, derived from the design of Hiroshima Bay's much-photographed Itsukushima shrine, epitomizes the striking yet serene mood here. Disney horticulturists deserve a hand for their achievement in constructing out of all-American plants and boulders a very Japanese landscape, complete with rocks, pebbled streams, pools, and hills. At sunset, or during a rainy dusk, the sharp edges of the evergreens and twisted branches of the corkscrew willows frame a perfect Japanese view of the five-story winged pagoda that is the heart of the pavilion. The peace is occasionally disturbed by performances on drums and gongs by the **Genroku Hanamai players.** Other entertainment, which takes place outdoors on the pavilion's plaza, includes demonstrations of traditional Japanese crafts, such as kite making or snipping brown rice toffee into intricate shapes. *Audience: Adults and older children. Rating:* ★★★

Mexico. Housed in a spectacular Mayan pyramid surrounded by a tangle of tropical vegetation, Mexico contains an exhibit of pre-Columbian art, a restaurant, and, of course, a shopping plaza, where you can unload many, many pesos. True to its name, the **El Río del Tiempo** boat ride takes you on a trip down the river of time. Your journey from the jungles of the Yucatán to modern-day Mexico City is enlivened by video images of feathered Toltec dancers; by Spanish-colonial, Audio-Animatronics, dancing puppets; and by film clips of the cliff divers in Acapulco, the speed boats in Manzanillo, and snorkeling around Isla Mujeres. *Audience: All ages. Rating:* ★

Morocco. You don't need a magic carpet to be instantaneously transported into an exotic culture—just walk through the pointed arches of the Bab Boujouloud gate. Koutoubia Minaret, a replica of the prayer tower in Marrakesh, acts as Morocco's landmark. Traditional, winding alleyways, each corner bursting with carpets, brasses, leather work, and other North African craftsmanship, lead to a beautifully tiled fountain and lush gardens. You can take a guided tour of the pavilion by inquiring of any cast member, check out the ever-changing exhibit in the **Gallery of Arts and History,** and entertain yourself examining the wares at such shops as Casablanca Carpets, Jewels of the Sahara, Brass Bazaar, and Berber Oasis. *Audience: Adults and older children. Rating:* ★★

Norway. Here you'll find rough-hewn timbers and sharply pitched roofs designed so the snow will slip right off, softened and brightened by bloom-stuffed window boxes, figured shutters, and lots of smiling, blond and blue-eyed young Norwegians, all eager to speak English and show off their country. The pavilion complex contains a 14th-century stone fortress that mimics Oslo's Akershus, cobbled streets, rocky waterfalls, and a wood stave church, modeled after one built in 1250, with wood dragons glaring from the eaves. The church houses an exhibit called "To the Ends of the Earth," which tells the story of two early 20th-century polar expeditions by using vintage artifacts. It all puts you in the mood to handle wood carvings, glass artworks, and beautifully embroidered woolen sweaters, which sell briskly despite Florida's heat, in the pavilion's shops. Norway also has a dandy boat ride: **Maelstrom,** in which dragon-headed longboats take a voyage through time that, despite its scary name and encounters with evil trolls, is actually more fascinating than frightening. *Audience: All ages. Rating:* ★★

United Kingdom. Never has it been so easy to cross the English Channel. A pastiche of "There-will-always-be-an-England" architecture, the United Kingdom rambles between the elegant mansions lining a London square to the bustling, half-timbered shops of a village High Street to the thatched-roof cottages of the countryside. Their thatch is made of plastic broom bristles in consideration of local fire regulations. And of course there's a pair of the scarlet phone booths that used to be found all over Great Britain, now on their way to being historic relics. The pavilion has no single major attraction. Instead, you can wander through shops selling tea and tea accessories, Welsh handicrafts, Royal Doulton figurines, and woolens and tartans from Pringle of Scotland. *Audience: Adults and older children. Rating:* ★★★

Entertainment

Above the lagoon every night, about a half hour before closing, don't miss the spectacular **IllumiNations** sound-and-light show, with fireworks, lasers, and lots of special effects to the accompaniment of a terrific score. Best viewing spots are on the bridge between France and the United Kingdom, the promenade in front of Canada and Norway, and the bridge between China and Germany.

Disney–MGM Studios Theme Park

❸ *Take the Epcot–Disney Village exit off I–4.*

When Walt Disney company chairman Michael Eisner opened Disney–MGM Studios in May 1989, he welcomed visitors to "the Hollywood that never was and always will be." Inspired by southern California's highly successful Universal Studios tour, an even more successful version of which is just down I–4, Disney-MGM combined Disney detail with MGM's motion-picture expertise. The result is an amalgamation that blends theme park with fully functioning movie and television production center, breathtaking rides with instructional tours, nostalgia with high-tech wonders.

Although some attractions will interest young children, Disney-MGM is best for teenagers old enough to catch all the cinematic references. Surprisingly, the entire park is rather small—only 110 acres, ¼ the size of Universal Studios—with barely a dozen major attractions. When the lines are minimal, the park can be easily covered in a day with time for repeat rides.

Animation Courtyard

The Backstage Studio Tour. This combination tram ride and walking tour takes you on a 25-minute trip through the back-lot building blocks of movies: set design, costumes, props, lighting, and the de rigueur Catastrophe Canyon. The tram's announcer swears that the film that's supposedly shooting in there is taking a break. Not! The next thing you know, the tram is bouncing up and down in a simulated earthquake, an oil tanker explodes in gobs of smoke and flame, and a water tower crashes to the ground, touching off a flash flood. *Audience: All but young children. Rating:* ★★★

Inside the Magic Special Effects and Production Tour. Currently based on *101 Dalmatians,* this walking tour explains how clever camera operators make illusion seem like reality through camera angles, miniaturization, matte backgrounds, and a host of other magic tricks. *Audience: Older children and adults. Rating:* ★★★

Magic of Disney Animation. This 30-minute self-guided tour through the Disney animation process is one of the funniest and most engaging attractions at the park. More than any backstage tour, more than any revelation of stunt secrets, this tour truly takes you inside the magic as you follow the many steps of animation from concept to charisma. From a designated lobby in the Animation Courtyard, you segue into the Disney Animation Theater for a hilarious eight-minute film in which Walter Cronkite and Robin Williams explain animation basics. From the theater, you follow walkways with windows overlooking the working animation studios, where you see salaried Disney artists at their drafting tables doing everything you just learned about. Their desks are strewn with finished drawings of Simba, Scar, Aladdin, Genie, and other famous characters, and you can peer over their shoulders at soon-to-be-famous characters. This is better than magic—this is real. *Audience: All but toddlers. Rating:* ★★★

Voyage of the Little Mermaid. A boxy building on Mickey Avenue invites you to join Ariel, Sebastian, and the underwater gang in this stage show, which condenses the movie into a marathon presentation of the greatest hits. *Audience: All ages. Rating:* ★★

Walt Disney Theater. Tucked behind the Voyage of the Little Mermaid is this movie theater, which usually runs *The Making of . . . ,* a behind-the-scenes look at Disney's latest smash hit. Each film was produced for the Disney Channel, so if you're a subscriber, you may have already seen it. Programs have included *The Lion King, Toy Story,* and *The Hunchback of Notre Dame. Audience: All ages. Rating:* ★★★

Echo Lake

In the center of this idealized California is cool, blue Echo Lake, an oasis fringed with trees and benches and ringed with landmarks: pink-and-aqua restaurants trimmed in chrome, presenting sassy waitresses and television sets at the tables; Min and Bill's Dockside Diner, which offers fast food in a shipshape atmosphere; and Gertie, a Sinclair gas station dinosaur that dispenses ice cream, Disney souvenirs, and the occasional puff of smoke in true magic-dragon fashion.

Indiana Jones Epic Stunt Spectacular. Don't leave Disney–MGM Studios without seeing this 30-minute show featuring the stunt choreography of veteran coordinator Glenn Randall (*Raiders of the Lost Ark, Indiana Jones and the Temple of Doom, E.T.,* and *Jewel of the Nile* are among his credits). Presented in a 2,200-seat amphitheater, it teaches how the most breathtaking movie stunts are pulled off, with the help of audience participants (go ahead, volunteer!). Arrive early because the theater does fill to capacity. *Audience: All but young children. Rating:* ★★★

Monster Sound Show. Despite its name, this show is anything but scary. Rather, it's a delightful, multifaceted demonstration of the use of movie sound effects. Volunteer Foley artists dash around trying to coordinate their sound effects with the short movie being shown simultaneously. "Foley artist," the movie name for sound effects specialists, was named for Jack Foley, the man who created the system. *Audience: All ages. Rating:* ★★★

Star Tours. Although the flight-simulator technology used for this ride was long-ago surpassed by other thrill rides, most notably Universal Studios' Back to the Future . . . The Ride, Star Tours is still a pretty good trip. Guarded by an otherworldly metallic monster, Star Tours is inspired by the *Star Wars* films. Piloted by characters R2D2 and C-3PO, the 40-passenger StarSpeeder that you board is supposed to take off on a routine flight to the moon of Endor. But with R2D2 at the helm, things quickly go awry. *Audience: Older children and adults. No pregnant women or guests with neck, back, or heart problems or motion sickness. Rating:* ★★★

SuperStar Television. Here, 28 volunteers are chosen and through judicious dubbing appear to play the starring roles on shows from "I Love Lucy" to "Gilligan's Island." While the volunteers are led off to makeup and costume, the audience files into a 1,000-seat theater reminiscent of the days of live television broadcasting. On 6-foot-wide monitors, the onstage action appears merged with clips from classic shows. *Audience: All but young children. Rating:* ★★

Hollywood Boulevard

With its palm trees, pastel buildings, and flashy neon, Hollywood Boulevard paints a rosy picture of Tinseltown in the 1930s. The sense of having walked right onto a movie set is enhanced by the art-deco storefronts, strolling brass bands, and roving actors dressed in costume and playing everything from would-be starlets to nefarious agents. Like Main Street, Hollywood Boulevard has souvenir shops and memorabilia collections galore. Oscar's Classic Car Souvenirs & Super Service Station is crammed with fuel pump bubble-gum machines and other automotive knickknacks. At Sid Cahuenga's One-of-a-Kind antiques and curios, you might find and acquire Liberace's table napkins or autographed stars' photos. Down the street at Cover Story, have your picture put on the cover of a major magazine.

Great Movie Ride. Housed in a fire-engine-red pagoda replica of Grauman's Chinese Theater, this 22-minute tour captures great moments in film—from Gene Kelly clutching that immortal lamppost as he sings the title song from *Singin' in the Rain* to some of the slimier characters from *Alien.* Disney cast members dressed in 1920s newsboy costumes usher you onto open trams and you're off—through Audio-Animatronics, scrim, smoke, and Disney magic. *Audience: All but young children, for whom it may be too intense. Rating:* ★★★

New York Street

Backlot Theater. This is where Disney animated films are brought to life. The productions rival Broadway in scope; in fact, the first show to be performed in the Backlot's original locale near the Brown Derby restaurant, *Beauty and the Beast: Live on Stage,* was actually a small-scale prototype for what eventually became the Broadway musical. *Audience: All ages. Rating:* ★★

Honey, I Shrunk the Kids Movie Set Adventure. Let the kids run free in this state-of-the-art playground based on the movie about Lilliputian kids in a larger-than-life world. They can slide down a gigantic blade of grass, crawl through caves, and climb a mushroom mountain. *Audience: Children and those who love them. Rating:* ★★★

Jim Henson's Muppet*Vision 3D. You don't have to be a Miss Piggyphile to get a kick out of this combination 3-D movie and musical revue. The theater was constructed especially for this show, with special effects built into the walls. *Audience: All ages. Rating:* ★★★

Sunset Boulevard

This newest of Disney-MGM's theme avenues pays tribute to famous Hollywood monuments.

Twilight Zone Tower of Terror. Ominously overlooking Sunset Boulevard is a 13-story structure that's reputedly the now-deserted Hollywood Tower Hotel. You take an eerie stroll, especially at night, through the dimly lit lobby and decaying library to the boiler room before boarding the hotel's giant elevator. As you head upward past seemingly deserted hallways, ghostly former residents appear around you, until suddenly—faster than you can say "Where's Rod Serling?"—the creaking vehicle abruptly plunges downward in a terrifying, 130-foot free-fall drop, and then it does it all over again! *Audience: Older children and adults. No pregnant women or guests with back, neck, or heart problems. Rating:* ★★★

The Disney Water Parks

Blizzard Beach

❹ **Blizzard Beach** promises the seemingly impossible—a seaside playground with an Alpine theme. The Disney Imagineers have gone all out to create a ski resort in the midst of a tropical lagoon. Playing with the snow-in-Florida motif, there are lots of puns and sight gags. The park centers on **Mt. Gushmore,** a 90-foot "snowcapped" mountain. After riding a chairlift to the top, "skiers" slide down the face of the mountain, tackling moguls, slalom courses, and toboggan and sled runs. At the base of the mountain, there's a sandy beach featuring the obligatory wave pool, a lazy river, and play areas for both young children and preteens.

Mt. Gushmore's big gun is **Summit Plummet,** which Disney bills as "the world's tallest, fastest free-fall speed slide." From the top, it's a wild 55-mph plunge straight down to a splash landing at the base of the mountain. **Teamboat Springs** is a "white-water raft ride" in which six-passenger rafts zip along a twisting series of rushing waterfalls. Of course, no water park would be complete without a flume ride; enter **Snow Stormers**—actually three flumes that descend from the top of Mt. Gushmore. Riders follow a switchback course through ski-type slalom gates. Slightly less adventurous swimmers take note: There are also rides for you, too.

River Country

Imagine a mountain in Utah's red-rock country. Put a lake at the bottom, and add a verdant fuzz of maples and pines here and there up the sides. Then plant some big water slides among the greenery, and call it a "good ol' fashioned swimmin' hole." The result is **River Country.** The first of Walt Disney World's water parks, it adjoins the Fort Wilderness Campground Resort. Whereas larger, glitzier Typhoon Lagoon is balmy and tropical, this is rustic and rugged. In summer, come first thing in the morning or in late afternoon to avoid crowds.

Walking from the dressing rooms brings you to the 330,000-gallon **pool,** bright blue and concrete-paved, like something out of a more modern Midwest; there are a couple of short, steep water slides here. **Bay Cove** is the roped-off corner of Bay Lake that's the main section of River Country. Rope swings hang from a rustic boom, and there are various other woody contraptions from which kids dive and cannonball. **White Water Rapids,** a series of short chutes and swirling pools, allows you to descend the mountain in jumbo inner tubes at a leisurely pace.

Typhoon Lagoon

Four times the size of River Country, **Typhoon Lagoon** offers a full day of activities: bobbing in 4-foot waves in a surf lagoon the size of two football fields, speeding down arrow-straight water slides and around twisty storm slides, and bumping through white-water rapids. The park is popular; in fact, in summer and on weekends, it often reaches capacity (7,200) by midmorning. If you must go in summer, head out for a few hours during the dreamy late afternoons or when the weather clears up after a thundershower. (Typically, rainstorms drive away the crowds, and lots of people simply don't come back.) If you plan to make a whole day of it, avoid weekends—Typhoon Lagoon is big among locals as well as tourists.

Activities include snorkeling in **Shark Reef,** a 360,000-gallon snorkeling tank (closed November–April) containing an artificial coral reef and 4,000 real tropical fish. Mellow folks can float in inner tubes along the 2,100-foot **Castaway Creek,** which circles the entire park. It takes about 30 minutes to do the circuit; you can stop as you please along the way. A children's area, **Ketchakiddie Creek,** replicates adult rides on a smaller scale (children must be accompanied by an adult). It's Disney's version of a day at the beach—complete with lifeguards in spiffy red-and-white stripe fisherman T-shirts.

Discovery Island

Discovery Island, in Bay Lake, was originally conceived as a re-creation of the setting of Robert Louis Stevenson's *Treasure Island,* complete with wrecked ship and Jolly Roger. Gradually it evolved into an animal preserve where visitors can see and learn about some 100 different species of exotic birds and animals amid 11½ lushly landscaped acres. Although it's possible to "do" Discovery Island in less than an hour, anything faster than a stop-and-start saunter would do it an injustice. You can wander along the shady boardwalks at your own pace, stopping to inspect the bougainvillea or visit with a rhinoceros hornbill. You can picnic on the beach or on one of the benches in the shade and watch trumpeter swans glide by. The only thing you may not do is go swimming—the Water Sprites and motor launches come just too close for safety.

Discovery Island Bird Show. These aviary "Animal Encounters" shows are presented in an open amphitheater equipped with benches and numerous perches. There's usually a show every hour from 11 to 4; most last about 15 minutes. *Audience: All ages. Rating:* ★★

Tips for Making the Most of Your Visit

- Line up for star attractions either first thing in the morning, during a parade, or at the end of the day.

- Whenever possible, eat in a restaurant that takes reservations, or have meals before or after mealtime rush hours (from 11 AM to 2 PM and again from 6 to 8 PM). Or leave the theme parks altogether for a meal in one of the hotels.

- Spend afternoons in high-capacity sit-down shows or catching live entertainment—or leave the park for a swim in your hotel pool.

- If you plan to take in Typhoon Lagoon, Blizzard Beach, or River Country, go early in your visit (but not a weekend). You may like it so much you'll want to go again.

- If a meal with the characters is in your plans, save it for the end of your trip, when your youngsters will have become accustomed to these large, looming figures.

- Familiarize yourself with all age and height restrictions to avoid having younger children get excited about rides they're too short or too young to experience.

- Call ahead to check on operating hours and parade times, which vary greatly throughout the year.

Walt Disney World A to Z

Admission Fees

Visiting Walt Disney World is not cheap, especially if you have a child or two along. Everyone 10 and older pays adult prices; reductions are available for children three through nine. Children under three get in free. No discounted family tickets are available.

TICKETS

In Disneyspeak, "ticket" refers to a single day's admission to the Magic Kingdom, Epcot, the Disney–MGM Studios, or Disney's Animal Kingdom. A ticket is good in the park for which you buy it only on the day you buy it; if you buy a one-day ticket and later decide to extend your visit, you can apply the cost of it toward the purchase of any pass (but only before you leave the park). Exchanges can be made at City Hall in the Magic Kingdom and at Guest Relations in Epcot, Disney-MGM, and Disney's Animal Kingdom.

PASSES

A number of options can save you money. (At press time, Disney's Animal Kingdom had not yet been added to any of the following combination passes. As prices and combinations change often, be sure to call for the most up-to-date information.) The **Four-Day Value Pass** allows you to visit one major park a day for three days and then one of the parks again on a fourth day. To visit more than one park on any day, you can get the **Four-Day Park Hopper,** a personalized photo-ID pass that allows unlimited admission to the parks on any four days. The

Five-Day World Hopper is also a photo ID; it includes unlimited visits to the major parks on any five days, plus seven consecutive days of admission to WDW's minor parks—Pleasure Island, Typhoon Lagoon, River Country, Blizzard Beach, and Discovery Island. Walt Disney World says it introduced the new park-hopping passes as photo IDs to prevent counterfeiting and the illegal resale of passes. (First, however, there was quite a controversy over an earlier decision to allow park hopping only to guests at hotels on WDW property.) Each time you use a pass the entry date is stamped on it; remaining days may be used years in the future. A variety of annual passes are also available, at a cost only slightly more than a World Hopper; if you plan to visit twice in a year, these are a good deal.

Guests at Disney resorts can also purchase **Length of Stay Passes,** which are good from the time of arrival until midnight of the departure day. Passes may be purchased at the front desks of all resorts as well as in Guest Services at the theme parks. Prices (not including tax) are based upon the number of room nights and range from $87.98 for a one-night/two-day adult pass to $288.32 for nine nights/10 days. The pass is good for all theme parks, as well as the three water parks, Pleasure Island, and Discovery Island.

PRICES

WDW changes its prices at least once a year and without any notice. At press time, the following rates were in effect (including 6% tax). For current information, call ahead.

One-day ticket: $42.14 adults, $33.92 children.
Four-Day Value Pass: $142.04 adults, $113.42 children.
Four-Day Park Hopper: $159 adults, $127.20 children.
Five-Day World Hopper: $217.30 adults, $173.84 children.
River Country: $16.91 adults, $13.25 children.
Discovery Island: $12.67 adults, $6.89 children.
Combined River Country/Discovery Island: $21.15 adults, $15.37 children.
Typhoon Lagoon: $26.45 adults, $20.67 children.
Blizzard Beach: $26.45 adults, $20.67 children.
Pleasure Island: $19.03 for all.

Tickets and passes to all Walt Disney World parks can be purchased at park entrances, at admission booths at the Transportation and Ticket Center (TTC), in all on-site resorts (if you're a registered guest), and at the Walt Disney World kiosk at Orlando International Airport (second floor, main terminal). American Express, Visa, and MasterCard are accepted, as are cash, personal checks (with ID), and travelers checks. Many offices of the American Automobile Association (AAA) sell discounted tickets. Check with your local office.

Getting Around

Walt Disney World has its own transportation system, which can get you wherever you want to go. It's fairly simple once you get the hang of it.

BY BOAT

Motor launches connect WDW destinations on lakes and waterways. Specifically, they operate between the Epcot resorts (except the Caribbean Beach) and Disney–MGM Studios and between Discovery Island and the Magic Kingdom, Wilderness Lodge, Grand Floridian, and the Fort Wilderness Campground, Polynesian, and Contemporary resorts (Discovery Island admission ticket, WDW resort ID, or multiday admission ticket required).

Buses provide direct service from every on-site resort to both major and minor theme parks, and express buses go direct between the major theme parks. You can go directly from or make connections at the TTC to Downtown Disney, Epcot, and the Epcot resorts, including the Beach and Yacht clubs, BoardWalk Inn, Caribbean Beach Resort, the Swan, and the Dolphin.

The elevated monorail serves many important destinations. It has two loops: one linking the Magic Kingdom, the TTC, and a handful of resorts, including the Contemporary, Polynesian, and Grand Floridian; and the other looping from the TTC direct to Epcot.

Monorails, launches, buses, and trams all operate from early in the morning until at least midnight. (Hours are shorter when the park closes earlier.) All transportation is free if you are staying at an on-site resort or if you hold a three-park ticket. If not, you can buy unlimited transportation within WDW for a small fee.

Guided Tours

A good way to get a feel for the layout of the Magic Kingdom and what goes on behind the scenes is to take the **"Keys to the Kingdom"** tour, a 3½- to 4-hour guided orientation tour ($45 adults and children 10 and up; no younger children allowed). Tours leave from City Hall daily between 9:15 and 9:30 AM.

Reserve up to three weeks in advance for one of the behind-the-scenes Epcot tours, led by knowledgeable Disney cast members and open to guests 16 and older (☎ 407/939–8687); the cost is $35 in addition to park admission. **"Hidden Treasures of World Showcase East,"** which runs on Tuesdays, offers a look at the eastern half of World Showcase; **"Hidden Treasures of World Showcase West"** runs on Saturdays and, you guessed it, features the other half of the countries. Both offer close-up views of the phenomenal detail involved in the planning and maintenance of Epcot.

Opening and Closing Times

Operating hours for the Magic Kingdom, Epcot, Disney–MGM Studios, and Disney's Animal Kingdom vary widely throughout the year and change for school and legal holidays. In general, the parks stay open longest during prime summer months and over the year-end holidays. During these peak seasons, the Magic Kingdom is open to midnight (later on New Year's Eve), Epcot is open to 11 PM, and Disney–MGM Studios is open until 9 PM. At press time, the hours for Disney's Animal Kingdom had not yet been determined. At other times, Epcot and Disney-MGM are open until 8 and the Magic Kingdom until 7. Always call ahead to make sure of closing times.

Note that though the Magic Kingdom, Epcot's Future World, and Disney-MGM officially open at 9 AM, visitors may enter at 8:30 and sometimes at 8. The parking lots open at least an hour earlier. Arriving at the Magic Kingdom turnstiles before Rope Drop, the official opening time, you can breakfast in a restaurant on Main Street, which opens before the rest of the park, and be ready to dash to one of the popular attractions in other areas as soon as officially possible. Arriving in Epcot or Disney–MGM Studios, you can make dinner reservations before the crowds arrive and take in some of the attractions and pavilions well before the major crowds descend, at about 10.

Parking

Every theme park has a parking lot—and all are huge. Always write down exactly where you park your car and take the number with you. (Repeating "Goofy, Goofy, Goofy" or something similar as a reminder of your Disney-themed locations doesn't always help; by the end of the day, you'll be so goofy with eating and shopping and riding that you'll be thinking "Sleepy, Sleepy, Sleepy.") Parking area trams deliver you to the park entrance. For each lot, the cost is $5 for cars and $6 for RVs and campers (free to WDW resort guests with ID). At Typhoon Lagoon, River Country, and Blizzard Beach, parking is free.

Visitor Information

For general information, contact **Walt Disney World Information** (✉ Box 10040, Lake Buena Vista 32830, ☎ 407/824–4321, TDD 407/827–5141) or the central **WDW switchboard** (☎ 407/824–2222). For accommodations and shows, call **WDW Central Reservations** (☎ 407/934–7639). For dining reservations at Walt Disney World there's a single phone number: ☎ 407/939–3463. To inquire about resort facilities, call the individual property. **Walt Disney Travel Co.** (✉ 1675 Buena Vista Dr., Lake Buena Vista 32830, ☎ 800/828–0228) can arrange packages, including cruises, car rentals, and hotels both on and off Disney property. People with disabilities can call **WDW Special Request Reservations** (☎ 407/939–7807, TDD 407/939–7670) to get information or book rooms. **Disney-MGM Production Information** (☎ 407/560–4651) can tell you how to be a member of the audience at a show being taped at Disney–MGM Studios.

THEME PARKS BEYOND DISNEY

Theme parks grow so well in the sandy central Florida soil that you might almost imagine a handful of seeds, scattered across the fertile I–4 belt, waiting for the right combination of money and vision. Growth engendered more growth. Whereas it used to be that you could do a whole park—any park—in about six hours, a thorough visit now can barely be contained in a day. As competition sharpened and tastes grew more sophisticated, a sort of me-too mentality became prevalent. If one park has a flight simulator attraction, then all parks must have one (the best are Disney-MGM's Star Tours and Universal Studios' Back to the Future . . . The Ride). Ditto for Broadway-style music-and-dance shows. A blessing for parents is that every park now has a sophisticated children's play area, with ball crawls, bouncing rooms, and the like.

Sea World

8 *Near the intersection of I–4 and the Bee Line Expressway; take I–4 to Exit 28 and follow signs.*

Aptly named, Sea World is the world's largest zoological park and is devoted entirely to the mammals, birds, fish, and reptiles living in the ocean and its tributaries. Every attraction is designed to demonstrate the beauty of the marine world and how it is threatened by human thoughtlessness. Yet the presentations are rarely dogmatic, never pedantic, and almost always memorable as well as enjoyable. The park rivals Disney properties for squeaky-cleanliness, courteous staff, and its clever attention to details.

Sea World is organized around a 17-acre central lake. As you enter, the lake is to your right. You can orient yourself by the Sky Tower, whose revolving viewing platform is generally visible even above the trees; it's directly opposite Shamu Stadium. Pick up an entertainment schedule when you come in.

Among Sea World's educational programs are **Backstage Explorations, Animal Lover's Adventure,** and **Animal Training Discoveries,** in which Sea World trainers discuss animal behavior and training techniques. Register at the guided tour center to the left of the Guest Relations/Information Center at the park entrance.

Clydesdale Hamlet. Stop by to visit the hulking Clydesdale horses, the trademark of park owner Anheuser-Busch. It's around the corner from Terrors of the Deep.

Journey to Atlantis. Opening in spring 1998, this isn't just any high-speed water ride/roller coaster. It's a sensory encounter with ancient statues that come to life and entire sets that metamorphose into Olympian vistas.

Key West. The region made famous by artists from Jimmy Buffett to Ernest Hemingway has been re-created here. Don't miss the up-close view of the dolphins and stingrays in the attached exhibits. Be a part of the fun by tossing a few smelt to the snack-happy stars that are the heart of these exhibits.

Manatees: The Last Generation? After a short film, you can watch manatees splash about in their 300,000-gallon tank (there's also a 30,000-gallon nursing lagoon for manatee moms and their babies).

Pacific Point Preserve. The fun-loving California sea lions and harbor and fur seals on these 2½ acres literally sing for their supper.

Penguin Encounter. Whip into this one early, to visit one of the most spectacular attractions at its least crowded time. This refrigerated re-creation of Antarctica is home to 17 species of penguins; a Plexiglas wall on the viewers side of the tank lets you see that the penguins are as graceful in the water as they are awkward on land.

Sea World Theatre. Between Penguin Encounter and the central lagoon, this theater features *The Mickey Finn Show,* a hand-clappin', foot-stompin' Dixieland extravaganza. After 5, the theater is turned into a giant wading pool for the **Water Fantasy,** during which 36 revolving nozzles spray water into fountains, waving plumes, and helices, all set to music and colored lights. It's great late in the afternoon.

Shamu: Close Up. This is a high point of every visitor's Sea World experience. Go as much as 45 minutes early to get a seat. Luckily, even the wait is fun. A camera plays along with the audience as you watch each other while watching the whales swim around their tank.

Shamu's Happy Harbor. If you've got kids, find the time to let them unwind at this 3-acre, state-of-the-art playground.

Terrors of the Deep. Videos and walk-through Plexiglas tunnels let you get acquainted with the world's largest collection of such dangerous sea creatures as eels, barracuda, venomous and poisonous fish, and sharks.

Tropical Reef. More than 1,000 tropical fish swim around a 160,000-gallon man-made coral reef in this soothing indoor attraction built around a cylindrical mega-aquarium.

Wild Arctic. The park's most ambitious attraction is a unique hybrid of a thrill ride and training center about the Arctic's most deceptively cuddly predators. It provides a chilly encounter with polar bears and some interesting interactive displays. To see it, follow the crowds across the bridge to Shamu Stadium; while they're watching Sea World's orca mascot perform, you can sneak in without a wait.

Sea World Information

✉ *7007 Sea Harbor Dr., Orlando 32821,* ☎ *407/351–3600 or 800/327–2424.* 🎫 *$40.95 adults, $33.90 children 3–9; educational* *programs: $5.95 adults, $4.95 children 3–9; parking: $5 per car, $7 per RV or camper. ⊙ Daily 9–7, until as late as 10 summer and holidays; educational programs daily 9–3, every 30 mins.*

Universal Studios Florida

9 *Near the intersection of I–4 and Florida's Turnpike. Take I–4 to Exit 29; turn onto Sand Lake Rd. (to the right if you've traveled west on I–4, to the left if you've traveled east) then turn right onto Turkey Lake Rd.*

Far from being a Disney–MGM Studios wannabe, Universal Studios Florida, which opened in 1990, is a theme park with plenty of personality of its own. It's saucy, sassy, and hip—and doesn't hesitate to invite comparisons with the competition. Disney–MGM's strolling actors are pablum compared to the Blues Brothers peeling rubber in the Bluesmobile. And let's face it, even Disney–MGM's Muppets are matched by E.T., Tickli Moot, and other inventions of Steven Spielberg, Universal's genius on call. They've even figured out a way to keep people entertained while they wait in line; from arcade games at Nickelodeon to news shows on overhead screens in the Jaws line, Universal makes the most of its video connection.

The lofty adult ticket prices raise expectations very high indeed. They are met most of the time, but resentment can set in if you're confronted by too many long lines and the price gouging at ubiquitous concession stands and snackeries. With Disney–MGM just down the road, is Universal worth the visit? The answer is an unqualified yes. Actually, Universal Studios and Disney–MGM dovetail rather than replicate each other. Universal's attractions are geared more to older children than to the stroller set.

Never wanting to be outdone by the House of the Mouse, Universal is adding new rides, centers, and even a new theme park—Islands of Adventure—by decade's end. At Universal Studios itself, a **Preview Center** will reveal the new park's themes, rides, shows, and attractions. Also new at Universal Studios, you can fight shoulder to shoulder with mythical heroes at the interactive **Hercules and Xena** attraction, based on the popular television series *Hercules: The Legendary Journeys* and *Xena: Warrior Princess*. Coming in summer 1998, **Twister** will let you experience the destructive nature of a tornado through a combination of special effects. **CityWalk**, debuting in mid-1998, will be Universal's entertainment complex, full of themed nightclubs with celebrity endorsements.

The 444 acres of Universal Studios are a bewildering conglomeration of stage sets, shops, reproductions of New York and San Francisco, and anonymous soundstages housing theme attractions as well as genuine moviemaking paraphernalia. On the map, these sets are neatly divided into six neighborhoods, surrounding a huge blue lagoon, which is the setting for the **Dynamite Nights Stunt Spectacular,** a shoot-'em-up stunt show (performed on water skis, no less!) presented nightly at 7. As you walk around the park, however, expect to get lost, and if you do, just ask directions of the nearest staffer.

The Front Lot

This is essentially a scene setter and the place to find many services. The main drag, the Plaza of the Stars, stretches from the marble-arch entrance gateway straight down to the other end of the lot.

Hollywood

Angling off to the right of Plaza of the Stars, Rodeo Drive forms the backbone of Hollywood.

The Gory, Gruesome & Grotesque Horror Make-Up Show. Although young children may be frightened, older kids and teens love this production, showing as it does what goes into and oozes out of the most mangled monsters in movie history.

Lucy: A Tribute. This walk-through collection of Lucille Ball's costumes, accessories, and other memorabilia is best for real fans of the ditzy redhead.

Terminator 2 3-D. Arnold is back in this 3-D adventure based on the popular movies. Lots of fun because the film features not only the muscle man himself but his original co-stars from the cinematic version.

Production Central

This area is composed of six huge warehouses containing working soundstages, as well as several attractions. Follow Nickelodeon Way left from the Plaza of the Stars.

Alfred Hitchcock's 3-D Theatre. This is a dandy 40-minute multimedia tribute to the master of suspense (young children may be frightened).

The Funtastic World of Hanna-Barbera. This combination ride–video–interactive display at the corner of Nickelodeon Way and Plaza of the Stars is always crowded. Using Hanna-Barbera animated characters (Yogi Bear, the Jetsons, the Flintstones), it shows how cartoons are made and gives you eight minutes of thrills in the process. (It may be too much for toddlers.)

Nickelodeon Studios. The Green Slime Geyser entices visitors into the home of the world's only television network designed for kids. A 30-minute tour shows how a television show is produced. The banks of lights, concrete floors, and general warehouse feel go a long way toward demystifying movie magic, but it's exactly that behind-the-scenes perspective that makes the tour interesting. About 90% of Nick's shows are made on its pair of soundstages. Lines are often long, however, so you may want to skip it if no shows are taping.

New York

Here the Big Apple is rendered with surprising detail, right down to the cracked concrete and slightly stained cobblestones. The **Blues Brothers Bluesmobile** regularly cruises the neighborhood, and musicians hop out to give impromptu performances at 70 Delancey.

Kongfrontation. A thriller, this very popular five-minute ride puts you on a tram for a joyous, scream-filled encounter with the beast.

San Francisco/Amity

This area combines two sets. One part is the wharves and warehouses of San Francisco's Embarcadero and Fisherman's Wharf district, with cable-car tracks and the distinctive redbrick Ghirardelli chocolate factory; the other is the New England fishing village terrorized by the shark in *Jaws*.

Beetlejuice's Graveyard Revue. A live 15-minute sound-and-light spectacle, this stars the ghoul of the same name, from the 1991 movie starring Michael Keaton. Its theme is rock and roll and monsters, and it's carried off with lots of noise, smoke, and wit.

Earthquake—The Big One. This is another headliner in Universal's Adrenaline Alley. The preshow reproduces choice scenes from the movie *Earthquake,* then takes you onto San Francisco Bay Area Rapid Transit subway cars to ride out an 8.3 Richter-scale tremor and its consequences: fire, flood, blackouts. Unlike Disney–MGM Studios' Disaster Canyon, this ride has no "safe" seats; it's not for younger children. It lasts 20 minutes, and lines are always long.

Jaws: **The Ride.** Stagger out of San Francisco into Amity and you can stand in line for this revamped, terror-filled boat trip with concomitant explosions, noise, shaking, and gnashing of sharp shark teeth.

The Wild, Wild, Wild West Stunt Show. Presented in a covered amphitheater at the very end of Amity Avenue, this extravaganza involves trapdoors, fistfights, bullwhips, water gags, explosions, shoot-outs, horseback riding, and jokes that skewer every other theme park in central Florida.

Expo Center

The southeastern corner of the park contains a treasure trove of attractions.

AT&T at the Movies. Here you can play high-tech computer games.

Back to the Future . . . **The Ride.** Universal's flight simulator ride is a flight simulator ride to beat all others, even (probably) those yet to be built. A seven-story, one-of-a-kind Omnimax screen surrounds your Delorean-shape simulator so that you lose all sense of perspective as you rush backward and forward in the space-time continuum—and there are no seat belts. You may have to wait up to two hours for this five-minute ride unless you make a beeline here first thing in the morning.

A Day in the Park with Barney. America's most famous purple dinosaur presides over a host of activities for children.

E.T. Adventure. This trip aboard bicycles mounted on a movable platform takes you through fantastic forests and across the moon in an attempt to help the endearing extraterrestrial find his way back to his home planet. You can wait hours to ride and (almost) be glad you did.

Fievel's Playland. For younger children, this is a true gift. Based on the adventures of Steven Spielberg's mighty-if-miniature mouse, this gigantic playground incorporates a four-story net climb, tunnel slides, water play areas, ball crawls, a 200-foot water slide, and a harmonica slide that plays music when you slide along the openings.

Universal Studios Florida Information

Tickets are available at the entrance, by mail from the park, and by mail through Ticketmaster (☎ 800/745–5000); discounted tickets are available at the Orlando/Orange County Convention and Visitors Bureau. ⊠ *1000 Universal Studios Plaza, Orlando 32819-7610,* ☎ *407/363–8000, TTY 407/363–8265.* 🎟 *One day: $39.75 adults, $32 children 3–9; two days: $59.75 adults, $49.75 children 3–9; parking: $5 cars, $7 campers.* ⊗ *Daily 9–7, until as late as 10 summer and holidays.*

Cypress Gardens

🔟 *Take I–4 to U.S. 27S exit and follow signs.*

A botanical garden, amusement park, and waterskiing circus rolled into one, Cypress Gardens is a uniquely Floridian combination of natural beauty and utter kitsch. A 45-minute drive from Walt Disney World, the park now encompasses more than 200 acres and contains more than 8,000 varieties of plants gathered from 75 countries. More than half of the grounds are devoted to flora, ranging from natural landscaping to cutesy-poo topiary to chrysanthemum cascades. Even at a sedate pace, you can see just about everything in six hours.

Botanical Gardens Cruise. This float through cypress-hung canals passes hoop-skirted Southern belles, flowering shrubs, 27 different

Pick up the phone.
Pick up the miles.

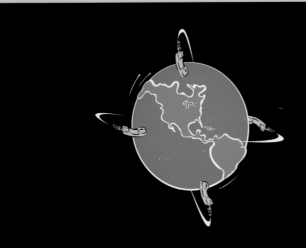

1-800-FLY-FREE

Now when you sign up with MCI you can receive up to 8,000 bonus frequent flyer miles on one of seven major airlines.

Then earn another 5 miles for every dollar you spend on a variety of MCI services, including MCI Card® calls from virtually anywhere in the world.*

You're going to use these services anyway. Why not rack up the miles while you're doing it?

Is this a great time, or what? :-)

Urban planning.

CITYPACKS

The ultimate guide to the city—a complete pocket guide plus a full-size color map.

species of palm, and the occasional baby alligator. Doing this as soon as you arrive in Cypress Gardens gives you a sense of the place.

Carousel Cove. Cypress Gardens' playground, at Southern Crossroads, has lots of ball rooms and bouncing pads plus a lovely old carousel.

Crossroads Arena. Here, in Southern Crossroads, you'll find a rotating collection of circus-theme acts, from acrobats to trained birds.

Exhibition Gardens. The path leading from the ski stadiums to the amusement-park area meanders through this expanse of landscaping, whose philosophy is heroic in intent and hilariously vulgar in execution.

Southern Crossroads. Many of the park's attractions are here: the bird show at the **Cypress Theatre;** a huge walk-through **butterfly conservatory;** a **museum of antique radios; Cypress Junction,** the nation's most elaborate model railroad exhibit; and **Cypress Roots,** a clapboard shack chock-full of fascinating memorabilia about the Gardens' founders, Dick and Julie Pope. **Kodak's Island in the Sky,** a 153-foot-high revolving platform, provides aerial views of the park. **Carousel Cove** is also here.

Water Ski Stadiums. Don't miss one of Cypress Gardens' true specialties, the stunt-filled water-ski revue. Unlike the splashy song-and-dance extravaganzas at other parks, the show at Cypress Gardens is purely athletic—and those sitting in the front rows don't get wet here!

Cypress Gardens Information

⊠ *Box 1, Cypress Gardens 33884,* ☎ *941/324–2111 or 800/237–4826; in FL, 800/282–2123.* ▣ *$26.95 adults, $16.45 children 6–12; parking free.* ☉ *Daily 9:30–5:30, later in summer.*

Splendid China

⓫ *12 mi from Orlando on U.S. 192, approximately 2½ mi west of I–4 Exit 25B.*

Splendid China is more a superlative open-air museum than a theme park. Here you can stroll among painstakingly re-created versions of China's greatest landmarks and watch artisans demonstrate traditional Chinese woodworking, weaving, and other crafts, while tinkling, meditative music plays in the background. It took $100 million and 120 Chinese craftspeople working for two years and using, whenever possible, historically accurate building materials and techniques to create the 60-plus replicas. Both man-made structures and natural phenomena are represented—some life-size, others greatly reduced in scale. (The bricks in the Great Wall, for example, are only 2 inches long.) To appeal to theme-park savvy western visitors, live entertainment and a playground are also on the grounds.

The park is at its most magical at night. Evenings kick off at 6:30 with a parade, so try to arrive after noon. As you come through the turnstile, you enter Splendid China's version of Main Street: **Suzhou Gardens,** a re-creation of a 14th-century Chinese village. Inside are most of the park's shops and restaurants, all a cut above those at typical theme parks. Check with Guest Services, inside the main entrance and to the right, for show times and any special events.

Before touring the park, stop at Harmony Hall to see the 15-minute film *This Is Splendid China,* which explains the park's history and construction. Then, when you're ready to see the monuments, head clockwise (rather than counterclockwise, as the exhibits are numbered), in order to save the best for last. Along the way you'll pass replicated stone grottoes, the originals of which are used as temples, and more.

Acrobatic Show. In the Golden Peacock Theater are some cheesy magic tricks followed by truly incredible feats of balance and flexibility. One woman stands on a bench about six feet off the ground and bends backward to pick up a coin with her mouth.

Great Wall. Although it can't compare to the original—the 1,500-mi-long behemoth that is the only man-made structure visible from space—it's nonetheless impressive, especially when you realize that the 6.5 million tiny bricks used to make the wall were mortared by hand.

Imperial Palace. A reproduction of the centerpiece of Beijing's Forbidden City is one of Splendid China's most impressive sights. The compound in Beijing, built in the early 1400s as the home of the royal family, was constructed with materials from all over China and decorated with centuries worth of loot. It housed so many people that as many as 6,000 cooks were needed to feed them. Even the scale model gives a feeling of its immense size and artistry.

Potala Palace. In the far back corner of the park is this reproduction of the traditional home of the Dalai Lama, Tibet's spiritual and political leader. The dusty rose-and-white structure seems even taller than it is, since the walls lean inward, creating a false perspective.

Stone Forest. The odd obelisks arranged mazelike here are replicas of limestone pillars whittled by aeons of erosion.

Temple of Light Amphitheater. This is Splendid China's live-action venue. A costume show and a demonstration of folk dances and music are presented on alternating hours. Both are slow-moving affairs (though the latter is considerably more interesting) and not improved by the mumbling Chinese announcer.

Terra Cotta Warriors. These figures, not far from the 1,000 Eyes and 1,000 Hands Guanyin Buddha Statue, are modeled after 7,000 life-size clay figurines unearthed in 1974; the originals, realistic portraits of servants, soldiers, and cavalry in the employ of Emperor Ch'in Shih Huang Ti, were buried with the emperor on his death 2,000 years ago.

1,000 Eyes and 1,000 Hands Guanyin Buddha Statue. After the acrobat show in the Temple of Light Amphitheater, stop here. The Buddha's many hands are said to ease the troubles of the world.

Splendid China Information

⊠ *3000 Splendid China Blvd., Kissimmee 34747,* ☎ *407/397–8800 or 800/244–6226.* ▨ *$23.55 adults, $13.90 children 5–12, $21.50 senior citizens; parking free.* ⊙ *Daily 9:30–7, later in peak seasons, Suzhou Gardens shops and restaurants until 9.*

WaterMania

⑫ *½ mi east of I–4 Exit 25.*

All the requisite rides and slides are at this 36-acre park—without Walt Disney World aesthetics. However, it's the only water park around to have **Wipe Out,** a surfing simulator, where you grab a body board and ride a continuous wave form. The giant Pirate Ship in the **Rain Forest,** one of two children's play areas, is equipped with water slides and water cannons. The **Abyss,** similar to Wet 'n' Wild's Black Hole, is an enclosed tube slide through which you twist and turn on a one- or two-person raft for 300 feet of deep-blue darkness. You'll also find a sandy beach, a picnic area, snack bars, gift shops, and periodic concerts, which can be enjoyed while floating in an inner tube. ⊠ *6073 W. Irlo Bronson Memorial Hwy., Kissimmee,* ☎ *407/239–8448, 407/396–2626, or 800/527–3092.* ▨ *$23.95 adults, $17.95 children 3–12 (½ price after 3, after 4 in summer); parking $3.* ⊙ *Daily with varying hrs; winter 11–5, summer 9:30–8. Call for exact hrs.*

Wet 'n' Wild

🔞 *Take I–4 Exit 30A and make a left.*

This park is probably best known for its outrageous water slides, especially the **Black Hole**—a 30-second, 500-foot, twisting, turning ride on a two-person raft through total darkness propelled by a 1,000-gallon-a-minute blast of water. There's also an elaborate **Kid's Park**—for those 4' and under—full of miniature versions of the bigger rides. The **Bubba Tub** is a six-story, triple-dip slide with a tube big enough for the entire family. Teens like the Top-40 concerts that take place frequently in summer. The park has snack stands, but visitors are allowed to bring their own food and picnic around the pool or on the lakeside beach. ⊠ *6200 International Dr., Orlando,* ☎ *407/351–3200.* 🎫 *$24.95 adults, $19.95 children 3–9 (half price after 3, after 5 in peak season); joint 5-day pass available with Sea World and Universal Studios; parking: $4 cars, $6 RVs.* ☉ *Daily 10–5, until 9 in summer. Call for exact hours.*

AWAY FROM THE THEME PARKS

Once you've exhausted the theme parks, or been exhausted by them, you can turn your attention to a wealth of other area offerings. Though you'll find plenty of other recreational activities of interest to kids, there are also museums and parks and gardens galore, highlighting the cultural and natural heritage of this part of the South.

Kissimmee

10 mi east of Walt Disney World.

Although Kissimmee is primarily known as the gateway to Walt Disney World, its non-WDW attractions just might tickle your fancy.

🔞 **Flying Tigers Warbird Air Museum.** Old warbirds never die—they just become attractions. This working aircraft restoration facility is nicknamed "Bombertown USA" because most of the planes here are bombers. Once they are operational, they are usually flown away by private collectors, but the museum also houses a permanent collection of about 30 vintage planes in its hangar, with a few big ones out on the tarmac. ⊠ *231 Hoagland Blvd.,* ☎ *407/933–1942.* 🎫 *$6 adults, $5 children 6–12.* ☉ *Mon.–Sat. 9–6, Sun. 9–5.*

🔞 **Gatorland.** Long before Walt Disney World, there was this campy attraction, which has endured since 1949 without much change, despite major competition. Through the monstrous aqua, gator-jaw doorway—a definite photo op—lie thrills and chills in the form of thousands of alligators and crocodiles, swimming and basking in the Florida sun. Don't miss the **Gator Jumparoo show,** in which gators leap out of the water for their food. There's also a **Gator Wrestling show,** and though there's no doubt who's going to win the match, it's still fun to see the handlers take on those tough guys with the beady eyes. In the educational **Snakes Alive show,** high drama is provided by the 30–40 rattlesnakes that fill the pit around the speaker. ⊠ *14501 S. Orange Blossom Trail, between Orlando and Kissimmee,* ☎ *407/855–5496 or 800/393–5297.* 🎫 *$10.95 adults, $7.95 children 3–11.* ☉ *Daily 8–sunset.*

OFF THE BEATEN PATH

BOK TOWER GARDENS – For those in need of a back-to-nature fix, this appealing but often overlooked sanctuary of plants, flowers, trees, and wildlife is definitely worth a trip. Shady paths meander through pine forests in this peaceful world of silvery moats, mockingbirds and swans, blooming thickets, and hidden sundials. The majestic, 200-foot Bok Tower is constructed of coquina (from seashells) and pink, white, and gray marble and houses a carillon with 57 bronze bells that ring every half hour after 10 AM. Each day at 3 there is a 45-minute recital, which may include Early American folk songs, Appalachian tunes, Irish ballads, or Latin hymns. There are also moonlight recitals. To reach the gardens, head south along U.S. 27, away from the congestion of Orlando and past quite a few of central Florida's citrus groves. ⊠ *Burns Ave. and Tower Blvd., Lake Wales,* ☎ *941/676–1408.* ☞ *$4 adults, $1 children 5–12, free Sat. if you arrive 8 am–9 am; Pinewood House $5 donation.* ☉ *Daily 8–6, Pinewood House tours Sept. 15–May 15, Tues. and Thurs. 12:30 and 2, Sun. 2.*

Near International Drive

7 mi northeast of Walt Disney World.

Between WDW and downtown Orlando are several attractions that kids adore. Unfortunately they may put some wear and tear on parents.

⑯ Mystery Fun House. There are a variety of ways to attack this place. You can just bring your quarters to the video arcade (for which there's no admission charge) or pay to walk through the 18-chamber **Mystery Maze**, which comes with the warning that it is "90% dark" and full of gory and distorted images. Outside, there's the 18-hole **Jurassic Golf**, a basic putt-putt course, laid out flat and simple, with, as you might expect, a dinosaur motif. The real highlight is the **Starbase Omega** laser-tag game. ⊠ *5767 Major Blvd., Orlando,* ☎ *407/351–3355.* ☞ *Maze $7.95, miniature golf $4.95, laser game $6.95, all 3 $13.85.* ☉ *Sun.–Thurs. 10–9, Fri. and Sat. 10–10, until midnight in peak seasons.*

⑰ Ripley's Believe It or Not! Museum. A 10-foot-square section of the Berlin Wall, a pain and torture chamber, a Rolls-Royce constructed entirely of matchsticks—these and almost 200 other oddities speak for themselves in this museum-cum-attraction in the heart of tourist territory. It is said that the fruits of Robert Ripley's explorations are to reality what Walt Disney World is to fantasy. ⊠ *8201 International Dr., Orlando,* ☎ *407/363–4418 or 800/998–4418.* ☞ *$9.95 adults, $6.95 children 4–12.* ☉ *Daily 9–11.*

Downtown Orlando

15 mi northeast of Walt Disney World.

This dynamic community is constantly growing and changing. Numerous lakes create lovely wide spaces that provide a pleasant relief from the tall office buildings. There are plenty of parks, some quiet museums, and bustling Church Street Station.

⑱ Harry P. Leu Gardens. The former estate of citrus entrepreneur Harry P. Leu provides a quiet respite from the artificial world of the theme parks. On the grounds' 50 acres are a collection of historical blooms, many varieties of which were established before 1900. ⊠ *1920 N. Forest Ave.,* ☎ *407/246–2620,* 🖷 *407/246–2849.* ☞ *$3 adults, $1 children 6–16.* ☉ *Garden daily 9–5; guided house tours Tues.–Sat. 10–4, Sun. and Mon. 1–4.*

⑲ Orange County Historical Museum. On Loch Haven Park, this storehouse of Orlando memorabilia, photographs, and antiques features displays of Native American and native Floridian culture, a country store, Victorian parlor, and print shop. Call for an update on the always-changing traveling exhibits. **Fire Station No. 3,** an actual 1926 brick firehouse behind the museum, houses antique fire trucks, fire-fighting memorabilia, and collectibles. ⊠ *812 E. Rollins St.,* ☎ *407/897–6350.* ⌨ *$2 adults, $1 children 6–12.* ☯ *Mon.–Sat. 9–5, Sun. noon–5.*

⑳ Orlando Museum of Art. The draw at this Loch Haven Park museum is the first-class **Art Encounter,** created with the help of Walt Disney World. Young children love it. Hands-on activities, such as dressing up in colorful handwoven clothing from South America, stimulate imaginations and enhance children's understanding of the works in the galleries. There's also a rather limited art collection, including 19th- and 20th-century American art. ⊠ *2416 Mills Ave.,* ☎ *407/896–4231.* ⌨ *$4 adults, $2 children 4–11.* ☯ *Tues.–Sat. 9–5, Sun. noon–5; tours Sept.–May, Wed. and Sun. 2; Art Encounter Tues.–Fri. and Sun. noon–5, Sat. 10–5.*

㉑ Orlando Science Center. Touching is encouraged at this action-packed spot, which moved in 1997 to a new 207,000-square-foot, four-level building with 10 themed display halls, numerous exciting interactive exhibits, and a giant-screen movie theater, **CineDome.** The **Tunnel of Discovery** has a variety of clever hands-on activities to teach the principles of physical science. Special traveling exhibits with themes ranging from dinosaurs to space travel all have interactive components. On weekend evenings, **Cosmic Concerts,** a local favorite, combine lasers and rock music in a psychedelic light show. ⊠ *777 E. Princeton St.,* ☎ *407/514–2000.* ⌨ *Exhibits $8 adults, $6.50 children 3–11; exhibits and either planetarium/astronomy show or CineDome film $12 adults, $9.50 children 3–11; all three $14 adults, $11.50 children 3–11.* ☯ *Mon.–Thurs. and Sat. 9–5, Fri. 9–9, Sun. noon–5; Cosmic Concerts Fri. and Sat. 9, 10, 11, and midnight.*

㉒ Terror on Church Street. Take a 25-minute walking tour through this showcase of horror in the heart of downtown, just a few blocks east of Church Street Station. The high-tech labyrinth features 23 scenes from horror films with live actors and state-of-the-art sound effects. ⊠ *Church St. and Orange Ave.,* ☎ *407/649–3327.* ⌨ *$12 adults, $10 students 17 and under.* ☯ *Sun.–Thurs. 7 PM–midnight, Fri. and Sat. 7 PM–1 AM.*

Winter Park

20 mi northeast of WDW; take Fairbanks Ave. 3 mi east of I–4.

A pleasant day in this upscale town can be spent shopping at chic boutiques, eating at a cozy café, visiting museums, and taking in the scenery along Park Avenue, with its hidden alleyways that lead to peaceful nooks and crannies. Away from the avenue, moss-covered trees form a canopy over brick streets, and old estates surround canal-linked lakes.

㉓ Central Park. This lovely shady green space with a stage and gazebo is Winter Park's gathering place, often the scene of concerts. If you don't want to browse in the shops across the street, a rest on a bench or a stroll through the park is a delightful alternative. ⊠ *Park Ave.*

㉔ Charles Hosmer Morse Museum of American Art. Here you'll see many of the works of Louis Comfort Tiffany, including stained-glass windows, lamps, watercolors, and desk sets. Many of the items were made for his mansion in Long Island, New York. ⊠ *445 Park Ave. N,* ☎

407/644–3686. ✆ $2.50 adults, $1 students. ⊙ Tues.–Sat. 9:30–4, Sun. 1–4.

㉕ Mead Gardens. The 55 acres in this unusual park have been intentionally left to grow as a natural preserve. Walkers and runners are attracted to the trails that wind around the creek. ✉ S. Denning Ave., ✆ 407/623–3334 ✆ Free. ⊙ Daily 8–sunset.

㉖ Rollins College. This private liberal arts school was once Mister (Fred) Rogers's neighborhood—yes, he's an alumnus. You'll see the **Knowles Memorial Chapel**, built in 1932, and the **Annie Russell Theatre**, a 1931 building that's often the venue for local theatrical productions. The **Cornell Fine Arts Museum** houses a small but interesting collection of 19th- and 20th-century American and European paintings, decorative arts, and sculpture. ✉ End of Holt Ave., ✆ 407/646–2526. ✆ Museum free. ⊙ Museum Tues.–Fri. 10–5, weekends 1–5.

OFF THE BEATEN PATH

CENTRAL FLORIDA ZOOLOGICAL PARK – If you're expecting a grand metro zoo, this will disappoint. However, there is a respectable display of about 230 animals tucked under pine trees, and, like the city of Orlando, 22 mi south, it continues to grow. Children love the **Animal Adventure,** containing domestic and farm animals to pet and feed. ✉ 3755 N. U.S. 17–92, Sanford, ✆ 407/323–4450. ✆ $7 adults, $3 children 3–12. ⊙ Daily 9–5; pony rides weekends 10–4.

DINING

Because tourism is king here, casual dress is the rule, and few restaurants require fancier attire. Reservations are always a good idea in a city where the phrase "Bus drivers eat free" could be emblazoned on the coat of arms. If you don't have reservations, the entire Ecuadorean soccer team or the Platt City High School senior class may arrive moments before you and keep you waiting a long, long time. Save that experience for the attractions.

For restaurants within Walt Disney World, reservations are especially easy to make, thanks to its central reservations line, ✆ 407/939–3463. In addition, you can make reservations for the very popular Epcot restaurants at any of the WorldKey Information System terminals in the park.

Orlando is not big, but getting to places is frequently complicated, so always call for directions. Some of the smaller, hungrier restaurant operators may offer to come get you. The other benefit of the competitive restaurant market is that prices have remained cheaper than elsewhere in Florida.

Epcot

British

$$ ✕ **Rose and Crown.** If you are an Anglophile and you love nothing more than a good, thick beer, this friendly pub is the place to soak up both the suds and the British street culture. "Wenches" serve up simple pub fare, such as steak-and-kidney pie and fish-and-chips. Dark wood floors, sturdy pub chairs, and brass lamps create a warm, homey atmosphere. At 4, a traditional tea is served. All things considered, it's one of the best bets in Epcot.

French

$$$ ✕ **Les Chefs de France.** To create this sparkling French café-restaurant,
★ three of France's most famous culinary artists came together: Paul Bo-

cuse, who operates one restaurant north of Lyon and two in Tokyo; Gaston Lenôtre, noted for his pastries and ice creams; and Roger Vergé, proprietor of France's celebrated Mougins, near Cannes. The three developed the menu, trained the chefs, and look in—apparently not as frequently as they should, according to some reviewers—to make sure the food and service stay up to snuff. Start with a chicken-and-duck pâté in a pastry crust, follow up with a classic coq au vin or broiled salmon with sorrel sauce, and end up with chocolate-doused, ice-cream-filled pastry shells.

$$–$$$ ✕ **Bistro de Paris.** The great secret at the France pavilion—and, indeed,
★ in all of Epcot—is this bistro, around the back of Les Chefs de France and upstairs. The sophisticated menu changes regularly and contains exciting offerings that reflect the cutting edge of French cooking. The dining salon is serene—and often filled with well-dressed French people, the mark of a successful transplant.

German

$$$ ✕ **Biergarten.** In this popular spot, Oktoberfest runs 365 days a year. The cheerful—some would say raucous—atmosphere is what you would expect in a place with an oompah band. Waitresses in typical Bavarian garb serve *breseln,* hot German pretzels made fresh daily on the premises. Other classic German fare includes sauerbraten, bratwurst, and stout pitchers of beer and wine, which patrons pound on their long communal tables—even when the yodelers, singers, and dancers aren't egging them on.

Italian

$$$ ✕ **L'Originale Alfredo di Roma Ristorante.** This is the most popular
★ restaurant at Epcot, and its namesake dish, made with mountains of butter flown in from Italy, is one of the principal reasons. The restaurant was created, with the help of Disney, by the descendants of Alfredo de Lelio, who in 1914 founded Rome's Alfredo all'Augusteo restaurant and invented the now-classic dish—fettuccine sauced with cream, butter, and loads of freshly grated, imported Parmesan cheese. But the true secret to the dish here is the butter. Insiders say the only Parmesan that goes into the mixture is what your waiter sprinkles on at the table. During dinner the Italian waiters skip around singing Italian songs and bellowing arias, a show in itself.

Japanese

$$–$$$ ✕ **Mitsukoshi.** This complex of dining areas overlooking tranquil gardens is actually three restaurants. The **Yakitori,** a fast-food stand in a small pavilion modeled on a teahouse in Kyoto's Katsura Summer Palace, offers broiled skewers of chicken basted with teriyaki sauce and *gyudon* (paper-thin beef simmered in a spicy sauce and served with noodles). At the **Tempura Kiku,** two dozen diners sit around a central counter and watch the chefs prepare sushi, sashimi, tempura, batter-dipped deep-fried shrimp, scallops, and vegetables. In the Mitsukoshi's third area—a series of five **Teppanyaki Rooms**—chefs skillfully chop vegetables, meat, and fish at lightning speed and then stir-fry them at grills set into communal dining tables.

Mexican

$$ ✕ **San Angel Inn.** The lush, tropical surroundings—cool, dark, and almost surreal—make this restaurant in the courtyard inside the Mexican pavilion perhaps the most exotic in Walt Disney World. It's popular among Disney execs as well as tourists, who treasure this place because it offers a great respite, especially when the humid weather outside makes central Florida feel like equatorial Africa. Don't expect to see a Disney employee, even off duty, ordering one of the margaritas: They are so bad as to be legendary. Candlelit tables are companionably close

together, and the restaurant is open to a midnight-blue "sky" in the inside of the pavilion and filled with the music of folk singers, guitars, and marimbas. On the roster of authentic dishes, one specialty is mole *poblano* (chicken simmered until tender in a rich sauce of different kinds of chilies, green tomatoes, ground tortillas, cumin, and 11 other spices mixed with cocoa).

Moroccan

$$–$$$ ✕ **Marrakesh.** This is the least popular of any of the World Showcase restaurants, possibly because the average American hasn't heard much about Moroccan food. Consequently, it's relatively easy to get seated, and once inside, you'll find belly dancers and a three-piece Moroccan band set a North African mood that feels almost like a set for a Disney Casablanca. The food is mildly spicy and relatively inexpensive. Try the couscous, the national dish of Morocco, served with vegetables, or *bastilla* (an appetizer made of alternating layers of sweet-and-spicy pork and a thin pastry, redolent of almonds, saffron, and cinnamon).

Norwegian

$–$$ ✕ **Restaurant Akershus.** Norway's tradition of seafood and cold-meat dishes is highlighted at the *koldtboard* (Norwegian buffet) in this restaurant, comprising four dining rooms that occupy a copy of Oslo's Akershus Castle. Hosts and hostesses explain the dishes and suggest which ones go together, then send you off to the buffet table. First, take your appetizers—usually herring, which comes several ways; then go for such cold seafood as gravlax, a cured salmon served with mustard sauce, and *fiskepudding,* a seafood mousse with herb dressing. Pick up cold salads and meats on your next trip, and then, on your last foray, fill up on hot lamb, veal, or venison. The selection of desserts, offered à la carte, includes cloudberries (a delicate fruit that grows on the tundra in season).

Elsewhere in Walt Disney World

American

$$$$ ✕ **Victoria and Albert's.** Servers work in man-woman pairs, calling themselves Victoria and Albert and reciting specials in tandem. But don't let the strange theatrics scare you away from this lavish, romantic dining room, considered the top restaurant by many Disney execs. The intimate 60-seat Victorian-themed room has a domed ceiling, fabric-covered walls, marbleized columns, and lots of flowers. A harpist adds an ethereal touch. The seven-course, prix-fixe menu ($80) changes day to day. Appetizers might include velvety veal sweetbreads and rare New Zealand venison or artichokes in a lusty *duxelles* (mushroom-based) sauce. Entrées range from sautéed breast of duck to well-prepared sirloin. Kosher and vegetarian meals can be ordered in advance. ⊠ *Grand Floridian, Magic Kingdom Resort Area,* ☎ *407/939–3463. Reservations essential. Jacket required. AE, MC, V.*

$$$ ✕ **Artist Point.** The Wilderness Lodge—a huge, jauntily brawny, hunting-lodge-style hotel—is definitely worth a look, and this excellent restaurant offers those not booked there a good excuse to see the place. The northwestern salmon sampler is a good start, but you might also try the smoked duck breast, maple-glazed steak, or sautéed elk sausage. Most meats are hardwood grilled. The house specialty is the "trail dust shortcake," a buttermilk biscuit with strawberries, vanilla-bean ice cream, and whipped cream. ⊠ *Wilderness Lodge, Magic Kingdom Resort Area,* ☎ *407/939–3463. AE, MC, V.*

$$–$$$ ✕ **California Grill.** Disney marketing executives cite this restaurant as an example of the culinary revolution that Dieter Hannig, vice presi-

dent of food and beverage for the resort, is bringing ab⊔ high-quality restaurants are serving original, one-of-a-kind n. The Grill, which flies in 23 varieties of tomatoes every day from a s⊔ cial farm in California, is a shining example of Hannig's master plan. Manager George Miliotes says the strategy is "fresh food, simply prepared," but those words hardly do justice to some of the excellent offerings, like the wood-oven pizza garnished with fresh veggies, the pan-seared tuna steaks, or the hearty grilled pork tenderloin. ⊠ *Contemporary Resort, Magic Kingdom Resort Area,* ☎ *407/393–3463. AE, MC, V.*

$$ ✕ **Planet Hollywood.** On weekend nights, when the nearby Pleasure Island clubs are jumping, so is this place. The wait is typically about two hours on most evenings. If you want to save time, go in midafternoon: The menu doesn't change. Food is secondary to the 20,000-square-foot building, complete with an indoor waterfall. The 110-foot-tall "planet" cost $15 million, as much as Disney or Universal Studios Florida might spend to add a new attraction. The menu is built around fresh, healthful dishes like turkey burgers, smoked and grilled meats, unusual pastas and salads, and a wide range of desserts. Among the better offerings are a Creole pizza with shrimp, chicken, and Cajun sausage, and a tasty $7.50 burger, a bargain in these parts. ⊠ *Pleasure Island,* ☎ *407/827–7827. Reservations not accepted. AE, DC, MC, V.*

$$ ✕ **Rainforest Café.** People start queuing up half an hour before the 11
★ AM opening of this 30,000-square-foot jungle fantasy. A pump system creates periodic "rain storms," and a 3½-story man-made volcano, forming the roof, erupts frequently, shaking the tables. The food, an eclectic mix of American fare with imaginative names, is also an attraction. Eyes of the Ocelot is a nice meat loaf topped with sautéed mushrooms. Other good choices are Rasta Pasta (bow-tie pasta with grilled chicken and pesto sauce) and Mojo Bones (tender, oven-roasted ribs with barbecue sauce). The big gleaming, neon Save the Rainforest globe in the fountain does resemble the Hard Rock Café's, but this place puts its money where its slogan is, donating to groups working to save forest land. ⊠ *Walt Disney Village Marketplace,* ☎ *407/827–8500. AE, D, DC, MC, V.*

Continental

$$$$ ✕ **Arthur's 27.** Though the 27th-floor view is breathtaking, you may be even more lightheaded when you get your check. Handle the fiscal traumas up front with one of three prix-fixe dinner options: $60 (excluding drinks and gratuities) for six courses, $55 for five, or $49 for four. If you order à la carte, you'll probably leave behind a couple of bills with Ben Franklin's picture on them. What you get, however, is a formal dining experience lasting two to three hours—time to savor the haute cuisine and the sun setting behind the Epcot dome. All entrées come with some kind of heavenly sauce, like the herb-rich garlic sauce with roast loin of lamb. Desserts include a chocolate cake to die for. ⊠ *Buena Vista Palace Hotel, Walt Disney World Village, Lake Buena Vista,* ☎ *407/827–3450. Reservations essential. Jacket required. AE, D, DC, MC, V.*

Italian

$$ ✕ **Portobello Yacht Club.** Operated by Chicago's venerable Levy brothers, this eatery has a much better lineage than the one Disney made up—that the building was the home of Merriweather Adam Pleasure, eponym of Pleasure Island. Of course, Pleasure is fictitious, but pleasurable dining is not. Start with something simple—chewy sourdough bread with roast garlic. Then move on to spaghettini *alla portobello* (a stick-to-your-ribs pasta dish with scallops, clams, shrimp, mussels, tomatoes, garlic, portobello mushrooms, and herbs). Since Pleasure Is-

...s in Disney's own nightclub district, where party animals are a ...ected species, the people-watching can be quite interesting, espe-...ly after a little sangria. This is a good spot for a late meal; it's open ...til midnight. ⊠ *Pleasure Island,* ☎ *407/934–8888. AE, MC, V.*

Mediterranean

$$–$$$ ✕ **Spoodles.** Chef David Reynoso, a native of Mexico who studied in
★ the United States and Italy, has blended all the best foods of the Mediterranean into a taste that can be sampled through the tapas-style menu (small portions on small plates, and a lot of them). Perhaps the best dish of all is *rotollo,* a Moroccan flat bread rolled up like a bur- rito and filled with succulent roasted vegetables, hummus, cucumbers, and *tzatziki* (a yogurtlike sauce). High recommendations also go to the barbecued Moroccan beef skewers with raisin and almond couscous, the spicy black mussel and pepperoni soup with Greek orzo and tomato fennel broth, and the duck sausage pizza. Fittingly, desserts, just like the rest of the meal, are from throughout the Mediterranean. The $21 sampler lets you taste them all. ⊠ *BoardWalk Inn, Epcot Resort Area,* ☎ *407/939–3463. AE, MC, V.*

Seafood

$$$ ✕ **Ariel's.** The centerpiece of this favorite of Disney executives, named for the Little Mermaid, is a 2,500-gallon saltwater tank. The finny fare comes from Florida, the Northeast, and the Northwest, and it's most often simply grilled over a hardwood fire. Want something more ex- otic? Start with the Tuckernut shellfish gumbo with andouille sausage and then have Ariel's strudel (chicken and ricotta wrapped in a flaky basil-perfumed pastry). There's no smoking. ⊠ *Disney's Beach Club Resort, Epcot Resort Area,* ☎ *407/949–3463. AE, MC, V.*

International Drive

American

$$ ✕ **Austin's.** That cameo on the front of the menu is Stephen F. Austin, kids, founder of the Republic of Texas and the inspiration for this er- satz Southwest eatery. Like many things in Orlando, Austin's is a fan- tasy, a Florida restaurant chain dedicated to Floridians' visions of what a Texas beef palace should be. But it's a good fantasy. The bar- becued ribs and chicken are quite tasty, and the Galveston Bay—half a pound of ribs and a skewer of hickory-grilled shrimp—should sat- isfy those buckaroos who can't settle the age-old surf vs. turf quandary for themselves. The hickory-grilled fish is also good, especially when Norwegian salmon is available. ⊠ *8633 International Dr.,* ☎ *407/363– 9575. AE, D, DC, MC, V.*

$$ ✕ **Beeline Diner.** This slick, 1950s-style diner in the Peabody Hotel is not exactly cheap, but the salads, sandwiches, and griddle foods are tops. They do the greatest combo ever—thick, juicy burgers; fries; and heavenly milk shakes—just right. Though very busy at times, it can be fun for breakfast or a late-night snack. And for just a little silver, you get to play a lot of old tunes on the jukebox. ⊠ *Peabody Hotel, 9801 International Dr.,* ☎ *407/352–4000. AE, D, DC, MC, V.*

$$ ✕ **Cafe Tu Tu Tango.** Multiple kitchens here bombard you with differ- ent courses, which arrive in waves if you follow the house custom and order a series of appetizers. Actually, you end up doing this anyway, since the entrées are appetizer-size. The menu gives the address—on International Drive—a new meaning. Try the Cajun chicken egg rolls, for instance, with blackened chicken, Greek goat cheese, Creole mus- tard, and tomato salsa, if you want to get a compendium of the major cuisines of the world at one go. For added atmosphere, or perhaps just for the surrealism factor, artists work on paintings on easels while diners watch and sip drinks like the Matisse margarita and the Renoir rum runner. ⊠ *8625 International Dr.,* ☎ *407/248–2222. Reservations not accepted. AE, D, DC, MC, V.*

Chinese

$$ ✕ **Ming Court.** Even though this place is on International Drive, a wall designed to look like a dragon's back gives an enclosed courtyardlike serenity to this Chinese palace of a restaurant. Diners look out through glass walls over a beautifully arranged series of floating gardens. Inside, little touches like rosewood chopsticks and linen tablecloths add to the classy feeling of the place. If you eat Chinese food often, the menu probably doesn't have any dishes you haven't heard of, but the versions here are expertly prepared. The jumbo shrimp in lobster sauce, flavored with crushed black beans, costs more than you may be used to paying ($15), but it's very worthwhile. ⊠ *9188 International Dr.,* ☎ *407/351–9988. AE, D, DC, MC, V.*

Japanese

$$ ✕ **Ran-Getsu.** The surroundings are definitely a Disney version of the Orient—but the food is fresh and carefully prepared. Sit at the curved, dragon-tail-shape sushi bar and order the *matsu* platter (an assortment of *nigiri-* and *maki*-style sushi). Or, unless you're alone, you can have your meal Japanese-style at the low tables overlooking a carp-filled pond and decorative gardens. Specialties include sukiyaki and *shabu-shabu* (thinly sliced beef prepared table side in a simmering seasoned broth and served with vegetables). If you feel more adventurous, try the deep-fried alligator tail. ⊠ *8400 International Dr.,* ☎ *407/345–0044. AE, DC, MC, V. No lunch.*

Mexican

$ ✕ **Don Pablo's.** If you're in dire need of an enchilada fix, this place is for you. Although the big, barnlike building doesn't actually look like a border cantina, the decor doesn't keep this eatery from qualifying as one of the best Tex-Mex places this far from the Rio Grande. Particularly worthwhile are the chicken enchiladas, made with slow-simmered chicken wrapped in corn tortillas, and the beef fajitas, marinated steak served sizzling on a cast-iron platter, with sides of frijoles, rice, and flour tortillas. An imaginative departure from traditional Tex-Mex are the tacos San Lucas—grilled tuna and cabbage wrapped in flour tortillas with lime yogurt sauce. ⊠ *8717 International Dr.,* ☎ *407/354–1345;* ⊠ *100 Towne Center Blvd., Sanford,* ☎ *407/328–1885;* ⊠ *900 E. Rte. 436, Casselberry,* ☎ *407/834–4421. Reservations not accepted. AE, DC, MC, V.*

Thai

$$ ✕ **Siam Orchid.** One of Orlando's several elegant Asian restaurants, Siam Orchid occupies a gorgeous structure a bit off I-Drive. Waitresses, who wear costumes from their homeland, serve authentic fare such as Siam wings (a chicken wing stuffed to look like a drumstick) and *plalad prig* (a whole, deep-fried fish covered with a sauce flavored with red chili, bell peppers, and garlic). If you like your food spicy, say "Thai hot" and grab a fire extinguisher. ⊠ *7575 Republic Dr.,* ☎ *407/351–0821. AE, DC, MC, V.*

Downtown Orlando

American

$$$$ ✕ **Manuel's on the 28th.** How's this for one-upmanship? For a decade,
★ Arthur's 27 was Orlando's loftiest restaurant in terms of altitude, with a spot on the 27th floor of the Buena Vista Palace Hotel. In 1994, Manuel's on the 28th—as in 28th floor of the downtown Barnett

Bank building—opened its doors and was almost immediately hailed by local dining critics as a culinary landmark. In many cases, restaurants with a view offer only that, but the cuisine here is excellent, with stellar offerings like seared loin of lamb in cayenne-Scotch-whiskey sauce, wood-roasted chicken and lobster in coconut-lime sauce, and hickory-grilled muscovy duck breast with plum-ginger sauce. ⊠ *390 N. Orange Ave.,* ☎ *407/246–6580. Jacket required. AE, D, DC, MC, V. Closed Sun. and Mon. No lunch.*

$$ ✕ **Harvey's Bistro.** In the Barnett Bank building, within walking distance of the arena and the Centroplex, this clubby café with panel walls and white tablecloths has collected an enthusiastic business crowd at lunch and concert-, theater-, and arena-goers after dark. The menu offers a good selection of bistro and comfort foods. Soups are good, as are the oven-roasted saffron scallops, the duck cassoulet with white and black beans, and the thin-crusted pizza with caramelized onions, fresh spinach, and goat cheese. ⊠ *390 N. Orlando Ave.,* ☎ *407/246–6560. AE, D, DC, MC, V. Closed Sun. No lunch Sat.*

Eastern European

$$–$$$ ✕ **Café Europa.** It tells you something about Orlando's diverse dining when you can sip a hot bowl of borscht in a cozy Eastern European eatery next door to a Hooter's restaurant. While this quaint little place with flagstone walls and artificial vines hanging from the ceiling may not make you swear you're in Budapest, the food makes a great European sojourn for the palate, and the quiet, sedate atmosphere makes a great change of pace from Orlando's hip and hoopla. The chef does wonderful things with potatoes, including excellent dumplings, which look like round morsels of pasta but have a lighter texture. They are served with the beef Stroganoff and the Hungarian goulash, both hearty, well-seasoned versions of these traditional stews. Good desserts include homemade apple strudel. ⊠ *Church Street Market, 55 W. Church St.,* ☎ *407/872–3388. AE, DC, MC, V.*

French

$$ ✕ **Le Provence Bistro Français.** This charming, two-story restaurant in the heart of downtown does a fine imitation of an out-of-the-way bistro on the Left Bank in Paris. Reasonable prices and first-rate service add to the delightful surroundings and excellent food. For lunch try the *salade Niçoise* (made with fresh grilled tuna, French string beans, and hard-boiled eggs), or the cassoulet *toulousain* (a hearty mixture of white beans, lamb, pork, and sausage). At dinner you can choose between a six-course prix-fixe menu, a less pricey four-course version, or à la carte options. ⊠ *50 E. Pine St.,* ☎ *407/843–1320. AE, DC, MC, V. Closed Sun. No lunch Sat.*

Elsewhere in Orlando

American

$$–$$$ ✕ **Chatham's Place.** This is one of Orlando's best. The Chatham broth-
★ ers, Culinary Institute of America graduates, prepare everything to order here, and the staff is genuinely concerned that every patron has a perfect experience. The professional office building that the restaurant calls home, across the street from the Marketplace shopping mall, lends nothing in the way of atmosphere; nor is the decor anything to get excited about—hanging plants; glass-topped, paisley tablecloths; and a view of the kitchen. But the meticulously prepared food rises above the setting. Try the black grouper with pecan butter, the rosemary-infused rack of lamb, or the duck breast, grilled to crispy perfection. ⊠ *7575 Dr. Phillips Blvd.,* ☎ *407/345–2992. AE, D, DC MC, V.*

$$ ✗ **Hard Rock Café Orlando.** The "Save the Planet" motto was set before founder Robert Earl jumped ship and moved on to found Planet Hollywood with a galaxy of star partners. Both chains purvey a similar fantasy: a few hours of being cool just for standing in line and getting inside. The huge, guitar-shape building is loaded down with memorabilia, including the collarless suits the Beatles wore on the "Ed Sullivan Show." Adjacent to Universal Studios Florida, it attracts a lot of Universal visitors and is a hangout for Orlando Magic players. And, yes, food is even served here. Best bets are the pig sandwich, made of pork shoulder hickory-smoked for 14 hours, and the ⅓-pound cheeseburger with all the trimmings. ⊠ *Universal Studios Florida, 5800 Kirkman Rd.,* ☎ *407/351–7625. Reservations not accepted. AE, DC, MC, V.*

$$ ✗ **Linda's La Cantina.** This place takes beef very seriously, as you can tell by the disclaimer on the menu: "We cannot be responsible for steaks cooked medium-well and well done." Despite that stuffy sounding caveat, this down-home eatery has been a favorite among locals since the Eisenhower administration, thanks to its straightforward approach to well-prepared, tender beef. The menu is short and to the point, including about a dozen steak dishes and just enough ancillary items to fill up a page. Among the best is the La Cantina large T-bone—more beef than most can handle, for $22. With every entrée you get a heaping order of spaghetti or a baked potato. ⊠ *4721 E. Colonial Dr.,* ☎ *407/894–4491. AE, D, MC, V.*

$$ ✗ **White Horse Saloon.** Cattle ranchers would love this, the only hoedown kind of place we know of in a four-star hotel. They would be mighty pleased at the way this western-theme saloon in the Hyatt Regency Grand Cypress sells their products: You can get a barbecued half-chicken for 20 bucks or pay a dollar more for prime rib. If you want to go for the 28-ounce beef-worshiper's cut—that's 1½ pounds of corn-fed beef—it's $46. All entrées come with sourdough bread, baked or mashed potatoes, and your choice of creamed spinach or corn on the cob. A hearty, hot apple pie with cinnamon-raisin sauce awaits those desperadoes who can still handle dessert. You also get music with your victuals. The Hand-Picked Trio, which has been here for years, plays in the evenings. ⊠ *Hyatt Regency Grand Cypress, 1 Grand Cypress Blvd.,* ☎ *407/239–1234. AE, DC, MC, V.*

Cuban

$ ✗ **Numero Uno.** To the followers of this long-popular Latin restaurant,
★ the name is quite appropriate. Downtowners have been filling the place up at lunch for years. It bills itself as "the home of paella," and that's probably the best dish. If you have time and a good appetite, try the paella *Valenciana* (with yellow rice, sausage, chicken, fish, Spanish spices, and a side order of plantains), which takes an hour and 15 minutes on special order. If you don't have that long, go for traditional Cuban fare like shredded flank steak or the dish that half of Latin America eats daily, arroz con pollo (chicken and rice). ⊠ *2499 S. Orange Ave.,* ☎ *407/841–3840. Reservations essential. AE, D, DC, MC, V.*

French

$$$ ✗ **La Coquina.** This gourmet restaurant bills itself as French with an Asian influence, and if you sample the pheasant and truffle wonton with foie gras and chives, you'll think this culture combo is quite worthwhile. The Hyatt Regency Grand Cypress culinary staff uses this restaurant as a showcase for its skills, and if you want a closer look, there's a special chef's table dining experience that can be arranged through the restaurant manager, in which your party eats in the kitchen. If your children can't quite scarf down all their wasabi-seared tuna with

soy or their glazed roast squab and foie gras, smaller portions at half the price are available for diners 12 and under. ⊠ *Hyatt Regency Grand Cypress, 1 Grand Cypress Blvd.,* ☎ *407/239–1234. Jacket required. AE, D, DC, MC, V.*

$$ ✕ **Le Coq au Vin.** Though Louis Perrotte could run a stuffed-shirt
★ kind of place—his food is as expertly prepared as any you'll find in town—instead he chooses the self-effacing route, running a modest little kitchen in a small but charming house in south Orlando. Perrotte and his wife, Magdalena, who acts as hostess, make the place warm and homey, and it is usually filled with friendly Orlando residents. The traditional French fare roused *Vogue's* restaurant critic to raves: homemade chicken liver pâté, fresh rainbow trout with champagne sauce, and Long Island duck with green peppercorns. For dessert, try crème brûlée, and pat yourself on the back for discovering a place that few tourists know about. Ask to be seated in the main dining room—it's the center of action. ⊠ *4800 S. Orange Ave.,* ☎ *407/851–6980. AE, DC, MC, V.*

Italian

$–$$ ✕ **Gargi's Italian Restaurant.** You can feel the building vibrate when Amtrak rolls by, but that just adds charm to this delightful, down-home ma-and-pa pasta place. If you crave old-fashioned spaghetti and meatballs, lasagna, or manicotti made with sauces that have been simmering all day, this hole-in-the-wall in Orlando's antiques district a little north of downtown is the place. If you want more than basic pasta, try the veal marsala or tasty shrimp with marinara sauce and peppers over linguine. Well-heeled Orlandoans eat here before Magic games; it's also a favorite of water-skiers from Lake Ivanhoe across the street. Off the beaten tourist track, but only a few hundred yards from I–4, it's a welcome change from I-Drive. The place is notorious for slow service—but worth it. ⊠ *1421 N. Orange Ave.,* ☎ *407/894–7907. MC, V. Beer and wine only. Closed Sun.*

$–$$ ✕ **Positano.** One side of this cheerful restaurant is a bustling family-
★ style pizza parlor; the other is a more formal dining room. Although you can't order pizza in the dining room, you can get anything on the entire menu in the pizzeria, which serves some of the best New York–style pies in central Florida. Try the unusual and piquant ziti *aum* (mozzarella, Parmesan, eggplant, and basil in a tomato sauce). ⊠ *8995 W. Colonial Dr., in Good Homes Plaza,* ☎ *407/291–0602. AE, D, DC, MC, V.*

Vietnamese

$ ✕ **Little Saigon.** The friendly folks here love to introduce novices to
★ their healthy and delicious national cuisine. Sample the spring rolls or the summer rolls (spring roll filling in a soft wrapper). Then move on to the grilled pork and egg, served atop rice and noodles, or the traditional soup, filled with noodles, rice, vegetables, and your choice of either chicken or seafood; ask to have extra meat in the soup if you're hungry, and be sure they bring you the mint and bean sprouts to sprinkle in. ⊠ *1106 E. Colonial Dr.,* ☎ *407/423–8539. MC, V. Beer and wine only.*

Outlying Towns

American

$$ ✕ **Pete's Bubble Room.** Based on a Captiva Island restaurant of the same name, this entertaining eatery has decor reminiscent of the Beatles' Sgt. Pepper album cover. Thousands of old movie star photos cover the walls of the pink and turquoise building hung year-round with Christmas lights and "bubbles"—colored glass ornaments. To add to the surrealism, servers are dressed in Boy Scout–style uniforms and silly hats. While the atmosphere is whimsical, the kitchen is dead serious. The trademark is well-prepared food in huge portions and tasty desserts in even larger portions. The specialty, "dem bones, dem bones," is a T-bone the size of a pot roast, served on an almost-glowing iron skillet. Another good choice is the Ingrid birdman, a Cornish game hen served with stewed vegetables. ⊠ 1351 S. Orlando Ave. (U.S. 17-92), Maitland, ☎ 407/628–3331. AE, D, DC, MC, V.

$–$$ ✕ **Dexter's.** This hip college bar is so nondescript on the outside that the facade almost blends into the coin laundry next door. But inside you'll find a popular, trendy eatery and winery sophisticated enough to offer its own wine label and publish a monthly newsletter for those who appreciate a good vintage. Much of the clientele comes from Rollins College, a block away, and the SoHo-like menu reflects that. If you are over 40, however, you won't feel out of place. One of the best entrées is chicken tortilla pie (a stack of cheese-laden tortillas that's more spaceship than pie); equally popular is the ratt pie (like the tortilla pie but filled with provolone and ratatouille). Jazz is frequently featured at night. ⊠ 200 W. Fairbanks Ave., Winter Park, ☎ 407/629–1150; ⊠ Dexter's of Thornton Park, 808 E. Washington St., Orlando, ☎ 407/648–2777. AE, D, DC, MC, V.

Continental

$$$$ ✕ **Chalet Suzanne.** If you like to drive or are returning from a day at
★ Cypress Gardens, consider making a dinner reservation at this family-owned country inn. Because of its charm and originality, Chalet Suzanne has earned praise from restaurant critics and might provide one of the most memorable dining experiences of your stay. Expanded bit by quirky bit since it opened in the 1930s, this unlikely inn looks like a small Swiss village right in the middle of orange groves. As an appetizer, try the broiled grapefruit, basted with a butter, cinnamon, and sugar mixture and served with a grilled chicken liver; then move on to shrimp curry, lobster Newburg, or filet mignon. Crepes Suzanne are a good bet for dessert. The restaurant is about 10 mi south of the Cypress Gardens turnoff on U.S. 27. ⊠ 3800 Chalet Suzanne Dr., Lake Wales, ☎ 941/676–6011. AE, DC, MC, V. Closed Mon. in summer.

Italian

$$$ ✕ **Enzo's on the Lake.** Enzo's is one of Orlando's most popular restau-
★ rants, even though it's on a tacky stretch of highway filled with used-car lots. The Roman charmer who owns the place, Enzo Perlini, has turned a rather ordinary lakefront house into an Italian villa. It's worth the trip, about 30 minutes from I-Drive, to sample the antipasto. Mussels, cooked in a heady broth of white wine and garlic, and the mild *buffalo* mozzarella cheese, flown in from Italy, make equally good starters. The *bucatini à la Enzo* (sautéed bacon, mushrooms, and peas served over long hollow noodles) is a very popular house specialty. Even people with reservations don't mind waiting at the bar; they simply get into the party mood. ⊠ 1130 S. U.S. 17–92, Longwood, ☎ 407/834–9872. Reservations essential. AE, DC, MC, V. Closed Sun.

$$–$$$ ✕ **La Scala.** Mirrored walls and gracious, sophisticated decor make this one of the area's most romantic restaurants. The fact that owner Joseph del Vento, a former opera singer who once worked in New York's Tre Scalini, breaks into song every so often only adds to the charm. For pasta, order the dish called Chop, Chop, Chop (fresh seafood sautéed table side, doused in marinara sauce, and served over fettuccine). ⊠ 205 Loraine Dr., Altamonte Springs, ☎ 407/862–3257. AE, DC, MC, V. Closed Sun. No lunch Sat.

$-$$ ✗ **Rosario's.** This little place, in a New England–style clapboard house that looks refreshingly out of place in the unsightly jumble of motels known as Kissimmee, is understated and cheerful. The above-average food includes spaghetti *aglio olio* (with fresh garlic, basil, and diced tomatoes sautéed in olive oil) and hearty pasta *e fagioli* soup (filled with Italian white beans, prosciutto, escarole, and pasta and flavored with both brandy and a touch of marinara sauce). ⊠ *4838 W. Irlo Bronson Hwy., Kissimmee,* ☎ *407/239–0118. AE, D, MC, V. Beer and wine only. No lunch.*

Seafood

$$ ✗ **Nick's on the Water.** The waterfront location is almost a technical-
★ ity; the postage stamp–size Crane's Roost Lake is actually across the street. But guests don't come for the proximity to the water. They come because the Italian seafood restaurant is one of the best way-too-small eateries around. It serves all sorts of tasty tuna, grouper, snapper, and salmon entrées, as well as some decent landlubber options. Veal dishes are a specialty, as are steaks cooked over wood on the open grill. Don't leave without trying the tasty vodka sauce, made with cream, herbs, and marinara. It's available on tasty rigatoni and on a gourmet pizza topped with scallops and fresh basil. Save room for another house specialty, the sweet and creamy cannoli, which, like all the desserts, is made on premises. ⊠ *309 N. Lake Blvd., Altamonte Springs,* ☎ *407/834–5880. AE, D, MC, V.*

LODGING

Your basic options come down to properties that are (1) owned and operated by Disney on WDW grounds, (2) not owned or operated by Disney but on Disney property, and (3) not on WDW property. There are advantages to each. If you are coming to Orlando for only a few days and are interested solely in the Magic Kingdom, Epcot, and the other Disney attractions, the resorts on Disney property—whether or not they're owned by Disney—are the most convenient. But if you plan to spend time sightseeing in and around Orlando, it makes sense to look into the alternatives. On-site hotels are generally more expensive, though there are now some moderately priced establishments on Disney property. But Orlando is not huge, and even apparently distant properties are only a half hour's drive from Disney entrance gates. As a rule, the greater the distance from Walt Disney World, the lower the room rates.

Reservations should be made several months in advance—as much as a year in advance for the best rooms during high season (historically, Christmas vacation, summer, and from mid-February through the week after Easter). Many hotels and attractions offer discounts up to 40% from September to mid-December. Orlando lodging prices tend to be a little higher than elsewhere in Florida, but in all but the smallest motels there is little or no charge for children under 18 who share a room with an adult.

In WDW: Disney-Owned Properties

For locations of these properties, *see* the Walt Disney World map. Reservations may be booked through **WDW Central Reservations** (⊠ Box 10100, Lake Buena Vista 32830, ☎ 407/934–7639); for same-day reservations, contact the number listed for the individual property.

Magic Kingdom Resort Area

$$$$ ⭐ 🏨 **Contemporary Resort.** The monorail runs through this awkwardly modern, 15-story, flat-topped pyramid, making it to look like an intergalactic docking bay. The high-class, ideally situated resort bustles from dawn until after midnight. Half the rooms are in the Tower, the main building, and you'll have to pay extra for their spectacular views. Those in front look out on Cinderella Castle and Space Mountain, flaming sunsets, and the fireworks show; those in back have ringside views of the Electrical Water Pageant and sunrise over misty Bay Lake. Avoid units with a "Magic Kingdom view"—they have a better view of the parking lot. All rooms have a small terrace. ☎ *407/824–1000,* FAX *407/824–3539. 1,041 rooms, 80 suites. 3 restaurants, 2 lobby lounges, snack bar, 3 pools, beauty salon, 6 tennis courts, health club, shuffleboard, volleyball, beach, boating, waterskiing, coin laundry, laundry service, concierge. AE, MC, V.*

$$$$ ⭐ 🏨 **Grand Floridian.** You might think a time machine transported this gilded-age masterpiece from some turn-of-the-century coastal hot spot to the shores of the Seven Seas Lagoon. Actually, the gabled red roof, brick chimneys, rambling verandas, and delicate gingerbread are grand-old yet brand-new. Loving attention was paid to each detail, from the crystal chandeliers and stain-glass domes to the ornate balconies and aviary. Although equipped with every modern convenience, the moss-green and salmon-pink rooms, with Victorian wallpaper, deep carpets, and wall hangings, have real vintage charm, especially the attic nooks up under the eaves. ☎ *407/824–3000,* FAX *407/824–3186. 965 rooms, 25 suites. 6 restaurants, 3 lobby lounges, pool, beauty salon, hot tub, 2 tennis courts, health club, beach, boating, baby-sitting, children's programs, playground, coin laundry, laundry service, concierge. AE, MC, V.*

$$$$ 🏨 **Polynesian Resort.** If it weren't for the kids in Mickey Mouse caps, you might think you were in Fiji. A three-story tropical atrium fills the lobby. Orchids bloom alongside coconut palms and banana trees, and water cascades from volcanic rock fountains. Arranged in 11 two- and three-story "longhouses" around the main building, rooms offer two queen-size beds and a twin bed in the living room, accommodating five. Most units have a balcony or patio. Both pools—one an extravagantly landscaped, free-form affair with rocks and caverns—are beloved by children; for quiet, head for the beach. Monorail, bus, and motor launch lines network at this always-popular resort. ☎ *407/824–2000,* FAX *407/824–3174. 848 rooms, 5 suites. 3 restaurants, lobby lounge, snack bar, 2 pools, volleyball, beach, boating, baby-sitting, children's playground, coin laundry, laundry service, concierge floor. AE, MC, V.*

$$$ ⭐ 🏨 **Walt Disney World Wilderness Lodge.** This seven-story hostelry was modeled after the turn-of-the-century lodges of national parks out west. Of course, Disney does everything bigger and grander than does history. Supported by great tree trunks, the towering, five-story lobby features a huge, three-sided fireplace made of rocks from the Grand Canyon, illuminated by enormous tepee-shape chandeliers. Rooms have western motifs—leather chairs, patchwork quilts, and cowboy art. Each has a balcony or a patio and two queen beds or, on request, a queen and two bunk beds. The hotel's showstopper is its Fire Rock Geyser, a sort of faux Old Faithful, near the large pool, which itself begins as a hot spring in the lobby, flows under a window wall to become Silver Creek, and then widens into a waterfall. Motor launches and buses connect here. ☎ *407/824–3200,* FAX *407/824–3232. 697 rooms, 31 suites. 3 restaurants, 2 lobby lounges, pool, wading pool,* *baby-sitting, children's programs, coin laundry, laundry service. AE, MC, V.*

$-$$$$ ⚠ **Fort Wilderness Resort and Campground.** For a calm spot amid the
★   theme-park storm, go no farther than the 700 acres of scrubby pine
and tiny streams known as Fort Wilderness, on Bay Lake and about a
mile from the Wilderness Lodge. Sports facilities abound; bike trails
are popular, and a marina rents sailboats. Bringing a tent or RV is one
of the cheapest ways to stay on WDW property, especially since sites,
with outdoor grills and picnic tables, accommodate up to 10. If you
don't have your own RV and don't want to camp out, you can rent
one of the fully equipped, air-conditioned trailers, known as **Wilder-
ness Homes;** they're perfectly comfortable. Larger trailers can accom-
modate four grown-ups and two youngsters; the bedroom has a double
bed and a bunk bed, and the living room has a double sleeper sofa or
Murphy bed. Smaller trailers, without the bunk beds, sleep four. Both
types come with full kitchen, dishes, linens, a comfortable bathroom,
daily housekeeping services, outdoor grill and picnic table, and cable
TV. ☎ 407/824–2900. *784 campsites, 408 60- and 80-foot trailers.
Cafeteria, grocery, snack bar, 2 pools, horseback riding, volleyball, beach,
boating, bicycles, coin laundry. AE, MC, V.*

Epcot Resort Area

$$$$ ▦ **BoardWalk Inn.** This Disney hotel, opened in 1996, brings back all
★   the candy-floss enchantment of America's great amusement piers.
Complete with New England–style verandas, painted marquee signs,
and saltwater-taffy touts, it comprises several buildings—ranging from
Victorian to Deco in style—all side by side on a lakeside boardwalk.
An inn-side view reveals WDW's smallest and most intimate deluxe
hotel, accented with courtyards and family-size garden cottages. Thanks
to the Muscles and Bustles health club, 10-piece bands, the dueling pi-
anos of Jellyrolls, and Luna Park—a pool with a 200-foot water slide
in the form of a classic wooden roller coaster—you will never be
bored. Bus, tram, and motor launch lines access the parks. ☎ 407/939–
5100 for inn, ☎ 407/939–6200 for villas, FAX 407/939–5150. *367 rooms,
378 villas. 4 restaurants, pool, tennis court, croquet, health club, night-
club, convention center. AE, MC, V.*

$$$$ ▦ **Walt Disney World Beach and Yacht Club Resorts.** Straight out of a
★   Cape Cod summer, these two properties on a 25-acre lake are coastal
inns on a grand Disney scale. The five-story Yacht Club recalls turn-
of-the-century New England seacoast resorts, with its hardwood floors,
lobby full of gleaming brass and polished leather, oyster-gray clapboard
facade, and evergreen landscaping; there's even a lighthouse on its pier.
Rooms are similarly nautical, with white-and-blue naval flags on the
bedspreads and a small ship's wheel on the headboard. Drawing on
similar inspiration is the blue-and-white, three- to five-story Beach Club,
where a croquet lawn; cabana-dotted, white-sand beach; and staffers'
19th-century Jams and T-shirts set the scene. Guest rooms are sum-
mery, with wicker and pastel furnishings. For the kids there's the Sand
Castle Club and Stormalong Bay, a 3-acre water-recreation area, com-
plete with a shipwreck to clamber over and a mast that is an exciting
water slide. Both hotels are accessible from Epcot via motor launch,
and trams and buses also stop here. *Beach:* ☎ 407/934–8000, FAX
407/934–3850; *Yacht:* ☎ 407/934–7000, FAX 407/934–3450. *1,192
rooms, 41 suites. 4 restaurants, 3 lobby lounges, snack bar, 3 pools,
beauty salon, 2 tennis courts, croquet, health club, volleyball, boat-
ing, baby-sitting, concierge. AE, MC, V.*

$$ ⛱ **Caribbean Beach Resort.** Talk about tropical punch! Awash in dizzy-
★ ing Caribbean colors, this hotel—the first of Disney's moderately
priced lodgings—was an instant smash. Surrounding 42-acre Barefoot
Bay, it comprises five palm-studded "villages" named for Caribbean
islands. Each has its own pool (one even has a pirate fort), but all share
a white-sand beach. Bridges over the lake connect to the 1-acre, path-
crossed Parrot Cay, where there's a play area. A 1-mi-long promenade
circling the lake is favored by bikers, joggers, and romantic strollers.
At the resort's hub, a complex called Old Port Royale, decorated with
pirates' cannons and tropical birds, has stores, a food court, and a trop-
ical lounge. Bus lines network to all parks. ☎ 407/934–3400, FAX
407/934–3288. 2,112 rooms. Restaurant, food court, lobby lounge,
7 pools, wading pool, hot tub, jogging, beach, boating, bicycles, baby-
sitting, playground, coin laundry, laundry service. AE, MC, V.

Downtown Disney/Disney Village Resort Area

$$ ⛱ **Dixie Landings Resort.** Disney's Imagineers drew inspiration from
the Old South for this sprawling, moderately priced resort northwest
of Disney Village Marketplace. Rooms, in three-story plantation-style
mansions and two-story, rustic, bayou dwellings, are all the same size
and accommodate up to four in two double beds. Elegantly decorated, they have wooden armoires and gleaming brass faucets. Guest
registration looks like a steamboat interior, and the quaint food court
offers burgers, sandwiches, breakfast items, and pizza. A 3½-acre, old-
fashioned swimming-hole complex called Ol' Man Island is, in fact, a
pool with slides, rope swings, and an adjacent play area. A marina rents
out Water Sprites and other craft. Alas, there's no children's program.
Transportation is provided by bus and motor launch. ☎ 407/934–6000,
FAX 407/934–5777. 2,048 rooms. Restaurant, food court, 6 pools,
wading pool, hot tub, boating, playground, coin laundry, laundry service. AE, MC, V.

$$ ⛱ **Port Orleans Resort.** Disney's version of New Orleans's French
Quarter emulates the charm and romance of the original. Ornate row
houses with wrought-iron balconies overgrown with vines are clustered
around squares lushly planted with magnolias. The food court serves
up such Crescent City specialties as jambalaya and beignets (fritters),
in addition to standards, and Bonfamille's Café offers varied Louisiana-
style fare. Kids love the large, free-form Doubloon Lagoon, one of Dis-
ney's most exotic pools. The body of Neptune twists through the
water and becomes a water slide; you zoom out through his mouth.
Most rooms have two double beds; book early for a king. Though more
costly, rooms looking over the garden are nicer. Buses and motor
launches access all parks. ☎ 407/934–5500, FAX 407/934–5353. 1,008
rooms. Restaurant, food court, lobby lounge, pool, wading pool, hot
tub, croquet, boating, bicycles, baby-sitting, coin laundry, laundry ser-
vice, concierge. AE, MC, V.

All-Star Village

$$ ⛱ **All-Star Sports and All-Star Music Resorts.** What could Americans
possibly love more than Mickey Mouse? Sports and music, perhaps.
The buildings at these resorts carry out five sports themes (baseball,
football, tennis, surfing, and basketball) and five music themes (Broadway, country, jazz, rock, and calypso). Don't worry about being able
to tell them apart; gargantuan exterior ornamentation defines each theme.
Stairwells shaped like giant bongos frame Calypso, while a three-story
silhouette of a sax player adorns Jazz. At Sports, you'll find 30-foot
tennis rackets striking balls the size of small cars, baseball bats as big
as oak trees, and football helmets you could climb into. These resorts
mark Disney's entry into the economy-priced hotel market, and so, be-

neath the elaborate packaging, the buildings are basically well-maintained motels. Each room has two double beds, a closet rod, an armoire, and a desk. The End Zone and Intermission food courts offer a predictable selection of fast foods. *Sports:* ☎ 407/939–5000, FAX *407/939–7333; Music:* ☎ *407/939–6000,* FAX *407/939–7222. 1,920 rooms at each. 2 food courts, 2 bars, 4 pools, baby-sitting, playground, coin laundry, laundry service. AE, MC, V.*

In WDW: Other Hotels

For locations of these properties, *see* the Orlando Lodging map. Epcot Resort Area hotels are also noted on the Walt Disney World map.

Epcot Resort Area

$$$$
★ ⊞ **Walt Disney World Dolphin.** Not everyone takes to this Sheraton-operated bit of whimsy, but no one denies that its wild, imaginative ambience has made it a Disney landmark. Outside, two mythical, 56-foot sea creatures—labeled dolphins by the hotel's noted architect, Michael Graves—bracket a 27-story pyramid. A waterfall cascades down from seashell to seashell into a 54-foot-wide clamshell supported by other giant dolphin sculptures. On the coral-and-turquoise facade, a mural sprouts giant banana leaves. Inside, monkey-shape chandeliers are matched by equally jocular palm tree–shape lamps in rooms. The best units overlook Epcot and its nightly fireworks. Buses, trams, and motor launches stop. ⊠ *1500 Epcot Resorts Blvd., Lake Buena Vista 32830-2653,* ☎ *407/934–4000 or 800/227–1500,* FAX *407/934–4884. 1,370 rooms, 140 suites. 5 restaurants, 3 lobby lounges, 4 pools, beauty salon, 4 tennis courts, exercise room, beach, boating, baby-sitting, children's programs, concierge. AE, D, DC, MC, V.*

$$$$
⊞ **Walt Disney World Swan.** Facing its twin, the Dolphin, across Crescent Lake, this is another example of the postmodern "Learning from Las Vegas" school of entertainment architecture characteristic of Michael Graves. Two 45-foot swans grace the rooftop of this coral-and-aquamarine hotel, connected to the Dolphin by a covered causeway. Guest rooms, in a 12-story main building and two seven-story wings, are quirkily decorated with floral and geometric patterns, pineapples painted on furniture, and exotic bird-shape lamps. As at the Dolphin, the atmosphere is more grown-up than at most on-site properties, though there are plenty of facilities for families. Bus, tram, and motor launch lines connect this Westin-managed hotel with the parks. ⊠ *1200 Epcot Resorts Blvd., Lake Buena Vista 32830,* ☎ *407/934–3000, 800/248–7926, or 800/228–3000,* FAX *407/934–4499. 717 rooms, 45 concierge rooms. 4 restaurants, 3 lobby lounges, 2 pools, 4 tennis courts, health club, beach, boating, baby-sitting. AE, DC, MC, V.*

Hotel Plaza Boulevard

$$$$
★ ⊞ **Buena Vista Palace Suite Resort and Spa at Walt Disney World Village.** This bold, sand-colored tower, the largest hotel at Lake Buena Vista, seems small and quiet when you enter. Don't be fooled. Better indications of its enormity are its sprawling parking lots and its huge roster of facilities, from a business center to a 10,000-square-foot spa with 14 treatment rooms. Bedrooms come with one king- or two queen-size beds and have private balconies or patios. In the adjacent Island Resort, suites accommodating up to eight people have queen-size sleeper sofas and dining areas with coffeemaker and microwave. ⊠ *1900 Buena Vista Dr., Lake Buena Vista 32830,* ☎ *407/827–2727 or 800/327–2990,* FAX *407/827–6034. 1,013 rooms. 3 restaurants, 4 lobby lounges, patisserie, snack bar, indoor-outdoor pool, wading pool, hot tub, spa, 3 tennis courts, health club, volleyball, boating, baby-*

Best Western Kissimmee, **23**

Buena Vista Palace Suite Resort and Spa at WDW Village, **18**

Courtyard by Marriott, **17**

Doubletree Guest Suites, **14**

Embassy Suites International Drive South, **5**

Embassy Suites Orlando–North, **2**

Embassy Suites Resort Lake Buena Vista, **13**

Enclave Suites at Orlando, **3**

Fairfield Inn by Marriott, **6**

Grosvenor Resort, **19**

Hilton at WDW Village, **20**

Holiday Inn Sunspree Resort Lake Buena Vista, **21**

Hyatt Regency Grand Cypress Resort, **12**

Inn at Maingate, **33**

Marriott's Orlando World Center, **28**

Parc Corniche Resort, **9**

Park Inn International, **27**

Park Plaza Hotel, **1**

Peabody Orlando, **7**

Perri House, **11**

Quality Suites Maingate East, **31**

Radisson Resort Parkway, **32**

Record Motel, **24**

Residence Inn by Marriott on Lake Cecile, **25**

Royal Plaza, **16**

Sevilla Inn, **26**

Sheraton Inn Lakeside, **34**

Summerfield Suites Hotel, **4**

Travelodge Hotel, **15**

Vistana Resort, **22**

WDW Dolphin, **29**

WDW Swan, **30**

Wyndham Garden Hotel, **10**

Wynfield Inn–Westwood, **8**

Note: For locations of Disney-owned accommodations, see the Walt Disney World map.

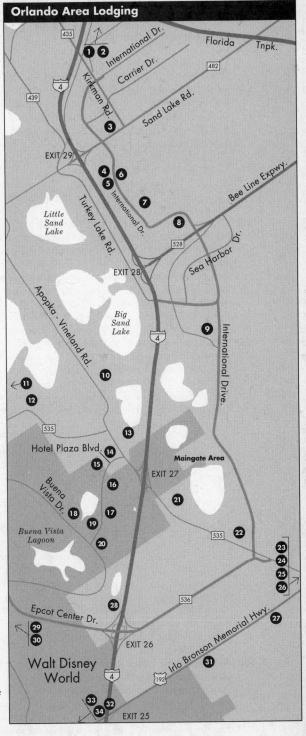

Orlando Area Lodging

sitting, children's program in summer, playground, coin laundry, laundry service, business services. AE, DC, MC, V.

$$$$ ⊞ **Hilton at Walt Disney World Village.** An ingeniously designed wa-
★ terfall tumbles off the covered entrance and into a stone fountain surrounded by palm trees so hefty you'd think they were on steroids.
Another fountain adorns the lobby, which is enlivened by floral carpeting, shell-shape cornices, and two large tanks of tropical fish. Guest
rooms sparkle in bright yellow and mauve and, although not huge, are
cozy and contemporary. Each has a king or two double beds, and amenities include a minibar, cable TV, and in-room movies. Prices vary dramatically from one location, floor, and season to another. ⊠ *1751 Hotel
Plaza Blvd., Lake Buena Vista 32830,* ☎ *407/827–4000 or 800/782–
4414,* FAX *407/827–6369. 787 rooms, 27 suites. 7 restaurants, 2 lobby
lounges, 3 pools, outdoor hot tub, 2 tennis courts, health club, baby-
sitting, children's program, coin laundry, laundry service, business
center. AE, DC, MC, V.*

$$$ ⊞ **Courtyard by Marriott.** A 14-story atrium accented with gazebos,
white-tile trim, and tropical gardens creates a tranquil place to enjoy
a gourmet breakfast under white umbrellas. By evening, you'll find the
energy center has shifted to the Tipsy Parrot, the hotel's welcoming
bar. Guest rooms are Marriott-modern and feature handy coffeemak-
ers. ⊠ *1805 Hotel Plaza Blvd., Lake Buena Vista 32830,* ☎ *407/828–
8888 or 800/223–9930,* FAX *407/827–4623. 323 rooms. Restaurant,
lobby lounge, 2 pools, wading pool, hot tub, exercise room, baby-sit-
ting, playground, coin laundry, laundry service. AE, DC, MC, V.*

$$$ ⊞ **Doubletree Guest Suites.** Lodgings in this modern, L-shape, concrete-
★ and-tinted-glass structure are all one- or two-bedroom suites, sleeping
six or 10, respectively, if not particularly comfortably. That extra room
can be a godsend when the kids—or the alleged grown-ups—decide
to spend all night recalling the day's adventures. Convenient for those
who want to avoid the hassle of cots and the expense of separate hotel
rooms, suites feature bedrooms with a king or two double beds and a
separate living area with sofa bed. There's a TV in each room plus one
in the bathroom, as well as a fridge, wet bar, and coffeemaker; microwaves are available on request. ⊠ *2305 Hotel Plaza Blvd., Lake
Buena Vista 32830,* ☎ *407/934–1000 or 800/222–8733,* FAX *407/934–
1011. 229 units. Restaurant, bar, ice cream parlor, lobby lounge, pool,
wading pool, hot tub, 2 tennis courts, exercise room, baby-sitting, coin
laundry, laundry service. AE, DC, MC, V.*

$$$ ⊞ **Grosvenor Resort.** Offering a wealth of facilities and comfortable
rooms for a fair price, this attractive member of the Best Western
chain is the best deal in the neighborhood. Rooms are average in size
but colorfully decorated and have many amenities, including minifridge,
coffeemaker, and VCR; rental movies are available in the lobby. Pub-
lic areas are spacious, with a Colonial-Caribbean decor. ⊠ *1850 Hotel
Plaza Blvd., Lake Buena Vista 32830,* ☎ *407/828–4444 or 800/624–
4109,* FAX *407/828–8192. 633 rooms, 6 suites. 2 restaurants, lobby
lounge, 2 pools, wading pool, hot tub, 2 tennis courts, basketball, vol-
leyball, playground, coin laundry, laundry service. AE, DC, MC, V.*

$$–$$$ ⊞ **Royal Plaza.** When in town, Burt Reynolds and Barbara Mandrell
stay here, in suites named after them. The rest of the time you can book
these rooms—complete with photos, gold records, and other memo-
rabilia. For the most part, this casual, lively establishment is popular
with families. Each of the generous rooms has a terrace or balcony,
and the best overlook the pool. If you want to sleep late or nap in the
afternoon, be sure your quarters aren't too close to the ground floor.
The Giraffe, the hotel's Top-40 nightclub, hops until the wee hours.
⊠ *1905 Hotel Plaza Blvd., Lake Buena Vista 32830,* ☎ *407/828–2828
or 800/248–7890,* FAX *407/828–8046. 394 rooms, 21 suites. Restau-*

rant, bar, lounge, pool, hot tub, sauna, 4 tennis
baby-sitting, children's program, laundry service. A

$$–$$$ ☐ **Travelodge Hotel.** An old, black London taxi is
entrance and the lobby is very British, with polishe
green carpet, a two-story winding staircase, and big, broad wicker ch.
Though otherwise unexceptional, this is a quality property and a good
choice for families. Each room comes with one king or two double beds
and private balcony. For nightly entertainment—and great vistas of
Epcot—head for Topper's, on the 18th floor. ⊠ *2000 Hotel Plaza Blvd.,
Lake Buena Vista 32830, ☎ 407/828–2424 or 800/348–3765; in FL,
800/578–7878; ℻ 407/828–8933. 325 rooms. Restaurant, lobby
lounge, 2 snack bars, pool, wading pool, baby-sitting, playground, coin
laundry, laundry service. AE, D, DC, MC, V.*

Orlando

International Drive

If you plan to visit other attractions besides Walt Disney World, the
sprawl of newish hotels, restaurants, and shopping malls known as International Drive—"I-Drive" to locals and "Florida Center" in formal
parlance—makes a convenient base. Parallel to I-4 and accessible from
Exits 28, 29, and 30, it's just a few minutes south of downtown Orlando. It's also near Sea World, Universal Studios, Wet 'n' Wild, and
several popular dinner theaters.

$$$$ ☐ **Peabody Orlando.** At 11 AM, the celebrated Peabody ducks exit a
★ private elevator into the enormous marble-floored lobby and waddle
across a red carpet to the little marble fountain where they pass the
day, basking in high-class fame: Eat your heart out, Donald. At 5, to
the crowd's delight, the marching mallards repeat the ritual in reverse.
Built by the owners of the landmark Peabody Hotel in Memphis, this
27-story structure looks like three high-rise offices from afar, but don't
be put off by its austere exterior. The interior is impressive and handsome. The most panoramic of the oversize beige-and-cream rooms have
views of WDW. Across from the Orange County Convention Center,
the hotel attracts rock stars and other performers, conventioneers and
duck lovers. ⊠ *9801 International Dr., 32819, ☎ 407/352–4000 or
800/732–2639, ℻ 407/351–9177. 891 rooms. 3 restaurants, 2 lobby
lounges, pool, wading pool, hot tub, spa, golf privileges, 4 tennis
courts, health club, baby-sitting, concierge. AE, D, DC, MC, V.*

$$$ ☐ **Embassy Suites International Drive South.** Another of the all-suite
chain of hotels, this member has an expansive lobby with marble
floors, pillars, hanging lamps, and old-fashioned ceiling fans. Tropi-
cal gardens with mossy rock fountains and palm trees add to the
atrium's distinctive southern ambience. Elsewhere, ceramic tile walk-
ways and brick arches complement the tropical mood. ⊠ *8978 Inter-
national Dr., 32819, ☎ 407/352–1400 or 800/433–7275, ℻
407/363–1120. 244 suites. Restaurant, lobby lounge, indoor pool, hot
tub, sauna, steam room, baby-sitting. AE, D, DC, MC, V.*

$$$ ☐ **Parc Corniche Resort.** A good bet for golf enthusiasts, the resort is
framed by a Joe Lee–designed course. Each of the one- and two-bed-
room suites is decked out in pastels and tropical patterns and has a
patio or balcony with a golf course view, as well as a kitchen. The largest
accommodations, with two bedrooms and two baths, can sleep up to
six. A complimentary Continental breakfast is served daily, and Sea
World is only a few blocks away. ⊠ *6300 Parc Corniche Dr., 32821,
☎ 407/239–7100 or 800/446–2721, ℻ 407/239–8501. 210 suites.
Restaurant, lobby lounge, pool, wading pool, hot tub, 18-hole golf
course, baby-sitting, playground, coin laundry, laundry service. AE, D,
MC, V.*

✓ **$$$** 🏨 **Summerfield Suites Hotel.** "Time to go to bed, kids—yes!—in your own room." How many times have you wanted to say that on your vacation? Sleeping from four to eight people, the one- and two-bedroom units at the all-suites Summerfield are a great option for families. Parents relish the chance for a little peace, and youngsters enjoy the feeling of grown-up privacy and, more importantly, the chance to control their own TV fate—there's a box in each room. Two-bedroom units, the most popular, have fully equipped kitchens, plus a living room with TV and VCR. Plush landscaping manages to give the place a secluded feel even though it's on International Drive. A Continental breakfast is included. ⊠ *8480 International Dr., 32819,* ☎ *407/352–2400 or 800/833–4353,* ℻ *407/352–4631. 146 suites. Grocery, lobby lounge, pool, wading pool, hot tub, exercise room, coin laundry, laundry service. AE, D, DC, MC, V.*

$$–$$$ 🏨 **Enclave Suites at Orlando.** With three 10-story buildings surrounding an office, restaurant, and recreation area, this all-suite lodging is less a hotel than a condominium complex. What you would spend for a room in a fancy hotel gets you a complete apartment here, with significantly more space than you'll find in other all-suite hotels. Accommodating up to six, the units have full kitchens, living rooms, two bedrooms, and small terraces. ⊠ *6165 Carrier Dr., 32819,* ☎ *407/351–1155 or 800/457–0077,* ℻ *407/351–2001. 321 suites. Grocery, indoor pool, 2 outdoor pools, hot tub, tennis court, exercise room, baby-sitting, playground, coin laundry, laundry service. AE, D, DC, MC, V.*

$–$$ 🏨 **Wynfield Inn–Westwood.** If you don't want a room with just the bare essentials yet don't have the budget for luxury, this two-story motel is a find. Its cheerful, contemporary rooms have colorful, floral-print bedspreads, peach walls, and understated wall hangings. The staff is friendly and helpful and acts more like the staff of a "do-anything-to-please" independent motel. ⊠ *6263 Westwood Blvd., 32821,* ☎ *407/345–8000 or 800/346–1551,* ℻ *407/345–1508. 299 rooms. Bar, 2 pools, coin laundry, laundry service. AE, D, DC, MC, V.*

$ 🏨 **Fairfield Inn by Marriott.** This understated, few-frills, three-story hotel—the Marriott Corporation's answer to the Motel 6 and Econolodge chains—is a natural for single travelers or small families on a tight budget. It's squeezed between International Drive and the highway and doesn't have the amenities of top-of-the-line Marriott properties, but nice perks such as complimentary coffee and tea, free local phone calls, and cable TV give a sense of being at a much fancier property. ⊠ *8342 Jamaican Ct., 32819,* ☎ *407/363–1944 or 800/228–2800,* ℻ *407/363–1944. 135 rooms. Pool. AE, D, DC, MC, V.*

Maingate

Outside the northernmost entrance to WDW, just off I–4, the Maingate area is full of large hotels unaffiliated with Walt Disney World. Most are sprawling, high-quality resorts catering to WDW vacationers.

$$$$ 🏨 **Hyatt Regency Grand Cypress Resort.** On more than 1,500 acres, ★ Orlando's most spectacular resort offers virtually every facility and then some—even a 45-acre nature preserve. Golf facilities, including a high-tech golf school, are first-class. The huge, 800,000-gallon pool resembles an enormous grotto, has a 45-foot water slide, and is fed by 12 waterfalls. As you'd expect of a Hyatt, a striking 18-story atrium is filled with tropical plants. Accommodations are divided between the Hyatt Regency Grand Cypress and the Villas of Grand Cypress. *Hyatt Regency Grand Cypress:* ⊠ *1 Grand Cypress Blvd., 32836,* ☎ *407/239–1234 or 800/233–1234,* ℻ *407/239–3800. 750 rooms. Villas of*

Grand Cypress: ✉ *1 N. Jacaranda, 32836,* ☎ *407/239–4700 or 800/835–7377. 146 villas. 5 restaurants, 4 lobby lounges, 2 pools, 4 hot tubs, 45 holes of golf, 12 tennis courts, croquet, health club, horseback riding, jogging, boating, bicycles, baby-sitting, children's program, laundry service. AE, D, DC, MC, V.*

$$$$ 🏨 **Marriott's Orlando World Center.** To call this hotel massive would be an understatement. The lineup of amenities and facilities seems endless. One of the four pools is Florida's largest, and the lobby is a huge, opulent atrium, adorned with 16th-century Asian artifacts. If you like your hostelries cozy, the size of this place is a definite negative; otherwise, its single unappealing aspect is the hordes of conventioneers it attracts. ✉ *8701 World Center Dr., 32821,* ☎ *407/239–4200 or 800/228–9290,* ℻ *407/238–8777. 1,419 rooms, 85 suites. 7 restaurants, 2 lobby lounges, 3 outdoor pools, indoor pool, wading pool, beauty salon, 4 hot tubs, 18-hole golf course, miniature golf, 7 tennis courts, health club, volleyball, baby-sitting, children's program, coin laundry, laundry service. AE, D, DC, MC, V.*

$$$$ 🏨 **Vistana Resort.** Consider this peaceful resort if you're interested in tennis. Its clay and all-weather courts can be used without charge, and private or semiprivate lessons are available for a fee. It's also a good bet if your family is large or you're traveling with friends. Spread over 95 landscaped acres, the spacious, tastefully decorated villas and town houses have two bedrooms each plus a living room and all the comforts of home, including a full kitchen and a washer and dryer. ✉ *13500 Rte. 535, 32821,* ☎ *407/239–3100 or 800/877–8787,* ℻ *407/239–3111. 722 units. 2 restaurants, grocery, lobby lounge, 6 pools, 5 wading pools, 6 hot tubs, miniature golf, tennis courts, basketball, health club, shuffleboard, baby-sitting, children's program. AE, D, DC, MC, V.*

Jeannette
200.⁹¹
w/tax
+300
428

$181.⁰ per night   2/24 - 3/3

$$$–$$$$ 🏨 **Embassy Suites Resort Lake Buena Vista.** Some locals have been shocked by the wild turquoise, pink, and yellow facade of this otherwise typical example of the all-suite chain. Clearly visible from I–4 and just 1 mi from WDW, 3 mi from Sea World, and 7 mi from Universal Studios, it has become something of a local landmark. The atrium lobby, loaded with tropical vegetation and soothed by the sounds of a rushing fountain, is a great place to enjoy the complimentary breakfast and evening cocktails. ✉ *8100 Lake Ave., Lake Buena Vista 32836,* ☎ *407/239–1144, 800/257–8483, or 800/362–2779,* ℻ *407/239–1718. 280 suites. Restaurant, deli, lobby lounge, indoor-outdoor pool, wading pool, hot tub, tennis court, basketball, exercise room, shuffleboard, volleyball, baby-sitting, children's program, playground. AE, D, DC, MC, V.*

$$–$$$ 🏨 **Holiday Inn Sunspree Resort Lake Buena Vista.** You might be impressed by the sweeping, covered entrance to the striking, terra-cotta-color facade, but what really earns the kudos is the focus on family fun. All employees, including managers, have to graduate from Clown College—an eight-week intensive course in balloonology, magic tricks, costume design, clown ethics, and the seven clown commandments. This ensures that Camp Holiday—a free children's program of magic shows, arts and crafts, movies, cartoons, and other supervised evening activities—is the finest program around. The hotel is an excellent value. ✉ *13351 Rte. 535, 32821,* ☎ *407/239–4500 or 800/366–6299,* ℻ *407/239–7713. 507 rooms. Restaurant, deli, lobby lounge, snack bar, pool, wading pool, 2 hot tubs, health club, billiards, children's program, playground. AE, D, DC, MC, V.*

$$–$$$ 🏨 **Radisson Resort Parkway.** This bright, spacious Radisson may offer
★ the best deal in the neighborhood: attractive setting, good facilities, and competitive prices. Its delicatessen comes in handy when you want to

assemble a picnic. Generously proportioned rooms are decked out in tropical patterns, with pastel colors and pineapple shapes carved in white, wooden furniture. Rooms with the best view and light face the pool. ⊠ *2900 Parkway Blvd., Kissimmee 34746,* ☎ *407/396–7000 or 800/634–4774,* FAX *407/396–6792. 712 rooms, 6 suites. Restaurant, deli, 2 lobby lounges, snack bar, 2 pools, wading pool, 2 hot tubs, sauna, 2 tennis courts, exercise room, volleyball, coin laundry, laundry service. AE, D, DC, MC, V.*

$$ ★ **Perri House.** Exactly 1 mi from the Magic Kingdom as the crow flies, this B&B on a serene side road is unique in build-it-bigger-and-they-will-come Orlando. Part-hostelry, part-bird preserve, Perri House is an Audubon Society–recognized bird sanctuary, complete with observation paths, a pond, feeding station, and a small birdhouse museum. About 200 trees and more than 1,500 bushes have been planted—many awaiting the addition of birdhouses. Nick and Angi Perretti planned and built the circular house so that each room has an outside entrance. The bird- and blossom-theme bedrooms come with either two queen- or one king-size four-poster bed, private bath, and TV. The furnishings are childproof, and kids are welcome. ⊠ *10417 Centurion Ct., Lake Buena Vista 32830,* ☎ *407/876–4830 or 800/780–4830,* FAX *407/876–0241. 8 rooms. Pool, hot tub. AE, D, MC, V.*

$$ ★ **Wyndham Garden Hotel.** After traipsing through theme parks and malls, what many visitors want most is to lounge around their living room as they do at home. This six-story complex lets you do just that: It provides a living room full of big couches, with a better-than-at-home, big-screen TV fitted with a Nintendo unit. Homey touches abound, and the in-room services and amenities, including hair dryers and coffeemakers, more than make up for the less-than-inspiring facade. A shuttle to WDW, Sea World, Universal Studios, and Wet 'n' Wild is available. ⊠ *8688 Palm Pkwy., 32836,* ☎ *407/239–8500 or 800/996–3426,* FAX *407/239–8591. 167 rooms. Restaurant, lobby lounge, pool, hot tub, health club. AE, D, DC, MC, V.*

Kissimmee

If you're looking for anything remotely quaint, charming, or sophisticated, move on. The U.S. 192 strip—aka the Irlo Bronson Memorial Highway, the Spacecoast Parkway, and Kissimmee—is a neon-and-plastic theme park crammed with mom-and-pop motels, bargain-basement hotels, and cheap restaurants. But if all you want is a decent room, this is Wonderland. Room rates start at $20 a night—lower at the right time of year, if you can cut the right deal—with most costing $30 to $70 a night, depending on facilities and proximity to Walt Disney World.

$$–$$$ **Quality Suites Maingate East.** This hotel, built in 1989, is an excellent option for a large family or group of friends. The spacious, green-and-mauve rooms, designed to sleep six or ten, come equipped with a microwave, refrigerator, and dishwasher. Suites have two bedrooms with two double beds each and a living room with a double pull-out couch. A complimentary Continental breakfast is offered, and free beer and wine are served afternoons at the poolside bar. As an added bonus, guests get one free admission per suite to Cypress Gardens, WaterMania, or Splendid China. ⊠ *5876 W. Irlo Bronson Memorial Hwy., 34746,* ☎ *407/396–8040 or 800/848–4148,* FAX *407/396–6766. 225 units. Restaurant, bar, lobby lounge, pool, wading pool, hot tub, playground, laundry service. AE, D, DC, MC, V.*

$$–$$$ **Residence Inn by Marriott on Lake Cecile.** Of the all-suite hotels on U.S. 192, this complex of four-unit town houses is probably the best. One side of the complex faces the highway; the other overlooks an attractive lake, where you can sail, water-ski, Jet Ski, and fish. Forty units

are penthouses accommodating four, with complete kitchens, small living rooms, loft bedrooms, and fireplaces. All others accommodate two and are laid out like studio apartments but still have full kitchens and fireplaces. Each suite has a private entrance. A Continental breakfast is complimentary. ✉ *4786 W. Irlo Bronson Memorial Hwy., 34746,* ☎ *407/396–2056 or 800/468–3027,* 🖷 *407/396–2296. 159 units. Pool, hot tub, basketball, playground, coin laundry, laundry service. AE, D, DC, MC, V.*

$$ 🖫 **Best Western Kissimmee.** Overlooking a nine-hole, par-three, executive golf course, this independently owned and operated three-story hotel is a hit with golf-loving senior citizens as well as families. The two pools in the garden courtyard are amply shaded to protect tender skin from the sizzling sun. Spacious rooms are done in soft pastels, with light wood furniture and attractive wall hangings. Units with king-size beds and kitchenettes are available. ✉ *2261 E. Irlo Bronson Memorial Hwy., 34744,* ☎ *407/846–2221 or 800/944–0062,* 🖷 *407/846–1095. 282 rooms. Restaurant, bar, lobby lounge, picnic area, 2 pools, playground. AE, D, DC, MC, V.*

$$ 🖫 **Inn at Maingate.** This sleek, twin-towered, seven-story hotel, just a
★ few minutes from WDW's front door, has cheerful guest rooms, large bathrooms, and plenty of extras for the price. It's not fancy, but it is perfectly adequate. The best rooms are those with a view of the pool. ✉ *3011 Maingate La., 34747,* ☎ *407/396–1400 or 800/239–6478,* 🖷 *407/396–0660. 578 rooms, 5 suites. Restaurant, deli, lobby lounge, pool, hot tub, 2 tennis courts, basketball, exercise room, jogging, baby-sitting, coin laundry, laundry service. AE, D, DC, MC, V.*

$$ 🖫 **Sheraton Inn Lakeside.** This comfortable, if undistinguished, resort, a complex of 15 two-story balconied buildings spread over 27 acres by a small man-made lake, offers quite a few recreational facilities. The nondescript beige rooms are available in the standard two double or one king-size bed configurations, and each has a refrigerator and safe. ✉ *7769 W. Irlo Bronson Memorial Hwy., 34747,* ☎ *407/396–2222 or 800/848–0801,* 🖷 *407/239–2650. 651 rooms. 2 restaurants, deli, lobby lounge, 3 pools, wading pool, miniature golf, 4 tennis courts, boating, fishing, children's program, coin laundry, laundry service. AE, D, DC, MC, V.*

$ 🖫 **Park Inn International.** The Mediterranean-style architecture of this property on Cedar Lake is not likely to charm you off your feet, but the friendly staff might. Ask for a room as close to the water as possible. ✉ *4960 W. Irlo Bronson Memorial Hwy., 34741,* ☎ *407/396–1376 or 800/327–0072,* 🖷 *407/396–0716. 197 rooms. Restaurant, grocery, pool, hot tub, beach, coin laundry. AE, D, DC, MC, V*

$ 🖫 **Record Motel.** This simple property is the kind of mom-and-pop operation with few frills and rock-bottom rates that made U.S. 192 famous. Clean rooms with free HBO, Continental breakfast, and a solar-heated pool are the basic attractions here. What the place lacks in luxuries and ambience, it more than makes up for with the friendliness of its staff, who'll gladly direct you to equally inexpensive restaurants. ✉ *4651 W. Irlo Bronson Memorial Hwy., 34746,* ☎ *407/396–8400, or 800/396–8000,* 🖷 *407/396–8415. 57 rooms. Pool. AE, D, MC, V.*

$ 🖫 **Sevilla Inn.** This family-operated motel built in 1985 and expanded
★ in 1990 is one of the best buys in the Orlando area. Stucco and wood on the outside, the three-story building has up-to-date rooms with colorful bedspreads, tasteful wall hangings, a fresh paint job, and cable TV. If you need a place just to drop your bags and get some rest between theme parks, this is a good bet. The pool area, encircled by palm trees and tropical shrubs, looks like something you'd find in a much fancier resort. ✉ *4640 W. Irlo Bronson Memorial Hwy., 34746,* ☎

407/396–4135 or 800/367–1363, ⅨX 407/396–4942. 46 rooms. Pool, coin laundry. AE, D, MC, V.

Orlando Suburbs

Travel farther afield and you can get more comforts and facilities for the money, and maybe even some genuine Orlando charm—of the warm, cozy, one-of-a-kind country inn variety.

$$$ **🏨 Embassy Suites Orlando–North.** What makes this hotel different from others in its chain is its location on the edge of Crane's Roost Lake. Otherwise, suites are up to the high Embassy Suites standard and look out on a lush, tropical atrium. Although the sound of the waterfalls is soothing, the same can't be said for that of the conventioneers at the tables around them. So for guaranteed quiet, choose a suite on an upper floor. Accommodations are spacious and flawlessly kept, the staff friendly and helpful, and the complimentary cooked-to-order breakfast makes a great send-off for your busy day. ✉ *225 E. Altamonte Dr., Altamonte Springs 32701,* ☎ *407/834–2400 or 800/362–2779,* ⅨX *407/834–2117. 210 suites. Restaurant, lobby lounge, indoor pool, exercise room, fishing, baby-sitting, coin laundry, laundry service, business services. AE, D, DC, MC, V.*

$$–$$$ **🏨 Park Plaza Hotel.** Small and intimate, this 1922-vintage establishment feels almost like a private home. The key to a special stay is getting a front garden suite with a living room. These open onto a long balcony usually abloom with impatiens and bougainvillea and punctuated by wicker tables and chairs to enhance people-watching on chic Park Avenue or Central Park. All rooms have either a double, queen-, or king-size bed, but those in the back can be small and cramped. Nice touches include a newspaper and complimentary Continental breakfast brought to your room. This old-fashioned spot is definitely not for people who want recreational facilities or other amenities—nor is it suitable for young children. ✉ *307 Park Ave. S, Winter Park 32789,* ☎ *407/647–1072 or 800/228–7220,* ⅨX *407/647–4081. 27 rooms. Restaurant, lobby lounge, jogging, laundry service, free valet parking. AE, DC, MC, V.*

NIGHTLIFE AND THE ARTS

Not too many years ago, downtown Orlando was deserted after office workers went home, but then club owners realized there was big money to be made by luring tourists into the city center. Nightspots sprang up and are thriving, fostering a diverse collection of nighttime activities that offer everything from cutting-edge palaces and quiet coffeehouses to jousting tournaments and murder-mystery buffets to a reasonably lively arts scene. Even locals who haven't ventured out in a few years are surprised.

The Arts

Check out the local fine arts scene in *The Orlando Weekly,* a local entertainment magazine, or "Calendar," which is printed every Friday in the *Orlando Sentinel.* They are available at most newsstands. Ticket prices for performing-arts events in the Orlando area rarely exceed $12 and are often half that.

Orlando has an active agenda of dance, classical music, opera, and theater, much of it taking place at the **Carr Performing Arts Centre** (✉ 401 W. Livingston St., Orlando, ☎ 407/849–2020). At **Civic Theater of Central Florida** (✉ 1001 E. Princeton St., Orlando, ☎ 407/896–7365), you can catch a variety of shows, with evening performances Wednesday–Saturday and Sunday matinees. **Orange County Convention and Civic Center** (⊠ South end of International Dr., ☎ 407/345–9800) is sometimes the venue for local concerts by top artists. The downtown **Orlando Arena** (⊠ W. Amelia St., ☎ 407/849–2020) plays host to many big-name performers. During the school year, **Rollins College** (⊠ Winter Park, ☎ 407/646–2233) has a choral concert series that is open to the public and usually free. The last week in February there is a **Bach Music Festival** (☎ 407/646–2182), a tradition for nearly 60 years. Also at the college, the **Annie Russell Theater** (☎ 407/646–2145) has a regular series of productions.

Nightlife

Bars, Lounges, and Nightclubs

IN WALT DISNEY WORLD

Every WDW hotel has its quota of bars and lounges. Jazz trios and bluegrass bands, DJs and rockers tune up and turn on their amps after dinner's done. Fancy drinks with even more fanciful names are a staple. And you can drink later here than off-property—WDW clubs serve as late as 2:45 AM.

A two-story inland answer to a beach party, **Baja Beach Club** (⊠ 8510 Palm Pkwy., Lake Buena Vista, ☎ 407/239–9629) plays hits from the 1960s to the 1990s. It has a sand volleyball court and an open deck that serves sandwiches and just-grilled burgers.

Many Disney clubs are at **Pleasure Island,** a 6-acre after-dark entertainment complex, connected to Disney Village Marketplace and the mainland by three footbridges. It's better than you might expect. Despite its location on Disney property, the entertainment has real grit and life. In addition to seven clubs, you'll find a few restaurants, shops, and a 10-screen AMC cinema that starts showing movies at 1:30 PM. The pay-one-price admission gets you into all the clubs and shows except the movie house. Children accompanied by an adult are admitted to all clubs except Mannequins.

Adventurer's Club whimsically re-creates a private club of the 1930s. Strange things happen, thanks to Disney wizardry and some clever scripting for a group of talented actors and actresses, who mingle with patrons. There's an improvisational setup at **Comedy Warehouse,** with five shows nightly. And not everything has been sanitized for your protection. At **8trax,** groove to the recorded music of Donna Summer or the Village People while light reflects from disco balls. **Rock & Roll Beach Club** throbs with live rock music of the 1950s and 1960s. ⊠ *Off Buena Vista Dr., ☎ 407/934–7781. ⊡ $19.61, shops and restaurants free. ☉ Clubs daily 7 PM–2 AM, shops daily 10 AM–1 AM, restaurants usually daily 11:30 AM–midnight.*

AROUND ORLANDO

Outside Walt Disney World, there's plenty going on, lots of it at Church Street Station but plenty in freestanding clubs as well. Nightclubs in Orlando proper have significantly more character than those in the areas around Walt Disney World, but they close earlier.

A two-level sports palace, **Coaches Locker Room** (⊠ 269 W. Rte. 436, Altamonte Springs, ☎ 407/869–4446) boasts six big-screen TVs and 12 smaller monitors and shows every pro football game, plus every other kind of sport imaginable. The food is not the major attraction, but the Buffalo wings are worth trying. It's in the strip mall behind the T. G. I. Fridays at the intersection of I–4 and Rte. 436. **Howl at the Moon** (⊠ Church St. Marketplace, 55 W. Church St., 2nd floor, Orlando, ☎

407/841–4695) provides the perfect solution to the problem of the rowdy barfly who insists on crooning loudly with the band. Orlando's only sing-along bar encourages its patrons to warble the pop classics of yesteryear or campy favorites like the Time Warp and Hokey Pokey (turn yourself around). Piano players keep the music rolling in the evening, and the World's Most Dangerous Wait Staff adds to the entertainment. No food is served, but the management encourages you to bring your own or order out; several nearby restaurants deliver. There's a cover charge of $2–$4 Wednesday–Saturday; Sunday–Tuesday it's free.

A jazz club with a gourmet menu, **Pinkie Lee's** (⊠ 380 W. Amelia Ave., Orlando, ☎ 407/872–7393) is among Orlando's most grown-up nightspots. The entertainment is usually top-notch, reflected in the $7.50 minimum and $11–$18 cover charge on weekends. People of all ages come to **Sullivan's Entertainment Complex** (⊠ 1108 S. Orange Blossom Trail [U.S. 441], Orlando, ☎ 407/843–2934), the city's only country-and-western dance hall, to strut their stuff. Big-name performers entertain on occasion; a house band plays Tuesday–Saturday. The cover charge runs $2 and up. In **Yab Yum** (⊠ 25 Wall St. Plaza, Orlando, ☎ 407/422–3322), a bohemian refuge from downtown's hustle and bustle, the crowd is heavy with aspiring-poet types hunched over espresso while giving form to their latest angst, but you don't have to be tormented to enjoy a sandwich, specialty coffee or stronger drink, or a hunk of fresh carrot cake along with the music of local bands. The sound system at **Zuma Beach** (⊠ 46 N. Orange Ave., Orlando, ☎ 407/648–8727), an art deco, beach-party dance club, is a real rainmaker; there's also an extensive light show. It draws a 30ish crowd most nights. The cover is $6.

In the **Church Street Station** entertainment complex, the old-fashioned saloons, dance halls, dining rooms, and shopping arcades are almost Disneyesque in their attention to detail. Unlike much of what you see at WDW, however, this place doesn't just look authentic—it is. The train on the tracks is an actual 19th-century steam engine; the whistling calliope was specially rebuilt to blow its original tunes. Just about everything down to the cobblestones that clatter under the horse-drawn carriages is the real McCoy. For a single admission, you can wander freely and stay as long as you wish. Food and drink cost extra and are not cheap. Parts of the complex are open during the day, but the place is usually quiet then; the pace picks up at night, especially on weekends, with crowds thickest from 10 to 11.

Quiet **Apple Annie's Courtyard** offers recorded easy-listening music from Jimmy Buffett to James Taylor. The immensely popular trilevel **Cheyenne Saloon and Opera House** was, in fact, an opera house and is now full of moose racks, steer horns, buffalo heads, and Remington rifles. The seven-piece country-and-western band that plays here darn near brings the house down, and an upstairs restaurant serves chicken-and-ribs fare. **Crackers Oyster Bar,** behind the Orchid Garden, is a good place to get a meal of fresh Florida seafood and pasta or slam down a few oysters with a beer chaser; it also has one of the largest wine cellars in Florida. Relaxed and wood-paneled, **Lili Marlene's Aviators Pub and Restaurant** feels like an English pub and has the best food on Church Street—hearty, upscale, and very American steaks, ribs, and seafood. Iron latticework, arch ceilings, and stained-glass windows create a striking Victorian setting at the **Orchid Garden Ballroom,** where visitors sit, drink, and listen to a first-rate band pounding out popular tunes from the 1950s to the present. **Phineas Phogg's Balloon Works** plays Top 40 tunes on a sound system that will blow your socks off. It draws a good-looking yuppie tourist crowd and a few young local singles; the place is jammed by midnight. **Rosie O'Grady's Good Time Emporium,** the original bar on Church Street, is a turn-of-the-century saloon with dark wood, brass trim, a full Dixieland band, banjo shows, tap dancers, and vaudeville singers. ✉ *129 W. Church St., Orlando,* ☎ *407/422–2434.* ⛶ *$16.95 adults, $10.95 children 4–12.* ◷ *Daily 11 AM–2 AM.*

Dinner Shows

For a single price, these hybrid eatery-entertainment complexes deliver a theatrical production and a multicourse dinner. Performances run the gamut from jousting to jamboree tunes and tend to be better than the rather forgettable meal. Unlimited beer, wine, and soda are usually included, but mixed drinks will cost you extra. What the shows lack in substance and depth they make up for in color and enthusiasm; children often love them. Most shows have seatings at 7 and 9:30, and at most you sit with strangers at long tables. Always call and make reservations in advance, especially for weekends and shows at Walt Disney World.

IN WALT DISNEY WORLD

An evening of song, dance, and food on Disney property goes for a fairly steep price, somewhere in the range of $30–$45 for adults, $15–$25 for children.

Staged at rustic Pioneer Hall, the **Hoop-Dee-Doo Revue** (✉ Fort Wilderness Campground Resort, ☎ 407/934–7639 in advance, ☎ 407/824–2748 day of show) may be corny, but it is also the liveliest show in Walt Disney World. A troupe of jokers called the Pioneer Hall Players stomp their feet, wisecrack, and otherwise make merry while the audience chows down on barbecued ribs, fried chicken, corn on the cob, strawberry shortcake, and all the fixin's. Shows sell out months in advance for busy seasons.

At the outdoor barbecue that is the **Polynesian Luau** (✉ Polynesian Resort, ☎ 407/934–7639), the entertainment is in keeping with the colorful, South Pacific setting. There are two shows nightly, plus an earlier wingding for children called **Mickey's Tropical Luau,** wherein Disney characters do a few numbers decked out in South Seas garb.

AROUND ORLANDO

Dinner shows are as immensely popular around Orlando as in Walt Disney World. Adult prices run $30–$39, fees for children $10–$28, depending on age.

The **Aloha! Polynesian Luau Dinner and Show** at Sea World's Bimini Bay Café is an Anheuser-Busch family version of *Blue Hawaii.* Scantily clad dancers undulate across the floor, bearing lei-draped platters of roast pig, mahimahi, piña coladas, and hula pie. Reservations may be made the same day either at the luau reservations counter in the information center at the entrance or by telephone. Although the restaurant is inside the park, you don't have to pay park admission to attend the feast. ✉ *Sea World, Orlando,* ☎ *407/363–2559 or 800/327–2424.* ⛶ *$29.95 adults, $19.95 children 8–12, $9.95 children 3–7. D, MC, V.*

An elaborate palace outside, **Arabian Nights** is more like an arena within, with seating for more than 1,200. The show features some 25 acts with more than 80 performing horses, music, special effects, and a chariot race; keep your eyes open for a unicorn. The three-course dinners are of prime rib or vegetarian lasagna. ✉ *6225 W. Irlo Bronson Memorial Hwy., Kissimmee,* ☎ *407/396–7400, 407/239–9223, or 800/553–6116; in Canada, 800/533–3615.* ⛶ *$34.95. AE, D, MC, V.*

Returning to gangland Chicago of 1931, **Capone's Dinner and Show** comes complete with mobsters and their dames. The evening begins in an old-fashioned ice-cream parlor; say the secret password and you'll be ushered inside Al Capone's private Underworld Cabaret and Speakeasy. Dinner is an unlimited Italian buffet heavy on pasta. Beer and sangria are included. ⊠ *4740 W. Irlo Bronson Memorial Hwy., Kissimmee,* ☎ *407/397–2378.* ⊠ *$31.99. AE, D, MC, V.*

In **King Henry's Feast,** jesters, jugglers, dancers, magicians, and singers ostensibly fête Henry VIII as he celebrates his birthday in this Tudor-style building. Saucy wenches serve forth potato-leek soup, salad, and chicken and ribs. ⊠ *8984 International Dr., Orlando,* ☎ *407/351–5151 or 800/883–8181.* ⊠ *$35.99. AE, D, DC, MC, V.*

Broadway musicals—such as *Oklahoma!, My Fair Lady, West Side Story,* and *South Pacific*—are performed at **Mark Two** throughout the year except during the Yuletide holidays, when there are musical revues chock-ablock with Broadway tunes. For about two hours before curtain, you can order from the bar and help yourself at buffet tables laden with institutional seafood Newburg, baked whitefish, meats, and salad; dessert arrives during intermission. Unlike other dinner theaters, the Mark Two offers only tables for two and four. ⊠ *Edgewater Center, 3376 Edgewater Dr., west of I–4 Exit 44, Orlando,* ☎ *407/843–6275 or 800/726–6275.* ⊠ *$37. AE, D, MC, V.*

In **Medieval Times,** no fewer than 30 charging horses and a cast of 75 knights, nobles, and maidens perform in a huge, medieval-style manor house. The two-hour tournament includes sword fights, jousting matches, and other games, and the bill of fare is heavy on meat and potatoes. ⊠ *4510 W. Irlo Bronson Memorial Hwy., Kissimmee,* ☎ *407/239–0214 or 800/229–8300.* ⊠ *$36.95. AE, D, MC, V.*

Held in the 22-acre Fort Liberty complex, **Wild Bill's Wild West Dinner Show** is a mixed bag of Indian dances, foot-stompin' sing-alongs, and acrobatics. The chow, served by a rowdy chorus of cavalry recruits, is beef soup, fried chicken, corn on the cob, and pork and beans. No smoking is allowed in the showroom. ⊠ *5260 W. Irlo Bronson Memorial Hwy., Kissimmee,* ☎ *407/351–5151.* ⊠ *$35.95. AE, DC, MC, V.*

OUTDOOR ACTIVITIES AND SPORTS

Basketball

The NBA **Orlando Magic** (⊠ Box 76, 600 W. Amelia St., 2 blocks west of I–4 Amelia St. exit, Orlando 32801, ☎ 407/839–3900) plays in the 15,077-seat Orlando Arena.

Biking

The Orlando area has a collection of city-constructed bike paths through downtown, and there are a few places suitable for cycling in the Winter Park area. Serious cyclists head to the rolling hills of nearby Lake County.

Dog Racing

Sanford Orlando Kennel Club (⊠ 301 Dog Track Rd., Longwood, ☎ 407/831–1600) has dog racing as well as South Florida horse-racing simulcasts, November–May. **Seminole Greyhound Park** (⊠ 2000 Seminola Blvd., Casselberry, ☎ 407/699–4510), open May–October, is a newer track.

Golf

Golf is extremely popular in central Florida. Be sure to reserve tee times well in advance.

Golfpac (✉ Box 162366, Altamonte Springs 32701, ☎ 407/260–2288 or 800/327–0878) packages golf vacations and prearranges tee times at more than 40 courses around Orlando. Rates vary based on hotel and course, and 60–90 days advance notice is recommended to set up a vacation.

Walt Disney World has five championship 18-hole courses—all on the PGA Tour route: **Eagle Pines** (Bonnet Creek Golf Club, 6,722 yds), **Lake Buena Vista** (Lake Buena Vista, 6,829 yds), **Magnolia** (Shades of Green, 7,190 yds), **Osprey Ridge** (Bonnet Creek Golf Club, 7,101 yds), and **The Palm** (Shades of Green, 6,957 yds). Except for **Oak Trail,** a nine-hole layout for novice and preteen golfers, these courses are among the busiest and most expensive ($100–$135) in the region.

The three original Disney courses—Lake Buena Vista, Magnolia, and The Palm—have the same fees and discount policies regardless of season and are slightly less expensive than Eagle Pines and Osprey Ridge, whose fees change during the year. All offer a twilight discount rate, $45–$68, which goes into effect at anywhere from 2 to 4, depending on the season.

Greens fees usually vary by season—the highest and lowest figures are listed, all including mandatory cart rental. For information on more area courses, *see* Chapter 2.

Cypress Creek Country Club (✉ 5353 Vineland Rd., Orlando, ☎ 407/351–2187) is a demanding 6,955-yard, 18-hole course with 16 water holes and lots of trees; greens fees run $34–$45. **Grenelefe Golf & Tennis Resort** (✉ 3200 Rte. 546, Haines City, ☎ 941/422–7511 or 800/237–9549), about 45 minutes from Orlando, has three excellent 18-hole courses, of which the toughest is the 7,325-yard West Course. Greens fees run $39–$110.

Horseback Riding

Fort Wilderness Campground (☎ 407/824–2832) offers tame trail rides through backwoods. Children must be over nine, and adults must be under 250 pounds. Trail rides cost $17 for 45 minutes. Rides are daily at 9, 10:30, noon, and 2.

Jai Alai

Orlando-Seminole Jai-Alai (✉ 6405 S. U.S. 17–92, Fern Park, ☎ 407/331–9191), about 20 minutes north of Orlando off I–4, offers South Florida horse-racing simulcasts and betting in addition to jai alai at the fronton (closed in May).

Jogging

Walt Disney World has several scenic jogging trails. Pick up jogging maps at any Disney resort. At the **Caribbean Beach Resort** (☎ 407/934–3400), there is a 1.4-mi jogging promenade around Barefoot Bay. **Fort Wilderness Campground** (☎ 407/824–2900) has a 2.3-mi course with plenty of fresh air and woods as well as numerous exercise stations along the way.

Water Sports

Marinas at the Caribbean Beach Resort, Contemporary Resort, Disney Village Marketplace, Fort Wilderness Campground, Grand Floridian, Polynesian Resort, and Beach and Yacht clubs rent Sunfish, catamarans, motor-powered pontoon boats, pedal boats, and tiny two-passenger Water Sprites—a hit with kids—for use on their nearby waters: Bay Lake, Seven Seas Lagoon, Lake Buena Vista, Club Lake, or Buena Vista Lagoon. The Polynesian Resort marina also rents outrigger canoes, and Fort Wilderness rents canoes for paddling along the placid canals in the area. For waterskiing reservations ($65 per hour), call 407/824–1000.

SHOPPING

Flea Market

Flea World (✉ 3 mi east of I–4 Exit 50 on Lake Mary Blvd., then 1 mi south on U.S. 17–92, between Orlando and Sanford) claims to be America's largest flea market under one roof. More than 1,600 booths sell only new merchandise—everything from car tires and pet tarantulas to gourmet coffee, leather lingerie, and beaded evening gowns. It's open Friday–Sunday 8–5. Kids love **Fun World,** next door, which offers miniature golf, arcade games, go-carts, bumper cars, bumper boats, kiddie rides, and batting cages.

Outlet Stores

The International Drive area is filled with factory outlet stores. At the northern tip of I-Drive, **Belz Factory Outlet World** (✉ 5401 W. Oakridge Rd., Orlando) is the area's largest collection of outlet stores—nearly 170, in two malls and four nearby annexes.

There are about 20 stores including Bass shoes and American Tourister at the **Kissimmee Manufacturers' Outlet Mall** (✉ 2511–2557 Old Vineland Rd., Kissimmee). It's off U.S. 192, 1 mi east of Route 535.

Shopping Areas and Malls

IN ORLANDO

Church Street Exchange (✉ Church Street Station, 124 W. Church St.) is a decorative, brassy, Victorian-theme marketplace with more than 50 specialty shops. Perhaps the best demonstration is at Augusta Janssen, where free candy samples are distributed during a lighthearted look at the process of making fudge. The necessities, such as a 24-hour grocery and pharmacy, post office, bank, and cleaners, are all at **Cross-roads of Lake Buena Vista** (✉ Rte. 535 and I–4, Lake Buena Vista), across from Disney Village Marketplace. While you shop, your offspring can entertain themselves at Pirates Cove Adventure Golf. **Florida Mall** (✉ 8001 S. Orange Blossom Trail), 4½ mi east of I–4 and International Drive, is the largest mall in central Florida. It includes Sears, JCPenney, Belk Lindsey, Gayfers, Dillards, 200 specialty shops, seven theaters, and one of the better food courts around. At **Mercado Mediterranean Village** (✉ 8445 International Dr.), there are over 60 specialty shops and a clean, quick, and large food court, which offers a selection of cuisines from around the world. A visitors bureau is open daily 8–8. **Orlando Fashion Square** (✉ 3201 E. Colonial Dr.), 3 mi east of I–4 Exit 41, has 130 shops including Burdines, JCPenney, Sears, Camelot Music, the Disney Store, the Gap, and Lerner.

ORLANDO SUBURBS

The airy, spacious, two-level **Altamonte Mall** (✉ 451 Altamonte Ave., Altamonte Springs) contains Sears, Gayfers, Burdines, and JCPenney department stores and 165 specialty shops. **Old Town** (✉ 5770 Irlo Bronson Memorial Hwy., Kissimmee) is a shopping-entertainment complex featuring a 1928 Ferris wheel, a 1909 carousel, and more than 70 specialty shops in a re-creation of a turn-of-the-century Florida village. **Park Avenue** (✉ Winter Park) has a collection of chic boutiques and bistros.

WALT DISNEY WORLD AND THE ORLANDO AREA A TO Z

Arriving and Departing

By Bus

Greyhound Lines (☎ 800/231–2222) buses stop in Orlando (✉ 555 N. Magruder Ave., ☎ 407/292–3422).

By Car

From I–95, which runs down Florida's east coast, you can turn off onto I–4 just below Daytona; it's about 50 mi from there to Orlando. If you're taking I–75 down through the middle of the state, get off at Wildwood and take Florida's Turnpike for about 50 mi. The scenic Beeline Expressway, a toll road, links Orlando and Cocoa Beach, about an hour away.

By Plane

More than 20 scheduled airlines and more than 30 charter firms operate in and out of **Orlando International Airport,** providing direct service to more than 100 cities in the United States and overseas. The most active carriers are **Delta** and **United.** Other airlines include **America West, American, Bahamasair, British Airways, Continental, Icelandair, KLM, Mexicana, Northwest, TransBrasil, TWA,** and **US Airways.**

BETWEEN THE AIRPORT AND THE HOTELS

Find out in advance whether your hotel offers a free airport shuttle; if not, ask for a recommendation.

Public buses operate between the airport and the main terminal of the **Tri-County Transit Authority** (✉ 1200 W. South St., Orlando, ☎ 407/841–8240). Though the cost is very low, other options are preferable since downtown is far from most of the hotels used by theme-park vacationers.

Mears Transportation Group (☎ 407/423–5566) has a meet-and-greet service—they'll meet you at the gate, help you with your luggage, and whisk you away, either in an 11-passenger van, a town car, or a limo. Vans run to Walt Disney World and along U.S. 192 every 30 minutes; prices range from $12.50 one-way to $22 round-trip for adults. Limo rates run around $50–$60 for a town car that accommodates three or four and $90 for a stretch limo that seats six. **Town & Country Limo** (☎ 407/828–3035) charges $30 to $40 one-way for up to seven, depending on the hotel.

Taxis take only a half hour to get from the airport to most hotels used by WDW visitors. They charge about $25 to the International Drive area, about $10 more to the U.S. 192 area.

By Train

Amtrak (☎ 800/872–7245) operates the Silver Star and the Silver Meteor to Florida. Both stop in Winter Park (✉ 150 Morse Blvd.), Orlando (✉ 1400 Sligh Blvd.), and Kissimmee (✉ 416 Pleasant St.).

Getting Around

Although the public transportation in Orlando could use some work and taxis are expensive because of the distances involved, it is by no means absolutely necessary to rent a car in Orlando.

If you are staying at a Walt Disney World hotel, or if you buy a four- or five-day pass instead of buying daily admission tickets to the Disney parks, your transportation within WDW is free.

Outside Walt Disney World, just about every hotel, and even many motels, are linked to one of several private transportation systems that shuttle travelers back and forth to most of the area attractions for only a few dollars. However, if you want to visit the major theme parks outside Walt Disney World, venture off the beaten track, or eat where most tourists don't, a rental car is essential. And if you are traveling with your family, you may spend more on these shuttles, which charge by the head, than on a rental car: Orlando offers some of the lowest rental-car rates in the entire United States.

By Bus

If you are staying along International Drive, in Kissimmee, or in Orlando proper, you can ride public buses to get around the immediate area. To find out which bus to take, ask your hotel clerk or call the **Tri-County Transit Authority Information Office** (☎ 407/841–8240) during business hours.

By Car

The most important artery in the Orlando area is I–4. This interstate highway, which links the Atlantic Coast to Florida's Gulf of Mexico, ties everything together, and you'll invariably receive directions in reference to it. The problem is that I–4, though considered an east–west expressway in our national road system (where even numbers signify an east–west orientation and odd numbers a north–south orientation), actually runs north and south in the Orlando area. So when the signs say east, you are usually going north, and when the signs say west, you are usually going south.

Another main drag is International Drive, aka I-Drive, which has many major hotels, restaurants, and shopping centers. You can get onto International Drive from I–4 Exits 28, 29, and 30B. The other main road, U.S. 192, cuts across I–4 at Exits 25A and 25B. This highway goes through the Kissimmee area and crosses WDW property, taking you to the Magic Kingdom's main entrance.

By Shuttle

Scheduled service and charters linking just about every hotel and major attraction in the area are available from **Gray Line of Orlando** (☎ 407/422–0744), **Mears Transportation Group** (☎ 407/423–5566), **Phoenix Tours** (☎ 407/859–4211), and **Rabbit Bus Lines** (☎ 407/291–2424). In addition, many hotels run their own shuttles especially for guests; to arrange a ride, ask your hotel concierge, inquire at the front desk, or phone the company directly.

One-way fares are usually $6–$7 per adult, a couple of dollars less for children 4–11, between major hotel areas and the WDW parks. Round-trip excursion fares to Cypress Gardens are $27 per person, including admission.

By Taxi

Taxi fares start at $2.45 and cost $1.40 for each mile thereafter. Call **Yellow Cab** (☎ 407/699–9999) or **Town and Country Cab** (☎ 407/828–3035). Sample fares are: to WDW's Magic Kingdom, about $20 from International Drive, $11–$15 from U.S. 192; to Universal Studios, $6–$11 from International Drive, $25–$30 from U.S. 192; to downtown Orlando's Church Street Station, $20–$25 from International Drive, $30–$40 from U.S. 192.

Contacts and Resources

Emergencies

Dial **911** for police or ambulance. All the area's major theme parks (and some of the minor ones) have first-aid centers.

HOSPITALS

Hospital emergency rooms are open 24 hours a day. The most accessible hospital, located in the International Drive area, is the **Orlando Regional Medical Center/Sand Lake Hospital** (⊠ 9400 Turkey Lake Rd., Orlando, ☎ 407/351–8500).

LATE-NIGHT PHARMACIES

Eckerd Drugs (⊠ 908 Lee Rd., off I–4 at Lee Rd. exit, Orlando, ☎ 407/644–6908) and **Walgreens** (⊠ 6201 International Dr., opposite Wet 'n' Wild, Orlando, ☎ 407/345–8311; ⊠ 4578 S. Kirkman Rd., north of Universal Studios, ☎ 407/293–8458).

Guided Tour

One of the most popular—and enduring—tours in the Orlando area is Winter Park's **Scenic Boat Tour,** which leaves hourly from the dock at the end of Morse Avenue. On this 45-minute tour you'll get to see lifestyles of the rich and famous—central Florida–style. The boat cruises by some of the area's most expensive waterfront homes. ⊠ *312 E. Morse Blvd., Winter Park,* ☎ *407/644–4056.* ⊡ *$6 adults, $3 children 2–11.* ☾ *Daily 10–4.*

Visitor Information

Kissimmee/St. Cloud Convention and Visitors Bureau (⊠ 1925 E. Irlo Bronson Memorial Hwy., Kissimmee 34744, ☎ 407/847–5000 or 800/327–9159). **Orlando/Orange County Convention and Visitors Bureau** (⊠ 8723 International Dr., Orlando 32819, ☎ 407/363–5871). **Winter Park Chamber of Commerce** (⊠ Box 280, Winter Park 32790, ☎ 407/644–8281).

9 The Tampa Bay Area

Tampa and St. Petersburg, on Florida's west coast, are eclectic and busy. Ybor City, in the heart of Tampa, reflects the city's Cuban flavor. Inland is typical suburban sprawl, while to the north are extensive nature preserves, parks, and such small towns as Tarpon Springs, known for decades for its Greek population. South of the bay along the gulf, communities are somewhat quieter and more resorty, although Sarasota is distinguished by a thriving arts scene.

WHILE GLITZY MIAMI and Mickey Mouse in Orlando grab most of the Florida tourism headlines, the rapidly growing Tampa Bay area has quietly become a favorite spot for pleasure-seeking visitors from the United States and around the world. Over the last 30 years the region has become fully developed, but at a much slower pace and with a less commercial atmosphere than the east coast. The resulting community has a varied economic base that is not entirely dependent upon tourism as well as excellent beaches and superior hotels and resorts.

Updated by
Pamela
Acheson

Native Americans were the sole inhabitants of the region for many years. (Tampa is a Native American word meaning "sticks of fire.") Spanish explorers Juan Ponce de León, Pánfilo de Narváez, and Hernando de Soto passed through in the mid-1500s, and the U.S. Army and civilian settlers arrived in 1824. A military presence remains in Tampa at MacDill Air Force Base, the U.S. Operations Command.

Today the region offers astounding diversity. Terrain ranges from the rolling, pine-dotted northern reaches to the coast's white-sand beaches and barrier islands. Communities run the gamut as well. Tampa is a full-fledged city with a high-rise skyline and highways jammed with traffic. Across the bay is a peninsula comprising the compact St. Petersburg downtown, which contains interesting restaurants, shops, and museums; a central residential area; and barrier islands on the western margin, with beaches, quiet parks, and little, laid-back beach towns. To the north are towns that celebrate their ethnic heritage and, farther still, mostly undeveloped land dotted with crystal-clear rivers and springs and nature preserves. To the south lie resort communities, including sophisticated and artsy Sarasota, which fills up in winter with snowbirds escaping the cold.

Pleasures and Pastimes

Beaches
Conditions on the Gulf of Mexico, which is fed by rivers and streams originating "up North," vary according to tides and storms. Though not all beaches are pristine, almost every barrier island from Clearwater to Venice has some great ones with excellent swimming. Don't swim in the bays, which boaters, marinas, and industry have polluted.

Biking
The Pinellas Trail, which follows the path of a former railroad, is 25 mi long and makes it possible to bike all the way from Tarpon Springs to Seminole Park in St. Petersburg. There are also many lovely rural areas to bike through and plenty of places to rent bikes, should you want to pedal along the streets. Be wary of traffic in downtown Tampa and on the congested areas of the Pinellas Trail.

Canoeing
Several inland rivers are good for canoeing, and several outfits rent canoes and provide guided tours.

Dining
Fresh seafood is plentiful. Raw bars serving fresh oysters, clams, and mussels are everywhere. The region's ethnic diversity is also well represented. Tarpon Springs adds a hearty helping of such classic Greek specialties as moussaka and baklava. In Tampa, the ethnic cuisine is Cuban, so you'll find black beans and rice and plenty of paella. In Sarasota, the emphasis is Continental, both in food and service.

Many restaurants, from family neighborhood spots to very expensive places, offer extra-cheap early-bird menus with seating before 6 PM. These are even more prevalent off-season, from May to October.

Fishing

Anglers flock to southwest Florida's coastal water to catch tarpon, king-fish, speckled trout, snapper, grouper, sea trout, snook, sheepshead, and shark. You can charter a fishing boat or join a group on a party boat for full- or half-day outings. Avoid fishing in polluted Tampa Bay.

Golf

There are dozens of good and even great golf courses in this part of Florida, most near Sarasota and Tampa/St. Petersburg.

Lodging

Historic hotels and ultramodern chrome-and-glass high-rises with excellent water views, sprawling resorts and cozy inns, and luxurious waterfront lodges and just-off-the-highway budget motels are among the options. In general, you'll pay more for a water view. Rates are highest between mid-December and mid-April; the lowest prices are available from May through November. Many hotels offer supervised children's programs in addition to reasonably priced two-bedroom, two-bath suites with full kitchens and facilities ranging from golf and tennis to boating to deep-sea fishing.

Shopping

Special souvenirs from this area include local natural sponges, which can be bought at reasonable prices along Dodecanese Boulevard, the main street in Tarpon Springs. In Tampa's Ybor City, many small shops sell hand-rolled cigars unlike any others north of Havana. Sarasota's upscale boutiques sell everything from antiques to resort wear. There are also flea markets throughout the region.

Exploring the Tampa Bay Area

Whether you feel like walking on white-sand beaches, watching sponge fishermen, or wandering through the upscale shopping districts, you'll find something to your liking in the remarkably diverse Tampa Bay area. Tampa is the area's commercial center, a bright, modern city. Peninsular St. Petersburg lies across the bay with a variety of attractions, including some good beach life. Tarpon Springs, to the northwest, was settled by Greek mariners and is still Greek in flavor. The Manatee Coast to the north is quite rural, with extensive nature preserves. To the south is Bradenton, with several museums; Sarasota, a sophisticated resort town; and small, canal-crossed Venice.

Numbers in the text correspond to numbers in the margin and on the Tampa/St. Petersburg and Bradenton/Sarasota maps.

Great Itineraries

IF YOU HAVE 3 DAYS

Florida Aquarium ①, in downtown ☷ **Tampa** ①–⑥, and Busch Gardens ④, 8 mi northeast of the city, are probably the two most popular attractions in the area. You'll need a half day for the aquarium and a full day for Busch Gardens. Then it's on to ☷ **Sarasota** ㉖–㉚, whose highlights include the Ringling Museums ㉖ and Bellm's Cars & Music of Yesterday ㉗.

IF YOU HAVE 4 DAYS

Start your time in ☷ **Tampa** ①–⑥ with a half day at the Florida Aquarium ①. Then it's just a short drive to Ybor City ②, where you can rest your feet over lunch before an hour or two of strolling through the shops. Busch Gardens ④ will take your whole second day and is worth a visit whether your preference is thrilling rides or seeing animals in their natural settings. One of the best spots for a day at the beach is pristine Fort De Soto Park ⑫, a perfect place for a picnic. Art lovers and circus buffs can spend their last day in Sarasota ㉖–㉚, traipsing through the Ringling Museums ㉖ and Bellm's Cars & Music of Yesterday ㉗, a delight if you love antique cars or music boxes.

IF YOU HAVE 10 DAYS

With this much time, you can linger five days in 🏨 **St. Petersburg** ⑦–⑫, which is centrally located for several engaging half- and full-day trips. You could easily spend a full day in downtown Tampa ①–⑥. Start with a morning visit to the spectacular Florida Aquarium ①, then head to Ybor City ② for a bit of exploring and lunch, and end the day with a visit to the Tampa Museum of Art ③. The next three attractions, clustered together northeast of Tampa, can be reached by car in 45–60 minutes from St. Petersburg. Spend a day at Busch Gardens ④, getting there early if you plan to see it all. Set aside another day for water fun at Adventure Island ⑤, Busch Gardens' water-park cousin. When Adventure Island is closed, or on a rainy afternoon or morning, visit the Museum of Science and Industry ⑥, or pick from the fascinating selection of museums in downtown St. Petersburg. Spend a day around Tarpon Springs ⑮–⑯, the sponge capital of the world. Fort De Soto Park ⑫ and Caladesi Island State Park, outside Dunedin ⑭, are both excellent for a day at the beach.

🏨 **Sarasota** ㉖–㉚ is a convenient base for the second part of your stay. One day, drive up to Bradenton ㉒–㉕ and take in its sights. If you feel like a boat ride, begin or end the day with a trip to Egmont Key ㉕. In Sarasota, allow about three hours to cover both the Ringling Museums ㉖ and Bellm's Cars & Music of Yesterday ㉗. In the afternoon, you might stop by the Sarasota Jungle Gardens ㉘, especially nice for children. Another day, visit the Marie Selby Botanical Gardens ㉙, quieter but still tropical, and give yourself a couple of hours to shop at St. Armand's Circle on Lido Key. Venice ㉛ makes an enjoyable half- or full-day trip, and, of course, sprinkle in some time on the beach.

When to Tour the Tampa Bay Area

Winter and spring are high season here; in summer there are huge, showy thunderstorms on many afternoons, and the temperatures are uniformly torrid, with humidity almost as high.

NORTH AND WEST AROUND TAMPA BAY

The core of the northern bay are the cities of Tampa and St. Petersburg. A semitropical climate and access to the gulf make Tampa an ideal port for the cruise industry—currently, Carnival and Holland America depart from the Port of Tampa—and the waters around St. Pete are often filled with pleasure and commercial craft.

It's fitting that an area with a thriving international port should also be populated by a wealth of nationalities. The center of the Cuban community is the east Tampa suburb of Ybor City, and north of St. Petersburg, in Dunedin, the heritage is Scottish. North of Dunedin, Tarpon Springs has supported a large Greek population for decades and is the largest producer of natural sponges in the world.

Inland, to the east of Tampa, it's all suburban sprawl, freeways, shopping malls, and—the main draw—Busch Gardens.

Tampa

84 mi southwest of Orlando.

The west coast's crown jewel as well as its business and commercial hub, Tampa has numerous high-rises and heavy traffic, but amid the bustle are all the delights you'd expect to find in a big city. The region's greatest concentration of restaurants, nightlife, stores, and cultural events are here as are some appealing extras.

★ ☺ ❶ The $84 million **Florida Aquarium** complex, with its 83-foot-high multitier glass dome, is a dazzling landmark. Included are more than 4,300 specimens of fish, other animals, and plants representing 550 species native to Florida. You follow the path of a drop of water from the freshwater springs and limestone caves of an aquifer through rivers and wetlands to beaches and open seas. Four major exhibit areas reflect the variety of Florida's natural habitats—springs and wetlands, bay and barrier beach, coral reef, and the Gulf Stream and open ocean. Perhaps the most spectacular is the full-scale replica of a Florida coral reef in a 500,000-gallon tank ringed with viewing windows, including an awesome 43-foot-wide panoramic opening; part of the tank is an acrylic tunnel through an underwater thicket of elk-horn coral teeming with tropical fish, where a dark cave reveals sea life you can ordinarily glimpse only on night dives. ⊠ *701 Channelside Dr.,* ☎ *813/273–4000.* ☜ *$13.95.* ☽ *Jan. 1–Labor Day daily 9–5, day after Labor Day–Dec. 31 9–6.*

★ ❷ Whether your interests run to spicy food, boutique shopping, or Latin music, **Ybor City,** Tampa's Cuban enclave, has it all. With cobblestone streets and wrought-iron balconies, this historic and lively neighborhood is one of only three National Historic Landmark districts in Florida. Cubans brought their cigar-making industry to Ybor (pronounced *Ee*-bore) City in 1866, and the smell of cigars—hand rolled by Cuban immigrants—still drifts through the heart of this east Tampa area. These days the neighborhood is emerging as Tampa's hot spot, as empty cigar factories are transformed into trendy boutiques, art galleries, restaurants, and nightclubs. There's even a microbrewery. Take a stroll past the ornately tiled **Columbia** restaurant and the stores lining 7th Avenue, or step back to the past at **Ybor Square** (⊠ 1901 13th St.), a restored cigar factory listed on the National Register of Historic Places that now houses boutiques, offices, and restaurants. Free guided walking tours of the area enable you to see artisans hand roll cigars following time-honored methods. ⊠ *Between Nuccio Pkwy. and 22nd St. from 7th to 9th Aves.,* ☎ *813/248–3712 for tours.* ☜ *Tours Thurs. and Sat. 10:30, also Jan.–Apr., Tues. 10:30.*

❸ The 35,000-square-foot **Tampa Museum of Art** has a permanent collection of more than 7,000 works, including the most comprehensive collection of Greek, Roman, and Etruscan antiquities in the southeastern United States and an excellent collection of 20th-century American art. In addition, it presents more than a dozen special exhibitions annually. The Florida Gallery showcases the state's well-known and emerging artists, and a sculpture garden and 7-acre park are also here. ⊠ *600 N. Ashley Dr.,* ☎ *813/274–8130.* ☜ *$5.* ☽ *Mon.–Tues. and Thurs.–Sat. 10–5, Wed. 10–9, Sun. 1–5.*

★ ☺ ❹ More than 3,400 animals are just part of the attraction of **Busch Gardens,** a sprawling, immaculately manicured site combining a zoolike setting with a theme park. Ten themed sections attempt to capture the spirit of turn-of-the-century Africa, and a monorail ride simulates an African safari—taking in free-roaming zebras, giraffes, rhinos, lions,

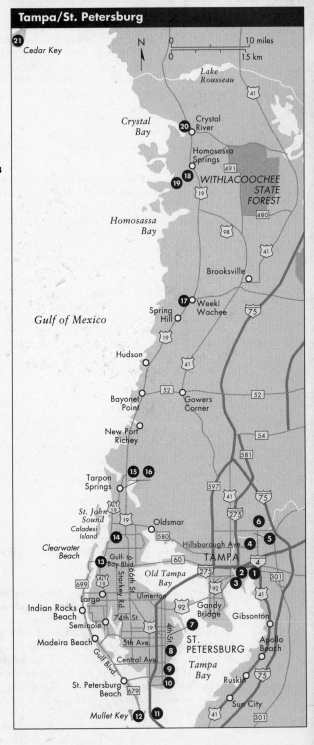

Tampa/St. Petersburg

and other exotic animals. The 335-acre park also has live entertainment, animal exhibits, shops, restaurants, games, and thrill rides. The heart-stopping Kumba and Montu are among the largest and fastest roller coasters in the Southeast, both reaching speeds of over 60 mph. You can also take a beer-tasting class. Allow six to eight hours. Parents take note: Although there's a small area of rides for littl'uns and the animals hold universal appeal, major rides are too wild for toddlers and young grade-schoolers—and the admission price for kids ages 3 through 9 approaches the cost of adult tickets. Busch Gardens is 18 mi northeast of downtown Tampa and 2 mi east of I–275. ⊠ *3000 E. Busch Blvd,* ☎ *813/987–5082.* ☞ *$38.45, parking $4.* ☉ *Daily 9:30–6.*

© **❺** Water slides, pools, and artificial wave pools create a 36-acre water wonderland at **Adventure Island,** a corporate cousin of Busch Gardens. Along with a championship volleyball complex, you'll find cafés, snack bars, changing rooms, and video games. The complex is less than a mile north of Busch Gardens. ⊠ *10001 Malcolm McKinley Dr.,* ☎ *813/987–5660.* ☞ *$20.95.* ☉ *Mar.–Oct., daily 10–5.*

❻ The **Museum of Science and Industry** is a thrilling scientific playground where you learn by doing as well as by seeing. The Gulf Coast Hurricane Exhibit re-creates the force of high-speed winds, Butterfly Encounter is an interactive garden inhabited by free-flying butterflies, the GTE Challenger Learning Center offers simulated flights, and the 100-seat Saunders Planetarium, Tampa Bay's only planetarium, has afternoon and evening shows daily, one of them a trek through the universe. There's also a spiffy IMAX theater. The museum is a mile north of Busch Gardens. ⊠ *4801 E. Fowler Ave.,* ☎ *813/987–6300.* ☞ *$11.* ☉ *Daily 9–5, longer in peak season.*

Dining and Lodging

$$$$ ✕ **Armani's.** Atop the Hyatt Regency Westshore, this award-winning ★ northern Italian restaurant has a great view of Old Tampa Bay and the city. Romantic lighting highlights the sophisticated almond and black decor. Service is impeccable and the food incredible. A feast in itself, the antipasto bar changes nightly. Pasta is excellent, and someone at your table should order the veal Armani (with mushrooms, cream, and cognac in black and white truffle sauce), the signature dish. ⊠ *6200 Courtney Campbell Causeway,* ☎ *813/281–9165. Jacket and tie. AE, DC, MC, V. Closed Sun. No lunch.*

$$$$ ✕ **Bern's Steak House.** Known well beyond the state line as perhaps ★ the best steak house in Florida, Bern's uses only finely aged prime beef. In fact, chef-owner Bern Lexer ages his own beef, grows his own organic vegetables, roasts his own coffee, and even maintains his own saltwater fish tanks. The wine list offers some 7,000 selections ranging in price from $10 to $10,000 a bottle. Sumptuous desserts are served upstairs in small, glass-enclosed rooms where you can tune in TV, radio, or the live entertainment in the lounge. ⊠ *1208 S. Howard Ave.,* ☎ *813/251–2421. AE, DC, MC, V. No lunch.*

$$$ ✕ **Kamy's.** Nouveau Italian cuisine is the hallmark of this cozy and ★ intimate spot. House specialties include linguine *alle Vongole Christoforo* (with clam sauce) and grouper *Arrabiatta* (in a spicy tomato sauce). At lunch try a grilled seafood salad or gourmet pizza. ⊠ *2832 S. MacDill Ave.,* ☎ *813/831–2939. AE, DC, MC, V.*

$$ ✕ **Castaway.** The water views are simply superb at this casual restaurant that overlooks gigantic Tampa Bay. Fresh local seafood—grilled, broiled, or blackened—is the specialty, but the menu also includes grilled steaks and several pasta dishes. You can choose to dine inside or outside on the expansive deck, which is particularly popular for lunch and at sunset. ✉ *7720 Courtney Campbell Causeway,* ☎ *813/281–0770. DC, MC, V. No lunch Sun.*

$$ ✕ **Colonnade.** The nautical decor suits the wharf-side location of this popular family restaurant. Seafood—particularly grouper, red snapper, and lobster—is a specialty, but steak and chicken are also well prepared. ✉ *3401 Bayshore Blvd.,* ☎ *813/839–7558. AE, DC, MC, V.*

$$ ✕ **Columbia.** A Spanish fixture in Ybor City since 1905, this magnif-
★ icent structure with ceramic murals, high archways, and ornate rail-ings occupies an entire city block and contains several airy, spacious dining rooms and a sunny atrium. Specialties include paella, black-bean soup, and the Columbia 1905 salad (with ham, olives, cheese, and gar-lic). There's also flamenco dancing. ✉ *2117 E. 7th Ave.,* ☎ *813/248–4961. AE, DC, MC, V.*

$ ✕ **Cactus Club.** Fajitas and other Southwestern dishes make up the bill of fare at this casual, fashionable restaurant. An alternative is the tasty pizza with a thin crispy crust or the famous Blues Burger. ✉ *1601 Snow Ave., Old Hyde Park Mall,* ☎ *813/251–4089. AE, DC, MC, V.*

$$$$ ⊞ **Hyatt Regency Westshore.** This large, business-oriented luxury hotel with a marble-accent lobby and a scattering of villas is convenient to downtown. Overlooking Tampa Bay, it also has spectacular views of a grassy, protected salt marsh and bird sanctuary. ✉ *6200 Courtney Campbell Causeway, 33607,* ☎ *813/874–1234,* ℻ *813/281–9168. 445 rooms. 3 restaurants, 4 lounges, 2 pools, tennis, jogging, racquetball. AE, D, DC, MC, V.*

$$$$ ⊞ **Saddlebrook Resort Tampa.** With 45 tennis courts and 36 holes of golf, this is arguably one of Florida's premier resorts of its type. Its heav-ily wooded grounds sprawl over 480 acres just 15 mi north of Tampa, offering varied accommodations, including two-bedroom, two-bath suites with kitchens. ✉ *5700 Saddlebrook Way, Wesley Chapel 33543,* ☎ *813/973–1111 or 800/729–8383,* ℻ *813/773–4504. 542 rooms. 3 restaurants, 2 lounges, pools, wading pools, saunas, 36 holes of golf, 45 tennis courts, health club, fishing, bicycles. AE, DC, MC, V.*

$$$$ ⊞ **Wyndham Harbour Island Hotel.** Thanks to dark wood paneling, substantial furniture, and attentive service, this 12-story hotel is an el-egant spot. The tennis facilities are excellent, and the location is con-venient to downtown and the convention center. ✉ *725 S. Harbour Island Blvd., 33602,* ☎ *813/229–5000,* ℻ *813/229–5322. 300 rooms. Restaurant, lounge, pool, tennis, health club, dock, boating. AE, DC, MC, V.*

$$$ ⊞ **Embassy Suites Hotel–Tampa Airport/Westshore.** In this modern hotel midway between Tampa International Airport and downtown, all rooms are suites and each has a kitchen. A complimentary breakfast is served. Pets are allowed. ✉ *555 N. Westshore Blvd., 33609,* ☎ *813/875–1555,* ℻ *813/287–3664. 221 suites. Restaurant, lounge, pool, health club, airport shuttle. AE, DC, MC, V.*

$$ ⊞ **Holiday Inn Busch Gardens.** This well-maintained family-oriented motor inn is a mile west of Busch Gardens, across the street from the University Square Mall, Tampa's largest. ✉ *2701 E. Fowler Ave., 33612,* ☎ *813/971–4710,* ℻ *813/977–0155. 398 rooms, 7 suites. Restaurant, lounge, pool, exercise room. AE, DC, MC, V.*

$ ⊞ **Tahitian Inn.** Comfortable rooms and budget prices are the draws at this two-story, family-run motel. It's five minutes from Tampa Sta-dium and 20 minutes from Busch Gardens. ✉ *601 S. Dale Mabry Hwy., 33609,* ☎ *813/877–6721,* ℻ *813/877–6218. 79 rooms. Restaurant, pool. AE, DC, MC, V.*

Nightlife and the Arts

THE ARTS

Occupying 9 acres along the Hillsborough River, the 290,000-square-foot **Tampa Bay Performing Arts Center** (⊠ 1010 W. C. MacInnes Pl., ☎ 813/229–7817 or 800/955–1045) is one of the largest such complexes south of the Kennedy Center in Washington, D.C. Included are a 2,400-seat festival hall, 900-seat playhouse, and 300-seat theater, which feature opera, concerts, drama, and ballet, including the **Tampa Ballet** (☎ 813/229–7827). The **Tampa Convention Center** (⊠ 333 S. Franklin St., ☎ 813/223–8511) hosts concerts throughout the year. The **Tampa Theater** (⊠ 711 N. Franklin St., ☎ 813/274–8981) presents shows, musical performances, and films.

NIGHTLIFE

For cry-in-your-cabernet blues, sail down to the **Blue Ships Cafe** (⊠ 1910 E. 7th Ave., ☎ 813/248–6097), in Ybor City, any Wednesday. On Friday and Saturday nights, crowds head to the noisy, boisterous **Dallas Bull** (⊠ 8222 N. U.S. 301, ☎ 813/985–6877) to stomp to down-home country sounds. Dance the night away at **Frankie's Patio Bar & Grill** (⊠ 1920 E. 7th Ave., ☎ 813/248–3337), which has entertainment nightly. The bar at the **Harbour Island Hotel** (⊠ Harbour Island, ☎ 813/229–5000) has a great bay view and a big-screen TV. **Skippers Smokehouse** (⊠ 910 Skipper Rd., ☎ 813/971–0666), a restaurant and oyster bar, has live reggae and blues.

Outdoor Activities and Sports

CANOEING

Just south of Tampa, **Canoe Outpost** (⊠ 18001 U.S. 301S, Wimauma, ☎ 813/634–2228) offers half-day, full-day, and overnight canoe trips on several area waters, including the Little Manatee River.

DOG RACING

Tampa Greyhound Track (⊠ 8300 N. Nebraska Ave., ☎ 813/932–4313) holds dog races from July to December.

FOOTBALL

NFL football comes in the form of the **Tampa Bay Buccaneers** (⊠ 4201 N. Dale Mabry Hwy., ☎ 813/870–2700 or 800/282–0683), who play at Tampa Stadium.

GOLF

Babe Zaharias Golf Course (⊠ 11412 Forest Hills Dr., ☎ 813/932–8932) has an 18-hole public course plus a driving range and a pro available for lessons. **Bloomingdale Golfers Club** (⊠ 4113 Great Golfers Pl., ☎ 813/653–1823) has 18 holes, a driving range, and a pleasant restaurant. You'll find an 18-hole course, a practice range, and a snack shop at the **Rocky Point Golf Course** (⊠ 4151 Dana Shores Dr., ☎ 813/884–5141). At the well-known **Saddlebrook Resort Tampa** (⊠ 5700 Saddlebrook Way, Wesley Chapel, ☎ 913/973–1111), there are 36 holes, a driving range, golf shop, and on-site pro.

HORSE RACING

Tampa Bay Downs (⊠ Race Track Rd., off Rte. 580, Oldsmar, ☎ 813/855–4401) holds Thoroughbred races from mid-December to early May.

ICE HOCKEY

The NHL's **Tampa Bay Lightning** (⊠ 401 Channelside Dr., ☎ 813/229–2658) plays at the Ice Palace, a classy $153 million downtown waterfront arena.

Tampa Jai-Alai Fronton (⊠ S. Dale Mabry Hwy. and Gandy Blvd., ☎ 813/837–2441) is open year-round.

The **City of Tampa Tennis Complex** (⊠ Hillsborough Community College, ☎ 813/870–2383), across from Tampa Stadium, has 12 clay courts and 16 hard courts.

Shopping

For bargains, stop at the **Big Top** (⊠ 9250 Fowler Ave.), open weekends 8–5, where vendors hawk new and used items at more than 600 booths. Over 120 shops, department stores, and eateries are in the **Brandon Town Center** (⊠ Grand Regency and Rte. 60), an attractively landscaped complex eight minutes from downtown. **Old Hyde Park Village** (⊠ Swan Ave., near Bayshore Blvd.) is an elegant outdoor shopping center stretching several blocks. The five-story bay-front **Pier** (⊠ 800 2nd Ave. NE), near the Museum of Fine Arts, looks like an inverted pyramid; inside are numerous shops and eating spots. The **Shops on Harbour Island** (⊠ 601 S. Harbour Island Blvd.) is a waterfront marketplace with stores, restaurants, and a food court.

St. Petersburg

21 mi west of Tampa.

St. Petersburg and the Pinellas Suncoast form the thumb of the hand jutting out of Florida's west coast, holding in Tampa Bay. There are two distinct parts of St. Petersburg—the downtown and cultural area, centered on the bay, and the beach area, on a string of barrier islands facing the gulf. Causeways link beach communities to the mainland.

❼ **Sunken Gardens** is one of Florida's most colorful attractions. Walk through an aviary full of tropical birds; stroll among more than 50,000 exotic flowers and other plants; stop to smell the rare, fragrant orchids; and take a peek into the antiques store. You'll also find gator wrestling and macaw bird shows several times a day. ⊠ *1825 4th St. N,* ☎ *813/896–3186.* 🎫 *$14.* ☉ *Daily 10–5.*

❽ Outstanding examples of European, American, pre-Columbian, and Far Eastern art line the walls of the **Museum of Fine Arts.** There are also photographic exhibits. ⊠ *255 Beach Dr. NE,* ☎ *813/896–2667.* 🎫 *$5.* ☉ *Tues.–Sat. 10–5, Sun. 1–5.*

❾ The world's most extensive collection of originals by Spanish surrealist Salvador Dali is found at the **Salvador Dali Museum.** Valued at more than $125 million, it includes 94 oils, more than 100 watercolors and drawings, and 1,300 graphics, sculptures, photographs, and objets d'art, including floor-to-ceiling murals. ⊠ *1000 3rd St. S,* ☎ *813/823–3767.* 🎫 *$8.* ☉ *Tues.–Sat. 10–5, Sun. and Mon. noon–5.*

❿ In **Great Explorations!** you'll never hear, "Don't touch." The museum is hands-on in every room: the Body Shop, where you can explore health; the Think Tank, featuring mind-stretching puzzles; the Touch Tunnel, a 90-foot-long, pitch-black, crawl-through maze; and Phenomenal Arts, where you can play a Moog synthesizer and explore neon-filled tubes that glow when touched. ⊠ *1120 4th St. S,* ☎ *813/821–8992.* 🎫 *$6.* ☉ *Mon.–Sat. 10–5, Sun. noon–5.*

★ ⓫ It costs $1 to travel southbound on the **Sunshine Skyway,** the 4.1-mi-long bridge connecting Pinellas and Manatee counties, a section of I–275. But it's money well spent. The roadway is 183 feet above Tampa Bay at its highest point, and the view out over the bay is spectacular. You'll see the several small islands that dot the bay if you're heading southeast, St. Petersburg Beach if you're going northwest.

⑫ Actually spread over six small islands, or keys, the 900-acre **Fort De Soto Park** lies at the mouth of Tampa Bay. It has 7 mi of beaches, two fishing piers, picnic and camping grounds, and a historic fort. The fort for which it's named was built on the southern end of Mullet Key to protect sea lanes in the gulf during the Spanish-American War. Roam the fort or wander the beaches of any of the islands within the park. ⊠ *Rte. 682 (54th Ave. S), no phone.* ☎ *Free.* ☉ *Daily sunrise–sunset.*

Beaches

Bay Beach (⊠ North Shore Dr. and 13th Ave. NE), on Tampa Bay, has showers and picnic shelters. **Fort De Soto Park** (⊠ Rte. 682), at the south end of the Pinellas Bayway (toll 85¢), has St. Petersburg's southernmost beaches. Facilities include two piers, picnic sites overlooking lagoons, a waterskiing and boating area, and miles of beaches for swimming. It's open daily until dark. **Maximo Park Beach** (⊠ 34th St. and Pinellas Point Dr. S, Madeira Beach) is on Boca Ciega Bay. It's unguarded, but there is a picnic area with grills, tables, shelters, and a boat ramp. **Pass-A-Grille Beach,** the southern part of St. Petersburg Beach, has parking meters, a snack bar, rest rooms, and showers. **St. Petersburg Municipal Beach** (⊠ 11260 Gulf Blvd.) is a free beach on Treasure Island. There are dressing rooms, metered parking, and a snack bar.

Dining and Lodging

$-$$ ✕ **Apropos Bistro.** Sit indoors or out at this little harbor-front café open all day. For breakfast try the delicious blueberry pancakes. For lunch, choose a light salad or one of the appealing sandwiches—filet mignon, tarragon chicken club, or ginger-marinated pork loin. Dinner entrées include salads, grilled meats, and pastas. ⊠ *300 2nd Ave. at beginning of pier,* ☎ *813/823–8934. MC, V. Closed Mon.*

$-$$ ✕ **Nick's on the Water.** Sitting at the end of the St. Petersburg Pier is this peaceful place with pretty water views. Wood-burning-oven-baked pizzas are a specialty, with toppings ranging from barbecued chicken to Philly cheese steak. Rigatoni à la vodka, the signature dish, headlines the pastas. ⊠ *800 2nd Ave. NE,* ☎ *813/898–5800. AE, MC, V.*

$ ✕ **Hurricane Seafood Restaurant.** Everyone loves this seafood joint on historic Pass-A-Grille Beach for its steamed shrimp, homemade crab cakes, and grilled, broiled, or blackened grouper. One of the few places in St. Petersburg with live jazz (Wednesday to Sunday), it also has a disco next door, Stormy's at the Hurricane. Crowds descend on the third-floor sundeck to see those gorgeous sunsets. ⊠ *807 Gulf Way,* ☎ *813/360–9558. MC, V.*

$ ✕ **Ted Peters Famous Smoked Fish.** The menu is limited to mackerel, mullet, and salmon, but all are smoked and seasoned to perfection and served with heaping helpings of German potato salad. All meals are served outdoors. ⊠ *1350 Pasadena Ave. S, Pasadena,* ☎ *813/381–7931. No credit cards. Closed Tues. No dinner.*

$$$$ ▥ **Don CeSar Beach Resort.** Still echoing with the ghosts of Scott and Zelda Fitzgerald, this sprawling, sybaritic, beachfront "Pink Palace" has long been a Gulf Coast landmark because of its remarkable architecture. It is steeped in turn-of-the-century elegance. ⊠ *3400 Gulf Blvd., St. Petersburg Beach 33706,* ☎ *813/360–1881,* ☎ *813/367–3609. 277 rooms. 3 restaurants, 3 bars, 2 pools, 2 spas, tennis courts, exercise room, beach, boating, jet skiing, parasailing, children's programs, meeting rooms. AE, DC, MC, V.*

$$$$ 🏨 **Stouffer Vinoy Resort.** More than $100 million was spent to renovate this 1925 hotel on the National Register of Historic Places, and it shows. The spacious rooms have three phones, two TVs, minibars, hair dryers, and bathrobes. Though rooms in the original building have more character, all are comfortable and stylish. Be sure to check out the frescoed ceilings in the dining room. Ron Garl designed the 18-hole, par-70 golf course. The hotel overlooks Tampa Bay, and a tiny beach does adjoin the property; however, in addition, transportation is provided to ocean beaches 20 minutes away. ⊠ *501 5th Ave. NE, 33701,* ☎ *813/894–1000,* FAX *813/822–2785. 360 rooms. 4 restaurants, 2 lounges, 2 pools, 18-hole golf course, tennis, croquet, health club, business services. AE, DC, MC, V.*

$$$$ 🏨 **Tradewinds on St. Petersburg Beach.** This beachfront complex feels a little like Old Florida. Rooms and suites (some with kitchens) are scattered among six buildings on manicured grounds. White gazebos, gondolas on canals, and swaying hammocks set the mood. ⊠ *5500 Gulf Blvd., St. Petersburg Beach 33706,* ☎ *813/367–6461,* FAX *813/367–4567. 577 rooms. 3 restaurants, ice cream parlor, lounge, pools, wading pool, sauna, putting green, tennis, exercise room, racquetball, beach, dock, windsurfing, boating, waterskiing, fishing, bicycles, playground. AE, DC, MC, V.*

$$ 🏨 **Islands's End Cottages.** These simply decorated, little one-bedroom cottages have water views and full kitchens. Outdoors, attractive wooden walkways lead to latticework sitting areas and peaceful gazebos. The grounds are nicely landscaped, and you can walk to the beach, restaurants, and shopping. Grills are available if you want to barbecue. ⊠ *1 Pass-A-Grille Way, St. Petersburg Beach 33706,* ☎ *813/360–5023,* FAX *813/367–7890. 6 cottages. Fishing. MC, V.*

Nightlife and the Arts

THE ARTS

The **St. Petersburg Concert Ballet** (⊠ 400 12th St. S., ☎ 813/892–5767) performs throughout the year, mostly at the Bayfront Center.

NIGHTLIFE

Carlie's (⊠ 5641 49th St., ☎ 813/527–5214) is hopping on Friday and Saturday nights, with plenty of dancing. At the popular **Cha Cha Coconuts** (⊠ City Pier, ☎ 813/822–6655), there is live contemporary music several nights a week and reggae on Sundays. **Coliseum Ballroom** (⊠ 535 4th Ave. N, ☎ 813/892–5202) offers ballroom dancing Wednesday and Saturday nights. **Harp & Thistle** (⊠ 650 Corey Ave., St. Petersburg Beach, ☎ 813/360–4104) presents live Irish music Wednesday through Sunday. **Hurricane Lounge** (⊠ 807 Gulf Way, Pass-A-Grille Beach, ☎ 813/360–9558) is a nice place to watch the sun go down and listen to jazz. Weekend crowds pack the noisy, boisterous **Joyland Country Music Night Club** (⊠ 11225 U.S. 19, ☎ 813/573–1919).

Outdoor Activities and Sports

BASEBALL

St. Pete's Lang Stadium is home to spring training camps for the **Baltimore Orioles** and **St. Louis Cardinals** (⊠ 1st St. and 2nd Ave., ☎ 813/822–3384).

BIKING

Cycle & Scooter Services of St. Pete Beach (⊠ 7116 Gulf Blvd., ☎ 813/367–3882) rents beach and mountain bikes.

DOG RACING

Dog races are held January–June at **Derby Lane** (⊠ 10490 Gandy Blvd., ☎ 813/576–1361).

GOLF

You'll find 18 holes and a practice range at **Mainlands Golf Course** (⊠ 9445 Mainlands Blvd. W, ☎ 813/577–4847). **Mangrove Bay Golf Course** (⊠ 875 62nd Ave. NE, ☎ 813/893–7800) offers a driving range as well as 18 holes.

WATER SPORTS

You can take sailing lessons and rent boats at **M & M Beach Service & Boat Rental** (⊠ 5300 Gulf Blvd., St. Petersburg Beach, ☎ 813/360–8295).

Shopping

John's Pass Village and Boardwalk (⊠ 12901 Gulf Blvd., Madeira Beach) features a collection of shops and restaurants in an old-style fishing village, where you can pass the time watching pelicans cavorting and dive-bombing for food. On weekends between 8 and 4, some 2,000 vendors set up a flea market on 100 acres at the **Wagonwheel** (⊠ 7801 Park Blvd., Pinellas Park).

Clearwater

13 *12 mi north of St. Petersburg.*

This sprawling town has many residential areas and small shopping plazas. The draw is the beaches along the barrier islands offshore.

OFF THE BEATEN PATH

SUNCOAST SEABIRD SANCTUARY – When pelicans become entangled in fishing lines, locals sometimes carry them to this nonprofit center dedicated to the rescue, repair, recuperation, and release of sick and injured birds. At times, there are 500 to 600 land and seabirds in residence, including pelicans, egrets, herons, gulls, terns, cranes, ducks, owls, and cormorants. Many of them are kept in open-air pens while they recover. The sanctuary backs up to the beach. ⊠ *18328 Gulf Blvd., Indian Shores,* ☎ *813/391–6211.* ⌨ *Donations welcome.* ⊙ *Daily sunrise–sunset, tours Wed. and Sun. 2.*

The Arts

Ruth Eckerd Hall (⊠ 1111 McMullen Booth Rd., ☎ 813/791–7400) hosts many national performers of ballet, opera, and music—pop, classical, or jazz.

Beaches

Clearwater Beach, on a narrow island between Clearwater Harbor and the gulf, is connected to downtown Clearwater by Memorial Causeway and is a popular hangout for teens and college students. Facilities include a marina, concessions, showers, rest rooms, and lifeguards. **Indian Rocks Beach** (⊠ Off Rte. 8, south of Clearwater Beach) attracts mostly couples. **North Shore Beach** (⊠ 901 North Shore Dr. NE, Belleair Beach) charges $1 admission and has a pool, beach umbrellas, cabanas, windbreaks, and lounges.

Dining and Lodging

$$–$$$ ✕ **Bob Heilman's Beachcomber.** Southern-fried chicken and mashed potatoes with gravy have long been the Sunday staple at this many decades–old restaurant otherwise known for its seafood, homemade desserts, and hearty portions. ⊠ *447 Mandalay Ave., Clearwater Beach,* ☎ *813/442–4144. AE, DC, MC, V.*

$$$$ ⊞ **Belleview Mido Resort Hotel.** This charming 21-acre Victorian re-
★ sort was built in 1896 and is on the National Register of Historic Places. Overlooking a narrow part of Clearwater Bay, the units are luxuriously

decorated, and there are recreational opportunities aplenty. ⊠ *25 Belleview Blvd., 34616,* ☎ *813/442–6171,* FAX *813/441–4173. 292 rooms. 2 restaurants, 3 lounges, 2 pools, saunas, spa, golf, tennis, health club, boating, bicycles, playground. AE, D, DC, MC, V.*

$$$ 🏨 **Sheraton Sand Key Resort.** This is a supreme spot for those searching for sun, sand, and surf. Balconies and patios overlook the gulf and well-manicured grounds. ⊠ *1160 Gulf Blvd., Clearwater Beach 33515,* ☎ *813/595–1611,* FAX *813/596–8488. 390 rooms. Restaurant, lounge, pool, wading pool, tennis, beach, windsurfing, boating, playground. AE, DC, MC, V.*

$$ 🏨 **Best Western Sea Wake Inn.** This white, concrete six-story hotel won't win any architectural awards, but it is right on the beach. Rooms are nicely decorated, and many have excellent views of the gulf. Some rooms have refrigerators. ⊠ *691 S. Gulfview Blvd., 34630,* ☎ *813/443–7652,* FAX *813/461–2836. 110 rooms. Restaurant, lounge, pool, beach, fishing. AE, DC, MC, V.*

Outdoor Activities and Sports

BASEBALL
The **Philadelphia Phillies** (⊠ Seminole St. and Greenwood Ave., ☎ 813/441–8638) get ready for the season at Jack Russell Memorial Stadium.

BIKING
D & S Bicycle Shop (⊠ 12073 Seminole Blvd., Largo, ☎ 941/393–0300) has bikes of all sizes for rent by the hour, day, or week.

GOLF
Clearwater Golf Park (⊠ 1875 Airport Dr., ☎ 813/447–5272) has 18 holes and a driving range. **Largo Municipal Golf Course** (⊠ 12500 131st St. N, Largo, ☎ 813/587–6724) is an 18-hole course.

TENNIS
Shipwatch Yacht & Tennis Club (⊠ 11800 Shipwatch Dr., Largo, ☎ 813/596–6862) has 12 clay courts, 10 with lights for night play.

Shopping
Hamlin's Landing (⊠ 401 2nd St. E, Indian Rocks Beach) has several shops and restaurants along the Intracoastal Waterway, in a Victorian-style setting.

Dunedin

⑭ *3 mi north of Clearwater.*

If the sound of bagpipes played by men in kilts appeals to you, head to this town, named by two Scots in the 1880s. In March and April, the Highland games and the Dunedin Heather and Thistle holidays pay tribute to the town's Celtic heritage.

OFF THE
BEATEN PATH

CALADESI ISLAND STATE PARK – One of Florida's few undeveloped barrier islands, this 600-acre preserve lies 3 mi off the coast, across Hurricane Pass, and is accessible only by boat. There's a beach on the gulf side, mangroves on the bay side, and a self-guided nature trail winding through the island's interior. Park rangers are available to answer questions. A good spot for swimming, fishing, shelling, boating, and nature study, the park has boardwalks, picnic shelters, bathhouses, and a concession stand. ⊠ *Dunedin Causeway to Honeymoon Island, then board ferry.* ☎ *813/734-5263.* 🎟 *Parking $3.25, ferry $4.* ☉ *Daily 8-sunset, ferry hourly 10-5 in fair weather.*

Dining and Lodging

$$ ✕ **Bon Appetit.** This restaurant with views of the Intracoastal Water-
★ way and the gulf is known for its creative cuisine. European-trained
chef-owners Peter Kreuziger and Karl Heinz Riedl change the menu
twice a month and offer salads and light entrées as well as fresh seafood
and more ambitious fare, such as peppered quail and scallops with figs
and raisins on fettuccine. This is an excellent place to catch a sunset.
✉ *148 Marina Plaza,* ☎ *813/733–2151. AE, MC, V.*

$$ 🏨 **Inn on the Bay.** A good value, this modest four-story motel has comfortable rooms and a small number of two-bedroom units. Check to
see if you can get one with an excellent gulf view. The inn has a fishing pier and rents bicycles, and good beaches and water sports rentals
are nearby, as is the ferry to Caladesi Island State Park. ✉ *1420
Bayshore Blvd., 34698,* ☎ *813/734–7689. 41 rooms. Lounge, pool,
fishing, bicycles. AE, MC, V.*

Outdoor Activities and Sports

BASEBALL

The **Toronto Blue Jays** (✉ 373 Douglas Ave., north of Rte. 88, ☎
813/733–9302) hold spring training at Grant Field.

GOLF

Dunedin Country Club (✉ 1050 Palm Blvd., ☎ 813/733–7836) has 18
holes and a driving range.

Tarpon Springs

10 mi north of Dunedin.

Decades ago, sponge divers from Greece moved to Tarpon Springs and
continued to pull riches from the sea, and by the 1930s it was the world's
largest sponge center. Although a bacterial blight wiped out the sponge
beds in the 1940s, the Greeks held on, and though it's not as strong
as it once was, the sponge industry has returned. Today, the Greek influence remains evident in the churches, the restaurants, and, often,
the language spoken on the streets.

⑮ Don't miss **St. Nicholas Greek Orthodox Church,** a replica of St. Sophia's
in Istanbul and an excellent example of New Byzantine architecture.
✉ *36 N. Pinellas Ave.* 🎫 *Donations welcome.* ☉ *Daily 9–5.*

⑯ **Spongeorama** offers an exhibit and film about the history of the
sponge industry. You'll come away converted to (and loaded up with)
natural sponges and loofas. ✉ *Dodecanese Blvd., off Rte. 19,* ☎
813/943–9509. 🎫 *Free.* ☉ *Daily 10–5.*

Beaches

Howard Park Beach (✉ Sunset Dr.) is one of two public beaches in
Tarpon Springs with lifeguards in spring and summer. **Sunset Beach**
(✉ Gulf Rd.) has rest rooms, picnic tables, grills, and a boat ramp.

Dining and Lodging

$$ ✕ **La Brasserie.** A bit of French cuisine in this highly Greek area makes
this little place noteworthy. Appetizers include escargot, frogs' legs, and
quiche, while entrées range from veal in a white sauce and veal *cor-
don bleu* to coq au vin and fondue. Onion soup is the house specialty.
✉ *200 E. Tarpon Ave.,* ☎ *813/942–3011. AE, MC, V.*

$$ ✕ **Louis Pappas' Riverside Restaurant.** The decor consists mainly of
★ wall-to-wall people who pour into this waterfront landmark for all man-
ner of Greek fare, especially the Greek salad. ✉ *10 W. Dodecanese Blvd.,*
☎ *813/937–5101. AE, DC, MC, V. No lunch Sun.*

$$$$ 🏨 **Innisbrook Hilton Resort.** This 1,000-acre resort is a pleasure.
★ Grounds are beautifully maintained, and the three 18-hole golf courses are highly rated and of championship caliber. All units are suites, all are roomy, and all have kitchens; some have balconies or patios as well. A good mix of restaurants and lounges compensates for the resort's isolation. ⊠ *U.S. 19, Box 1088, 34689,* ☎ *813/942–2000,* FAX *813/942– 5576. 1,200 units. 4 restaurants, pools, saunas, 63 holes of golf, miniature golf, tennis, health club, racquetball, nightclub, children's programs, playground. AE, DC, MC, V.*

$$ 🏨 **Inness Manor.** Built in the late 1800s, this B&B was home to the well-known American painter George Inness, Jr. Highlights of the house are natural cypress beams, a magnificent staircase, and burled yellow-pine panels. There are currently five casually decorated guest rooms, four with balconies. Picnic lunches are available, and smoking is not permitted. ⊠ *34 W. Orange St., 34689,* ☎ *813/938–2900. 5 rooms (2 share bath). AE, MC, V.*

Outdoor Activities and Sports

GOLF

Innisbrook Hilton Resort (⊠ U.S. 19, ☎ 813/942–2000) offers 63 holes of golf, driving ranges, and putting greens.

THE MANATEE COAST

The coastal area north of Tampa is aptly called the Manatee Coast. Of these gentle vegetarian water mammals, distantly related to elephants, only 1,200 are alive today, and they are threatened by development and speeding motor boats. Extensive nature preserves and parks have been created to protect them and other wildlife indigenous to the area and are among the best spots to view manatees in the wild. Although they are far from mythical beauties, it is believed that manatees inspired ancient mariners' tales of mermaids.

U.S. 19 is the prime route through rural manatee country, and traffic flows freely once you've left the congestion of St. Petersburg. If you are planning a day trip from the bay area, pack a picnic lunch before leaving, since most of the sights are outdoors.

Weeki Wachee

27 mi north of Tarpon Springs.

⑰ The highlight here is **Weeki Wachee Spring,** which flows at the remarkable rate of 170 million gallons a day with a constant temperature of 74°. The spring has long been famous for its live mermaids, and nowadays, clever breathing makes possible performances of *Pocahontas* and *The Little Mermaid* in the underwater theater. A nature trail threads through the subtropical wilderness, and a jungle boat cruises to view local wildlife. You'll need four hours to see everything. ⊠ *U.S. 19 and Rte. 50,* ☎ *352/596–2062.* 🎟 *$16.95.* ☉ *Daily 9:30–5:30.*

Homosassa Springs

20 mi north of Weeki Wachee.

⑱ At the **Homosassa Springs State Wildlife Park** you may see manatees, but the main attraction is the Spring of 10,000 Fish, a clear spring with many species of fish that can be easily watched through a floating glass observatory. A walk along the park's paths leads you to alligator, other reptile, and exotic bird shows. Jungle boat cruises on the Homosassa River are available across Fish Bowl Drive from the entrance.

⊠ *1 mi west of U.S. 19 on Fish Bowl Dr.,* ☎ *352/628–2311.* 🎟 *$7.95.*
🕑 *Daily 9–5:30.*

⑲ The **Yulee Sugar Mill State Historic Site,** the ruined remains of a 5,100-
acre sugar plantation owned by Florida's first U.S. Senator, David
Levy Yulee, make for pleasant picnicking. ⊠ *Rte. 490A,* ☎ *352/795–
3817.* 🎟 *Free.* 🕑 *Daily sunrise–sunset.*

Dining and Lodging

$$$ ✕ **K. C. Crump.** This 1870 Old Florida residence on the Homosassa
River was restored in 1986 and opened as a restaurant serving meat
and seafood in 1987. In addition to the large, airy dining rooms,
there's outdoor dining, a lounge, and a marina on the river. ⊠ *11210
Halls River Rd.,* ☎ *352/628–1500. AE, MC, V.*

$$ 🏨 **Ramada Inn Downtown.** This is a simple motor inn with queen-size
beds in most rooms. It accepts pets. ⊠ *U.S. 19 at Rte. 490A, 34448,*
☎ FAX *352/628–4311. 104 rooms. Restaurant, lounge, pool, tennis
courts, playground. AE, D, DC, MC, V.*

$$ 🏨 **Riverside Inn.** This rustic little inn is intimately set beside the Ho-
mosassa River and across from Monkey Island—residence of six such
mammals. Though it has its own restaurant and lounge, the Riverside
is within walking distance of three local restaurants, and two others
are accessible by boat. Rent bicycles to get a feel for the lovely sur-
roundings. ⊠ *Box 258, 32687,* ☎ *352/628–2474,* FAX *352/628–5208.
76 rooms. Restaurant, lounge, pool, tennis courts, bicycles. AE, MC,
V.*

$ 🏨 **Homosassa River Retreat.** On the banks of the Homosassa River,
with two docks and nearby boat and pontoon rentals, this resort of
one- and two-bedroom cottages with kitchens is well situated for out-
door adventuring. ⊠ *10605 Hall's River Rd., 32646,* ☎ *352/628–7072.
9 cottages. Docks, coin laundry. MC, V.*

Crystal River

7 mi north of Homosassa Springs.

⑳ The **Crystal River National Wildlife Refuge** is a U.S. Fish and Wildlife
Service sanctuary for the endangered manatee. The main spring, around
which manatees congregate in winter, feeds crystal-clear water into the
river at 72° year-round. In warmer months, when manatees scatter, the
main spring is still fun for a swim. Manatee season runs from Octo-
ber to April. Though accessible only by boat, the refuge provides nei-
ther tours nor boat rentals. For these, contact marinas in the town of
Crystal River. ⊠ *1502 S. Kings Bay Dr.,* ☎ *352/563–2088.* 🎟 *Free.*
🕑 *Daily 9–4, office weekdays 7:30–4.*

Dining and Lodging

$ ✕ **Charlie's Fish House Restaurant.** This popular, no-frills seafood spot
serves fish caught locally as well as oysters, crab claws, and lobster. ⊠
224 U.S. 19 N, ☎ *352/795–3949. MC, V.*

$$ 🏨 **Plantation Inn & Golf Resort.** Set on the banks of Kings Bay, this
rustic two-story plantation-style resort sits on 232 acres near several
nature preserves and rivers. Rooms are decorated in soft pastels, and
the furniture is blond wood. ⊠ *9301 W. Fort Island Trail, 34423,* ☎
352/795–4211 or 800/632–6262, FAX *352/795–1368. 136 rooms.
Restaurant, lounge, 2 pools, saunas, 27 holes of golf, tennis, boating,
fishing. AE, DC, MC, V.*

$ 🏨 **Best Western Crystal River Resort.** This cinder-block roadside motel
is close to Kings Bay and its manatee population. A marina is steps

away, with dive boats departing for scuba and snorkeling excursions. Only two rooms view the water: 114 and 128. ✉ *614 N.W. U.S. 19, 34428,* ☎ *352/795–3171,* 🖷 *352/795–3179. 96 rooms, 18 efficiencies. Restaurant, lounge, pool. AE, DC, MC, V.*

Outdoor Activities and Sports

GOLF

Plantation Inn & Golf Resort (✉ 9301 W. Fort Island Trail, ☎ 352/795–7211) features 27 holes and a putting green.

Cedar Key

57 mi northwest of Crystal River; follow Rte. 24 southwest from U.S. 19 to the end.

Up in the area known as the Big Bend, Florida's long, curving coastline north of Tampa, you won't find many beaches. But you will find an idyllic collection of small cays and a little island village tucked in among the marshes and scenic streams feeding the Gulf of Mexico. Once a strategic port for the Confederate States of America, remote Cedar Key is today a commercial fishing center. Don't be surprised if you don't see another car on your way there, despite the fact that Route 24 is the only route to the island.

㉑ The **Cedar Key Historical Society Museum** displays photographs and exhibits that focus on the area's development. ✉ *Rte. 24 and 2nd St.,* ☎ *352/543–5549.* 🖻 *$1.* 🕑 *Mon.–Sat. 11–5, Sun. 2–5.*

Lodging

$ 🖭 **Park Place Motel.** Views of the gulf are lovely from the private balconies off many units at this three-story motel within walking distance of stores and restaurants. On the top floor are bilevel units with sleeping lofts, but there's no elevator. ✉ *211 2nd St. at A St., 32625,* ☎ *352/543–5575. 34 rooms. MC, V.*

SOUTH OF TAMPA BAY

The southern end of Tampa Bay is anchored by Bradenton and Sarasota, two cities bordered by a string of barrier islands with fine beaches. Sarasota County has no less than 35 mi of gulf beaches, as well as two state parks, 22 municipal parks, and more than 30 golf courses, many open to the public.

Sarasota has a thriving cultural scene, thanks mostly to John Ringling, founder of the Ringling Brothers Barnum & Bailey Circus, who chose this area for the winter home of his circus and his family. Bradenton, to the north, maintains a lower profile, while Venice, a few miles south on the Gulf Coast, claims some of Sarasota County's best beaches and the world's only clown college.

Bradenton

49 mi south of Tampa.

This city on the Manatee River is home to some 20 mi of beaches and is well sited for access to fishing, both fresh- and saltwater. It also has its share of golf courses and historic sites dating to the mid-1800s.

㉒ The real thing, the **Manatee Village Historical Park** consists of an 1860 courthouse, 1887 church, 1903 general store and museum, and 1912 settler's home. The Old Manatee Cemetery, which dates back to 1850, contains the graves of early Manatee County settlers. An appointment is necessary for a cemetery tour. ✉ *Rte. 64 at 6th Ave. E,* ☎ *941/749–*

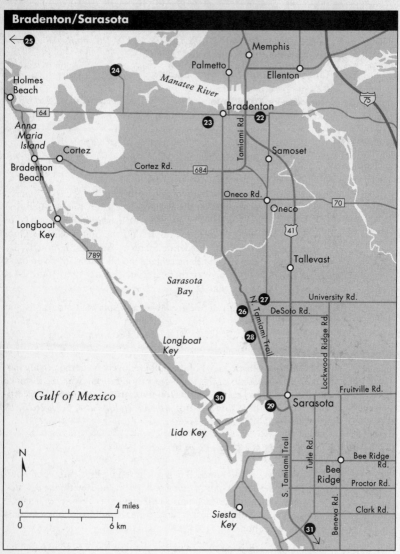

Bradenton/Sarasota

Holmes Beach
Palmetto
Memphis
Ellenton
Manatee River
I-75
64
Anna Maria Island
Cortez
Bradenton
Samoset
Tamiami Rd.
Bradenton Beach
Cortez Rd.
684
Oneco Rd.
Oneco
70
Longboat Key
41
789
Tallevast
Sarasota Bay
University Rd.
DeSoto Rd.
Longboat Key
S. Tamiami Trail
Lockwood Ridge Rd.
Gulf of Mexico
Fruitville Rd.
Sarasota
Lido Key
N
Bee Ridge Rd.
Tutle Rd.
Bee Ridge
Proctor Rd.
0   4 miles
0   6 km
Siesta Key
Beneva Rd.
Clark Rd.

7165. ☎ Free. ⊙ Sept.–June, weekdays 9–4:30, Sun. 1:30–4:30; July and Aug., weekdays 9–4:30.

㉓ Showcased at the **South Florida Museum and Bishop Planetarium** are Florida artifacts, including displays relating to Native American culture and an excellent collection of Civil War objects. The museum is also home to Snooty, the oldest living manatee in captivity. He likes to shake hands and perform other tricks at feeding time in his 60,000-gallon home. At the domed Bishop Planetarium, you can see star shows and laser-light displays. ⊠ *201 10th St.,* ☎ *941/746–4132.* ☎ *$6.* ⊙ *Mon.–Sat. 10–5, Sun. noon–5; star shows Tues.–Sun. at 1:30 and 3.*

Hernando de Soto, one of the first Spanish explorers, set foot in Florida in 1539 near what is now Bradenton; that feat is commemorated at

★ **㉔** the **De Soto National Memorial.** In the high season (late December–early April), park employees dressed in 16th-century costumes demonstrate period weapons and show how European explorers prepared and preserved food for their journeys over the untamed land. Films, demonstrations, and a short nature trail are on the grounds. ⊠ *75th St. NW,* ☎ *941/792–0458.* ☎ *Free.* ⊙ *Daily 9–5.*

Just off the northern tip of Anna Maria Island, Bradenton's barrier island to the west, lies **Egmont Key.** On it is **Fort Dade,** a military in-

㉕ stallation built in 1900 during the Spanish-American War, and Florida's sixth-brightest lighthouse. The primary inhabitant of the 2-mi-long island is the threatened gopher tortoise, and the only way to get here is by the *Miss Cortez,* an excursion boat (☞ Guided Tours *in* Tampa Bay Area A to Z, *below*). Shellers will find the trip rewarding.

OFF THE   **GAMBLE PLANTATION AND CONFEDERATE MEMORIAL** – Built in 1850,
BEATEN PATH   this, the only pre–Civil War plantation house in South Florida, still displays some of the original furnishings. The Confederate secretary of state took refuge here when the Confederacy fell to Union forces. ⊠ *3708 Patten Ave., Ellenton,* ☎ *941/723–4536.* ☎ *$3.* ⊙ *Thurs.–Mon. 8–5, tours at 9:30, 10:30, 1, 2, 3, 4.*

Beaches

Anna Maria Island boasts four public beaches. **Anna Maria Bayfront Park** (⊠ N. Bay Blvd., adjacent to municipal pier, Anna Maria Island) is a secluded beach fronting both the Intracoastal Waterway and the Gulf of Mexico. Facilities include picnic grounds, a playground, rest rooms, showers, and lifeguards. In the middle of Anna Maria Island, **Manatee County Beach** (⊠ Gulf Dr., at 44th St., Holmes Beach) is popular with all ages. It has picnic facilities, a snack bar, showers, rest rooms, and lifeguards. **Cortez Beach** (⊠ Gulf Blvd., Bradenton Beach) is popular with those who like their beaches without facilities—nothing but sand, water, and trees. **Coquina Beach** (⊠ Southern end of Anna Maria Island) is big with singles and families. Facilities here include a picnic area, boat ramp, playground, refreshment stand, rest rooms, showers, and lifeguards.

Greer Island Beach, at the northern tip of Longboat Key, is accessible by boat or via North Shore Boulevard. The secluded peninsula has a wide beach and excellent shelling but no facilities.

Manatee Avenue runs from the mainland to Anna Maria Island over the **Palma Sola Causeway,** adjacent to which is a long, sandy beach fronting Palma Sola Bay. There are boat ramps, a dock, and picnic tables.

Dining and Lodging

$$ ✕ **Crab Trap and Crab Trap II.** Rustic decor, ultrafresh seafood, gator tail, and wild pig are among the trademarks of these casual and very popular restaurants. ⊠ *U.S. 19 at Terra Ceia Bridge, Palmetto,* ☎ *941/722–6255;* ⊠ *4814 Memphis Rd., Ellenton,* ☎ *941/729–7777. D, MC, V.*

$$$ 🏨 **Holiday Inn Riverfront.** This Spanish Mediterranean–style motor inn near the Manatee River is easily accessible from I–75 and U.S. 41. One-third of the rooms are suites. ⊠ *100 Riverfront Dr. W, 34205,* ☎ *941/747–3727,* ℻ *941/746–4289. 153 units. Restaurant, lounge, pool. AE, DC, MC, V.*

Outdoor Activities and Sports

BASEBALL

The **Pittsburgh Pirates** (⊠ 17th Ave. W and 9th St., ☎ 941/748–4610) have spring training at McKechnie Field.

BIKING

Ringling Bicycles (⊠ 3324 Manatee Ave., ☎ 941/749–1442) rents bicycles by the hour and the day.

GOLF

Manatee County Golf Course (⊠ 6415 53rd Ave. W, ☎ 941/792–6773) features a driving range as well as 18 holes of golf. **Peridia Golf & Country Club** (⊠ 4950 Peridia Blvd., ☎ 941/753–9097) has 18 holes and a driving range.

Shopping

Some vendors at the **Red Barn** (⊠ 1707 1st St. E), a flea market in the requisite big red barn, do business during the week (often Tuesday–Sunday 10–4), but the number of vendors skyrockets to 1,000 on weekends, when many open as early as 8.

Sarasota

16 mi south of Bradenton.

Despite its circus reputation, Sarasota is a sophisticated resort town with cultural events scheduled year-round. Across the water from Sarasota lie the barrier islands of **Siesta Key, Longboat Key,** and **Lido Key,** with myriad beaches, shops, hotels, condominiums, and houses.

Decades ago, circus tycoon John Ringling found this area an ideal spot for his clowns and performers to recuperate from their months of travel while preparing for their next journey. Along Sarasota Bay, Ringling built himself a fancy home, patterned after the Palace of the Doges

★ ㉖ in Venice, Italy. Today, the **Ringling Museums** include that **mansion,** as well as his **art museum** (with a world-renowned collection of Ruben

🅒 paintings and 17th-century tapestries) and a **museum of circus memorabilia.** ⊠ *½ mi south of Sarasota-Bradenton Airport on U.S. 41,* ☎ *941/355–5101.* 🎟 *$8.50.* ⊙ *Daily 10–5:30.*

㉗ You could say they are rocking and rolling at **Bellm's Cars & Music of Yesterday.** On display are both 175 restored antique automobiles—including Rolls-Royces, Pierce Arrows, and Auburns—and more than 1,200 old-time music makers, such as hurdy-gurdies, calliopes, and music boxes. ⊠ *5500 N. Tamiami Trail,* ☎ *941/355–6228.* 🎟 *$8.* ⊙ *Daily 9:30–5:30.*

🅒 ㉘ It takes a couple of hours to stroll through the 10-acre spread of tropical plants at the **Sarasota Jungle Gardens.** Also on site are a petting zoo and playground, a shell and butterfly museum, and reptile and bird shows. ⊠ *3701 Bayshore Rd.,* ☎ *941/355–5305.* ☞ *$9.* ⊙ *Daily 9–5, shows daily 10, noon, 2, and 4.*

㉙ At the 9-acre **Marie Selby Botanical Gardens,** you can stroll through a world-class display of orchids, see air plants and colorful bromeliads, and wander through 14 garden areas along Sarasota Bay. There is also a small museum of botany and art in a gracious restored mansion. ⊠ *811 S. Palm Ave.,* ☎ *941/366–5730.* ☞ *$6.* ⊙ *Daily 10–5.*

�℃ ㉚ The 135,000-gallon shark tank at **Mote Marine Aquarium** lets you see its inhabitants from above and below the water's surface. Additional tanks show off sharks, rays, and other marine creatures native to the area. A neat touch tank lets you handle rays, guitar fish, horseshoe crabs, and sea urchins. ⊠ *1600 City Island Park, Lido Key,* ☎ *941/388–2451.* ☞ *$8.* ⊙ *Daily 10–5.*

OFF THE BEATEN PATH **MYAKKA RIVER STATE PARK –** With 28,900 acres, this outstanding wildlife preserve is absolutely lovely and great for bird-watching and gator sighting. Tram tours explore natural hammocks, airboat tours whiz over the lake, and there are hiking trails and bike rentals. ⊠ *17 mi southeast of Sarasota on Rte. 72,* ☎ *941/361–6511.* ☞ *$2 for 1 person, $4 per vehicle for 2–8 people; tours $6.* ⊙ *Daily 8–sunset.*

Beaches

Siesta Beach (⊠ 600 Beach Rd., Siesta Key) and its 40-acre park contain nature trails, a concession stand, soccer and softball fields, picnic facilities, a playground, rest rooms, and tennis and volleyball courts. **South Lido Park** (⊠ Ben Franklin Dr., Lido Key), at the southern tip of the island, has one of the largest and best beaches in the region. The sugar-sand beach offers little for shell collectors, but the interests of others are served well, resulting in a mix of people. Try your luck at fishing, take a dip in the waters of the bay or gulf, roam the 130-acre park, or picnic as the sun sets through the Australian pines into the water. Facilities include nature trails, a volleyball court, playground, horseshoe pits, rest rooms, and picnic grounds. Only 14 acres, **Turtle Beach** (⊠ Turtle Beach Rd., Siesta Key) includes boat ramps, horseshoe pits, picnic and play facilities, a recreation building, rest rooms, and a volleyball court.

Dining and Lodging

$$$ ★ ✕ **Bijou Cafe.** Wood, brass, and sumptuous green carpeting surround diners in this 1920 gas station-turned-restaurant. Chef-owner Jean Pierre Knaggs's Continental specialties include superb crab cakes with rémoulade sauce, crispy roast duckling with tangerine brandy sauce or cassis and blackberry sauce, rack of lamb for two, and crème brûlée. ⊠ *1287 1st St.,* ☎ *941/366–8111. AE, DC, MC, V.*

$$$ ★ ✕ **Cafe L'Europe.** On fashionable St. Armand's Circle, this greenery- and art-filled café specializes in fresh veal and seafood. Menus change frequently but might include fillet of sole Picasso, Dover sole served with a choice of fruits, or Wiener schnitzel sautéed in butter and topped with anchovies, olives, and capers. ⊠ *431 St. Armand's Circle, Lido Key,* ☎ *941/388–4415. AE, DC, MC, V.*

$$$ ✕ **Marina Jack.** Eat in the restaurant overlooking Sarasota Bay or, Wednesday through Sunday, take a dinner cruise on the *Marina Jack II,* a paddle wheeler that cruises for two romantic hours with entertainment. Either place, fresh seafood prevails. ⊠ *2 Marina Plaza,* ☎ *941/365–4232. MC, V.*

$$–$$$ ✕ **Michael's on East.** Prices are reasonable despite the elegant setting of this favorite in downtown Sarasota. The cuisine is contemporary, ranging from penne with grilled summer vegetables and black olives

to grilled fillet of beef served with a house specialty—mashed potatoes. A light menu is served in the intimate bar, where there's always piano music or jazz in the evening. The lunch menu includes unusual sandwiches—grilled portabello mushrooms with gouda, for example—and an excellent assortment of fresh salads. ⊠ *1212 East Ave. S,* ☎ *941/366–0007. AE, MC, V.*

$$ ✕ **Ophelia's on the Bay.** Sample mussel soup, eggplant crepes, chicken pot pie, or cioppino, among other things, at this waterfront restaurant. ⊠ *9105 Midnight Pass Rd., Siesta Key,* ☎ *941/349–2212. AE, D, DC, MC, V. No lunch.*

$ ✕ **Trolley Station.** This spot looks and feels like a trolley station, inside and out. Long benches frame the entrance, the cashier sits behind an old-fashioned ticket counter, and people line up for dinner as for the trolley. Offerings range from a salad and baked-potato bar to roast beef, fish, chicken, and pastas. Prices are remarkably low. ⊠ *1941 Stickney Point Rd.,* ☎ *941/923–2721. AE, MC, V.*

$$$$ 🏨 **Colony Beach and Tennis Resort.** If tennis is your game, this is the
★ place to stay—such tennis greats as Björn Borg make the Colony their home court, and for good reason. Ten courts are clay hydro-surfaced (the others are hard), and pros are all USPTA-certified. They run clinics and camps at all levels, do video analyses of your game, and play with guests when no one else is available. They even have scaled-down rackets for children. Other activities include ecology-oriented trips and deep-sea fishing. All accommodations are suites, some sleeping up to eight; private beach houses that open onto sand and sea are also available. ⊠ *1620 Gulf of Mexico Dr., Longboat Key 34228,* ☎ *941/383–6464 or 800/237–9443; 800/282–1138 in FL;* 🅵🅰🆇 *941/383– 7549. 235 suites. 3 restaurants, bar, pool, 21 tennis courts, health club, children's programs. AE, D, MC, V.*

$$$$ 🏨 **Hyatt Sarasota.** The Hyatt is contemporary in design and conveniently located in the heart of the city, across from the Van Wezel Performing Arts Hall. All of the spacious rooms overlook Sarasota Bay or the marina. ⊠ *1000 Blvd. of the Arts, 34236,* ☎ *941/953–1234,* 🅵🅰🆇 *941/952–1987. 297 rooms. 2 restaurants, lounge, pool, sauna, health club, dock, boating. AE, DC, MC, V.*

$$$$ 🏨 **Resort at Longboat Key.** This beautifully landscaped, 1,000-acre property is one of *the* places to golf in the state and one of the top tennis resorts in the country. Water is the test on both golf courses, which have excellent pro shops, lessons, and clinics. Tennis courts are Har-Tru–surfaced. Hobie Cats, kayaks, Sunfish, deep-sea charters, and ecology trips are also available. Suites, for four or six, are done in tropical motifs and light woods; huge private balconies overlook a golf course, beach, or private lagoon where manatees are occasionally seen. Some suites have kitchens. ⊠ *301 Gulf of Mexico Dr., Box 15000, Longboat Key 34228,* ☎ *941/383–8821 or 800/237–8821; 800/282–0113 in FL;* 🅵🅰🆇 *941/383–0359. 228 suites. 4 restaurants, pool, 45 holes of golf, 38 tennis courts, beach, library, meeting rooms. AE, DC, MC, V.*

$$$ 🏨 **Radisson Lido Beach Resort.** The newest addition to Lido Key is this classy beachfront resort with superb views of the gulf. Units are decorated in soft blue and pink pastel print fabrics. All have a refrigerator, and many have a full kitchen. Beachfront minisuites, at the western end of the building, have balconies. A large rectangular pool is right on the beach. ⊠ *700 Ben Franklin Dr., Lido Beach 34236,* ☎ *941/388– 2161,* 🅵🅰🆇 *941/388–3175. 116 units. Restaurant, lounge, pool, beach. AE, DC, MC, V.*

$$ 🏨 **Best Western Midtown.** This three-story motel is clean, comfortable, and very affordable. Set back from U.S. 41 and somewhat removed from traffic noise, it is within walking distance of a shopping center

and several restaurants—including the popular Michael's on East—and is central to area attractions and downtown. Rooms, which have seating areas, are done in pale pastel fabrics and blond wood. ⊠ *1425 S. Tamiami Trail, 34239,* ☎ *941/955–9841,* ℻ *941/954–8948. 100 rooms. Pool. AE, DC, MC, V.*

$$ 🖵 **Days Inn Sarasota-Siesta Key.** Good value is the strong point of this modest but comfortable and well-maintained motel on U.S. 41. Rooms are decorated in earth tones. Beaches are just a mile away, and many restaurants and shopping centers are close by. ⊠ *6600 S. Tamiami Trail, 34231,* ☎ *941/924–4900,* ℻ *941/923–7774. 132 rooms. Pool. AE, DC, MC, V.*

Nightlife and the Arts

THE ARTS

Among the many theaters in Sarasota, the $10 million **Asolo Center for the Performing Arts** (⊠ 5555 N. Tamiami Trail, ☎ 941/351–8000) mounts productions nearly year-round. The small, professional **Florida Studio Theatre** (⊠ 1241 N. Palm Ave., ☎ 941/366–9796) presents contemporary dramas, comedies, and musicals. **Golden Apple Dinner Theatre** (⊠ 25 N. Pineapple Ave., ☎ 941/366–5454) serves up a standard buffet along with musicals and comedies. A long-established community theater, the **Players of Sarasota** (⊠ U.S. 41 and 9th St., ☎ 941/365–2494) has launched such performers as Montgomery Clift and Pee-Wee Herman. The troupe performs comedies, thrillers, and musicals. The **Van Wezel Performing Arts Hall** (⊠ 777 N. Tamiami Trail, ☎ 941/953–3366) is easy to find—just look for the purple shell rising along the bay front. It hosts some 200 performances each year, including Broadway plays, ballet, jazz, rock concerts, symphonies, children's shows, and ice skating.

Florida West Coast Symphony Center (⊠ 709 N. Tamiami Trail, ☎ 941/953–4252) consists of a number of area music groups that perform in Manatee and Sarasota counties regularly: the Florida West Coast Symphony, Florida String Quartet, Florida Brass Quintet, Florida Wind Quintet, and New Artists String Quartet. The **Sarasota Concert Band** (⊠ Van Wezel Performing Arts Hall, 777 N. Tamiami Trail, ☎ 941/955–6660) includes 50 players, many of them full-time musicians. The group performs monthly concerts.

The **Sarasota Opera** (⊠ 61 N. Pineapple Ave., ☎ 941/953–7030) performs February through March in a historic theater downtown. Internationally known artists sing the principal roles, supported by a professional chorus of 24 young apprentices.

The **Sarasota Film Society** (⊠ 506 Burns La., ☎ 941/388–2441) operates year-round, showing foreign and art films daily at 2, 5:45, and 8 at the Burns Court Cinema.

NIGHTLIFE

In Extremis (⊠ Sarasota Quay, ☎ 941/954–2008) has laser-light shows and high-energy disco and alternative music. The **Patio** (⊠ Columbia Restaurant, St. Armand's Circle, Lido Key, ☎ 941/388–3987), a casual lounge, has live music Wednesday through Sunday.

Outdoor Activities and Sports

BASEBALL

The **Chicago White Sox** (⊠ 2700 12th St., ☎ 941/954–7699) have spring training at Ed Smith Stadium.

BIKING

CB's (✉ 1249 Stickney Point Rd., ☎ 941/349–4400) rents bikes hourly and daily. **Village Bike Shop** (✉ 5101 Ocean Blvd., ☎ 941/346–2111) is a source for rental by the hour or the day.

CANOEING

At **Myakka River State Park** (✉ 17 mi southeast of Sarasota on Rte. 72, ☎ 941/361–6511), you can rent canoes, paddles, and life vests.

DOG RACING

The greyhounds run late December through June at the **Sarasota Kennel Club** (✉ 5400 Bradenton Rd., ☎ 941/355–7744).

FISHING

Marina Jack's (✉ U.S. 41 on bay front, ☎ 941/366–3373) has several boats that can be chartered for deep-sea fishing and offers scheduled group trips.

GOLF

Bobby Jones Golf Course (✉ 1000 Circus Blvd., ☎ 941/955–8097) has 18 holes and a driving range. **Forest Lakes Golf Club** (✉ 2401 Beneva Rd., ☎ 941/922–1312) features a practice range and 18 holes. Known for its golf, **Resort at Longboat Key** (✉ 301 Gulf of Mexico Dr., Longboat Key, ☎ 941/383–8821) offers 45 holes and several putting greens.

TENNIS

If you love tennis and aren't staying at one of the tennis resorts, you might want to play at the **Forest Lakes Racket Club** (✉ 2401 Beneva Rd., ☎ 941/922–0660), which has six courts.

WATER SPORTS

Don and Mike's Boat and Jet Ski Rental (✉ 520 Blackburn Point Rd., ☎ 941/966–4000) has water skis, Jet Skis, pontoon boats, and instruction for all activities. For sailboard rentals and lessons try **Gulf Water Sports** (✉ Colony Beach and Tennis Resort, 1620 Gulf of Mexico Dr., Longboat Key, ☎ 941/383–7692).

Shopping

St. Armand's Circle (✉ Lido Key) is a cluster of oh-so-exclusive shops and restaurants.

Venice

③ *18 mi south of Sarasota.*

This small town is crisscrossed with even more canals than the city for which it was named. Venice beaches are good for shell collecting, but they're best known for their wealth of sharks' teeth and fossils.

The Arts

Theatre Works (✉ 1247 1st St., ☎ 941/952–9170) presents professional, non-Equity productions at the Palm Tree Playhouse. **Venice Little Theatre** (✉ 140 W. Tampa Ave., ☎ 941/488–1115) is a community theater offering comedies, musicals, and a few dramas during its October–May season.

Beaches

Along with a plentiful mix of shells, observant beachcombers are likely to find sharks' teeth on Venice beaches, washed up from the ancient shark burial grounds just offshore. At **Blind Pass Beach** (✉ Manasota Beach Rd., Manasota Key), you can fish and swim but will find no amenities. **Caspersen Beach** (✉ Beach Dr., South Venice) is the county's largest park. It has a nature trail, fishing, picnicking, rest rooms, and lots of beach for those who prefer space to a wealth of amenities. **En-**

glewood Beach, near the Charlotte–Sarasota county line, is popular with teenagers, although beachgoers of all ages frequent it. In addition to a wide and shell-littered beach, there are barbecue grills, picnic facilities, boat ramps, a fishing pier, playground, and showers. There's a $1 charge for parking. **Manasota Beach** (⌂ Manasota Beach Rd., Manasota Key) has a boat ramp, picnic area, and rest rooms. **Nakomis Beach** (⌂ Albee Rd., Casey Key) is one of two notable beaches on the island. Just north of North Jetty Park, it offers rest rooms, a concession, picnic equipment, play areas, two boat ramps, a volleyball court, and fishing. **North Jetty Park** (⌂ Albee Rd., Casey Key), at the south end of the key, is a favorite for family outings, and fossil hunters may get lucky here. Facilities include rest rooms, a concession stand, play and picnic equipment, horseshoes, and a volleyball court.

Dining and Lodging

$$ ✕ **Sharky's on the Pier.** Gaze out on the beach and sparkling waters while dining on fresh, grilled seafood at this popular and very casual eatery. There's an outdoor veranda and tables indoors as well. ⌂ *1600 S. Harbor Dr.,* ☎ *941/488–1456. MC, V.*

$$ ⊡ **Days Inn.** This simple but well-kept motel is on the main business route through town—but it's only 10 minutes from the beach. Rooms are comfortable, and pets are allowed. ⌂ *1710 S. Tamiami Trail, 34293,* ☎ *941/493–4558,* FAX *941/493–1593. 73 rooms. Restaurant, lounge, pool. AE, MC, V.*

$$ ⊡ **Veranda Inn-Venice.** A landscaped pool is the focal point of this small but spacious inn on U.S. 41. All rooms look out on the pool and courtyard. ⌂ *625 S. Tamiami Trail, 34285,* ☎ *941/484–9559,* FAX *941/484–8235. 38 rooms. Restaurant, pool. AE, DC, MC, V.*

Outdoor Activities and Sports

BIKING

Bicycles International (⌂ 744 Tamiami Trail S, ☎ 941/497–1590) rents its varied stock weekly as well as hourly and daily.

FISHING

Gulfwater Marine (⌂ 215 Tamiami Trail S, ☎ 941/484–9044) is a good place to try for deep-sea fishing.

GOLF

Bird Bay Executive Golf Course (⌂ 602 Bird Bay Dr. W, ☎ 941/485–9333) has 18 holes. **Plantation Golf & Country Club** (⌂ 500 Rockley Blvd., ☎ 941/493–2000) boasts 36 holes and a driving range.

Shopping

If you like flea markets, check out the **Dome** (⌂ Rte. 775 west of U.S. 41), where dozens of sheltered stalls sell new and recycled wares. It's open October–August, Friday–Sunday 9–4.

THE TAMPA BAY AREA A TO Z

Arriving and Departing

By Bus

Service to and throughout the state is provided by **Greyhound Lines** (☎ 800/231–2222; in Tampa, ☎ 813/229–2112; St. Petersburg, ☎ 813/898–1496; Sarasota, ☎ 941/955–5735).

By Car

I–75 spans the region from north to south. Once you cross the Florida border from Georgia, it should take about three hours to reach Tampa and another hour to reach Sarasota. If coming from Orlando, you're likely to drive west into Tampa on I–4.

By Plane

Several carriers serve **Tampa International** (☎ 813/870–8700), 6 mi from downtown, including **Air Canada** (☎ 800/776–3000), **Air Jamaica** (☎ 800/523–5585), **American** (☎ 800/433–7300), **Bahamasair** (☎ 800/222–4262), **British Airways** (☎ 800/247–9297), **Canadian Holidays** (☎ 800/661–8881), **Cayman Airlines** (☎ 800/422–9626), **Continental** (☎ 800/956–6680), **Delta** (☎ 800/241–4141), **Mexicana** (☎ 800/531–7921), **Northwest** (☎ 800/225–2525), **TWA** (☎ 800/222–2000), **United** (☎ 800/241–6522), **US Airways** (☎ 800/428–4322), and **Virgin Atlantic** (☎ 800/862–5621). **Central Florida Limousine** (☎ 813/396–3730) provides airport service to and from Hillsborough and Polk counties. **The Limo** (☎ 813/572–1111 or 800/282–6817) serves Pinellas County. Expect taxi fares to be about $12–$25 for most of Hillsborough County and about twice that for Pinellas County.

Sarasota's airport, **Sarasota-Bradenton** (☎ 941/359–5200), lies just north of the city. It is served by American, Continental, Delta, Northwest, TWA, United, and USAir. Transportation to and from the airport is provided by **Airport Shuttle** (☎ 941/355–9645) and **West Coast Executive Sedan** (☎ 941/359–8600). The average cab fare between airport and downtown is $15–$25.

By Train

Amtrak (☎ 800/872–7245) trains run from the Northeast, Midwest, and much of the South to the Tampa station.

Getting Around

By Bus

Around Tampa, the **Hillsborough Area Regional Transit** (HART, ☎ 813/254–4278) serves the county. In Sarasota, the public transit company is **Sarasota County Area Transit** (SCAT, ☎ 941/951–5850).

By Car

I–75 and U.S. 41 (which runs concurrently with the Tamiami Trail for much of the way) stretch the length of the region. U.S. 41 links the business districts of many communities, so it's best to avoid it and all bridges during rush hours, 7–9 AM and 4–6 PM. U.S. 19 is St. Petersburg's major north–south artery; traffic can be heavy, and there are many lights, so use a different route when possible.

I–275 heads west from Tampa across Tampa Bay to St. Petersburg, swings south, and crosses the bay again on its way to Terra Ceia, near Bradenton. Along this last leg—the Sunshine Skyway and its bright-yellow suspension bridge—you'll get a bird's-eye view of bustling Tampa Bay.

The Bayshore Boulevard Causeway also yields a spectacular view of Tampa Bay, and Route 679 takes you along two of St. Petersburg's most pristine islands, Cabbage and Mullet keys. Route 64 connects I–75 to Bradenton and Anna Maria Island. Route 789 runs over several slender barrier islands, past miles of blue-green gulf waters, beaches, and waterfront homes. The road does not connect all the islands, however; it runs from Holmes Beach off the Bradenton coast south to Lido Key, then begins again on Siesta Key and again on Casey Key south of Osprey, and runs south to Nokomis Beach.

By Trolley

One good way to get around Tampa is via the **Tampa-Ybor Trolley** (50¢), which runs from 7:30 until 5:30; it makes 17 stops between Ybor City, the Florida Aquarium, and Harbour Island.

Contacts and Resources

Emergencies

Dial **911** for police and ambulance.

HOSPITALS

There are 24-hour emergency rooms at **Bayfront Medical Center** (✉ 701 6th St. S, St. Petersburg), **Manatee Memorial Hospital** (✉ 206 2nd St. E, Bradenton), **Sarasota Memorial Hospital** (✉ 1700 S. Tamiami Trail, Sarasota), and **University Community Hospital** (✉ 3100 E. Fletcher Ave., Tampa).

LATE-NIGHT PHARMACY

Eckerd Drugs (✉ 11613 N. Nebraska Ave., Tampa, ☎ 813/978–0775).

Guided Tours

AIR TOURS

Tours of the bay area and Gulf Coast, given by **Helicopter Charter & Transport Co.** (✉ 9000 18th St., ☎ 813/933–2686), leave from Tampa International. **West Florida Helicopters** (✉ Albert Whitted Airport, ☎ 813/823–5200) offers bay area tours.

BOAT TOURS

The *Lady Anderson* (✉ St. Petersburg Causeway, 3400 Pasadena Ave., St. Petersburg Beach, ☎ 813/367–7804) combines sightseeing with lunch and dinner cruises, October–May. The *Miss Cortez* (✉ Cortez, ☎ 941/794–1223) departs for Egmont Key from just north of Bradenton every Tuesday, Thursday, and Sunday. **Myakka Wildlife Tours** (✉ Myakka River State Park, Rte. 72 southeast of Sarasota, ☎ 941/365–0100) runs four daily hour-long tours of the wildlife sanctuary aboard the *Gator Gal,* a large airboat. The *Starlite Princess* (✉ Hamlin's Landing, Indian Rocks Beach, ☎ 813/595–1212), an old-fashioned paddle wheeler, makes sightseeing and dinner cruises.

Visitor Information

Greater Clearwater Chamber of Commerce (✉ 128 N. Osceola Ave., Clearwater 34615, ☎ 813/461–0011). **Greater Dunedin Chamber of Commerce** (✉ 301 Main St., Dunedin 34698, ☎ 813/736–5066). **Greater Tampa Chamber of Commerce** (✉ Box 420, Tampa 33601, ☎ 813/228–7777; ☎ 813/223–1111 Visitors Information Department). **Gulf Beaches on Sand Key Chamber of Commerce** (✉ 501 150th Ave., Madeira Beach 33701, ☎ 813/595–4575 or 813/391–7373). **St. Petersburg Chamber of Commerce** (✉ 100 2nd Ave. N, St. Petersburg 33701, ☎ 813/821–4069). **St. Petersburg/Clearwater Area Convention & Visitors Bureau** (✉ Thunderdome, 1 Stadium Dr., Suite A, St. Petersburg 33705-1706, ☎ 813/582–7892). **Sarasota Convention and Visitors Bureau** (✉ 655 N. Tamiami Trail, Sarasota 34236, ☎ 941/957–1877 or 800/522–9799). **Tampa/Hillsborough Convention and Visitors Association** (✉ 111 Madison St., Suite 1010, Tampa 33601-0519, ☎ 800/826–8358; ☎ 800/448–2672 information and hotel reservations; ☎ 800/284–0404 vacation packages). **Tarpon Springs Chamber of Commerce** (✉ 210 S. Pinellas Ave., Suite 120, Tarpon Springs 34689, ☎ 813/937–6109). **Treasure Island Chamber of Commerce** (✉ 108th Ave., Treasure Island 33706, ☎ 813/367–4529).

10 Southwest Florida

Most noted for Sanibel Island, a low-key spot home to beautiful beaches and world-class shelling, and Naples, a once-sleepy fishing village that's developed fast, this region is subtropical to the core. Unlike the east coast, much of the development here has been inland of the mangrove swamps, and the area prides itself on the number of access points along its 41 mi of sand.

THE SOUTHWEST FLORIDA COAST is often called "Florida's Florida" because its natural subtropical environment has made it a favorite vacation spot for

Updated by
Pamela
Acheson

Florida natives as well as visitors. There's lots to do here, and although much activity centers on sun and surf, there are several distinctly different travel destinations in a relatively compact area.

Fort Myers is a small and pretty inland city built along the Caloosahatchee River. It got its nickname, "the City of Palms," from the hundreds of towering royal palms that inventor Thomas Edison planted along McGregor Boulevard, the main residential street and site of his winter estate. Edison's idea caught on, and there are now more than 2,000 royal palms on McGregor Boulevard alone.

Off the coast west of Fort Myers, more than 100 barrier islands range in length from just a few feet to over 20 mi. Here you'll find Sanibel and Captiva, two thoughtfully developed resort islands. Connected to the mainland by a 3-mi causeway, Sanibel is known for its world-class shelling, fine fishing, luxury hotels and restaurants (mostly at the south end of the island), and its wildlife refuge. You won't be able to see most of the houses, which are shielded by tall Australian pines, but the beaches and tranquil gulf waters are readily accessible.

Down the coast is Naples, once a small fishing village and now a thriving and sophisticated town—something like a smaller version of Palm Beach. There are a number of fine restaurants and several upscale shopping complexes, including the gracious, tree-lined 3rd Street South area. The number of golf courses per capita in Naples is said to be the highest in the world, a 1,200-seat performing arts hall attracts world-class performers, and the town is the west coast home of the Miami City Ballet. Unlike Palm Beach, the Naples area offers easy access to its many miles of sun-drenched white beach.

East of Naples stretches the Big Cypress National Preserve, and a half hour south is Marco Island, with several large resorts, good beaches, restaurants, and shops. Farther southeast is Everglades City, the western gateway to Everglades National Park (☞ Chapter 4).

Pleasures and Pastimes

Baseball
For a more relaxed and intimate view of major-league baseball, catch any of several teams' exhibitions during spring training, in March and April. For information or for guides, available around the first of each year, call the Florida Sports Foundation at ☎ 904/488–8347.

Beaches
Southwest Florida has gorgeous white sand beaches along the coast and on many barrier islands. Many beaches are prime shelling spots.

Biking
There are excellent opportunities for biking in less populated areas. Boca Grande, a barrier island about an hour from Fort Myers, has good bike paths. Sanibel Island's well-maintained bike lanes run throughout the island but away from traffic, providing safe routes and enabling riders to enjoy the scenic waterways and wildlife.

Canoeing
Sanibel Island's J. N. "Ding" Darling National Wildlife Refuge is a popular spot for canoeing. There are also many opportunities to canoe in-

land in the less developed areas of the region; several outfits offer half-
and full-day trips and overnighters.

Dining

In Fort Myers and Naples, seafood reigns supreme. Expect ample fresh
fish on the menu. A particular treat is a succulent claw of the native
stone crab, usually served with drawn butter or a tangy mustard sauce
and in season from mid-October through mid-May. Many restaurants
offer early-bird menus with seating before 6 PM.

Fishing

Tarpon, kingfish, speckled trout, snapper, grouper, sea trout, snook,
sheepshead, and shark are among the species found in coastal waters.
You can charter a boat or join a group for full- or half-day outings.

Golf

The area has one of the highest concentrations of courses in the nation. In fact, Naples has more than 40 courses (new ones open all the
time) and *Golf Digest* named it the "Golf Capital of the World."

Lodging

Generally, inland rooms are considerably cheaper than those on the
islands or along the shore, with waterfront accommodations being on
the upper end of the price scale. Recent years, however, have seen the
creation of many apartment-motels that bring great savings for families or groups, especially if dining costs are cut by cooking some of your
own meals. Rates are highest between mid-December and mid-April.
The lowest prices are available from May to November.

Shopping

Prepare to shell out some cash for at least one kitschy crustacean creation. As one of the world's premier shelling grounds, Sanibel Island
has numerous shops seriously selling shells (try to say that three times
fast)—from lamps to jewelry. Naples has many unique but expensive
shops and boutiques carrying gift items, men's and women's clothing,
shoes, linens, and lingerie. There are also numerous art galleries.

Exploring Southwest Florida

Vacationers to southwest Florida tend to spend most of their time outdoors—swimming, sunning, shelling, or playing tennis or golf. Fort
Myers is the only major inland destination; it is situated along a winding river and has a number of interesting museums. The offshore barrier islands vary from tiny undeveloped islands to popular vacation spots
with numerous hotels and restaurants. Sanibel and Captiva, connected
to each other and to the mainland by causeways, offer beaches known
for shelling and a superb wildlife preserve. Naples is a sophisticated
town with art galleries, fine dining, and upscale shopping and rapid
development along its north shore. Nearby is Marco Island, where you
can take an airboat to see tight clusters of tiny undeveloped islands.
While high-rises line much of Marco Island's waterfront, many natural areas have been preserved, including the tiny fishing village of
Goodland, an outpost of Old Florida.

Great Itineraries

Visitors to southwest Florida are generally in search of warm sun, white
sand, and an outdoor diversion such as tennis or golf. For those who
want more to do, there are numerous appealing attractions that can
take anywhere from an hour to a full day.

Numbers in the text correspond to numbers in the margin and on the
Southwest Florida map.

IF YOU HAVE 2 DAYS

⊞ **Fort Myers** ① is a good base for a short visit. It's not directly on the beach, but its central location makes day trips easy. On the morning of your first day, visit Thomas Edison's Winter Home, in downtown Fort Myers, and then take beautiful McGregor Boulevard to Sanibel Island ⑥ for the rest of the day. Once on the island, stop by the new Bailey-Matthews Shell Museum and the J. N. "Ding" Darling National Wildlife Refuge before heading to Bowman's Beach for shelling and swimming the rest of the afternoon. The next day, drive down I–75 to Naples ⑩, where you can check out Caribbean Gardens's tropical flora and exotic wildlife. Those with a soft spot for teddy bears should stop by the Teddy Bear Museum of Naples before hitting Olde Naples for some shopping and relaxing on the nearby beach.

IF YOU HAVE 4 DAYS

With a little extra time for getting around, you'll be able to stay near the water, on **Sanibel Island** ⑥. Spend your first day shelling and swimming, with a stop at the Bailey-Matthews Shell Museum. On day two, head into Fort Myers ① to Thomas Edison's Winter Home and Henry Ford's Mangoes. Then drive to Babcock Wilderness Adventures, northeast of the city, for a swamp-buggy ride. Why not spend your third day back on Sanibel, dividing your time between the beach and the J. N. "Ding" Darling National Wildlife Refuge? You could even try early morning or evening bird-watching. On day four, drive south to Naples ⑩ and the sights mentioned in the two-day itinerary, or, for even more wildlife, head to the Corkscrew Swamp Sanctuary, a nature preserve east of Bonita Springs ⑨.

IF YOU HAVE 10 DAYS

An extended stay will enable you to move your base from area to area and explore each in more depth by adding the following activities to those listed above. With two days in the ⊞ **Fort Myers** ① area, you can get a taste of southern viticulture at the Eden Vineyards Winery and Park, or, if the Babcock Wilderness Adventures has whetted your ecological appetite, head to the Calusa Nature Center and Planetarium. An extra day on ⊞ **Sanibel Island** ⑥ allows you to visit an isolated key, such as Cabbage Key ⑤ or Boca Grande, on Gasparilla Island ④. For the second half of your trip, relocate to ⊞ **Naples** ⑩, where you can combine beach activities with days of wandering through art galleries and shops in Olde Naples. The Caribbean Gardens and the Corkscrew Swamp Sanctuary are good bets for kids; to try your hand at paddling, rent a canoe or kayak at the Naples Nature Center.

When to Tour Southwest Florida

In winter, this is one of the warmest areas of the United States, though there is occasional cold weather. From January through April you may find it next to impossible to find a hotel room in this hugely popular destination. Fewer people visit in the off-season, but there really is no bad time to come. Ocean breezes keep the coast cool even in summer.

FORT MYERS AND NORTH

Fort Myers is one of the prettiest cities in Florida. The broad, flat Caloosahatchee River forms its northern shoreline, and water views soften the businesslike cluster of downtown office buildings. Between rows of stately palms you can catch glimpses of old Southern mansions. North of Fort Myers are several small fishing communities, including Port Charlotte, on the north side of the Caloosahatchee River, and Punta Gorda, at the convergence of the Peace River and Charlotte Harbor.

Fort Myers

❶ *90 mi southeast of Sarasota, 140 mi west of Palm Beach.*

Although the nearest beach is a half hour away, there is still plenty to do in this small, inviting inland city that stretches along the Caloosahatchee River. The town is best known as the winter home of inventors Thomas A. Edison and Henry Ford.

One of the region's most scenic stretches of highway, **McGregor Boulevard** is lined with majestic palm trees, some planted by Thomas Edison. It runs from downtown to the Gulf of Mexico.

Thomas A. Edison's Winter Home, Fort Myers's premier attraction, contains a laboratory, botanical gardens, and a museum. A remarkable showpiece, the house was donated to the city by Edison's widow. As a result, the laboratory is not merely reconstructed but just as Edison left it. The property straddles McGregor Boulevard about a mile west of U.S. 41, near downtown. The inventor spent his winters on the 14-acre estate, developing the phonograph and teletype, experimenting with rubber, and planting some 600 species of plants collected around the world. Next door is **Mangoes,** the more modest winter home of fellow inventor and longtime friend, automaker Henry Ford. It is said that the V-8 engine was primarily designed on the back porch. ✉ *2350 McGregor Blvd.,* ☎ *941/334–3614.* 🎫 *Edison home and Mangoes (combined) $10.* ☉ *Tours Mon.–Sat. 9–3:30, Sun. noon–3:30.*

Housed in a restored railroad depot, the **Fort Myers Historical Museum** showcases the area's history dating back to 1200 BC. Displays include prehistoric Calusa artifacts, a reconstructed *chickee* hut, canoes, clothing and photos from Seminole settlements, and the Ethel Cooper collection of decorative glass. A favorite attraction is the *Esperanza,* a 1930s private rail car. ✉ *2300 Peck St.,* ☎ *941/332–5955.* 🎫 *$2.50.* ☉ *Tues.–Thurs. 9–4:30, Fri.–Sat. 10–4.*

For a look at frequently changing exhibits on wildlife, fossils, and Florida's native animals and habitats, head to the **Calusa Nature Center and Planetarium.** Rustic boardwalks lead through subtropical wetlands, an aviary, and a village. There are snake and alligator demonstrations several times daily. The planetarium offers star shows, laser light shows, and Cinema-360 films in its 90-seat theater. ✉ *3450 Ortiz Ave.,* ☎ *941/275–3435.* 🎫 *Nature center $4, planetarium $3, laser light and music shows $5 per person.* ☉ *Nature center Mon.–Sat. 9–5, Sun. 11–5; planetarium Wed.–Sun. 9–5.*

OFF THE
BEATEN PATH

EDEN VINEYARDS WINERY AND PARK – Even connoisseurs can't resist a stop here, reputed to be the southernmost bonded winery in the United States. Besides half a dozen kinds of traditional wine, the vineyard puts its own spin on the trade with carambola (starfruit) wine. The family-owned winery offers tours and tastings. Reservations are needed for groups of 12 or more. ✉ *10.2 mi east of I–75 on Rte. 80, Alva* ☎ *941/728–9463.* 🎫 *$2.50; complimentary tasting.* ☉ *Daily 11–4.*

Dining and Lodging

$$$ ✕ **Peter's La Cuisine.** Smack in the middle of downtown Fort Myers,
★   two blocks off the river, is this charming restaurant in a restored brick building. The dining room's extra-high ceiling gives a spacious feel, and exposed brick walls, dim lighting, and a refined atmosphere provide a pleasant background for Continental cuisine with a twist. After din-

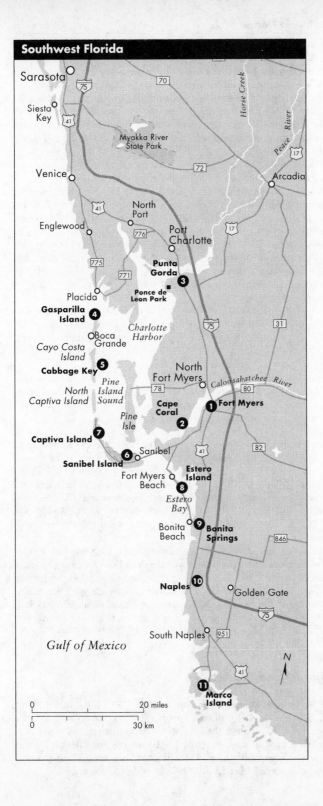

Southwest Florida

Sarasota

Siesta Key

Venice

Englewood

Placida

Gasparilla Island **4**

Boca Grande

Cayo Costa Island

Cabbage Key **5**

North Captiva Island

Pine Island

Captiva Island **7**

6 Sanibel

Sanibel Island

Fort Myers Beach

Estero Bay

Bonita Beach

Naples **10**

Golden Gate

South Naples

11 Marco Island

Gulf of Mexico

North Port

Port Charlotte

Punta Gorda **3**

Ponce de Leon Park

Charlotte Harbor

North Fort Myers

Cape Coral **2**

1 Fort Myers

Estero Island

8

9 Bonita Springs

Myakka River State Park

Arcadia

Horse Creek

Peace River

Caloosahatchee River

Pine Island Sound

Pine Isle

75

70

41

72

17

41

776

17

775

771

31

78

80

41

82

846

951

41

75

0   20 miles

0   30 km

N

ner wander upstairs for a cordial and some great blues. ⊠ *2224 Bay St.,* ☎ *941/332–2228. AE, MC, V. No lunch weekends.*

$$$ ✕ **Prawnbroker Restaurant and Fish Market.** Ads for this restaurant
★   urge you to scratch and sniff—there is no odor, says the ad, because truly fresh fish has none. The dyed-in-the-wool establishment has an abundance of seafood seemingly just plucked from gulf waters, plus some selections for culinary landlubbers. This place is almost always crowded, for good reason. ⊠ *13451 McGregor Blvd.,* ☎ *941/489–2226. AE, MC, V. No lunch.*

$$ ✕ **The Veranda.** An imaginative assortment of American regional cuisine, with an emphasis on Southern cooking, is turned out in this sprawling turn-of-the-century home. This is a popular place for business and government bigwigs. Courtyard and indoor dining is available. ⊠ *2122 2nd St.,* ☎ *941/332–2065. AE, DC, MC, V. Closed Sun. No lunch Sat.*

$ ✕ **Mel's Diner.** During peak hours you have to wait for a table, but it's
★   worth it at this 1950s-style diner, which serves real mashed potatoes, homemade soups, spicy chili, and blue-plate specials. For dessert, try the popular mile-high pies. ⊠ *4820 Cleveland Ave.,* ☎ *941/275–7850. No credit cards.*

$ ✕ **Miami Connection.** If you hunger for choice chopped liver, lean-but-tender corned beef, and a chewy bagel, this kosher-style deli can fill the bill. The sandwiches are huge. It is, as a local restaurant critic aptly said, "the real McCohen." ⊠ *11506 Cleveland Ave.,* ☎ *941/936–3811. No credit cards. No dinner.*

$ ✕ **Mill Bakery, Eatery, and Brewery.** Homemade beer is just one of the draws (draughts?) at this popular spot. People flock to dine on freshly baked breads, pizzas, deli-style stacked sandwiches, and prime rib. ⊠ *11491 S. Cleveland Ave.,* ☎ *941/939–2739. AE, MC, V.*

$$$ ▦ **Radisson Inn Fort Myers.** Rooms have been recently spiffed up at this hotel, which is conveniently located close to I–95, about 7 mi south of downtown Fort Myers and 12 mi from Fort Myers Beach. Units, many with balconies, are in both a two- and a five-story building, and an inviting courtyard dotted with palm trees surrounds the free-form pool. ⊠ *12635 Cleveland Ave., 33907,* ☎ *941/936–4300,* 𝔽𝔸𝕏 *941/936–2058. 192 rooms. Restaurant, lounge, pool, tennis, horseshoes, volleyball, billiards. AE, DC, MC, V.*

$$$ ▦ **Sheraton Harbor Place.** This modern, pink high-rise has a commanding spot in the downtown skyline, rising above the river and yacht basin. Well-furnished rooms have panoramic views of the water and the city. An unusual indoor/outdoor bar is complete with waterfalls. Restaurants, the Harborside Convention Center, and Thomas Edison's home are all within easy walking distance. ⊠ *2500 Edwards Dr., 33901,* ☎ *941/337–0300 or 800/325–3535,* 𝔽𝔸𝕏 *941/337–1530. 417 rooms. Bar, pool, hot tub, tennis, exercise room, dock, game room. AE, DC, MC, V.*

Nightlife and the Arts

THE ARTS

The **Barbara B. Mann Performing Arts Hall** (⊠ 8099 College Pkwy. SW, ☎ 941/481–4849) presents plays, concerts, musicals, and dance programs. Call or check the Friday entertainment section of the local newspapers for upcoming events. The **Broadway Palm Dinner Theater** (⊠ 1380 Colonial Blvd., ☎ 941/278–4422) serves up buffet dinner along with some of Broadway's best comedies and musicals.

NIGHTLIFE

Laugh-In Comedy Club (⊠ Springs Hotel, 1 S. Aleiko͡ 6127) features MTV, HBO, and Comedy Networ͡ Friday and Saturday. **Shoeless Joe's Sports Cafe** (⊠ ͡ 13051 Bell Tower Dr., ☎ 941/482−2900) plays Top 40 tunes, usua͡, with live bands every night but Monday. Musicians play nightly at **Up-stairs at Peter's** (⊠ 2224 Bay St., ☎ 941/332−2228). The music is usually blues, but about once a week there's jazz.

Outdoor Activities and Sports

BASEBALL

The **Boston Red Sox** (⊠ 2201 Edison Ave., ☎ 941/334−4700) play in Fort Myers during their spring-training sojourn. The **Minnesota Twins** (⊠ Lee County Sports Complex, 1410 Six Mile Cypress Pkwy., ☎ 941/768−4278) play exhibition games in March and April.

BIKING

The best path in Fort Myers is along Summerlin Road; for rentals, try **Trikes & Bikes & Mowers** (⊠ 3224 Fowler St., ☎ 941/936−4301).

FISHING

Party-boat and private charters can be arranged at **Deebold's Marina** (⊠ 1071 San Carlos Blvd., ☎ 941/466−3525).

GOLF

The **Eastwood Golf Club** (⊠ 4600 Bruce Herd La., ☎ 941/275−4848) has a driving range and an 18-hole course. The **Fort Myers Country Club** (⊠ 3591 McGregor Blvd., ☎ 941/936−2457) offers golf lessons and an 18-hole course. A practice range and 18-hole course can be found at the **Cypress Pines Country Club** (⊠ Lehigh Acres, ☎ 941/369−8216), southeast of town.

WATER SPORTS

For sailing lessons or bareboat or captained sail cruises, contact **Fort Myers Yacht Charters** (⊠ Port Sanibel Yacht Club, South Fort Myers, ☎ 941/466−1800). **Southwest Florida Yachts** (⊠ 3444 Marinatown La. NW, ☎ 941/656−1339 or 800/262−7939) has a fleet of sailboats for charter and also offers lessons.

Shopping

Bell Tower (⊠ U.S 41 and Daniels Rd., South Fort Myers), an outdoor shopping center catering to upscale tastes, has about 50 boutiques and specialty shops, a large department store, and three multiplex cinemas. Historic downtown **1st Street** has been renovated and features charming restaurants and stores as well as street musicians and artists. **Royal Palm Square** (⊠ Colonial Blvd. between McGregor Blvd. and U.S. 41) has more than two dozen shops and restaurants set amid waterways and tropical foliage. **Sanibel Factory Outlets** (⊠ McGregor Blvd. and Summerlin Rd.) has 35 brand-name outlets, including Dexter, Van Heusen, Maidenform, and Corning/Revere.

Just east of Fort Myers, **Fleamasters Fleamarket** (⊠ 1 mi west of I−75 Exit 23 on Rte. 82) features covered walkways and hundreds of vendors selling new and used items. It's open Friday−Sunday 8−4.

Cape Coral

❷ *13 mi from Fort Myers via North Fort Myers.*

Though this relaxed residential community is just across the Caloosahatchee River from Fort Myers, to reach it you have to head north to North Fort Myers and then swing back southwest along the river.

★ ℭ Nature walks, bubblebins, xeriscape displays, mazes, optical tricks, mind-benders, and brain twisters are just some of the attractions at **Children's Science Center.** ⊠ *2915 N.E. Pine Island Rd.,* ☎ *941/997–0012.* ⊡ *$4.* ⊘ *Tues.–Fri. 9:30–4:30, weekends noon–5.*

ℭ **Sun Splash Family Waterpark** has more than two dozen wet and dry attractions, including three large water slides; the Lilypad Walk, where you step from one floating "lilypad" to another; an arcade; and Squirt-works, a special play area for very young children. ⊠ *400 Santa Barbara Blvd.,* ☎ *941/574–0558.* ⊡ *$8.50.* ⊘ *Mid.-Mar.–May, Wed.–Fri. 11–5, weekends 10–5; June–Aug., Sun.–Wed. and Fri. 10–6, Thurs. and Sat. 10–9; Aug.–Oct., weekends 10–5.*

OFF THE
BEATEN PATH

ECHO – Educational Concerns for Hunger Organization is a small Christian ministry group striving to solve the world's hunger problems. It offers tours of its gardens (which feature the largest collection of tropical food plants in Florida), walks through a simulated rain forest, and looks at crops such as sesame and rice grown without soil. ⊠ 17430 Durrance Rd., North Fort Myers, ☎ 941/543-3246. ⊡ Free. ⊘ Tours Tues., Fri., and Sat. at 10 or by appointment.

Dining and Lodging

$$$
★ ✕ **Dario's Restaurant and Lounge.** This casual yet quiet and intimate place, with candlelight and tablecloths, serves gourmet northern Italian and Continental cuisine. People head here for the delicious chicken Dario (chicken breast in a garlic and white wine sauce) and for the other excellently prepared entrées, including several nightly specials. Save room for the homemade desserts. It's tough to choose between the tiramisù and the Cappuccino Commotion. ⊠ *1805 Del Prado Blvd.,* ☎ *941/574–7798. AE, MC, V. No lunch weekends.*

$$ ✕ **Cape Crab and SteakHouse.** Crabs are served Maryland-style—heaped on a tablecloth of newspaper and with a mallet on the side. Don't want to whack out your frustrations on your dinner? A more refined second dining room has linen tablecloths and a piano player. ⊠ *Coralwood Mall, Del Prado Blvd.,* ☎ *941/574–2722. AE, MC, V.*

$ ✕ **Siam Hut.** Thai music pings and twangs in the background while your taste buds do the same. Specialties are *pad thai* (a mixture of noodles, crushed peanuts, chicken, shrimp, egg, bean sprouts, and scallions) and crispy Siam rolls (spring rolls stuffed with ground chicken, bean thread, and vegetables). Get it fiery hot or extra mild. ⊠ *1873 Del Prado Blvd., Coral Pointe Shopping Center,* ☎ *941/772–3131. AE, MC, V.*

$–$$ ⌂ **Cape Coral Golf & Tennis Resort.** Aimed at golf and tennis enthusiasts, this resort is a good value. The main clubhouse houses a reception area and restaurant, while comfortably furnished rooms are in a two-story, motel-like building. Understated decor reflects the sporty atmosphere. ⊠ *4003 Palm Tree Blvd., 33904,* ☎ *941/542–3191,* FAX *941/542–4694. 100 rooms. 3 restaurants, lounge, pool, driving range, golf, tennis, baby-sitting. AE, DC, MC, V.*

$–$$ ⌂ **Quality Inn–Nautilus.** Conveniently near parks, beaches, restaurants, and malls, this downtown motel offers no-smoking and wheelchair-accessible rooms with complimentary breakfast and newspaper. Pets are permitted. ⊠ *1538 Cape Coral Pkwy., 33904,* ☎ *941/542–2121,* FAX *941/542–6319. 146 rooms. Pool. AE, DC, MC, V.*

Outdoor Activities and Sports

GOLF

Cape Coral Golf & Tennis Resort (⊠ 4003 Palm Tree Blvd., ⊠ 941/542-7879) features an 18-hole course, a practice range, and a putting green.

Coral Oaks Golf Course (⊠ 1800 N.W. 28th Ave., ✆ 941/283–4100) has an 18-hole course and a practice range.

TENNIS
Cape Coral Golf & Tennis Resort (⊠ 4003 Palm Tree Blvd., ✆ 941/542–3191) features eight Har-Tru courts. Lochmoor Country Club (⊠ 3911 Orange Grove Blvd., North Fort Myers, ✆ 941/995–0501) has two Har-Tru clay courts; lessons are available.

Shopping
The Shell Factory (⊠ 2787 N. Tamiami Trail, North Fort Myers, ✆ 941/995–2141) claims to have the world's largest display of seashells and coral.

Punta Gorda

❸ *30 mi north of Cape Coral, 23 mi north of Fort Myers.*

This small town is at the mouth of the Peace River, where it empties into Charlotte Harbor. Although both it and its slightly larger neighbor, Port Charlotte, are on the water, they are not on the ocean, and the closest beach is about 20 minutes away. This is a good destination if you're interested in canoeing, walking through the Florida wilderness, and most of all, escaping the crowds.

The **Florida Adventure Museum** features mounted animal specimens from Africa and North America, as well as a rotating exhibit on local artifacts. A variety of programs entertain and educate the kids. ⊠ *260 W. Retta Esplanade, ✆ 941/639–3777. ⬚ $1. ⊙ Weekdays 8–5, Sat. 10–3.*

OFF THE BEATEN PATH **BABCOCK WILDERNESS ADVENTURES** – To see what Florida looked like centuries ago, visit the 90,000-acre Babcock Crescent B Ranch, southeast of Punta Gorda, and take a 90-minute swamp-buggy excursion through the Telegraph Cypress Swamp. Among its inhabitants are turkey, deer, bobcats, alligators, cows, and a herd of bison. Reservations are essential. ⊠ *800 Rte. 31, ✆ 941/489–3911. ⬚ $15.95. ⊙ 4 tours daily, weather permitting; closed Mon. May–Dec. and Sun.*

Dining and Lodging
$$ ✕ **Salty's Harborside.** Although seafood is the specialty, including some of the freshest mahimahi and grouper around, you'll also find grilled filet mignon, rosemary chicken, and various salads. The dining room looks out on Burnt Store Marina and Charlotte Harbor. ⊠ *Burnt Store Rd., ✆ 941/639–3650. AE, DC, MC, V.*

$$$ ⌂ **Burnt Store Marina Resort.** For boating, golfing, and getting away from it all, this sprawling resort and marina fill the bill. Modern one- and two-bedroom apartments are situated along a relatively undeveloped stretch of vast Charlotte Harbor. All have kitchens, and some face the water. ⊠ *3150 Matecumbe Key Rd., 33955, ✆ 941/575–4488 or 800/859–7529. 39 1-bedroom suites, 1 2-bedroom suite. Restaurant, lounge, pool, tennis, boating. AE, DC, MC.*

Outdoor Activities and Sports
BASEBALL
The Texas Rangers (⊠ Charlotte County Stadium, Rte. 776, Port Charlotte, ✆ 941/625–9500) play games during spring training.

CANOEING
With several Florida locations, **Canoe Outpost** (⊠ 2816 N.W. Rte. 661, Arcadia, ✆ 941/494–1215) conducts all-day and overnight canoe trips, camping equipment included. The outfit has riverside picnic/camp-

ing areas just for their customers, some with great hiking trails. Up the Peace River, about 25 mi from Punta Gorda, **Canoe Safari** (✉ 3020 N.W. Rte. 661, Arcadia, ☎ 941/494–7865) runs half- and full-day trips, plus overnights including camping equipment.

FISHING

King Fisher Charter (✉ Fishermen's Village, ☎ 941/639–0969) offers deep-sea fishing on full-day trips.

GOLF

The Burnt Store Marina Resort (✉ 3150 Matecumbe Key Rd., ☎ 941/332–7334) has 27 holes of golf, and lessons are available. There are 18 holes of golf at the **Deep Creek Golf Club** (✉ 1260 San Cristobal Ave., Port Charlotte, ☎ 941/625–6911).

TENNIS

Port Charlotte Tennis Club (✉ 22400 Gleneagles Terr., Port Charlotte, ☎ 941/625–7222) features four lighted hard-surface courts.

THE BARRIER ISLANDS

Forming a backwards "J," dozens of islands curve toward Fort Myers and Cape Coral, separated from the mainland by Pine Island Sound. Though Sanibel and Captiva, the most-visited spots, are reached by causeway, you need a boat to reach many of the other islands. (If you cut through Pine Island Sound, you have a good chance of being escorted by bottlenose dolphins.) Many of the tiny and uninhabited islands are excellent spots for bird-watching and nature walks.

The tourist-pampering hotels on Sanibel and Captiva have counterparts in such neighboring islands as Cabbage Key and Pine Island, which have older properties and a sleepier atmosphere. When exploring the beaches, keep one eye on the sand; shelling is a major pursuit in these parts.

South of Pine Island Sound's barrier islands and just 18 mi away from Fort Myers is Estero Island, casual home of Fort Myers Beach.

Gasparilla Island (Boca Grande)

❹ *43 mi northwest of Fort Myers, 23 mi southwest of Punta Gorda.*

Before roads to southwest Florida were even talked about, wealthy northerners came by train to spend the winter at the **Gasparilla Inn,** built in 1912 in Boca Grande on Gasparilla Island. While condominiums and modern sprawl creep up on the rest of Gasparilla, much of the town of Boca Grande looks as it has for a century or more. The mood is set by the old Florida homes, many made of wood, with wide, inviting verandas and wicker rocking chairs. The island's relaxed atmosphere is disrupted only in the spring, when tarpon fishermen descend with a vengeance on Boca Grande Pass, considered among the best tarpon-fishing spots in the world.

Cabbage Key

❺ *5 mi south of Boca Grande.*

You'll have to take a boat from Bokeelia on Pine Island to get to this island, which sits at Marker 60 on the Intracoastal Waterway. Here, atop an ancient Calusa Indian shell mound is the friendly, six-room **Cabbage Key Inn,** built by novelist and playwright Mary Roberts Rinehart in 1938. The inn also offers several guest cottages, a marina, and a dining room papered in thousands of dollar bills, signed and posted by patrons over the years.

Sanibel and Captiva Islands

23 mi southwest of downtown Fort Myers.

❻ Popular **Sanibel Island** and its quieter northern neighbor, Captiva, are reached via the Sanibel Causeway. There is a $3 round-trip bridge toll (collected on the way over), but avid shell collectors and nature enthusiasts will get their money's worth, for Sanibel's beaches are rated among the best shelling grounds in the world. For the choicest pickings, arrive as the tide is going out or just after a storm—you'll probably see plenty of other shell-seekers with the telltale "Sanibel stoop."

❼ **Captiva Island** has more private development than Sanibel, and its resorts reflect this sense of seclusion.

At Sanibel's southern tip stands the historic wooden **Sanibel Lighthouse** (⊠ Old Lighthouse Beach, Sanibel), a frequently photographed landmark. It was built in 1884, when the entire island was a nature preserve. While you can't enter the lighthouse itself, the adjacent beach is especially good for shell collecting.

★ Footpaths, winding canoe routes, and the 5-mi, dirt Wildlife Drive meander through the beautiful **J. N. "Ding" Darling National Wildlife Refuge.** Visitors can drive, walk, bicycle, canoe, or ride a specially designed open-air tram with a naturalist on board. With 5,030 acres, the area covers about a third of the island and is home to raccoons, otters, alligators, and numerous exotic birds, such as roseate spoonbills, egrets, ospreys, and herons. Walk among sea grape, wax and salt myrtles, red mangrove, sabal palms, and other flora native to Florida. An observation tower along the road is a prime bird-watching site, especially in the early morning and just before dusk. ⊠ *Refuge: Sanibel-Captiva Rd., Sanibel,* ☎ *941/472–1100; Tarpon Bay Recreation Center, 941/472–8900.* ⊠ *$4 per car, $1 per pedestrian/bicyclist, duck stamp $15 (covers all national wildlife refuges), tram $6.75.* ☉ *Visitor center daily 9–5, Wildlife Dr. Mon.–Thurs. and Sat. 7–5:45, tram Mon.–Thurs. and Sat. 10:30, 1, 3:15; Sun. 2.*

★ As though to one-up the nearby beaches, the **Bailey-Matthews Shell Museum** contains more than a million shells from around the world. The centerpiece, a 6-foot revolving globe, shows visitors where in the world the museum's shells are found. Novice collectors can identify their beach finds by comparing their own shells with the numerous local specimens displayed. ⊠ *3075 Sanibel-Captiva Rd., Sanibel,* ☎ *941/395–2233.* ⊠ *$5.* ☉ *Tues.–Sun. 10–4.*

Beaches

Bowman's Beach, on Sanibel's northwest end, is mainly a family beach. Off of Sanibel-Captiva Road, **Gulfside Park** is a lesser known and less populated beach, ideal for those who seek solitude and who do not require facilities. Off Casa Ybel Road at Sanibel's southern end is **Old Lighthouse Beach** (⊠ East end of W. Gulf Dr.), which attracts a mix of families, shellers, and singles; rest rooms are available, and a plus is the historic lighthouse.

Dining and Lodging

$$$ ✕ **Bubble Room.** It's hard to say which is more eclectic here, the atmosphere or the menu. Waiters and waitresses wearing Boy Scout uniforms race amid a dizzying array of art deco, while music from the 1940s sets the mood. The aged prime rib is ample enough to satisfy two hearty eaters—at least. Chances are you'll be too full for dessert, but it can be wrapped to go. The Red Velvet cake is an unforgettable meal in itself. ⊠ *Captiva Rd., Captiva,* ☎ *941/472–5558. AE, DC, MC, V.*

$$$ ✕ **Greenhouse at Thistle Lodge.** Take a seat at the copper-topped bar
★ to look into the full-view kitchen and try to pick out the day's specials.
The menu reflects Continental, Asian, and Southwestern cuisine and
includes rack of lamb, red snapper with wild mushrooms, homemade
sausage, fresh seafood, and an excellent assortment of desserts. ⊠ *Captiva Rd., Captiva,* ☎ *941/472–6066. DC, MC, V.*

$$$ ✕ **Jean-Paul's French Corner.** The food here is finely seasoned with everything but the highfalutin attitude often dished up in French establishments. Excellent onion soup, salmon in a creamy dill sauce, veal
medallions in a cream sauce with mushrooms, and roast duckling in
fruit sauce are among the few but well-prepared choices on the menu.
⊠ *708 Tarpon Bay Rd., Sanibel,* ☎ *941/472–1493. MC, V. Closed
Sun. No lunch.*

$$ ✕ **McT's Shrimphouse and Tavern.** This lively and informal gathering
spot features a host of fresh seafood specialties, including numerous
oyster and mussel appetizers, shrimp prepared all kinds of ways, and
all-you-can-eat shrimp and crab. Landlubbers will enjoy the black-bean
soup, prime rib, and blackened chicken. There's always a dessert du
jour, but most people end up choosing the Sanibel mud pie, a delicious
concoction heavy on the Oreos. ⊠ *1523 Periwinkle Way, Sanibel,* ☎
941/472–3161. AE, DC, MC, V.

$ ✕ **Lighthouse Cafe.** Sanibel's oldest restaurant looks pretty much like
a plain old coffee shop, but it consistently wins the local award for best
breakfast on the island. Whole-wheat pancakes, fresh-baked muffins,
fritatta, and bubbly mimosas bring people in the morning and beyond,
since breakfast is served until closing. Hamburgers, grilled cheese sandwiches, and fresh salads are popular luncheon items. ⊠ *362 Periwinkle Way, Sanibel,* ☎ *941/472–1033. MC, V.*

$$$$ ▦ **Casa Ybel Resort.** This time-share property faces the gulf on 23 acres
of tropical grounds, complete with palms, ponds, a footbridge, and gazebos dotting the lawns. Early this century, this was the site of a lodge,
but current buildings are built in a Victorian style. Contemporary one-
and two-bedroom apartments with full kitchens are brightly furnished
in tropical prints, and big screened-in porches look out to the beach.
There is a well-respected restaurant on site. ⊠ *2255 W. Gulf Dr.,
Sanibel 33957,* ☎ *941/472–3145 or 800/237–8906,* ℻ *941/472–2109.
40 1-bedroom units, 74 2-bedroom units. Restaurant, lounge, pool,
tennis, shuffleboard, windsurfing, boating, bicycles, game room, babysitting, playground. AE, DC, MC, V.*

$$$$ ▦ **Sanibel Harbour Resort & Spa.** At the last mainland exit before the
causeway, this high-rise resort has large, well-decorated rooms—all with
sweeping views of island-studded San Carlos Bay. A wooden walkway
leads through woods and across a pond to an exceptional spa. The beach
is only fair (and it's on the Inland Waterway, not the gulf), but there
is a large free-form pool and free transportation to Sanibel beaches.
The Kids Klub keeps children busy, and the staff is exceptionally helpful. ⊠ *17260 Harbour Pointe Dr., Fort Myers 33908,* ☎ *941/466–
4000 or 800/767–7777,* ℻ *941/466–2150. 320 rooms, 80 2-bedroom
condominiums. 3 restaurants, 3 lounges, indoor pool, outdoor pool,
spa, tennis, exercise room, racquetball, children's programs. AE, DC,
MC, V.*

$$$$ ▦ **South Seas Plantation Resort and Yacht Harbour.** This busy 330-
★ acre property at Captiva's far end is more neighborhood than resort.
Nine types of accommodations include tennis and harborside villas,
gulf cottages, and private homes. Pursue outdoor activities or visit the
new nature center, which has an exhibit of marine life and seashore
and shelling programs. From the posh restaurant's servers to water-

skiing instructors, the staff is generally five-star. Rates can drop up to 40% off-season. ⊠ *South Seas Plantation Rd., Captiva 33924,* ☎ *941/472–5111 or 800/237–1260,* FAX *941/472–7541. 620 rooms. 4 restaurants, 2 lounges, pools, beauty salon, golf, putting green, tennis, docks, windsurfing, boating, parasailing, waterskiing, fishing, game room, children's programs, playground. AE, DC, MC, V.*

$$$ 🏠 **Sanibel Seaside Inn.** A pleasant alternative to large full-service resorts is this quiet inn that is right on the beach. Choose from studios, one-bedrooms, and individual cottages. All are decorated in bright tropical prints and have rattan furniture. Some units have much better views than others so be sure to ask. Outdoor grills are available. ⊠ *541 E. Gulf Dr., Sanibel 33957,* ☎ *941/472–1400,* FAX *941/472–6518. 32 units. Pool, shuffleboard, beach. DC, MC, V.*

$$ 🏠 **Shalimar Motel.** Well-maintained grounds and an inviting beach make this small property appealing. Units (all with full kitchen) are in small two-story cottages set back from the beach amid tropical greenery. There's a courtyard pool and barbecue facilities. ⊠ *2823 W. Gulf Dr., Sanibel 33957,* ☎ *941/472–1353 or 800/645–4092,* FAX *941/472–6430. 21 efficiencies, 10 1-bedroom units, 2 2-bedroom units. Pool, shuffleboard, beach. DC, MC, V.*

Outdoor Activities and Sports

BIKING

On Sanibel, rent bicycles by the hour at **Bike Route** (⊠ 2330 Palm Ridge Rd., ☎ 941/472–1955). On Captiva, rent bikes by the hour or day from **Jim's Bike & Scooter Rental** (⊠ 11534 Andy Rosse La., ☎ 941/472–1296).

BOATING

Boat House of Sanibel (⊠ Sanibel Marina, 634 N. Yachtman Dr., Sanibel, ☎ 941/472–2531) rents powerboats. **Jensen's Marina** (⊠ Captiva, ☎ 941/472–5800) rents little powerboats perfect for fishing and shelling.

CANOEING

Tarpon Bay Marina (⊠ 900 Tarpon Bay Rd., Sanibel, ☎ 941/472–8900) has canoes and equipment for exploring the wildlife refuge.

FISHING

Fishing is popular in this part of the world, and anglers head out to catch mackerel, pompano, grouper, reds, snook, bluefish, and shark. Call **Captain Pat Lovetro** (⊠ Sanibel Marina, 634 N. Yachtman Dr., Sanibel, ☎ 941/472–2723) for half-day, six-hour, and full-day trips.

GOLF

You can rent golf clubs and take lessons as well as play at **The Dunes** (⊠ 949 Sand Castle Rd., Sanibel, ☎ 941/472–2535), which has 18 holes.

TENNIS

At **The Dunes** (⊠ 949 Sand Castle Rd., Sanibel, ☎ 941/472–3522), there are seven clay courts and two tennis professionals ready to give lessons. The **City Recreation Complex** (⊠ 3840 Sanibel-Captiva Rd., Sanibel, ☎ 941/472–0345) has five lighted tennis courts.

Shopping

The largest cluster of shops on Sanibel, **Periwinkle Place** (⊠ 2075 Periwinkle Way), has 55 shops and several restaurants. **Aboriginals** (⊠ 2340 Periwinkle Way, ☎ 941/395–2200) sells textiles, baskets, pottery, and jewelry from Native Americans, Australians, and Africans. At **She Sells Sea Shells** (⊠ 1157 Periwinkle Way, ☎ 941/472–6991), everything imaginable is made out of shells, from decorative mirrors and lamps to Christmas ornaments.

Estero Island (Fort Myers Beach)

❽ *18 mi southwest of Fort Myers.*

This laid-back island lined with motels, hotels, and restaurants serves as one of Fort Myers's more frenetic ocean playgrounds. The marina at the north end of the island is the starting point for much boating, including sunset cruises, sightseeing cruises, and deep-sea fishing.

OFF THE BEATEN PATH **CARL E. JOHNSON RECREATION AREA –** To the south, on two small islands between Estero Island and Bonita Beach, you'll find this area devoted to recreation. Shelling, bird-watching, boating, fishing, canoeing, and nature walks in an unspoiled setting are the main attractions. Admission covers the round-trip tram ride from the park entrance in Bonita Beach. There are also rest rooms, picnic tables, a snack bar, and showers. ⊠ *Rte. 865, Black Island, no phone.* 🖭 *$1.50.* ☉ *Daily 8–sunset.*

Beach

Lynn Hall Memorial Park (⊠ Estero Blvd.) is in the more commercial northern part of Estero Island. The shore slopes gradually into the usually tranquil and warm gulf waters, providing safe swimming for children. Since the beach is for the most part lined with houses, condominiums, and hotels, you're never far from civilization. A number of nightspots and restaurants are also close. There's a free fishing pier, picnic tables, barbecue grills, playground equipment, and a bathhouse with rest rooms. Though the beach is open 7 am–10 pm, lifeguards are only on duty 10–5:45.

Dining and Lodging

$$ ✗ **Mucky Duck.** Yes, there are two restaurants by this name—one on the Captiva waterfront, the other a slightly more formal restaurant in Fort Myers Beach. Both concentrate on fresh, well-prepared seafood. The bacon-wrapped barbecued shrimp is popular, and local grouper prepared any number of ways is the house specialty. ⊠ *2500 Estero Blvd.,* ☎ *941/463–5519;* ⊠ *Andy Rosse La., Captiva,* ☎ *941/472–3434. MC, V.*

$$ ✗ **Snug Harbor.** You can watch boats coming and going whether you sit inside or out at this dockside restaurant on stilts. The secret of its success is absolutely fresh seafood, courtesy of the restaurant's private fishing fleet. This place is a favorite of year-round residents and seasonal visitors alike. ⊠ *645 San Carlos Blvd.,* ☎ *941/463–4343. MC, V.*

$$$ 🏨 **Outrigger Beach Resort.** This informal, family-oriented resort is set on a wide beach overlooking the gulf. Rooms and efficiencies are decorated in bright prints. Views vary, so ask when making reservations. The resort also has a broad sundeck, tiki huts to sit under to escape the heat, sailboats, and a beachfront pool. ⊠ *6200 Estero Blvd., 33931,* ☎ *941/463–3131 or 800/749–3131. 144 units. Pool, shuffleboard, volleyball, beach, jet skiing, bicycles. MC, V.*

$$–$$$ 🏨 **Best Western Pink Shell Beach Resort.** Set on 12 acres, this beachfront and family-focused resort's accommodations range from cottages on stilts to rooms and apartments in a five-story building. There are children's, social, and recreation programs. ⊠ *275 Estero Blvd., 33931,* ☎ *941/463–6181,* FAX *941/463–1229. 208 units. 3 pools, tennis courts, shuffleboard, volleyball, beach, windsurfing, jet skiing, parasailing, fishing, children's programs. AE, MC, V.*

Outdoor Activities and Sports

BIKING

Beach Cycle and Repair (⌧ 1901 Estero Blvd., ☎ 941/463–8844) rents bicycles by the day and the week.

FISHING

Getaway Bait and Boat Rental (⌧ 1091 San Carlos Blvd., ☎ 941/466–3200) rents motorboats and fishing equipment, sells bait, and offers half- and full-day charters.

GOLF

The **Bay Beach Club Executive Golf Course** (⌧ 7401 Estero Blvd., ☎ 941/463–2064) offers 18 holes, a practice range, and lessons.

TENNIS

You'll find six Har-Tru clay courts plus private and group lessons at the **Bay Beach Racquet Club** (⌧ 120 Lenell St., ☎ 941/463–4473).

NAPLES AREA

Driving U.S. 41 south from Fort Myers you'll pass through Bonita Springs on your way to the Naples and Marco Island area, sandwiched between the Big Cypress Swamp and the Gulf of Mexico. The land east of Naples is undeveloped all the way to Fort Lauderdale. Most of it is swampland and forms the northern border of the Florida Everglades—making it excellent territory for visiting nature preserves and parks.

Naples is a major vacation spot, having sprouted a bevy of high-end restaurants and shops. A similar, but not as thorough, change has occurred on Marco Island, once a quiet fishing community.

Bonita Springs

9 *24 mi south of Fort Myers.*

Though the town is not on the gulf, there are several sizable, popular beaches to its west and south. **Bonita Beach** is the gateway to the Carl E. Johnson Recreation Area (☞ Estero Island, *above*).

The **Everglades Wonder Gardens,** one of the first attractions of its kind in the state, captures the feral beauty of untamed Florida. Zoological gardens contain Florida panthers, black bear, crocodiles and alligators, tame Florida deer, flamingos, and trained otters and birds. There's also an eclectic natural history museum on site. ⌧ *Old U.S. 41,* ☎ *941/992–2591.* ☷ *$8.* ☺ *Daily 9–5.*

OFF THE
BEATEN PATH

CORKSCREW SWAMP SANCTUARY – To get a feel for what this part of Florida was like before civil engineers began draining the swamps, drive 13 mi east of Bonita Springs (30 mi northeast of Naples) to this 11,000-acre sanctuary. Managed by the National Audubon Society, it protects 500-year-old trees and endangered birds, such as wood storks, which often nest high in the bald cypress. Visitors taking the 1¾-mi self-guided tour along the boardwalk, which takes about two hours, may glimpse alligators, graceful wading birds, and air plants that cling to the sides of trees. ⌧ *16 mi east of I–75 on Rte. 846 ,* ☎ *941/657-3771.* ☷ *$6.50.* ☺ *Dec.–Apr., daily 7–5; May–Nov., daily 8–5.*

Beaches

Bonita Springs Public Beach (⌧ Bonita Beach Rd.) is at the southern end of Bonita Beach. There are picnic tables, free parking, and nearby refreshment stands and shopping. **Barefoot Beach Preserve** (⌧ Lely Beach

Rd.), between Naples and Bonita, is a popular spot. It has picnic tables, a nature trail, refreshment stands, and other comforts.

Outdoor Activities and Sports

BIKING

You can rent bicycles at **Pop's Bicycles** (⌧ 3685 Bonita Beach Rd., ☎ 941/947–4442).

BOATING

Bonita Beach Resort Motel (⌧ 26395 Hickory Blvd., ☎ 941/992–2137) rents motorboats by the hour or day.

CANOEING

Estero River Tackle and Canoe Outfitters (⌧ 20991 Tamiami Trail S, Estero, ☎ 941/992–4050) has canoes and equipment for use on the meandering Estero River.

DOG RACING

There is dog racing year-round at the **Naples/Fort Myers Greyhound Track** (⌧ 10601 Bonita Beach Rd., ☎ 941/992–2411).

Naples

➓ *21 mi south of Bonita Springs.*

Naples is fast becoming Florida's west-coast version of Palm Beach. Twenty-story condominiums now line the north shore, and many sophisticated (and expensive) restaurants have opened, as have a number of upscale shopping areas, including the tree-lined 3rd Street South. Though golf, tennis, and miles of beach draw visitors to this area year-round, the winter months are by far the most crowded.

Teddy bear lovers of all ages delight in the more than 2,500 teddy bears on display at the **Teddy Bear Museum of Naples.** Built by oil heiress and area resident Frances Pew Hayes, the $2 million museum also has a reading library—stocked with books just about bears—and a life-size Three Bears House. ⌧ *2511 Pine Ridge Rd.,* ☎ *941/598–2711.* 🎫 *$6.* 🕙 *Wed.–Sat. 10–5, Sun. 1–5.*

Originally a botanical garden planted in the early 1900s, **Caribbean Gardens & Zoological Park,** a 52-acre junglelike educational park, now houses exotic wildlife including African lions, mandrills, Bengal tigers, lemurs, antelope, and monkeys. The Primate Expedition Cruise takes you through islands of monkeys and apes living in natural habitat. There are elephant demonstrations and alligator feedings, and kids particularly enjoy the petting zoo. ⌧ *1590 Goodlette Rd.,* ☎ *941/262–5409.* 🎫 *$12.95.* 🕙 *Daily 9:30–5:30.*

On 13 acres bordering a tidal lagoon teeming with wildlife, the **Naples Nature Center** includes an aviary, a wildlife rehabilitation clinic, a natural science museum with a serpentarium, and a 3,000-gallon marine aquarium. Free guided walks and miniboat tours are scheduled several times daily, and there are canoes and kayaks for rent. ⌧ *1450 Merrihue Dr.,* ☎ *941/262–0304.* 🎫 *Free.* 🕙 *Daily 9:30–5:30.*

Beaches

Clam Pass Park is a glistening stretch of particularly pristine white sand. A 3,000-foot boardwalk winds through tropical mangroves to the beach. ⌧ *Seagate Dr.,* ☎ *941/353–0404.* 🎫 *Free.* 🕙 *Daily 8–sunset.*

Delnor-Wiggins Pass State Recreation Area is a well-maintained park with 100 acres with sandy beaches, lifeguards, barbecue grills, picnic tables, boat ramp, observation tower, rest rooms with wheelchair access, lots of parking, bathhouses, and showers. Fishing is best in Wiggins Pass, at the north end of the park. Alcohol is prohibited. ⊠ *West end of 111th Ave. N.* 🖃 *$3.25 per vehicle with up to 8 people, boat launching $1.* ☉ *Daily 7–sunset.*

Stretching along Gulf Shore Boulevard, **Lowdermilk Park** has over 1,000 feet of beach, volleyball courts, a playground, rest rooms, showers, a pavilion, vending machines, and picnic tables. No alcoholic beverages or fires are permitted. ⊠ *Gulf Shore Blvd. at Banyan Blvd.* 🖃 *Free.* ☉ *7–sunset.*

Dining and Lodging

$$$ ✕ **Bistro 821.** The decor for this trendy restaurant is spare but sophisticated. Fairly bright, the long, narrow room is mostly white and black. Entrées range from marinated leg of lamb with basil mashed potatoes to snapper baked in parchment, wild-mushroom pasta, vodka penne, risotto, and a seasonal vegetable plate. The menu accommodates appetites of all sizes, with little plates, big plates, and half portions. ⊠ *821 5th Ave. S,* ☎ *941/261–5821. Reservations essential on weekends. AE, DC, MC, V. No lunch.*

$$$ ✕ **Ristorante Ciao.** One block north of 5th Avenue's "Restaurant
★ Row," this elegant, award-winning Northern Italian restaurant is packed all winter long. Veal is excellent: Try the veal picatta, veal marsala, or whatever the nightly special is. A hearty minestrone or the garlicky Caesar salad are good bets for a first course, and the extensive wine list includes some fine Italian selections. ⊠ *835 4th Ave. S,* ☎ *941/263–3889. AE, D, DC, MC, V. No lunch.*

$–$$ ✕ **Busghetti Ristorante.** Despite the cutesy name and the affordable prices,
★ this eatery serves excellent Italian cuisine in an appealing, upscale setting. Choose to eat inside in a cozy poster-decorated room or outside on a quiet patio. The menu includes a wide range of pastas, from traditional lasagna to "busghetti" with everything from Gorgonzola to ratatouille. There are also many veal, steak, chicken, and seafood selections and a good wine list. ⊠ *1181 3rd St. S,* ☎ *941/263–3667. AE, MC, V.*

$ ✕ **Old Naples Pub.** From Robinson Court, walk up a few stairs to this comfortable pub, open 11 AM until late at night. Sample from 20 kinds of beer and the not-so-traditional pub menu, with fish-and-chips, burgers, bratwurst, pizza, and chicken Caesar salad as well as a selection of snacks: nachos, fries smothered in chili, and cheese-stuffed, deep-fried jalapeños. There's piano entertainment Monday–Saturday. ⊠ *255 13th Ave. S,* ☎ *941/649–8200. AE, MC, V.*

$$$$ 🏨 **Edgewater Beach Hotel.** At the north end of fashionable Gulf Shore Boulevard stands this compact, high-rise, waterfront resort. The brightly decorated units are either one- or two-bedroom suites and have full kitchens, and patios or balconies. Many have exquisite views of the gulf. Dine by the pool or in the elegant restaurant, or enjoy piano music in the lounge during happy hour. Shopping, golf, and tennis are close by. Some units are being converted to time-shares. ⊠ *1901 Gulf Shore Blvd. N, 33940,* ☎ *941/262–6511 or 800/821–0196; in FL, 800/282–3766;* 🖷 *941/262–1243. 124 units. Restaurant, lounge, pool, exercise room, beach, bicycles. AE, DC, MC, V.*

$$$$ 🏨 **Registry Resort.** From the elegant marble and oak lobby to the ex-
★ ceptional service, this high-rise is the essence of luxury. Inside are rooms that feel more like someone's house than a hotel. Outside are unique, free-form swimming pools with waterfalls. Walk through a mangrove forest to 3 mi of glistening white beach, or take an open-air tram. Try canoeing around a lagoon. The Caddymaster service arranges tee times at the area's finest golf clubs months in advance, and the tennis

program is especially strong. The outstanding Sunday brunch has table after table of exquisitely prepared selections. Most guests dress up for it. ⊠ *475 Seagate Dr., 33940,* ☎ *941/597–3232,* ℻ *941/566–7919. 395 rooms, 29 suites, 50 tennis villas. 4 restaurants, 2 lounges, 3 pools, golf, tennis, health club, bicycles, shops, children's programs. AE, DC, MC, V.*

$$$$ 🖬 **Ritz-Carlton.** Equally fabulous hotel rooms can be had elsewhere, but the extensive network of lavishly appointed public rooms is astounding, with a dozen meeting rooms of varying shapes and sizes and an estimable collection of 19th-century European oils. Though you might feel a little uncomfortable traipsing through the lobby in tennis shoes, you will be graciously welcomed. Guests have access to a nearby 27-hole golf course. ⊠ *280 Vanderbilt Beach Rd., 33941,* ☎ *941/598–3300,* ℻ *941/598–6690. 463 rooms. 4 restaurants, lounge, pool, saunas, 6 tennis courts, health club, beach, windsurfing, boating, children's programs. AE, D, DC, MC, V.*

$$$ 🖬 **La Playa Beach & Racquet Inn.** Nestled between a bay and the gulf, this large hotel stretches along the beach. A recent multimillion-dollar renovation has refurbished the bright, spacious rooms with stylish print fabrics. Rooms and efficiencies are in a three-story low-rise, and one- and two-bedroom suites are in a 14-story high-rise. All have patios or balconies with excellent gulf views. Kayaks are available. ⊠ *9891 Gulf Shore Blvd., 33963,* ☎ *941/597–3123,* ℻ *941/597–6278. 172 units. 2 restaurants, lounge, 2 pools, tennis, shuffleboard, volleyball, beach, dock, boating. AE, MC, V.*

$$$ 🖬 **Naples Beach Hotel & Golf Club.** This appealing resort, owned and
★   operated by the same family since it opened in 1946, sprawls along the gulf. Comfortable rooms and suites, furnished in rattan and tropical prints, are in several buildings. Quite a few have spectacular water views, and orchids, grown on site, are placed in rooms daily. The beach and pool stretch along the western edge of the property, while the championship golf course and tennis courts flank the eastern edge. The new Tennis Center features six Har-Tru courts and a clubhouse. Among the eateries is the only beachfront bar and restaurant in Naples, built prior to strict zoning laws. ⊠ *851 Gulf Shore Blvd. N, 33940,* ☎ *941/261–2222 or 800/237–7600,* ℻ *941/261–7380. 315 units. 3 restaurants, 2 bars, deli, pool, 18-hole golf course, 6 tennis courts, beach. AE, MC, V.*

$$ 🖬 **Best Western Naples Inn & Suites.** You'd never know you were anywhere near busy U.S. 41 at this two-story spot, which is set back in lush tropical gardens with waterfalls. It is a ½-mi walk to gulf beaches and an easy walk to shopping and restaurants. ⊠ *2329 9th St. N, 33940,* ☎ *941/261–1148 or 800/528–1234,* ℻ *941/262–4684. 80 rooms. Restaurant, lounge, 2 pools, shuffleboard. AE, D, DC, MC, V.*

Nightlife and the Arts

THE ARTS

Naples is the cultural capital of this stretch of coast. The **Naples Philharmonic Center for the Arts** (⊠ 5833 Pelican Bay Blvd., ☎ 941/597–1111) has two theaters and two art galleries offering a variety of plays, concerts, and exhibits year-round. It's home to the 80-piece **Naples Philharmonic**, which presents both classical and pop concerts; the **Miami Ballet Company** also performs during its winter season. Halfway between U.S. 41 and I–75, the **Naples Dinner Theatre** (⊠ Immokalee Rd., ☎ 941/597–6031) features professional companies performing mostly musicals and comedies, October–August; admission includes a candlelight French buffet. The **Naples Players** (⊠ 399 Goodlette Rd., ☎ 941/263–7990) has winter and summer seasons—winter shows often sell out well in advance.

NIGHTLIFE

The casual **Backstage Tap & Grill** (⊠ 5535 U.S. 41 N, ☎ 941/598–1300) has great jazz a few nights each week. **Club Zanzibar** (⊠ 475 Seagate Dr., North Naples, ☎ 941/597–3232), at the Registry Resort, is a light and airy multilevel nightclub where DJs pump out Top 40 hits from 9 PM until 2AM. It's packed on weekends. Stop at the **Silver Dollar Saloon** (⊠ Gulf Gate Shopping Plaza, ☎ 941/775–7011) for open country dancing Tuesday–Sunday. There are free lessons Wednesdays 7–9. **Witch's Brew** (⊠ 4836 N. Tamiami Trail, ☎ 941/261–4261) is a lively location for nightly entertainment. There is a happy hour weekdays 4–6 and excellent Continental cuisine. The upstairs lounge at Witch's Brew's sister restaurant, **Seawitch** (⊠ 179 Commerce St., Vanderbilt Beach, ☎ 941/566–1514), overlooks Vanderbilt Bay and is a relaxing spot for casual dining. Bands play Top 40 music Tuesday–Sunday.

Outdoor Activities and Sports

BIKING

Try the **Bicycle Shop** (⊠ 941 Vanderbilt Beach Rd., ☎ 941/566–3646) for rentals by the hour, day, or week.

BOATING

Port-O-Call (⊠ 550 Port-O-Call Way, ☎ 941/774–0479) rents 16- to 25-foot powerboats.

FISHING

If you want to attempt to catch some fish, ask for Captain Tom at **Deep Sea Charter Fishing** (⊠ Boat Haven, ☎ 941/263–8171). The **Lady Brett** (⊠ Tin City, ☎ 941/263–4949) makes fishing and sightseeing trips twice daily.

GOLF

The **Ironwood Golf Club** (⊠ 205 Charity Ct., ☎ 941/775–2584) has an 18-hole course, a practice range, lessons, and rentals. **Naples Beach Hotel & Golf Club** (⊠ 851 Gulf Shore Blvd. N., ☎ 941/261–2222) features 18 holes, a golf pro, and a putting green. **Naples Golf Center** (⊠ 7700 E. Davis Blvd., ☎ 941/775–3337) has a 300-yard driving range and offers private and group lessons by a PGA teaching staff; it even has computerized swing analysis.

TENNIS

Cambier Park Tennis Courts (⊠ 775 8th Ave. S, ☎ 941/434–4694) offers clinics and play on nine hard-surface and five Har-Tru courts; 11 are lighted. **Naples Racquet Club** (⊠ 100 Forest Hills Blvd., ☎ 941/774–2442) has seven Har-Tru clay courts.

Shopping

The largest shopping area is **Olde Naples,** with more than 100 shops and restaurants. Shoppers stroll along broad, tree-lined walkways in an eight-block area bordered by Broad Avenue on the north and 4th Street South on the east. **Old Marine Market Place at Tin City** (⊠ 1200 5th Ave. S), in a collection of former fishing shacks along Naples Bay, has 40 boutiques, artisans' studios, and souvenir shops with everything from scrimshaw to Haitian art. Classy **Village on Venetian Bay** (⊠ 4200 Gulf Shore Blvd.) has more than 50 shops and restaurants built over the bay. **Waterside Shops** (⊠ Seagate Dr. and U.S. 41) are built around a courtyard with a series of waterways. Anchored by a Saks Fifth Avenue boutique and Jacobson's Department Store, Waterside houses 50 shops and several eating places.

Gattle's (⊠ 1250 3rd St. S, ☎ 941/262–4791) is the place for beautifully made (and pricey) linens. **Marissa Collections** (⊠ 1167 3rd St.

S, ☎ 941/263–4333) showcases designer women's wear, including Louis Féraud, Donna Karan, and Calvin Klein. Stop at **Mettlers** (⊠ 1258 3rd St. S, ☎ 941/434–2700) for high-fashion men's and women's sportswear, including full lines of clothing by Giorgio Armani and Polo. At the **Mole Hole** (⊠ 1201 3rd St. S, ☎ 941/262–5115), every surface is covered with gift items large and small, from glassware to paperweights to knick-knacks.

Marco Island

⑪ *20 mi south of Naples.*

Another island connected to the mainland by causeways, this one stubbornly retains its isolated feeling despite the high-rises that line parts of its shore. Many natural areas have been preserved, and the fishing village of **Goodland** resists tourism-induced change. Surfing, sunning, swimming, golf, and tennis are the primary activities.

OFF THE
BEATEN PATH

TEN THOUSAND ISLANDS – There aren't really 10,000, but it sure looks like it. The best way to see this cluster of small, undeveloped, protected islands—and their remarkable wildlife—is by airboat. Cruises last about two hours, and you'll probably see many birds, including pelicans and hawks, as well as dolphins swimming alongside the boat. ⊠ *1079 Bald Eagle Dr., at Factory Bay Marina,* ☎ *941/642-6717.* ☞ *$20.* ☉ *Departures daily at 10 and 2.*

Beaches

Tigertail Beach is on the southwest side of the island. Facilities include parking, a concession stand, a picnic area, sailboat rentals, volleyball, rest rooms, and showers. ⊠ *480 Hernando Ct.,* ☎ *941/642-0818.* ☉ *Daily sunrise–sunset.*

Resident's Beach is right in the middle of the south side of the island. Facilities include parking, a concession stand, picnic areas, rest rooms, and showers. ⊠ *618 Collier Blvd., no phone.* ☉ *Daily sunrise–sunset.*

Dining and Lodging

$$-$$$ ✕ **Old Marco Inn.** This turn-of-the-century home is now a beautifully
★ decorated spot for intimate dinners. The menu covers a cross section of cuisines—such old-world German specialties as Wiener schnitzel plus grilled steaks and chops and fresh seafood. The piano bar opens nightly at 8. ⊠ *100 Palm St.,* ☎ *941/394-3131. Jacket required in season. AE, MC, V. No lunch weekends.*

$$ ✕ **Cafe de Marco.** This cozy little award-winning bistro serves some of the best food on the island. It specializes in combining fresh local fish with original sauces, so listen carefully to the selections of the day. Landlubbers can enjoy steaks, chicken, and pasta. ⊠ *244 Royal Palm Dr.,* ☎ *941/394-6262. AE, DC, MC, V. Closed Sun.*

$$ ✕ **Marco Lodge Waterfront Restaurant & Lounge.** Built in 1869, Marco's oldest landmark is a tin-roofed, wood building on the waterfront. Boats (up to 35 feet) tie up dockside, and you can dine on a wide veranda overlooking the water. Fresh local seafood and Cajun entrées are featured. One specialty is a wooden bowl of blue crabs in rich garlic butter. ⊠ *1 Papaya St., Goodland,* ☎ *941/642-7227. AE, DC, MC, V. Closed Mon.*

$$$$ ☷ **Marco Beach Hilton.** With fewer than 300 rooms and wisely apportioned public areas, the Hilton is smaller than the other big-name resorts in the area, and facilities tend to be a little less crowded. All of the rooms in this 11-story beachfront hotel are spacious and have private balconies with unobstructed gulf views, a sitting area, wet bar, and refrigerator. There is golf nearby. ⊠ *560 S. Collier Blvd., 33937,* ☎ *941/394–5000 or 800/443–4550,* FAX *941/394–5251. 298 rooms. 2 restaurants, snack bar, pool, tennis, health club, beach, windsurfing, parasailing, waterskiing. AE, D, DC, MC, V.*

$$$$ 🏨 **Marriott's Marco Island Resort and Golf Club.** A circular drive leads to this big beachfront resort hotel and its manicured grounds. Large rooms are plush, have good to exceptional water views from their balconies, and come with a multitude of amenities, including coffeemaker, small refrigerator, movie channels, and minibar. Serious shell seekers will delight in the beachside shell-washing spigot, and golf is not far away. ⊠ *400 S. Collier Blvd., 33937,* ☎ *941/394–2511 or 800/438–4373,* FAX *941/394–4645. 736 rooms, 6 penthouse suites, 30 lanais, 8 private villas. 6 restaurants, lounge, 3 pools, golf, miniature golf, tennis, health club, beach, windsurfing, boating, waterskiing, bicycles, children's programs. AE, DC, MC, V.*

$$$ 🏨 **Radisson Suite Beach Resort.** There's something for everyone at this full-service, beachfront property designed for families. Tastefully decorated rooms and one- and two-bedroom suites in this medium high-rise contain fully equipped kitchens. Though rooms are a bit tight, suites have plenty of space. ⊠ *600 S. Collier Blvd., 33937,* ☎ *941/394–4100 or 800/333–3333,* FAX *941/394–0419. 55 rooms, 214 suites. 3 restaurants, 2 lounges, pool, exercise room, beach, parasailing, bicycles, game room, children's programs. AE, DC, MC, V.*

Outdoor Activities and Sports

BIKING

Rentals are available at **Scootertown** (⊠ 845 Bald Eagle Dr., ☎ 941/394–8400).

FISHING

Blue Runner Charters (⊠ 951 Bald Eagle Dr., ☎ 941/642–7585) offers offshore fishing charters. Bait, tackle, and license are supplied. **Factory Bay Marina** (⊠ 1079 Bald Eagle Dr., ☎ 941/642–6717) has fishing-boat rentals as well as charters.

WATER SPORTS

For sailing lessons or bareboat or captained sail cruises, contact **Marco Island Sea Excursions** (⊠ 1281 Jamaica Rd., ☎ 941/642–6400).

SOUTHWEST FLORIDA A TO Z

Arriving and Departing

By Bus

Greyhound Lines (☎ 800/231–2222) has service to Fort Myers (⊠ 2275 Cleveland Ave., ☎ 941/334–1011) and Naples (⊠ 2669 Davis Blvd., ☎ 941/774–5660).

By Car

I–75 spans the region from north to south. Once you cross the border into Florida, it's about five hours to Fort Myers and another hour to Naples. Alligator Alley, a section of I–75, is a two-lane toll road (75¢ at each end) that runs from Fort Lauderdale through the Everglades to Naples. The trip takes two hours.

By Plane

The area's airport is **Southwest Florida International Airport** (☎ 941/768–1000), about 12 mi southwest of Fort Myers, 25 mi north of Naples. It is served by **Air Canada** (☎ 800/776–3000), **American** (☎ 800/433–7300), **Canadian Holidays** (☎ 800/282–4751), **Continental**

(☎ 800/525–0280), **Delta** (☎ 800/221–1212), **Northwest** (☎ 800/225–2525), **TWA** (☎ 800/221–2000), **United** (☎ 800/241–6522), and **US Airways** (☎ 800/428–4322). A taxi to Fort Myers, Sanibel, or Captiva costs about $30; it's about twice that to Naples. Other transportation companies include **Aristocrat Super Mini-Van Service** (☎ 941/275–7228), **Personal Touch Limousines** (☎ 941/549–3643), and **Sanibel Island Limousine** (☎ 941/472–8888).

The **Naples Airport** (☎ 941/643–6875), a small facility east of downtown, is served by **American Eagle** (☎ 800/433–7300), **Comair** (☎ 800/282–3424), and **US Airways Express** (☎ 800/428–4322). Shuttle service to Naples is generally $15 to $25 per person. Once you have arrived, call **Naples Taxi** (☎ 941/643–2148) or, for Marco Island, try **Marco Transportation, Inc.** (☎ 941/394–2257).

Getting Around

By Bus
The **Lee County Transit System** (☎ 941/939–1303) serves most of the county.

By Car
I–75 and U.S. 41 run the length of the region. U.S. 41, also known as the Tamiami Trail, goes through downtown Fort Myers and Naples and is also called Cleveland Avenue in the former and 9th Street in the latter. McGregor Boulevard (Route 867), Fort Myers's main road, heads southwest toward Sanibel-Captiva. San Carlos Boulevard runs southwest from McGregor Boulevard to Fort Myers Beach, and Pine Island–Bayshore Road (Route 78) leads from North Fort Myers through northern Cape Coral onto Pine Island.

Contacts and Resources

Emergencies
Dial **911** for police or ambulance.

HOSPITALS
The following hospitals have 24-hour emergency rooms: **Lee Memorial Hospital** (⊠ 2776 Cleveland Ave., Fort Myers), **Naples Community Hospital** (⊠ 350 7th St. N, Naples), and **North Collier Hospital** (⊠ 1501 Imokolee Rd., Naples).

LATE-NIGHT PHARMACIES
Walgreen (⊠ 70703 College Pkwy., Fort Myers, ☎ 941/939–2142; ⊠ 8965 Tamiami Trail, North Naples, ☎ 941/597–8196).

Guided Tours

AIR TOURS
Boca Grande Seaplane Service (⊠ 4th and Bayou Sts., Boca Grande, ☎ 941/964–0234) operates sightseeing tours in the Charlotte Harbor area. **Classic Flight** (☎ 941/939–7411) flies an open cockpit biplane for sightseeing tours of the Fort Myers area, leaving from the Fort Myers Jet Center (⊠ 501 Danley Rd.).

BOAT TOURS
Adventure Sailing Charters (☎ 941/472–7532) offers captained, half- and full-day sailing cruises and sunset cruises for groups of six or fewer. Boats leave from South Seas Plantation on Captiva. **Estero Bay Boat Tours** (☎ 941/992–2200) takes you on guided tours of waterways once inhabited by the Calusa Indians. You'll see birds and other wildlife and may even spot some manatees or dolphins. **Everglades Jungle Cruises** (☎ 941/334–7474) explores the Caloosahatchee and Or-

ange rivers of Lee County. From mid-November through mid-April, there are a variety of cruises along the Caloosahatchee River conducted on the *Capt. J. P.,* a stern paddle wheeler, and there is a manatee-watching cruise on a smaller boat. Brunch, lunch, and dinner cruises are available, departing from the Fort Myers Yacht Basin.

Island Rover (☎ 941/765–7447), a 72-foot schooner that leaves from Gulf Star Marina in Fort Myers Beach, takes morning, afternoon, and sunset sails in the Gulf of Mexico. In Fort Myers Beach, **Jammin' Sailboat Cruises** (☎ 941/463–3520) offers 2½-hour champagne cruises and four-hour shrimp and seafood cruises on a 30-foot sailboat. Call for reservations. **King Fisher Cruise Lines** (☎ 941/639–0969) has half-day, full-day, Sunday brunch, and sunset cruises in Charlotte Harbor, the Peace River, and the Intracoastal Waterway. Boats depart from Fishermen's Village, Punta Gorda. **Tarpon Bay Recreation Center** (☎ 941/472–8900) operates guided canoe tours through the J. N. "Ding" Darling Wildlife Refuge's mangroves.

TROLLEY TOUR

Naples Trolley Tours (☎ 941/262–7300) has five narrated tours daily, covering more than 100 points of interest. The tour ($9) lasts about 1¾ hours, but you can get off and reboard at no extra cost.

Visitor Information
The following are open weekdays 9–5: **Charlotte County Chamber of Commerce** (✉ 2702 Tamiami Trail, Port Charlotte 33950, ☎ 941/627–2222), **Lee County Visitor and Convention Bureau** (✉ 2180 W. 1st St., Fort Myers 33901, ☎ 941/338–3500 or 800/533–4753), **Naples Area Chamber of Commerce** (✉ 3620 N. Tamiami Trail, Naples 33940, ☎ 941/262–6141), and **Sanibel-Captiva Chamber of Commerce** (✉ Causeway Rd., Sanibel 33957, ☎ 941/472–1080).

11 The Panhandle

With its magnolias, live oaks, and loblolly pines, northwest Florida has more in common with the Deep South than with the Florida of the Everglades. Even the high season is different: Things in the Panhandle are just gearing up by May, as activities are winding down south of Tampa. Like the rest of the state, however, fabulous beaches are a Panhandle staple.

Updated by
Ann Hughes

FLORIDA'S LONG, GREEN, NORTHWEST CORNER snuggles up between the Gulf of Mexico and the Alabama and Georgia state lines. Known as the Panhandle, some call it "the other Florida," since instead of palm trees, what thrives here are the magnolias, live oaks, and loblolly pines common in the rest of the Deep South. As South Florida's season is winding down in May, action in the northwest is just picking up. The area is even in a different time zone: the Apalachicola River marks the dividing line between eastern and central times.

Others call this section of the state "Florida's best-kept secret." Until World War II, when activity at the Panhandle air bases took off, it really was. But by the mid-1950s, the 100-mi stretch along the coast between Pensacola and Panama City was dubbed the "Miracle Strip" because of a dramatic rise in property values. In the 1940s this beachfront land sold for less than $100 an acre; today that same acre can yield tens of thousands of dollars. Still, the movers and shakers of the area felt this sobriquet fell short. So to convey the richness of the region, with its white sands and sparkling green waters, swamps, bayous, and flora, they coined the phrase "Emerald Coast."

It's a land of superlatives: It has the biggest military installation in the Western Hemisphere (Eglin Air Force Base), arguably the oldest city in the state (Pensacola, claiming a founding date of 1559), and the most productive fishing waters in the world (off Destin). It has resorts that out-glitz the Gold Coast's, campgrounds where possums invite themselves to lunch, and every kind of lodging in between. Students of the past can wander the many historic districts or visit archaeological digs. For sports enthusiasts, there's a different golf course or tennis court for each day of the week, and for nature lovers, there's a world of hunting, canoeing, biking, and hiking. And anything that happens on water happens here: surfing, scuba diving, and plenty of fishing, both from a deep-sea charter boat and the end of a pier.

Pleasures and Pastimes

Beaches
Thanks to restrictions against commercial development imposed by Eglin Air Force Base (AFB) and the Gulf Islands National Seashore, the Emerald Coast has been able to maintain several hundred miles of unspoiled beaches. A 1996 study by the University of Maryland's Laboratory for Coastal Research named Perdido Key State Recreation Area, St. Joseph Peninsula State Park, and St. George Island State Park among the top 20 beaches in the United States.

Biking
Some of the nation's best bike paths run through northwest Florida's woods and dunelands, particularly on Santa Rosa Island, where you can pedal for almost 20 mi and never lose sight of the water. Eglin AFB Reservation presents cyclists with tortuous, wooded trails.

Canoeing
Both beginners and veterans get a kick out of canoeing the area's abundant waterways. The shoals and rapids of the Blackwater River in the Blackwater River State Forest, 40 mi northeast of Pensacola, challenge even seasoned canoeists, while the gentler currents of sheltered marshes and inlets are less intimidating.

Dining

Because the gulf is only an hour's drive from any spot in the Panhandle, restaurants from modest diners to elegant cafés feature seafood, most served the same day it is hauled out of the water. Native fish such as grouper, red snapper, amberjack, catfish, and mullet are the regional staples. Prices are generally reasonable, but if you visit during the off-season, watch for dining discounts, such as two-for-one meal deals and early-bird specials.

Fishing

Options range from fishing for pompano, snapper, marlin, and grouper in the saltwater of the gulf to angling for bass, catfish, and bluegill in freshwater. Deep-sea fishing is immensely popular on the Emerald Coast, so there are boat charters aplenty. A day costs about $575, a half day about $300.

Lodging

For the most part, you won't have to worry about far-in-advance reservations in this part of the state; most accommodations accept walk-ins. To be on the safe side, though, you can reserve a spot through a property management service. Note that summer is high season for this part of Florida and you can expect to pay a premium for rooms then; winters are chilly—if you want to get warm, you need to head south.

Scuba Diving and Snorkeling

In the Panama City Beach area, you can investigate the wreckage of sunken tanker ships, tugboats, and cargo vessels. For snorkelers and beginning divers, the jetties of St. Andrews State Recreation Area, where there is no boat traffic, are safe.

Exploring the Panhandle

There are sights to see in the Panhandle, but sightseeing is not the principal activity here. The area is better known for its ample opportunities for such sports as fishing and diving and for just plain relaxation.

Pensacola, with its antebellum homes and historic landmarks, is a good place to start your trek through northwest Florida. After exploring the museums and preservation districts, head east on U.S. 98. Don't overlook the deserted beaches along the Gulf of Mexico, where the sugar-white quartz-crystal sand crunches underfoot like snow on a sub-zero night. Farther east are Fort Walton Beach, the Emerald Coast's largest city; neighboring Destin, where sportfishing is king; and the twin cities of Valparaiso and Niceville. An interesting side trip along Route 20— a road that twists along Choctawhatchee Bay past bait shacks and catfish restaurants—allows an up-close look at the other Florida.

The next resort center along the coast is Panama City Beach, while to the far southeast is Apalachicola, an important oyster-fishing town. Inland, a number of interesting towns and state parks lie along I–10 on the long eastward drive to the state capital, Tallahassee.

Numbers in the text correspond to numbers in the margin and on the Panhandle map.

Great Itineraries

IF YOU HAVE 3 DAYS

History and nature are the two biggest calling cards of this part of the Sunshine State. Visit ⚐ **Fort Walton Beach** ③ or Eglin Air Force Base, depending on whether your heart lies on the seas or in the skies. Kids might enjoy a stop at the Indian Temple Mound Museum. On day two drive to the capital, ⚐ **Tallahassee** ⑭, and soak up some of Florida's past. On day three you can make a trip to nearby Wakulla Springs State Park ⑯, where you'll find one of the world's deepest springs.

IF YOU HAVE 5 DAYS

Start with a visit to the Palafox Historic District in ⛅ **Pensacola** ① and spend the day enjoying a glimpse of Old Florida, as well as visiting the National Museum of Naval Aviation. Next move on to ⛅ **Fort Walton Beach** ③, and stop by Eglin Air Force Base and the antebellum mansion at the Eden State Gardens, set amid moss-draped live oaks. Be sure to spend an afternoon at the Grayton Beach State Recreation Area, one of the most scenic spots along the Gulf Coast. Moving inland, go spelunking at the Florida Caverns State Park ⑬ before heading to ⛅ **Tallahassee** ⑭. From there you can make day trips to Wakulla Springs State Park ⑯ and St. Marks Wildlife Refuge and Lighthouse ⑰, where you can hike, swim, or have a leisurely picnic.

IF YOU HAVE 7 DAYS

From a base in ⛅ **Pensacola** ①, take a couple of side trips: to the Gulf Islands National Seashore, paying special attention to Fort Pickens, and to the Zoo in Gulf Breeze. Swing north to Milton, do the walking tour of its historic downtown, and then spend two days taking an Adventures Unlimited canoe trip on the Blackwater River and roughing it in an outdoor cabin. Proceed to ⛅ **DeFuniak Springs** ⑪, where must-sees are the quaint Walton DeFuniak Public Library and the Chautauqua Winery. Head south to ⛅ **Destin** ④ for a day of deep-sea fishing or a shopping spree at Silver Sands. Wind up your expedition through the other Florida at the beaches and amusement parks of ⛅ **Panama City Beach** ⑦, via an afternoon's stopover at the legendary planned community of Seaside ⑥.

AROUND PENSACOLA BAY

In the years since its founding, Pensacola has come under the control of five nations, earning this fine, old Southern city its nickname, "the City of Five Flags." Spanish conquistadors, under the command of Don Tristan de Luna, landed on the shores of Pensacola Bay in 1559, but discouraged by a succession of destructive tropical storms and dissension in the ranks, De Luna abandoned the settlement two years after its founding. In 1698, the Spanish once again established a fort at the site, and during the early 18th century, control jockeyed back and forth between the Spanish, the French, and the British. Finally, in 1819, Pensacola passed into U.S. hands, though during the Civil War, it was governed by the Confederate States of America and flew yet another flag.

The city itself has many historic sights, while across the bay lies Santa Rosa Island, where pristine coastline provides a delightful setting for beaching and other recreational activities.

Pensacola

❶ *59 mi east of Mobile, Alabama.*

Historic Pensacola consists of three distinct districts—Seville, Palafox, and North Hill—though they are easy to explore as a unit. Stroll down streets mapped out by the British and renamed by the Spanish, such as Cervantes, Palafox, Intendencia, and Tarragona. Be warned, though, that it is best to stick to the beaten path; Pensacola is a port town and can get rough around the edges, especially at night.

The best way to orient yourself is to stop at the **Pensacola Visitor Information Center** (⊠ 1401 E. Gregory St., ☎ 904/434–1234), located

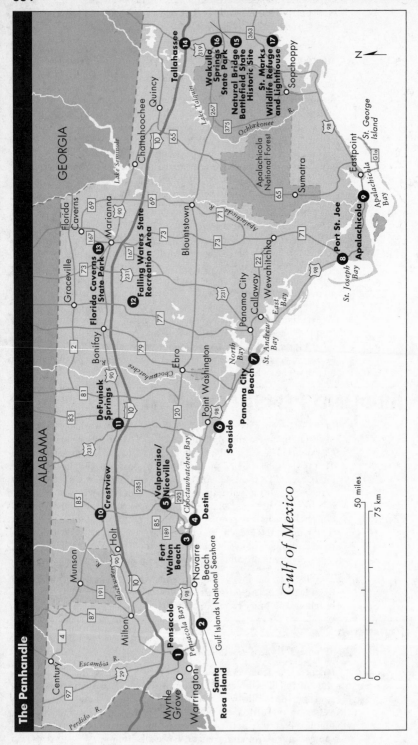

The Panhandle

GEORGIA

ALABAMA

Gulf of Mexico

Century

Myrtle Grove

Warrington

Santa Rosa Island

Pensacola

Pensacola Bay

Escambia R.

Perdido R.

Milton

Munson

Holt

Gulf Islands National Seashore

Navarre Beach

Fort Walton Beach

Destin

Crestview

Valparaiso/Niceville

Choctawhatchee Bay

Choctawhatchee R.

DeFuniak Springs

Bonifay

Graceville

Florida Caverns State Park

Falling Waters State Recreation Area

Marianna

Florida Caverns

Quincy

Chattahoochee

Lake Seminole

Lake Talquin

Tallahassee

Wakulla Springs State Park

Natural Bridge Battlefield State Historic Site

St. Marks Wildlife Refuge and Lighthouse

Sopchoppy

Ochlokonee R.

Apalachicola National Forest

Sumatra

Blountstown

Apalachicola R.

Ebro

Point Washington

Seaside

Panama City Beach

Panama City

Callaway

Wewahitchka

St. Andrew Bay

North Bay

East Bay

Port St. Joe

St. Joseph Bay

Apalachicola

Apalachicola Bay

Eastpoint

St. George Island

St. George Island

Lake Talquin

50 miles

75 km

Gulf of Mexico

at the foot of the Pensacola Bay Bridge. Here you can pick up maps of the self-guided historic district tours.

The **Seville** historic district is the site of Pensacola's first permanent Spanish colonial settlement. Its center is Seville Square, a live oak–shaded park bounded by Alcaniz, Adams, Zaragoza, and Government streets. Roam these brick streets past honeymoon cottages and bay-front homes. Many of the buildings have been converted into restaurants, commercial offices, and shops.

Palafox Street is the main stem of the **Palafox Historic District,** which was the commercial and government hub of old Pensacola. Note the Spanish Renaissance–style **Saenger Theater,** Pensacola's old movie palace, and the **Bear Block,** a former wholesale grocery with wrought-iron balconies that are a legacy from Pensacola's Creole past. On Palafox between Government and Zaragoza streets is a **statue of Andrew Jackson** that commemorates the formal transfer of Florida from Spain to the United States in 1821.

Pensacola's affluent families, many made rich in the turn-of-the-century timber boom, built their homes in the **North Hill Preservation District,** where British and Spanish fortresses once stood. Residents still occasionally unearth cannonballs in their gardens. North Hill occupies 50 blocks with over 500 homes in Queen Anne, neoclassical, Tudor revival, and Mediterranean styles. Take a drive through this community, but remember these are private residences. Places of general interest include the 1902 Spanish mission–style **Christ Episcopal Church; Lee Square,** where a 50-foot obelisk stands as a tribute to the Confederacy; and **Fort George,** an undeveloped parcel at the site of the largest of three forts built by the British in 1778.

More than a half dozen historical museums and buildings are clustered together in the **Historic Pensacola Village.** The Museum of Industry, housed in a late-19th-century warehouse, hosts permanent exhibits dedicated to the lumber, maritime, and shipping industries—once mainstays of Pensacola's economy. A reproduction of a 19th-century streetscape is displayed in the **Museum of Commerce,** and the city's historical archives are kept in the **Pensacola Historical Museum—** what was once one of Florida's oldest churches. Also in the village are the **Julee Cottage Museum of Black History, Dorr House, Lavalle House,** and **Quina House.** ⊠ *Zaragoza and Tarragona Sts.,* ☎ *904/444–8905.* 🎫 *Free.* ☉ *Mon.–Sat. 10–4.*

In the days of the horse-drawn paddy wagon, the two-story mission revival building housing the **Pensacola Museum of Art** served as the city jail. Now it offers international fine art, rotating its two exhibits about every six weeks. ⊠ *407 S. Jefferson St.,* ☎ *904/432–5682.* 🎫 *$2, free Tues.* ☉ *Tues.–Fri. 10–5, Sat. 10–4, Sun. 1–4.*

Pensacola's old City Hall, built in 1908, has been refurbished and reopened as the **T. T. Wentworth, Jr. Florida State Museum,** where some 150,000 artifacts ranging from Civil War weaponry to bottle caps are on display. ⊠ *330 S. Jefferson St.,* ☎ *904/444–8905.* 🎫 *$6.* ☉ *Mon.–Sat. 10–4.*

The **Pensacola Naval Air Station,** established in 1914, is the nation's oldest such facility. On display in its **National Museum of Naval Aviation** (☎ *904/452–3604*) are more than 100 aircraft that played an important role in aviation history. Among them are the NC-4, which in 1919 became the first plane to cross the Atlantic; the famous World War II fighter, the F6 *Hellcat*; and the *Skylab Command Module.* A recent attraction is a 14-seat flight simulator. ⊠ *1750 Radford Blvd., ☎ 904/452–2311. ☞ Free. ☉ Daily 9–5.*

Dating from the Civil War, **Fort Barrancas** now has picnic areas and a ½-mi woodland nature trail on its grounds. The fort is part of the Gulf Islands National Seashore, maintained by the National Park Service. ⊠ *Navy Blvd., ☎ 904/455–5167. ☞ Free. ☉ Dec.–Jan., Wed.–Sun. 10:30–4; Feb.–Nov., daily 9:30–5.*

OFF THE
BEATEN PATH

THE ZOO – The local zoo is home to plants, animals, and 30 acres of ponds, lakes, and open plains. ⊠ *5701 Gulf Breeze Pkwy., Gulf Breeze, ☎ 904/932–2229. ☞ $9.25. ☉ Daily 9–5.*

Beach

Johnson Beach, on Perdido Key, is about 20 mi southwest of Pensacola's historic districts.

Dining and Lodging

$$ ✕ **Jamie's.** Dining here is like spending the evening in the antiques-
★   filled parlor of a fine old Southern home. If a visit to Florida has you oystered and shrimped out, the chef recommends the roasted pork loin with apples, sun-dried tomatoes, and pine nuts. The wine list has more than 200 labels. ⊠ *424 E. Zaragoza St., ☎ 904/434–2911. AE, D, MC, V. Closed Sun. No lunch Mon.*

$ ✕ **McGuire's Irish Pub.** Drink beer brewed right on the premises in copper and oaken casks, and eat your corned beef and cabbage while an Irish tenor croons in the background. Located in an old firehouse, the pub is replete with antiques, moose heads, Tiffany lamps, and Erin-go-bragh memorabilia. More than 100,000 dollar bills signed and dated by the pub's patrons flutter from the ceiling. The waitresses are chatty and aim to please. Menu items run from kosher-style sandwiches to chili con carne to pecan pie. ⊠ *600 E. Gregory St., ☎ 904/433–6789. AE, D, DC, MC, V.*

$ ✕ **Mesquite Charlie's.** Stop by for the best gol' darn steaks east (or west) of the Mississippi. You can watch 'em broil over mesquite charcoal in a pit just inside the door. Got a hankerin' for sumpin' else? Try baby-back ribs barbecued with a tangy house sauce. No neckties allowed— "We cut 'em off." ⊠ *5901 N. W St., ☎ 904/434–0498. AE, D, MC, V. No lunch.*

$$$–$$$$ ⌂ **Pensacola Grand Hotel.** The lobby will instantly tell you that this hotel is actually the renovated Louisville & Nashville train depot. Ticket and baggage counters are still intact, and old railroad signs remind guests of the days when steam locomotives chugged up to these doors. The old train station connects with a 15-story tower via a canopied two-story galleria. Here's where the spittoons and hand trucks give way to upholstered furniture and deep-pile carpet; standard doubles are up-to-date and roomy. Bi-level penthouse suites have snazzy wet bars and whirlpool baths. ⊠ *200 E. Gregory St., 32501, ☎ 904/433–3336, ℻ 904/432–7572. 212 rooms. Restaurant, lounge, pool, airport shuttle. AE, D, DC, MC, V.*

$$$–$$$$ ⌂ **Perdido Sun.** This high-rise is the perfect expression of gulf-side resort living. One-, two-, and three-bedroom decorator-furnished units all have seaside balconies with spectacular water views. You can choose to make this your home away from home—accommodations include fully equipped kitchens—or you can pamper yourself with daily maid service. ⊠ *13753 Perdido Key Dr., 32507, ☎ 904/492–2390 or 800/227–2390, ℻ 904/492–4135. 93 units. Indoor pool, outdoor pool, spa, health club. AE, D, MC, V.*

$$ ★ 🏨 **New World Inn.** This is Pensacola's hush-hush hotel, the one where celebrities are likely to stay. Photos of dozens of famous guests (Lucille Ball, Shirley Jones, Charles Kuralt) hang behind the front desk. Exquisite furnishings take their inspiration from the five periods of Pensacola's past: French or Spanish provincial, early American, antebellum, or Queen Anne. Baths are handsomely appointed. ⊠ *600 S. Palafox St., 32501,* ☎ *904/432–4111,* FAX *904/432–8939. 15 rooms, 1 suite. Restaurant, lounge. AE, DC, MC, V.*

$–$$ 🏨 **Ramada Inn North.** Near the airport, this is a good bet if you've got an early flight. Suites have game tables and entertainment centers; some have whirlpools. ⊠ *6550 Pensacola Blvd., 32505,* ☎ *904/477–0711 or 800/272–6232,* FAX *904/477–0711, Ext. 611. 106 rooms. Restaurant, lounge, pool, airport shuttle. AE, D, DC, MC, V.*

Nightlife and the Arts

THE ARTS

Productions at the **Saenger Theatre** (⊠ 118 S. Palafox St., ☎ 904/433–6737) include touring Broadway shows and three locally staged operas a year. The **Pensacola Little Theatre** (⊠ 400 S. Jefferson St., ☎ 904/432–2042) presents plays and musicals during a fall–spring season. **Pensacola's Symphony Orchestra** (☎ 904/435–2533) offers five concerts each season at the Saenger Theatre.

NIGHTLIFE

After dark, **McGuire's Irish Pub** (⊠ 600 E. Gregory St., ☎ 904/433–6789) particularly welcomes those of Irish descent. If you don't like crowds, stay away from McGuire's on Friday night and nights when Notre Dame games are televised. **Mesquite Charlie's** (⊠ 5901 N. W St., ☎ 905/434–0498) offers country music and all the trappings of a Wild West saloon. The **Seville Quarter** (⊠ 130 E. Government St., ☎ 904/434—6211) has seven fabulous bars and features music from disco to Dixieland; it's Pensacola's equivalent of the New Orleans French Quarter.

Outdoor Activities and Sports

AUTO RACING

Billed as the fastest ½-mi track in the country, **Five Flags Speedway** features action-packed racing with top-name stock-car drivers. ⊠ *7451 Pine Forest Rd.,* ☎ *904/944–0466.* 🎟 *$8.* ☉ *Racing late Mar.–Sept., Sat. 8.*

CANOEING

Canoe rentals for the versatile Blackwater River are available from **Blackwater Canoe Rental** (⊠ U.S. 90E, Milton, ☎ 904/623–0235). **Adventures Unlimited** (⊠ Rte. 87, 12 mi north of Milton, ☎ 904/623–6197) provides a variety of light watercraft as well as camping accommodations.

DOG RACING

Rain or shine, year-round, there's live racing at the **Pensacola Greyhound Track.** Lounge and grandstand areas are fully enclosed and air-conditioned and have instant-replay televisions throughout. ⊠ *951 Dog Track Rd., West Pensacola,* ☎ *904/455–8595 or 800/345–3997.* 🎟 *$1, kennel club $2.50.* ☉ *Racing: Tues., Wed., and Fri–Sat. 7, also weekends 1.*

FISHING

Fishing tackle is available at **Penny's Sporting Goods** (⊠ 1800 Pace Blvd., ☎ 904/438–9633). In a pinch, you can drop a line from **Old Pensacola Bay Bridge.**

GOLF

There are several outstanding golf courses in and around Pensacola. The **Perdido Bay Resort** (⊠ 1 Doug Ford Dr., ☎ 904/492–1223) has an 18-hole course. **Tiger Point Golf & Country Club** (⊠ 1255 Country Club Rd., Gulf Breeze, ☎ 904/932–1333) has 36 holes.

TENNIS

Tennis courts are available in more than 30 locations in the Pensacola area; among them is the **Pensacola Racquet Club** (⊠ 3450 Wimbledon Dr., ☎ 904/434–2434).

Shopping

Cordova Mall (⊠ 5100 N. 9th Ave.) is anchored by four department stores, plus specialty shops and a food court. **Harbourtown Shopping Village** (⊠ 913 Gulf Breeze Pkwy., Gulf Breeze) has trendy shops and the ambience of a wharf-side New England village.

Santa Rosa Island

❷ *5 mi south of Pensacola via U.S. 98 to the Rte. 399 (Bob Sikes) Bridge.*

The site of beaches, natural areas, and the town of Pensacola Beach, this barrier island draws visitors for more than seascapes and water sports. It's also a must for cyclists and bird-watchers. Since 1971 more than 280 species of birds, from the common loon to the majestic osprey, have been spotted here. Two caveats for visitors: "Leave nothing behind but your footprints," and "Don't pick the sea oats" (natural grasses that help keep the dunes intact).

Dotting the 150-mi stretch between Destin and Gulfport, Mississippi, is **Gulf Islands National Seashore** (☎ 904/934–2600), managed by the National Park Service. A number of the beach and recreational spots along this beautiful stretch of island coast are part of the national seashore. Check with the park service for any restrictions that might apply.

The most famous resident of **Fort Pickens** was imprisoned Apache chief Geronimo, who was reportedly fairly well liked by his captors. Located at the western tip of Santa Rosa Island (now part of the Gulf Islands National Seashore), Fort Pickens has a museum, nature exhibits, aquariums, and a large campground. ⊠ *Ranger station at Ft. Pickens Rd.,* ☎ *904/934–2635.* ☑ *$4 per car.* ☉ *Daily 8:30–sunset.*

Beaches

Areas within the Gulf Islands National Seashore that have good beaches include **Fort Pickens,** at the west end of Santa Rosa Island. The **Santa Rosa Day Use Area**, 10 mi east of Pensacola Beach, is yet another part of the national seashore.

At **Pensacola Beach** (☎ 904/932–2258), 5 mi south of Pensacola, beachcombers and sunbathers, sailboarders and sailors keep things going at a fever pitch in and out of the water.

Lodging

$$–$$$ 🏨 **Holiday Inn/Pensacola Beach.** Renovated throughout in 1996, this hotel has a new lobby furnished with white wicker and accented with beiges and greens. Outside, there's 1,500 feet of private beach. From the ninth-floor Penthouse Lounge, you can watch the goings-on in the gulf, which is especially nice when the setting sun turns the western sky to lavender and orange. ⊠ *165 Ft. Pickens Rd., Pensacola Beach 32561,* ☎ *904/932–5361 or 800/465–4329,* FAX *904/932–7121. 150 rooms. Lounge, pool, tennis courts, beach. AE, D, DC, MC, V.*

Outdoor Activities and Sports

BIKING

To take advantage of the island's great cycling, rent a bike from **Dinah's Shore Shop** (⊠ 715 Pensacola Beach Blvd., Pensacola Beach, ☎ 904/934–0014).

FISHING

Dinah's Shore Shop (⊠ 715 Pensacola Beach Blvd., Pensacola Beach, ☎ 904/934–0014) is a one-stop shop for fishing tackle. For a full- or half-day deep-sea charter, try the **Moorings Marina** (⊠ 655 Pensacola Beach Blvd., Pensacola Beach, ☎ 904/932–0305).

GOLF

The **Club at Hidden Creek** (⊠ 3070 PGA Blvd., Navarre, ☎ 904/939–4604) has 18 holes.

WATER SPORTS

When you rent a sailboat, Jet Ski, or catamaran from **Bonifay Water Sports** (⊠ 460 Pensacola Beach Blvd., Pensacola Beach, ☎ 904/932–0633), you'll also receive safety and sailing instructions.

CHOCTAWHATCHEE BAY

There's a handful of interesting towns around the western end of Choctawhatchee Bay, two of which have had sudden growth spurts, and two of which are on the brink of expansion. Fort Walton Beach got its jump start during World War II; now greater Fort Walton Beach has more than 78,000 residents, making it the largest urban area on the Emerald Coast. Destin, on the southern side of the strait that connects Choctawhatchee Bay to the Gulf of Mexico, boomed in the 1930s, when its rich fishing waters were recognized. The twin cities of Valparaiso and Niceville are still relatively tranquil but have become more popular with tourists since the opening of the Mid-Bay Bridge, which links the cities with beaches across the bay.

Fort Walton Beach

❸ *46 mi east of Pensacola.*

This coastal town dates from the Civil War but had to wait more than 75 years to come into its own. Patriots loyal to the Confederate cause organized Walton's Guard (named in honor of Colonel George Walton, onetime acting territorial governor of West Florida) and camped at a site on Santa Rosa Sound, later known as Camp Walton. In 1940 fewer than 90 people lived in Fort Walton Beach, but within a decade the city became a boomtown, thanks to New Deal money for roads and bridges and the development of Eglin Field during World War II. The military is now Fort Walton Beach's main source of income, but tourism runs a close second.

Encompassing 728 sq mi of land, **Eglin Air Force Base** (⊠ Rte. 85, ☎ 904/882–3931) includes 10 auxiliary fields and a total of 21 runways. Jimmie Doolittle's Tokyo Raiders trained here, as did the Son Tay Raiders, a group that made a daring attempt to rescue American POWs from a North Vietnamese prison camp in 1970.

★ The collection at the **Air Force Armament Museum,** just outside the Eglin Air Force Base's main gate, contains more than 5,000 Air Force armaments from World Wars I and II and the Korean and Vietnam wars. Included are uniforms, engines, weapons, aircraft, and flight simulators; larger craft such as transport planes are exhibited on the grounds outside. A 32-minute movie about Eglin's history and its role in the development of armaments plays continuously. ⊠ *Rte. 85, Eglin Air Force Base,* ☎ *904/882–4062.* ▣ *Free.* ⊙ *Daily 9:30–4:30.*

🐥 Kids especially enjoy the **Indian Temple Mound Museum,** where they can learn all about the prehistoric peoples who inhabited northwest Florida up to 10,000 years ago. The funerary masks and weaponry on display are particularly fascinating. The museum is adjacent to the 600-year-old **National Historic Landmark Temple Mound,** a large earthwork built over saltwater. ⊠ *139 Miracle Strip Pkwy. (U.S. 98),* ☎ *904/833–9595.* ▣ *$2.* ⊙ *Sept.–May, weekdays 11–4, Sat. 9–4; June–Aug., Mon.–Sat. 9–4.*

When the weather drives you off the beach, the **Gulfarium** is a great place to spend your time. Its main attraction is its Living Sea, a 60,000-gallon tank that simulates conditions on the ocean floor. It also features performances by trained porpoises, sea-lion shows, and marine-life exhibits. Don't overlook the extensive gift shop, where you can buy anything from conch shells to beach toys. ⊠ *U.S. 98E,* ☎ *904/244–5169.* ▣ *$12.* ⊙ *May–Sept. daily 9–6; Oct.–Apr. daily 9–4.*

Beaches

John C. Beasley State Park (no phone) is Fort Walton Beach's seaside playground on Okaloosa Island. A boardwalk leads to the beach, where you'll find covered picnic tables, changing rooms, and freshwater showers. Lifeguards are on duty in summer. **Eglin Reservation Beach** (no phone) is on 5 mi of undeveloped military land, about 3 mi west of the Brooks Bridge. This beach is a favorite haunt of local teenagers.

Dining and Lodging

$$ ✕ **Staff's.** Sip a Tropical Depression or a rum-laced Squall Line while you peruse a menu tucked into the centerfold of a tabloid-size newspaper filled with snippets of local history, early photographs, and family memorabilia. Since 1931, people have been coming to this garage-turned-eatery for steaks broiled as you like them and seafood dishes like freshly caught Florida lobster and char-grilled amberjack. The grand finale is a trip to the delectable dessert bar; try a generous wedge of cherry cheesecake. ⊠ *24 S.E. Miracle Strip Pkwy.,* ☎ *904/243–3482. AE, D, MC, V. No lunch.*

$ ✕ **Pandora's.** On the Emerald Coast the name Pandora's is synony-
★ mous with prime rib. On the outside, this waterfront restaurant appears gray and weather-beaten, but inside it's decorated in warm, cozy earth tones and filled with alcoves and tables for four that lend an air of intimacy. You can order your prime rib regular or extra cut; fish aficionados should try the char-grilled yellowfin tuna, bacon-wrapped and topped with Jamaican sauce. The mood turns a bit more gregarious in the lounge, where there is live entertainment several evenings a week. ⊠ *1120 Santa Rosa Blvd.,* ☎ *904/244–8669. AE, D, DC, MC, V. No lunch.*

$$–$$$ ⊡ **Holiday Inn.** This U-shape hotel consists of a seven-story tower flanked by three-story wings. Rooms have a pastel green-and-peach decor and face either gulf or pool, though even poolside rooms have some sea view. ⊠ *1110 Santa Rosa Blvd., 32548,* ☎ *904/243–9181 or 800/732–4853,* 𝖥𝖠𝖷 *904/664–7652. 380 rooms. Restaurant, lounge, 3 pools, tennis courts, beach. AE, D, DC, MC, V.*

$$–$$$ ⊡ **Ramada Plaza Beach Resort.** Activity centers on a pool with a grotto and swim-through waterfall; there's also an 800-foot private beach. ⊠ *U.S. 98E, 32548,* ☎ *904/243–9161, 800/874–8962, or 800/447–0010,* 𝖥𝖠𝖷 *904/243–2391. 335 rooms. 3 restaurants, 2 lounges, 3 pools, exercise room, beach. AE, D, DC, MC, V.*

Nightlife and the Arts

THE ARTS

The **Okaloosa Symphony Orchestra** (☎ 904/244–3308) performs a series of concerts featuring guest artists at the Fort Walton Beach Civic Auditorium (⌧ U.S. 98W). **Stage Crafters Community Theatre** (⌧ U.S. 98W, ☎ 904/243–1102) stages five first-rate amateur productions a year at the Fort Walton Beach Civic Auditorium. The **Northwest Florida Ballet** (⌧ 101 S.E. Chicago Ave., ☎ 904/664–7787) has a repertoire of the classics and performs throughout the Panhandle.

NIGHTLIFE

Catch the action at **Cash's Faux Pas Lounge** (⌧ 106 Santa Rosa Blvd., ☎ 904/244–2274), where anything goes.

Outdoor Activities and Sports

BIKING

Eglin Air Force Base Reservation has plenty of challenging, twisting, wooded trails. Biking here requires a $3 permit, which can be obtained from the **Jackson Guard** (⌧ 107 Rte. 85N, Niceville, ☎ 904/882–4164). Rentals are available from **Bob's Bicycle Center** (⌧ 415 Mary Esther Cutoff, ☎ 904/243–5856).

FISHING

Get outfitted with a license and tackle at **Stewart's Outdoor Sports** (⌧ 4 S.E. Eglin Pkwy., ☎ 904/243–9443).

GOLF

Island Golf Center (⌧ 1306 Miracle Strip Pkwy., ☎ 904/244–1612) has 36 holes of miniature golf, a nine-hole par-3 course, and video games. The **Fort Walton Beach Municipal Golf Course** (⌧ Rte. 189, ☎ 904/833–9529), which has 36 holes, is rated as one of Florida's best public layouts. **Shalimar Pointe Golf & Country Club** (⌧ 302 Country Club Dr., Shalimar, ☎ 904/651–1416) has 18 holes.

SCUBA DIVING

You can arrange for diving lessons or excursions at the **Scuba Shop** (⌧ 348 Miracle Strip Pkwy., ☎ 904/243–1600).

TENNIS

You can play tennis on seven Rubico and two hard courts at the **Fort Walton Racquet Club** (⌧ 23 Hurlburt Field Rd., ☎ 904/862–2023). The **Municipal Tennis Center** (⌧ 45 W. Audrey Dr., ☎ 904/243–8789) has 12 lighted Laykold courts and four practice walls.

WATER SPORTS

Pontoon-boat rentals are available at **Consigned RV's** (⌧ 101 W. Miracle Strip Pkwy., ☎ 904/243–4488).

Shopping

Stores in the **Manufacturer's Outlet Center** (⌧ 127 and 255 Miracle Strip Pkwy.) offer well-known brands of clothing and housewares at a substantial discount. There are four department stores in the **Santa Rosa Mall** (⌧ 300 Mary Esther Cutoff, Mary Esther), as well as 118 other shops and 15 bistro-style eateries.

Destin

❹ *8 mi east of Fort Walton Beach.*

Fort Walton Beach's neighbor lies on the other side of the strait that connects Choctawhatchee Bay with the Gulf of Mexico. Destin takes its name from its founder, Leonard A. Destin, a Connecticut sea captain who settled his family here sometime in the 1830s. For the next

100 years, Destin remained a sleepy little fishing village until the strait, or East Pass, was bridged in 1935. Then, recreational anglers discovered its white sands, blue-green waters, and abundance of some of the most sought-after sport fish in the world. More billfish are hauled in around Destin each year than from all other gulf fishing ports combined. But you don't have to be the rod-and-reel type to love Destin. There's plenty to entertain the sand-pail set as well as senior citizens, and there are many gourmet restaurants.

The highlight at the **Destin Fishing Museum** is a dry aquarium, where lighting and sound effects create the sensation of being underwater. You can get the feeling of walking on a sandy bottom broken by coral reef and dotted with sponges. It's a good place for the marine enthusiast to get an overview of aquatic life in the gulf. ⊠ *20009 Emerald Coast Pkwy.,* ☎ *904/654–1011.* ☞ *$1.* ۩ *Weekdays 12:30–5, Sat. 11–2.*

To get an idea of the rampaging growth that's occurred in the Destin area, visit the **Old Destin Post Office Museum.** This tiny facility was a working post office until 1954; its display of old photographs and office machines reflects the fishing-hamlet character of Old Destin. ⊠ *Stahlman Ave.,* ☎ *904/837–8572.* ☞ *Free.* ۩ *Wed. 1:30–4:30 or by special appointment.*

℃ In addition to a seasonal water park, **Big Kahuna's Lost Paradise** has year-round family attractions, including miniature golf, two go-cart tracks, an arcade, a kiddy land with a scaled-down Ferris wheel and merry-go-round, and an amphitheater. ⊠ *U.S. 98E,* ☎ *904/837–4061.* ☞ *Grounds free, water park $24.50, miniature golf $6, go-carts $8.50.* ۩ *Sept.–Apr., daily 10–4:30; May–Aug., daily 10–6.*

Beach
Crystal Beach RV Park (☎ 904/837–6447) has something to appeal to just about everyone. This sanctuary, located just 5 mi east of Destin, is protected on each side by undeveloped state-owned land.

Dining and Lodging
$$ ✕ **Marina Café.** A harbor-view setting, impeccable service, and uptown
★   ambience have earned this establishment a reputation as one of the finest dining experiences on the Emerald Coast. The decor's oceanic motif is expressed in shades of aqua, green, and sand accented with marine tapestries and sea sculptures. Diners have a choice of classic Creole, Italian, or Pacific Rim cuisine. Try a regional specialty, such as the award-winning black pepper–crusted yellowfin tuna with braised spinach and spicy soy sauce. The wine list is extensive. ⊠ *404 U.S. 98E,* ☎ *904/837–7960. AE, D, DC, MC, V. No lunch.*

$ ✕ **Flamingo Café.** This café serves up two different atmospheres. The pink and teal color scheme, carried through to the teal cummerbunds and bow ties on the waiters, creates a tropical ambience the proprietor calls "Floribbean," while the panoramic view of Destin harbor seen from every seat in the house lends an airy, seaside feel. Chef's specialties include a delicious Floribbean grilled swordfish with papaya chutney butter, wilted spinach, black beans, and roasted sweet peppers. ⊠ *414 U.S. 98E,* ☎ *904/837–0961. AE, D, DC, MC, V.*

$ ✕ **Harbor Docks.** An unimposing gray clapboard building in front fans out into a series of dining areas behind, all within the sights and sounds of the fishing boats and jet skis in Destin Harbor. Char-grilled, sautéed, or blackened fish include such regional favorites as snapper, cobia, and triggerfish, fresh from the restaurant's own wholesale market. ⊠ *538 U.S. 98E,* ☎ *904/837–2506. AE, D, DC, MC, V.*

$$–$$$$ 🏨 **Sandestin Beach Resort.** This 2,600-acre resort of villas, cottages,
★ condominiums, and an inn seems to be a town unto itself. All rooms
have a view, either of the gulf, Choctawhatchee Bay, a golf course, la-
goon, or natural wildlife preserve. This resort accommodates an as-
sortment of tastes, from the simple to the extravagant, and offers
special rates September through March. ✉ *9300 U.S. 98W, 32541,* ☎
904/267–8000 or 800/277–0800, FAX *904/267–8222. 175 rooms,
375 villas. 4 restaurants, 11 pools, 3 golf courses, 16 tennis courts, health
club, beach, pro shops. AE, D, DC, MC, V.*

$–$$ 🏨 **Holiday Beach Resort.** You can lounge on sugar-white sands, get to
several golf courses with ease, and walk to some of Destin's amuse-
ment parks. Common areas jazzed up with skylights and greenery are
spacious and eye-pleasing. Standard motel appointments don't vary
much, but prices do, depending on the view. ✉ *U.S. 98E, 32541,* ☎
904/837–6112 or 800/874–0402, FAX *904/837–1523. 230 rooms.
Restaurant, lounge, 2 pools. AE, D, DC, MC, V.*

$–$$ 🏨 **Summer Breeze.** White picket fences and porches or patios outside
each unit make this condominium complex look like a summer place
out of the Gay '90s. One-bedroom suites have full kitchens and sleep
up to six in queen-size beds, sleeper sofas, or bunks. It's halfway between Destin and the Sandestin Beach Resort area, across from a roadside park that gives it a secluded feel. ✉ *2384 Old Hwy. 98, 32541,*
☎ *904/837–4853, 800/874–8914, or 800/336–4853,* FAX *904/837–
5390. 35 units. Pool, hot tub. AE, D, MC, V.*

$–$$ 🏨 **Village Inn of Destin.** Only minutes away from the gulf, this prop-
erty was built in 1983 with families in mind. A variety of amenities,
including entertainment, is provided to occupy each member of the family. Rooms have serviceable dressers and queen- or king-size beds. ✉
215 U.S. 98E, 32541, ☎ *904/837–7413,* FAX *904/654–3394. 100
rooms. Pool. AE, D, DC, MC, V.*

Nightlife

Nightown (✉ 140 Palmetto St., ☎ 904/837–6448) has a dance floor
with laser lights and a New Orleans–style bar with a live band. At **Yesterday's** (✉ 1079 U.S. 98E, ☎ 904/837–1954), you can relive a juke-
box Saturday night with an evening of '60s-style rock 'n' roll.

Outdoor Activities and Sports

FISHING

Among the deep-sea fishing charters in this acclaimed fishing area is
Miller's Charter Services (✉ Off U.S. 98 on docks next to A. J.'s
Restaurant, ☎ 904/837–6059). **East Pass Charters** (✉ East Pass Marina, 288 U.S. 98E, ☎ 904/654–2022) has a deep-sea charter service
for avid sportsmen as well as pontoon rentals for leisurely cruising close
to shore. You can always pier fish from the 3,000-foot-long **Destin Cat-
walk,** along the East Pass Bridge.

GOLF

The **Indian Bayou Golf & Country Club** (✉ Airport Rd., off U.S. 98,
☎ 904/837–6192) offers a 27-hole course. For sheer numbers of
holes, the **Sandestin Beach Resort** (✉ 9300 U.S. 98W, ☎ 904/267–
8211) tops the list with 63. The **Santa Rosa Golf & Beach Club** (✉ Rte.
30A, Santa Rosa Beach, ☎ 904/267–2229) has 18 holes.

SCUBA DIVING

Diving instruction and outings are available through **Aquanaut Scuba
Center, Inc.** (✉ 24 U.S. 98W, ☎ 904/837–0359).

TENNIS

Sandestin Beach Resort (✉ 9300 U.S. 98W, ☎ 904/267–7110), one
of the nation's five-star tennis resorts, has 16 courts with grass, hard,

and Rubico surfaces. The **Destin Racquet & Fitness Center** (⊠ 995 Airport Rd., ☎ 904/837–7300) has six Rubico courts.

Shopping

The **Market at Sandestin** (⊠ 9375 U.S. 98W) has 28 upscale shops that peddle such goods as gourmet chocolates and designer clothes in an elegant minimall with boardwalks. **Silver Sands Factory Stores** (⊠ 5021 U.S. 98E) has more than 106 shops featuring top-name merchandise that ranges from gifts to kids' clothes to menswear.

Valparaiso and Niceville

5 *15 mi north of Destin across the Mid-Bay Bridge (Rte. 293).*

On the northern side of Choctawhatchee Bay are the twin cities of Valparaiso and Niceville, granted their charters in 1921 and 1938, respectively. Niceville evolved from a tiny fishing hamlet called Boggy, whose sandy-bottom bays were rich in mullet. Valparaiso was founded by an entrepreneurial Chicagoan named John B. Perrine, who envisioned it as an ideal city by the sea, or "vale of paradise." Together, the cities have maintained a serene existence, more or less untouched by the tourist trade farther south. Although their character hasn't changed since the Mid-Bay Bridge opened, the link to the beaches of south Walton County has enhanced their viability as a vacation destination.

At the **Heritage Museum,** you can take a long step back in time among 8,000-year-old stone tools and early 20th-century iron pots and kettles. A rarity on display here is a steam-powered, belt-driven cotton gin. The museum also maintains a reference library of genealogical and historical research materials and official Civil War records. ⊠ *115 Westview Ave.,* ☎ *904/678–2615.* ☜ *Free.* ☉ *Tues.–Sat. 11–4.*

In the **Fred Gannon Rocky Bayou State Recreation Area,** east of Niceville off Route 20 on Rocky Bayou, there are 50 excellent picnic areas, nature trails, boat ramps, and uncrowded campsites with electrical and water hookups. It's quiet and secluded, yet easy to find, and a great venue for serious bikers. ⊠ *Rte. 20,* ☎ *904/833–9144.* ☜ *$2 per vehicle for day use; campsites $8.56, with electricity $10.70.* ☉ *Daily 8–sunset.*

Dining and Lodging

$ ✕ **Nicometo's.** Wedged between a jeweler's and a sporting-goods store, this shopping plaza restaurant dishes up steamed shrimp that makes even the most jaded of diners sit up and take notice. Fried shrimp and char-grilled grouper also go over big with the regulars, but the only concession to red-meat eaters is a New York strip. The decor in the dimly lit dining room is plain and simple—fishing trophies and advertising memorabilia. If you want a jazzier setting, pick a table in the sports bar, where you can throw darts or watch TV. ⊠ *1027 John Sims Pkwy., Niceville,* ☎ *904/678–5072. D, MC, V.*

$$–$$$ ☷ **Bluewater Bay Resort.** This upscale resort is carved out of 1,800
★   acres of pines and oaks on the shores of Choctawhatchee Bay. It's still woodsy around the edges, but showcase homes are surrounded by tenderly manicured gardens. Rentals run the gamut from motel rooms to villas (some with fireplaces and fully equipped kitchens) and patio homes. Checkout information in the rental units is translated into German for the benefit of international visitors, who flock to this golf course–rich region. ⊠ *1950 Bluewater Blvd., Niceville 32578,* ☎ *904/897–3613 or 800/874–2128,* ℻ *904/897–2424. 106 units. Restaurant, lounge,*

3 pools, 36 holes of golf, 19 tennis courts, beach, boating, playground. AE, D, DC, MC, V.

Outdoor Activities and Sports

FISHING

Licenses and tackle are available at **Outdoor Sports** (⊠ 1025 Palm Plaza, Niceville, ☎ 904/678–4804).

GOLF

Bluewater Bay Resort (⊠ 1950 Bluewater Blvd., Niceville, ☎ 904/897–3241), 6 mi east of Niceville on Route 20E, offers 36 holes of championship golf on courses designed by Jerry Pate and Tom Fazio.

TENNIS

There are 19 courts (12 lighted) featuring two different playing surfaces at **Bluewater Bay Resort's tennis center** (⊠ Rte. 20E, Niceville, ☎ 904/897–3679).

THE GULF COAST

From Choctawhatchee Bay southeast to Apalachicola Bay, there is an enormous variety of towns strung along the shoreline on U.S. 98. Seaside, a town less than 20 years old, is an interesting experiment; residents hope that a strong sense of community will be inspired by old-fashioned architecture and civic planning. Farther south on U.S. 98 is Panama City Beach, its "Miracle Strip" crammed with classic boardwalk entertainment and junk food. An alternative to neon-lit tourist havens is the quiet, blue-collar town of Apalachicola, Florida's main oyster fishery, where many oystermen still fish by hand, using long-handled tongs to bring in their catch.

Seaside

★ ❻ *26 mi east of Destin off U.S. 98 on Rte. 30A.*

Unlike most developments with their contemporary architecture, the Seaside community is all Victorian-style fretwork, white picket fences, front-porch rockers, and captain's walks. The resulting effect is like being magic-carpeted to Cape May or Cape Cod. Seaside is the brainchild of Robert Davis, who dictated certain architectural elements that he felt would promote a neighborly, old-fashioned lifestyle. All houses are on small lots, so none is more than ¼ mi from the center of town, and it's easy to get about on foot. Though there isn't enough moss in the brick sidewalks to give that "historic district" look (building didn't start until 1981), this architectural-social experiment is a visual stunner nonetheless.

OFF THE BEATEN PATH

EDEN STATE GARDENS – Scarlett O'Hara might be at home here on the lawn of an antebellum mansion set amid an arcade of moss-draped live oaks. Furnishings in the spacious rooms date from as far back as the 17th century. The surrounding gardens are beautiful year-round, but they're nothing short of spectacular in mid-March, when the azaleas and dogwoods are in full bloom. ⊠ *Rte. 395, Point Washington,* ☎ *904/231-4214.* ☛ *Gardens free, mansion tour $1.50.* ☉ *Daily 8–sunset, mansion tours Thurs.–Mon. hourly 9–4.*

Beach

★ **Grayton Beach State Recreation Area** is, without a doubt, one of the most scenic spots along the Gulf Coast. It has blue-green waters, white-sand beaches, salt marshes, and swimming, snorkeling, and campground facilities. ⊠ *357 Main Park Rd.,* ☎ *904/231–4210.* ⊡ *$3.25 per vehicle with up to 8 people.* ⊙ *Daily 8–sunset.*

Dining and Lodging

$ ✕ **Bud & Alley's.** This roadside restaurant grows its own herbs—rose-
★ mary, thyme, basil, fennel, and mint. The inside room is down-to-earth, with hardwood floors, ceiling fans, and 6-foot windows looking onto the garden. There is also a screened-in porch with a gulf view. Daily salad specials are tangy introductions to such entrées as roasted game hen with sourdough thyme dressing and roasted root vegetables. ⊠ *Rte. 30A,* ☎ *904/231–5900. MC, V. Closed Tues. Sept.–May.*

$$$–$$$$ **Josephine's Inn.** These charming accommodations contain four-poster beds, fireplaces, and claw-foot tubs. The daily breakfast is delicious. ⊠ *101 Seaside Ave., 32459,* ☎ *904/231–1939,* ℻ *904/231–2446. 15 rooms. AE, MC, V.*

$$$–$$$$ ⌂ **Seaside.** One- to six-bedroom porticoed faux Victorian cottages are
★ furnished down to the vacuum cleaners, and decor reflects the own-
ers' personalities. Gulf breezes blowing off the water remind you of the unspoiled, sugar-white beaches a short stroll away. ⊠ *Rte. 30A, 32459,* ☎ *904/231–2992, 800/865–8895, or 800/475–1841,* ℻ *904/231–4196. 40 units. 2 pools, 6 tennis courts, badminton, croquet, boating, bicycles. AE, MC, V.*

Panama City Beach

❼ *21 mi southeast of Seaside.*

In spite of the shoulder-to-shoulder condominiums, motels, and amuse-
ment parks that make it seem like one big carnival ground, this coastal resort has a natural beauty that excuses its overcommercialization. The incredible white sands, navigable waterways, and plentiful marine life that attracted Spanish conquistadors today lure family vacationers.

☾ Enjoy dozens of rides at **Miracle Strip Amusement Park,** from a tradi-
tional Ferris wheel to a roller coaster with a 65-foot drop. ⊠ *12000 Front Beach Rd.,* ☎ *904/234–5810.* ⊡ *$16.* ⊙ *Mid-Mar.–Labor Day, daily starting June; hours vary.*

☾ There are 6 acres of water rides at **Shipwreck Island,** from speedy slides and tubes to the Lazy River. ⊠ *12000 Front Beach Rd.,* ☎ *904/234–0368.* ⊡ *$18.* ⊙ *Late Apr.–Labor Day, daily starting June; hours vary.*

☾ Come to **Gulf World** to see bottle-nosed dolphin, sea lions, and otters perform. ⊠ *15412 Front Beach Rd.,* ☎ *904/234–5271.* ⊡ *$13.50.* ⊙ *June–Aug., daily 9–7; Sept.–May, daily 9–5.*

Beaches

At the **Panama City Beaches** (☎ 800/722–3224), public beaches along the Miracle Strip combine with the plethora of video-game arcades, miniature golf courses, sidewalk cafés, souvenir shops, and shopping centers to lure people of all ages.

☾ At the eastern tip of Panama City Beach, the **St. Andrews State Recre-
ation Area** includes 1,260 acres of beaches, pinewoods, and marshes. There are complete camping facilities here, as well as ample opportu-
nities to swim, pier fish, or hike the dunes along clearly marked na-
ture trails. You can board a ferry to **Shell Island**—a barrier island in the Gulf of Mexico that offers some of the best shelling north of Sani-
bel Island. An artificial reef creates a calm, shallow play area that is perfect for young children. ⊠ *4607 State Park La.,* ☎ *904/233–5140.* ⊡ *$4 per vehicle with up to 8 people.* ⊙ *Daily 8–sunset.*

Dining and Lodging

$–$$ ✕ **Boar's Head.** An exterior that looks like an oversize thatch-roof cottage sets the mood for dining in this ersatz-rustic restaurant and tavern. Prime rib has been the number-one people-pleaser since the house opened in 1978, but blackened seafood and broiled shrimp with crabmeat stuffing are popular, too. ⌧ 17290 Front Beach Rd., ☎ 904/234–6628. AE, D, DC, MC, V. No lunch.

$–$$ ✕ **Capt. Anderson's.** Come early to watch the boats unload the catch of the day on the docks, and be among the first to line up to eat in this noted restaurant. The atmosphere is nautical, with tables made of hatch covers. The Greek specialties aren't limited to feta cheese and shriveled olives; charcoal-broiled fish and steaks have a prominent place on the menu as well. ⌧ 5551 N. Lagoon Dr., ☎ 904/234–2225. AE, D, DC, MC, V. Closed Nov.–Jan.; Sun. May–Sept. No lunch.

$ ✕ **Montego Bay.** Line up with vacationers and natives to enjoy the swift service and good food. Some dishes, such as red beans and rice or oysters on the half shell, are no surprise. Others, such as shrimp rolled in coconut and served with a honey mustard and orange marmalade sauce, are real treats. ⌧ 4920 Thomas Dr., ☎ 904/234–8686; ⌧ 9949 Thomas Dr., ☎ 904/235–3585; ⌧ Shoppes at Edgewater, ☎ 904/233–6033. AE, D, DC, MC, V.

$$–$$$$ 🏨 **Edgewater Beach Resort.** Luxurious one-, two-, and three-bedroom
★ units in beachside towers and golf-course villas are elegantly furnished with wicker and rattan. The resort centerpiece is a Polynesian-style lagoon pool with waterfalls, reflecting ponds, footbridges, and more than 20,000 species of tropical plants. ⌧ 11212 Front Beach Rd., 32407, ☎ 904/235–4044 or 800/874–8686, FAX 904/233–7529. 520 units. Restaurant, lounge, golf, 12 tennis courts, shuffleboard, game room. AE, D, DC, MC, V.

$$–$$$$ 🏨 **Marriott's Bay Point Resort.** Sheer elegance is the hallmark of this
★ pink stucco property on the shores of Grand Lagoon. Wing chairs, camelback sofas, and Oriental carpets in the common areas recall an English manor house, as do the Queen Anne guest room furnishings. Gulf view or golf view—take your pick. Kitchen-equipped villas are a mere teeshot away from the hotel. ⌧ 4200 Marriott Dr., 32408, ☎ 904/234–3307 or 800/874–7105, FAX 904/233–1308. 355 rooms and suites. 5 restaurants, lounges, indoor pool, 4 outdoor pools, hot tub, 2 golf courses, 12 lighted tennis courts, boating, fishing. AE, D, DC, MC, V.

$–$$$ 🏨 **Boardwalk Beach Resort.** This mile of beachfront has been staked out by a group of four family-oriented hotels: Howard Johnson and Comfort, Gulfwalk, and Beachwalk inns. All share the long beach, and group parties are given regularly by all four hotels. Each has its own pool. ⌧ 9450 S. Thomas Dr., 32408, ☎ 904/234–3484 or 800/874–6613, FAX 904/233–4369. 627 units. Lounge, 4 pools, beach. AE, D, DC, MC, V.

Nightlife and the Arts

THE ARTS

Broadway touring shows, top-name entertainers, and concert artists are booked into the **Marina Civic Center** (⌧ 8 Harrison Ave., Panama City, ☎ 904/769–1217).

NIGHTLIFE

Pineapple Willy's (⌧ 9900 S. Thomas Dr., ☎ 904/235–0928) alternately features big-band and rock music for a post-college crowd.

Outdoor Activities and Sports

CANOEING

Rentals for a trip down Econofina Creek, "Florida's most beautiful canoe trail," are supplied by **Econofina Creek Canoe Livery** (⊠ Strickland Rd., north of Rte. 20, Youngstown, ☎ 904/722–9032).

DOG RACING

There's pari-mutuel betting year-round and live greyhound racing five nights and two afternoons a week at the **Ebro Greyhound Park.** Simulcasts of Thoroughbred racing from the Miami area are also shown throughout the year. Schedules change periodically, so call for details. ⊠ *Rte. 20 at Rte. 79, Ebro,* ☎ *904/535–4048; outside FL, 800/345–4810.* ☞ *$1, clubhouse $2.*

GOLF

The **Hombre Golf Club** (⊠ 120 Coyote Pass, ☎ 904/234–3673) has an 18-hole course. **Marriott's Bay Point Resort** (⊠ 100 Delwood Beach Rd., ☎ 904/235–6909 or 800/874–7105), open to the public, has 36 holes.

TENNIS

The tennis center at **Marriott's Bay Point Resort** (⊠ 100 Delwood Beach Rd., ☎ 904/235–6910) has 12 Har-Tru tennis courts.

Shopping

Stores in the **Manufacturer's Outlet Center** (⊠ 105 W. 23rd St., Panama City) offer well-known brands at a substantial discount. The **Panama City Mall** (⊠ U.S. 231 and Rte. 77, Panama City) has a mix of more than 100 franchise shops and national chain stores.

Port St. Joe

8 *50 mi southeast of Panama City Beach.*

Florida's first constitution was drafted here in 1838. Most of the old town, including the original hall, is gone—wiped out by hurricanes—but the exhibits in the **Constitution Convention State Museum** recall the event. There are also provisions for camping and picnicking in a small park surrounding the museum. ⊠ *200 Island Memorial Way,* ☎ *904/229–8029.* ☞ *$1.* ☉ *Thurs.–Mon. 9–noon and 1–5.*

Outdoor Activities and Sports

GOLF

St. Joseph's Bay Country Club (⊠ 650 Country Club Rd., ☎ 904/227–1751) offers an 18-hole course.

Apalachicola

9 *15 mi southeast of Port St. Joe.*

Meaning "land of the friendly people" in the language of its original Native American inhabitants, Apalachicola lies on the Panhandle's southernmost bulge. Settlers began arriving in 1821, and, by 1847, the southern terminus of the Apalachicola River steamboat route was a bustling port town. Though the town is now known as the Oyster Capital of the World, oystering only became king after the sponge colonies were depleted and the sponge industry moved down the coast. So if you like oysters or you want to go back in time to the Old South of Gothic churches and spooky graveyards, Apalachicola is a good place to start. Drive by the **Raney House**, circa 1850, and **Trinity Episcopal Church**, built from prefabricated parts in 1838.

Stop in at the **John Gorrie State Museum,** which honors the physician credited with inventing ice-making and air-conditioning. Exhibits of

Apalachicola history are displayed here as well. ⊠ *Ave. D and 6th St.,* ☎ *904/653–9347.* ▣ *$1.* ⊙ *Thurs.–Mon. 9–5.*

OFF THE
BEATEN PATH **ST. GEORGE ISLAND STATE PARK –** Here you can drive toward the sea along a narrow spit of land full of dunes, sea oats, and abundant bird life. A boardwalk trail winds through the dunes, which seem to be constantly moving. Pine trees have been almost buried here by windblown sand. The park can be reached by a causeway over the Apalachicola River from Eastpoint, east of Apalachicola. ☎ *904/927–2111.* ▣ *$3.25 per vehicle with up to 8 people.* ⊙ *Daily 8–sunset.*

Dining and Lodging

$ ✕ **Boss Oyster.** Eat your oysters fried, Rockefeller, or on the half shell at this laid-back eatery overlooking the Apalachicola River. Eat 'em alfresco at picnic tables or inside in the anything-goes atmosphere of the rustic dining room. If you're allergic to seafood, don't worry. The menu also features such staples as steak and pizza. ⊠ *123 Water St.,* ☎ *904/653–9364. AE, D, DC, MC, V.*

$ ✕ **Gibson Inn.** You can hobnob with Apalachicola aristocracy as you dine in a serene, Edwardian setting at the town's traditional hotel. The dining room's a bit formal—crisp, creased linen tablecloths and fresh-cut flowers on the tables—and the food's impeccable. Sip a margarita in the adjacent bar. Then sample grouper Rockefeller; shrimp, scallop, and crab Dijon; or oysters Remick, in a horseradish-laced chili sauce with chopped Swiss cheese. ⊠ *51 Ave. C,* ☎ *904/653–2191. AE, MC, V.*

$$ ▦ **Coombs House Inn.** Nine fireplaces and an ornate oak staircase with leaded-glass windows on the landing lend authenticity to this restored 1905 mansion. No two guest rooms are alike, but all are appointed with Victorian-era settees, poster or sleigh beds, English chintz curtains, and Asian rugs on polished hardwood floors. Continental breakfast is served in the dining room. ⊠ *80 6th St., 32320,* ☎ *904/653–9199,* ℻ *904/653–2785. 18 rooms. AE, MC, V.*

$$ ▦ **Gibson Inn.** One of a few inns on the National Register of Historic Places still operating as a full-service facility, this turn-of-the-century hostelry in the heart of downtown is easily identified by its wraparound porches, fretwork, and captain's watch. Rooms are furnished with period pieces, such as four-poster beds, antique armoires, and pedestal lavatories that have wide basins and porcelain fixtures. ⊠ *51 Ave. C, 32329,* ☎ *904/653–2191,* ℻ *904/653–3521. 31 rooms. Restaurant, lounge. AE, MC, V.*

LOWER ALABAMA

Near Florida's border with Alabama, in "Lower Alabama," as the locals have labeled it, are several towns worth visiting. Small and unassuming, they often have surprising cultural attributes, such as the voluminous collections at the Robert L. F. Sikes Public Library in Crestview and the Walton-DeFuniak Public Library in DeFuniak Springs. The area also has its share of geologic oddities, such as the plunging pit of the Falling Waters Sink.

Crestview

🔟 *18 mi north of Valparaiso/Niceville.*

This is the sort of small town where the mayor rides shotgun with the police patrol on a Saturday night and folks enjoy the simpler pleasures, such as roller skating and playing softball. At 235 feet above sea level

(quite high by Florida standards), Crestview was dubbed by survey-
ors of the Louisville & Nashville Railroad Company, which completed
a line through northwest Florida in 1882. There has been a settlement
of sorts here since the days of the conquistadors, when it was a crossroads on the Old Spanish Trail.

The **Robert L. F. Sikes Public Library** (⊠ 805 U.S. 90E, ☎ 904/682–
4432) and its research center, housed in an imposing Greek revival building, contain more than 44,000 volumes as well as the private papers
of its eponym, a former U.S. congressman.

Dining and Lodging

$ ✕ **McLain's Family Restaurant.** Assorted Wal-Mart art, piped-in coun-
try music, and a fireplace with a raised hearth give this mom-and-pop
establishment a folksy feel that carries right over to the menu. The owners offer an all-you-can-eat buffet three times a day, always with a
poached or broiled entrée. All steaks are hand-cut. On weekends, a
seafood buffet draws customers from as far away as Alabama. ⊠
2680 S. Rte. 85, ☎ 904/682–5286. AE, D, MC, V.

$ ⌂ **Crestview Holiday Inn.** The simple sandstone-and-stucco motel has
typical Florida decor: shell-shape ceramic lamps, seashell-print bedspreads, and oceanic art on the walls. It's a bit south of downtown and
is the "in" place for local wedding receptions. ⊠ Rte. 85 and I–10,
Box 1358, 32536, ☎ 904/682–6111, FAX 904/689–1189. 120 rooms.
Restaurant, lounge, pool. AE, D, DC, MC, V.

DeFuniak Springs

⓫ 28 mi east of Crestview.

In 1848, the Knox Hill Academy was founded in this small town, and
for more than half a century it was the only institution of higher learning in northwest Florida. In 1885, the town was chosen as the location for the New York Chautauqua educational society's winter
assembly. The Chautauqua programs were discontinued in 1922, but
DeFuniak Springs attempts to revive them, in spirit at least, by spon-
soring a county-wide Chautauqua Festival in April.

By all accounts, the 16-foot by 24-foot **Walton-DeFuniak Public Library**
is Florida's oldest library continuously operating in its original building. Opened in 1887 and added to over the years, it now contains nearly
30,000 volumes, including some rare books, many older than the
structure itself. The collection also includes antique musical instruments
and impressive European armor. ⊠ 3 Circle Dr., ☎ 904/892–3624.
☉ Mon. 9–7, Tues.–Fri. 9–6, Sat. 9–3.

The **Chautauqua Winery** (⊠ I–10 and U.S. 331, ☎ 904/892–5887)
opened in 1989, but already its award-winning wines have earned raves
from oenophiles nationwide. Take a free tour to see how ancient art
blends with modern technology; then retreat to the tasting room.

Falling Waters State Recreation Area

⓬ 35 mi east of DeFuniak Springs.

This is the site of one of Florida's most recognized geological features—
the Falling Waters Sink. The 100-foot-deep cylindrical pit provides the
background for a waterfall, and there's an observation deck for viewing this natural phenomenon. ⊠ Rte. 77A, Chipley, ☎ 904/638–
6130. ☑ $3.25 per vehicle with up to 8 people. ☉ Daily 8–sunset.

Florida Caverns State Park

⑬ *13 mi northeast of Falling Waters off I–10 on U.S. 231.*

Take a ranger-led spelunking tour to see an array of stalactites, stalagmites, and "waterfalls" of solid rock at this expansive park. There are also hiking trails, campsites, and areas for swimming and canoeing on the Chipola River. ⊠ *Rte. 167, Marianna,* ☎ *904/482–9598.* 🎟 *Park $3.25 per vehicle with up to 8 people, caverns $4.* ⊘ *Daily 8–sunset, cavern tours daily 9:30–4:30.*

TALLAHASSEE

⑭ *61 mi southeast of Florida Caverns.*

I–10 rolls east over the timid beginnings of the Appalachian foothills and through thick pines into the state capital, with its canopies of ancient oaks and spring bowers of azaleas. Home to Florida State University, the city has more than a touch of the Old South.

Tallahassee maintains a tranquil atmosphere quite different from the sun-and-surf hedonism of the major coastal towns. Vestiges of the city's colorful past are found throughout; for example, in the Capitol Complex, the turn-of-the-century Old Capitol building is strikingly paired with the New Capitol skyscraper. Tallahassee's tree-lined streets are particularly memorable—among the best canopied roads are St. Augustine, Miccosukee, Meridian, Old Bainbridge, and Centerville, all dotted with country stores and antebellum plantation houses.

Downtown

A Good Walk

Most of the sights of the downtown area are compact enough for walking, though it's also served by a free, continuous shuttle trolley. Start at the Capitol complex, which contains the **Old Capitol** and its counterpoint, the **New Capitol.** Across the street from the older structure is the restored **Union Bank Building,** and two blocks west of the new statehouse you'll find the **Museum of Florida History,** with exhibits on many eras of the state's history and prehistory.

If you really want to get a feel for old Tallahassee, walk the **Downtown Tallahassee Historic Trail** as it wends its way from the Capitol complex through several of the city's historic districts.

TIMING

You can't do justice to the Capitol complex and downtown area in less than two hours. Allow four hours to walk the 8-mi stretch of the historic trail. If you visit between March and April, you'll find flowers in bloom and the Springtime Tallahassee festival in full swing.

Sights to See

Downtown Tallahassee Historic Trail. A route originally mapped and documented by an eager Eagle Scout as part of a merit-badge project, this trail has since become a Tallahassee sightseeing staple. The starting point is the Old Capitol, where you can pick up maps and descriptive brochures. You'll walk through the **Park Avenue and Calhoun Street historic districts,** which will take you back to Territorial days and the era of postwar Reconstruction. The trail is dotted with landmark churches and cemeteries, along with outstanding examples of Greek Revival, Italianate, and prairie-style architecture. Some houses are open to the public, including the **Brokaw-McDougall House,** which is a superb example of the Greek Revival and Italianate styles, and the

Meginnis-Monroe House, which served as a field hospital during the Civil War and is now an art gallery.

Museum of Florida History. Here the long, intriguing story of the state's past—from mastodons to space shuttles—is told in lucid and entertaining ways. ⊠ *500 S. Bronough St.,* ☎ *904/488–1484.* ☐ *Free.* ☉ *Weekdays 9–4:30, Sat. 10–4:30, Sun. noon–4:30.*

★ **New Capitol.** This modern skyscraper looms up 22 stories directly behind the low-rise Old Capitol. On a clear day, you can catch a panoramic view of Tallahassee and surrounding countryside from the top floor. To pick up information about the area, stop at the Florida Visitors Center, on the plaza level. ⊠ *Duvall St.,* ☎ *904/488–6167.* ☐ *Free.* ☉ *Hourly tours weekdays 9–3, visitor center weekdays 8–5.*

★ **Old Capitol.** The centerpiece of the Capitol complex, this pre–Civil War structure has been added to, and subtracted from, several times. Its restored jaunty red-and-white striped awnings and combination gas-electric lights make it look much as it did in 1902. ⊠ *Monroe St. at Apalachee Pkwy.,* ☎ *904/487–1902.* ☐ *Free.* ☉ *Self-guided or guided tours weekdays 9–4:30, Sat. 10–4:30, Sun. noon–4:30.*

Union Bank Building. Built in 1833, this is Florida's oldest bank building. Since it closed in 1843, it has played many roles, from ballet school to bakery. It has been restored to what is thought to be its original appearance. ⊠ *Monroe St. at Apalachee Pkwy.,* ☎ *904/487–3803.* ☐ *Free.* ☉ *Tues.–Fri. 10–1, weekends by appointment.*

Away from Downtown

Sights to See

Lake Jackson Mounds State Archaeological Site. Here are waters to make bass fishermen weep. For sightseers, Indian mounds and the ruins of an early 19th-century plantation built by Colonel Robert Butler, adjutant to General Andrew Jackson during the siege of New Orleans, are found along the shores of the lake. ⊠ *Indian Mound Rd.,* ☎ *904/562–0042.* ☐ *Free.* ☉ *Daily 8–sunset.*

Maclay State Gardens. In spring the grounds are afire with azaleas, dogwood, and other showy or rare plants. Allow half a day to wander past the reflecting pool, into the tiny walled garden, and around the lakes and woodlands. The Maclay residence, furnished as it was in the '20s; picnic areas; and swimming and boating facilities are open to the public. ⊠ *3540 Thomasville Rd.,* ☎ *904/487–4556.* ☐ *$3.25 per vehicle with up to 8 people.* ☉ *Daily 8–sunset.*

San Luis Archaeological and Historic Site. This museum focuses on the archaeology of 17th-century Spanish mission and Apalachee Indian town sites. In its heyday, in 1675, the Apalachee village here had a population of at least 1,400. Threatened by Creek Indians and British forces in 1704, the locals burned the village and fled. ⊠ *2020 W. Mission Rd.,* ☎ *904/487–3711.* ☐ *Free.* ☉ *Weekdays 9–4:30, Sat. 10–4:30, Sun. noon–4:30; 1-hr tours weekdays noon, Sat. 11 and 3, and Sun. 2.*

Tallahassee Museum of History and Natural Science. The eclectic collection features old cars and carriages, a red caboose, nature trails, a snake exhibit, and a restored plantation house. ⊠ *3945 Museum Rd.,* ☎ *904/576–1636.* ☐ *$6.* ☉ *Mon.–Sat. 9–5, Sun. 12:30–5.*

Dining and Lodging

$$ ✗ **Andrew's 2nd Act.** Part of a smart complex in the heart of the po-
★ litical district, this is classic cuisine: elegant and understated. If you like
pub hopping, there's Andrew's Upstairs and the Adams Street Cafe (also
by Andrew) next door. For dinner, the tournedos St. Laurent and the
peppered New York strip are both flawless. ⊠ *228 S. Adams St.,* ☎
904/222–2759. AE, DC, MC, V.

$ ✗ **Anthony's.** Often confused with Andrew's, this is the locals' choice
for uncompromising Italian classics. Try Italian-style grouper or salmon.
⊠ *1950 Thomasville Rd.,* ☎ *904/224–1447. AE, MC, V.*

$ ✗ **Barnacle Bill's.** The seafood selection is whale-size, and it's steamed
★ to succulent perfection before your eyes, with fresh vegetables on the
side. This popular hangout is famous for pasta dishes and home-
smoked fish, too. Children eat for free on Sunday. ⊠ *1830 N. Mon-
roe St.,* ☎ *904/385–8734. AE, MC, V.*

$ ✗ **Nicholson's Farmhouse.** The name says a lot about this friendly, in-
formal country place with an outside kitchen and grill. Hand-cut steaks
and chops are specialties of the house. ⊠ *From U.S. 27 follow Rte. 12
toward Quincy and look for signs,* ☎ *904/539–5931. AE, D, MC, V.
BYOB. Closed Sun. and Mon.*

$$$ 🏨 **Governors Inn.** Only a block from the Capitol, this plushly restored
★ historic warehouse is abuzz during the week with politicians, press, and
lobbyists. It's a perfect location for business travelers and, on weekends, for tourists who want to visit downtown sites. Rooms are a rich
blend of mahogany, brass, and classic prints. The VIP treatment includes airport pickup, breakfast, cocktails, robes, shoe shine, and a daily
paper. ⊠ *209 S. Adams St., 32301,* ☎ *904/681–6855; in FL, 800/342–
7717;* 𝐅𝐀𝐗 *904/222–3105. 40 units. Airport shuttle, free valet parking.
AE, D, DC, MC, V.*

$$ 🏨 **Doubletreee Hotel Tallahassee.** Bustling and upscale, the hotel hosts
heavy hitters from the worlds of politics and media, who can walk from
here to the Capitol. ⊠ *101 S. Adams St., 32301,* ☎ *904/224–5000,*
𝐅𝐀𝐗 *904/513–9516. 244 rooms. Restaurant, bar, lounge, pool. AE, D,
DC, MC, V.*

$$ 🏨 **Shoney's Inn.** The quiet courtyard with its own pool and the darkly
welcoming cantina (where a complimentary Continental breakfast is
served) convey the look of old Spain. Rooms are furnished in heavy
Mediterranean style. ⊠ *2801 N. Monroe St., 32303,* ☎ *904/386–8286
or 800/222–2222,* 𝐅𝐀𝐗 *904/422–1074. 112 rooms. Lounge, pool. AE,
D, DC, MC, V.*

Nightlife and the Arts

The Arts

Florida State University annually hosts 400 concerts and recitals given
year-round by its **School of Music** (☎ 904/644–4774) as well as performances of the **Tallahassee Symphony Orchestra** (☎ 904/224–0461)
from October through April. The **Monticello Opera House** (⊠ U.S. 90E,
Monticello, ☎ 904/997–4242) presents operas in a restored gaslight-
era playhouse. The **Tallahassee Little Theatre** (⊠ 1861 Thomasville Rd.,
☎ 904/224–8474) has a five-production season that runs from September through May.

Nightlife

Monday through Saturday nights, stop by **Andrew's Upstairs** (⊠ 228
S. Adams St., ☎ 904/222–3446) to hear contemporary jazz. Top-
name entertainment is booked into the **Tallahassee–Leon County Civic
Center** (⊠ 505 W. Pensacola St., ☎ 904/487–1691).

Outdoor Activities and Sports

Golf
Killearn Country Club & Inn (⊠ 100 Tyron Circle, ☎ 904/893–2144) has 27 holes.

Side Trips

South to the Gulf
South of the capital and east of the Ochlockanee River are several fascinating natural and historical sites. Since they're near each other, you can string several together on an excursion from Tallahassee.

⑮ Natural Bridge Battlefield State Historic Site marks the spot where, in 1865, Confederate soldiers stood firm against a Yankee advance on St. Marks. The Rebs held, saving Tallahassee—the only southern capital east of the Mississippi that never fell to the Union. Ten miles southeast of Tallahassee, the site is a good place for a hike and a picnic. If you visit the first week in March, you can watch a reenactment of the battle. ⊠ *Natural Bridge Rd., off Rte. 363, Woodville,* ☎ *904/922–6007.* ⌧ *Free.* ⊙ *Daily 8–sunset.*

★ **⑯** Known for containing one of the deepest springs in the world, **Wakulla Springs State Park** remains relatively untouched, retaining the wild and exotic look it had in the 1930s, when Tarzan movies were made here. Take a glass-bottom boat deep into the lush, jungle-lined waterways to catch glimpses of alligators, snakes, nesting limpkin, and other waterfowl. An underground river flows into a pool so clear that you can see the bottom, more than 100 feet below. The park is 15 mi south of Tallahassee on Route 61. ⊠ *250 Wakulla Park Dr., Wakulla Springs,* ☎ *904/922–3632.* ⌧ *$3.25 per vehicle with up to 8 people, boat tour $4.50.* ⊙ *Daily 8–sunset, boat tours hourly 9–4.*

⑰ As its name suggests, **St. Marks Wildlife Refuge and Lighthouse** is of both natural and historical interest. The once-powerful Fort San Marcos de Apalache was built here in 1639, and stones salvaged from the fort were used in the lighthouse, which is still in operation. In winter the refuge is home to thousands of migratory birds. The visitor center has information on more than 75 mi of marked trails. Located 25 mi south of Tallahassee, the refuge is reached on Route 363. ⊠ *1255 Lighthouse Rd., St. Marks,* ☎ *904/925–6121.* ⌧ *$4 per car.* ⊙ *Refuge daily sunrise–sunset; visitor center weekdays 8–4:15, weekends 10–5.*

Spreading north of Apalachicola and west of Tallahassee and U.S. 319 is the **Apalachicola National Forest** (☎ 904/643–2282). Here you can camp, hike, picnic, fish, or swim.

CANOEING
Contact **TNT Hideaway** (⊠ U.S. 98 at the Wakulla River near Crawfordville, St. Marks, ☎ 904/925–6412) to canoe the Wakulla River.

DINING
$ ✕ **Wakulla Springs Lodge and Conference Center.** Located on the grounds of Wakulla Springs State Park, this facility serves three meals a day in a sunny, spartan room that seems little changed from the 1930s. Schedule lunch here to sample the famous bean soup, home-baked muffins, and a slab of pie. ⊠ *550 Wakulla Park Dr., Wakulla Springs,* ☎ *904/224–5950. MC, V.*

THE PANHANDLE A TO Z

Arriving and Departing

By Bus
The principal common carrier throughout the region is **Greyhound Lines** (☎ 800/231–2222), with stations in Crestview (☎ 904/682–6922), DeFuniak Springs (☎ 904/892–5566), Fort Walton Beach (☎ 904/243–1940), Panama City (☎ 904/785–7861), Pensacola (☎ 904/476–4800), and Tallahassee (☎ 904/222–4240).

By Car
The main east–west arteries across the top of the state are I–10 and U.S. 90. Pensacola is about an hour's drive east of Mobile. Tallahassee is 3½ hours west of Jacksonville.

By Plane
The **Pensacola Regional Airport** is served by **ASA–The Delta Connection** and **Comair** (☎ 800/221–1212), **Continental** (☎ 800/525–0280), **Delta** (☎ 800/221–1212), **Northwest Airlink** (☎ 800/225–2525), and **US Airways** and **US Airways Express** (☎ 800/428–4322). A trip from the airport via **Yellow Cab** (☎ 904/433–1143) costs about $9 to downtown and $17 to Pensacola Beach.

Fort Walton Beach/Eglin AFB Airport/Okaloosa County Air Terminal is served by ASA–The Delta Connection, **Northwest** (☎ 800/225–2525), USAir Express, and **ValuJet** (☎ 800/825–8538). A ride from the Fort Walton Beach airport via **Checker Cab** (☎ 904/244–4491) costs $10 to Fort Walton Beach, Niceville, or Valparaiso and $18 to Destin. **Bluewater Car Service** (☎ 904/897–5239) charges $12 to Fort Walton Beach and $22 to Destin.

Panama City–Bay County Airport is served by ASA–The Delta Connection, Northwest Airlink, and USAir Express. **Yellow Cab** (☎ 904/763–4691) charges about $15–$27 to the beach area, depending on where your hotel is. **DeLuxe Coach Limo Service** (☎ 904/763–0211) provides van service to downtown Panama City and to Panama City Beach for $1.25 a mile.

Tallahassee Regional Airport is served by ASA–The Delta Connection, Delta, **Gulfstream** (☎ 800/992–8532), and US Airways Express. **Yellow Cab** (☎ 904/222–3070) travels to downtown for $10–$13. Some Tallahassee hotels provide free shuttle service.

By Train
Amtrak (☎ 800/872–7245) has a Los Angeles–to–Panhandle route; its stops include Pensacola, Crestview, and Chipley.

Getting Around

By Boat
The Emerald Coast is accessible to yacht captains and sailors from the Intracoastal Waterway, which turns inland at Apalachicola and runs through the bays around Panama City to Choctawhatchee Bay and into Santa Rosa Sound.

By Car
It takes about four hours from Pensacola to Tallahassee. Driving along I–10 can be monotonous, but U.S. 90 piques your interest by routing you along the main streets of several county seats.

U.S. 98 snakes eastward along the coast, splitting into 98 and 98A at Inlet Beach before rejoining at Panama City and continuing down to Port St. Joe and Apalachicola. The view of the gulf from U.S. 98 can leave you oohing and ahhing if the sun is out to distract you. If not, the fast-food restaurants, sleazy bars, and tacky souvenir stores are a little too noticeable.

Route 399 between Pensacola Beach and Navarre Beach takes you down Santa Rosa Island, a spit of duneland that juts out into the turquoise and jade waters of the Gulf of Mexico. It's a scenic drive if the day is clear; otherwise, it's a study in gray.

Major north–south highways that weave through the Panhandle are (from east to west) U.S. 231, U.S. 331, Route 85, and U.S. 29. From U.S. 331, which runs over a causeway at the east end of Choctawhatchee Bay between Route 20 and U.S. 98, the panorama of barge traffic and cabin cruisers on the twinkling waters of the Intracoastal Waterway will get your attention.

Contacts and Resources

Emergencies
Dial **911** for police or ambulance.

HOSPITALS

The following hospitals have 24-hour emergency rooms: **Columbia Fort Walton Beach Medical Center** (⊠ 1000 Mar-Walt Dr., Fort Walton Beach, ☎ 904/862–1111), **Columbia Gulf Coast Medical Center** (⊠ 449 W. 23rd St., Panama City, ☎ 904/769–8341), **Columbia West Florida Regional Medical Center** (⊠ 8383 N. Davis Hwy., Pensacola, ☎ 904/494–4000), and **Tallahassee Regional Medical Center** (⊠ Magnolia Dr. and Miccosukee Rd., Tallahassee, ☎ 904/681–1155).

Visitor Information
Offices below are open from between 8 and 9 to between 4 and 5 unless otherwise stated. **Apalachicola Bay Chamber of Commerce** (⊠ 84 Market St., Apalachicola 32320, ☎ 904/653–9419) is open weekdays 9:30–4, Saturday 10–3. **Crestview Area Chamber of Commerce** (⊠ 502 S. Main St., Crestview 32536, ☎ 904/682–3212) is open weekdays. **Destin Chamber of Commerce** (⊠ 1021 U.S. 98E, Destin 32541, ☎ 904/837–6241 or 904/837–0087) is open weekdays. **Emerald Coast Convention & Visitors Bureau** (⊠ 1540 U.S. 98E, Fort Walton Beach 32548, ☎ 904/651–7131 or 800/322–3319) is open daily. **Niceville/Valparaiso/Bay Area Chamber of Commerce** (⊠ 170 John Sims Pkwy., Valparaiso 32580, ☎ 904/678–2323) is open weekdays. **Panama City Beach Convention & Visitor Bureau** (⊠ 12015 W. Front Beach Rd., Panama City Beach 32407, ☎ 904/233–6503 or 800/722–3224) is open daily. **Pensacola Visitor Information Center** (⊠ 1401 E. Gregory St., Pensacola 32501, ☎ 904/434–1234 or 800/874–1234) is open daily. **Tallahassee Area Convention and Visitors Bureau** (⊠ 200 W. College Ave., Tallahassee 32302, ☎ 904/413–9200 or 800/628–2866) is open weekdays. **Walton County Chamber of Commerce** (⊠ 95 W. Circle Dr., DeFuniak Springs 32433, ☎ 904/892–3191) is open weekdays. The **Information Center** on U.S. 331 at U.S. 98 (☎ 904/267–3511) is open daily.

12 Northeast Florida

The northeast corner of the state is an area of remarkable diversity. Only a short drive separates the 400-year-old town of St. Augustine from the spring-break and auto-racing mecca of Daytona Beach. The entire coast is dotted with slender barrier islands—some relatively pristine, all with fabulous beaches. Inland is the university town of Gainesville, the horse country around Ocala, and the backwoods scrub.

Updated by
Pamela
Acheson

I N NORTHEASTERN FLORIDA YOU'LL FIND some of the oldest settlements in the state—indeed in all of the United States—though this region didn't get much attention until the Union Army came through during the Civil War. The soldiers' rapturous accounts of the mild climate, pristine beaches, and lush vegetation captured the imagination of folks up North. First came the speculators and the curiosity seekers. Then the advent of the railroads brought more permanent settlers and the first wave of winter vacationers. Finally, the automobile transported the full rush of snowbirds, seasonal residents escaping from harsh Northern winters. They still come, to sop up sun on the beach, to tee up in this year-round golfer's paradise; to bass fish and bird-watch in forests and parks, and to party in the clubs and bars of Daytona (which has the dubious honor of replacing Fort Lauderdale as a top spring break destination).

This region of Florida is an area of remarkable diversity. Towering, tortured live oaks, plantations, and antebellum-style architecture recollect the Old South. The mossy marshes of Silver Springs and the St. Johns River look as untouched and junglelike today as they did generations ago. Horse farms around Ocala resemble Kentucky's bluegrass country or the hunt clubs of Virginia. St. Augustine is a showcase of early U.S. history, and Jacksonville is a young but sophisticated metropolis. Yet these are all but light diversions from northeastern Florida's primary draw—absolutely sensational beaches. Hugging the coast are long, slender barrier islands whose entire eastern sides comprise a broad band of spectacular sand. Except in the most populated areas, development has been modest, and beaches are lined with funky, appealing little towns.

Pleasures and Pastimes

Beaches

Beaches in northeastern Florida are luxuriously long. Some are hard-packed white sand, while others have sand with a fine, sugary texture. Surf is normally gentle, and many areas are safe for swimming. The very fragile dunes, held in place by sea grasses, are responsible for protecting the shore from the sea. Florida law mandates that you neither pick the sea oats nor walk on or play in the dunes. A single afternoon of careless roughhousing can destroy a dune forever.

The area's most densely developed beaches, with rows of high-rise condominiums and hotels, are in Daytona and Cocoa Beach. Elsewhere, coastal towns are still mostly small and laid-back, and beaches are crowded only on summer weekends.

Canoeing

Opportunities for canoeing are excellent here. Inland, especially in Ocala National Forest, sparkling clear spring "runs" may be mere tunnels through tangled jungle growth. Near the coast, grassy marshes and the maze of shallow inlets along the inland waterway side of Canaveral National Seashore are other favored canoeing spots.

Dining

Between the ocean, Intracoastal Waterway, and numerous lakes and rivers, seafood is prominent on local menus. In coastal towns, catches often come straight from the restaurant's own fleet. Shrimp, snapper, swordfish, and grouper are especially popular.

Fishing

From cane-pole fishing in a roadside canal or off a pier to deep-sea fishing from a luxury charter boat, options abound. There's no charge (or a nominal one) to fish from many causeways, beaches, and piers. Deep-sea fishing charters are available up and down the coast.

Horseback Riding

Ocala's bluegrass country can be explored on trail rides. Amelia Island is famous for horseback riding on the beach.

Lodging

Accommodations range from splashy beachfront resorts and glitzy condominiums to cozy inns nestled in historic districts. In general, the closer you are to the center of activity, the more you'll pay. You'll save quite a bit if you stay across from the beach rather than on it, even more if you select a place that's a bit removed.

Scuba Diving and Snorkeling

Inland, divers can explore freshwater caves and snorkelers can swim over "boils"—naturally bubbling water that sometimes occurs when an underground spring comes to the surface.

Skydiving

Deland is the skydiving capital of the world. Spectators can watch high-flying competitions, while those interested in swooping down from an airplane that's thousands of feet up can try tandem jumping.

Water Sports

For a lazy day drifting along the St. John's River, rent a pontoon boat, houseboat, or bass boat. Or catch an ocean wave on a boogie board, surfboard, or sailboard, all of which can be rented along the beaches.

Exploring Northeast Florida

Much of this region's tourist territory lies along the Atlantic coast, both on the mainland and on the barrier islands that lie just offshore. A1A (mostly called Atlantic Avenue) is the main road on all the barrier islands, and it's here that you'll find the best beaches. The region defies any single description. In the far northeast are both the remote resort of Amelia Island, just south of the Georgia border, and Jacksonville, the only real high-rise city in northeast Florida. St. Augustine is the historic capital of this part of Florida. Coastal towns range from the spring-break bustle of Daytona Beach to the sleepy appeal of neighboring New Smyrna Beach. Inland are charming small towns and the sprawling Ocala National Forest, but even here the quiet is broken in Gainesville, home of the University of Florida.

Great Itineraries

Even with 10 days, northeast Florida is too large to cover in depth, and even for a brief regional overview, you'd have to spend most of your time in the car. A better plan is to pick some spots that interest you and explore them more thoroughly.

Numbers in the text correspond to numbers in the margin and on the Northeast Florida and St. Augustine maps.

IF YOU HAVE 3 DAYS

Spend your first night in 🖼 **Jacksonville** ①, using it as a base to explore both the Jacksonville Museum of Contemporary Art and Amelia Island's Fort Clinch State Park, which contains one of America's best-preserved brick forts. Take I–95 south to **St. Augustine** ⑤–⑰, and see the restored Spanish Quarter Museum ⑧ before continuing down the coast. Enjoy Canaveral National Seashore, accessible from either 🖼

New Smyrna Beach ⑳ or ⛱ Cocoa Beach ㉑, and if the movie *Apollo 13* captured your attention, don't miss Spaceport USA.

IF YOU HAVE 5 DAYS
From ⛱ **Jacksonville** ①, visit the Amelia Island Historic District as well as Fort Clinch State Park; in town, see both the Jacksonville Museum of Contemporary Art and the Museum of Science and History. Going south on I–95, stop in ⛱ **St. Augustine** ⑤–⑰, where you can follow the Old City Walking Tour suggested by the Visitor Information Center ⑤ and stroll through the restored Spanish Quarter Museum ⑧. Consider taking the slightly longer but more scenic Route A1A to ⛱ **Daytona Beach** ⑲, where you can visit the Museum of Arts and Sciences and the famous beaches. For your last night, stay in ⛱ **New Smyrna Beach** ⑳ or ⛱ **Cocoa Beach** ㉑, within reach of the Cape Canaveral National Seashore and Spaceport USA at the Kennedy Space Center.

IF YOU HAVE 10 DAYS
As in the previous itineraries, start in ⛱ **Jacksonville** ① and visit the attractions mentioned above; by staying three nights, however, you can also see the Kingsley Plantation, Florida's oldest remaining plantation, and hike or picnic in Fort Clinch State Park on Amelia Island ④. Next, head to ⛱ **St. Augustine** ⑤–⑰. Three days here will enable you to conduct a more leisurely exploration of the extensive historic district and to take in the Lightner Museum ⑫, housed in one of Henry Flagler's fancy hotels. Another three-day stay, this time based at either ⛱ **Daytona Beach** ⑲, ⛱ **New Smyrna Beach** ⑳, or ⛱ **Cocoa Beach** ㉑, allows you to cover Daytona's Museum of Arts and Sciences, drive along the shoreline, spend some time at the beach, and see the Canaveral National Seashore and Spaceport USA. Then head inland for a day in the Ocala National Forest, a beautiful wilderness area.

When to Tour Northeast Florida

In December and January, northeast Florida can get a bit chilly and tends to fill up with Canadians escaping much colder temperatures. Auto-racing enthusiasts should be sure to visit Daytona in February, the height of the racing season. The ocean warms up by March, and college kids on spring break pack the beaches—but this is also the best month to see the azalea gardens in full bloom. Midsummer is breezy and hot but not as hot as in a northern city, as long as you stick to the beaches; inland, the summer heat and humidity can be stifling.

JACKSONVILLE TO AMELIA ISLAND

The northeasternmost corner of Florida is a land of tall pine trees, red earth reminiscent of neighboring Georgia, and coastal marshes. It can be 20 degrees colder than Miami in winter, and the "season" here (and the most expensive rooms) actually runs from April to September. Our discussion of the area starts in its hub—Jacksonville. From there we head to the coast, starting in the communities to the east, which serve as Jacksonville's beaches, and continuing north to Amelia Island and its old seaport town, Fernandina Beach.

Jacksonville

❶ *399 mi north of Miami, 120 mi south of Savannah, Georgia.*

One of Florida's oldest cities and, in terms of square miles (730), the largest U.S. city, Jacksonville makes for an underrated vacation spot. You'll find appealing downtown riverside areas, handsome residential neighborhoods, the region's only skyscrapers, and a thriving arts scene.

Remnants of the Old South flavor the city, as does the sense of sub-tropical paradise for which Florida is famous.

Because Jacksonville was settled along both sides of the twisting St. Johns River, many attractions are on or near a riverbank, and the plentiful shoreline yields pretty vistas across the wide waterway. It helps to plan your trip carefully. Both sides of the river, which is spanned by a myriad of bridges, have downtown areas and waterfront complexes of shops, restaurants, parks, and museums. Some attractions can be reached by water taxi, a handy alternative to driving back and forth across the bridges, but a car is generally necessary.

☼ Permanent exhibits at the **Museum of Science and History** range from those on pre-Columbian history and the ecology and history of the St. Johns River to the Maple Leaf Civil War Collection and the hands-on Kidspace section. New this year is a display on whales, dolphins, and manatees. There are also excellent special exhibits and a popular 3-D laser show in the Alexander Brest Planetarium. Physical science shows are held weekends in the science theater. ⊠ *1025 Museum Circle,* ☎ *904/396–7062.* ☜ *$5.* ☉ *Weekdays 10–5, Sat. 10–6, Sun. 1–6.*

The **Jacksonville Museum of Contemporary Art** includes contemporary and classic art, including the Koger collection of Oriental porcelains, works by Pablo Picasso, and rare pre-Columbian artifacts. Special exhibits, film and lecture series, and workshops are also held. ⊠ *4160 Boulevard Center Dr.,* ☎ *904/398–8336.* ☜ *$3.* ☉ *Tues., Wed., Fri. 10–4, Thurs. 10–10, weekends 1–5.*

The world-famous Wark Collection of early 18th-century Meissen porcelain is just one reason to see the **Cummer Gallery of Art.** Set amid leafy formal gardens, this former baron's estate includes 12 permanent collection galleries, displaying over 2,000 items covering over 4,000 years, and an interactive teaching gallery for kids and adults. ⊠ *829 Riverside Ave.,* ☎ *904/356–6857.* ☜ *$3. Free Tues. 4:30–9:30.* ☉ *Tues. 10–9:30, Wed.–Fri. 10–4, Sat. noon–5, Sun. 2–5.*

Fine collections of Boehm, Royal Copenhagen, Bing, and Grondahl porcelains are found at the **Alexander Brest Museum,** at Jacksonville University. Also on display are Steuben glass, cloisonné, pre-Columbian artifacts, and an extensive collection of ivories. The home of composer Frederick Delius, also on campus, has tours on request. ⊠ *2800 University Blvd. N,* ☎ *904/744–3950, ext. 3371.* ☜ *Free.* ☉ *Weekdays 9–4:30, Sat. noon–5. Closed school holidays.*

☼ A 10-year expansion and renovation of the **Jacksonville Zoo,** known for its outstanding collection of rare waterfowl, is well under way. The new African Veldt is home to alligators, elephants, and white rhinos, among other species of African birds and mammals. ⊠ *8605 Zoo Rd., off Heckscher Dr. E,* ☎ *904/757–4462.* ☜ *$6.50.* ☉ *Daily 9–5.*

OFF THE
BEATEN PATH

FORT CAROLINE NATIONAL MEMORIAL – Spread over 130 acres along the St. Johns River, 13 mi northeast of downtown Jacksonville via Route 113, this spot holds both historical and recreational interest. The original fort was built in the 1560s by French Huguenots, who were later slaughtered by the Spanish in the first major clash between European powers for control of what would become the United States. An oak-wooded pathway leads to a replica of the original fort—a great, sunny place to picnic (bring your own food and drink), stretch your legs, and explore a small museum. ⊠ *12713 Fort Caroline Rd.,* ☎ *904/641–7155.* ☜ *Free.* ☉ *Museum daily 9–5.*

Northeast Florida

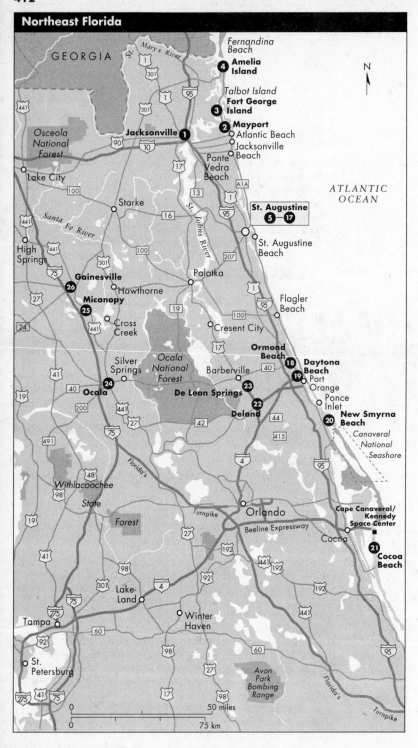

Dining and Lodging

$$$ ✕ **24 Miramar.** This stylish restaurant, with its long, narrow room minimally decorated in black and white, is hidden in a small shopping center on the south side of the river. The superb cuisine captures the essence of Californian, Asian, Latin, and Italian cooking, and it's difficult to choose among the inventive nightly specials. Try the Thai crab cakes, Caribbean cannelloni, or roast duckling crepes. A 16% service charge is automatically added to your bill. ⊠ *Miramar Shopping Center, 4446 Hendricks Ave.,* ☏ *904/448–2424. AE, MC, V. No lunch.*

$$$ ✕ **Wine Cellar.** Thought by many to be the finest restaurant in Jack-
★ sonville, this elegant, candlelit spot specializes in classic Continental fare. Enjoy the rack of lamb (the house favorite), or choose grilled salmon with dill mustard sauce, veal chop with morel sauce, or chicken topped with crabmeat, asparagus, and béarnaise sauce. Desserts include a bittersweet-chocolate mousse cake and a traditional cheesecake. ⊠ *314 Prudential Dr.,* ☏ *904/398–8989. Jacket required. AE, MC, V.*

$$ ✕ **River City Brewing Company.** There are now two of these popular brew pubs: one overlooking the river on the south bank and the other on the city's south side, in Baymeadows. Take one of the daily brewery tours; then sample the day's brew. Sandwiches and salads are featured at lunch, while dinner brings shrimp, fresh fish, grilled steaks, and seafood jambalaya. There's live jazz for Sunday brunch. ⊠ *835 Museum Circle Dr., Southbank Riverwalk,* ☏ *904/398–2299;* ⊠ *9810-3 Baymeadows Rd.,* ☏ *904/642–6310. AE, MC, V.*

$ ✕ **Crawdaddy's.** Take it Cajun or cool. This riverfront fish shack, just off I–10 at I–95, is the place for seafood, jambalaya, and country chicken. Lunch is a sumptuous buffet, and there's a very popular Sunday brunch. Dig into the house specialty, catfish—all you can eat— then dance to a *fais-do-do* (Cajun dance) beat. ⊠ *1643 Prudential Dr.,* ☏ *904/396–3546. AE, D, DC, MC, V.*

$$$ 🏨 **Jacksonville Hilton.** This completely renovated hotel reopened in 1997
★ as a brand-new Hilton. On the south side of the St. Johns River, it's within easy walking distance of museums, restaurants, and the water taxi. Rooms are spacious, and many have outstanding river views and balconies. ⊠ *1201 Riverplace Blvd., 32207,* ☏ *904/398–8800,* 𝖥𝖠𝖷 *904/398–5570. 292 rooms. 3 restaurants, lounge, pool, spa, exercise room. AE, D, MC, V.*

$$$ 🏨 **Jacksonville Omni Hotel.** This 16-story ultramodern facility is in the
★ heart of downtown. The splashy, marble-floored lobby leads to the reception area, an upscale bar and lounge, and a restaurant with cozy banquettes and tables that look up to a soaring atrium. Sunday brunch is popular here. Extra-large rooms, many with spectacular river views, are stylishly decorated and include minibars. ⊠ *245 Water St., 32202,* ☏ *904/355–6664,* 𝖥𝖠𝖷 *904/354–2970. 354 rooms. Restaurant, lounge, pool, exercise room. AE, D, DC, MC, V.*

$$–$$$ 🏨 **Radisson Riverwalk Hotel.** This bustling five-story hotel, connected to the Riverwalk complex, has modern rooms with either a king-size or two double beds. It's within walking distance of four restaurants, a museum, and water taxis to Jacksonville Landing. Units overlooking the St. Johns River command the highest prices. ⊠ *1515 Prudential Dr., 32207,* ☏ *904/396–5100,* 𝖥𝖠𝖷 *904/396–7154. 304 rooms, 19 suites. 3 restaurants, lounge, no-smoking rooms, pool, 2 tennis courts. AE, DC, MC, V.*

$$ 🏨 **Comfort Suites Hotel.** In Baymeadows, near some currently "in" restaurants, clubs, and shops, this all-suites hotel is a real value. Units, decorated in breezy, radiant Florida hues, include refrigerators and sleep sofas. Microwaves and VCRs come with master suites. Rates include daily Continental breakfast and cocktails on weekdays. ✉ *8333 Ellis Trail, 32256,* ☎ *904/739–1155,* FAX *904/731–0752. 128 suites. Pool, spa, coin laundry. AE, DC, MC, V.*

$$ 🏠 **House on Cherry St.** This early 20th-century treasure is furnished with pewter, Oriental rugs, antique canopy beds, and other remnants of a rich past. Fresh flowers in rooms add a nice touch, and Carol Anderson further welcomes guests to her riverside home with wine and hors d'oeuvres. Full breakfast is served. You can walk to the parks and gardens of the chic Avondale district. ✉ *1844 Cherry St., 32205,* ☎ *904/384–1999. 4 rooms. Bicycles. MC, V.*

Nightlife and the Arts

THE ARTS

Broadway touring shows, top-name entertainers, and other major events are booked at the **Florida Theater Performing Arts Center** (✉ 128 E. Forsyth St., ☎ 904/355–5661). The **Jacksonville Civic Auditorium** (✉ 300 W. Water St., ☎ 904/630–0701) draws various popular entertainment; check local publications for schedules. The **Alhambra Dinner Theater** (✉ 12000 Beach Blvd., ☎ 904/641–1212) serves up professional theater with menus that change with each play. The oldest continuously producing community theater in the United States, **Theatre Jacksonville** (✉ 2032 San Marco Blvd., ☎ 904/396–4425) features productions from Shakespeare to programs for children. The **Jacksonville Symphony Orchestra** (☎ 904/354–5479) presents a variety of concerts around town.

NIGHTLIFE

Cafe on the Square (✉ 1974 San Marco Blvd., ☎ 904/399–4422) has live local blues, jazz, and rock bands Tuesday through Saturday. At **Club 5** (✉ 1028 Park Ave., ☎ 904/355–1119), there is alternative high-energy techno and disco dance music nightly. At the **Diamond Boots Saloon** (✉ 797 Blanding Blvd., ☎ 904/264–0611), crowds dance to live country bands. **River City Brewing Company** (✉ 835 Museum Circle Dr., Southbank Riverwalk, ☎ 904/398–2299; ✉ 9810-3 Baymeadows Rd., ☎ 904/642–6310) has live local jazz or blues bands on Friday and Saturday nights as well as Sunday brunch.

Outdoor Activities and Sports

DOG RACING

Race seasons are split among three tracks. In town, the **Jacksonville Kennel Club** (✉ 1440 N. McDuff Ave., ☎ 904/646–0001) runs races May–September. **Orange Park Kennel Club** (✉ ½ mi south of I–295 on U.S. 17, ☎ 904/646–0001) has racing November–April. Dogs race at the **St. Johns Greyhound Park** (✉ 7 mi south of I–95 on U.S. 1, ☎ 904/646–0001) March–April.

FOOTBALL

The region's blockbuster event is the **Gator Bowl** (☎ 904/396–1800), on New Year's Day. The NFL **Jacksonville Jaguars** (☎ 904/633–6000) play scheduled games all season.

Shopping

For a huge group of specialty shops and a number of restaurants, roam around the downtown **Jacksonville Landing** (✉ 2 Independent Dr. at Main Street Bridge), on the north side of the river. **Riverdale/Avondale Shopping Center** (✉ 12 Riverside Ave.), in the heart of historic Avondale, is a quiet two-block area of one-of-a-kind art galleries, restaurants, and boutiques. Stop at the **San Marco Shopping Center** (✉ 25 San Marco Blvd.), and wander through interesting stores and restaurants in 1920s Mediterranean revival–style buildings.

Jacksonville Beaches

20 mi east of Jacksonville on U.S. 90 (Beach Blvd.).

Jacksonville's main beaches run along the barrier island that includes the popular, laid-back towns of Jacksonville Beach and Atlantic Beach and the area around Ponte Vedra Beach. The large number of private homes along Ponte Vedra's beaches make access difficult, however.

Atlantic Beach is a favored surfing area. Around the popular Sea Turtle Inn, you'll find catamaran rentals and instruction. Five areas have lifeguards on duty in the summer 10–6. **Jacksonville Beach** is the liveliest of the long line of Jacksonville beaches. Young people flock here, and there are all sorts of games to play, beach concessions, rental shops, and a fishing pier. **Neptune Beach,** on the north end of Jacksonville Beach, is more residential than its neighbor and offers easy access to quieter beaches. Surfers consider it one of the area's two best surfing sites, the other being Atlantic Beach.

Dining and Lodging

$$–$$$ ✕ **Gio's Cafe.** At this sophisticated art-deco spot, the cuisine is described as "Continental Italian with California flair." The many pasta dishes share the menu with Beef Wellington with a smoked lobster filling and roast rack of lamb, prepared differently each night. The most popular dessert is the wild berry fruit tart. ⊠ *900 Sawgrass Village, Ponte Vedra Beach,* ☎ *904/273–0101. AE, MC, V.*

$–$$ ✕ **Ragtime.** A New Orleans theme threads through everything from
★ the Sunday jazz brunch to the beignets at this loud spot, popular with a sophisticated young bunch. If you aren't into Creole and Cajun, have a simple po'boy sandwich or fish sizzled on the grill. Bouillabaisse, conch salad, and baked brie are also good. ⊠ *207 Atlantic Blvd., Atlantic Beach,* ☎ *904/241–7877. AE, DC, MC, V.*

$ ✕ **Homestead.** A down-home place that has been around forever and is always busy, this country-cooking restaurant specializes in skillet-fried chicken with rice and gravy. Chicken and dumplings, deep-fried chicken gizzards, buttermilk biscuits, and strawberry shortcake also draw the locals. There are several dining rooms and a huge fireplace. ⊠ *1712 Beach Blvd., Jacksonville Beach,* ☎ *904/249–5240. AE, D, MC, V. No lunch. Brunch Sun.*

$$$ 🏨 **Lodge at Ponte Vedra Beach.** White stucco and Spanish roof tiles yield a look that's Mediterranean villa grand luxe. The lodge caters to a clientele whose passions are golf and tennis. Though it doesn't have its own tennis courts, it does provide shuttle service. Rooms, designed with a country-French flair, have private balconies and cozy window seats. Some have a whirlpool and fireplace. ⊠ *607 Ponte Vedra Blvd., Ponte Vedra Beach 32080,* ☎ *904/273–9500,* FAX *904/273–0210. 66 rooms, 24 suites. 2 restaurants, bar and grill, lounge, 3 pools, 54 holes of golf, exercise room, horseback riding, boating, fishing. AE, D, DC, MC, V.*

$$$ 🏨 **Marriott at Sawgrass.** The grounds are beautifully manicured, but the main building and lobby areas feel more like a functional, business hotel than a plush resort. Rooms are spacious and well-appointed, with deep-color carpets and drapes, wood furniture, and roomy bathrooms. This is truly a full-service resort, and whether you've come to laze about or to spend your days busy with activities, you'll only need to leave the property to hit the beach. ⊠ *1000 TPC Blvd., Ponte Vedra Beach 32082,* ☎ *904/285–7777,* FAX *904/285–0906. 546 units. 3 restaurants, 2 pools, wading pool, 99 holes of golf, putting green,*

lighted tennis courts, exercise room, horseback riding, bicycles, children's programs. AE, D, DC, MC, V.

$$ 🏨 **Comfort Inn Oceanfront.** Every room in this oceanfront hotel has a private balcony and a view of the Atlantic. Four waterfalls cascade into a giant free-form heated pool and there is a rock grotto and spa. ⊠ *1515 N. 1st St., Jacksonville Beach 32250,* ☎ *904/241–2311 or 800/654–8776,* 🗗 *904/249–3830. 177 rooms. Deli, lounge, pool, spa, exercise room, beach, airport shuttle. AE, D, DC, MC, V.*

Nightlife

Ragtime Taproom Brewery (⊠ 207 Atlantic Blvd., Atlantic Beach, ☎ 904/241–7877) resonates with live local jazz and blues bands Thursday through Sunday.

Outdoor Activities and Sports

FISHING

One popular spot is **Jacksonville Beach Fishing Pier,** which extends 1,200 feet into the Atlantic; the cost to fish is $3, 50¢ just to watch.

GOLF

Ponte Vedra Beach is home of the PGA Tour. **Ponte Vedra Inn & Club** (⊠ 200 Ponte Vedra Blvd., Ponte Vedra Beach, ☎ 904/285–1111 or 800/234–7842) offers 36 holes. **Ravines Golf & Country Club** (⊠ 2932 Ravines Rd., Middleburg, ☎ 904/282–7888) has 18 holes. The 99-hole **Tournament Players Club at Sawgrass** (⊠ 110 TPC Blvd., Ponte Vedra Beach, ☎ 904/273–3235 or 800/457–4653) hosts the Tournament Players Championship in March.

TENNIS

Ponte Vedra Beach is the headquarters of the Association of Tennis Professionals (ATP). The **Marriott at Sawgrass** (☎ 904/285–7777) offers 19 courts. The **Ponte Vedra Inn & Club** (☎ 904/285–3856) has 15 Har-Tru courts.

Mayport

❷ *20 mi northeast of Jacksonville.*

Dating back more than 300 years, Mayport is one of the oldest fishing communities in the United States. Today it's home to several excellent and very casual seafood restaurants and a large commercial shrimp-boat fleet. It's also the Navy's fourth-largest home port.

Kathryn Abbey Hanna Park is the area's showplace park. It offers beaches, showers, and snack bars that operate April–Labor Day.

En Route   You can take your car on a fun **ferry** ride between Mayport and Fort George Island. ☎ *904/270–2520.* 🎫 *$2.50 per car, pedestrians 50¢.* ☉ *Daily 6:20 AM–10 PM every ½ hour.*

Fort George Island

❸ *25 mi northeast of Jacksonville.*

★   Reachable by ferry or bridge, the **Kingsley Plantation** was built by an eccentric slave trader in 1792 and is the oldest remaining cotton plantation in the state. Slave quarters, as well as the modest Kingsley home, are open to the public. ☎ *904/251–3537.* 🎫 *Free.* ☉ *Daily 9–5; guided tours Thurs.–Mon. 9:30, 11, 1:30, and 3.*

At the **Talbot Island State Parks,** you'll find 17 mi of gorgeous beaches, sand dunes, and golden marshes that hum with birds and bugs. Come to picnic, fish, swim, snorkel, or camp. ⊠ *12157 Heckscher Dr., Tal-*

bot Island, ☎ 904/251–2320. 🖃 $3.25 per vehicle with up to 8 people. ☉ Daily 8–sunset.

Amelia Island (Fernandina Beach)

❹ *35 mi northeast of Jacksonville.*

Although this island at the northeasternmost reach of Florida is a bit out of the way, it is worth the trip. Here you'll find 13 mi of beautiful beaches with enormous sand dunes along the island's eastern flank, a state park with a Civil War fort, sophisticated shops and restaurants, accommodations that range from bed-and-breakfasts to luxury resorts, and the quaint town of Fernandina Beach, on the northern end of the island, with its enchanting historic district.

★ Stroll through the **Amelia Island Historic District,** containing more than 50 blocks of homes and other buildings listed on the National Register of Historic Places. Here 450 ornate structures built prior to 1927 offer some of the nation's finest examples of Queen Anne, Victorian, and Italianate mansions. Many date back to the haven's glory days in the mid-19th century. Pick up a map for a self-guided tour at the chamber of commerce in the old railroad depot, once a stopping point on the first cross-state railroad.

Founded in 1859, **St. Peter's Episcopal Church** (🖃 801 Atlantic Ave., ☎ 904/261–4293) is a Gothic Revival structure with Tiffany glass–style memorials and an original, turn-of-the-century L. C. Harrison organ with magnificent hand-painted pipes. It once served as a school.

You'll probably recognize the **Amelia Island Lighthouse** (🖃 1 Lighthouse La., ☎ 904/261–3248) at first glance. This frequently photographed landmark, built in 1839, is one of the oldest structures on the island. It is still in operation and is visible 19 mi out to sea. The inside, however, is not open to the public.

One of the country's best-preserved and most complete brick forts can
★ be found at **Fort Clinch State Park.** Fort Clinch was built to discourage further British intrusion after the War of 1812 and was occupied in 1863 by the Confederacy; a year later it was retaken by the North. During the Spanish-American War, it was reactivated for a brief time but for the most part was not used. Today the 1,086-acre park offers camping, nature trails, carriage rides, swimming on a pristine beach, surf fishing, picnicking, and living-history reenactments showing life in the garrison at the time of the Civil War. 🖃 N. 14th St., ☎ 904/277–7274. 🖃 $3.25 per vehicle with up to 8 people. ☉ Daily 8–sunset.

Beaches

Amelia Island's **eastern shore** is one giant 13-mi stretch of white-sand beach edged with dunes, some 40 feet high. It's one of the few beaches where you are allowed to go horseback riding.

Fort Clinch State Park, on the island's northern tip, includes a beach and pier; you pay a state-park entrance fee to reach them. Broad and lovely, the beach is close to parking, bathhouses, picnic areas, and all other park facilities, including the fort.

Dining and Lodging

$$$–$$$$ ✕ **The Grill.** This award-winning signature restaurant of the Ritz-Carl-
★ ton Amelia Island is quietly elegant and truly outstanding. Chef Matthew Medure has created an unusual menu, and thanks to his talent, it works. Dine on grilled bison tenderloin with stewed Vidalia onions in tuna sauce or salmon escallop with angel-hair pasta in tomato-basil oil. The daring can choose the Adventurous Guest menu, a multi-

course meal created on the spot by the chef. ✉ *4750 Amelia Island Pkwy.,* ☎ *904/277–1100. Reservations essential. Jacket required. AE, DC, MC, V. No lunch.*

$$–$$$ ✕ **Beech Street Grill.** The hardwood floors, high ceilings, and marble fireplaces in the many rooms of this lovingly restored 1889 sea captain's house create a pleasant environment for a meal, but don't be surprised if small children are running about. An extensive menu includes such house favorites as roasted duck with raspberry sauce, braised rack of lamb with fresh mint salsa, and swordfish with mustard cognac sauce. A blackboard lists four or five fresh fish specials nightly. The outstanding wine list includes some coveted Californians. As this is an extremely popular restaurant, reservations are advised on weekends. ✉ *801 Beech St.,* ☎ *904/277–3662. AE, MC, V. No lunch.*

$–$$ ✕ **O'Kane's Irish Pub.** Stop here for authentic Irish fare: shepherd's pie,
★   steak and Guinness pie, or fish-and-chips. Also on the menu are sandwiches, ribs, and pasta and an amazing soup that's served in a bowl of sourdough bread—you eat the whole thing! This is one of the few bars in the United States that still prepares Irish coffee the way they do in Ireland—with very cold, barely whipped heavy cream floated on top. ✉ *318 Centre St.,* ☎ *904/261–1000. AE, MC, V.*

$$$$ 🏨 **Amelia Island Plantation.** This sprawling resort, one of the first to be "environmentally sensitive," encompasses ancient live-oak forests, marshes, lagoons, and some of the state's highest dunes. Some homes are occupied year-round, and a warm sense of community prevails. Accommodations range from home and condo rentals to a full-service hotel; honeymoon villas have private indoor pools. Though the resort is best known for golf and tennis, hiking and biking trails thread through the 1,300 acres. ✉ *3000 First Coast Hwy., 32034,* ☎ *904/261–6161 or 800/874–6878,* 𝔽𝔸𝕏 *904/277–5159. 1,100 units. 6 restaurants, 1 18-hole and 3 9-hole golf courses, 25 tennis courts, health club, racquetball, boating, fishing, bicycles, pro shops, children's programs. D, MC, V.*

$$$$ 🏨 **Ritz-Carlton Amelia Island.** Considered by many Florida's finest re-
★   sort, this hotel woos guests with its stylish elegance, superb comfort, excellent service, and exquisite beach. All units in the eight-story building have balconies and ocean views. Suites and rooms are spacious and luxurious. Public areas are exquisitely maintained, grounds are beautifully manicured, and fine cuisine can be had at a choice of restaurants, including the award-winning Grill. ✉ *4750 Amelia Island Pkwy., 32034,* ☎ *904/277–1100. 449 units. 3 restaurants, 3 bars, indoor and outdoor pools, 18-hole golf course, 9 tennis courts, health club, beach, bicycles. AE, D, DC, MC, V.*

$$ 🏨 **Elizabeth Pointe Lodge.** Built to resemble a Nantucket shingle-style house but blown up to the proportions of a lodge, this inn is set just behind the dunes. Oceanside units have great water views, albeit through disappointingly small windows. A chair-filled porch offers everyone a chance to rock in ocean breezes, and on cold nights guests can cluster around the living room fireplace. Two adjacent cottages have suites. ✉ *98 S. Fletcher Ave., 32034,* ☎ *904/277–4851. 25 rooms and suites. Beach. AE, MC, V.*

Outdoor Activities and Sports

GOLF

Designers Pete Dye and Tom Fazio created 45 challenging holes at the **Amelia Island Plantation** (✉ 3000 First Coast Hwy., ☎ 904/261–6161 or 800/874–6878). At the **Ritz-Carlton Amelia Island** (✉ 4750 Amelia Island Pkwy., ☎ 904/277–1100), live oaks, palm trees, and sand dunes frame 18 holes.

Amelia Island Plantation (☎ 904/277–5145 or 800/486–8366) has 25 tennis courts and is the site of the nationally televised, top-rated Women's Tennis Association Championships in April and the Men's All-American Tennis Championship in September. The **Ritz-Carlton Amelia Island** (☎ 904/277–1100) has nine Har-Tru tennis courts.

Shopping

Within the Amelia Island Historic District are numerous shops, art galleries, and boutiques, many of which are clustered along cobblestoned **Centre Street.** The **Island Art Association Co-op Gallery** (⌂ 205 Centre St., ☎ 904/261-7020) displays and sells paintings, prints, and other artwork by local artists.

ST. AUGUSTINE

35 mi south of Jacksonville.

Founded in 1565, St. Augustine claims to be the oldest U.S. city and has a wealth of historic buildings and attractions. Once you've visited the historic sites on the mainland, however, you haven't exhausted this city's charms; it also has 43 mi of beaches on two barrier islands to the east, both reachable by causeways. Several times a year St. Augustine holds historic reenactments, such as December's Grand Christmas Illumination, which marks the town's British occupation.

Exploring St. Augustine

The core of any visit is a tour of the historic district, a showcase for more than 60 historic sites and attractions, plus 144 blocks of historic houses listed on the National Register of Historic Places. You could probably spend several weeks exploring these treasures, but don't neglect other, generally newer, attractions found elsewhere in town. Pick the sights that interest you, as your time allows.

A Good Walk

A good place to start is the **Visitor Information Center** ⑤, where you can pick up maps, brochures, and information. It's on San Marco Avenue between Castillo Drive and Orange Street, right across from the big fort. From there, cross Orange Street to reach the **City Gate** ⑥, the entrance to the city's popular restored area. Walk south on St. George Street to the **Oldest Wooden Schoolhouse** ⑦. Directly across from it is the **Spanish Quarter Museum** ⑧, a state-operated living-history village. Go out Fort Alley and cross San Marco Avenue to the impressive **Castillo de San Marcos National Monument** ⑨, a wonderful fort for exploring.

Now head west on Cuna Street and turn left on Cordova Street. Walk south three blocks to Valencia Street and turn right. At the end of the block you'll come to the splendid **Flagler Memorial Presbyterian Church** ⑩. Head one block south on Sevilla Street and turn left on King Street to find the **Museum of Historic St. Augustine Government House** ⑪ and two more of Henry Flagler's legacies: the **Lightner Museum** ⑫ and **Flagler College** ⑬. Continue two blocks east on King Street and turn right onto St. George Street to reach the **Ximenez-Fatio House** ⑭. For a taste of the turn of the century, head east on Artillery Lane to the **Oldest Store Museum** ⑮. Finally, head back north to the Bridge of Lions, the **Plaza de la Constitution** ⑯, and the **Basilica Cathedral of St. Augustine** ⑰.

TIMING

Though most sights keep the same hours (daytime only), a few are not open on Sundays, so it's best to visit Monday–Saturday. Besides, weekday mornings generally have the smallest crowds.

Sights to See

⑰ Basilica Cathedral of St. Augustine. The cathedral holds the country's oldest written parish records, dating to 1594. Restored in the mid-1960s, the current structure (1797) had extensive changes after an 1887 fire. ⊠ *40 Cathedral Pl.,* ☎ *904/824–2806.* ☒ *Donation welcome.* ☉ *Weekdays 5:30–5, weekends 5:30–7.*

❾ Castillo de San Marcos National Monument. This massive structure looks every century of its 300 years. Park rangers provide an introductory narration, after which you're on your own to explore the moat, turrets, and 16-foot-thick walls. The fort was constructed of coquina, a soft limestone made of broken shells and coral. Built by the Spanish to protect St. Augustine from British raids (English pirates were handy with a torch), the fort was used as a prison during the Revolutionary and Civil wars. Garrison rooms depict the life of the era, and special cannon-firing demonstrations are held on weekends from Memorial Day to Labor Day. Children under 17 must be accompanied by an adult. ⊠ *1 Castillo Dr.,* ☎ *904/829–6506.* ☒ *$2.* ☉ *Daily 8:45–4:45.*

❻ City Gate. The gate is a relic from the days when the Castillo's moat ran westward to the river and the Cubo Defense Line (defensive wall) protected against approaches from the north. ⊠ *St. George St.*

⑬ Flagler College. Originally one of two posh hotels Henry Flagler built in 1888, this building is a riveting structure replete with towers, turrets, and arcades decorated by Louis Comfort Tiffany. Now a small liberal arts college, the building is not open for tours, but you can look at the front courtyard. ⊠ *78 King St.,* ☎ *904/829–6481.*

❿ Flagler Memorial Presbyterian Church. To look at a marvelous Venetian Renaissance structure, head to this church, built by Flagler in 1889. The dome towers more than 100 feet and is topped by a 20-foot Greek cross. ⊠ *Valencia and Sevilla Sts.* ☉ *Weekdays 8:30–4:30.*

Fountain of Youth Archeological Park. Well north of St. Augustine's main sights is this tribute to explorer Ponce de León, marking the location of the legendary spring that flowed through folklore as the Fountain of Youth. In the complex is a springhouse, an explorer's globe, a planetarium, a Native American village, and exhibits about early Timucuan Indian inhabitants. ⊠ *155 Magnolia Ave.,* ☎ *904/829–3168.* ☒ *$4.75.* ☉ *Daily 9–5.*

★ ⑫ Lightner Museum. In his quest to turn Florida into an American Riviera, Henry Flagler built two fancy hotels in 1888—the Ponce de León, which became Flagler College, and the Alcazar, which now houses this museum. The building showcases three floors of furnishings, costumes, and Victorian Art glass plus a collection of ornate antique music boxes (demonstrations daily at 11 and 2). The Lightner Antiques Mall perches on three levels of what was the hotel's grandiose indoor pool. ⊠ *75 King St.,* ☎ *904/824–2874.* ☒ *$5.* ☉ *Museum daily 9–5, mall Tues.–Sun. 10–4.*

Mission of Nombre de Dios. This site, north of the historic district, commemorates where America's first Christian mass was celebrated. A 208-foot stainless-steel cross marks the spot where the mission's first cross was planted. ⊠ *San Marco Ave. and Old Mission Rd.,* ☎ *904/824–2809.* ☒ *Donation requested.* ☉ *Daily 9–6.*

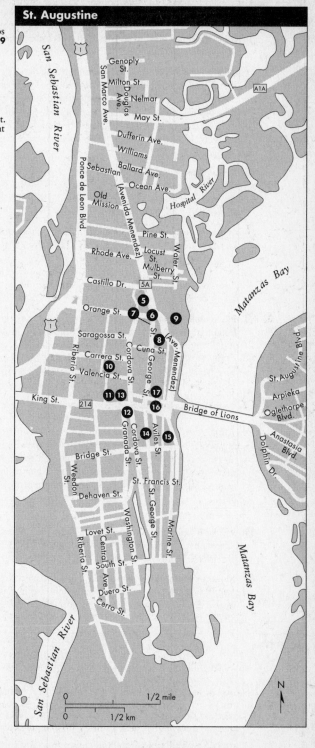

St. Augustine

⓫ **Museum of Historic St. Augustine Government House.** Featuring a collection of over 300 artifacts from both archaeological digs and Spanish shipwrecks off the Florida coast, this museum reflects five centuries of history. ⊠ *48 King St.,* ☎ *904/825–5033.* ☞ *$2.* ☉ *Daily 10–4.*

Oldest House. Though the current building dates from the early 1700s, there has been a structure on this site since the early 1600s. Much of the city's history is seen in the building's changes and additions, from the coquina blocks used instead of wood soon after the town burned in 1702 to the house's enlargement during the British occupation. The house is a few blocks south of the Oldest Store Museum. ⊠ *14 St. Francis St.,* ☎ *904/824–2872.* ☞ *$5.* ☉ *Daily 9–5.*

⓯ **Oldest Store Museum.** There are high-button shoes, lace-up corsets, patent drugs, and confectionery specialties at this re-creation of a turn-of-the-century general store. ⊠ *4 Artillery La.,* ☎ *904/829–9729.* ☞ *$4.* ☉ *Mon.–Sat. 9–5, Sun. 10–5.*

❼ **Oldest Wooden Schoolhouse.** Automated mannequins of a teacher and students relate the school's history. This tiny 18th-century building is built of cypress and cedar and thought to be one of the nation's oldest schoolhouses. Because it was the closest structure to the city gate, it served as a guardhouse and sentry shelter during the Seminole Wars. ⊠ *14 St. George St.,* ☎ *904/824–0192.* ☞ *$2.* ☉ *Daily 9–5.*

⓰ **Plaza de la Constitution.** The central area of the original settlement was laid out in 1598 by decree of King Philip II, and little has changed since. At its center is a monument to the Spanish constitution of 1812, while at the east end is a public market dating from early American days. Just beyond is a statue of Juan Ponce de León, who "discovered" Florida in 1513. ⊠ *St. George St. and Cathedral Pl.*

❽ **Spanish Quarter Museum.** You can wander through the narrow streets at your own pace in this village comprising eight sites. Along your way you may see a blacksmith building his shop (a historic reconstruction) or artisans busy at candle dipping, spinning, weaving, and cabinetmaking. They are all making reproductions that will be used within the restored area. You'll find period artifacts and an orientation center in the Triay House, but buy your tickets at the Museum Store. ⊠ *Triay House, 29 St. George St., Museum Store, 33 St. George St.;* ☎ *904/825–6830.* ☞ *$5.* ☉ *Daily 9–5.*

❺ **Visitor Information Center.** An entertaining film on the founding of St. Augustine, *Dream of an Empire* is shown hourly 9–4. ⊠ *10 Castillo Dr.,* ☎ *904/824–1000.* ☞ *$3.* ☉ *Daily 9–5.*

⓮ **Ximenez-Fatio House.** Originally built as a merchant's house and store in 1797, it became a tourist boardinghouse in the 1800s and is now restored as it was when it was an inn. ⊠ *20 Aviles St.,* ☎ *904/829–3575.* ☞ *Free.* ☉ *Mon. and Thurs.–Sat. 11–4, Sun. 1–4.*

Beaches

Stretching between St. Augustine and the Ormond/Daytona Beach area are miles of empty beaches. The young gravitate to the public beaches at **Vilano Beach,** at the southern tip of the barrier island just north of St. Augustine. The very popular **St. Augustine Beach,** the closest beach to downtown, is on the northern end of Anastasia Island, directly east of town. Containing 1,700 protected acres of bird sanctuary, the **Anastasia State Recreation Area** draws families who like to hike, bike, camp, swim, and play on the beach.

Dining

$$ ✕ **King's Head British Pub.** Bangers and mash, fish-and-chips, steak and kidney pie, and other English pub fare are the order here as well as a superb selection of fine English beers on tap. ⊠ *6460 U.S. 1N,* ☎ *904/823–9787. AE, DC, MC, V.*

$$ ✕ **La Parisienne.** Tiny and attentive, pleasantly lusty in its approach
★ to honest bistro cuisine, this little place is a true find (that everyone has unfortunately now found). Weekend brunches are available, too. Try the roast duck or chicken provençale, but save room for the pastries at this excellent, very French restaurant. ⊠ *60 Hypolita St.,* ☎ *904/829–0055. Reservations essential. AE, MC, V. Closed Mon.*

$–$$ ✕ **Columbia.** An heir to the original Columbia, founded in Tampa in 1905, this one serves time-honored Cuban and Spanish dishes: arroz con pollo, filet *salteado* (with a spicy sauce), and a fragrant paella. Sunday's Fiesta Brunch has everything from cheeses and cold meats to Belgian waffles. ⊠ *98 St. George St.,* ☎ *904/824–3341; in FL, 800/227–1905. AE, D, MC, V.*

$–$$ ✕ **Raintree.** The oldest home in its part of the city, this building has been lovingly restored and is worth a visit even though the food is generally not outstanding. The buttery breads and pastries are baked on the premises. Try the rainbow trout, filet of salmon, the new vegetarian dishes, or the Maine lobster special. The Raintree's madrigal and champagne dinners are especially fun. The wine list is impressive, and there are two dozen beers to choose from. Courtesy pickup is available from any lodging in the city. ⊠ *102 San Marco Ave.,* ☎ *904/824–7211. AE, DC, MC, V. No lunch.*

$–$$ ✕ **Santa Maria.** This ramshackle landmark, run by the same family since the 1950s, perches over the water beside the colorful city marina. Seafood is the focus, but there are also steaks, chicken, prime rib, and a children's menu. From the open-air porch you can feed the fish and try to spot a manatee. ⊠ *135 Avenida Menendez,* ☎ *904/829–6578. AE, DC, MC, V. No lunch Wed.*

$ ✕ **Zaharias.** A short drive from downtown across the Bridge of Lions, this restaurant is big, busy, and buzzing with an air of open hospitality. Serve yourself from an enormous buffet instead of, or in addition to, ordering from the menu. Greek and Italian specialties include homemade pizza, a big gyro dinner served with a side of spaghetti, and shish kebabs, steaks, seafood, and sandwiches. ⊠ *3945 Rte. A1A S,* ☎ *904/471–4799. AE, MC, V. No lunch.*

Lodging

$$$ 🏨 **Radisson Ponce de León Golf and Conference Resort.** Radisson bought and completely refurbished this resort late in 1996, and the rooms, which needed help, now sparkle. The lavish grounds are a spacious contrast to the narrow streets and crowds in the old city. You can loll in the sun or seek the shade of century-old live oaks, but the location is a bit out of the way if you intend to spend time sightseeing. ⊠ *4000 U.S. 1N, 32095,* ☎ *904/824–2821,* 𝖥𝖠𝖷 *904/824–8254. 200 rooms, 99 condos. Restaurant, lounge, pool, 18-hole golf course, 18-hole putting course, 6 tennis courts, horseshoes, jogging, shuffleboard, volleyball. AE, D, DC, MC, V.*

$$ 🏨 **Carriage Way Bed and Breakfast.** A grandly restored Victorian
★ mansion, this B&B is within walking distance of the old town. Innkeepers Diane and Bill Johnson see to such welcoming touches as fresh flowers, home-baked breads, and evening cordials. A full breakfast is included in the rate. Special-occasion breakfasts, flowers, picnic lunches, romantic dinners, or a simple family supper can be arranged with ad-

vance notice. ⊠ *70 Cuna St., 32084,* ☎ *904/829–2467 or 800/908–9832. 9 rooms. Bicycles. D, MC, V.*

$$ 🏨 **Kenwood Inn.** For over a century this stately Victorian inn has wel-
★ comed wayfarers, and the Constant family continues the tradition. In
the heart of the historic district, the inn is near restaurants and sight-
seeing. A Continental buffet breakfast of home-baked cakes and breads
is included. ⊠ *38 Marine St., 32084,* ☎ *904/824–2116. 10 rooms, 4
suites. Pool. D, MC, V.*

$$ 🏨 **Monterey Inn.** Location—right across from the Castillo de San Marcos National Monument—is the draw of this modest two-story motel.
It's within walking distance of many restaurants, museums, and shops.
⊠ *16 Avenida Menendez, 32084,* ☎ *904/824–4482,* FAX *904/829–8854.
59 rooms. Coffee shop, pool. AE, D, DC, MC, V.*

$–$$ 🏨 **St. Francis Inn.** If the walls could whisper, this late 18th-century house
would tell tales of slave uprisings, buried doubloons, and Confeder-
ate spies. The inn, a guest house since 1845, now offers rooms, suites,
an apartment, and a five-room cottage. Furnishings are a mix of antiques and just plain old. It's located in the historic district, and rates
include Continental breakfast. ⊠ *279 St. George St., 32084,* ☎
904/824–6068. 16 units. Pool, bicycles. MC, V.

Nightlife

Something is always happening at **Scarlett O'Hara's** (⊠ 70 Hypolita
St., ☎ 904/824–6535). Some nights it's live blues, jazz, or reggae bands;
on others it might be disco, Top 40, or karaoke; and many nights the
early and late-night entertainment are completely different. **Trade
Winds** (⊠ 124 Charlotte St., ☎ 904/829–9336) showcases live bands
every night, from country and western to rock. Call for a schedule.
Crowds head to **White Lion** (⊠ 20 Cuna St., ☎ 904/829–2388) for a
variety of live music on Fridays, Saturdays, and Sundays.

Outdoor Activities and Sports

Fishing
Charter the *Sea Love II* (☎ 904/824–3328) or sign up to join a half-
or full-day fishing trip.

Golf
The **Radisson Ponce de León Golf and Conference Resort** (⊠ 4000 U.S.
1N, ☎ 904/824–2821) offers 18 holes on a Donald Ross–designed
championship course. You'll find 72 holes at the **Sheraton Palm Coast**
(⊠ 300 Clubhouse Dr., Palm Coast, ☎ 904/445–3000).

Tennis
The **Radisson Ponce de León Golf and Conference Resort** (⊠ 4000 U.S.
1N, 32095, ☎ 904/824–2821) has six courts.

Water Sports
Surfboards and sailboards can be rented at the **Surf Station** (⊠ 1002
Anastasia Blvd., ☎ 904/471–9463).

Side Trips

Marineland
🕐 *18 mi south of St. Augustine.*

One of the first aquarium attractions with shows ever built in the United
States, Marineland is still a magic place. Dolphins grin, sea lions bark,
and seals slither seductively to everyone's delight. ⊠ *Rte. A1A,* ☎
904/471–1111; in FL, 800/824–4218. 💲 *$14.95.* ⊙ *Daily 9–5:30.*

Ravine State Gardens
35 mi southwest of St. Augustine.

For a great picnic spot, make your way to one of the state's great azalea gardens, which began during the Depression as a WPA project. The ravines are atypical of flat Florida. They're steep and deep, threaded with brooks and rocky outcroppings, and floored with flatlands. Although any month is a good time to hike the shaded glens here, the azaleas are in full bloom February and March. ⊠ *Off Twig St. from U.S. 17 S, Palatka,* ☎ *904/329–3721.* ☞ *$3.25 per vehicle with up to 8 people.* ☉ *Daily 8–sunset.*

ALONG THE COAST

Daytona to New Smyrna Beach to Cocoa Beach

This section of coast covers only 75 mi, yet comprises distinctly different areas, primarily because it includes three separate barrier islands. At the northern end are the small city of Daytona Beach and its neighbor to the north, Ormond Beach. Daytona is primarily known for auto racing and spring break, and its beach, at the southern end of the same barrier island that includes St. Augustine Beach, is fronted with a mixture of tall condos and apartments, hotels, and low-rise motels.

To the south is the small town of New Smyrna Beach. Its beach, which is lined with private houses, some empty land, and an occasional taller condominium, shares the next barrier island with the Cape Canaveral National Seashore and, farther south, the northern and inaccessible boundaries of the John F. Kennedy Space Center. As a result, the island is unusually unpopulated.

The towns of Cape Canaveral, Cocoa, and Cocoa Beach are still farther south and include the northern end of the next barrier island. Cocoa Beach is a laid-back beach town, but it gets crowded on weekends all year, as it's the closest beach to Orlando.

Ormond Beach

⑱ *60 mi south of St. Augustine.*

This town got its reputation as the birthplace of speed because early car enthusiasts such as Alexander Winton, R. E. Olds, and Barney Oldfield raced their autos on the sands here. The Birthplace of Speed Antique Car Show and Swap Meet is held every Thanksgiving, attracting enthusiasts from across the nation.

Ormond Beach borders the north side of Daytona Beach on both the mainland and the barrier island—nowadays you can't tell you've crossed from one to the other unless you notice the sign.

The scenic **Tomoka State Park** is a perfect location for fishing, camping, hiking, and boating. It is the site of a Timucuan Indian settlement discovered in 1605 by Spanish explorer Alvaro Mexia. Wooded campsites, bicycle and walking paths, and guided canoe tours on the Tomoka and Halifax rivers are the main attractions. ⊠ *2099 N. Beach St.,* ☎ *904/676–4050.* ☞ *$3.25 per vehicle with up to 8 people; campsite $8 per day June–Dec., $16 per day Jan.–May; additional $2 for electric campsite.* ☉ *Daily 8–sunset.*

The Casements, the restored winter retreat of John D. Rockefeller, now serves as a cultural center and museum. Take a tour through the period Rockefeller Room, which displays some of the family's memorabilia. The estate and its formal gardens host an annual lineup of special events and exhibits; there is also a permanent exhibit of Hungarian folk art, musical instruments, and other utilitarian objects. ✉ *25 Riverside Dr.,* ☎ *904/676–3216.* 🎫 *Donation welcome.* ⏱ *Mon.–Thurs. 9–7, Fri. 9–5, Sat. 9–noon.*

Take a walk through nearly 5 acres of lush tropical gardens, past fish ponds and fountains, at the **Ormond Memorial Art Museum and Gardens.** Inside the museum are historical displays, a collection of symbolic religious paintings by Malcolm Fraser, and exhibits by Florida artists. ✉ *78 E. Granada Blvd.,* ☎ *904/676–3347.* 🎫 *Free.* ⏱ *Tues.–Fri. 11–4, weekends noon–4 Sept.–July.*

Dining and Lodging

$$$ ✕ **La Crepe en Haut.** Outside stairs lead up to this quiet and elegant
★   classic French restaurant with several dining rooms and many window tables. Start with the onion soup, then try the filet of beef with burgundy sauce or the roasted duck with berries, but leave room for a sweet fruit tart or a slice of creamy cheesecake from the dessert tray. The wine list includes many excellent French wines. ✉ *142 E. Granada Blvd.,* ☎ *904/673–1999. AE, DC, MC, V. Closed Mon. No lunch Sat.*

$ 🏨 **Mainsail Motel.** Although there is an attempt at a nautical motif, this three-story, U-shaped building right on the beach is rather plain looking. Rooms and suites are basic but comfortably furnished, rates are very reasonable, and management is caring. ✉ *281 S. Atlantic Ave., 32176,* ☎ *904/677–2131,* 📠 *904/676–0323. 48 rooms, 13 two-bedroom suites. Pool, wading pool, sauna, exercise room, beach. AE, D, DC, MC, V.*

Daytona Beach

⑲   *65 mi south of St. Augustine.*

Best known for the Daytona 500, Daytona has been the center of automobile racing since cars were first raced along the beach here in 1902. February is the biggest month for race enthusiasts, and there are weekly events at the International Speedway. During race weeks, the now notoriously popular spring breaks, and summer holidays, expect heavy traffic along the strip of garishly painted motels, inexpensive restaurants, and tacky souvenir shops as well as on the beach itself, since driving on the sand is allowed. On the mainland, near the Inland Waterway, several blocks of Beach Street have been recently "street-scaped," and shops and restaurants open on an inviting brick walkway.

Racing enthusiasts make **Daytona USA** their first stop. The interactive motor-sports attraction lets visitors participate in a pit stop on a NASCAR Winston Cup stock car, design their own race car, and talk to their favorite competitors through video. There's also an exhibit of the history of auto racing. ✉ *1801 International Speedway Dr.,* ☎ *904/947–6800.* 🎫 *$10.* ⏱ *Daily 9–7.*

One of only 12 photography museums in the country, the **Southeast Museum of Photography,** located at Daytona Beach Community College, contains changing historical and contemporary exhibits. ✉ *1200 W. International Speedway Blvd.,* ☎ *904/254–4475.* 🎫 *Free.* ⏱ *Tues. 10–3 and 5–7, Wed.–Fri. 10–3, weekends 1–4.*

With the recent addition of the Humanities Wing, the **Museum of Arts and Sciences** is now one of the five largest museums in Florida. The humanities section includes displays of Chinese art and glass, silver, gold, and porcelain examples of decorative arts. The museum also has a large collection of pre-Castro Cuban art and an eye-popping complete skeleton of a giant sloth that is 13 feet long and 130,000 years old. ☒ *1040 Museum Blvd.,* ☏ *904/255–0285.* ☜ *$4.* ☉ *Tues.–Fri. 9–4, weekends noon–5.*

Memorabilia from the early days of beach automobile racing are on display at the **Halifax Historical Society Museum,** as are historic photographs, Native American artifacts, a postcard exhibit, and a video that details city history. There's a shop for gifts and antiques, too. ☒ *252 S. Beach St.,* ☏ *904/255–6976.* ☜ *$2.* ☉ *Tues.–Sat. 10–4.*

OFF THE
BEATEN PATH
PONCE INLET – At the southern tip of the barrier island that includes Daytona Beach is this sleepy town, where you'll find a small marina, a few bars, and informal restaurants specializing in very fresh fish. Boardwalks traverse delicate dunes and provide easy access to the beach, although recent storms have caused serious erosion. Marking this prime spot is the bright red, century-old **Ponce de León Lighthouse,** now a historic monument and museum. ☒ *4931 S. Atlantic Ave.,* ☏ *904/761–1821.* ☜ *$4.* ☉ *Daily 10–5.*

Beach

Daytona Beach, which bills itself as the "World's Most Famous Beach," permits you to drive your car right up to your beach site, spread out a blanket, and have all your belongings at hand; this is especially convenient for beachgoers who are elderly or have disabilities. However, heavy traffic during summer and holidays makes it dangerous for children, and families should be extra careful. The speed limit is 10 mph. To get your car on the beach, look for signs on Route A1A indicating beach access via beach ramps. Sand traps are not limited to the golf course, though—cars can get stuck.

Dining and Lodging

$$$ ╳ **Gene's Steak House.** This family-operated restaurant, located a bit west of town, has long upheld its reputation as *the* place for steaks. The setting is quiet and intimate, and the wine list is one of the state's most comprehensive. Though the menu does include seafood specialties, it's basically a meat-and-potatoes paradise for beef-eaters. ☒ *4½ mi west of I–95/I–4 interchange on U.S. 92,* ☏ *904/255–2059. AE, DC, MC, V. Closed Mon.*

$$ ╳ **Anna's Trattoria.** White table linens and flowers set the scene for
★ delightful Italian fare. Choose from two pages of delicious pasta items: spaghetti with Italian sausage and onions, angel hair with fresh chopped tomatoes and garlic, and spinach ravioli stuffed with spinach. There are also many veal and chicken dishes. ☒ *304 Seabreeze Blvd.,* ☏ *904/239–9624. AE, MC, V. Closed Mon.*

$$ ╳ **Frappe Downtown.** This cozy second-floor restaurant across from
★ a park on newly "street-scaped" Beach Street cooks up such unusual appetizers as a papaya and brie quesadilla. Entrées include beef tenderloin sautéed with herbs and peppers, shrimp in an Asiago-Romano cream sauce, and fresh salmon. A little porch with several tables offers outside dining. ☒ *174 N. Beach St.,* ☏ *904/254–7999. AE, DC, MC, V. No dinner Sun. and Mon., no lunch weekends.*

$$ ╳ **Ristorante Rosario.** Chef Rosario Vinci has owned several successful restaurants in Florida, and Daytona is lucky that he chose this area for his latest venture. From the outside, the building is not much to look at, but inside candlelight creates an intimate atmosphere. The real draw, however, is the excellent northern Italian cuisine, the best in Volusia County. Come here for tender veal marsala, *pollo pepperonata* (chicken breast sautéed in wine with roasted peppers and onions), or

fresh local grouper poached in white wine. Pasta lovers can choose from a full page of selections, including tortellini *alla Rosario* and spaghetti *putanesca* (with sun-dried tomatoes, olives, capers, and anchovies). Save room for the sweet cannoli. ⊠ *5548 S. Ridgewood Ave., Port Orange,* ☎ *904/756–8800. AE, MC, V.*

$–$$ ✕ **McK's Tavern.** Crowds fill up the bar, the tables in the bar, and the cozy booths. The fare is simple but hearty—juicy cheeseburgers, spicy chili, homemade meat loaf and mashed potatoes, onion rings, and a long list of stuffed sandwiches. ⊠ *218 S. Beach St.,* ☎ *904/238–3321. AE, DC, MC, V.*

$ ✕ **Aunt Catfish's on the River.** This popular place on the southwest bank of the Intracoastal Waterway (off U.S. 1, just before you cross the Port Orange Causeway), just south of Daytona, is crowded day and night. Locals and visitors flock here for the great salad bar, the hot cinnamon rolls and hush puppies that come with any entrée, the Southern-style chicken, and the freshly cooked seafood—fried shrimp, fried catfish, and crab cakes are specialties. ⊠ *4009 Halifax Dr., Port Orange,* ☎ *904/767–4768. AE, MC, V.*

$$$$ ★ 🏨 **Adam's Mark Resort.** Daytona's most luxurious high-rise hotel (15 stories) is set right on the beach, near the convention center and the band shell. Every room has a great ocean view and is comfortably furnished in pleasing pastels and blond oak. Guests can lounge around the pool on the spacious deck or head to the beach. There is an elegant restaurant, a poolside bar, and numerous other amenities. ⊠ *100 N. Atlantic Ave., 32118,* ☎ *904/254–8200 or 800/872–9269,* 🖷 *904/253–0275. 402 rooms. 3 restaurants, bar, lounge, indoor-outdoor pool, wading pool, beauty salon, health club, beach, playground. AE, DC, MC, V.*

$$$ 🏨 **Daytona Beach Hilton.** Most rooms in this beachside high-rise have balconies; some have a kitchenette, patio, or terrace. Convenient touches include a hair dryer, lighted makeup mirror, and a bar with refrigerator. ⊠ *2637 S. Atlantic Ave., 32118,* ☎ *904/767–7350 or 800/525–7350,* 🖷 *904/760–3651. 214 rooms. 3 restaurants, lounge, pool, wading pool, hot tub, sauna, exercise room, game room, playground, coin laundry. AE, D, DC, MC, V.*

$$$ ★ 🏨 **Live Oak Inn.** This lovely B&B is in a restored home that is listed on the National Register of Historic Places. Each room is different, but all are beautifully furnished with antiques. Some have long, enclosed porches and look out over the marina or onto gardens. Three have whirlpools. Downstairs is a fine restaurant and a small lounge and reception area. ⊠ *488 S. Beach St., 32114,* ☎ *904/252–4667. 13 rooms. Restaurant, lounge. AE, MC, V.*

$$–$$$ 🏨 **Captain's Quarters Inn.** It may look like just another mid-rise hotel, but the antique desk, Victorian love seat, and tropical greenery in the lobby will change your mind. At this beachfront, all-suite inn, fresh-baked goodies and coffee are served in the Galley, which overlooks the ocean and resembles a family kitchen with a few extra tables and chairs. Each guest suite features rich oak furnishings, a complete kitchen, and private balcony. Penthouse suites have fireplaces. ⊠ *3711 S. Atlantic Ave., Daytona Beach Shores 32127,* ☎ *904/767–3119,* 🖷 *904/760–7712. 25 suites. Pool. AE, D, MC, V.*

$$ 🏨 **Perry's Ocean-Edge.** Long regarded as a family resort, Perry's is famous for its free homemade doughnuts and coffee—a breakfast ritual served in the lush solarium. Three-quarters of the rooms are efficiencies, and most have great ocean views. Choose from several pools, a wide beach, and a putting green. ⊠ *2209 S. Atlantic Ave., 32118,* ☎ *904/255–0581 or 800/447–0002; in FL, 800/342–0102;* 🖷 *904/258–7315. 204 rooms. Café, indoor pool, 2 outdoor pools, putting green, beach, game room. AE, D, DC, MC, V.*

Nightlife and the Arts

THE ARTS

Broadway touring shows, symphony orchestras, international ballet companies, and popular entertainers appear at the **Ocean Center** (⊠ 101 N. Atlantic Ave., ☎ 904/254–4545; in FL, 800/858–6444). **Peabody Auditorium** (⊠ 600 Auditorium Blvd., ☎ 904/255–1314) is used for concerts and programs year-round. **Seaside Music Theater** (⊠ Box 2835, ☎ 904/252–3394) presents musicals in two venues, January–March and June–August.

NIGHTLIFE

Crowds flock to **Billy Bob's** (⊠ 2801 S. Ridgewood Ave., ☎ 904/756–0448) to dance to live country music nightly. Popular **La Playa Penthouse Cocktail Lounge** (⊠ 2500 N. Atlantic Ave., ☎ 904/672–0990), on the top floor of the Best Western La Playa Resort, has a dance floor and live entertainment most nights. Acts range from contemporary musicians in their 20s to the original Platters, from the 1950s. If you're ready to twist, head to the **Memory Lane Rock and Roll Cafe** (⊠ 2424 N. Atlantic Ave., ☎ 904/673–5389), where DJs spin music from the '50s and '60s. **Razzles** (⊠ 640 N. Grandview St., ☎ 904/257–6236) is the hottest spot in Daytona. DJs play high-energy dance music from early evening to early morning.

Outdoor Activities and Sports

AUTO RACING

The massive **Daytona International Speedway,** on Daytona's major east–west artery, has year-round auto and motorcycle racing, including the Daytona 500 in February and Pepsi 400 in July. ⊠ U.S. 92, ☎ 904/254–2700. ☉ *20-minute tours daily 9–5 except race days.*

DOG RACING

You can bet on the dogs every night but Sunday year-round at the **Daytona Beach Kennel Club** (⊠ U.S. 92, near International Speedway, ☎ 904/252–6484).

FISHING

Contact **Critter Fleet Marina** (⊠ 4950 S. Peninsula Dr., ☎ 904/767–7676) for full- or half-day deep-sea party trips.

GOLF

Indigo Lakes Golf Club (⊠ 312 Indigo Dr., ☎ 904/254–3607) offers 18 holes of golf. **Spruce Creek Golf & Country Club** (⊠ 1900 Country Club Dr., ☎ 904/756–6114) has an 18-hole course, a practice range, a driving range, and a pro shop.

WATER SPORTS

You can rent sailboards, surfboards, or boogie boards at the **Salty Dog** (⊠ 700 E. International Speedway Blvd., ☎ 904/258–0457). For Jet Ski rentals, try **J&J Jet Ski** (⊠ 841 Ballough Rd., ☎ 904/255–1917).

Shopping

The **Volusia Mall** (⊠ 1700 W. International Speedway Blvd., ☎ 904/253–6783) has four anchor stores, including Burdines and Sears, plus many specialty shops. Daytona's **Flea Market** (⊠ I–4 at U.S. 92) is one of the South's largest.

New Smyrna Beach

20 *19 mi south of Daytona Beach.*

This small town has a long dune-lined beach that abuts the Canaveral National Seashore. Behind the dunes sit beach houses, small motels, and an occasional high-rise. (Except at the extreme northern tip, none is higher than seven stories.) Canal Street, on the mainland, has been recently "street-scaped" and now has wide brick sidewalks. Flagler Avenue, the main beachside street, is in the process of being restored.

Changing every two months, the gallery exhibits at the **Atlantic Center for the Arts** feature the works of internationally known artists. Mediums include sculpture, mixed media, video, drawings, prints, and paintings. Intensive, three-week workshops are periodically run by visual, literary, and performing master artists such as Edward Albee, James Dickey, and Beverly Pepper. ⊠ *1414 Art Center Ave.,* ☎ *904/427–6975.* ⊠ *Free.* ☉ *Weekdays 9–5, Sun. 2–5.*

Smyrna Dunes Park is on the northern tip of its barrier island. Here 1½ mi of boardwalks crisscross sand dunes and delicate dune vegetation as they lead to beaches and a fishing jetty. Botanical signs identify the flora, and there are picnic tables and an information center. ⊠ *N. Peninsula Ave.* ⊠ *Free.* ☉ *Daily 7–sunset.*

★ Miles of grassy, windswept dunes and a virtually empty beach await you at **Canaveral National Seashore,** a remarkable 57,000-acre park with 24 mi of undeveloped coastline. But be warned: The dunes are endangered and it's against the law to walk on or play in them or to pick the sea grass. Stop at any of the six parking areas and follow the wooden walkways to the beach. Ranger-led weekly programs range from canoe trips to sea turtle talks. Call for a schedule. ⊠ *South end of Rte. A1A,* ☎ *904/428–3384.* ⊠ *Free.* ☉ *Daily sunrise–sunset.*

Beach
New Smyrna Beach has 7 mi of public beach with hard-packed white sand. Cars are allowed on certain parts from sunrise to sunset; the speed limit is 10 mph.

Dining and Lodging
$$–$$$ ✕ **Riverview Charlie's Seafood Grill.** A brick walkway winds through tropical foliage to this popular spot, whose two cozy dining rooms look out over the Intracoastal Waterway. You can also dine in the high-ceiling bar, which has entertainment Friday and Saturday nights, or eat outside on the spacious waterfront deck. Fresh local grouper is the specialty, sandwiches and salads are available for lunch, and there is a late-night tapas menu on weekends starting at 9. ⊠ *101 Flagler Ave.,* ☎ *904/428–1865. AE, MC, V.*

$$–$$$ ✕ **Skyline.** Watch private airplanes land and take off at the New
★ Smyrna Beach airport as you dine on secretly seasoned Tony Barbera steaks, veal, shrimp, chicken, and fish. Both dining rooms are dimly lit and elegant, and the new lounge is a favorite spot for cocktails. A pianist plays music to dine by six nights a week, and there is a tiny dance floor. Prices are high for the area, but the fresh fish is excellent. ⊠ *2004 N. Dixie Fwy.,* ☎ *904/428–5325. AE, MC, V. No lunch.*

$–$$ ✕ **Chase's On the Beach.** Eat on a deck beneath the stars—overlooking either ocean or pool—or dine indoors. This place is popular day and night. Barefooted beachgoers wander up for beverages, hamburgers, and salads during the day (shoes required inside), whereas the evening crowd comes for fried shrimp and weekend entertainment. ⊠ *3401 S. Atlantic Ave.,* ☎ *904/423–8787. AE, MC, V.*

$ ✕ **Norwood's Seafood Restaurant.** This casual New Smyrna Beach landmark has been open since 1945, and though it recently doubled its size with the addition of an airy high-ceiling dining room, it's still just as busy. Fresh local fish and shrimp are the specialties here, but you can also order steak, blackened chicken breast, or pasta. The mashed potatoes and onion rings (both homemade) are outstanding. Prices are incredibly low, and the extensive wine list is extraordinary. ⊠ *400 E. 2nd Ave.,* ☎ *904/428–4621. AE, MC, V.*

$ ✕ **Sam's Italian Seafood.** New Smyrna's best-kept secret is this hide-
★ away on U.S. 1. Sam's the chef; his wife, Celeste, is the manager. Pasta dishes are superb, particularly the eggplant rollatini, and you can count on absolutely fresh seafood. House specialties include flounder primavera and seafood crepes. The extensive menu is augmented by nightly specials, and there is a small but good wine list (beer and wine only). Four small dining rooms and some private rooms with just two tables ensure a quiet evening. ⊠ *2392 N. Dixie Fwy.,* ☎ *904/427– 1462. AE, MC, V.*

$ ✕ **Teddy's.** You wouldn't expect to find a New York–style Greek cof-fee shop in a small Florida town, but here's a great one. The menu runs the gamut from homemade soups to sandwiches, hamburgers, fresh salads, and steaks plus gyros, Greek salads, and an absolutely superb spinach pie. Early risers flock here for French toast, blueberry pancakes, and western omelets. ⊠ *812 3rd Ave.,* ☎ *904/428–0443. No credit cards. No dinner mid-Apr.–mid-Dec.*

$ ✕ **Toni and Joe's.** This longtime ultra-casual favorite opens right onto
★ the beach and has a large terrace perfect for people-watching. Head here (no shoes required) for the famous "hoagies," long rolls of fresh bread stuffed with slices of steak, cheese, sweet peppers, and onions and heated until the cheese is perfectly melted. ⊠ *309 Buenos Aires,* ☎ *904/427–6850. No credit cards.*

$$–$$$ ▥ **Holiday Inn Hotel Suites.** Families tend to like these comfortable suites, which sleep four, six, or eight people. Bedrooms are raised and set be-hind the living room, which opens out to a balcony and a spectacular view of the ocean. The furnishings are contemporary, and each unit has a full kitchen. ⊠ *1401 S. Atlantic Ave., 32169,* ☎ *904/426–0020. 102 suites. Restaurant, bar, pool. AE, MC, V.*

$$–$$$ ▥ **International Properties.** There are lots of condos and houses avail-able for rent that are on either the ocean or the Intracoastal Water-way. Units, which all have full kitchens, can be rented from three days to a week, a month, or a season. ⊠ *4166 S. Atlantic Ave.,* ☎ *904/424– 9173 or 800/227–5581,* ℻ *904/427–0470. 220 units, most with pools. MC, V.*

$$–$$$ ▥ **Riverview Hotel.** A landmark since 1886, this former bridge tender's
★ home is set back from the Intracoastal Waterway at the edge of the North Causeway, which to this day has an operating drawbridge. Rooms open out to plant-filled verandas and balconies, and views look either through trees to the Intracoastal or onto the private courtyard and pretty pool. Each room is furnished differently with charming an-tique touches, such as an old washbasin, a quilt, or a rocking chair. A complimentary Continental breakfast is served in your room, and the inn is near many interesting shops. ⊠ *103 Flagler Ave., 32169,* ☎ *904/428–5858 or 800/945–7416,* ℻ *904/423–8927. 18 rooms. Restaurant, pool, bicycles. AE, D, DC, MC, V.*

Shopping

Flagler Avenue (North Causeway) is the major entranceway to the beach, and art galleries, gift shops, and surf shops line the street. The 3rd Av-enue Shopping Center contains a number of specialty stores, includ-ing the popular **Snow Goose Gift Shop** (⊠ 721 3rd Ave., ☎ 904/423–3100), where you'll need to check out the ceiling and floor to catch everything on display. Art lovers will want to stop at **Arts on Douglas** (⊠ 123 Douglas St., ☎ 904/428–1133), displaying works by 50 artists plus a solo exhibit, which changes monthly.

Cocoa and Cocoa Beach

50 mi south of New Smyrna Beach.

㉑ The town of **Cocoa,** on the mainland, includes the quaint shopping area known as Olde Cocoa Village. Cocoa's neighbor on the barrier island is **Cocoa Beach,** a popular year-round escape for folks who live in central Florida. Motels and inexpensive restaurants line the beach, and Kennedy Space Center is just 10 minutes away.

★ ☾ **Spaceport USA** is perhaps the best entertainment bargain in Florida. There are two narrated bus tours: One passes by some of NASA's office and assembly buildings, including current launch facilities and the space shuttle launching and landing sites. The other goes to Cape Canaveral Air Force Station, where early launch pads and unmanned rockets that were later adapted for manned use illuminate the history of the early space program. Even more dramatic is the IMAX film *The Dream Is Alive,* shown hourly in the Galaxy Theater. Projected onto a 5½-story screen, this overwhelming 40-minute film, most of which was shot by the astronauts, takes you from astronaut training, through a thundering shuttle launch, and into the cabins where the astronauts live while in space. (Two other exciting films capture footage from nine Space Shuttle flights and focus on the earth from 200 mi up.) ✉ *Kennedy Space Center, Cocoa Beach,* ☎ *407/452–2121; outside FL, 800/432–2153.* ⊞ *Free, bus tours $7, IMAX film $4.* ☉ *Daily 9–6, last tour 2 hours before dark; closed certain launch dates (call ahead).*

At the entrance to Spaceport USA, the **United States Astronaut Hall of Fame** focuses not only on the milestones of the space program but on the personal stories of the astronauts. Board a space shuttle replica to view videos of historic moments. ✉ *Kennedy Space Center, Cocoa Beach,* ⊞ *$9.95.* ☉ *Daily 9–5.*

☾ Don't overlook the hands-on discovery rooms and the Taylor Collection of Victorian memorabilia at the **Brevard Museum of History and Natural Science.** Its nature center has 22 acres of trails encompassing three distinct ecosystems—sand pine hills, lake lands, and marshlands. ✉ *2201 Michigan Ave., Cocoa,* ☎ *407/632–1830.* ⊞ *$3.* ☉ *Tues.–Sat. 10–4, Sun. 1–4.*

☾ Exhibits of contemporary art; presentations of decorative arts, ethnographic works, photography, and experimental art forms; and hands-on activities for children are the draw at the **Brevard Museum of Art and Science.** ✉ *1463 Highland Ave., Melbourne,* ☎ *407/247–0737.* ⊞ *$3.* ☉ *Tues.–Sat. 10–5, Sun. 1–5.*

Beaches

Cocoa Beach (✉ Rte. A1A, ☎ 407/868–3274) has showers, playgrounds, changing areas, picnic areas with grills, snack shops, and plenty of well-maintained, inexpensive surf-side parking lots. Beach vendors offer a variety of necessities for sunning and swimming.

North of Cocoa, **Playalinda Beach,** part of the **Canaveral National Seashore** (☎ 407/267–1110), is the longest stretch of undeveloped coast on Florida's Atlantic Seaboard. Hundreds of giant sea turtles come ashore here May through August to lay their eggs, and the extreme northern area is favored by nude sun worshipers. There are no lifeguards, but park rangers patrol. Take Exit 80 from I–95, and follow Rte. 406 east across the Indian River, then Rte. 402 east for 12 more mi.

Dining and Lodging

$$$ ✕ **Mango Tree Restaurant.** Dine in elegance amid orchid gardens, with piano music playing in the background. House favorites include fresh grouper with shrimp and scallops glazed in hollandaise sauce and veal *française à la* Mango Tree (scallopini, very lightly breaded and glazed with a mushroom sauce). ⊠ *118 N. Atlantic Ave., Cocoa Beach,* ☎ *407/799–0513. AE, MC, V. Closed Mon. No lunch.*

$$ ✕ **Black Tulip.** Two cozy rooms create an intimate setting for elegant
★ cuisine in lovely Cocoa Village. Starters include tortellini bolognese, crab-stuffed mushrooms, and a delicious black-bean soup. Choose from such entrées as roast duckling with apples and cashews, steak au poivre, or linguini with chicken in a garlic and white wine sauce. Lunch selections are lighter and include sandwiches and salads. ⊠ *207 Brevard Ave., Cocoa,* ☎ *407/631–1133. AE, DC, MC, V.*

$$ ✕ **Cafe Margaux.** Choose indoor or outdoor seating at this romantic spot in restored Cocoa Village. The menu features an eclectic mix of classical French and Italian cuisine. Try the roast duck with berries or the filet of beef with port wine sauce. ⊠ *220 Brevard Ave., Cocoa,* ☎ *407/639–8343. AE, DC, MC, V. Closed Tues.*

$ ✕ **Herbie K's.** This diner is a 1950s rock-and-roll landmark. The juke box plays golden oldies and the servers dress, walk, talk, and even dance in the spirit of the times. You'll see saddle shoes and revisit expressions such as "daddy-o" and "doll-face." Famous for its burgers, Herbie K's also serves old-fashioned blue plates and ice cream desserts. ⊠ *2080 N. Rte. A1A, Cocoa Beach,* ☎ *407/783–6740. AE, D, DC, MC, V.*

$ ✕ **Lone Cabbage Fish Camp.** The natural habitat of wildlife and local characters, this one-of-a-kind spot sits on the St. Johns River, 9 mi north of Cocoa city limits and 4 mi west of I–95. Catfish, turtle, country ham, and alligator make the drive worthwhile. You can also fish from a dock here, buy bait, rent a canoe, or take an airboat ride (reservations essential). Check out the gator souvenirs behind the bar and the Swamp Monster stuffed and mounted on the wall; it was "caught" by one of the owners, Charlie Jones. ⊠ *8199 Rte. 520, Cocoa,* ☎ *407/632–4199. No credit cards.*

$$$ ☷ **Cocoa Beach Hilton.** It's easy to pass by the Hilton, as its sign is sometimes hidden by the dense natural foliage that grows right out to the edge of Route A1A. Once you turn into the parking lot, however, it's impossible to miss. At seven stories, it's one of the tallest buildings in Cocoa Beach. Just a small strip of sand dunes separates this resort from a wide stretch of excellent beach. Most rooms have ocean views, but for true drama get a room on the east end directly facing the water. The floor-to-ceiling windows really show off the scenery. ⊠ *1550 N. Atlantic Ave., Cocoa Beach 32931,* ☎ *407/799–0003 or 800/526– 2609. 300 rooms. Restaurant, lounge, pool. AE, D, DC, MC, V.*

$$-$$$ ☷ **Inn at Cocoa Beach.** The finest accommodations in Cocoa Beach are
★ in this charming oceanfront inn. Each spacious room is decorated differently, but all have some combination of reproduction 18th- and 19th-century armoires, four-poster beds, and comfortably upholstered chairs and sofas. There are several suites, some with whirlpool baths. All units have balconies or patios and views of the ocean. Included in the rate are an evening spread of wine and cheese and a sumptuous Continental breakfast with delicious homemade muffins and breads, served in the sunny breakfast room. ⊠ *4300 Ocean Beach Blvd., Cocoa Beach 32931,* ☎ *407/799–3460; outside FL, 800/343–5307. 50 rooms. Pool, beach. AE, D, DC, MC, V.*

$$ ☷ **Wakulla Motel.** This popular motel is clean and comfortable and just two blocks from the beach. The bright rooms are decorated in tropical prints. Completely furnished five-room suites, designed to sleep six, are great for families; they comprise two bedrooms, living room, dining room, and fully equipped kitchen. Outdoor grills are available.

✉ *3550 N. Atlantic Ave., Cocoa Beach 32931,* ☎ *407/783–2230. 116 suites. 2 pools, shuffleboard. AE, D, DC, MC, V.*

Outdoor Activities and Sports

FISHING

Cape Marina (✉ 800 Scallop Dr., Port Canaveral, ☎ 407/783–8410) has half- and full-day charter fishing trips.

Shopping

Ron Jon Surf Shop (✉ 4151 N. Atlantic Ave., Cocoa Beach, ☎ 407/799–8840) is a local attraction in its own right—a castle that's purple, pink, and glittery as an amusement park, plunked right down in the middle of the beach community. This multilevel store is packed with swimwear and surfboards and is open 24 hours a day. It's worth a stop just to see what all those billboards are about. In downtown Cocoa, cobblestone walkways wind through **Olde Cocoa Village,** a cluster of restored turn-of-the-century buildings now occupied by restaurants and specialty shops purveying crafts, fine art, and clothing.

INLAND TOWNS

Inland you'll find peaceful little towns separated by miles and miles of two-lane roads running through acre upon acre of dense forest and flat pastureland and skirting one lake after another. Here you'll see cattle and not much else, but you'll also catch a glimpse of the few hills found in the state. Gentle and rolling, they're hardly worth noting to folks from true hill country, but they're significant enough in Florida for much of this area to be called the "hill and lake region."

Deland

㉒ *21 mi southwest of Daytona Beach.*

This quiet university town is home to Stetson University, established in 1886 by Stetson hat magnate John Stetson. Other than the university, there isn't much to see, but several inviting state parks are nearby. As for other activities, there's great manatee-watching during the winter as well as skydiving for both spectators and participants.

One of the largest private collections of gems and minerals in the world can be found in the **Gillespie Museum of Minerals** on the Stetson University campus. ✉ *Michigan and Amelia Aves.,* ☎ *904/822–7330.* 🎟 *Donation welcome.* ☉ *Weekdays 9–noon and 1–4.*

February is the top month for sighting manatees, but they begin to head here in November, as soon as the water gets cold enough (below 68°F). **Blue Spring State Park,** once a river port where paddle wheelers stopped to take on cargoes of oranges, also contains a historic homestead that is open to the public. You can hike, camp, or picnic here. Your best bet for spotting a manatee is to walk along the boardwalk. ✉ *2100 W. French Ave., Orange City,* ☎ *904/775–3663.* 🎟 *$3.25 per vehicle with up to 8 people.* ☉ *Daily 8–sunset.*

Dining and Lodging

$$ ✕ **Pondo's.** You lose about 50 years as you step into what was once a romantic hideaway for young pilots who trained in Deland during the war. The owner-chef specializes in whimsical veal dishes, but he also does fish, beef, and chicken. The old-fashioned bar will remind you of "Cheers," and a pianist entertains Friday and Saturday. ✉ *1915 Old New York Ave.,* ☎ *904/734–1995. AE, MC, V.*

$ ✕ **Original Holiday House.** This, the original of what has become a small chain of buffet restaurants, is enormously popular with seniors, families, and especially college students. (It's right across from the Stetson University campus.) Patrons can choose from three categories: salads only, salads and vegetables only, or the full buffet. ⊠ *704 N. Woodland Blvd.,* ☎ *904/734–6319. MC, V.*

$$ ☷ **Holiday Inn Deland.** Picture a snazzy, big-city hotel in a little college town, run by friendly, small-town folks with city savvy. An enormous painting by nationally known local artist Fred Messersmith dominates the plush lobby. Rooms are done in subdued colors and styles; prestige suites have housed the likes of Tom Cruise. Tennis and golf privileges at the Deland Country Club are offered. ⊠ *350 E. International Speedway Blvd. (U.S. 92), 32724,* ☎ *904/738–5200 or 800/826–3233,* ℻ *904/734–7552. 149 rooms. Restaurant, bar, pool, nightclub. AE, D, MC, V.*

$–$$ ☷ **The 1888 House.** Spacious rooms, fireplaces, family heirlooms, and whirlpool baths make this a particularly enjoyable retreat. The building is of the distinctive Classic Revival style, with steep roofs and broad porches, excellent for rocking. Restaurants and historic sights are within easy walking distance. ⊠ *124 N. Clara Ave., 32720,* ☎ *904/822–4647. 3 rooms. Bicycles. AE, MC, V.*

$ ☷ **University Inn.** For years this has been the choice of business travelers and visitors to Stetson University. Conveniently located on campus, and next door to the popular Holiday House restaurant, this motel has clean, comfortable rooms and offers a Continental breakfast each morning. Some rooms have kitchenettes. ⊠ *644 N. Woodland Blvd., 32720,* ☎ *904/734–5711 or 800/345–8991,* ℻ *904/734–5716. 60 rooms. Pool. AE, D, DC, MC, V.*

Outdoor Activities and Sports

BOATING

Pontoon boats, houseboats, and bass boats for the St. Johns River are available from **Hontoon Landing Marina** (⊠ 2317 River Ridge Rd., ☎ 904/734–2474).

FISHING

One of the most savvy guides to St. Johns River bass fishing is **Bob Stonewater** (☎ 904/736–7120). He'll tow his boat to meet clients at the launch best for the day's fishing. **Hontoon Landing Marina** (⊠ 2317 River Ridge Rd., ☎ 904/734–2474) rents bass boats and offers fishing guide service.

SCUBA DIVING

For spring and freshwater diving and scuba instruction, try **Dive Tour Inc.** (⊠ 1403 E. New York Ave., ☎ 904/736–0571).

SKYDIVING

In addition to hosting competitions, Deland is home to tandem jumping. You are attached at the hip—literally—to an experienced instructor-diver, enabling even novices to take their maiden voyage after one day. For lessons, contact **Skydive Deland** (⊠ 1600 Flightline Blvd., ☎ 904/738–3539), open daily 8–sunset.

De Leon Springs

㉓ *7 mi northwest of Deland, 26 mi southwest of Daytona Beach.*

This town (population 1,500) is a small spot on the map just outside the eastern edge of the Ocala National Forest.

Near the end of the last century, **De Leon Springs State Recreation Area** was promoted as a fountain of youth to winter tourists, but visitors are now content to swim, fish, and hike the nature trails. ⊠ *Off U.S. 17,* ☎ *904/985–4212.* ⊠ *$3.25 per vehicle with up to 8 people.* ☉ *Daily 8–sunset.*

Dining

$ ✕ **Karlings Inn.** A sort of Bavarian Brigadoon, set beside a forgotten highway, this restaurant is decorated like a Black Forest inn. Karl Caeners oversees the preparation of the sauerbraten, red cabbage, and succulent roast duckling, as well as charcoal-grilled steaks, seafood, and fresh veal. The menu features Swiss, German, French, and Italian selections. Ask to see the dessert tray. ⊠ *4640 N. U.S. 17,* ☎ *904/985–5535. AE, MC, V. Closed Sun. and Mon. No lunch.*

Ocala National Forest

★ *Eastern entrance 40 mi west of Daytona Beach, northern entrance 52 mi south of Jacksonville.*

This delightful 366,000-acre wilderness with lakes, springs, rivers, hiking trails, campgrounds, and historic sites offers three major recreational areas. From east to west they are: **Alexander Springs** (⊠ Off Rte. 40 via Rte. 445 south), featuring a swimming lake and campground; **Salt Springs** (⊠ Off Rte. 40 via Rte. 19 north), which has a natural saltwater spring where Atlantic blue crabs come to spawn each summer; and **Juniper Springs** (⊠ Off Rte. 40), with a picturesque stone waterwheel house, campground, natural-spring swimming pool, and hiking and canoe trails. ⊠ *Visitor center, 10863 E. Rte. 40, Silver Springs,* ☎ *352/625–7470.* ⊠ *Free.*

Lodging

$ ⛺ **Ocala National Forest.** Close to 30 campsites are sprinkled throughout the park and range from bare sites to those with electric hook-ups, showers, and bathrooms. Some have canoe runs nearby. Prices range from $3 to $12.75 per night. ☎ *352/625–7470 for campsite locations. No credit cards.*

Outdoor Activities and Sports

CANOEING

The 7-mi **Juniper Springs run** is a narrow, twisting, and winding canoe ride, which, though exhilarating, is not for the novice. You must arrange with the canoe rental concession (⊠ Rte. 40, ☎ 352/625–7470) for rehaul—getting picked up and brought back to where you started—but it's included in the rental price.

FISHING

Rental boats and motors are available from **Blair's Jungle Den Fish Camp** (⊠ 1820 Jungle Den Rd., Astor, ☎ 904/749–2264).

Ocala

㉔ *78 mi west of Daytona Beach, 123 mi southwest of Jacksonville.*

This is horse country. Here at the forest's western edge are dozens of horse farms with grassy paddocks and white wooden fences. Rolling hills and sweeping fields of bluegrass make the area feel more like Kentucky than Florida, which is entirely appropriate. The peaceful town is considered a center for Thoroughbred breeding and training, and Kentucky Derby winners have been raised in the region's training centers. Sometimes the farms are even open to the public.

The **Appleton Museum of Art,** a three-building cultural complex, is a marble-and-granite tour de force with a serene esplanade and reflecting pool. The collection lives up to its surroundings, thanks to more than 6,000 pre-Columbian, Asian, African, and 19th-century objets d'art. ⊠ *4222 E. Silver Springs Blvd.,* ☎ *352/236–5050.* ⬛ *$3.* ⊙ *Tues.–Sat. 10–4:30, Sun. 1–5.*

OFF THE
BEATEN PATH

SILVER SPRINGS – The world's largest collection of artesian springs can be found outside Ocala at the western edge of the Ocala National Forest. The state's first tourist attraction, it was established in 1890 and is listed on the National Register of Historic Landmarks. Today, the park presents wild-animal displays, glass-bottom boat tours in the Silver River, a jungle cruise on the Fort King Waterway, a Jeep safari through 35 acres of wilderness, an antique and classic car museum, and walks through natural habitats. A great place to cool off, **Silver Springs Wild Waters** has the park's giant wave pool and seven water-flume rides. ⊠ *Rte. 40,* ☎ *352/236–2121.* ⬛ *Park $26.95; Wild Waters $9.95.* ⊙ *Park daily 9–5:30; Wild Waters late Mar.–July, daily 10–5; Aug., daily 10–7; Sept., weekends 10–5.*

Dining and Lodging

$$$ ✕ **Arthur's.** Don't pass up this elegant restaurant in the Ocala Hilton. Filet mignon with port sauce and chicken breast stuffed with spinach and sun-dried tomatoes are favorites, and the Sunday brunch is a must. ⊠ *3600 S.W. 36th Ave.,* ☎ *352/854–1400. AE, D, DC, MC, V.*

$$–$$$ ✕ **Fiddlestix, Edibles, & Libations.** This casual spot is extremely popular with locals and visitors alike. The menu offers everything from hamburgers and overstuffed sandwiches to open-pit-grilled steaks, chops, and chicken. ⊠ *1016 S.E. 3rd Ave.,* ☎ *904/629–8000. AE, MC, V. Closed Sun.*

$$$ ⊞ **Seven Sisters Inn.** This showplace Queen Anne mansion is now an
★ award-winning B&B. Each room has been glowingly furnished with period antiques and has its own bath. Some have a fireplace, some a canopy bed. A wicker-furnished loft sleeps four. Rates include a gourmet breakfast and afternoon tea. ⊠ *820 S.E. Fort King St., 32671,* ☎ *904/867–1170. 8 rooms. AE, MC, V.*

$$–$$$ ⊞ **Ocala Hilton.** A winding, tree-lined boulevard leads to this nine-story pink tower, nestled in a forested patch of countryside just off I–75 and a bit removed from downtown. The marble-floored lobby, with a piano bar, greets you before you enter your spacious guest room, decorated in deeply colored, contemporary prints. ⊠ *3600 S.W. 36th Ave., 32674,* ☎ *352/854–1400,* ℻ *904/854–4010. 200 rooms. Restaurant, pub, pool, outdoor hot tub, tennis courts. AE, D, DC, MC, V.*

Outdoor Activities and Sports

GOLF

Golden Ocala Golf Club (⊠ 7340 U.S. 27 NW, 34482, ☎ 352/622–0172) has 18 holes.

HORSEBACK RIDING

Ocala's bluegrass horse country can be explored during trail rides organized by **Oakview Stable** (⊠ S.W. 27th Ave., behind Paddock Mall, ☎ 352/237–8844).

JAI ALAI

The speediest of sports, jai alai is played year-round at **Ocala Jai Alai** (⊠ Rte. 318, Orange Lake, ☎ 352/591–2345).

Micanopy

㉕ *36 mi north of Ocala.*

Though this was the state's oldest inland town, site of both a Timu-cuan Indian settlement and a Spanish mission, there are few traces left from before white settlement, which began in 1821. Micanopy (pro-nounced micka-*no*-pee) does still draw those interested in the past, how-ever. The beautiful little town, its streets lined with live oaks, is a mecca for antiquers. The main street has quite a few antiques shops, and in fall roughly 200 antiques dealers descend on the town for the annual Harvest Fall Festival.

★ A 20,000-acre wildlife preserve with ponds, lakes, trails, and a visitor center with museum, **Paynes Prairie State Preserve** is a wintering area for many migratory birds and home to alligators and a wild herd of American bison. There was once a vast lake here, but a century ago it drained so abruptly that thousands of beached fish died in the mud. The remains of a ferry, stranded in the 1880s, can still be seen. Swim-ming, boating, picnicking, and camping are permitted. ⊠ *Off U.S. 441, 1 mi north of Micanopy,* ☎ *352/466–3397.* ⌸ *$3.25 per vehicle with up to 8 people.* ☉ *Daily 8–sunset.*

OFF THE
BEATEN PATH

MARJORIE KINNAN RAWLINGS STATE HISTORIC SITE – Rawlings's readers will feel the writer's presence permeating this home, where the type-writer rusts on the ramshackle porch, the closet where she hid her booze during Prohibition yawns open, and clippings from her scrapbook re-veal her legal battles and marital problems. Bring lunch and picnic in the shade of one of Rawlings's trees. Then visit her grave a few miles away at peaceful Island Grove. ⊠ *Rte. 325,* ☎ *352/466–3672.* ⌸ *Grounds free, tours $2.* ☉ *Daily 9–5; tours Oct.–July, hourly 10–11 and 1–4.*

Gainesville

㉖ *11 mi north of Micanopy on U.S. 441.*

This sprawling town is home to the University of Florida. Visitors are mostly Gator football fans and parents with kids enrolled at the uni-versity, so styles and prices of accommodations are geared primarily to budget-minded travelers rather than luxury-seeking vacationers. In the surrounding area are several state parks and interesting gardens and geologic sites.

☾ Located on the campus of the University of Florida, the **Florida Mu-seum of Natural History** has several interesting replicas, including a Maya palace, a typical Timucuan household, and a full-size replica of a Florida cave. There are outstanding collections from throughout Florida's history, so spend at least half a day here. ⊠ *Museum Rd. at Newell Dr.,* ☎ *352/392–1721.* ⌸ *Free.* ☉ *Tues.–Sat. 10–5, Sun. and holidays 1–5.*

☾ The **Fred Bear Museum** is a showcase for the many items that Fred Bear, an avid bow hunter who bagged an impressive array of big-game tro-phies, collected on his trips around the world. The museum also has archery artifacts dating to the Stone Age and a wealth of natural his-tory exhibits. Kids will enjoy seeing the life-size animals and the an-cient spears, shields, and arrowheads. ⊠ *Fred Bear Dr. at Archer Rd.,* ☎ *352/376–2411.* ⌸ *$3.50.* ☉ *Wed.–Sun. 10–6.*

About 10,000 years ago an underground cavern collapsed and created a geological treat. Today at **Devil's Millhopper State Geological Site,** you can see the botanical wonderland of exotic, subtropical ferns and trees that has grown in the 500-foot-wide, 120-foot-deep sinkhole. You pass a dozen small waterfalls as you head down 232 steps to the bottom. ⊠ *4732 Millhopper Rd., off U.S. 441,* ☎ *352/955–2008.* 🖅 *$2 per vehicle, pedestrians $1.* ⊘ *Daily 9–5.*

Dining and Lodging

$$ ✕ **Sovereign.** Crystal, candlelight, and a jazz pianist set a tone of re-
★ strained elegance in this 1878 carriage house—one of the area's fanciest restaurants. Veal specialties are notable, particularly the saltimbocca. Duckling and rack of baby lamb are dependable choices, too. ⊠ *12 S.E. 2nd Ave.,* ☎ *352/378–6307. AE, D, DC, MC, V.*

$ ✕ **Market Street Pub.** This British-style pub brews its own beer as well as serving up homemade sausage, fish-and-chips, salads, and hearty sandwiches. Dine indoors or outdoors in the sidewalk café. ⊠ *120 S.W. 1st Ave.,* ☎ *352/377–2927. AE, MC, V. No lunch weekends.*

$$ 🏨 **Residence Inn by Marriott.** Studios and two-bedroom suites with a kitchen and fireplace make a cozy pied-à-terre. Cocktails, Continental breakfast, and a daily paper are part of the hospitality. The central location is convenient for the university or business traveler. ⊠ *4001 S.W. 13th St. (at U.S. 441 and Rte. 331), 32608,* ☎ *352/371–2101 or 800/331–3131,* 🖷 *904/371–2101. 80 suites. Pool, exercise room, coin laundry. AE, D, DC, MC, V.*

$ 🏨 **Cabot Lodge.** Included in the rate are a Continental breakfast and a chummy two-hour cocktail reception. Spacious rooms and a club-like ambience make this a favorite with business and university travelers. ⊠ *3726 S.W. 40th Blvd., 32608,* ☎ *904/375–2400; outside FL, 800/843–8735;* 🖷 *352/335–2321. 208 rooms. Pool. AE, D, DC, MC, V.*

Nightlife

DJ Chaps (⊠ 108 S. Main St., ☎ 352/377–1619) is Gainesville's only country-western dance club; it's always hopping. Crowds head to the **Hardback Cafe** (⊠ 232 S.E. 1st St., ☎ 352/756–0048) for the newest local bands playing live music.

Outdoor Activities and Sports

AUTO RACING

Hot-rod auto racing goes on at the Gatornationals, championship competitions of the **National Hot Rod Association** (☎ 818/914–4761). They're held each year in late winter at the **Gainesville Raceway** (⊠ 1121 N. Rte. 225).

FOOTBALL

The games of the **University of Florida Gators** (☎ 352/375–4683) are extremely popular, and tickets are very hard to get.

NORTHEAST FLORIDA A TO Z

Arriving and Departing

By Bus

Greyhound Lines (☎ 800/231–2222) serves the region, with stations in Jacksonville (☎ 904/356–9976), St. Augustine (☎ 904/829–6401), Gainesville (☎ 352/376–5252), Daytona Beach (☎ 904/255–7076), and Deland (☎ 904/734–2747).

By Car

East–west traffic travels the northern part of the state on I–10, a cross-country highway stretching from Los Angeles to Jacksonville. Farther south, I–4 connects Florida's west and east coasts. Signs on I–4 designate it an east–west route, but actually the road rambles northeast from Tampa to Orlando, then heads north–northeast to Daytona. Two interstates head north–south on Florida's peninsula: I–95 on the east coast (from Miami to Houlton, Maine) and I–75 to the west.

By Plane

The main airport for the region is **Jacksonville International.** It is served by **American** and **American Eagle** (☎ 800/433–7300), **Comair** (☎ 800/354–9822), **Continental** (☎ 800/525–0280), **Delta** (☎ 800/221–1212), **TWA** (☎ 800/221–2000), **United** (☎ 800/241–6522), and **US Airways** (☎ 800/428–4322). Vans from the Jacksonville airport to area hotels cost $16 per person. Taxi fare is about $20 to downtown, $40 to the beaches and Amelia Island. Among the limousine services, which must be booked in advance, is **Classic Limousine & Charters** (☎ 904/645–5466), which charges $27 for one to four people going downtown ($9 for each additional person) and $40 for one to four people going to the Jacksonville beaches or Amelia Island.

Daytona Beach International Airport is served by American, Continental, Delta, and USAir. Taxi fare to beach hotels is about $10–$12; cab companies include **Yellow Cab** (☎ 904/252–5555), **Checker Cab** (☎ 904/258–6622), and **A&A Cab** (☎ 904/677–7777). **DOTS Transit Service** (☎ 904/257–5411) has scheduled service connecting the Daytona Beach airport to Orlando International Airport, the Sheraton Palm Coast area, Deland, Deland's Amtrak station, New Smyrna Beach, Sanford, and Deltona; fares are $26 one-way and $46 round-trip between the Daytona and Orlando airports, $20 one-way and $36 round-trip from the Orlando airport to Deland or Deltona.

Gainesville Regional Airport is served by **ASA–The Delta Connection** (☎ 800/282–3424), Comair, Delta, and USAir. Taxi fare to the center of Gainesville is about $10; some hotels provide free airport pickup.

Although Orlando is not part of the area, visitors to northeastern Florida often choose to arrive at **Orlando International Airport** because of the huge number of convenient flights. Driving east on the Beeline Expressway brings you to Cocoa Beach in about an hour. You can reach Daytona, about a two-hour drive, by taking the Beeline Expressway to I–95 and driving north.

By Train

Amtrak (☎ 800/872–7245) schedules stops in Jacksonville, Deland, Waldo (near Gainesville), Ocala, and Palatka. The Auto Train carries cars between Sanford and Lorton, Virginia (just south of Washington D.C.). Schedules vary depending on the season.

Getting Around

By Bus

Daytona Beach has an excellent bus network, **Votran** (☎ 904/756–7496), which serves the beach area, airport, shopping malls, and major arteries. Exact fare (75¢) is required.

By Car

Chief north–south routes are I–95, along the east coast, and I–75, which enters Florida south of Valdosta, Georgia, and joins the Sunshine Parkway toll road at Wildwood.

If you want to drive as close to the Atlantic as possible, and are not in a hurry, stick with A1A. It runs along the barrier islands, changing its name several times along the way. Where there are no bridges between islands, cars must return to the mainland via causeways; some are low, with drawbridges that open for boat traffic on the inland waterway, and there can be unexpected delays. The Buccaneer Trail, which overlaps part of Route A1A, goes from St. Augustine north to Mayport (where a ferry is part of the state highway system), through marshlands and beaches, to the 300-year-old seaport town of Fernandina Beach, and then finally into Fort Clinch State Park.

Route 13 runs from Jacksonville to East Palatka along the east side of the St. Johns River, through tiny hamlets. U.S. 17 travels the west side of the river, passing through Green Cove Springs and Palatka.

Route 19 runs north–south and Route 40 runs east–west through the Ocala National Forest, giving a nonstop view of stately pines and bold wildlife. Short side roads lead to parks, springs, picnic areas, and campgrounds.

By Water Taxi

Connecting the banks of the St. Johns River, the **Bass Marine Water Taxi** (☎ 904/730–8685) runs from 11 to 10 daily (except during rainy or other bad weather) between several locations, including Riverwalk and Jacksonville Landing. The one-way trip takes about five minutes. Round-trip fare is $3; one-way fare is $1.50.

Contacts and Resources

Emergencies

Dial **911** for police or ambulance.

HOSPITALS

The following hospitals have 24-hour emergency rooms: **Alachua General** (✉ 801 S.W. 2nd Ave., Gainesville, ☎ 904/372–4321), **Fish Memorial Hospital** (✉ 401 Palmetto St., New Smyrna Beach, ☎ 904/424–5152), **Halifax Medical Center** (✉ 303 N. Clyde Morris Blvd., Daytona, ☎ 904/254–4100), **Munroe Regional Medical Center** (✉ 131 S.W. 15th St., Ocala, ☎ 352/351–7200), and **St. Luke's Hospital** (✉ 4201 Belfort Rd., Jacksonville, ☎ 904/296–3700).

LATE-NIGHT PHARMACIES

Eckerd Drug (✉ 4397 Roosevelt Blvd., Jacksonville, ☎ 904/389–0314) and **Walgreen Drug Stores** (✉ 4150 N. Atlantic Ave., Cocoa, ☎ 407/799–9112; ✉ 1500 Beville Rd., Daytona, ☎ 904/257–5773) stay open 24 hours.

Guided Tours

City tours of Jacksonville are offered by **Jacksonville Historical Society Tours** (☎ 904/396–6307) for groups and by arrangement.

In New Smyrna Beach, **Coastal Cruise Lines** (☎ 813/428–0201) runs lunch, dinner, sunset, and special-occasion cruises through wetlands. You can often see herons, manatees, and dolphins. **La CRUISE** (☎ 800/752–1778) has day and evening cruises from Mayport, with live bands, dancing, and gambling. In Jacksonville, **River Entertainment** (☎ 904/396–2333) has dinner and dancing cruises on five different boats; schedules vary with the season. **Riverwalk Cruise Lines** (☎ 904/398–0797) offers sightseeing, lunch, dinner, and party cruises of Jacksonville.

Suwannee Country Tours (✉ White Springs, ☎ 352/397–2347), run by the Florida Council of American Youth Hostels, organizes bicycle and canoe trips on some of the state's most unspoiled and unusual roads and waters. Stay overnight in country inns, picnic in ghost towns, eat at country churches, and explore forgotten sites.

Visitor Information

Most offices are open weekdays from between 8 and 9 to 5. **Amelia Island–Fernandina Beach Chamber of Commerce** (✉ 102 Centre St., Amelia Island 32034, ☎ 904/261–3248). **Cocoa Beach Area Chamber of Commerce** (✉ 400 Fortenberry Rd., Merritt Island 32952, ☎ 407/459–2200). **Destination Daytona!** (✉ 126 E. Orange Ave., Daytona 32120, ☎ 904/255–0415 or 800/854–1234). **Gainesville Visitors and Convention Bureau** (✉ 10 S.W. 2nd Ave., Suite 220, Gainesville 32608, ☎ 352/374–5231). **Jacksonville and Its Beaches Convention & Visitors Bureau** (✉ 6 E. Bay St., Suite 200, Jacksonville 32202, ☎ 904/353–9736). **Ocala–Marion County Chamber of Commerce** (✉ 110 E. Silver Springs Blvd., Ocala 32671, ☎ 352/629–8051). **St. Augustine Visitor Information Center** (✉ 10 Castillo Dr., St. Augustine 32084, ☎ 904/825–1000) is open daily 8:30–5:30.

INDEX

NOTES

Fodor's Travel Publications

Available at bookstores everywhere, or call 1–800–533–6478, 24 hours a day.

Gold Guides

U.S.

Alaska	Florida	New Orleans	Seattle & Vancouver
Arizona	Hawai'i	New York City	The South
Boston	Las Vegas, Reno, Tahoe	Pacific North Coast	U.S. & British Virgin Islands
California		Philadelphia & the Pennsylvania Dutch Country	USA
Cape Cod, Martha's Vineyard, Nantucket	Los Angeles		
	Maine, Vermont, New Hampshire		Virginia & Maryland
The Carolinas & Georgia		The Rockies	Walt Disney World, Universal Studios and Orlando
	Maui & Lāna'i	San Diego	
Chicago	Miami & the Keys	San Francisco	
Colorado	New England	Santa Fe, Taos, Albuquerque	Washington, D.C.

Foreign

Australia	Europe	Montréal & Québec City	Scotland
Austria	Florence, Tuscany & Umbria	Moscow, St. Petersburg, Kiev	Singapore
The Bahamas			South Africa
Belize & Guatemala	France	The Netherlands, Belgium & Luxembourg	South America
Bermuda	Germany		Southeast Asia
Canada	Great Britain	New Zealand	Spain
Cancún, Cozumel, Yucatán Peninsula	Greece	Norway	Sweden
	Hong Kong	Nova Scotia, New Brunswick, Prince Edward Island	Switzerland
Caribbean	India		Thailand
China	Ireland		Toronto
Costa Rica	Israel	Paris	Turkey
Cuba	Italy	Portugal	Vienna & the Danube
The Czech Republic & Slovakia	Japan	Provence & the Riviera	
	London		
Eastern & Central Europe	Madrid & Barcelona	Scandinavia	
	Mexico		

Special-Interest Guides

Adventures to Imagine	Fodor's Gay Guide to the USA	Halliday's New Orleans Food Explorer	Rock & Roll Traveler USA
Alaska Ports of Call			
Ballpark Vacations	Fodor's How to Pack	Healthy Escapes	Sunday in San Francisco
Caribbean Ports of Call	Great American Learning Vacations	Kodak Guide to Shooting Great Travel Pictures	Walt Disney World for Adults
The Official Guide to America's National Parks	Great American Sports & Adventure Vacations	National Parks and Seashores of the East	Weekends in New York
Disney Like a Pro	Great American Vacations	National Parks of the West	Wendy Perrin's Secrets Every Smart Traveler Should Know
Europe Ports of Call	Great American Vacations for Travelers with Disabilities	Nights to Imagine	
Family Adventures		Rock & Roll Traveler Great Britain and Ireland	

Fodor's Special Series

Fodor's Best Bed & Breakfasts

America

California

The Mid-Atlantic

New England

The Pacific Northwest

The South

The Southwest

The Upper Great Lakes

Compass American Guides

Alaska

Arizona

Boston

Chicago

Colorado

Hawaii

Idaho

Hollywood

Las Vegas

Maine

Manhattan

Minnesota

Montana

New Mexico

New Orleans

Oregon

Pacific Northwest

San Francisco

Santa Fe

South Carolina

South Dakota

Southwest

Texas

Utah

Virginia

Washington

Wine Country

Wisconsin

Wyoming

Citypacks

Amsterdam

Atlanta

Berlin

Chicago

Florence

Hong Kong

London

Los Angeles

Montréal

New York City

Paris

Prague

Rome

San Francisco

Tokyo

Venice

Washington, D.C.

Exploring Guides

Australia

Boston & New England

Britain

California

Canada

Caribbean

China

Costa Rica

Egypt

Florence & Tuscany

Florida

France

Germany

Greek Islands

Hawaii

Ireland

Israel

Italy

Japan

London

Mexico

Moscow & St. Petersburg

New York City

Paris

Prague

Provence

Rome

San Francisco

Scotland

Singapore & Malaysia

South Africa

Spain

Thailand

Turkey

Venice

Flashmaps

Boston

New York

San Francisco

Washington, D.C.

Fodor's Gay Guides

Los Angeles & Southern California

New York City

Pacific Northwest

San Francisco and the Bay Area

South Florida

USA

Pocket Guides

Acapulco

Aruba

Atlanta

Barbados

Budapest

Jamaica

London

New York City

Paris

Prague

Puerto Rico

Rome

San Francisco

Washington, D.C.

Languages for Travelers (Cassette & Phrasebook)

French

German

Italian

Spanish

Mobil Travel Guides

America's Best Hotels & Restaurants

California and the West

Major Cities

Great Lakes

Mid-Atlantic

Northeast

Northwest and Great Plains

Southeast

Southwest and South Central

Rivages Guides

Bed and Breakfasts of Character and Charm in France

Hotels and Country Inns of Character and Charm in France

Hotels and Country Inns of Character and Charm in Italy

Hotels and Country Inns of Character and Charm in Paris

Hotels and Country Inns of Character and Charm in Portugal

Hotels and Country Inns of Character and Charm in Spain

Short Escapes

Britain

France

New England

Near New York City

Fodor's Sports

Golf Digest's Places to Play

Skiing USA

USA Today The Complete Four Sport Stadium Guide

CNN✈
Airport Network

Your
Window
To The
World
While You're
On The
Road

Keep in touch when you're traveling. Before you take off, tune in to CNN Airport Network. Now available in major airports across America, CNN Airport Network provides nonstop news, sports, business, weather and lifestyle programming. Both domestic and international. All piloted by the top-flight global resources of CNN. All up-to-the-minute reporting. And just for travelers, CNN Airport Network features intriguing segments such as "Travel Facts." With an information source like Fodor's this series of fascinating travel trivia will definitely make time fly while you're waiting to board. SO KEEP YOUR WINDOW TO THE WORLD WIDE OPEN. ESPECIALLY WHEN YOU'RE ON THE ROAD. TUNE IN TO CNN AIRPORT NETWORK TODAY.

WHEREVER YOU TRAVEL, *H*ELP IS NEVER FAR AWAY.

From planning your trip to providing travel assistance along the way, American Express® Travel Service Offices are always there to help.

Florida

American Express Travel Service
32 Miracle Mile
Coral Gables
305/446-3381

American Express Travel Service
330 Biscayne Boulevard
Miami
305/358-7350

American Express Travel Service
3312-14 N.E. 32nd Street
Fort Lauderdale
305/565-9481

American Express Travel Service
2 West Church Street, Suite 1
Orlando
407/843-0004

American Express Travel Service
9908 Baymeadows Road
Jacksonville
904/642-1701

American Express Travel Service
1390 Main Street
Sarasota
941/365-2520

American Express Travel Service
Epcot Center
Walt Disney World Resort
Lake Buena Vista
407/827-7500

American Express Travel Service
One Tampa City Center
Tampa
813/273-9380

Travel

http://www.americanexpress.com/travel

American Express Travel Service Offices are located throughout Florida. For the office nearest you, call 1-800-AXP-3429.

Wet'n Wild ®

$3 OFF

Present this coupon and save $3.00 off the regular all-day adult or child admission price. Coupon good for up to six people. Not to be used in conjunction with any other discounted offer or afternoon pricing.

Expires 12/31/98

Wet 'n Wild®

$3 OFF

Present this coupon and save $3.00 off the regular all-day adult or child admission price. Coupon good for up to six people. Not to be used in conjunction with any other discounted offer or afternoon pricing.

Expires 12/31/98

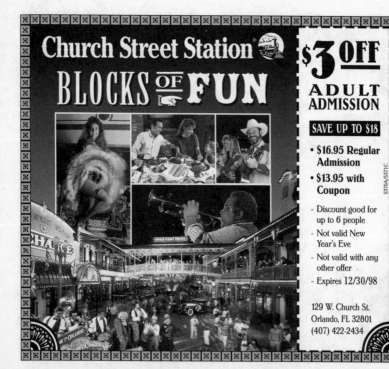

$3⁰⁰ OFF

All-Day Studio Pass

Regular admission price $38.50 (plus tax)

RIDE THE MOVIES®!

Universal Studios Florida®, the only place on earth where you can Ride The Movies®. Guests can thrill to Back To The Future®...The Ride™, Kongfrontation®, Earthquake®, E.T.®, A Day In The Park With Barney™ and TERMINATOR 2: 3-D BATTLE ACROSS TIME™!

20% OFF

Food and beverages purchased for your party (up to six) at Studio Stars Restaurant or Finnegan's Pub after 4pm.

$3⁰⁰ OFF

All-Day Studio Pass

$3.00 discount valid through 12/31/98. Coupon valid for up to 6 people and must be presented at the time of purchase. This offer has no cash value and is not valid with any other special discounts. Subject to change without notice. Parking Fee not included.

6183920001990

DINE HOLLYWOOD-STYLE

Be a part of the scene at the Studio Stars Restaurant (across from Ghostbusters®) or drop into Finnegan's Pub for Irish spirits, ales and entertainment. Your 20% discount is good for a party of six after 4pm! Remember to present this coupon when ordering.

Cannot be used in conjunction with any other promotion - including happy hour pricing.